*The Bear Tribe's*

# SELF RELIANCE BOOK

*Sun Bear, Wabun & Nimimosha*

*BEAR TRIBE PUBLISHING*
*P.O. Box 9167*
*Spokane, Washington 99209*

First Printing - 1977
Second Printing - 1981
Third Printing - 1983
Fourth Printing - 1984
Revised Edition - 1986

CONTENTS: Native American medicine, philosophy, prophecy
and religion.  Self reliance and survival skills.  Poetry
and legends.


Cover painting by Linda Legman.  Illustrations signed KVG
are done by Ken von Geldern, L are done by Lynne Van Mansum,
Y are done by Yarrow, N are Nimimosha, and KC are Ken C.

ISBN 0-943404-00-2

# TABLE OF CONTENTS

# *Thanks*

We offer thanks to Great Spirit for letting us serve his will.

We offer thanks to Earth Mother for her patience, understanding, perception, acceptance, gentleness and beauty.

We give thanks to those who have been our teachers, and to those who came to learn, and thus taught us.

We give thanks to our relatives in the mineral, plant and animal Kingdoms for teaching us, feeding us and needing our praise.

We offer thanks for this opportunity to share some of the things we've learned.

We thank all those who have ever come to the Tribe for sharing themselves and their learning. We give special thanks to the following people who have put their best love and energy into preparing the first edition of this book; Yarrow McDonald, Ken, Mondamin and Soon-kaax-kwe, Jim, Leon, Mary Kay, Wolf, Barbara, Brad, Carla, Yarrow Goding, Bobby and Red Bear. We thank Gregory, Stan and Whispering Leaf for writings they contributed. We thank all of the poets and artists who have contributed work. We thank Bill Durrell and Jean Terra for helping with printing and photo information. We thank those who dropped by and pitched in. We thank Linda Legman for the cover painting.

We thank Simon Henderson with his valuable knowledge and experience in organic gardening, for his help in this revised version of this book, and we thank him for the part he plays in our lives. We thank Cougar for his love of the Earth and his insights about acquiring and living on land. We thank Nimimosha who has remained with Bear Tribe Publishing these past 10 years, and has added her growing wisdom and perspective into the revision of the Self Reliance Book.

We also thank those who are working with the Tribe as the revised edition is published: Sun Bear, Wabun, Shawnodese, Gaia, Raven, Cougar, Nimimosha, Donna Singing Pipe Woman, Ruth Blue Camas, Casey, Yarrow, Thunderbird Woman, Michelle Odayinquae, Beth Earthseeker, Simon Henderson, Marc Creller, Mary Fallahay, Matt Ryan, Elisabeth Robinson, Tom Wilson, Saundra Pathweaver, Gail Buckner, Cheryl and Tricia Crombie.  They, along with many other good people, including Sun Bear's 250 apprentices, have greatly added to our knowledge of self reliance, and of life, over these years.

We thank you for buying and reading this book.

# Preface to the Second Edition

It has been nearly ten years since the Self Reliance Book was first published. During that time, we have seen many changes in our environment. The weather patterns are changing. There have been unprecedented extremes in our temperatures and humidity levels. We have discovered that chemicals we formerly saw as relatively safe are killing people. There have been two frightening nuclear disasters -- one at Three Mile Island, and one in Chernobyl in the Soviet Union. We do not yet know the extent of the effect these will have upon each of our lives.

There is much we don't yet know about our environment and the effects of our various technologies upon it. It often seems that our "research", our environmental impact statements, are simply empty but expensive gestures to give ourselves permission to do things that we will regret later. Indeed, it appears that our serious mistakes teach us more than our "research" does.

The last ten years have brought increasing awareness of the importance of this planet to our lives. Excellent books on the environment have become more popular. Natural health practices have proliferated everywhere. Readers and audiences have become more discriminating, and more research is required of speakers and authors. Alternatives in lifestyle are becoming more available and less "eccentric". In terms of pocketbook alone, more people are finding that the best ways to do things are often the most economical, and that prevention is worth immeasurably more than cure. Even public schools have shifted their focus from a high-tech, high-income program, to one giving attention to the natural sciences.

We have seen another important change since the first edition. In the seventies people tended to have a feeling of powerlessness of which we yet feel the vestiges. The desperation of those times led many to say "I'm only one person. What can I do?" That sense of helplessness, born of an unwillingness to live in a powerless state while not yet knowing how to gather our power, is dissolving in the eighties as we discover that, despite all we've done to the earth, there is hope!

This book is not a comprehensive guide to all self reliance skills. We could easily have added ten times the length to any topic in the section on practical skills. There are already many fine books available which give complete and accurate technical information on such skills as raising livestock, solar energy and so forth. These are valuable sources, and can be found in our own book catalog (write and ask us for one).

What we aim to do in this book is to give an overview, to focus on the point of being consciously self reliant, and to promote the attitude of nurturing the earth and affirming life in the way we live. The intention of this book is for it to be an introductory overview for people just beginning to learn self reliance, and a reaffirming expression for those who have already lived with a degree of self reliance.

In Sun Bear's book SUN BEAR: THE PATH OF POWER, he says, "When we see problems that require new answers, think of the Power that created the Universe." That very thought can serve us well, added to the experience and outlook we aim to share with you in this book.

It is important to know that everything you do matters. Each time you treat the Earth with care and sensitivity, She responds. Each time we change our behavior from the old destructive habits to new, gentler ways, no matter how small the difference, Earth responds. The Earth has a remarkable capacity for regeneration, if we will but cooperate, fully and from our hearts.

Nimimosha
June 1986

# *Fable of the Water Clan*

Once upon a time a long time ago some people travelled across the Great Water in canoes that had giant sails upon them. These strange canoes were able to haul the many people coming in search of new land because the rulers in their old lands had become evil and selfish, and had taught the people to hate those who had a different language, or a different way of worshipping the Great Spirit. The rulers encouraged wars that made them profit but caused suffering and death to the people.

When they came to the land of our ancestors our people welcomed them and sat down with them in council and treated them as brothers and sisters. They passed the pipe, smoked, shared good thoughts and words together, and our people and the strangers gave gifts to each other. There was much happiness in the land.

The people who came across the water said they had need of new homes. Our people said, "Come live with us and share our land and our ways and you shall be called people of the Water Clan." The people from across the Great Water looked at the ways of our people and saw that there was peace and plenty and that each man could worship the Great Spirit according to his own vision so they accepted, with warm gratitude, the offer of our people. The people of the Water Clan learned how to raise crops in the new land and their sons and daughters married with our people. They learned to respect our system of government where chiefs and counselors sat together and made good decisions for the people.

The Water Clan told horrible tales of other lands where men ruled for money and became corrupt. They said, "This shall not happen here. Our chiefs, like yours, shall counsel for love of the people and they shall work together in the hunt or the fields with their brothers and sisters."

They told other stories of how people were put in prison because they stole when they were hungry or killed or committed injury against their fellow humans when there were sicknesses in their minds. And they said, "This is bad. It is better if we do as you do and feed the hungry and send people who are sick in these ways to spend time with counselors and medicine chiefs who can help them become well."

As the country grew we founded warm-up centers together where people who felt upset or had problems could go and rest and be warmed up with love from the wise counselors who helped them to expand and find their balance.

As people moved Westward they met more tribes of people who had other visions and they said, "This is the vision for this part of the land. We must respect it. There are different chiefs here and they are loved by their people so we will accept their knowledge and counsel."

The chiefs there told the people to take of the buffalo only what they needed for food, and the people saw that this was good wisdom that would always leave buffalo for the children yet to come. A chief named Sitting Bull said he had had a bad dream that white men in blue coats came with fire sticks to kill and murder his people. The Water Clan people assured him this would not be since this was a sickness they had happily left behind when they reached the shores of this new land.

As the Water Clan, along with members of some other clans, moved across the land they continued to meet new people until finally the people knew of each other from sea to sea. In some places people had large villages but always they raised their food together about the village so that they remembered their balance with the Earth Mother. Each area had a council of chiefs who measured the value of any new ideas according to how they would benefit the people, the Earth Mother and the Great Spirit.

When a man called Ford discovered an invention that could move people about and cultivate land they said, "This is good if we use it well. We can raise food to feed hungry people in other lands, and we can move necessary items more quickly within our own land. This will enable the people of one area to visit with people from other areas so that we may learn from each other and our hearts may beat more as one." The Water Clan people thought of many inventions that became useful for the good of the people, and which worked in harmony with the land, and the other clans said, "It is good that our new brothers and sisters came from across the water to join with us."

When the Water Clan members heard that the people in their old lands had gone crazy and made weapons that killed many people they asked if they might bring these people to the counselors. This was done and they were placed in warm-up centers until they learned a balance. Then they were sent back to their own lands and they taught this balance to others while they worked to rebuild the things their madness had destroyed. Certain of our people visited with the traditional leaders in countries even farther to the East, and the chiefs of all the tribes on the planet counseled together and found a way for all the people to live in peace and plenty.

Everyone learned a balance with the Earth Mother and she became green and bountiful in her joy. The Great Spirit looked to the Earth where all creatures knew their place and purpose and was glad to see their happiness. It is good.

This is how it could have been. This is how it still might be for those people who learn to walk in love and balance on the Earth Mother.

# I. THE VISION

*Sun Bear's Vision*

The vision is something that is hoped for but not yet seen.
The vision is that which leads you on, that which directs you,
and points the way. The vision is the quest that each young
Native man was encouraged to seek, and Native women were free
to do so also. In seeking the vision, one would go out and pray,
"What shall my purpose be in life, Great Spirit? How can I best
serve the needs of my people? What is my part in the universe?"
I had my vision when I was very young. With the vision comes
the power of direction.

I saw the time when people would come together, when they
would learn to live together as brothers and sisters. This would
be in a real manner. I saw people living together in groups
sharing and helping each other, Indian and non-Indian alike. I
saw the Earth Mother being healed as people began to show real

love for the land. But first I saw whole cities become desolate
because there was no way left for people to support themselves.
I wondered at this when this nation seemed to be all-powerful.
Then I saw the vision of the great drought years, a time when
the Earth Mother would withhold all increase. I saw great black
birds like vultures hovering over withered grain fields, and
hungry bands of people travelling across the land in search of
food. I knew I must teach people to be self-reliant.

At first, I worked with only Indian people, but in time
my work took me to California, and my medicine told me that it
was time to start my main work, The Bear Tribe Medicine Society.
The vision I had was of people working and sharing together,
living on the land, raising their own food, building their own
shelters, and at the same time teaching other people the same
responsibility to the land, rather than complaining about the
things that the over-all society does. I would rather that we
teach people how to support their families by living closer to
the land, and thereby take away their dependence on city living.

In my vision I saw people returning to the land with a new
humbleness and respect for the Earth Mother. I saw new ceremonies
coming out of the old. The pipe of peace was there being used
in a proper manner, and people came together in an old way that
was new again. There was a real sense of sharing. I saw camps
of people around natural water, such as rivers, creeks, and
springs, working hard to produce their food, but thankful to be
alive  for only here and there  were small bands of people alive,
and they were thankful to the Great Spirit that they were. When
people came together they embraced with love, even those who
were strangers before that moment, because they knew.

There were only a few people surviving these changes. I've
seen major destruction, and people fleeing great cities, and
other people dying from pollution, and cities abandoned, and I
wondered how, until these last few years when I see California
and other places which no longer have the water, electricity,
or natural gases to care for their cities.
Then I understood what I saw before. We were told that our people would lay as if dead in the dust, and then we would rise up on
the land again. We were told that the sons and daughters of the
possessors of our land would come to us and accept our ways,
and that we would live together as one people sharing the land
and showing love and understanding for each other.

My medicine directed me to seek out a place that would
have a natural water supply. Here we have a spring that supplies
our water and needs. It runs out of the mountainside and there
is no need for electric pumps that would stop if there was

nothing to power them. We are far enough up the hill that nothing can pollute it, as there is no one above us. Where we lived before the Irrigation District would put a poison in the irrigation ditch to kill the weeds that grew in the ditch, killing off the fish and frogs and polluting the water. We have no dams to burst above us here. We found the pine trees and great rocks of our vision, and so here we live in northeastern Washington. If our vision or medicine told us to move again, we would do that, because we cannot be arrogant. We must accept what our vision tells. In the mountains we will hold out our hands and teach and help our fellow beings on the planet Earth. It is good to walk in Balance on the Earth Mother.

It gives me great happiness to look at the ten years since we first wrote this book about harmony with the Earth. It gives me happiness to see that we are living our vision, and that that vision continues to grow, along with our ever-growing awareness.  It is a good thing to see the work we did a decade ago remain good, solid, and harmonious while seeing that we didn't stop our sacred journey there, but grew in knowledge.  We strive to continue that growth so that the Earth might live.

## MEDICINE POWER

In the past medicine people and societies were an important part of all tribal life. They made medicine and prayers for good crops, and for success in the hunt. If the tribe was faced with going to war, the medicine people were consulted. In times of sickness or drought, prayers and ceremonies were made to the Great Spirit.

In the Southwest there are today many kivas and pueblo medicine societies and they function in much the same way as they did in the past. The members go down into their kivas, and the prayers, chants and medicine made there are known only to them. When the Green Corn ceremony is held in the Pueblo the preparation is first made in the kiva. The Hopi Snake priests make medicine with their people before they dance with the rattlesnakes and ask for rain for their crops. The medicine people are busy as they prepare for the kachina ceremonial. They make prayers asking for the blessing of the Great Spirit on the people.

The individual medicine people today have different medicines they serve. Some work with herbs. They make their prayers and gather herbs to cure those with sickness. Others see with the inner seeing. They search out the future and tell people what is to come in their lives. Others are earth prophets. They ask and seek out what is to happen on the Earth Mother. Others have the responsibility of teaching the old ways. Some use their medicine to help people with alcohol or drug problems.

Medicine to Indian people is many things. It can be what is seen through a dream or vision. It can be prayers or herbal knowledge. With true medicine people, each one respects the power or knowledge of the other. No one puts down another or exults themselves. They feel that each one has something to give to the whole. They do not boast of their power. The doing of the deed is enough in itself.

If a person goes to learn from a teacher, he learns to accept and respect that person's way of teaching.  Some people teach by talking and showing.  Many watch and listen.  And when you can understand and do it, then it's real.  Many old medicine people had an apprentice or more, who was there as long as their teacher lived.  When he passed on, they they could start practicing the medicine that they had learned. That is part of the reason I have my apprentice program. Spirit told me to pass on my wisdom while I still live so I could be filled with new knowledge.

Today many people are coming alive with the medicine ways. Great Spirit, let it grow, and help them to walk in balance.

FOR LACK OF LOVE

For lack of love the world died. Today we see the reaping of the harvest. All the selfishness of this nation and all the others is coming to its just reward. Those responsible for taking the natural resources of the earth without concern for future generations; those whose only thought was to make a profit; those responsible for the great wastefulness and destruction of natural resources; and those who murdered people in Cambodia and elsewhere will be punished by forces far beyond their reach.

In Asia this nation murdered many of the inhabitants, destroyed their rice fields, and rice supplies, and sprayed their lands with chemicals so no food can grow.  America grew fat from their exploitation of people all over the world, just as, in their earlier days, they stole from the Indians and ignored and mocked their hunger.  When they bombed hospitals and murdered people with contract killers, they said "God is dead, no one will see."  But the Great Spirit saw all that happened both in this country and abroad.

While the president of this country paraded himself as the great law and order man who said "we should stop coddling criminals" his own people were busy committing every crime in the book.  Then, when he was caught in his lies, he tried to cover them over with other lies.  But now, all of his lies and the other lies of this society are being exposed.  How can anyone show love or patriotism for this country?  The unions strike and struggle with each other for more money while big business increases prices.  Wherever we look we see greed masquerading as love and concern.  More than 3/4 of the wheat produced in this country has been sold overseas, because the money was right. As a result commodity food programs have been discontinued in most places because there are no foods left to give out.

How long will your policemen and firemen be there? Just as long as there is a paycheck in it for them. They have already developed what is called "blue flu" in most big cities. They stay home if their wage demands are not met. The truck drivers will stop hauling to the cities if there's no money involved.

The energy and other crises already have made many people unemployed.  There are major **food** shortages around the world.

All of this suffering and more yet to come because the majority of the people in the world today have been and continue to be selfish.  They show no concern or love for anyone but themselves.  We see coming the destruction of the major cities where people today walk in fear with black pitted against white, middle class against the poor.  When the transportation system breaks down completely there will be no food in the cities and hungry street gangs will wander, looting and worse.

Brothers and Sisters, I can give you good advice.  Find people who you can love and live with; people who share the same direction.  Then prepare food resources.  There will be

very little wild game or food available in the next few years.
In recent years there have been no acorns or pine nuts in many
places. There are more deer hunters than deer. The Earth
Mother will withhold her increase until after the great cleansing and purification. We will live because we believe our old
prophecies and our faith is in the Great Spirit. We will learn
to live in love and harmony upon the land.

## MAKING GOOD MEDICINE

Things come about in this way. We see our needs and then
make our prayers for good medicine. Each day we work toward
our goal and thank the Great Spirit for the gifts of that day.
We accept and acknowledge our place in the universe, and we
take our responsibility for it.

We know that there are major changes coming on the Earth
Mother, and that we should expect them, prepare for them, and
accept them. Knowing your place in the universe, and knowing the
time of history in which you are living is one way to help your
medicine always be good.

Good medicine is something that should serve you every day
of your life. It is not something that you make only on Sunday.
In the past our people lived very close to nature. They had a
sense of blending and belonging. When they wanted a good corn
harvest they made prayers and then worked toward it. The same
was true when they went on a buffalo hunt or took care of any
other need.

When you move in harmony with the universe and the Earth
Mother, then you will have a oneness with all things. Each
person, creature or plant becomes an extension of yourself. When
you make prayers or offer the pipe, you offer it for all things,
because all things are part of you and your universe. This is why
you show respect for all things.

Part of one Ghost Dance prayer is "When all of the little
dreams of horse, buffalo and man are gone, then we shall be as
one." When you feel the true sense of sharing a stream with a
fish, or sharing the sky with an eagle, or the land with a
prairie dog or deer, then you will not pollute her. When people
have this respect in their hearts, then their prayers are good
and they make good medicine.

# Hopi Prophecy

The following Hopi prophecies are largely from messages of the Hopi elders.

In the Hopi religion, the name applied to the Creative force is Taiowa (The Infinite). This Force, in the Beginning, conceived of the individual Sotuknang (The Finite) and commanded him to create "Lesser Beings." Sotuknang created the twins, Poqanghoya (North Pole) and Palonqawhoya (South Pole). He also created Kokyangwuti (Spider Woman). She created man, out of earth that was in four colors: Yellow, Red, White, and Black. Another tool used in the creation of man was tuchvala (saliva). Over her creations she spread the Cloak of Creative Wisdom and breathed life into them.

There were three phases of Creation at the Dawn of Creation. The first phase is the Time of the Dark Purple Light, known as Quganguptu. Here was the basic physical creation without life. Only the physical forms were established—there was, as yet, no life.

The second phase is the Time of the Yellow Light, known as Sikangnuya. Here the Breath of life was introduced into these physical forms.

The third phase is the Time of the Red Light, known as Talawva. Here the life forms were fully completed and began to develop.

The People have lived, since the Dawn of Creation, on Four Worlds. The First World was TOKPELA (Endless Space). The direction is considered to be West and the color associated with the world is Sikyangpu (Yellow). The mineral related to Tokpela is Sikyasvu (Gold) and the chief life forms were Katoya (The Great Headed Snake), Wisuko (Bird Who Eats Fat), and Muha (The Plant With Four Leaves). This World was lived upon by the People for quite some time until they began to lose sight of their origin. They lost the use of the Vibratory Center on the top of the head (Kopave) and the

Soft Spot that was the doorway between the body and the spirit
began to harden. Taiowa decided that would never do, and so he
ordered Sotuknang to destroy the world, but to save a few people
from destruction. He led them into the center of the World where
they were recieved by the Ant People. The Ant People fed them
so well that they, themselves, began to grow thin. It is said
that this is the reason why today the Ant People have such thin
waists. As the People stayed underground, the volcanoes on the
surface of the First World erupted, and the whole world caught
fire. After the fires subsided, the People came up from their
shelter and began to move to the Second World that had been
prepared for them.

The Second World was called TOKPA (Dark Mid-Night). The
direction is considered to be South and the color, blue. The
related mineral was Qochasiva (Silver), and the chief life forms
were Salave (Spruce), Kwahu (Eagle), and Kolichigan (Skunk).
Here, again, the People lived until they forgot their origin
and grew cold and hard to the ways of the Good Life. And, so,
once again, Sotuknang was ordered to destroy the World. This
time, he ordered the Twins, Poqanghoya and Palongawhova, to
leave their stations at the North and South Poles and let the
World be destroyed.  They did this, after the People had, once
again hidden with the Ant People underground.  After the twins
left their stations the world's stability was removed and so
it flipped end over end and everything on it was destroyed by
ice. The World froze over completely. In this legend we see
evidence of two ideas now held by scientists: Polar Reversals
and the Glaciation of the last Ice Age. After the ice had
melted enough to make the world inhabitable, the People came
up from their shelter and began to move into the Third World.

The Third World was called KUZKURZA (a word for which
it is said there is no modern meaning). The direction is considered to be East, the color red. The related mineral was
Palasiva (Copper) and the chief life forms were the Piva (Tobacco),
Aungwusi (Raven), and Chuvio (Antelope). Here the People
established great cities and a great technology. Much of what
is considered to be modern inventions were in use there, such
as airplanes. The People, however, lost sight once again of
their origin and that which had been taught to them at the time
of their creation. They flew in the flying machines, called
Patowavta, to other cities and there attacked them at night
when they could not be seen. Such evil things as war and the
establishment of boundaries and fences came into being. Again,
the People turned evil and Taiowa ordered the destruction of the
Third World. This time the Chosen People were sealed into hollow
tubes and set to float upon the water, for the World was to be

destroyed by water. Legend says that the waves grew taller and taller and eventually began to sweep over the land--they are said to have been higher than the mountains.

Before that happened the Faithful ones asked and received permission from the Great Spirit to live with Him in this new land. Great Spirit said: "It is up to you, if you are willing to live according to my Teachings and Instructions and will never lose faith in the life I shall give you, you may come and live with me." The Hopi and all who were saved from the great flood made a Sacred Covenant with the Great Spirit. They made an oath that they will never turn away from him.

The Fourth World, known as Tuwaquachi (World Made Complete) is considered to be in the direction north. The color is Sikyangpu (yellow, nearly white). The related mineral is Sikyapala (Many minerals mixed) and the chief life forms are Tohopko (Puma), Kneumapee (Juniper), and Mongwau (Owl, Sacred Messenger).This is the present world where the Hopi live now.

To the Hopi the Great Spirit is ALL powerful. He appeared to the first people and taught them how to live, to worship. In order to safeguard his land and life He made a set of Sacred Stone Tablets into which he breathed all teachings, instructions, prophecies and warnings. Before the Great Spirit hid himself He placed before the leaders of different groups different colors and sizes of corn for them to choose which shall be their food in this world. Hopi waited last and picked up the smallest one. By this means Hopi showed himself to the Great Spirit as intelligent. The Great Spirit said that he had done well, obtaining the real corn while the others got imitations inside of which were hidden seeds of different plants. Because of this the Great Spirit placed in his hands the Stone Tablets, Tiponi, symbol of power and authority over all land and life to guard, protect, and hold in trust for the Great Spirit until he returns in later days.

The Chief who led the Faithful Ones to this new land and life fell into evil ways and died.  His two sons, brothers of the same mother, scolded their father for the mistake he had made and, after he died they took over the responsibilities of Leadership. To these two brothers a set of Sacred Stone Tablets were given and both were instructed to carry them to a place the Great Spirit had instructed them. The Older Brother was to go immediately to the East, to the Rising and upon reaching his destination was to immediately start back to look for his younger brother who remained in the land of the Great Spirit. His mission was to help his younger brother bring about Purification Day at which time all wicked or wrong doers shall be punished or destroyed after which real peace, brotherhood and everlasting life shall be brought about. He'll restore to his brother the land that the Evil One among white man shall have taken from him. He will also come to look for the Sacred Stone Tablets and to fulfill the Sacred Mission given him by the Great Spirit.

The Younger Brother was instructed to cover all land, to mark well his footprints as he goes about in this land.  Both of the Brothers were told that a great White Star would appear in the sky as the people moved about in this land, and in other lands. They were told that when that happened ALL people shall know that Older Brother has reached his destination and thereupon all people were to settle wherever they may be at that time, until the older brother returned to him. It is said that the Older Brother after many years may change in color of skin which may become white but his hair will remain black. He will also have the ability to write things down and will be the only one to read the Sacred Stone Tablets. When he returns to this land and finds his younger brother these Stone Tablets will be placed side by side to show all the world that they are TRUE BROTHERS.

In ancient times it was prophesied by our forefathers that this land would be occupied by the Original Peoples, who have received permission from the Great Spirit Massau'u and then from another land a white brother would come, supposedly to help his brothers, who are here taking care of the land and life in a spiritual way with prayer, ceremonies and humility. He would come either with a strong faith and righteous religion which Massau'u had given him, or he would come after he had abandoned the great life plan and fallen to a faith of his own personal ideas which he invented before coming here. It was known that the white man is an intelligent person, an inventor of many words and material things, a man who knows how to influence people because of his sweet way of talking. He would use many of these things upon us when he came. The white brother would do many things that will be good for our Native Brother.

When it becomes the sole purpose of getting control of this land and he lives only for his own self-glory, then we must not listen to his sweet tongue, but watch his deeds.  If he mistreats us, lies, and starts to force our people off their lands, we must wait for our true brother who has the other set of sacred stone tablets.

The Hopi has not listened to the first white **brother**.  We Hopi have been faithful to the instructions of the Great Spirit,

Massau'u up to this time. We have followed our life plan. We are still carrying on our sacred rites and ceremonies -- we are still living in accordance with the pattern of life Massau'u has given us. We have not lost our faith in Massau'u. He has given us many prophecies. He told us the white Brother would come and be a very intelligent man, bringing to us many things he would invent. One invention, that our forefathers spoke of, was a machine, or object that would move on the land with animals pulling it---the wagon. Our forefathers also talked of a machine which would afterwards move with nothing pulling it--when we saw the automobile we understood. Then they said that the land would be cut up and that there would be many roads. Today we see pavement all over the land. Later there would even be roads in the sky, where people will travel. Now we see airplanes. It was said by Massau'u that if and when a gourd of ashes is dropped upon the earth, that many men will die and that the end of the materialistic way of life is near at hand. We interpret this as the dropping of atomic bombs on Hiroshima and Nagasaki. We do not want to see this happen again, here or any place on our Earth Mother, instead we should now turn all this energy for peaceful uses, not for war.

The white brother up to the present time, through his insensitivity to the way of nature, has desecrated the face of Mother Earth. The white brother's advanced technological capacity has occurred as a result of his lack of regard for the spiritual path and for the way of all living things. The white brother's desire for material possessions and power has blinded him to the pain he has caused Mother Earth by his quest for what he calls natural resources. And the path of Massau'u has become difficult to see by almost all men, even by Native First People who have been forced into white brothers Educational systems and now have chosen to follow the path of the white brother. We are coming to the time of the purifiers, who were commissioned by the Great Spirit, to stop man's destruction of self and nature.

It is known that our true White Brother when he comes will be all powerful and he will wear a red cap or red cloak. He will be large in population and belong to no religion but his very own. He will bring with him the Sacred Stone Tablets. Great will be his coming. None will be able to stand against him. All power in this world will be placed in his hand and he will come swiftly and in one day get control of this whole continent. Hopi has been warned never to take up arms.

With him there will be Two Great Ones, both very intelligent and powerful, one of which will have a symbol or sign 卐

which represents purity, and is a male. Also ✠ which represents purity and is a female, a producer of life. It is also known that he will wear a cap similar to the Horned Toad ⌒. The third or second one of the helpers to our True White Brother will have a sign or a symbol of Sun ✺ . He too will be many people, and very intelligent and powerful.

The Hopis say that these signs together represent the world and that when the time of Purification Day is near those with these signs will shake the earth two times then it will fall upon the Third One, with whom these two will join together and they will come as One to bring on Purification Day and to help his younger Brother who waits in this land.

It is also prophesied that if these three failed to fulfill their mission then the ONE from the West will come like a big storm. He will be many, many people, and unmerciful. When he comes he will cover the land like ants. The Hopi people have been warned not to get up on house tops to watch as he will come to punish all people.

Then if none of these fulfill their mission in this life the Hopi leaders will place their prayer feathers to the four corners of the Earth in an appeal to the Great Spirit. He will cause lightning to strike the Earth People. Only the righteous ones will revive. Then if all people turn away from the Great Spirit he will cause the great waters to cover the Earth again. We humans shall have lost the change to enter Everlasting Life. They say the ANTS may inhabit the Earth after that.

But if the THREE fulfill their sacred mission and if One or Two or Three Hopi remained fast to the last on these Ancient Teachings or Instructions then the Great Spirit, Massau'u will appear before all that will be saved and the THREE will lay out a new life plan that leads to Everlasting Life. This Earth will become new as it was from the beginning. Flowers will bloom again, wild game will come home and there will be abundance of food for all. Those who are saved will share everything equally. They will all recognize the Great Spirit and they may intermarry and may speak ONE TONGUE. A new religion will be set up if the people desire it.

Today almost all the prophecies have come to pass. Great roads like rivers pass across the landscape; man talks to man through the cobwebs of telephone lines; man travels along the roads in the sky in his airplanes; two great wars have been

waged by those bearing the Swastika and the sun symbol; as
prophesied by our Religious Elders; man is tampering with the
moon and the stars. Hopi and other Native Brothers were warned
no man should bring anything down to earth from the moon. It
will create unbalance of natural and universal laws and create
more severe earthquakes, floods, hail storms, season changes
and famines. This is now happening. Most men have strayed from
their life plan shown them by Massau'u. These signs tell us we
are nearing the end of our life patterns.

This is what the Hopi know and wait for by adhering to
their way of life and in spite of hardship they have been
faithful up to this day. For they are upholding this land
and life for all Righteous people.

# Iroquois Prophecy

The following prophecy, attributed to Deganawida, was related by the late Mad Bear Anderson, an Iroquois medicine person.

When Deganawida was leaving the Indians in the Bay of Quinte in Ontario, he told the Indian people that they would face a time of great suffering. They would distrust their leaders and the principles of peace of the League. A great white serpent was to come upon the Iroquois that, for a time, would intermingle with the Indian people and would be accepted by the Indians, who would treat the serpent as a friend. This serpent would in time become so powerful that it would attempt to destroy the Indian, and the serpent is described as choking the life's blood out of the Indian people. Deganawida told the Indians that they would be in such a terrible state at this point that all hope would seem to be lost. He told them that when things looked their darkest a red serpent would come from the north and approach the white serpent, which would be terrified. Upon seeing the red serpent he would release the Indian, who would fall to the ground almost like a helpless child, and the white serpent would turn all its attention to the red serpent.

The bewilderment would cause the white serpent to accept the red serpent momentarily. The white serpent would be stunned and take part of the red serpent and accept him. Then there will be a heated argument and fight. Then the Indian revives and crawls toward the land of the hilly country, where he assembles his people together, and they renew their faith and the principles of peace that Deganawida had established. There would be at the time among the Indians a great love and forgiveness for his brother. In this gathering would come streams from all over -- not only the Iroquois but from all over -- and they would gather in this hilly country, and would renew their friendship. And they would remain neutral in the fight between the white serpent and the red serpent.

While they were watching the two serpents locked in battle a message comes to them which makes them ever so humble. When they become that humble they will be waiting for a young leader, an Indian boy, possibly in his teens, who would be a choice seer. Nobody knows who he is or where he comes from, but he will be given great power, and would be heard by thousands. He would give them guidance and the hope to refrain them from going back to their land and he would be the accepted leader. And Deganawida said that they will gather in the land of the hilly country, beneath the branches of an elm tree, and they should burn tobacco and call upon Deganawida by name when facing our darkest hours, and he will return.

Deganawida said that as the choice seer speaks to the Indians that number as the blades of grass, being heard by all at the same time, and as they gather watching the fight, they notice from the south a black serpent coming from the sea, and he is described as dripping with salt water, and, as he stands there, he rests for a spell to get his breath, all the time watching to the north to the land where the white serpent and the red serpent are fighting. It is said that the battle between the white and the red serpents opened real slow but that it became so violent that the mountains would crack and the rivers would boil and the fish would turn up on their bellies. Then there would be no leaves on the trees in that area, and no grass, and strange bugs and beetles would crawl from the ground and attack both serpents, and a great heat would cause the stench of death to sicken both serpents. Then, as the boy seer is watching this fight, the red serpent reaches around the back of the white serpent and pulls from him a hair which is carried toward the south by a great wind into the waiting hands of the black serpent. As the black serpent studies this hair it suddenly turns into a woman, a white woman who tells him things that he knows to be true, but he wants to hear them again. When this white woman finishes telling these things, he takes her and gently places her on a rock with great love and respect, and then he becomes infuriated at what he has heard, so he makes a beeline for the north and enters the battle between the red and white serpents with such speed and anger that he defeats the two serpents, who have already been battleweary.

When he finishes, he stands on the chest of the white serpent, and he boasts and puts his chest out like he's the conqueror, and he looks for another serpent to conquer. He looks to the land of the hilly country and then he sees the Indian standing with his arms folded and looking ever so noble so that he knows that this Indian is not the one he should fight. The next direction that he will face will be eastward and at that time he

will be momentarily blinded by a light that is many times brighter
than the sun.   The light will be coming from the east to the west
over the water, and when the black serpent regains his sight he
becomes terrified and makes a beeline for the sea.   He dips
into the sea and swims away in a southerly direction, and
shall never be seen again by the Indians.   The white serpent
revives and he, too, sees this light and he makes a feeble
attempt to gather himself and go toward that light.   A portion
of the white serpent refuses to remain but instead makes its
way toward the land of the hilly country, and there he will
join the Indian People with a great love like that of a lost
brother.   The rest of the white serpent would go to the sea
and dip into the sea and be lost out of sight for a spell.
Then suddenly the white serpent would appear again on the top
of the water and he would be slowly swimming toward the light.
Deganawida said that the white serpent would never be a trouble-
some spot for the Indian people.   The red serpent would revive
and he would shiver with great fear when he sees that light.   He
would crawl to the north and leave a bloody shaky trail north-
ward, and he would never be seen again by the Indians.   Deganawida said that as this light approaches he would be that light,
and he would return to his Indian People.   When he returns, the
Indian people would be a greater nation than they ever were
before.

# *Other Prophecies*

I'm always interested in Indian prophecy, and I learned of one from the Manitoba Indians which I'd like to share with all of you.

It seems that the Indians up there knew about the white man coming to their land, and that he would be like a plague of locusts. Many warnings would be given to the white man to be good to his red brother and our Earth Mother. He would be warned to change his ways and if he did not change the Creator would cause many natural catastrophes over which the white man could have no control. Great winds would sweep across the prairies taking everything with them. Nothing would be left standing. The Indian people would band together to help one another. The mountains would have great landslides and earthquakes would crack the land near the sea. Destruction would be everywhere. The earth will change. Great huge animals will also be returning (a sea serpent has already been seen in one of the lakes). The land of ice and snow would grow warmer and Greenland will be green again. The Indian people will once more be in control of their country.

While I was in Canada I talked with some Northern Crees and Chippawayans. They said the ice floes are changing, something different is happening to the ice lands. They can't explain it but a change is happening there.

Makes one think, heh?

The Sly Ole Fox-1973

At night I made my prayers and asked to see what would happen on the Earth Mother. I dreamed I saw hungry groups of people roving in search of food. I saw them in desperation throwing their lives against people who were even armed to try and take food. Then, in their anger, they set fire to the homes and buildings of the people.

I saw people in cities who thought they were safe trapped in concrete vaults, destroyed by great floods of water.

I saw wheat fields being destroyed by rust and I saw some men deliberately using some kind of deformed plants that spread a sickness. I saw people trying to harvest wheat that was so full of rusty type sickness that the grains stuck together like syrupy candy. There were crows and vultures sitting together on the rotting crop.

Gheezis Mokwa - 1974

Tribe follows tribe
And nation follows nation
Like the waves of the sea.
It is the order of nations
And regret is useless.
Your time of decay may be distant
But it will surely come.

For even the whiteman whose God
Walked and talked with him
As friend to friend
Cannot be exempt from the
Common destiny.
We may be brothers after all
We shall see.---Chief Seattle

# A Gift of the Four Directions

The following poems have been shared with us by Whispering Leaf With Blue Jacket, a Shawnee man who had a traditional camp in Tennessee in the 1970's.

As we once again turn our faces toward the daybreak star, and our fear of the darkness lessens, may the teachings and instructions of Great Spirit illuminate our hearts. This is a time of awakening, and as we pray to Great Spirit for guidance, many sacred ceremonies and traditions are returned to us through dreams and visions. One sacred gift which has been renewed is the medicine or peace shield. Of this gift I would now speak:

The Great Spirit
Sensing much confusion among Earth
    Mother's children as they
    struggled through daily life,
Prepared a special gift.

Taking a rainbow, Great Spirit formed
    it into a blanket and spread it
    upon the breast of Mother Earth.
Then with the whispering of the wind,
And the roar of thunder,
The brightness of the morning star,
And the warmth of the summer's sun,
The clearness of the autumn sky,
And the depth of the great sea,
The suppleness of a spring sapling,
And the strength of the mighty oak,
The vision of the eagle,
And the stamina of the bear,
The wisdom of the ages,
And the great silence of the sky,
With these things,
The Great Spirit created forty-four
    warriors of the rainbow.
To each one,
He gave a special shield,
And because these shields could pierce
    darkness and drive fear before
    them,
They were called sacred medicine shields.

Now these forty-four warriors, who
    were called peace chiefs,
Were instructed to ride to the four
    directions and to count coup on
    fear, ignorance, deceit and
    jealousy,
The four warriors of darkness.

So even tho' these peace chiefs carry
    no war lance,
They are easy to recognize:
For besides the special shields,
They wear white buckskins of justice
    through wisdom,
Ride upon golden ponies of truth and
    light,
And smoke the sacred pipe of love and
    understanding.

Whispering Leaf With Blue
Jacket, Blades of Grass,
and Butterfly in front of
their wegiwa.

So now once again around small campfires throughout the land,
the teachings of the sacred medicine shields may be heard. Fire-
light flickers and in the dancing light, the painted symbols
of the medicine shield seemingly come to life. It is a time of
renewal and hearts are filled with new hope and strength.

First let me put a few more sticks upon the fire, and then
I will tell you a story of how one of these shields was returned
to the people.

Not so many winters ago, a young warrior sought to place
his feet upon the good red road. Now his people were few and
scattered like leaves before the wind, and many of these had now
forgotten the original instructions. So alone with this spiritual
hunger, he set out upon his quest. First he travelled toward the
setting sun, the place of looks within. As the cold moons were
approaching, he made camp in the mountains, and each day he would
climb a sacred mountain and ask Moneto "Who am I?" After many
moons of daily climbing the snow covered mountain to ask his
question, Moneto spoke to him. In a soft voice upon the wind came
his answer.

"Young warrior, you are a son of Mother Earth and Father
Sky and your breath is of the Great Universal Mystery of Creation."

page 32

With this new understanding, the young warrior broke camp and resumed his journey. This time he travelled to the north, the place of wisdom. And after making camp, he began to fast and pray.

"Oh Mother Earth
And Father Sky!
I pray to Moneto
Why am I?
Alone I stand
Upon holy ground
On a vision quest
I am bound!
Oh spirit of the north
hear my plea,
I'm seeking your wisdom
To truthfully guide me."

And after he had sung this prayer many times to the four directions, he began to notice something about the trees and grasses, the winged and the insects. It seemed as if all of creation was honoring the master of life through song and dance. He watched the trees and grasses sway to and fro as they sang with rustling leaves. The winged would pour forth great song to the rising and setting sun, while insects kept up a steady song day and night. And he began to wonder if perhaps he too should not honor this spirit. Then clear and strong came his inner voice speaking to his heart. "Yes, oh child of the Mother Earth and Father Sky, you are alive that you may know, love and serve the Great Spirit which is in all things and beyond all things."

Having learned this new truth, he once again resumed his journey, this time toward the rising sun, the place of illumination. Finally he reached a very tall mountain, and, climbing to the top, he spread his blanket and sat down. Now he prayed: "Oh Moneto I am of your breath. You have given me life so that I may honor you. How may I best serve your will?"

Now it became night and the sky was filled with clouds and a light rain began to fall. After awhile grandmother moon in all her fullness appeared. She spoke in a gentle voice to the young warrior. "You must make peace with your past, for the path ahead can only be walked in the spirit of life. Chase away all shadows from your heart." Then grandmother moon once again hid herself behind the clouds and rain fell as before. At dawn, the warrior descended to the valley so that he might make peace in

page 33

his heart.  And when he had done this, a mockingbird sang to
him.  The winged messenger instructed this new peace warrior to
paint a sacred shield.  When it was finished, he was told to
carry it to the south so that he might be of service to Moneto.

Thus began the last and longest part of the journey to
the place of love and compassion.  As he began to walk in this
direction many voices tried to lure him astray from his goal.
In the night came the voices of fear and doubt urging him to
turn back.  Oftentimes he would stop and wonder if he was strong
enough to continue his journey.

Now we may see how the gift of the medicine shield can be
of help.  Each time we falter in our journey, a look at our
shield reminds us of who we are, why we are and what our duty
is in this life. It erases the seeds of doubt and confusion
which are sprouting all around us during these troubled times.
The shield reminds us that we seek to become a whole medicine
circle and to turn in harmony with the four seasons of life while
carrying the gifts of the four directions within our hearts.

When I first received the shield I felt a sense of despair.
How was I to revive this medicine that had been lost for 100 years?
Since I could not answer this question, I had to let the breath
of Great Spirit guide me. This Whispering Leaf was blown and
tossed for many moons until at last he came to rest on a little
stream in the hills of Central Tennessee. This stream we call
Singing Sweetwater Creek and it is here that a small camp of
the medicine shield has been established.  With the strength of
the medicine shield we have been able to sustain this camp and
its traditional way of life for 19 moons.

Living on the barest of subsistence levels, we have been
able to call on the help of our ancestors who speak to us through
the wind and waters and teach us how to build quonset wigewas,
plant corn and beans in small hills, gather and dry herbs for
healing, and how to think and act with a family awareness. By
this family awareness, I mean the act of sharing ourselves and
our energies with our brothers and sisters so we can all grow
in the spirit.

Our time has not been easy in this new camp as ignorance of
the natural world was an obstacle to growth. We had to learn to
Walk in Balance with our Mother before she would yield her wisdom
and abundance. Through all this, when the doubts and fears and
frustrations would attack the heart, it was the strength within
the shield that would sustain our effort. It is a constant re-

minder that we are of the Creation and our sole purpose is to know,
love and serve the Creator. It is this service to Great Spirit
in a hostile world that has turned away from the instructions
of Creation that makes the journey to the place of love and
compassion the longest and most difficult. It is here that the
warriors of light with their sacred medicine shields must conquer the fear, ignorance, deceit and jealousy spread by the
warriors of the darkness.

It is a good day to begin the struggle.  I have spoken.

## *Rebirth of the Spirit*

These thoughts come from Wabun, one of Sun Bear's medicine helpers.

When we sit quietly to reflect, we all know the feelings the words in this article seek to express. At those times we are free to feel in our hearts our connection to the rest of the circle of the universe. We experience the peace that comes from knowing, as the traditional Indian does, that you are one part of the whole universe, and not <u>the</u> whole universe. We know then that the world is flowing, changing as it should and that we are progressing as we should.

Indian societies were designed to reinforce these feelings at all times. The world was considered sacred--plants, animals, people and their actions were all sacred. People were taught to respect all things for their implicit, natural beauty and holiness. The world was seen as an ocean of balanced energies, all running along their proper courses.

Sadly, little we find in the daily life of the society built by the people who tried to destroy the religion and culture of the Indian peoples is designed to allow us to remember that feeling of being one with the world around us. From cradle to casket, competition is stressed. As infants in this society

we learn that even love comes with a price tag.  We sense that
people fussing over us in many cases aren't doing it to make us
happy.  They're doing it so we'll smile and laugh and make them
feel good and look good to others. In a short period of time we
learn how to manipulate those around us so we can look good
too. Our lifelong affection and approval sweepstakes--that which
we usually call love -- has begun.  We've entered the Great American Rat Race.

By the time that most of us get to school, we're set up
for the "socialization" process there. Our already insecure
young minds eagerly accept America's golden rule "He who is on
top is best." We begin to shove and push to get to the top: to
be first in the class, the teacher's pet, the best athlete,
mama's little angel. Always and in everything--school, family,
church, music, television, literature--we are given the message
that the winner, automatically, is a good guy, and, even more, a
person who feels he belongs.  Throughout, this emotional message
is backed by the economic system which rewards  the best compet-
itor.  To the victor went the spoils and few people seemed to
care how the victory was won.

Eventually, growing up, some of us began to question whether
the end of winning justified all of the dirty means being used.
Those of us who had won found that while our image might be improved, we still had no sense of belonging, of contentment.  If
you were president of the senior class, you really wanted to be
president of the student body. And if you were that you still
envied the scholarship to Harvard the president of your rival
high school got. Rats on a treadmill, running toward an unde-
fined home.

In the sixties when most of us had full bellies, we called
time out to look at where we were headed, individually and as
a society.  Some of us were so disgusted that we followed the
lead of a few dissatisfied radicals, bohemians and utopians
of the past and dropped out of playing the game by the rules
we had been taught.  We formed what was called "The Movement",
"the counter-culture." This alternate culture was never the
unified group that the government's paranoia painted.  It was
composed of radicals, revolutionaries, rock heads, plain heads,
women's libbers, communards, collectivists, and a lot of hangers
on, the people so bruised by the battle of life that they seemed
unable to ever commit themselves to anything. Being a member
of the counter-culture was, at first, exciting.  Black, white,
red, brown, yellow, together we were going to overcome the evil
system that discriminated, maimed and killed to serve its own

greed. We demonstrated, sat in, campaigned, debated. Eventually, the excitement ebbed, money dwindled and we became discouraged. Many of our veterans turned to drugs, a more vicious mind killer than the fears they used them to forget; or to hedonism; or to the system they despised.

Others graduated from the political movement into the communal one. These people said that they felt if they couldn't change the dominant system they could create a viable and pleasant alternative. They felt that if they couldn't change the world for everyone, they could try to change themselves. Unfortunately, in a very important respect many communards emulate the system they condemn. As it was in the movement, so in most communes our brothers and sisters value above all the freedom to "do their own thing." And doing your own thing is nothing more than competing. Rather than trying to prove our worth by being the best kid in class or the rising young executive we try to prove it by being the most original mind, the best craftsperson, the natural leader, the most liberated woman, the most spiritually advanced. While we have dropped out of competing for money and the power this society has to give, most of us have not stopped trying to achieve the grand prize in the affections and approval sweepstakes. We still try to achieve a sense of belonging built on being better at something, anything. And for us to be better, a brother or sister has to be proven worse.

Without comparisons there would be no competition and, without both, there'd be no greed, envy, war. If we could make our communal societies work like the traditional Indian ones did, we'd be glad for the happiness and achievements of our brothers and sisters. We wouldn't try to top them. We'd know that we were all important parts of the universe and so we wouldn't compete to get feelings of belonging and being loved. We'd be free to truly love, to free others from their cages built of fear.

Emotional habits--especially negative ones--die hard. Being insecure, unhappy, complaining, competing is familiar emotional ground. Being secure, happy, and cooperative is not. Most of us rather stick with the familiar, even if we hate it, just because we're afraid of the unknown. To make our own fledgling societies work we have to learn to effectively dispose of our own negativity. To do that we have to watch ourselves as we live our lives, seeing and accepting our actions without judgement or fear. Eventually we will see enough good that we'll begin to really like our self. As this liking grows, so does our confidence and security. When we find enough real love in ourself

for our own spirit we can begin to live with real balance and
to create the kind of tribal society that will make us all free
to be what we are--joyful creatures of the universe.

What you believe you become.  Believe in beauty for the
Earth Mother is covered with beauty.  Believe in love, for your
Earth Mother and Sky Father love you.  Believe in magic, and you
release your soul from the prison your mind tries to build
around it. Above all, don't be afraid. The Great Spirit provides
all that is needed. Believe in your medicine. Believe in the
work you are doing to become an instrument of the Great Spirit's
will. Believe that you are where you should be. Believe that
your life is progressing to its proper destiny. Believe in
beauty, believe in love, believe in magic, and you will realize
you are beautiful, loving and magical.

Hey--hey yo hey--he yo--HO!

Grandfathers and Grandmothers
Great Spirit
We give thanks for this day
We give thanks for your Light.

The Light you have put within
    each of us grows brighter.
It shines through us, reaching out
    to Light our paths,
Illuminating for others their own
    spark of Light.

The People are
    bathed in this Light
Soon they will be complete
    once again.

As the Spirit grows,
    as your Light spreads,
The People will grow
    Oppression will end.

Greed will go, taking with it
All of its dark helpers:
    hatreds, envies, fears,
    violence, sicknesses, wars.

In your Light all darknesses
of the Soul disappear.

Eagles soon will soar across the land,
telling of your Light.
In their talons they hold--
    for all to see--
The mended hoop of the Nation.

Brothers, Sisters, two-leggeds,
four-leggeds, the people of the air,
those of the water, those who live
within the womb of earth mother,
and grow upon her--

All will gather
    To celebrate Your light.

All the differences, divisions,
    and fears
will disappear.

All will be truly One.

It is good.

HO!

                Wabun
                For the Bear Tribe

# II. RELATING TO
# THE EARTH MOTHER

## Coming Into Harmony

    We must learn to love our Earth Mother and the other beings
who dwell with us on her with the emotional force we usually
reserve for loving our dearest human friends. When you learn to
do this you will transform yourself, and help the transformation
of the Earth. Some people are able, naturally, to love the Earth
in this manner. Others have to learn how to give themselves
the space to do it. It is helpful to find an area that feels
really good to you: one in which you feel safe, protected and loved.
Go to visit this area whenever your heart tells you to. Always
thank the area for giving you such good feelings. Take the area
presents of tobacco or corn meal. Pray there. Sing there. Dance
there. Feel yourself merging with this part of the Earth Mother.
Feel her merging with you. Be patient. Don't resist your feelings. If it is meant to happen,one day you will feel your heart
fill with that place. You will yearn to see it, as you once
yearned to see a loved one's face. You will know that you've
taken the first step in learning to really love Mother Earth,
and the rest will come.

## PRAYING

Too many of us have forgotten how to pray for anything outside of our own wants. We have forgotten that the Earth Mother and our fellow creatures also need our prayers. We have forgotten that praying for these others is one of our responsibilities as human beings. How often do you tell the trees they are beautiful? How often do you compliment the birds on the beauty of their song? How often do you thank the spirit of the water for the many gifts she brings you? How often do you thank Earth Mother for sustaining your life?

Prayers don't need to be the complicated, eloquent prose offerings many of us have grown up with. All they need to be is sincere. If your heart speaks in eloquent language, fine. If your heart speaks as a child, that is beautiful too. Pray often. Pray when you feel it. Be abundant with your thanks. Explain to other forces of nature what you need when you have need of them.

If you are planting something, go to the area beforehand, and tell those of the mineral kingdom what it is you wish to do. Ask them for their help and support. Ask them to feed the plant people you will be putting there. Thank them for being there. Thank them for all that they have to give. Thank them for working with you. Tell them of your need for them, and of your appreciation.

If you must disturb them, ask them to understand. If you must destroy some rocks, tell them why. Assure them that you, too, will someday be food for the Mother Earth.

It is the same when you deal with your brothers and sisters in the plant and animal kingdom. Always show them love and respect. Always treat them as equal partners in the work you are doing--whether it is planting a garden, harvesting, birthing a lamb or butchering a cow. If your attitude is sincerely prayerful, loving and respectful, your fellow beings will help you in whatever it is that you have to do.

## NATURE SPIRITS

If you show a good attitude to the beings who work with us on the physical plane, the beings from other planes will note what you are doing, and will try to help you. The spirits of the planet are very much present. They are willing to help, they are willing to re-establish their proper relationship with human beings. All they need is to know of your sincerity, of your respect.

Don't have expectations about what it will be like contacting nature spirits. Don't expect to see elves and leprechauns sitting on all of your plants. Different spirits take different forms. Many don't take form at all. Some humans are capable of seeing spirits; others, of hearing them; others, of sensing their presence. Have faith in your way of making contact. Believe in those things that you feel to be true. When you are sailing in uncharted territory -- and dealing with spirits today is surely that -- the heart is the most reliable navigator. Move gently among the spirits. Accept them. Understand them as best you can. And have patience. What seems impossible today may seem like the most natural thing in the world a month or a year from now.

# *Celebrations*

   One of the best ways to show our love for Mother Earth
and the Great Spirit is through celebrations of their unity,
and the unity of all creation.  Our celebrations are based upon
our knowledge of the traditional way, but they are not copies of
old celebrations.  We feel that this is a new time, and that our
celebrations must reflect the time we are in and the heart feelings that we have.  While we respect the old ways we know that
feelings are more important than form.  And that is how it was
in the even older way that is remembered in the hearts of a few.


## THE CIRCLE

   We use the circle several times each day. When we pray in
the morning and evenings, we come together in a circle. Before
eating, we join hands in a circle. Before sweating we gather in
a circle. When we council, we sit in a circle.

   The circle reminds us that all life is continuous, that
there is no beginning or end, that all flows together in perfect harmony.

   We also have a medicine wheel on our land. At this circle
we make our special prayers and give thanks for our connections
with the universe, and with the power that such special circles
can bring.

We use the pipe at many times. When we are about to council, when we have another celebration, when we pray for healing, when we pray with thanks we make smoke. We are blessed to have several pipes to use for medicine. We have our tribal pipe. We have the pipe of Yellow Hand, a Cheyenne chief killed by Buffalo Bill. This came to us from another medicine man. Sun Bear has his own pipe for special medicine, and we have another pipe used only for particular kinds of medicine. Several of our members also have their own pipes.

The pipe represents the universe. The bowl is made of stone from the mineral kingdom. The stem is made of wood from the plant kingdom. When we bring out the pipe, we acknowledge our relationship to all of these other kingdoms. The tobacco is the ritual victim which gives itself so that our prayers may rise to the Great Spirit. When we place the tobacco in the pipe we offer a pinch for each of these kingdoms, for the spirit world, for our fellow two-leggeds, for the powers of the four directions, and for any special healing or prayer we are making. After lighting the pipe we then offer smoke for each of the directions, for the Earth Mother, and for the Great Spirit.

Using the pipe helps us to remember our connection with all of the universe.

## THE SWEAT

In the sweat lodge we are cleansed in our bodies, our minds, our hearts and our spirits. Through the marriage of earth, fire, water and air, this cleansing comes about. We enter in our ignorance and fear, and, through grandfather and grandmother's breath we come out as new beings, better able to know the love of the Great Spirit and the compassion of the Earth Mother.

The sweat lodge is built from any young hardwood sapling. After proper prayers, the trees are cut, and then bent into a dome shape, and lashed together. The lodge is covered with canvas or blankets or sleeping bags, or with mats woven from grasses, or with mud. The door of the lodge faces East. A fire pit is built outside. Rocks are obtained from a river bed or volcanic area, as these rocks will not break when they are heated. Be careful not to get granite rocks as they'll explode.

Before the sweat the firekeeper puts the rocks in the fire pit then builds a fire over them. When they are really hot, the sweat is ready to begin. The firekeeper takes a rock from the fire for each of the directions, for the Earth Mother and Great Spirit. He or she carries them in a sun-wise direction around the fire pit, and then places them in a pit in the center of the lodge. Additional rocks may be put inside. The people enter the lodge in a sun-wise direction. Water is placed on the rocks and the sweat ceremony begins. If there is a leader, he or she makes

prayers for each of the directions. They may also open the flap
to invite in the power of the directions. They make prayers for
Earth Mother and Great Spirit. Songs may be offered. Others
may offer their prayers. Water is passed around the circle. When
the time feels right, we exit in the opposite direction from
that in which we entered. We give thanks for the sweat, for
feeling clean and good, and for the time we have been able to
share together.

## PLANTING AND HARVESTING

We celebrate the time of planting by giving thanks to the
Earth Mother for the season in which she brings forth in such
abundance. The sisters offer corn meal and make their prayers,
and they then circle the fields that will be planted, asking
that the power of creation that they have been given will join
with the creative power of Earth Mother.

After our harvest, we give thanks for all the goodness
that the Earth Mother and our plant brothers and sisters have
given us. We pray that the time of rest for the earth and the
spirits will be good and refreshing.

## EARTH RENEWAL

Our biggest celebration of the year comes at the time of
the winter solstice, the time of earth renewal. At this time,
when the sun is at its furthest point away from us, we have four
days of fast.  During these days we remember that without the
warmth and light of Father Sun returning to heat the Earth
Mother and make her grow, life would not continue.  We fast and
pray that Father Sun will return, that the cycle of life will
continue.  On the day that the sun begins its return, we take
a sweat to cleanse ourselves of all the old so that we may greet
the new year as new humans. On this day the sisters join together
to grind the sacred corn meal for the year in the old way, with
a stone grinding bowl and pestle. This corn meal is used during
the year when we wish to make an offering for fertility and
abundance. On Earth Renewal day we offer some corn meal and ask
that the year coming be a good one for the Earth Mother, and for
all people. We then have a day of feasting and fun, and we invite
all of our friends to come and join with us.

It is important to remember the life-giving sources of
Creation, and the reality that we can't create them ourselves.
The traditional Native didn't take the return of the sun for
granted, but was thankful and joyful each time it happened.
Because of the way most of us were educated, we are taught to

expect the beginning of winter as a given, not as a gift. This has changed our attitude from one of thankfulness, to one of expectation, allowing us to extract from the Earth's resources without acknowledgement or return. The ceremonies of Earth Renewal are one of the ways we say Thank You.

There is a growing awareness of ceremony in the last decade. More and more workshops, seminars and lectures are being given on its importance. More people are organizing groups that meet together for a variety of homemade and learned ceremonies, songs and dances honoring earth and her resources.

We celebrate the summer solstice, and the spring and autumn equinox by fasting, sweating, doing pipe ceremony, having a spirit feast, praying and giving thanks for the turning of the wheel of life.

## SINGING, DRUMMING, DANCING

The whole universe dances to the song of creation. When we sing and dance we join in this union. When we drum we hear the merging of the heartbeat of our body, with that of the earth mother, and of the drum. It is good to give thanks in these ways.

# Freeing the Sister Within

Following is Wabun's personal account of learning to free the sister within her.

Until I was thirty, I always harbored a secret wish to be a man. I remember as a child I always envied the little boys. They seemed so much freer. Growing older, I learned well to emulate the men I saw around me. I became competitive, and I pushed to excel at any of the things I chose to do. I did not have a strong physical body, and so I developed my mind. I was an excellent student. I learned to manipulate, and I became a student leader. I went into politics, and knew how to be elected to any offices I wanted to hold, up to a point, that point being when I threatened the men I worked with too much. Then they put me down. After one such incident, I stopped being political. I turned to writing, which I had always been good at doing. I went to the best journalism school in the States, and I did well. When I tried to get a job, after over $20,000 worth of education, I found that, as a woman, I only qualified as an assistant to a man. This was before woman's lib, and jobs were not being equally doled out. I found a man I could enjoy working with, and helped start several new magazines. Finally, I was made editor of one. Still, all my decisions were censored by the men backing the magasine. I felt powerless.

I free-lanced, writing about what interested me, mainly radical politics and the human potential movement. I wrote a book, published by a major New York publisher. By that time, I had realized that my satisfaction had to come from within, not without. I became involved in searching for a spiritual teacher, someone who could tell me how to become free. While involved with a Sufi oriented group in New York, I met Sun Bear and decided I wanted to write about him and the Bear Tribe. Because of the love I felt for him and his work I left New York and came to live with the Tribe. I became his medicine helper.

What a learning experience that was and is. Being in such close assiciation with a strong man, I had to really fight to keep any sense of my own identity, my own worth. We both had to learn to work with each other without losing our separate balances.

I felt that the struggle was worthwhile since he was a man who was not afraid of my energy and my strength. He encouraged me to develop all the skills I had, to develop my powers. Still, things did not feel quite right. There was a missing element.

Within the last years, I have found what that is. It is my femininity -- my true essence of womanhood. I had always been a highly intuitive person, though, until recently, I could not have even found the words to express that. I just knew that sometimes I thought differently from people around me, and that, sometimes this got me into trouble. I'd know things that other people couldn't see, and I would know them from some source of knowing that I could not explain. I remember one man friend once listening to me expound on how I felt about things and then saying, "You're impossible. You have no comprehension of the basis of Western civilization." He was right, and I thank the Great Spirit for sparing me that.

The past years have been a time for many to realize that female energy must be allowed to develop and strengthen. I have been helped in my search to find my essence by others who are also seeking. Many beautiful sisters have helped me, by finding the beauty and ability to carry on, and by reflecting my own beauty and strength back to me. The Earth Mother has helped me, as I have finally been able to open myself to her. Spirits wishing to correct the imbalance between male and female energies have helped also.

A medicine man who is a friend of ours has also helped greatly. He is a young man of great gentleness, compassion, beauty and clarity. He feels deeply the female energy within himself, his sisters, and the Earth Mother. Because of his deep feelings he is able to express some things many of us know, but have had a hard time verbalizing. He has helped many sisters to feel and begin to express their own power.

Following are excerpts from some talks he has given on the subject of women.

"You need an enormous amount of acceptance to let a child follow the vision that they have received. You need an enormous amount of patience to see how long it takes to do that, how long it takes for them to grow. You need an enormous amount of understanding to be able to explain to them the things of the world and the things of their life. You need an enormous amount of perception in order to know how things come, how things go for them or for life, in order to tell those things to the children. Does this make sense? To raise children you need understanding,

acceptance, patience, and perception.  At some point in life it
has been decided that women will give birth.  Because of that they
have been given those qualities.  They have been given patience,
they have been given perception, they have been given understanding, they have been given acceptance.  Throughout history, for
whatever reason or other, those things have been turned down into
weaknesses.  Somebody who is accepting is a coward, somebody who
is patient is not aggressive enough.  Somebody who is perceptive
has become a witch in time.  Somebody who is understanding often
too has become a weak person.  You have to be very aware of these
things.  It's very powerfully imprinted inside of us.  This is
something that is absolutely essential in order for life to
happen.  This is something that is very powerful inside of each
and every woman.  Anybody that's got 5 ounces of common sense
and good eyes can see that very obviously even if the woman herself forgets it.

"Most men think they're on top of it.  They go around trying
to more or less control the world or saying what it's all about.
Most women out of habit of cultural history think that the men
know what it's all about.  But it's exactly the opposite.  For a
man to learn he has to have those qualities, most men are too
scared to have them.  So what a man has to do at one point or
another -- I'll make for this time a broad sweeping generalization
-- it's a must to be able to listen to a woman.  Whomever the
woman is, that doesn't matter so much.  But to really listen, to
really watch, to really accept that something has to be learned
if life wants to go on, from women.  Does this make sense?  It's
a very important thing.  It's very difficult for men to do that
because it goes completely opposite to all the culture that a man
has ever lived in.

"Somebody asked me about the future.  I say there will never
be peace on the face of the Earth as long as it's not women who
rule it.  There will never be peace on the face of the earth as
long as men have not accepted that they have to learn from women
in order to go back to themselves.  That's a pretty hard pill to
swallow for a lot of us.

"Relationships are really intricate between man and woman
because they are exactly opposite of what they really should be;
the man listening and the woman talking.  Most of the time.

"One thing I know is that man is going to find peace with
himself only with the help of women."

What Gabriel knows is what many sisters are now beginning to feel. This feeling is allowing us to gather the strength we have within ourselves. It is allowing us to see our own gentleness, love and patience. It is helping us to realize that we must not be ashamed of what we are, or of how we do things. This feeling is helping us to connect with the Earth Mother in a real and honest way. This helps with the healing. This helps to bring balance.

I know that you cannot really love the Earth Mother unless you also love and respect her human daughters. I am now strong enough to tell this to my sisters, and brothers, and to be patient if they do not understand right away. I know that I must increase my strength, my patience, my understanding, my acceptance and my perception so that I can most effectively serve the Great Spirit and the Earth Mother. I know that in the coming cleansing all those who survive -- whether their bodies are female or male -- must be open to the lessons I am learning now. I know that those of us who can open now must do so, so that we can be there to help others through the pain of freeing the sister within themselves. And I have a glimmering of the joy that will eventually come through this freeing.

# III. COMMUNITIES

## Rebirth of Medicine Societies

Many people today are looking for ways to restore the spiritual values and traditional ways of people. They know that Native Americans were a people who had a strong reverence for and belief in the Great Spirit.

As they look around in these times and see the continuous deterioration of this system, they are looking for stronger values. They see that the way the white man's Sunday religion works is that people go to church on Sunday and then they steal and cheat each other all the rest of the week. They see a nation that claims to be Christian and yet plunders Native lands and continues to hold back justice from many people.

Native prophecies predicted this time thousands of years ago. The time will come, the ancient teachings say, when the sons and daughters of our oppressors will return to us and say, "Teach us so that we might survive; for we have almost ruined the Earth now." Many modern people are now examining the values of the old ones, the values that were life-affirming. These people search the old ways asking themselves, "What were the ideals of old that kept Natives strong and true in their hearts?"

One answer is that medicine people and medicine societies were the center of a tribe. Before the crop was planted proper prayers and medicine for success were made, prayers and ceremonies of thanksgiving were done. In every major undertaking of the tribe, the medicine was first consulted. The consideration was always, is this act in harmony with Creation? Is it in harmony with life? Is it in harmony with the sacred journey we are on?

To get back to the old values, people must learn to live together in strong tribal groups which are interdependent with each other. It is not simply a matter of copying the outward forms practiced centuries ago. It is not a matter of rejecting technological developments or social structures. To re-establish decent values people need to learn love and harmony for each other and for the Earth. They must listen to their own medicine, to the voice within, the voice which is in harmony with life. They must learn all they can, and then let go of it all, to learn NEW ways of relating to our Earth Mother, new ways of relating to each other, new ways of responding to the changing needs of the Earth. They have to learn that they can't lean on the past, but must allow the Earth Mother and the race called humanity to continue their paths of destiny. They must release themselves from the idea that all will be as it once was. Life continues to move forward. In these conditions, medicine societies will become alive again and they will allow the peaceful, gentle forces to work at establishing true harmony on our Earth Mother.

# History of the Bear Tribe

People who are drawn to medicine societies and communities are often motivated by wanting to be part of something
larger than themselves.  In coming to such an alternative,
they find they have chosen a way that will sometimes be painful, sometimes challenging, sometimes exhilerating, and always
growth producing.  They can no longer hide from their old
attitudes, wounds, limitations and fears.  They can no longer
pursue "personal freedom" as though nobody else existed.  In
community they must learn the meaning of responsibility to
themselves, to Spirit, to the Earth, and the others with whom
they share their lives.  The following is Wabun's account of
her experience in opening to the Tribe, during her first four
years of community, with some updates as to the Tribe's
structure in 1986.

The Bear Tribe is This One's vehicle for learning how to
work, and how to believe.  The Bear Tribe is a modern day
medicine society composed of Indian and non-Indian people.  We
have been brought together by the medicine and the vision of
Sun Bear, a medicine man of Chippewa heritage, and by our own
visions.  Sun Bear believes, because of his visions and dreams,
that people must learn again how to be in harmony with each
other and the Earth Mother.

As of 1986 the Bear Tribe consists of more than 20 people
who live and work together on Vision Mountain or at our Circle
Center in Spokane, and of 250 apprentices who work with us from
their homes all around the world.  We have been together for
varying lengths of time, from 8 months to 21 years.  During
these years many other people have come to the Tribe and left,
either at our request, or because they felt we asked too much of
them, or because their path was elsewhere.  We have few laws
that people pledge themselves to when they take their oath to
the Tribe.  We promise to try to build a relationship of true
love, and responsibility to our brothers and sisters, and to
abstain from the use of drugs.  We also commit ourselves to a
goal of non-possessiveness and gentleness.  We give a portion
of our resources to the Tribe, and in return, the Tribe assumes
responsibility for many of our needs: physical, mental, emotional and spiritual.

Our aim is to be in harmony with ourselves, with each other, with the Earth Mother, and with the will of the Great Spririt.

To accomplish our aims we must first learn to be in harmony with ourselves and each other. To do this we live and work together. Learning to live and work with a group of people is not as easy as it may sound. All of us now in the Tribe came to it tainted by the dominant society which teaches competitiveness and possessiveness. It teaches us that we must be number one, no matter what the cost to those who are around us, to those we profess to love. It teaches us that our "personal freedom" is paramount. It teaches us that love, trust, and responsibility are commodities to be sold to the highest bidder. It teaches us to be insecure, fearful and cynical. It teaches us that the law is there to oppress people who are inherently bad.

To live in harmony with ourselves and with a group of people we must constantly work to un-learn all of the things the dominant society has taught us. We must work to learn to cooperate instead of compete, to share instead of possess. We must learn that we are one unique and important part of the whole, but not the only one. We learn to surrender "personal freedom"--doing our own thing--when our own thing will be destructive to the Society. We must learn that love, trust and responsibility are real feelings that grow with time, with work shared, and respect earned. We work to learn to be secure from within, knowing that we are a part of the Earth Mother, and of a Medicine we all respect and cherish. We learn to trust our medicine, so we have no need of fear. We learn to always look at the wonders of the Earth Mother and each other with fresh and open eyes, so there is no room for cynicism.

We learn to see our laws as something we must measure up to in our own hearts, not as things that oppress us. We strive to see that to build a true medicine society, our words and actions must always be measured by how they will affect the Earth Mother, the Great Spirit's will, the Society, and our brothers and sisters. We learn to listen to the council of our brothers and sisters, and to the consensus of our council circle. We learn to trust that our circle, and the others in it, can sometimes see truths about ourselves that we don't want to see.

To put all of this into practice in our daily lives with each other we must learn to be happy, no matter what we are doing. We must learn to see that all work -- seeking medicine, doing dishes, digging cesspools, building houses, writing articles, answering letters, drawing pictures, doing craft work, teaching children, growing gardens -- is a way of developing our selves, and our strength as a circle. We must learn that different people have different gifts, and different levels of energy, and that we are not being "exploited" if, at some times, we are doing more outward work that the others in the circle. We must learn to share our gifts, rather than hoarding them, and to be happy if some other one excels at something we previously had done "best". We must learn to take responsibility, and then to give it away when another is ready to have it. We must learn to be proud of our accomplishments, yet humble in knowing that everything that allows us to accomplish is a gift from the Great Spirit.

To live in harmony we must practice the age-old virtues of charity, humility, love, patience and compassion for others and ourselves. This is a big order to fill, considering the backgrounds most of us come from. Twentieth century survival and "success" do little to support such virtues as compassion, or letting go of anything without first acquiring a replacement for it.

One key to letting go is trust, most often trust that a decision to let go will bring about higher good. The caution we need to exercise here is not to confuse "higher good" with personal wishes, or with our preconceived notions of the outcome. If this confusion exists, the act of "letting go" can become a manipulation -- just the opposite of letting go. Most of us still fear the sense of loss we expect to feel if we let go of something or someone. How will we re-fill the void left within us? Will we become unimportant and unfulfilled? The things we have to let go of are difficult -- fear, hiding in our "privacy", being a particular kind of person, old habits and attitudes, and our expectation that we can make these changes quickly and completely simply by wanting to. This process requires compassion, a skill we each have to learn for ourselves as well as others.

While striving to be in harmony with each other, we must also learn to be in harmony with our common Earth Mother and all of her other children. This too, takes work, practice and patience. The society that we have come from teaches that nature is a fearful thing, something to be harnessed and controlled by man. It also teaches that mankind is supreme, and has rightful dominion over the four-leggeds, the people of the air, and the people of the water.

Consequently most of us have some fear of the Earth Mother and her creatures. It takes time to become as at ease with the sounds of the country as we are with those of the city. It takes work to realize that the climatic changes on the Earth are necessary for her development, and not something to curse when they foil our plans. We must learn to enjoy the sounds of the many winds, the roar of the thunder beings, the clash of lightning bolts. We must learn to see a snowstorm as a thing of beauty, not an inconvenience. We must learn to fall on ice, and slide in mud, and trust the Earth Mother to catch us.

Especially in this time of earth changes, we must trust that the sudden floods, the unexpected tornadoes, the droughts, the earthquakes are all necessary happenings that will return the Earth Mother to a state in which she can bloom again cleansed of the poisons with which man has polluted her.

We strive to learn love and respect for our little brothers and sisters who fly in the air, swim in the water, walk on four legs, and grow on the Earth. We learn, through observation, that they too have a place on our Mother, and functions they must perform for her. We learn that no creature is a pest, although some are destined to bring pestilence to those two-leggeds who have no respect for our Mother. We learn from these little ones, for often they have knowledge or instincts that we lack. We can learn what berries are good to eat, and which are poisonous by watching whether our little brothers eat them. We can be forewarned of floods, storms, even earthquakes if we have learned to be in harmony with the little brothers.

We learn that killing for anything other than necessity is wrong. We always pray and offer smoke before taking the life of our little brothers. In our prayer we tell our brother that we need his flesh to feed our own, that we realize our flesh, too, will become food for the Mother and her creatures, and we pray for his spirit to quickly go to our common Father. We always try to use every part of the brother we have killed.

We learn to extend the same respect to those in the plant kingdom. We never pick the wild plants without leaving an offering of kinnickinnik, and telling them why we need them, and how they will help us. We never pick all of the plants growing in one area, for we realize that they must continue to grow and perform the work for which they were designed.

We learn to always offer prayers, and, sometimes, ceremonies, before using a part of the Mother to grow those plants we need to eat.  We offer the seeds to the Earth Mother, and ask her blessing so they may be fruitful.  We also offer prayers to the seeds, asking them to grow, and telling them of our need for them.  When we harvest any of our brothers in the plant kingdom we offer prayers of thanksgiving to them, and to the Earth Mother who has helped them to grow.

By learning respect for, and harmony with ourselves, each other, and the Earth Mother, we prepare ourselves to become instruments of the Great Spirit's will; to become medicine people of and for this time. Many times Sun Bear has told us that the mistake most people make when they want to learn medicine is that they just want to go right to the mountain, before they have learned to walk with any balance on the Earth Mother.

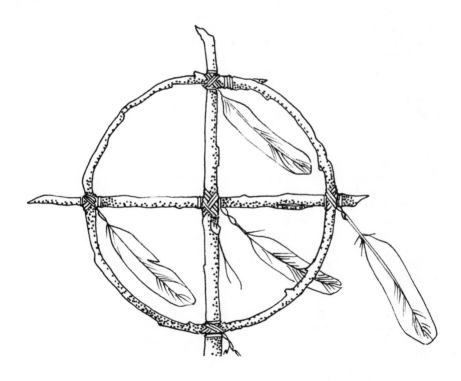

"What would the Great Spirit want with a bunch of ding-a-lings who want to shake the rattle, but who don't even know how to be together without bashing each other's heads in, and scattering beer cans all over the Earth Mother?" he asks.

In the years that our group has been together we have learned through work, suffering and struggles to be in better harmony with ourselves, and with each other. It is often a pleasure now to sit in our council circle. We are learning to love, to respect and to trust each other. On even the most difficult problems facing us, we no longer need to struggle so much with each other. The Medicine flows smoothly.

We have all come a lot closer to being in harmony with the Earth Mother, though we still have to work to do in that direction. As long as we still get mosquito bites, and have to scratch them, we are not in perfect harmony. But this, too, may come in time.

Daily, we are preparing ourselves to be instruments of the Great Spirit's will. We pray a lot, separately, and in a group, and our prayers, most often, are ones of thanksgiving. We have much to be thankful for. Often now, we sing together, and some of us dance old dances that have been given to us. Daily, we feel the medicine growing stronger in the circle, and in each of us who compose the circle. Each day we grow more receptive to the will of the Great Spirit, and to the voices of his helpers in the spirit world.

Before we were able to come to our degree of harmony, we, as individuals, and the Tribe, as an entity had to experience difficult times. The Tribe began in California in 1970 when Sun Bear took the message of his vision to several universities and colleges in the Sacramento area. The response was so great that he soon had 200 people living in 17 base camps that had been given to the Tribe to use. In the summer of 1971 Sun Bear's medicine directed him to carry his message across the land. He did, with good results.

Upon his return to California he found that some camps were now using psychedelics. Since people joining the Tribe vowed to abstain from drugs, he felt sad. He went to a mountaintop to seek an answer.

As Sun Bear tells the story in THE PATH OF POWER, "...I saw a golden eagle. It circled around me while I lay there on the hilltop.

"I made my prayers, and I asked for a sign, for a direction. The eagle came and went, and he looked into my soul; I almost wept. I was joyful to have a sign from the Great Spirit, but I didn't know what it really meant.

"I stayed there; I prayed harder and harder. Suddenly, a huge white cloud came over me; it was the only cloud in a sky of perfect blue. As I prayed, the cloud came closer and closer; then a small puff of it separated off from the rest. A whirlwind came, and spun the little puff of cloud away. Part of it dissolved, but a fluff of it joined back with the large cloud. I knew, then, what would happen with the Bear Tribe, and I felt better.

"The Great Spirit had given me a sign; the people who were with me were not quite ready to live by my vision. Some would go back to the cities. Some would grow, and eventually find their balance. And some, the vision told me, would only split off from the Bear Tribe for a while; they were the little puff of cloud, and they would return. The large cloud, the Bear Tribe itself, would then blossom once again. I felt this in my heart."

Sun Bear then told people that he was leaving, as he could not compromise his medicine. He invited those who wanted to follow his medicine to come with him. Some did. Others stayed, mouthing his ideals and hoping he'd change his mind. Eventually these camps broke apart.

Over the next few years Sun Bear, Wabun, Nimimosha and some others worked to build a solid foundation for the Tribe. We moved back onto the land, this time in Oregon. In 1975, because of the direction of the medicine, we moved to Washington.

Yarrow, the first child born into the Tribe, with Nimimosha.

page 61

The Tribe now has 60 acres outside of Spokane. We have a large house, a cabin, a root cellar, tipis, storage sheds and animals.

We also have the Circle Center in town, where the outreach activities of the Tribe are administered. All our business functions take place there, including our bookstore, the planning for Medicine Wheel Gatherings (which we put on 3 or 4 times a year, drawing up to 1000 people to each), for speaking and the apprentice program, for our magazine Wildfire, for Bear Tribe Publishing, for fundraising and for self-help projects.

# Some Things We've Learned

A community is a spiritual entity.  It is a being with a
birth, life, and death, reason, emotion, perception, the ability
to grow and reproduce.  It exists as such because the spiritual
energy of individuals is channelled into it, merging with the
energy of the spirits guiding it, creating its life force.

Love is the force that holds things together. Among people,
it gives birth to families, communities, and nations. Without
love, the harmonious energy of mutual enrichment is replaced
with a perverted, choatic energy of divisiveness. We can see
this process happening all around us.

Perhaps it is necessary to explain what is meant by "Love",
since we seem to have lost this understanding. It is not sex,
although physical touching may be involved. It is not romance
or sentimental attachment.  It is the force of Nature, by which
all things can live together in harmonious abundance.  It is
the force of Creation, through which we gain our existence.  It
is the energy of positive mutual interest, which comes from the
sharing of purpose.

For a community to survive, it is important to maintain a
loving relationship among its members.  We must always remember that we're here together for our mutual benefit.  If we
allow possessiveness or negativity to be expressed in our in-
terpersonal relationships, or in our work, we create an energy
field which weakens us.  Neither should we deny our negative
feelings, as they will then tend to come out in subtle ways.
In cooperation and positivity we create a healthy atmosphere
in which we can bring out and get rid of these divisive traits.
This is a function of a healthy community.

Because we live so closely in our community/medicine society, we have had to create healthy ways to prevent conflict,
and to resolve conflict when it occurs.  We agree that we do
not wish to live with conflict as a daily reality with people
we love, and so we ask a great deal of ourselves and each other.
We ask each person to set aside his/her own sense of safety,
and, using both honesty and compassion, resolve the conflict as

soon as possible.  We do not want our personal energies tied up
in frustration, resentment, confusion, or anything negative.
By resolving these feelings, our energy is then free to use for
the life-affirming purposes for which we're together.

During the day we make medicine to strengthen our love as
a community.  Before each meal we join hands and give thanks
for our nourishment and for our sharing as brothers and sisters.
In the evening we sometimes form a circle to make prayers and
re-assert our togetherness.  We share the pipe and sweat ceremony each week, and join together to celebrate the full moon,
the equinoxes and solstices.

It is also important to maintain a loving relationship with
nature and our fellow beings.  The trees, rocks, animals, sky
soil and other beings need to share their love with us, and we
need to love them.  When we refuse, they are sad.  The balanced
energy flow is upset.  Divisiveness replaces harmony, and the
Earth Mother becomes ill.  An example of this divisiveness is
found in the concepts of property ownership and trespassing.
Because property ownership is seen as a right, many property
owners also assume the "right" to abuse "their" land, and keep
other people away. This kind of possessive ownership is not in
harmony, or in loving relationship with people or nature, and
the result is most often disfiguring to the Earth, and dispirit-
ing to other beings.  If we break our bond with the Earth, we
can easily be thrown off when this illness is discharged.  When
the uniting energy of love is maintained, we can all share in
nature's abundance.

Love of the Spirit is necessary to continue our mutually
beneficial relationship with those spiritual beings who give us
help.  During our ceremonies we call together the spirits of
the four winds, the plant, animal and mineral kingdoms, asking
for their guidance and help.  We do this in a loving atmosphere,
with an attitude of respect.  By losing this reverent attitude
for the spiritual beings, for the Spirit itself, modern people
have forfeited this beneficial relationship.  They are divided
without and within.  Relinquish the Spirit, relinquish your
heart and the mind and body fight for control.  Love of the
Spirit gives us internal strength, guiding us in the quest
to achieve higher spiritual awareness.

COMMON VISION

Members must be in agreement on the purpose of a community,
its goals, methods, and priorities.  This common vision is nec-

essary so that our energy is not dispersed in conflicting directions, but channeled toward a specific goal. The democratic
system fails on this point. Forty-nine percent of the people
can be in disagreement, thus undermining the effectiveness of
the group. There should be a forum whereby each person has
the chance to express his or her feelings and ideas.

For us, this forum is our council circle. It is our way
of governing ourselves on a daily basis, and for dealing with
issues and decisions that must be made. When we have an issue
that needs clarification or a decision that affects us all, or
any matter we need to discuss, we have Council. We usually
meet once a week, but if our need changes, we may have more or
fewer meetings of Council. In this Council, we bring our best
selves, and observe a tacit agreement to listen well as each
person speaks, not interrupting for any reason. In the early
days, we often used a talking stick that the speaker held in
his or her hand as a reminder to stay on subject, to speak the
truth, to avoid filibustering, and to remind others that it is
time for them to listen. We no longer need to use the talking
stick. We have developed the ability to employ these skills
without the stick.

In Council, everyone is given the opportunity to speak,
though we discourage ourselves from becoming windbags. Everyone
participates by making a contribution in the decision-making
process. We no longer need it to be a lengthy process. We talk
until we reach consensus. We remember that it is the medicine
that guides us, not our individual throughts or desires.

Being able to receive the guidance of the Medicine takes a
great amount of trust, especially when we are first learning.
Trust is the first quality one must attain in living the life
of the Spirit, the first stepping-stone on the Pathway of Peace.
We must come to the realization that we always get what we need.
If we are not experiencing joyful success, we are being sent a
lesson. This happens by way of the balancing of natural forces.
The energy which we put out is balanced by that which we receive.
Nobody gets ahead of the game. There is no free lunch. Once we
have this understanding, we can begin to see what the lessons
are, and accept our guidance.

Sometimes it is difficult to hold onto our trust. In painful times we fall in despair, striking out at whatever is closest
to us. When we begin to come back up, trust is right there, the
first thing we have to learn, and accept.

Today many people still have faith in the medicine of the modern world, but many are beginning to lose it. That world no longer provides the needs of its subjects, nor guides them in a positive manner. It is important to realize that when we lose our trust in that society we don't have to lose the ability to have trust in anything. The true medicine is waiting to help us whenever we seek it.

## KEEPING ORDER

One thing we can observe quite obviously when watching the workings of nature is that she is orderly. Everything has a place and a purpose. There is no waste, nothing is ever lost. By maintaining this order the greater whole, the Earth Mother, can function in a healthy manner, providing the needs for all of her subjects. If the order is broken, the balance is upset, and the needs are no longer met.

This principle can be practically applied within the community. The land, animals, buildings, equipment, tools, etc. have been placed here under our care and for our benefit. Fire hazards should be removed, animals should be fed and watered regularly, buildings maintained, work areas kept neat and convenient, tools put away.

The energy invested in establishing and keeping order is well worthwhile, as it makes for happier people and more efficient work of better quality. When we make a chair, cook a meal, or write an article, we are creating order from disorder. This can be more easily done in an organized environment, as it takes more energy to overcome the vibrations of chaotic surroundings. For brothers and sisters to live together harmoniously we should have a well-kept home. This makes for happier people in a stronger community.

Things should also be kept in order out of respect for the spirits of the things themselves. The kitchen should be bright and happy, not cluttered with messes and gloom. No self-respecting hammer wants to lie outside in the rain. If we truly care for it, we will place it in its proper resting place with a word of thanks. The spirit of the water hole doesn't mind our getting in to cool off, if we act with respect, but she certainly doesn't want all that poisonous soap in her home. One should walk carefully among chickens, thanking them for their eggs and their energy.

Respect for one another is one of our greatest needs when

living close together.  When someone fails to pick up after themselves or do their share of the chores, it's a drain on someone
else.  Someone who is sloppy in appearance and actions detracts
from the good feelings of others.  Balance must be maintained
among those who don't care about neatness and those who do most
of the cleaning up.

Many communities respond to this situation by setting up
schedules and delegating responsibility, but we find that this
interferes with the working of the Medicine.  Each person must
learn to see what needs to be done to balance out the load.
Each person must participate by choice.  It is Sun Bear's belief
that the least governed are the best governed.  This is an ideal
we have all had to learn.  This ideal will not be learned through
criticism or scheduling, but through positive support, and
through learning to see the larger picture of our relationship
with each other.  We have agreed on a high standard of neatness
and quality workmanship, and we keep drawing our attention to
this agreement.  Learning to live with this agreement is a process, not an event.  With plenty of tolerance, patience and
positivity, we are learning to achieve what we want.

When we move into a communal living situation we become
painfully aware of our various problems left over from living in
the modern world.  These problems keep us from living harmoniously, and block our higher levels of awareness.  There are many
different theories about how to deal with these problems, and
better live together, and so there are many doctrines concerning
organization, communication, cooperation, health, etc.  Different communities are based on different theories, which serve to
focus attention on a certain area of our improvement.  Eventually,
though, too rigid systems of thought will block individual expression and community growth.

We have frequently seen and felt the contradiction present
in so many people, that while "lost" without an authority above
us, or a visible chain of command, we feel the impulse to rebel
against any form of heirarchy.  Because of the culture and society that has formed us, we seldom know how to appropriately
relate to authority, either in responding to it, or in taking it
ourselves.

It has taken the exercise of patience to answer new visitors who first complain about our "disorganization", then complain
when we do display organization.  They wanted to know how they
could fit in, but they didn't really want to be told.  Had they
been able to take note of the real authority -- the order of
Creation -- they may have seen the need to be clean, to wash the

dishes and sweep the floor, before seeking the special experiences that come when a person is ready. As Sun Bear puts it, "How are you going to go to the mountain to meet the Creator if you can't get your dishes washed?"

We find it important to get along with the minimum of rules. People who are unwilling to do their fair share of the ordinary work cannot be allowed to stay. Daily chores, like washing dishes and farm maintenance, should be shared in some way that is equal, and it is each one's responsibility to make sure he or she does his or her own share. Some of us here have grown to have particular skills and knowledge for which the Tribe has great need -- skills such as writing, typesetting, computer programming, administration -- and are called upon at times, to put most of their energy into these areas. These same people make sure that they do take part in the daily sharing of work whenever they can, so they don't forget the basics of their own home/community. For the most part, they have given most generously of their energies at the daily level.

We agree on priorities, and people are encouraged to do whatever is most important to them, or whatever is most in harmony with who they are. From time to time, we all do something we don't enjoy because there is a need for it, but we try to allow each person to do the work they enjoy most, where positive spirit and pleasure in work can produce a positive and supportive environment.


## DISCIPLINE

One quality we must have if we are to accomplish our goals, both personally and communally, is discipline. This may sound bad at first, because "discipline" has negative connotations. Dsicipline often has been forced upon us and has been unfair or irrational. In our reaction to this, many of us shun all concepts of discipline.

Discipline is the ability to set certain limitations, and stick to them. It can be used to overcome forces which may attempt to sidetrack us from our chosen path. When we have a goal, we plan ahead how to work toward materializing it. While carrying out the plan, we may meet up with new desires or ideas which make us think that some other activity is better. Discipline enables us to resist being sidetracked, and keep on with our work.

When some members of a group lack self-discipline, hence

responsibility, it is important for others to assert enough leadership to keep the group on track.  They supply the discipline for the group, to insure that projects are finished, standards met, guidelines adhered to, and lessons learned.

## RESPONSIBILITY

What we are striving for is to get free of planned existence, of leader-follower relationships.  To do this, we must learn to take responsibility.  Individuals must become clear-minded enough to be able to see what needs to be done, and to act on it in a positive way.  We are each responsible for our own survival and well-being.  If an individual cannot handle responsibility, he or she makes it necessary for someone or something else to lead them.  The more we need to be led, the less we can hear the voices of our guidance or reach the higher levels of our creative expression.  Without responsibility, one cannot attain medicine power.

At the same time, we need to turn loose our desires and expectations of others.  If we try to assert our will too much over others, or over occurrences, the medicine cannot work. Other people cannot learn to hear the inner voices, and our own lessons cannot be received.  We should be able to put our full attention into every task without worrying if something else is being done right (or our way).  Then we can feel the approval of the Great Spirit in each of our accomplishments. The result of assuming responsibility and dropping expectations is freedom -- not having to be led, nor to lead others.  When we have achieved this, we will have achieved self-reliance, and we will be able to live together in harmony.

## PATIENCE

It is important to remember that it takes time to change. This is especially true for people who are coming to an alternative way of being.  They need to adjust not only to new ways of thinking, acting and perceiving, but to a whole different speed.  It is important for all involved to give the process time to work.  Putting oneself or others down for their shortcomings is one of the biggest things blocking improvement. This is part of learning compassion for ourselves and others. A good healer would avoid adding trauma to a wound.  In the same way, demanding rapid change from a person often makes them cling more tightly to their old ways of being.  In such situations patience allows time for healing and for change.

page 69

By placing ourselves in a healthier environment, we ask to be guided toward health. We receive cleansing and lessons when we need them. If we try to force the changes before we're ready, we upset the balance, creating negativity which must itself be overcome. Make sure that the change is in a positive direction, ask for help when it is needed, and wait for the process to work. Be guided not by concepts, but by the Spirit.

While you're waiting for yourself and others to change, develop your sense of humor. Laughter is always good medicine.

Be gentle to yourself and to others. Remember how gentle the Earth Mother is to all of us.

*Other Folks*

This chapter is a note of honor from us to others who are
striving to serve the Great Spirit, and our Earth Mother.   We
have heard about a lot of folks who are doing this, and we are
honored to know some of them personally.  We pray for all those
we know, and those we've yet to encounter.  It is so important
to support the efforts of others on the same path on all of the
levels that we can.  Even if others walk with a different step,
we support them for being on the good path.

### THE RAINBOW CLAN

Two friends who taught us a special way to pray and to
spread the light are Joyce Rainbow  and Richard Rainbow.   He
passed into the spirit world in 1985.  They made their living
selling turquoise and silver jewelry made by their clan.

"The whole clan believes in the old, traditional way," said
Richard.  "We are brothers to all living things.  Everything is
as important as we are, and we are as important as everything.
We feel that the Grandfather Spirit guides our hands as we work
so that we put the right stone with the right piece of silver
to bring the maximum good or healing to the person who wears one
of our pieces of jewelry."

The oldest members of the clan, Richard and his brother,
Ted Bear, Sr., were both raised on the Miwuk tribal allotment
in Tuolumne City, California.  One hundred of the tribe's 1800
members now live on this 300 acre allotment.  Their mother,
almost a full-blood, was a member of the first tribal council
back in 1935.  Their father was Greek.

"When we were growing up on the reservation we were considered the Greeks.  When we went into town we were considered
the Indians.  It was good because it was a growing situation.
While we were growing up we were tutored by an old Miwuk medicine man who taught about herbs and about mentally making medicine.  Our silverwork, too, started when we were kids.  We
used to tap coins into conchos or rings and then give the stuff
away or sell it for a quarter."

Rainbow went to the Sherman Indian Institute in Riverside, then into the Navy, then to work for the Greek side of the family where he remained for 10 years learning about business and the white world. He went into business for himself, and continued until he got sick for eight months and lost everything. He made application for reinstatement as a tribal member, asked for an assignment and was given 15 acres. When he, Joyce and their four children went to the reservation, Ted Bear, Sr. led him back into silversmithing. He also taught the craft to his own wife, Ramona, to their children and grandchild. The clan all works together now in a shop they own, the Tepee, located in the Tuolumne City Plaza.

When Rainbow returned to the reservation, he also began to work for an Office of Economic Opportunity-funded alcoholism program there.

"It wasn't hard for me to relate to the problems," Richard said. "I'd been a heavy drinker for thirty years before I quit that. But when I'd been doing alcoholism counselling for about six months, I got frustrated with the structured program. I was going to quit because I felt that I was doing no good. I worked with a hundred people, and had one success. I started looking for the common denominator of why Indian people drank. The thing that stuck out was that Indian people lacked spiritual expression. Where this did occur, like where people were heavy into Christianity, the alcoholism rate was low. I wrote a proposal for a program that would give Indian people the expression they lacked, and it was funded. I started talking to different medicine men. The first one I met was Ray Stone, a Paiute who conducts sweats. He came to the reservation three times, and he set up a sweat lodge on my assignment. Then David Villasenor who does sandpainting came to demonstrate that. At the 1973 Acorn Festival they both came. Ray ran the sweat for four days and better than 300 people were involved. David gave two sandpainting sessions, and 600 people were there. And, for the first time, there was no drunken-ness at the Festival, which would seem to show that the program is on the right track."

During his work with this program, the name Rainbow was given to Richard by a medicine man who told him his medicine comes from the Rainbow. He sees a real connection between his medicine work and his clan's work on silversmithing.

"To make our jewelry authentic, we've mixed our medicine work with our silversmithing. When we work we ask that our hands be guided to make jewelry that will bring the wearer the happiness and harmony they seek, and we ask that every piece of jewelry will go to the right person."

As Richard and Joyce travelled around the country to shows, they looked for people their medicine told them were ready to open to what they had to teach, and they taught them what they were capable of learning. Basically, they taught people their special way of praying and connecting themselves to the universe. They used the image of the rainbow, and the light in their prayers. They sometimes invited people to their home, to sweat with them. Joyce Rainbow continues with the work she and Richard began.

## SENECA WOLF CLAN LODGE

Another friend who has generously shared her medicine with us is Twylah Hurd Nitsch, Wolf Clan Mother of the Seneca Nation. Yeh-weh-node, her Seneca name means "echo" or "the voice that rides on the wind".

Twylah is both a powerful and peaceful woman. She grew up steeped in the wisdom of the Seneca way. Moses Shongo, one of the great Seneca medicine people, was her grandfather. Before her birth, he had worried about who was to take over the teachings. When Twylah was born he had said that since she had both Native and white blood, she would be able to walk on two paths, to move from the Indian to the white. When she was two, she became very ill with whooping cough. When she was choking one night, Moses Shongo revived her with what we now call mouth to mouth resuscitation. After he told her mother, Blue Flower, "Now she will carry on my work, because my breath is her breath."

True to her grandfather's predictions, Twylah did live in two worlds. Following a childhood of instruction in the Seneca way, and an adolescence of learning both the way of the Native and the non-Native, Twylah married Robert Nitsch, a man of German descent. With their four children, they lived in Buffalo, New York until the polio epidemic of the 1950's. They moved back then to her family home and land on the Cattaraugus Reservation, to protect their family. They have lived there since. Robert Nitsch was a successful businessman in the area. Twylah worked for many years as a recreational therapist.

While Twylah never forgot the teachings of her grandfather, nor the responsibilities that they gave her, she was hesitant to discuss them with groups of people. One night Blue Flower saw Moses Shongo, her brother and grandmother standing at the foot of her bed. They told her that she had to tell Twylah that it was all right, that she must do the teaching and sharing she was thinking of doing. "She has got to do it," they told Blue Flower. "We have given this knowledge to her, and we are helping her."

Shortly after this experience, Twylah made a tobacco offering in a class that she was teaching, and it felt so right, that she opened herself to all of the teachings that were waiting to come through her. Since that time, many people have been opened and enriched by their contact with this understanding and gentle woman.

One of the first things Twylah's pupils learn are four questions that helped the Seneca people to walk always in harmony and balance. They are:

1. Are you happy doing what you are doing?

2. Is what you are doing adding to the confusion?

3. What are you doing to further peace and contentment?

4. How will you be remembered after you are gone -- in absence or in death?

These questions can help anyone to evaluate their actions in a way that can bring them into greater harmony with the Earth Mother, and all of their fellow beings. Phrased in a slightly different way they are a marvelous tool to teach children to take responsibility for their own actions and happiness.

Twylah stresses that to the Seneca, "Self-knowledge was the need, Self-understanding was the desire, Self-discipline was the way, and Self-realization was the goal."

In her book, 'ENTERING INTO THE SILENCE THE SENECA WAY', Twylah writes of how the Seneca learned of himself and nature.

"In the very beginning, the early Seneca was drawn close to Nature. Legends related the wonders of Nature and its effects upon all creatures and plants. It was not long before the ancestors of the Senecas sensed a Powerful Force all around them. Everyone saw the results of this Force; some were able to feel it; still others were able to receive impressions from it. They

page 74

believed it was in everything, everywhere, at all times, for time eternal. They called this Force the Great Mystery and vowed to learn all they could about it.

"Legends related that the Indian emerged from the deep and, as he evolved, he increased his awareness by being a student of Nature, recognizing Mother Earth as his caretaker and all creatures of the Great Mystery, his teachers. For this reason, he devoted his life to learning about the secrets that governed Nature. In this way, he began to understand his role in Nature's plan.

"Living within the peace and quiet of Nature taught the Indian self-control. He moved slowly, spoke softly, and was habitually silent. Controlled silence was acquired and signified perfect harmony in spirit, mind, body, and action. It was an earned virtue and revered as an honorable trait. To master this trait, the Indian recognized the need for functioning harmonious- ly in his own environment. His instruction began at an early age and was uniform among all the Indian Nations. There was no need to question the Indian "Way of Life" -- it was an accepted fact.

"Ancient Seneca instruction introduced a simple but efficient understanding of symbolism. Early routines of daily living re- volved around the number four, thus, "4" became a symbolic number and established traditions that held families and Nations to- gether. Its symbolism included the first four Creations, the four stages of learning, the four principles of development and the four guidelines toward attaining wisdom.

"Learning about oneself meant learning how to communicate. One cannot communicate with others unless there is a reasonable amount of self-knowledge, was the belief of the early Senecas.

"Communicating means understanding, Understanding leads toward peace of mind, Peace of mind leads toward happiness, Happiness is communicating."

"How well do we communicate?" was the question asked. "We learn to measure happiness by the depth of our self-awareness and recognize it by the peace and contentment we enjoy within our environment."

"Entering into the Silence" meant communing with Nature in Spirit, mind, and body. Nature's atmosphere radiated the Spiritual Essence of the Supreme Power and provided the path that led the early Seneca into the "Great Silence."

The legend of the First Messenger, tells of the encounter with the Spiritual Essence that was responsible for the practice of "Entering into the Silence."

"Two men and two women of great age, honored among their people for their wisdom, sat in the woodlands on the warm earth near a brooklet rippling under a canopy of leaves and branches. They had come to reminisce of their kindred experiences gleaned through their advancing years, when suddenly the heavens opened:

> "A GLORIOUS BEAM OF LIGHT,
> IN ALL ITS BRILLIANT SPLENDOR,
> GENTLY DRIFTED OVER THEM,
> SEEDING PEACE AND SOLEMNITY
> ON EVERYTHING IT TOUCHED."

They watched in wonderment, spellbound by its Sublime Magnificence. It filtered into their bodies, cleansing them, throughout, of all infirmities. Presently, they felt themselves being borne aloft to a place of Divine Ecstasy, where the "Secret of the Ages" was revealed telling them of things to be. They saw the "First Messenger of the Great Mystery", the Spiritual Hand with outstretched fingers and thumb. The message meant "It comes through". This was the first experience of "Entering into the Silence."

"Its symbolism imparts; as the thumb assists the four fingers in life, equality, unity and eternity, so does the Great Mystery assist all things in Creation. From that time on, the symbolic number "4" became an integral part of the Indian "Way of Life." Following the revelation, the wisdom of the four aged ones increased and people came from many nations to listen to their Spiritual counseling. From this Divine Experience the entire custom of sitting in Council evolved. It developed that the messengers of the Great Mystery wore many faces. They could be any manifestation in Nature, in creatures and in earthly forces."

Teaching others how to go into the silence, how to gently walk the pathway of peace is Twylah's lifework, as her grandfather knew it would be. Twylah has also revitalized the Wolf Clan Lodge, and begun the Seneca Indian Historical Society. Through her lecturing, teaching, and writing, Twylah is indeed the voice that rides on the wind. We are happy that she has worked with us in many ways, including being a sacred teacher at many of our Medicine Wheel Gatherings.

Whispering Leaf With Blue Jacket, whose vision appears in Section One, is a brother who has learned to live on Earth Mother in the most simple way. People who came to visit his camp found him and his two children living in wegiwas of simple, local materials. Their brothers and sisters in the plant and animal kingdoms provided their food. The Beauty of Earth Mother provided their entertainment, and brought them happiness. In the time since the first edition of this book Whispering Leaf's path has taken him elsewhere. Because of the historical relevance of his clan, we have still included this material.

The Goat Clan was organized to be a moder day warrior society based upon the old ways. Following is their Constitution:

PREAMBLE: The Goat Clan Warrior Society is a small campfire, kindled and nurtured within the hearts of brothers and sisters, which, above all else, seek to follow the original instructions of the Creation. It is a small family that exists within the larger universal family of mankind. It is a warrior society which seeks through prayer, self-discipline and simple living, to maintain a healthy, happy, and exemplary existence upon the earth mother. Toward this goal, it is guided by the following constitution, which was written, not to limit the actions or thoughts, nor to infringe upon basic human rights of people, but to help establish a common path toward self-awareness and discovery of the intimate and eternal link between man and the Great Universal Mystery of Creation.

1. MEMBERSHIP: Membership in the GCWS is offered to all brothers and sisters who are able to embrace the spirit of the Goat Clan and its constitution without undue qualification, and no restriction toward membership shall be placed upon any person because of age, race, or physical effect. All members agree to the following:

a. To abstain from the consumption of alcohol and/or the use of drugs.
b. To strive to be a true witness of life by sharing and receiving in a spirit of universal brotherhood without possessive attachment.

c.   To work and live in harmonious union with the forces of
Creation, and to exemplify the highest ideals of mind, heart
and spirit.
d.   To put the good of the Clan, the Tribe, and the Nation above
personal ambition, desire or gain, and to work unceasingly for
the renewal of the Sacred Hoop and the healing of our Earth
Mother.
e.   To walk in a sacred and balanced manner by following the
eight guides through daily life.  They are: 1) right ideals-
universal laws 2) right motive - love of God 3) right speech
4) right action through honesty and truth 5) right means of
livelihood 6) right effort through self-discipline 7) right
remembrance of the self 8) right realization - unity with God.

All those persons who are able to embrace the spirit of membership of the GCWS are then eligible for adoption into the clan
as a full family member.

2.   ADOPTION: Those wishing to be adopted into the goat clan
may call a special council through the Okema.  At this council,
each member shall speak for or against adoption, but adoption
shall only be through unanimous decision of all members.  Adoption as a full member in the GCWS is accomplished through a
sacred, traditional ceremony known as the making of our relatives.  During this ceremony, the brother or sister, if not in
possession of a natural spirit name, will receive one, and
thereafter is to be known through this name only, and in keeping with the Great Law of Peace, no question of origin is to
arise among clan members.

3.   PROPERTY:  Since we are of one universal family, and having
the same Earth Mother and Sky Father, we will act as true brothers and sisters and share that which has been given to us
from the Great Spirit through her children.  There will be one
cookfire and all will eat together around this fire, sharing
whatever food is available.  Each member will be given a wooden
bowl and spoon for their own continued use.  The Clan Mother
will be the keeper of common property and will distribute all
gifts of bedding, clothing and cloth material so that each
person shall have adequate clothing and bedding to be comfortable and warm during the cold moons.  Lodges should be shared
whenever possible, and the little ones should be invited to
visit all lodges so as to learn of their relationship within
the family.  The ownership of the lodges rests in the hands of
the women.  Horses, rifles, bows, knives, shields, medicine
bundles and clothing are to belong to an individual and not to
the clan.  The disposition of material gifts to the clan is to
be decided upon in general council.

4.  The GCWS maintains an open council lodge, and the fire is ever lit.  Any member with good cause may call the camp together in special council.  The business of the council will be preceded by the silent smoking of the clan pipe, the touching of which will signify that all are pledged to speak the truth.  The person then calling the council is given first opportunity to speak.  In council, all voices will be equal and all decisions affecting the existence of the camp will be based on unanimous decision of the clan members.  Visitors may attend council by invitation, or may call a council through the Okema or Clan Mother to discuss adoption.  The Okema will call general council.  In addition to the msi-kah-mi-qui, the Okema and Clan Mother will maintain an open lodge door for counsel, complaint, suggestion or discussion at all times.

5.  WORK:  Much of our original instructions have been forgotten through the loss of essential livelihood.  It is through the cultivation of crops that we relearn of the eternal link between man and the sun, moon, rain and soil.  It is through the gathering of nuts and berries, herbs and roots that we are made aware of the bounty spread upon our Earth Mother for our wise use by the Master of Life.  It is through the construction of our lodges that we learn the true meaning of shelter, and a respect for our earth home.  Because the necessities of food, clothing and shelter were meant as teachings and not as burdens, all should participate in camp work with willingness to learn how to care and provide for oneself, and to share that knowledge with others who seek to learn.  Work should not be divided by age or sex, but should be mutually shared energy for thanksgiving to the Master of Life who sustains us in our every need.  Let us share our knowledge, our skills and our gifts with each other so our work becomes joyous living.

6.  INTERACTION WITH DOMINANT SOCIETY:  Our Earth Mother is sick, and her children are responsible.  For this reason, we of the GCWS have severed ourselves from the day to day functions and dependencies of that society.  It is our purpose to re-establish the moral, spiritual and physical environment necessary in order to become instruments of the Great Spirit's will.  To this end, we see our work as being contained within the framework of a traditional peoples' village.  We do not seek employment for monetary wages, nor will we sell our knowledge, skills or time.  We do not maintain motor vehicles.  We seek the life of aboriginals and seek independence from U.S. Government aid in the forms of welfare, food stamps, medicaid, education or claims settlements.  We do not want our little ones to be educated by the dominant society.  It is our goal to become less dependent on trade goods and more aware of the ecosystem economy in which

we live.

7.   INTERACTION WITH EARTH MOTHER:  All warriors of the Goat Clan
must revere and respect the grasses and trees, the waters and
sands, the rocks and holy mountains.  We must revere and respect all things that live, and all things that do not live.
All creatures that walk or crawl, or swim or fly.  We must revere
and respect the sacred spirit that dwells in all things and
beyond all things.  With this understanding, we will construct
our lodges and shelters with beauty and lightness using the
grasses, reeds and cane indigenous to our land base.  Our lodges
will be quonset shaped wegiwas with frames of cedar saplings
and cane.  Consumption of food from glass or metal containers
that are not reusable should be a terminal practice.  Use of
petroleum products should be minimized to the maximum possible
cutback.  We must always remember that the Master of Life is the
only real owner of the land, and that we are simply caretakers
for the unborn generations that will follow us.  The land is
a sacred trust from Moneto to his children and we do not sell,
buy or rent our Earth Mother or the gifts which grow upon her
for the benefit of all creation.


## OTHER PEOPLE, CLANS AND CAMPS

     In Nevada are two traditional camps we know about.  One
was founded by Rolling Thunder, the well-known Cherokee medicine man, and his late wife, Spotted Fawn, a Shoshone.  The
other is Frank Thunder's, and consists of a camp, and a unique
museum.  In California is Grandfather Csimu's Red Wind Foundation.  These are all traditional camps, with similarities to
the Bear Tribe and to the camp of Whispering Leaf.

     We have many friends who live in cities, but often visit
their home places to recharge themselves with the traditional
ways.  These folks are in the cities to teach others of the
way of harmony.  Lee Piper, the Bird Clan Mother of the Overhill
Band of Cherokees lives in Seattle and works as minority affairs
director of a college there.  She actively helps the Native people in the Seattle area, and in her home in the South. Archie
Fire, Lame Deer's son, lives outside of Los Angeles and works
with people when they are in need of help and medicine.  Ernie
Peters is also active helping people there, particularly through
the sweat lodge.

     Crow Dog is a Sioux medicine man who has helped many in the
American Indian Movement to return to tradition.  He has suffered
great harassment from the dominant society because of his work,

yet he remains steadfast in the faith. The late Mad Bear was an Iroquois medicine person who has also studied Native religions in many other parts of the world. Osapana Powhatan is a medicine man now living in New Mexico. He has served his people in all the ways he can for many years now.

Gabriel, spoken of in Section Two, is a medicine man who helps people to see more clearly themselves and their relation to the universe. Kwi-tsi-tsa-las is a Kwakiutl medicine woman who runs the Greenvale Herbal College in Canada. Oh Shinnah Fastwolf is an Apache woman who takes the message of the Earth Mother, and her cleansing, to many people via her talks and music.

Adolf and Beverly Hungry Wolf have shared the traditional Blackfoot message with many people through their series of GOOD MEDICINE books.

There are many teachers, both Native and non-Native, who have participated in our Medicine Wheel Gatherings. All of them have shared generously with those attending the Gatherings. The following list honors only some of the teachers who have worked with us. Our thanks go to all of the teachers.

-Grey Antelope is a Tewa Pueblo medicine man, a healer, chanter and dancer. He has come to the Gatherings with his Humbios Clan Dancers, an inter-racial group. They have performed the sacred Buffalo, Eagle, Bow and Corn dances.

-Bear Heart is a Muskogee Indian who trained under two tribal elders and is now a tribal medicine chief. He has Sundanced with both the Northern and Southern Cheyenne people, and is a respected leader in the Native American church.

-Dr. Frans Bakker is the Director of the Radiant Life Clinic in California. He is a specialist on rejuvenation health techniques and teacher of radical spiritual healing.

-John Bradshaw of Houston is an educator, theologian and counselor.

-Dr. Paul Brenner is the author of LIFE IS A SHARED CREATION, and other books. He is the Health Director for the Center for the Healing Arts, a lecturer, holistic teacher and physician.

-Tom Brown, Jr. is author of THE TRACKER, THE SEARCH, and THE FIELD GUIDE TO WILDERNESS SURVIVAL. He is one of the foremost survival instructors and trackers in the world.

-Page Bryant, Sun Bear's first apprentice, is a psychic, radio personality, teacher and lecturer who teaches the integration of the psychic and intuitive self. She is the author of several books including THE EARTH CHANGES SURVIVAL HANDBOOK.

-Red Cloud is a Cree teacher who studied Indian medicine with his grandmother and with Nauskeechask, a noted shaman. He is the former President of the Metis Association of Alberta, Canada.

-Norma Cordell (Eagle Morning Star) is the Director of the Eugene (Oregon) Center of the Healing Arts. She is a healer and spiritualist trained by a Nez Perce shaman. She is the author of EARTH DANCE.

-Prem Das is the Director of the Mishakai Center for the Study of Shamanism, in Northern California. He has studied with the Huichol shaman Don Jose Matsuwa, and is the author of THE SINGING EARTH.

-Brooke Medicine Eagle is the great-great grandniece of Chief Joseph, the Nez Perce holy man and leader. She is trained both in the traditions of her people, and in Western psychology and body work. She lectures throughout the world.

-J.C. Eaglesmith is a Creek/Shawnee Indian who is a pipeholder in the Straight Pipe Society. He conducts seminars about the sacred pipe and the healing sweat.

-Evelyn Eaton (Mahad'yuni), who died in 1983, was a pipe woman, healer and teacher. She was a tribal grandmother to the Bear Tribe. She was the author of I SEND A VOICE, SNOWY EARTH COMES GLIDING, THE SHAMAN AND THE MEDICINE WHEEL and twenty other books.

-Wallace Black Elk is a Lakota holy man who has been trained since childhood in the traditional and sacred knowledge of the Earth people. Black Elk has been chosen by the Spirit to be a spiritual guide for all of the people. He is the grandson of the famed Lakota holy man Black Elk, whose vision was shared with the world in BLACK ELK SPEAKS.

-Oh Shinnah Fastwolf is a Scottish, Apache and Mohawk eclectic person whose teachings come from various ancient traditions. Oh Shinnah dedicates her work to the healing of Mother Earth.

-Steven Foster and Meredith Little are the founders and former co-directors of Rites of Passage, a teaching organization which guides people along the medicine path. They are now directing the School of Lost Borders in the Owens Valley of California. They co-authored THE BOOK OF THE VISION QUEST — PERSONAL TRANSFORMATION IN THE WILDERNESS.

-Adele Getty is co-director, with Sunwater, of Medicine Ways, a teaching organization in Petaluma, California. She is a wilderness leader, and a ritual consultant who works with re-connecting people with the earth through self-generated ritual.

-Rosemary Gladstar is the founder and director of the California School of Herbal Studies. She is an herbalist, a teacher, and an organizer of holistic health seminars.

-Joan Halifax is the Director of the Ojai Foundation in Ojai, California. She is the author of SHAMAN: THE WOUNDED HEALER, and SHAMANIC VOICES.

-Hawk Little John is a teacher and healer of Cherokee descent. He lectures to many people about the traditional Native ways of healing. He is also a farmer.

-Dr. Elisabeth Kubler-Ross is the Director of Shanti Nilaya in Escondido, California, a world renowned teacher and lecturer, and a founding member of the American Holistic Medical Association. She is the author of seven books including ON DEATH AND DYING and LIVING WITH DEATH AND DYING.

-Winona LaDuke, Sun Bear's daughter, is an internationally-known anti-nuclear activist, and the former director of the Circle of Life Survival School on the White Earth Reservation in Minnesota.

-Barry McWaters, Ph.D., is the co-director of the Institute for the Study of Conscious Evolution and editor of "Humanistic Perspectives". He is also the author of several books, including CONSCIOUS EVOLUTION — PERSONAL AND PLANETARY TRANSFORMATION, and THE COUPLE'S JOURNEY (with Susan Campbell).

-Manitonquat (Medicine Story) is a Keeper of the Lore of the Wampanoag people, director of "Another Place" in New Hampshire, founder of the Mettanokit community, and author of RETURN TO CREATION.

-Frank Mola is the founder and director of Alpha Logics in Bristol, Connecticut, a psychic, teacher and healer, and a successful businessman.

-Norma Meyers is a well-known herbalist and healer of Mohawk descent. She is the Director of the Tsonqua Herbal Center in British Columbia, Canada.

-Don Perrote is an Earth Man of Pottawatomi descent who presents the sacred teachings as being alive and well and relevant to today's needs. He works with the sacred pipe and the sweatlodge.

Lee Piper is the Bird Clan Mother of the Eastern Cherokee Overhill Band. She is the author of traditional Native children's stories, a teacher and a counselor.

-Joan Price works in media, and has presented a slide presentation she developed on Native American sacred areas, and the Hopi.

-Starhawk is a ritualist, counselor, writer and political activist. She is the author of DREAMING THE DARK: MAGIC, SEX AND POLITICS and THE SPIRAL DANCE.

-Brant Secunda has completed his apprenticeship with Don Jose Matsuwa, the Huichol Shaman. He is the ceremonial leader and director of the Dance of the Deer Foundation: Center for Shamanic Studies.

-Grandfather Sky Eagle is a Chumash teacher and elder.

-Grace Spotted Eagle is Wallace Black Elk's wife. She teaches about women and the traditional way.

-Brad Steiger is an internationally-known author and teacher. He has written MEDICINE POWER, MEDICINE TALK, STAR PEOPLE, THE CHINDI and many other books. He is teaching people how to find their multi-dimensional self.

-Hyemeyohsts Storm is the author of SEVEN ARROWS and SONG OF HEYOEHKAH. He is the founder of the National American Metis Association.

-Harley Swiftdeer is a Cherokee/Metis medicine man, founder of the Deer Tribe, and teacher of the Sun Dance way, and of White Crystal Medicine.

-Jim Swan is the former director of Life Systems Educational Foundation in Seattle. He is an environmental psychologist specializing in sacred places.

-Slow Turtle (John Peters) is a medicine man for the Wampanoag Nation, and Director of Indian Affairs for the State of Massachusetts.

-John White is a well-known teacher, lecturer and author. He has written many books and edited many anthologies. He is the author of POLE SHIFT.

-Dhyani Ywahoo is the director of the Sunray Meditation Society, in Vermont. She is the lineage holder of the medicine traditions of the Anigadoah-Catawaba People, and a Planetary teacher and guide.

-Yehwehnode (She Whose Voice Rides on the Wind) or Twylah Nitsch speaks with the voice of her ancestors on the wisdom, prophecy and philosophy of the Seneca people.

-Jack Zimmerman/Jaquelyn McCandless are the focalizers of the Heartlight Community and School outside of Los Angeles. They teach about relationships in the New Age.

These brothers and sisters are helping others to see the light and love of the Great Spirit. They are part of the network of light formed by people of all true traditions that is now covering our Earth Mother, helping to heal her, and to remind us of our connection with the Great Spirit. We are glad to honor them and their work.

# IV. PRACTICAL SKILLS

## Focalizing Community

In the 60's it was common practice to bask in the illusion that being idealistic was enough to ensure that a utopian new alternative would emerge when people drew together for that purpose. A few realistic individuals dared to differ with that point of view. The idealistic/realistic conflict is still being cultivated in the mainstream, but as we've matured, we've seen how counterproductive that is. We were lucky to avoid that pitfall of the angry 60's, especially lucky in light of the fact that that's when we began all this.

The key word in focalizing community has been Responsibility. In an attempt to avoid the pitfalls of heirarchy and red tape, many a sincere group has fallen into other pitfalls, particularly that of avoidance. Perhaps it took a try or two before some communities could work. Perhaps experience has allowed a few people to begin again with their eyes wide open. For us, our eyes opened after we were already committed to this vision of an alternative way to live.

Vision is a compelling force. Like any other experience, vision is something already seen, that can never return to being unknown. We all act upon what we know, upon what life has taught us. Vision is what makes it possible to embark upon a path that is not romantic, not glamourous, not easy, and has none of the rewards we are taught to value. The rewards of community are personal growth, vision, greater courage, creativity and joy in life. Joy in nurturing life. Joy in participating in life. Joy in all aspects of life. Few of us were taught the maturity required to value these things adequately.

Focalizing community can be thought of as a "thankless task", although it isn't, once we let go of old attitudes about freedom versus committment, work versus happiness, risk versus security, responsibility versus fun. You will at times work more hours than you ever thought a person could. You will cover work left

page 84

undone by people you thought you could rely on.  You will take
risks, not just for yourself, but for your whole community, and
you will bear the strain of the unknown outcome.  You will make
a few unpopular decisions, and feel the resentment of people in
whose interest you are acting.  Others will expect you to manifest the changes they want, come up with the money for things
they regard as important.  You will be called upon to do tasks
too difficult or complicated for anyone else.  You will not always have enthusiastic response to your need for help.

You will be unpopular when you make people face unpleasant
facts.  You will sometimes doubt your own perception, especially
when, in spite of your total commitment to doing your best,
things aren't going well.  You will feel inadequate when the cash
flow isn't flowing.  You will feel loneliness when you perceive
that others can or will not be individually or adequately motivated, experienced, educated or wise to give you the relief you
feel you need.  You then ask yourself exactly why you hang in
there, still praying, still looking within, still loving the
task you've set out to do.

The answer must be that your work is important, and that
it is your path.

## HAVING WHAT IT TAKES

Shared purpose is the only reason for having a community.
Shared purpose is important before anything else.  Purpose is
more important than having a home together, or having land, or
sharing your knowledge and experience, or having money.  This
purpose must be strong, and shared truly from deep within.  This
purpose must be able to survive difficult times, times of doubt,
times of careful self-examination.  Shared purpose is so important that we are compelled to express it as clearly as possible
to each other, and to know, not assume, agreement.

The Tribe has a written statement of purpose.  This statement changes as our purpose becomes larger, and as our vision
grows.  Our purpose is alive, not rigid and unchanging.  This
reality reflects our growth at all levels.  All of us have
participated in stating our written purpose.

One of the most important things that a stated purpose gives,
especially in the early growth of a community, is a guideline by
which to make decisions.  It makes it possible to answer such
questions as, what decision will be in harmony with our vision
and purpose?  Are we serving our purpose?  Later, it helps new
people know whether or not they belong in your community.  It

becomes a guideline by which to discriminate between what is essential, and what is disruptive. Ultimately, when the world knocks on your door to question your departure from the American Dream, you will have a way to explain yourself, and you and your community will be able to present an example of agreement, unity and shared priority.

## POSITIVE ATTITUDE

Three attitudes work well toward achieving a positive, constructive community: wanting to do (not just achieve) the work of building community, believing in this work as life-affirming and good, and knowing that it's possible for you to do. Seeing the larger picture of your relationship to the world is immeasurably valuable, and vital. It does much to dispel loneliness and the illusion of separation from other people, and from the world.

Regardless of your stated purpose, your activities and lifestyle will have an impact on the world in some way. The people in your community are directly affected by it, and they, in turn, touch others with their individual energies. Your community energy will have its impact on the immediate environment and on the neighborhood or local area. Simple activities like recycling, protecting wildlife habitat, growing a garden, all have far-reaching effects just as much as harmful activities do. You are part of Creation, and it is an illusion to pretend that you are somehow above it or separate from it.

## LISTENING

Listening is one of the lost arts. It was a part of the recent enough past, however, that we are able to retrieve it. Among the Native American people, the elders were listened to in a way that's hard to explain. In modern America, we learn to listen shallowly, enough to memorize facts, or to detect points we want to refute, or enough to make someone feel respected as duty requires. So often we listen to the words but not the message. We hear the notes, but not the music, see the lines but not the art. It is truly our loss, that we cannot see anew through the eyes of another.

There are two kinds of listening that are essential in a community: listening to the voice of spirit, and listening to the voice of individual and collective need within the community. When members learn to listen, both they and the community experience miraculous growth.

No one community can be all things to all people. Learning what you reasonably can and cannot do is essential, and difficult. Many people coming to community want to change everything in their lives at once. This doesn't work. To survive and prosper a community needs to limit itself, and be clear about its limits. Members need to learn to say a rational "no" to new goals or projects that could overwhelm them, to unsought advice, and to potential members who are not in harmony with their purpose.

# *Land*

There are many ways to get land.  The Bureau of Land Management puts land up for sale.  These are cash deals, but reasonable.  Contact the office for the area in which you are interested.  Mining claims can also be useful to some people.  You
can stake a claim on 20 acres of public land providing you can
prove that there are minerals there.  Sometimes you can get the
use of existing mining claims by looking after them for the owners.  You can also camp in national forests on a temporary basis,
and on Bureau of Land Management land, but you cannot put up any
permanent shelters.  Of course, if you have the money, there are
a lot of deals available through private parties.  In this case,
it is best to scout the area you are interested in.  Sometimes
people have land they bought for speculation or to retire on and
they will let you live on it.  Check on property taxes.  Check
everything.

In looking at land, remember that the water supply is very
important, especially in the Western states.  Be sure you have
a water supply for drinking, and a steady supply for animals
and irrigation.  If you have to have a well put in, it could cost
you $5000 or more.  Check on local land restrictions as to septic
tanks, or whether they'll let you get by with an out-house.

In the past we were involved in acquiring land in many of
these ways.

We thought of land as something to use, but not to own.
We felt that ownership of the Earth Mother should only be vested in the Great Spirit.  During past years we used land, but
didn't own it.  This way was successful when we dealt with
people with true hearts and spirits.  When we dealt with some
who spoke with forked tongues, they made it impossible for us
to continue using land that we did not own.

Several times, we have put much energy and money into
someone else's land, and buildings we created on it, only to
find that the owners had both forked tongues and crooked hearts.
We had to move on at their whim.

In the fall of 1975 we decided that to have a stable

land base during this time of change, we would have to purchase land ourselves. We felt the need to be the "legal" owners, according to the customs of this society, of the land we would be caring for. At this time, we felt, this would be the only way we could bring some land, and our lives, into the balance that we feel is necessary.

So we went in search of land. We knew that we wanted to be in the foothills of the Rocky Mountains. We wanted land with a natural water supply, and with areas where we could raise a garden, keep some chickens, and pasture a milk cow. We wanted an area that was isolated, yet accessible by road.

We found that realtors have an odd language that they use in newspaper ads. "Reasonable" can mean anything from $350 to $1500 per acre. "Gently sloping" seemed to describe land that is accessible only in the summer, and only then in a four-wheel drive vehicle. "Good water" often meant that the water would be good if you could afford to drill 150 feet down for a well.

When looking for land, you must consider all of these things, and more. Generally, well-drilling costs at least $30 per foot. Bringing power in costs at least $2 per foot, and you may have to sign a $20 per month minimum contract for a five-year period. You must also check out legal access that allows you to drive in and out, utilities, zoning laws, the building code, and how much houses will cost. It's sad that it is this way, but true, and, as long as this system exists, we feel better about complying with its laws than about getting caught up in its court system because the foundation of our house isn't proper.

The medicine was good to us again, and we found some beautiful acreage within our price range. It has a natural spring, two ponds, pasture, trees, and wilderness for the back yard. Wild fruit and herbs abound, there are fishing streams nearby, and we've seen tracks of deer, coyote and elk. To us, the spring was very important since if you have only a well, you are usually dependent on electricity to pump the water.

One day, we know, the land will be free to those who would live on it in harmony with the way of the Great Spirit. Until then, it is sometimes good to follow the example of our brothers, the fox, and coyote, and to move further from the cities, back in the brush and silent land.

# *Shelters*

The kind of shelter you need depends on climate, water supply, available materials, and how long you plan to be in one place. Following is a listing of different shelters, and our suggestions.

## BRUSH LEAN-TO

This is made of a basic frame of poles or stripped branches, and covered with brush, grass thatching or reeds. This gives shade and some protection from wind. A little canvas or plastic adds protection from rain and snow.

## TIPI or TENT

The tipi was used a lot by the Plains Indians. Theirs were made of heavy buffalo hides and had liners in them. The modern canvas ones are alright for warm climates, but we wouldn't recommend them for wintering in cold areas. If you buy or make a tipi, make sure that it's waterproof or water-proof it yourself. We recommend tipi-living because it helps people experience the sacred circle of life. We only point out one disadvantage of the tipi and that is that it sticks out and shows up for miles in most country which isn't help-ful if you're trying to be inconspicuous.

One of the Bear Tribe tipis.
page 90

These begin with a framework of poles anchored in the ground and bent over and lashed to form a small dome.  At this stage the wickiup looks like a bare sweat lodge.  Other poles can be added horizontally.  Many Eastern Woodland tribes laced on birchbark, but bark and other materials can be used. A layer of plastic or canvas under the covering will keep things a lot cleaner inside.

## EARTH LODGE

This type of dwelling is suitable in places where it isn't too rocky or rainy.  One type is dug into the earth 3 or 4 feet with 2 or 3 feet of wall above ground, then a roof added.  These blend nicely into a wilderness background.  Other dwellings can be built out of sod, like the ones built by the settlers on the prairies where money and materials were short.  Strips of sod were arranged like bricks to make a house that was warm in winter and cool in summer.  Rammed earth also makes blocks suitable for building, but it should be carefully done and tested before it is relied upon to hold up in severe weather.  The same is true of adobe blocks.  These must be cured for at least two weeks, and are best used in mainly dry climates.

## LOG CABIN

A sturdy cabin can be built with reasonable effort in areas where the materials are available.  Logs of uniform size need less hewing to match them.  Notching is very important as the notches take the place of nails.  They must line up. Cured logs should be used for any permanent dwelling.  Green ones may crack, ooze pitch, warp, and do all kinds of things. Cracks between the logs can be chinked with a number of materials from mud to sod to concrete.

Roofs are difficult because of all the lifting needed. The main roof beams should be one pole, strongly fixed to the walls.  The pitch of the roof will depend on what kind of weather it must withstand.  A good framework is important for supporting the roof.  It is wise to inspect roofs of other structures before you decide how to build yours.  A number of materials can be used to cover the basic framework, such as slab wood, birch bark, thatching.  Be sure to think in advance of such things as water resistance and insulation.  Sometimes these are more easily incorporated in the building than added later.

Log cabins are attractive for their lasting value, and for the builder's independence from lumber mills. They are, however, quite work-intensive. It is a long process to select and fell trees, and the work of stripping off the bark, and waiting for the logs to cure, is a major test of patience. It's satisfying to complete one of these when the shelter harmonizes with the surrounding terrain, is solid, and needs no paint or siding.

## ROCK HOUSE

For someone who has the time, rock construction is good. It's lasting, and it has beauty. It's fire resistant and never needs to be painted. Some people combine rock with railroad ties. A small investment in mortar is necessary, and a good foundation.

## DOMES

These are good, cheap housing. Our objection is that without good maintenance, they quickly become an eyesore. Dome kits can be bought, or you can follow a  plan and build out of wood.

## HOUSE

The Bear Tribe lives in a large house (24' x 64' with an addition, two-story), which was built by our own people. It is mainly built out of materials which were considered to be of inferior quality, and we got them free or cheap. If you can salvage, re-cycle, scrounge, bargain and improvise, you might get what you need within a very limited budget. This means you may have to consider using materials which you had not considered before. We've always been willing to combine standard materials with others we find. The materials we find fall into two basic groups -- natural materials like rock (also very labor-intensive and not very warm) and wood (for cabinet handles, towel racks and curtain rods, table legs, etc.) and substandard building supplies like salvaged siding, insulation, fixtures, door, windows, stairs and discarded materials which were warped, splintered or odd sizes.

There are a number of factors to consider when you select materials. If you want a house that will look clean when you've cleaned it -- not dingy -- and be easy to take care of, you will have to be more selective about wall and floor coverings. Bare, natural wood is very nice when it's new, but once it's stood a

while, it tends to absorb dust and smoke to shower down upon
your dining room table at a later time.  The amount of attention
paid to detail (such as finishing a garment you have made) will
make a great deal of difference in the feeling of quality of the
dwelling.  The same applies to outbuildings -- woodsheds and
tool sheds.  If you take the time to hang the doors right, they
will always open and shut.

The Bear Tribe's longhouse under construction.


When we first built the longhouse at Vision Mountain, we
had little money, a newborn infant, animals and gardens that
needed immediate attention, business to attend, a tiny work
force, and a limit of 24 hours in a day.  Because of our circumstances, we needed a home, cheap and in a hurry.  We cut lots
of corners in cost and construction.  We did live to regret
some of the decisions we made.  We now wish we had a home with
washable walls, insulation in the subfloor, more windows.  However, we avoided perpetual debt.  We own the place, and we have
been able to add a wing and lift part of a roof.  We could do
it because we understood (by then) how building components go
together, and how ours was built.

We've found that it's hard to over-estimate your needs in
terms of space.  While it's true that a smaller dwelling is
easier and cheaper to heat, we have found that we sometimes have
insufficient work space for all projects -- baking bread, beadwork, canning the garden, sewing, office work, carving, music,
holding programs and ordinary activities.  On the one hand, we
did underestimate future space needs.  On the other hand, we
didn't overbuild and overbudget.

Floor plans must take into account the immediate needs of the group, and individual needs for privacy. If there are children, there must be room in your home for them. Comfort and cleanliness are so important that we stress the need to acquire some experience in building, or research it well, at least. Insulate well. Allow for circulation of oxygen. Yet budget realistically. It is a good idea to write two budgets, one you hope to adhere to, and another showing the cost of building the traditional way. Be prepared to pay the bill either way. This will allow you to change your mind about floor coverings, for instance. Furthermore, if you are unprepared to foot the bill, your project will be interrupted when it is partially done. Any house left unoccupied always ages badly, compared to an occupied dwelling. It is important to get the house liveable.

Safety is another important aspect of building -- both during the work of building with power tools, and long distances to fall, and after the building is complete. Your research into wood stoves, for instance, should occur before you build. You need sufficient clearance for even the safest metalbestos roof packs, and you absolutely must check on insurance and fire marshall regulations. Then you will build according to your needs, and not have to change things later.

Carefully check local building codes and electrical codes before beginning the construction of your house. Begin with a good foundation, literally, and information-wise. Most of the time, you can build your house with no hassle from the county if you simply buy a building permit and adhere to the county guidelines. They only want your fee, and they want to know how to assess the value of your property so they can tax your property. Our longhouse was designated a "low-quality dwelling", and our taxes are very low.

Anything you want in your house is easier to do in the first place, if you can afford it. Additionally, you need to look at the surrounding terrain to see if there are things you need to do to protect your house. Do you need rain gutters? Do you need to build a little earth berm to keep rainwater from flooding your kitchen?

The electrical codes will be much more strict, and for good reason. Poor wiring causes many tragic fires. If your mind fails to comprehend this code, don't hesitate to get help from a friend you KNOW can do it. The power company will NOT hook you up until everything is according to their specifications. Addi-

tionally, insurance companies take a dim view of insuring anything at all, especially if it doesn't look "right". Quality in
this respect is absolutely essential.

We feel it is wise to have an alternative to electric heating even if you equip your house for that. We heat with wood.
One centrally located stove heats almost the entire house. We
built the house with space around the stairs so that the heat
from the downstairs effectively heats the second story. Again,
the word is SAFETY. We can't emphasize it enough. Buy fire
extinguishers. Keep flammables far away from fires.

## OTHER HINTS

There are any number of excellent books available from
libraries which show the detail of building traditional or
alternative shelters. It is well worth the time spent to
read 10 or 12 books on building -- you are thinking about
making a major investment in time and money (counting transportation, materials, time off from work), and you can't
afford many mistakes. If you do make mistakes, take the time
to correct them, rather than covering them up or hoping it
isn't very important. You want to have a house that will bear
the weight of whatever roofing you have, and snow, and solar
water heating, or whatever will be going on your roof.

When you pick a location for your dwelling, be sure to
consider your water source, access (for purposes of bringing in
electricity, phone [if desired], supplies, wood, food), fire
danger, beauty, climate and safety from possible flooding.
It is good to have an overall plan for your camp or community,
with projected sites for outhouse, woodshed, barn, root cellar,
gardens, well or springhouse. This can save a lot of steps in
daily chores, and also avoid mistakes such as putting an outhouse too close to a water source.

## INTERIOR

In a permanent house, beauty and comfort are as important
as function, and they tie in together. An organized area will
automatically be more attractive and appear larger than an un-
planned one. But you also have to think about such things as
light and warmth, cleanliness, and color. All these things
can contribute much to your happiness and energy for other
things. Here are some of the things we have found helpful:

Plan the kitchen.  The kitchen, or the hearth, is the center of the home.  It reflects the condition of the family. It's condition is also reflected in the family.  The food which nourishes us is prepared here.

Cleanliness is of utmost importance.  Plan where you want your water supply to be kept.  Go to adequate measures to get good containers for it.  Where will you dispose of used water? Where will you stack dirty dishes?  Where will you keep the clean ones?  Take the time daily to keep your house clean. People who live in pigpens often act like pigs.

It is good to organize firewood so that it is near the door and near (but not too near) the stove.  There should be adequate space so that wood can be dried out if necessary.

The cook stove will be the center of the kitchen on hot days as well as cool, so plan accordingly.  It is where food is canned and cooked, where water is heated for all hot water needs (unless you plan to have electric, gas or solar equipment), and where people will go to thaw out.

If there will be stoves in other parts of the house, designate places for firewood.  Build boxes for it.  Make it easy to use.  Plan for ease in housekeeping, and for beauty. Curtains, plants, flowers, attractive furniture - purchased or home-made - make a big difference in how the house looks and how you feel living in it.  Carpeting or linoleum brightens a house up and helps to insulate.

Adequate light is crucial, especially in the winter.  Plan to have sufficient windows, and good lighting from electric or other sources.  We strongly recommend NOT having fluorescent bulbs as they tend to agitate people.

Furniture and cabinets are more a necessity than a luxury, as you will quickly learn when times get busy.  It is wise to plan your projected needs, then custom build for versatility. If you need temporary kitchen shelves, build them shallow enough to serve later as a bookcase, or deep enough to use as pantry shelves or linen storage.  Wasting work is as bad as wasting materials.  You can build cupboards a lot cheaper than buy them, and they are more attractive.  The inside of cabinets is a simple shelf, which can be built into the wall.  For nice looking cabinets use facer boards that match the doors and produce an even surface.  Obtain good hinges and latches.

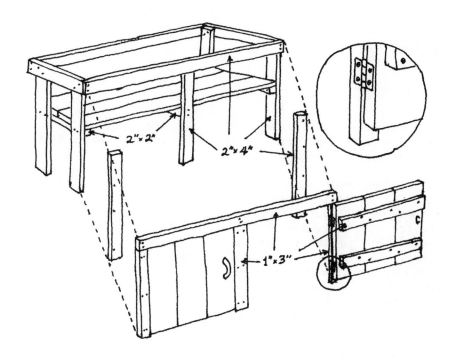

Refer to the accompanying sketch of the kitchen cabinets we use in the longhouse. Remember that cupboards are essential if you have toddlers in the family.

Plan for adequate storage and closet space. We've found that a loft bed about 5' high is a good bedroom space-saver as your closet and dressers can go underneath.

# *Water*

Having your own water source is a blessing. Daily prayers to the spirits that guard it are important and are most effectively made by sisters.

Before you buy land with a well or spring it is good to test for any toxic materials that may have polluted it. Either test it yourself or have it tested through the county. The fee will be reasonable. In any case, it will be more reasonable than an illness caused by drinking contaminated water. If you have a stream, find out what is upstream that could get into the water. If you have a well or a spring, maintain it. We drain our wood spring box once or twice a year and spray it with clorox. We also cover it with screen in the summer as it seems more effective than a wood top in keeping insects out. We always ask permission of the spring spirit before making changes.

Contamination is the worst threat to water storage. Realize that ANYTHING added to water reduces its quality. This includes material from the container or reservoir. Invest whatever is required to protect your water supply. It's impossible to live without an adequate supply of good water.

Changes in weather and season sometimes affect the quantity and quality of water. Become familiar with the lay of the land and how it relates to the water supply.

We try to use water sparingly, and for as many uses as it will stand. Become aware of all the uses water is put to, like drinking, cooking, bathing, livestock, gardening, cleaning, canning, dishwashing, house plants, etc. Most people use more water than they think for all these. It is good standard practise to use as little as possible for everything.

Alternatives to using a lot of water for bathing are bathing in a basin most of the time, or using a sauna or sweat lodge. Gardens can be irrigated with the runoff from other projects, if there are no foreign substances in the water. Laundry should be done only when necessary. Let the sun freshen your out-of-season clothing. Use less soap, and less rinse water. Do more than one load of clothing in wash water.

If you are lucky and have enough water for a system, decide what your needs will be over a projected period.

Can you have a gravity flow system? This is best if you can. Otherwise, is electric power dependable in your area? Do you plan to use a pump in your well? If so, try to design it so you can also dip water.

Make sure you take steps in warm weather to keep all your water from freezing when it's cold. This means burying any hose or pipe below the frost line and insulating it with straw or insulation and soil. Use the best quality pipe you can afford. Cheap pipes spring leaks in about five years.

If you decide to install plumbing, be sure you have enough water to make it practical and be sure you take measures to prevent freezing, or your system will be destroyed and you will lose many gallons of water through burst pipes. Keep track of the amount of water being used. A common result of having plumbing is that people use more water as it is easier to get.

Part of our economy is looking at the ways we use water. At Vision Mountain, we have some of the best water that exists. Because the spring is located in such a magic-feeling place we were immediately aware of what a sacrament it is. We have been unwilling to dishonor it by using it stupidly. In the days when we had to carry every drop, we made sure the water was used first for dishes, then for a few very dirty clothes, then for floors. We learned to bathe in six quarts of water which sufficed for washing hair first. Now that we have gravity-flow water into the house, we find we still don't take that gift for granted. We use it more generously, yes. We take an occasional therapeutic bath in a tub, and we drain dishwater when it has been thoroughly used. We still flush only when necessary, though. We don't take clean drinking water for washing the floor.

A good wringer washer is an excellent way to make more honest use of water. We use an automatic washer now, with justifications we feel alright about, but we use a machine that has a water level control. It still wastes some water, but not as much as other machines. We use a clothesline instead of a dryer whenever we can.

A little hard work gives good perspective on water. When our youngest child was an infant, we discovered, counting the price of cloth diapers, laundry soap, quarters for laundramat machines and dryers, pins, pails, pants, we still saved $700.00 per child by using cloth diapers instead of disposable. This means we washed cloth ones. First we split firewood, then found a bucket with a handle to go get water. We had a hand-operated wringer washer. We could adjust our own temperature according to how much wood we were willing to split, give the paddle 100 churns, run the diapers through the wringer, and drop them into the pot of rinse water, then use the sudsy water for the next round of diapers. It was a heck of a lot of work. It was worthwhile for reasons at two levels: one, water was in limited supply and was needed everywhere on the farm, and two, it gave us perspective about how water was handled in the good old days when there was plenty of water. It helps us appreciate the peoples of the Third World countries who must carry their water many miles for drinking and cooking.

Following are some suggestions for conserving water:

1.  Keep a jar of water in the refrigerator so people won't run the faucet just to get a cool drink.

2.  Showers use less water than baths.

3.  On-off showers where you wet yourself down, shut off the water, soap up and then turn on the water to rinse off use even less.

4.  Flush only when necessary. Be sure your fixtures are working properly, not leaking.

5.  If you have a reservoir-type toilet, put a quart bottle or a brick in the tank and you'll use less each time you flush.

6.  Wash only clothing which is dirty. Automatic washers are wasteful. Wash some things by hand.

7.  Do not use harsh or chemical cleaning agents -- soaps like Ivory are the gentlest and are better for the Earth Mother than detergents.

8.  Recycle water. Use dish rinsing water for another job, like washing the floor or an article of clothing.

9.  Don't let the water run while you are shaving or brushing your teeth.

10. Find some way to catch rainwater (barrels under the rain gutters). This can be used for washing and watering.

11. Keep plumbing in good repair.

12. Give up your lawn and grow vegetables.

13. Water your garden by hand. Don't walk away and leave water running. Don't water driveways.

# *Waste*

You will need a way to dispose of human and kitchen waste without defiling the portion of the Earth Mother given into your care. For human waste you may use an outhouse, a composting toilet, a methane producing toilet, an incinerating toilet or a toilet hooked into a septic system. Digging holes isn't realistic for a group of people on a permanent land base. We've seen some good plans for methane and composting toilets but they aren't practical with the number of people we have. You need propane for incinerating toilets. We've chosen to have an outhouse, and a septic system.

We make sure the outhouse is away from any water or gardens. We use ashes from our stoves and lye in the summer to keep the outhouse fresh. We move it every four to six months depending on the number of people here. To build a septic system you need the proper permits and a backhoe or a lot of time. You also need the tank and gravel and straw for the leach lines. To have a system installed costs at least $1500, materials and labor considered.

Unless you are sure of your water supply's abundance, a septic system isn't a good investment. Without adequate water to keep the system moving, the septic tank turns into an accidental methane generator that is unpleasant to have around.

Although a septic system is the most responsible way of disposing of kitchen waste water (which often should not be used on plants because of dirt or grease or detergents), you can just throw dirty water on an arid area such as a driveway, and use whatever water you can recycle on plants or trees. Do use bio-degradable cleansers, and be cautious as even some of these harm trees and plants.

Another important aspect of disposing of waste products is recycling. Recycling is more than taking cans, paper and glass to a recycling center. It is an attitude of boycotting the consumerism addiction of most people. It is recyling your thoughts so you don't need to buy a new coat or appliance just because it's on sale. Real recycling is realistic economics. Group recycling activities and large weekend projects have their important place, but recycling is for every day. Anyone who survived the Great Depression of the 30's can tell you all about it.

Most recycling is still done by individuals who turn scraps into quilts, cans into flowerpots, or garbage into compost. Ironically, in some circles these same conscientious people become targets of criticism from others who consider them lax for using disposable diapers one weekend or having an electric heater to supplement their wood heat. Yet these are some of the people who usually do more recyling than any commercial industry has yet attempted to do.

We advocate that everyone begin a daily recycling program that is realistic for their own lifestyle - a pattern that they can continue to improve upon - rather than an enormous project which they can't ever hope to maintain. The following suggestions are only a few ideas. Select the ones that are useful to you.

## SHOPPING

Things cost so much these days that most of us need to be selective about what we buy new and what we buy second-hand. When buying used items, you don't pay for advertising, brand name and style. Being able to find good deals is a skill worth developing, and buying this way is often a lot of fun.

Thrift stores and garage sales are good places to find used items. Children's items which are quickly outgrown can usually be found cheaply and in good condition. New luggage is expensive, so if you seldom go on trips, a thrift store is a good place to shop for it. Eyeglass frames are ridiculously expensive, but in a thrift store, they can often be bought for less than $1.00.

Rummage sales are a good place to shop if you get there early, but most of the bargains will be snapped up in the first hour. Get there early, examine all items carefully, and wash them before you use them. Try out appliances to be sure they work and will continue to work.

The dump is usually the last place to look for things you need. Yet many horse-watering troughs have been picked up there. Washing machines may still have good motors worth money. Just be wary of the filth that accompanies anything from the dump.

Classified ads list goods and equipment of all kinds. Many of these items must be left behind when people move. Bankruptcy auctions are usually listed in the legal column. Watch for them.

Re-selling your own unused articles is also important. Turning an unused piano into a washing machine is financially and aesthetically sound.

## AROUND THE HOUSE

We can learn through separating the garbage what it is we can do as "only one person", for our environment and our economy. We have recycled aluminum as well as we could. Surprisingly, we found that the recycling center was not interested in foil. The center was interested in cans only, and in aluminum siding, enamel and all, if the nails are pulled out.

If you balk at paying outrageous prices for food storage containers that quickly stain and split at the corners, you can save cottage cheese and yogurt containers for other foods. If you make your own dairy products, you can collect containers from your friends. They may be good for only a few uses, but they work, and more containers can be accumulated at no additional cost. Plastics are products of the petroleum industries, and they are not biodegradable. They do not readily melt down to be re-made into other things. Their fumes are toxic. It therefore behooves us to use all plastics for as long as we can. Even us plastics-haters should be taking care of the plastics that already exist, so that fewer will need to be manufactured later to supply consumer habits. Yes, it will take some time and energy, and it will use some space. However, it is a far greater thing to recycle than it is to throw up our hands in despair over the brutalization of Earth by industry.

Separating the trash is basic, but requires space. Household garbage can be separated into meat and grease for dogs and cats; vegetable scraps for chickens, pigs and rabbits; compost; paper; and plastic for the dump. Paper, glass and cans should be taken to a recycling center.

Saving containers saves money. Plastic bags are the first things we save. We use them for dried foods, home made bread and rolls, covering leftovers, shoe bags and many other things. Paper bags are natural for re-use. Milk cartons are good pots for tomato seedlings and other plants which must be started indoors. They are also good for freezing fish and other food in large amounts, or block ice. Large cans are easily converted into flowerpots or canisters (coffee cans are the best). Baking powder and cocoa cans are useful in a workshop or sewing area. Spice jars work neatly for buttons, beads, hair pins, and other odd stuff.  Large jars can be used for food storage when metal is not advisable, and smooth-edged cans can be used for feeding dogs and cats.  Almost any container has possibilities, and as long as we pay so dearly for packaging, we should get as much mileage from it as we can.

How to make a scoop from
a plastic bleach jug.

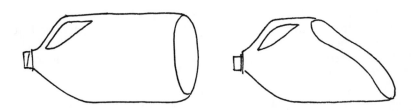

We have been able to use every kind of fabric scrap, from nylon to canvas to fake leather.  We've made quilt tops, pot holders, pin cushions, lampshades, toys, slippers, pouches, and we've used the tiny snips for stuffing.  Again, the possibilities are endless.

Newspapers are a valuable resource.  They start fires, wrap dishes for storage, mulch gardens, cushion items for mailing, and house break puppies.  They catch spills, insulate, clean up.  Don't throw them away.

Dog food bags have insulation qualities and are strong. Egg boxes can be used for sound and temperature insulation. Scraps of rug, linoleum or tile are valuable in pet or doorway areas.

Leftovers in the kitchen should always be re-heated for another meal.  Left over leftovers are a harder problem, but can be managed.

Worn out sheets and towels can be a real life-saver if they are clean.  Finding enough rags for odd jobs or emergencies (slings and such) can be a challenge.  They are good for all kinds of equipment maintenance, draping clothing in storage. Always useful for cleaning, they are also good to keep in a vehicle for cleaning windows, checking oil  and for mopping up spills.

Most farm people are great recyclers who find uses for vegetable parings, egg shells, coffee grounds, ashes and soap chips. We find that getting the most out of everything will cut down the shopping list.

## OUTDOORS

Outdoors, there's plenty of opportunity to recycle junk that is otherwise an eyesore and maybe even a hazard. Discarded scrap iron can be added to rusty baling or fencing wire and used for stablizing concrete. This is done by pouring the cement over all this junk right in the form.

Used motor oil can be used for a number of things. It can be used with a worn-out paintbrush for conditioning hooves. It can be used for oiling a very dusty driveway, for preventing rot on fenceposts, or for weed control around a pumphouse, so long as it can do no harm to animals or water source. Do not try to use it on leather.

Manure from livestock should be collected and used. It is far better than chemical fertilizer and is very expensive if you have to buy it. Leaves, wet straw which can't be used for animal bedding, and lawn clippings can all be composted or used in a garden as mulch. Mulching cuts back the growth of weeds, and therefore insects, and it conserves moisture.

Sawdust makes good insulation where some temperature control is important. Feed sacks can be re-used for insulation, fire control, and other things. Ashes can be sprinkled on icy paths.

Many of these recycling ideas will be useful and convenient for you. You doubtless have ideas of your own.

Over the years, we've used uncountable wood for the construction and heating of our homes. This brings to us the awareness that we therefore share some of the responsbility to care for our trees and forests. These particular plant people have protected us from exposure to the elements, kept us comfortable, fueled our ceremonial fires, cooked our food. These trees also provided beauty to the land where we live, showed us where to find water, freshened the air, shaded us and provided a natural windbreak. They sheltered the animals here, both wild and domestic. We therefore feel that we must take a role in caring for whatever part of the forest we can, by removing fire hazards, using safe practices with our fires, and being thankful for whatever we take. We pause to be thankful, make a prayer, leave tobacco when we take the dead relatives of the plant people for our own use.

On a more mundane level, we have also become more aware of the real cost of firewood. Even if we pick up slash for our use, it isn't "free". We must count the costs of driving a truck (the cost goes much further than the price of the gasoline), buying and running a chainsaw, building a woodshed, acquiring permits when those are needed, and the human costs of time and energy.

Remember wood is not an unlimited resource. Nor should trees be treated merely as fuel. They are fellow beings and should be treated with respect. Thank them for giving themselves so you can be warm and continue to live. Continue showing respect by having adequate arrangements to maintain and contain your fire area.

Prevention of spreading fire is a major consideration. Have a fire extinguisher near every stove or fireplace, even if it is only a 5-gallon container of water that is easy to reach. Do not try to camouflage it because of its appearance. Learn to accept it. Do not pile things on it. Check it often to be sure it is available and full, and workable if it is a regular fire extinguisher. Be sure you know how to open or use it. And don't hesitate to use it the minute fire gets out of hand.

If you are heating with wood, search out your area and find good, fallen dead timber. Never cut green wood unless you absolutely must, and you are prepared to let it dry for about six months to cure it as it will not burn green. Gathering dead trees gives both you and the forest extra fire protection. A bow saw or buck saw is your best bet for a camp wood supply. Also get a single or double bit axe or a small sledge hammer and wedge. Hatchets are okay only for boy scouts and weekend campers. If you're going into the woods for permanent living, you should have a minimum wood supply for two weeks ahead. Cut out the dead timber near your camp first, then fan out.

You will need to keep your wood dry. Properly stacked wood will stay fairly dry, but it is better to put up a woodshed -- just a simple roof on four posts will do in a pinch. Even a tarp or plastic sheet helps a lot.

You will find that different wood burns differently. All wood is usable for burning in the day. But small pieces burn quickly and need to be replaced often. Some kinds of wood burn hot and fast -- others burn long and evenly. You will learn what kind you prefer for what purpose. Some people burn pine in the daytime when they are there to re-stoke the stove, but burn tamarack at night so the house will stay warm. It is important to find out what woods are plentiful in your area, and where to look for dead trees. In a house where wood is the only fuel, a great deal of wood is burned over one winter. Estimate your needs from the experience of others, and by scrutinizing your own needs and the size of your home. It's better to over-, rather than under-estimate.

Keep flammable things well away from the fire area -- like rugs, coats, wet laundry, chairs, bedding, toys, and above all, flammable liquids and vapors. Keep firewood in its own container, and make sure the wood can't slide down against the side of the stove. Do not let children play in the area. Plan your traffic pattern through the house with safety in mind.

Have adequate equipment for cleaning stoves, and clean stoves and chimneys often. Caked-on soot is the usual cause of roof fires. Chimneys must be clean in order to draw well, and stoves full of ashes do not work. In the winter, cleaning ashes will need to take place every two or three days. In the summer, it will be less often.

Under no circumstances leave a fire unattended. Open

fireplaces are charming, but are less practical than a stove which can be banked for long burning with relative safety, and can be used for many needs.

In fireplaces, always use a screen to keep flying sparks in the fire area. Don't encourage children to feed any fire. Wood stoves should not be placed too close to walls or furniture. Cover walls in these areas with asbestos or foil.

When camping, always clear a large area around your fire, clear down to the mineral earth. Put your fire out at night. Never burn quantities of paper in an open fireplace, as burning paper easily flies out.

Never start any fire by using gasoline or oil.

When using a chain saw or motorcycle in the woods or brush, be sure it is equipped with a spark arrestor, and watch it. Never smoke while walking in the woods.

Fire is a wonderful friend, but an uncontrolled fire is one of man's and Mother Earth's worst enemies.

# Vegetables

The gardener's basic attitude toward the earth, his plants and himself as a gardener, and about his garden as a whole, all have a definite effect on the growth and productivity of the garden.

Respect for the Earth Mother herself is very important. When you first begin your garden and start to develop the land, explain to the spirits of the area why you break the Earth, kill the weeds, and why you are disturbing the natural balance of the area.

The individual plants of the garden deserve respect as well, for they work hard to produce a crop for you.  Respect for the plants entails attention throughout the growing season. Plants should be checked for parasites, for moisture, and for whether they need cultivation.  Many gardeners have a tendency to plant their crops, water, and otherwise leave them to struggle along on their own until the crop is ready.  Another thing you must remember is that all the crop must be used, be- cause it is disrespectful to the individual plant, the species, and the garden as a whole to waste any part of the crops yielded.  If you can't handle the abundance of your garden, sell or give the excess to someone who can.

Thinning and weeding is attention plants need.  Some gar- deners fear thinning plants as they don't want to kill them. Plants need space, however, to produce their best.  Without space to grow, they are subject to disease, parasites, molds, and they produce less fruit of poorer quality.  Many annuals tend to bolt when crowded, such as spinach, lettuce, and many annual root crops like radishes and turnips.

While we used to think that weeds in the garden were not good, we have found in more recent studies that weeds can be our friends and helpers.  As some herbalists say: weeds are plants we have not found a use for.  Indeed many are coming into knowledge and useage in our very own garden, including in our biodynamics, our compost pile, and as edible food sources. Contrary to popular opinion, weeds do not necessarily sap nutri- ents and water from the soil, nor do they necessarily crowd out the plants.  In reality, many weeds with long tap roots, such as burdock and dandelion bring nutrients and trace minerals up to the surface of the soil and enhance the shallow rooted plants around them.  So unless a "weed" is in direct competition with a plant, has noxious chemicals or hormones being emitted from it, such as wormwood and deadly nightshade, we would reconsider pulling it and, in fact, would welcome it into our garden.

Some plants that are beneficial in ways I've mentioned are burdock, dandelion and pig weed (also known in our area as lambs quarters) which is one of the best weeds for pumping nutrients from the sub-soil and is a beneficial plant for potatoes, onions and corn.  It is also very edible and we boil it or steam it in a similar manner to cooking spinach.  Burdock root can be eaten. So can dandelion greens in salads.  Stinging nettle, as a companion plant, or "weed companion" with tomatoes will enhance the flavor, protect them from insect pests, and release nitrogen enhancing hormones into the soil around the tomato plant.  It is also an excellent plant for the compost pile as it is a nitrogenous plant, as is comfrey.  They both will speed up the heating of your compost pile.

I would also urge you to re-think what "weed" means.  I believe it was Ralph Waldo Emerson who said, "What is a weed?  A weed is a plant whose virtues have not yet been discovered." James Russell Lowell said, "A weed is no more than a flower in disguise."  A weed is simply an unloved flower so we must learn to love them more.  They grow wild with no help from us.  No planting, fertilizing or cultivating is necessary and in the spring they can be worked back into the soil and they become valuable as mulch.  They help to regulate the soil temperature and the winter covering of weeds on the soil will help protect and increase the earthworm population.  Weeds also help to hold nutrients in the soil.  Without the natural ground cover of weeds many nutrients would be leached away or blown away by the wind. In other words, they are good for erosion control when you are not using that space for your vegetables or flower garden.  Weeds are also very important companion crops for your garden and for field plants.

The gardener should feel respect for himself, and for his abilities as a gardener, for without this self-respect, he can feel no real respect for anything else: the Earth Mother, the plants, or the soil.  Without self-respect, the gardener will do poor work, and  his attitude alone will have a bad effect on the plants.  Thinking in a positive manner toward the success of your garden will help to bring it about: your work will be better and more joyful, the plants will feel encouraged, and a positive attitude can only attract good spirits.

People coming into a garden area that has been consecrated should be made aware that they need to leave their negative attitudes, their egos, arrogance and bad vibes on the compost pile or at the garden gate. The garden is a refuge where we raise our food and meditate on our relationship with the Earth Mother. It is a sacred place and should be celebrated as such.

## PLANNING YOUR GARDEN

The work of raising a garden can be eased considerably by good planning. The health and well-being of your garden plants is affected, as well as the surrounding land, by the way your garden is planned and executed.

An ideal spot would be a gentle south slope (sun and drainage) just below a water source, with loamy soil, not shaded by trees. However, ideal spots are hard to come by, and most of us are forced to compromise. The only thing that must be available is water. Everything else can be changed. Sandy soil can be improved by the addition of organic matter, shade (unless from rocks) can be removed, and the gardener can always walk a little farther.

Near the garden should be the compost heap. This is to avoid the time and energy spent on trucking or hauling finished compost to the garden.

Your watering system should be well planned, too, to do the job well without wasting valuable water. There are several watering systems a gardener can use, according to what is available, and the type of climate he lives in.

The first of these methods is irrigation. This involves allowing large quantities of water to flow between the rows of vegetables and soak into the soil. This is a good method to use if plentiful water is available; it also takes a lot of work. Irrigating takes a lot of water, more than any other method, and the gardener has to put a lot of care into laying out his garden with carrying ditches so that the garden is watered evenly; it is very easy with irrigation to flood some parts of the garden and leave other parts dry. Despite its drawbacks, irrigation is the most commonly used watering system because once the system is set up it takes very little attention: letting the water in through a headgate or pump and periodic maintenance of the ditches. Care must also be taken to avoid erosion of the surrounding area because of the volume of water that must be used.

The second method for watering is sprinkling. This is a good system  because it washes the plants while it waters them, and also cools them off.  In very hot or dry climates, sprinkling should be done in the evening or at night, both to conserve water and to avoid burning the plants.  Water staying on the leaves of plants in hot sunlight will collect heat and burn leaves.  The major drawbacks to sprinkling are: 1.  expense (pipes, sprinklers, pump); 2.  power (electricity for a pump, or, as an alternative, a collection tank for gravity feed pressure); and 3.  waste (much water, as much as 20% in hot, dry climates, will evaporate before the plants can use it). The only thing to remember is that  sprinkling must be started before the ground begins to dry out in the spring.

The third system is drip irrigation.  This is very similar to the first system, except that with drip irrigation  the water is let into the ground very slowly and almost constantly.  The ground is never allowed to become dry, as this will break the capillarity of the soil, meaning water can't get from the source to the plants without first flooding the garden.  The chief advantage  of drip irrigation is that very little water is wasted.

Sub-irrigation is very similar to drip irrigation  except that no water at all runs over the surface of the ground.  Perforated pipes are laid out <u>under</u> the ground, and water is sent into the system under low pressure, going up through the ground to the plants (capillary action).  Again, great care must be taken not to allow the soil to dry out.

All four of these irrigation systems should be combined with a thick layer of mulch, for conservation of water and to prevent erosion.  Mulch does many other things, too, and will be discussed later.

Planning is required in deciding what to plant, as well as when to plant it, and where in the garden.

First, consider your available space.  If you have only a small garden area, you won't want to fill it with something which takes up a lot of space with a relatively low yield, such as corn, potatoes, or cabbages.  One cabbage plant, yielding a five-pound cabbage, takes up a square yard.  On the other hand, pole beans in the same space could yield up to 20 pounds.  Check out how much space each plant needs for a good yield; a hint: roots take less space for a good yield, and many produce greens as well.

It is important not to overplant, as this creates waste; plants and spirits resent this, seeing fruit they worked hard to produce being wasted. Care must be taken in planting heavy-yield plants such as tomatoes, zucchini, or things you would use little of, such as radishes. One tomato plant (medium-size tomato) can yield up to 30 pounds, one zucchini produces as much as 20 squashes. A 20-foot row of radishes will yield 10 pounds, more than most families would use.

Where, and next to what, should be considered also. Cole family plants (cabbages, kale, broccoli, etc.) should be planted together, so that when you rotate the second year, they are all moved to an area where none of that family has grown for 2 years. Also, companion planting should be considered. This is planting combinations of plants which grow well together and repel each other's parasites: a good example of this is the Three Sisters, corn, squash and beans, which have been grown together by Native people for many centuries.

Different areas and climates have differing companion combinations. Something universal, though, is that members of the onion family (onion, leek, garlic) will repel many, but not all, parasites.

## SOIL PREPARATIONS

Soil preparation, BEFORE you plant, is perhaps the most important part of your garden work. How the soil is prepared affects the garden throughout its growth, and how well it resists disease and parasites.

For a first-year garden, the first step is to get rid of the wild plants (weeds). Many of these are edible (lambs quarters, wild mustard, tumbleweeds) or useful (yarrow, St. John's wort) but will crowd out your domestic, not-so-hardy vegetables. There are several ways of doing this: 1. Spading: dig and pull, composting the weeds. 2. Double-tilling: in warm, long-season areas. Not practical for those with short summers. Till in very early spring, wait one month so weeds will grow up in fresh soil, then till again to kill the weeds, plowing them into the soil. 3. Slash-and-burn; the way many gardeners do it has both good and bad points. It kills weeds, seeds, and many insect eggs, but fails to kill roots of many perennial weeds. When combined with spading and caution, though, burning is a good method of getting rid of the weeds. However, we don't recommend it because of the adverse effect of the smoke on the atmosphere.

The next step in development of the garden is composting
-- adding organic matter to the soil. You shouldn't expect the
soil to feed you unless you feed it. Composted, rotten horse
or cow manure is ideal for a first-year garden. Lay it on
about six inches thick and mix it well with the top foot of soil.

This must be done at least once a year, preferably twice:
before planting and after harvest. I will speak more of compost later.

The other part of soil building is mulch, and this is a
maintenance procedure carried on throughout the growing season.
Mulching means covering the ground between the plants with a
layer of straw, dead leaves, or other organic matter. You can
also use newspaper or black plastic, but these add nothing to
the soil. A good cover of mulch helps retain moisture, retard
weed growth, and keeps the soil from eroding or becoming
packed hard. Mulch the garden well in the spring, after the
ground is warmed up and the plants are well established and
after all the first batch of weeds is pulled. Mulch will
retard weed growth, but not stop it. Renew the mulch midway
in the growing season, and again after the fall compost is dug
in, to keep winter rain and snow from washing soil and nutrients
away. Rake back the mulch before planting to allow the dark
soil to collect heat.

## PLANTING THE GARDEN

We will start with early-season, or frost-resistant vegetables. These can be planted as soon as the ground thaws in
the early spring; many are also late-season, or fall planted
crops.

1. Peas: plant 6 inches apart and 1 inch deep; provide
something for them to climb on. Peas are good for the soil:
they fix nitrogen, an essential for plant growth.

2. Chard: plant thinly and shallow, then start thinning
and eating as soon as they are 4 inches high; cook for greens,
or use raw for salad.

3. Spinach: Same as chard, except it grows faster.

4. Carrots: should be sown a little more thickly, as the
delicate seedlings have trouble breaking through the soil.
Thin them when 3 inches high, then to 6 inches apart when first
roots are edible.

5.  Radishes:  Sow 1 inch apart, ¼ inch deep, thin to 2 inches when the fourth leaf appears, and use the greens.

6.  The Cole family:  cabbages, broccoli, kale, collards, and brussels sprouts.  You may plant these either as seeds in early spring (most are frost-resistant) or as plants.  Space about 12 inches apart in rows 2 feet apart or more.  Thin to three feet apart when 4 inches high.

7.  Roots:  rutabagas, turnips and beets are all frost-resistant.  Sow thinly in rows or beds; thin to 4 inches apart when the third leaf appears, then eat the greens.

8.  Tubers:  potatoes, sweet potatoes and Jerusalem artichokes, can all be planted in cold weather.  Mulch over them immediately, as all these will grow right through mulch.  Plant potatoes about 18 inches apart; Jerusalem artichokes about 2 feet apart.

9.  Onions:  plant seeds or sets as soon as ground is thawed, 6 inches apart.

A final note on cold-weather planting: often seeds won't germinate until much later, sometimes waiting a full month until temperature and sunlight are right.

## STARTING PLANTS EARLY

Many plants which aren't frost-resistant must be started early indoors, especially in northern climates.  Sow in flats (shallow wooden boxes) in rows 3-4 inches apart.  Thin plants as soon as the third leaf appears.  Be sure that the plants get enough sunlight: a south-facing window is sometimes enough.

Tomatoes, peppers, lettuce, the squash family and the cole family may all be started indoors in this manner.  Onions, leeks and scallions, as well as many others, get a good start this way.  These can all be transplanted outside as soon as frost danger is past.  We start ours in February, giving a good margin in case we lose two or three flats.

## MID-SEASON PLANTING

Mid-season crops are planted in late spring after the last frost, and usually (except greens) harvested in fall.

1.   Three Sisters: corn, squash and beans have been planted the same way for centuries.  Hills, three feet apart, a foot high and wide, are planted with seeds of the sisters.  You may want to soak the seeds overnight first so they get a head start of about four days.  Well watered and cultivated, these three help keep each other healthy and pest-free.

2.   Tomatoes and peppers:  tomatoes should be planted 3-4 inches apart, then thinned to 18 inches when five inches high. Peppers should be started early indoors in most areas of the U.S., and planted outdoors, a foot apart, when four inches high.

3.   Melons:  plant in hills, 3-4 seeds to a hill.  Make hills three feet apart, and thin to two strong plants per hill when four inches high.

4.   Lettuce and other greens can be planted fairly thickly in rows a foot apart, or in beds.  Thin when large enough to eat, and all season long.  Head lettuce is difficult to grow without pesticides; we prefer leaf lettuce.

5.   Potatoes, peanuts, more beans, cucumbers, zucchini, pumpkins and many other things can be planted in late spring.

## FALL PLANTING

There are many crops that can be planted after the first harvest.  These include many of the early spring crops: peas, chard, lettuce (hot summer not being good for growing lettuce), spinach, etc.  This isn't a good time for roots because if they don't mature before the ground freezes, they go to seed in the spring.  On the other hand, fall is a good time to plant garlic and onion sets, onion seed, and to replant some tubers like Jerusalem artichokes, for a crop the next fall.  Garlic, if planted in spring, takes two full summers to come to maturity; but if planted in the fall, takes only one year.

This is also a good time to lay on a good thick layer of horse or cow manure, or finished compost, with a layer of mulch on top for the winter.

## MAINTENANCE AFTER PLANTING

Proper care of the soil and plants ensures a bigger and better quality harvest, and helps to control pest damage.

Water is the highest priority.  Without sufficient water, plants become stunted and much more vulnerable to insects.

## COMPOSTING

Composting is the most important part of the gardener's work, for without good, rich compost, the soil will fail after one or two seasons, and the garden will fail before that, from pests or stunted plants.

We have seen many complex systems for making large quantities of finished compost, but we have found a very simple way that works well and fairly quickly. Start with a 4 foot by 6 foot wood structure that is a little more than four feet high. Make sure that the slats in your compost bin are about one-half inch apart to allow for aeration. Into this, place all the weeds you gathered clearing the garden. If you have nettles or comfrey growing nearby, add these as they will heat up the compost and speed decomposition. These are both nitrogenous plants and nitrogen will make your compost hot. Coffee grounds or blood meal, which can be purchased at any nursery or plant supply place, also speed up decompostion.

EARTH –
MANURE –
VEGETABLE
MATTER –
ASHES –
MANURE –
WEEDS –

Use a foot or more of the weeds and other materials mentioned above as the first layer in your compost. If you don't have enough weeds you can supplement with straw, grass clippings or pine needles. Cover this first layer with manure of some kind -- either chicken, horse or cow. Add a layer of wood ashes of any kind, then add another layer of vegetable matter, then more manure. Cover the whole pile with earth, seasoned manure from horse or cow, or rotten sawdust. Don't use fresh sawdust as it ties up the nitrogen in the soil which is one of the main ingredients in making compost. Fresh sawdust can delay the decomposition of your compost by a year or more. Your completed pile should be about four feet high.

Cover it with a piece of plastic after saturating the pile with water. This keeps the water in and the chickens out. Anywhere in there except right on top can be your kitchen

wastes, feathers from butchered chickens, or other miscellan-
eous organic matter. Let it cook (it really does: about 100
to 150 degrees) for about six weeks, then turn it and let it
go another three weeks, after which it is ready to put on the
garden.

## MORE MAINTENANCE

Weeding is also important. Some weeds crowd and shade
plants when they are in direct competition with them. Weeds
also attract insects. We nearly had our potatoes wiped out one
year by a swarm of tiny beetle larvae that are a natural para-
site on deadly nightshade, a close relative of the potato and
a very common weed in the area.

Insect control is another priority. Much of this can be
done by companion planting, soil maintenance, and weeding, but
sometimes you have to go out and pick bugs off by hand.

There are other pests besides bugs; if you raise chickens,
you'll have to fence the garden -- or the chickens. Dogs likewise: we once had a whole zucchini and cucumber patch wiped out
by one St. Bernard in a single trip across the garden.

Other pests are more difficult: moles, mice, and gophers.
Rotating plastic garden daisies which create a vibration uncomfortable for burrowing rodents are some help. We have seldom
been bothered by birds -- on the contrary, birds in the garden
are usually after bugs. If they are a problem for you, we suggest you get a good mouse-eating cat. She'll scare off the
birds, and she'll keep the mice out of your stored harvest in
the root cellar too.

Cultivating, or hoeing up earth around such plants as the
coles, potatoes, and corn, is important too. This aerates the
soil, softens it, and conserves water. An easier way is to lay
on two or three layers of mulch through the season. This is
especially important with potatoes: if young spuds are exposed to light, they turn green and poisonous, like the leaves.

Mulch is a vital part of garden maintenance. Moisture is
retained better, plants stay healthier, and erosion is stopped.
Plants like broccoli, Swiss chard, and lettuce can be kept
growing until the ground is frozen hard, by putting 6-8 inches
of straw or leaf mulch over the soil and plant.

## THE HARVEST

Harvesting, and the care of your crops, is the last part of the year's gardening cycle.

Harvest plants like beets, turnips, rutabagas when young and tender. Then place them in boxes of earth in your root cellar or back room. Onions and garlic should be allowed to dry in the sun for 2-3 days, then hung by the tops or stored in a dry place in mesh bags. Potatoes can be stored in sacks or bins in your root cellar. We also suggest freezing, canning, and drying for all of your garden vegetables. Waste nothing: feed excess and trimmings to your animals, or put them in the compost for the next year's garden.

Celebrate the harvest, and offer prayers of thanks for the bounty of Mother Earth, for if she is respected she feeds the spirit as well as the body.

It is good to get fruit trees planted as soon as possible
after moving to the country.  It takes three to five years to
get most varieties established.  In the meantime, the trees
will have to be protected from gnawing animals, both wild and
domestic.  They may even need extra watering.

Wild varieties of trees may be moved too.  That way, you
can be sure the tree is native to your area, but you will want
to locate the trees in a place very similar to the old one.  It
is best not to transplant during the winter months when the sap
is down because any damaged roots would cause the tree to bleed
to death.  Care should be used to prevent transplant shock.
The trees should be handled gently, and great care taken not to
damage the roots or expose them to harsh sunlight.  The ball of
earth around the root system should be kept intact if possible,
and kept from drying out.

In planting, dig an adequate hole for the root structure of
the tree.  Put a cone or mound of earth back in the hole before
setting the tree in.  This step is to avoid air pockets which
will prevent the tree from growing.  Pour in water to be sure
moisture will be near the roots when the tree is planted.  Then
set the tree on top of the cone and spread the roots evenly over
it, as much in their natural position as possible.  Fill in the
dirt, a little at a time, making sure there are no clods or
chunks to create air pockets.  Water the tree again, soaking it
thoroughly.  Do not water it again for a week unless the weather
is extremely hot and dry.

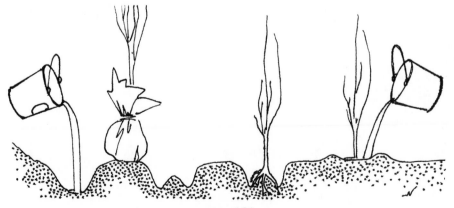

page 121

Berry shoots can be moved anytime after berries are harvested and before the leaves fall.  They are extremely hardy and
can withstand more handling and root breaking than most fruits.
As long as the tap root isn't broken and the plants get enough
water, the bushes will grow.  Some kinds of berries will grow
and take over your land.  Find out what bushes do that so you
can be selective.  They are next to impossible to remove once
established.

If you plan on extensive tree-planting, or if you want to
establish a little orchard, it is always best to learn all you
can about the characteristics of different varieties of fruit.
Seed nurseries will send you catalogs free which will describe
them.  If you still aren't sure, or if the words confuse you
(like hybrid, F1, etc.) go to a garden center or other seed-
man, and ask him to help you understand the differences.

Like a garden, fruit trees require your care and love.
At first they will need watering and a collar made from a can
or milk carton to keep rabbits from chewing off the bark.  When
the trees grow older, they will need pruning.  Sometimes the
branches will need support when they become loaded with fruit.
Always, the trees need to feel that you respect them and their
spirits.

# *Livestock*

After you've had the satisfaction of planting and raising your own vegetables, you may want to go further, and produce more of the things you need to survive. If you intend to eat meat you might want to consider raising animals for this. We feel it is irresponsible now to depend on hunting for meat as our wild four-legged brothers have already been too depleted. Home grown meat is better for you than supermarket meat, as it hasn't been injected with toxic chemicals and hormones, and the animals have been raised with love and butchered with respect.

## RABBITS

Putting aside the fact that a few people keep a rabbit or two for pets, let's consider raising rabbits for food. Rabbits are famous for being prolific, so they are a steady source of meat. Aside from that, there are other advantages to raising rabbits as they require very little care and don't need much space to live in.

Rabbits can be raised in hutches (small screened-in box structures) or in wire mesh cages in a rabbit house. We started out with pens made of chicken wire with just the ground for a floor, but had to change the fence to small gauge wire because even after they were pretty big, the rabbits would squeeze right through the fence. As for the ground, they started digging out so fast that we soon had to install wooden floors in the pen too. We also discovered that the wood had to be hard enough and thick enough so that the rabbits couldn't chew through it. At present our rabbits are housed in hanging all-mesh wire cages in a rabbit house.

Our rabbit cages are hung about three feet off the ground and the floor area directly below the cages has a layer of sawdust which combines with the liquid and solid wastes from these four-leggeds, and eventually becomes the best manure compost our garden gets. Rabbit manure is the only manure than can be used directly on the soil with having to cure before use.

page 123

We had been told that the buck rabbits would fight if they were kept in the same area. They didn't. We were informed that the bucks and does wouldn't breed if they were kept in the same area all the time. They did. We were told that other adult rabbits would eat the newborn ones if they were all together. They didn't. There were little rabbits of all different sizes living with the full-grown ones. All these things had been explained to us by a man who had been raising rabbits for years. The only reason we can think of for all these rabbits doing so well is that we got them when they were young and let them grow up together.

Rabbits need feed at least twice a day, although they'll eat almost any time there's food. A grain or farm supply store usually carries bags of rabbit ration and salt spools. They also need a constant supply of clean water. Rabbits eat a lot and they'll eat anything green. During the summer months, we pick up dandelions and alfalfa, wild oats, and quite a few other things and feed them these as well as the ration. In the cold seasons, the produce man at a supermarket usually has lettuce trimmings and greens that anyone can get free for the asking.

If you don't want too many rabbits, it's a good idea to separate the bucks from the does. As for young ones, a doe rabbit generally always knows how to make a nest and take care of babies. As long as there's enough dry straw, she'll take care of the rest. Baby rabbits can squeeze through anything, so make sure their accommodations are designed to order. If a nest box approximately 12" x 15" x 6" deep is provided for the doe a few days before she is due, and maintained half full of clean dry hay or straw, the babies will remain warm and content in the enclosure until old enough to hop out on their own.

When you have rabbits, one thing is inevitable; they'll get out. When domestic rabbits are out, you won't be the only one trying to catch them. Owls, hawks, stray dogs, coyotes, and quite a few other animals like to eat rabbits, so keep a close watch on your hutch.

## CHICKENS

Chickens provide a good supply of meat and eggs if they're properly cared for.

The most economical way to raise them is to start with
baby chicks since they don't cost much.  Your first concern
should be building a chicken coop that is insulated well
enough to protect the chicks from rain, wind, and cold weather.
It should also be built well enough to protect chickens from
rats, skunks, and various other predators.  It should have at
least one window.  Chickens don't need a wooden floor, but the
ground should be covered with straw.  Your coop should have
enough space so they don't get crowded, a minimum of 2 square
feet per chicken.

While they're young, chicks can be kept warm at night and
during cold weather by two 200 watt lamps about a foot off the
floor.  They should be provided with a constant supply of clean
water, and fed an adequate amount of chick scratch once each
morning and evening.

As they grow larger and get their heavy feathers, the food
can be changed to your own organic mix of corn, wheat, barley,
soy beans, oats and oyster shell, and the heat source can be
reduced to one 200 watt bulb raised higher off the ground.  Not
long after this, chickens will show a tendency to sit (roost)
on something higher above the ground.  A roost can be built by
constructing a rectangular framework of one inch slats about six
inches apart and eighteen inches above the floor.

About this time your chickens can be let outside in the
morning to scavenge.  When it gets dark they'll come back inside to roost.  It is inevitable that you'll lose some chickens
to predators, injury or disease.  Do not hesitate to destroy a
hurt or sick bird.  It will release it from suffering and it
will protect the rest of the flock from the same disease.  Because of possible losses, it's a good idea to start with about
10% more chickens than you expect to end up with.

As far as chicken diseases go, there are more of them than
can be mentioned in this book.  But don't worry!  Chicken
diseases are regional and each area usually is affected by only
two or three.  Also, most of the diseases are very rare.  The
best source of information on diseases in your area is your
local feed-grain farm supply store, not a veterinarian.

As your chickens get older, you'll be able to see very
definitely which are roosters and which are hens.  You don't
need a lot of roosters, but you should keep at least one for
each ten hens if you want fertile eggs.  Of course this means
the hens will need nests about a foot square and a foot off

the ground. Wooden nest boxes with open fronts will work well
so you don't need to crawl around on the floor to look for eggs.
The reason you won't want to do this is because the floor will
be covered with chicken manure, but most of it should accumulate under the roost.

After the manure builds up, it can be removed with a
shovel and used as compost (fertilizer). It should be cleaned
out every time it builds up to a few inches deep. It's good
for your garden since it's a natural source of nitrogen.

After the chickens reach the adult stage, you need only
feed them twice a day and collect eggs in the evenings. If
you decide you need more chickens, just let a hen or two keep
all her eggs. She'll do all the rest, until the chicks hatch,
then you start all over with the lights, chick scratch and
such.

After a certain age, chickens will eat almost anything
that grows from the Earth Mother. It is from the energy of
the Earth Mother that they grow and produce, the same as you.
Just take care of a few things for them and the Earth Mother
will take care of them and you as well.

## CARE OF A COW

Have you ever thought about having a cow? One cow can
give a couple of gallons of milk a day. What does that mean?
Well, even figuring at $1.80 a gallon, that's $3.60 a day or
almost $1100 a year after subtracting the two months when
she has her calf. If she has a heifer calf, you've got another potential milk cow. If it's a bull calf, you've got
your own meat supply.

When a cow has a calf, milk production will increase to
about four gallons a day. That's enough so you can have 1½
to 2 gallons after the calf gets its share. If that's more
milk than you can use, you can make cheese, cottage cheese,
yogurt, butter, buttermilk, and whipped cream from it. If
you're lucky like us and have an ice cream churn, you can make
superior ice cream.

If you use the calf for meat, this can account for 24% to
40% of your total food bill -- and that's all from one cow.

A healthy cow might cost between $600 and $800. Then
she'll need a shelter which shouldn't cost more than $100 if

you use inexpensive materials.  Ours didn't cost anything.

You'll need straw for the floor of her barn, about $25 worth per year.  It will take about two acres of pasture.  You will probably need oats (never barley) and sometimes a milk-producing supplement, but that shouldn't cost over $300 a year. You'll also need about two tons of alfalfa hay at $50 to $75 per ton.

There may be some veterinary bills, up to $75 to $100 a year, but a very reasonable sum to insure the health of the cow.  It's a good thing to get your cow from someone you know so you'll know you're getting a healthy cow to begin with.  If you don't know anyone in the business, cows do sell very cheaply at auction yards, but be cautious.  There is bound to be a reason why they're being sold.  Have her checked by a vet as soon as you have her home.

With a cow, you must be willing to take the time she requires.  She needs two milkings and two feedings a day -- 12 hours apart is ideal.  A six-inch plug of hay and a quart and a half of oats or grain supplement will hold her through each milking.

You will need a few simple pieces of equipment.  One is a stainless steel milk bucket, to be thoroughly cleaned with dairy detergent, then scalded after each use.  Also cheese-cloth for straining the milk.  You'll also need a rope halter and a lead rope and a watering trough and feed box.  These things shouldn't cost over $50.

A cow project might cost up to $1600 to get started, but it will produce $1100 per year in milk, plus 24% to 40% of your food bill if your cow has a bull calf.

A former Bear Tribe Holstein cow, Snow, and her calf Harry.

# Preserving Food

In this day and age, we have several choices open to us
for food preservation.  Almost any of these is preferable to
buying manufactured food at a supermarket at inflated prices.
If you have a garden of your own, have fruit trees, or raise
your meat, you will be able to feed your family much better for
much less money than city people can.  If you don't raise all
your own food, there are other ways of getting quantities of
it, such as gleaning, buying directly from the grower, and
trading.  You must be willing to invest your time, and learn
the best methods for certain foods to preserve their flavor
and quality and keep them safe for consumption.

It is possible to preserve foods by canning, freezing,
drying, smoking, and root cellar storage.

## Freezing

Today, people are discovering that freezing food, both raw
and cooked, is easier than canning and preserves nutrients, color,
texture and flavor better.  It makes it possible to take advantage
of quantity buying when foods are in season, or when special sales
are available.  It is possible to freeze leftovers for use at
another time or to prepare in advance for holiday and company
meals.  Wise use can make it possible for any family to eat better
on less money and conserve the time of the people for other activities.

Some fruits and vegetables should be blanched (steamed
quickly or boiled for 2 or 3 minutes, then immersed in cold
water) before freezing.  It is best to check in the freezer
manual for the correct amount of time to blanch each type
of food.

Meat should be ready to use before being wrapped.  It is
very difficult to do anything with a frozen solid piece of meat.
Be sure to wrap it twice to prevent freezer burn.  Take care to
rotate the food in the freezer every month or two.  Put dates
on your labels.

There is a disadvantage to freezing.  If the electricity is
out for any length of time, you're out of luck.

## Canning

There are different methods of canning different foods: cold packing, pressure canning, and open kettle canning. Be sure to follow the correct directions since the bacteria causing botulism may now be present in your soil even if they weren't in the past. Botulism can be carried from place to place and infect the soil, and if your canned food contains this bacteria, it will grow in the presence of moisture to become very poisonous, often deadly. Many times in the past people have eaten vegetables or meat improperly processed and not become ill because the soil was not infected BUT YOU CAN NOT BE SURE.

Most agricultural extension services have good free books on canning. Most cookbooks have canning sections. You can also buy the BALL BLUE BOOK or the Kerr Company canning book. These are reputable firms. Follow the instructions exactly. Have the book open as you can the food.

Before starting any canning process, inspect your jars carefully and discard any with even a tiny nick. Wash and rinse them thoroughly. Some canning methods require you to sterilize the jars. This is done by boiling them in a pan with some water in the pan and in each jar, for 20 minutes. The rings and seals should also be sterilized. Before you begin, read the specific instructions for what you are canning, and be sure you have everything you need, and that it is in good condition.

After each batch has been canned, lift it out of the canner and put it where it can stay undisturbed while it cools. There should be good air space around each jar so it can cool evenly and seal properly. Then test the seals. The cooling of the jar causes a vacuum to form inside and pull the "dome" lid down. If this does not happen, the jar hasn't sealed, and most likely won't if the jar has cooled off. You'll have to either eat the food right away, or can it again with a new seal. Under no circumstances should you try to use a seal a second time.

When you get ready to use your canned foods, you will be able to tell that they have a good seal by inspecting them, pushing on the lid or hitting it with metal. If you hear a hollow thump, throw it out. If you are in doubt, throw it out. Botulism poisoning is serious, sometimes fatal.

The basic steps in canning are these: choose good, firm fruit or vegetables, unless you are trying to save a crop; wash, cut, peel, pit, whatever is appropriate; cut out any bad spots; pack the fruit or vegetables into the jars no higher than one-half inch from the top; add water or syrup; wipe the rims of the jars clean then put the seals and rings on tight. Next you process the jars, either under pressure or in a canning kettle according to complete instructions.

We are fairly experienced at home drying and have run the gamut of successes and failures. We know what works for us, and wish to share it here.

From our point of view, drying is the most practical way of preserving food. Almost any fruit, vegetable, meat, or grain can be dried. We have heard of local Indians drying duck eggs.

The main thing to remember in ANY method of storage is the list of things that affect the overall quality of food -- and they are MOISTURE, LIGHT, PESTS and TEMPERATURE.

We don't sulphur anything. Some say that sulphuring saves the vitamin C in fruit (but destroys the B complex). It does preserve the color. We're willing to lose the color to preserve the natural taste. People have been drying things for at least 5000 years without sulphur.

Basically drying is the removal of MOISTURE which is the growth medium for bacteria, fungi, and molds. Sufficiently dried foods keep very well. They eventually deteriorate, but so do foods preserved by any other means.

We have found that it takes a real group effort to prepare large quantities of fruit or vegetables for drying. Removal of pits and cores requires a good sense of humor, endurance, and a willingness to get sticky. Unblemished fruit and vegetables dry best, but we've dried "culls" (seconds) with success after cutting the blemishes out. If you suspect pesticides have been used, wash whatever you want to dry.

We dry most things in the sun on cardboard flats. We spread the fruit or vegetables out in a single layer making sure the pieces don't touch (that causes rot), turn it sometimes for even drying, and let the sun do the work. This method works if there are no flies (PESTS), you don't have chickens, and your area doesn't get much rain or heavy dew (MOISTURE). Cheesecloth held down with clothespins takes care of the fly problem. A fence, either around the fruit or around the chickens, will take care of the pecking and other poultry problems. And a team of fast people can bring the fruit in the house every night or if it rains.

Most fruits dry easily by the methods already described.
Some notable exceptions are watermelon and non-raisin grapes.
We have dried strawberries and other berries by sewing them
together in garlands and hanging them by both ends. We know
that Pueblo Indians dry melons by quartering them and peeling
them, then hanging them on line in the sun. We haven't tried
it yet.

Most fruits are quite edible in dry form if you have good
teeth, but they can all be reconstituted by soaking several
hours in water or by boiling, with or without sweetener.

In the vegetable department, we've dried zucchini, celery,
cut corn, onions, cabbage, carrots, peppers, and string beans.
String beans must be dried slowly in the shade. We strung
them on thread and decorated our office with them for almost a
month. These are called Leather Britches beans and you cook
them several hours with a hambone if you have one. Unless
you're drying a stringless variety, it is wise to string them
before drying.

Meats and fishes are easily dried. Jerky is made by cutting the meat in thin strips and sewing it together. The whole
string can be boiled rapidly for 3 minutes in very salty water
(10% solution, one that floats an egg) and hung to dry for 3 to
10 days, depending on the moisture in the air. Meat strips can
also be put in a pan with salt packed between the layers for a
day before you string them. Small fish filets can be salted
well and hung until dry. Fish and meat can also be smoked,
but we haven't tried it yet.

The STORAGE of dried foods is just as important as the
drying. Be sure all the food is completely dry. The drier it
is, the longer it will keep. Package it in small plastic bags
and seal them tightly with twister seals. The reason for the
small batches is that if spoilage does begin, it will stay
within the one bag. The MOISTURE will not spread easily to
others. We freeze each bag for at least 48 hours to kill any
bugs - bacteria, larvae, or whatever. Then we put the little
bags in airtight containers, as the lack of OXYGEN  retards
the growth of some bacteria. Then we store the whole works
in a fairly dark, cool place.

One life-saver has been rotating the food every two months
or so. This gives you a better idea of how fast you're using
certain foods and what you have left. You can discard any bags
that might have spoiled. It is also an opportunity to see
whether or not you need mousetraps in your storage area. It is

a good idea to have a reminder that our enemies are MOISTURE, LIGHT, HEAT, and PESTS.  Although light, heat, and oxygen helped us to dry the foods to begin with, they do nothing to improve the flavors and nutrition of the food once it is dry.

## Smoking

Smoking meat and fish is a slow process for removing the moisture which causes spoilage, and for permeating it with smoke which acts as a natural preservative.  A smouldering fire is built of hardwood, and a low temperature (never over 90 degrees F.) is maintained in the smoke chamber.

Remember that it takes time, not heat, to dry the meat.

Meat is cleaned and prepared by cutting it in slices and hanging it in an enclosure where smoke can reach all surfaces. Uneven smoking will not preserve the meat.  Fish may be smoked whole if they are not too large, but they must be opened out so that smoke reaches every inside and outside surface.  No piece of fish or meat should be touching anything.

The fire should be made with hardwood, such as hickory or alder.  Soft woods are not suitable.  A smoke tunnel is needed to conduct the smoke, but not the heat, from the fire to the smoking chamber.  It is sometimes best to install a simple baffle to distribute the smoke evenly in the smoke chamber.

Cool smoking will preserve the meat.  If the meat becomes too hot, it will cook, and then it must be frozen, canned, or eaten immediately.

Northwest Native people have used cool smoking to preserve their salmon and other meat for many centuries, and many of them have impressive smokehouses just for that purpose.

# Root Cellars

A root cellar is very important when you raise your own vegetables and fruits. It functions in several ways. It is used to store your tuberous vegetables, fresh and canned food, and in some cases, serves as a storm cellar. It is comparatively simple to construct, although it takes a lot of hard work with a shovel.

First you dig a pit about the size of an average room in a house, if this will be adequate for your needs, with a slightly sloping floor for drainage. The walls can be lined with rock and mortar or other materials if you choose, or if you are uncertain of the lasting value of the walls otherwise. Rock is a good material to use in a root cellar because it gives the desired coolness.

Be sure there is adequate drainage from your root cellar. Stagnant water is not something you want in with your food.

The pit should be covered except for the entrance, with a cover that will support the weight of the earth that will cover it to give it its insulated qualities. An insulated door is necessary, and a ladder or steps. When you have shelves for canned goods, and bins lined with good wheat straw, your cellar is finished.

The purpose of the cellar is to preserve your food. Milk and eggs can be set there as well as potatoes, rutabagas, carrots, cabbage, beets, onions, pumpkins, squash and melons. Winter apples do extremely well there. Be sure to pack everything but potatoes and carrots in straw. The potatoes and carrots should be packed in boxes of earth. Be careful to pack vegetables well so they do not touch each other, because they will rot where they touch if they are left for long enough. During summer months your root cellar can preserve many vegetables and fruits you would otherwise have to refrigerate.

It is very important to check your stored foods every few weeks to remove any that might be bad. Ultimately, this effort will reduce spoilage.

# *Storing for Survival*

It is our belief that mainly those people living on the land in groups in harmony with each other and the Earth Mother will survive the coming cleansing of the earth. For these groups to survive, they must be prepared. That means that they must have stored enough supplies to sustain the group for a period of three or more years.

What will you need to survive? First of all, water. If you have chosen your land well, you will have a good natural water supply that will flow without interruption. A spring or well is the best alternative. If you get your water from a stream it might be cut off or become unsafe during certain periods of the cleansing of the earth. To make sure you'll have some water if such periods arise you should fill some glass or plastic containers with fresh water, store in a safe place, and check every few months for leaks and freshness. Figure on a minimum of one half gallon of water per person per day for drinking. To use water that is unsafe, purify it by boiling for one to three minutes then pour it from one container to another several times to get some air and flavor back in. You may also purify it by adding any bleach that has hypochlorite as its only active ingredient (8 drops to a gallon of clear water, 16 if the water is cloudy), letting the water sit for half an hour and checking that the chlorine smell is still there. If it isn't, add another dose of the bleach and let stand for another 15 minutes. You may also use 3 percent tincture of iodine. Add 12 drops to a gallon of clear water, and twice that to cloudy. Or you can use water purification tablets if you have them. These methods are useful when the water is unsafe because of bacteria or other organisms. They will not help with chemical pollution or radioactivity.

Alternatively, you can use granular activated charcoal (GAC). It can be used by pouring water through the GAC in a coffee melita with a coffee filter.

Next you should have on hand a large supply of any herbal or prescription medication needed by members of your group: birth control pills, heart pills, allergy pills, insulin, etc. Then, of course, you'll need food, and seeds, canning and drying equipment, fishing and hunting gear. Having a varied diet is very essential to keeping your balance so we really urge any of you who think you can live completely off the land to re-think your plan. While you can get your meat through hunting, and forage for wild greens, berries, herbs and fruits, we believe that this can be irresponsible as it puts too much strain on the Mother Earth at this time. If you have a good supply of seeds you can grow your own vegetables then can or dry them for the fall, winter and spring when you can't get them fresh. Besides canning equipment (remember to have 3 or 4 times the number of lids as jars and rings) you'll need sugar or honey for canning fruits and jams, salt for vegetables, and vinegar, dill and spices for pickling.

Because growing a garden may be difficult or impossible for a year or two we suggest that you have canned foods, and dried ones on hand. For a family of five you'll need on the average 2 cans of soups per day, 2 of vegetable, 1 meat, and 2 fruit, plus 5 cans of juice per week. In addition for a year you'll need at least 12 three-pound cans of shortening, 6 cans of baking powder, and 8 gallons of clorox for water and other purification.

Besides your fruits, juices and vegetables, you'll also need some staples. With a mixed diet an adult will use 300 pounds of wheat per year, or 100 pounds of flour. Wheat is cheaper to get and easier to store than flour. Make sure to get a hand powered grinder with a stone buhr to grind the wheat. Each adult will also need 80 pounds of powdered milk, 150 pounds of dried beans and peas (including soybeans, your best non-meat source of protein), 60 pounds of honey, and 50 pounds of peanut butter per year. In addition to the above store any itmes that you're used to having in your diet: for instance coffee, tea, herbs for tea, oats, rice, barley, nuts, hard candies, salt, pepper, spices, vinegar, oil, desserts, corn meal, potatoes, syrup, molasses. To figure out how much you need to store, mark boxes or jars and see how much you use over a 2-week period and figure that amount times 26 for a year's supply. Store things that will keep well and store them in moisture-, mouse-, and insect-proof containers whenever possible.

What hunting and fishing gear you'll need depends on what you are used to and can use. Unless you think you want to be vegetarian (which may not be practical in a period when vegetables may not grow well) you should know how to use something. A .22 is a good all around rifle, but you have to be a good shot to get small game with it. Shotguns are good for that. Get the right ammunition for the guns you have and get plenty of it. For fishing get plenty of line, an assortment of hooks, flies, sinkers, and a float.  You can make your own pole, and later, your own flies.  In case you hit a period where no game is available to you we suggest having a supply of jerky, dried fish and canned meat and fish on hand.

You should also have in storage (or in use) tools that you are likely to need.  These should include a good case skinning knife, a sharpening stone, a double bit axe, a saw, shovel, hammer, screw drivers, nails, screws, hoe, spade, pliers, pots, pans, plates, bowls, silverware, long handled fork, towels, sheets, matches, several canvas tarps or large pieces of heavy plastic, a fire grill, canteens, washboard, rope, pails, can openers and other utensils for cooking and eating.  And you should stock up on sanitary and personal items: soaps of all kinds, disinfectants, cleaning solutions, toilet paper, sufficient bedding for everyone, personal clothes, sweaters, heavy jackets and rain ponchos, sewing equipment, craft supplies, good hiking or woodsman boots, boots or overshoes for winter, work gloves, tooth equipment (include dental floss), sanitary napkins, extra underwear, alcohol, ammonia, aspirin, bandages, band-aids, cotton, ear drops, epsom salt, paragoric, safety pins, shampoo, thermometers, tweezers, antihistimine, linament, calamine lotion, vaseline, smake bite kits, insect repellent, and vitamins.  You'll probably also want reading and writing material, cards and other games.

You'll also need to store different fuels to combat the present fuel shortages, and the worse ones that we'll face in the future.  Gasoline is a good fuel that can not only power your car but also generators and various other things.  It can be stored in the metal gasoline cans made specifically for that purpose, or in metal drums.  For reasons of both safety and security it is probably best to bury the drums, and not let people see what you are doing.  Unleaded gasoline can also be used to fuel coleman stoves and lanterns.  We don't feel that either natural or propane gas will be available for use for an indefinite period, nor do we recommend storing them.  Other than gasoline, the only other fuel we feel will be relevant is wood (or possibly coal if you're in an area where it is available).  Wood is a good fuel for both heating and cooking, and it is easily available in most areas.  We think that you'll be safe if you just have a year's supply ready in advance.  In any case, you should always get in your winter's supply before it gets too wet and cold to do so.  Four to eight cords of wood should be enough for the heating and cooking needs of a four-room cabin, depending on the area where the cabin is located. For additional light needs you should have a good supply of

candles, flashlights, batteries, kerosene lanterns and kerosene.

We know that we've suggested storing a substantial amount
of goods of all kinds and that it will be costly to do so.
However, we can't think of any safer investment you can make.
While we are geared to having small groups together on the land,
we feel that you should start storing these supplies wherever
you are and whatever your family structure. We do urge city
dwellers to at least think of places in the country where they
might be able to store some of their supplies. We think you
should start gathering your storage supplies now. While we
can't put a date on when we think this system will destroy
itself completely, we don't think there is much time left.
And it's better to have your survival supplies ready a year
too early than an hour too late.

# Making Meat

For those who like to eat meat, hunting is an essential skill. There may be times when vegetarians will have to eat meat or starve, so everyone should know how to hunt if they have to. Before beginning, always pray to the guardian spirit of the animal you seek. Explain that you have need of one of its sons or daughters to continue your life, and that you, too, will someday feed the Earth Mother. When you make a kill, always thank the animal for giving its life and pray for its spirit to go quickly to the Great Spirit.

When we have to hunt in hot weather we catch fish and hunt small animals like ground squirrels, woodchucks, etc. (although care must be taken with small, furry animals during the summer because of rabies and because cases of the plague have been reported in the Southwest and West). We hunt big game in the fall and winter. In cold climates if you hunt in November you can freeze your meat and it will keep outside in a shed all winter. Do cut the meat before it freezes.

In hunting, especially still hunting, patience is important. If you find a water hole where game comes to water you may have to come back and sit more than one evening to get meat. In deer country if you put out salt near one of their runways you can get them coming there regularly. If you make a kill, clean up all of the blood and cover it over so as not to scare off other game. Late afternoon or early evening is the best time to hunt deer and rabbit. In stalking game, try to blend into the surrounding country as much as possible. Placing grass on your hat and binding brush to your arms will change your appearance enough to enable you to get close to game. Wear brown, grey, greens, black or levi blue, no white or bright colors. The Indian bowman knew he had to get close in order to get meat with his bow and arrow. Sometimes it might take half a day of stalking but time wasn't the important factor. Food was. So if it takes all day to get meat, fine. At the same time you're enjoying the countryside.

A 45 or 50 pound bow with blade head hunting arrows is good for the bowman. And you can learn how to shape your arrowheads from obsidian or flint using a deer antler or nail to flake them off, and then, by feathering your own shafts, you are one step closer to self reliance.

If you want to use guns, two of the best are the 20-gauge over under, or the 410 gauge 22 over under. A 22 rifle is a good all around gun. A 22 repeater long rifle with hollow point shells is best. Shotguns are good and they'll keep you in small game like ducks, grouse and rabbits. Buy good ammunition.

Get yourself a good case skinning knife. You don't need a big machete on your hip if you get a good knife. Keep it sharp, and know how to use it.

To skin rabbits, squirrels and other small game, cut around the back legs by the feet and then cut down the inside of the legs to the rectum. It's best to put the point of the knife under the skin and cut. Then work the skin free from the body using both your fingers and knife. Pull the skin over the body toward the front legs. Cut carefully around the legs cutting the skin free at the wrist of the paw. Take your time around the ears and eyes if you want to save the whole hide. On rabbits you can just cut the skin off at the neck. Use wire coat hangers bent into shape to stretch the pelts. Now, to prepare the carcass of small game for cooking, cut off the feet and the head then cut into the stomach and draw out the entrails. You can then reach up into the rib cage and draw out the heart and liver, both of which make good eating. Wash the meat in water. If it's bloody, let it sit overnight in cold water.

In skinning deer and other big animals first cut the throat to bleed the meat. Cut the skin around the back legs then cut down the inside of the legs to the rectum, cut around the rectum, then cut down the belly between the front legs to the throat. Cut around the front legs and then work the hide off. If you can, hang the animal from a tree by the hind legs as it's easier to skin. Otherwise, skin it out by using your hands to pull and cut with your knife where necessary. Keep the carcass on the skin if skinning on the ground. Cut through the belly and remove the entrails. Cut into the chest cavity and remove lungs, heart and liver. Cook up the heart and liver the first night. Give the lungs to your pets. Wiggle the legs and you can see where to cut at the joints. Cut through the meat around the backbone then cut the ribs loose by first splitting the breast plate with either a heavy knife or a hatchet and then cut the ribs away from the backbone. Cut chops and steaks from the legs and back.  The rest of the meat is good for roasting, stew meat or soup bones.  Remember to use all of the meat.  Don't waste the gifts that the four-leggeds have given to you.

## FISHING

Hook and line is probably the most-used method of fishing. You should have the fishing equipment you are used to, but if you don't, you can improvise.  The point is to catch food, not the sport of game fishing.  A variety of hooks will equip you for different kinds of fish, depending on where you plan to fish.  A pole can be made of a switch from a large bush, or from a branch.  All it does is enable you to get your baited hook to the fish.

Suitable bait is anything that looks good to a fish.  It can be a piece of cheese, corn, worms, or a fly that looks juicy. Learn where the fish hang out (on the bottom, in the shady eddies, etc.).  Do not think you can't catch fish without the usual equipment.  A little imagination and prayer go a long way.

Nets can be used for catching fish, either by scooping them out of the water when they run heavy, or by securing a net in a body of water where fish are likely to be.

Don't take the lives of fish unless you need to.  Be sure you understand the law in your state with regard to fishing.  In some places, the use of nets is illegal, and the catch limit will vary according to what kind of fish you're after.  Remember to make your prayers, the same as you would when you take any other animal or plant life.

# *Wild Plants*

While we feel that relying solely on wild plants is irresponsible at this time because they have been reduced dangerously in numbers by human carelessness, we do feel they can be used sparingly to supplement one's diet.

When we need to pick an herb or plant, we always approach it with humility and respect. We tell the herbs why we need them, and how we plan to use them. We never pick the first of any herb or other wild food that we see. Rather, we make an offering of tobacco, corn-meal, or of a special prayer. We never take from the Earth Mother and our fellow creatures without giving also.

We always harvest the plants quickly, but carefully, so as not to prolong the trauma of picking. While harvesting, we continually give thanks in our hearts. We never "clear cut" a plant patch. It is important to leave enough plants growing so that they can replace themselves and multiply, so that there will be plentiful wild plants for this generation, and all generations to come.

When picking wild plants it is always wise to be cautious. Some poisonous plants closely resemble edible ones. Following are some safety hints on edible plants:

1.   There is no general reliable test for poisonous plants such as milky juice being present or absent. For instance, the dandelion has milky juice and is edible whereas some of the most poisonous plants do not have it.

2.   Wild animals eat various poisonous plants. However, they have a different digestive system and these same plants may poison humans.

3.   Livestock usually avoid toxic plants if others are available but in the spring and when they are hungry they will graze on poisonous plants, sometimes with fatal results.

4.   Some plants are poisonous when they are wilted such as chokecherry twigs and some grasses. Therefore, use fresh plants.

5.   The toxic property may be concentrated or even confined to one part of the plant such as the elderberry where all parts are poisonous with the exception of the RIPE purplish-black berries.

6.   In some cases cooking tends to destroy the poison in the plant, but this doesn't hold true in all cases.

7.   Don't use any wild plants that look like wild carrot or parsley unless you're absolutely sure of your species.  It may be poison hemlock.

8.   Don't eat white or red colored berries without being absolutely sure of the plant.  Use caution on blue or black berries, even some of them are poisonous.

9.   It is best to avoid all mushrooms and toadstools (except the ones that you buy at the store) as even experts have been fooled as to which ones are poisonous and which are edible. Caution: The edibility test is not reliable on mushrooms as some species do not show symptoms of poisoning for up to three days.  A pea-sized portion of some mushrooms can kill you.   It only takes one mistake.

10.  Don't eat any plants from soil that is known to contain selenium or from soil where plant "indicators" of selenium grow.

11.  Some plants such as lambs quarters absorb toxic levels of nitrates from commercial fertilizers.  Avoid these plants in commercially fertilized areas.

12.  Avoid plants close to main roadsides as many times they are sprayed with toxic weed control chemicals as well as the exhaust of cars.

13.  Be sure you know the plant in its very young stages as well as other stages of growth.

14.  A wild plant is not necessarily edible just because it looks somewhat like a well known species.

15.  Always use caution in trying an unknown plant even if you think you know you're sure; some poisonous effects are cumulative.

16.  Many plants are toxic if they are moldy.  Use fresh plants.

17.  The fungus, ergot, is poisonous and will affect several types of grain.  Avoid grain that has turned a dark color and is several times the size of other individual grains.

18.  Learn the common poisonous plants of the area, particularly those that may be mistaken for edible plants.

19.  Build your recognition list of edible plants with great care so that you are familiar with them at all stages of growth. It is better to be too cautions than to end up in the hospital or cemetery.

20.  Don't gorge yourself on unfamiliar food until your system becomes used to it.

21.  Whenever possible, eat the plants raw since prolonged boiling tends to get rid of vitamins and enzymes very quickly.

22.  When boiling wild plants it is wise to use several changes of water.  Throw away the first one as it may be too bitter.

23.  Don't eat wild plants when you know radiation levels are high in the area.


There are many varieties of plants you can eat safely. Following are some common ones we like which grow in most areas of the country.  The list just gives you a few ideas of the many plants that are edible.  If you want to know more, consult the many good books now available on the subject.

ACORNS - The Indians are very fond of these nuts.  We gather them in the fall as they drop from the trees.  If left on the ground they will get wormy.  We shell them and then leach out the bitterness by pouring hot water over them and draining them repeatedly.  Then we grind them and use them as flour mixed with other meal, or we add them to beans and soups.

BURDOCK - Young tender shoots can be peeled and eaten raw or fried in butter or oil.  They can also be mashed and made into cakes and fried in butter.

CAT TAILS - Young shoots can be cleaned and eaten raw like celery, or they can be steamed with other vegetables.  The "sausage" top can also be steamed and eaten like corn on the cob.

DANDELION - Young leaves can be used in a salad, or older leaves can be boiled in two waters to remove the bitterness for a green vegetable similar to spinach or beet tops.  These greens have a large amount of Vitamin A.

page 145

LAMBS QUARTERS - These make a fine summer potherb. They grow almost anywhere. They should be boiled in two waters which does away with any bad taste they may have picked up.

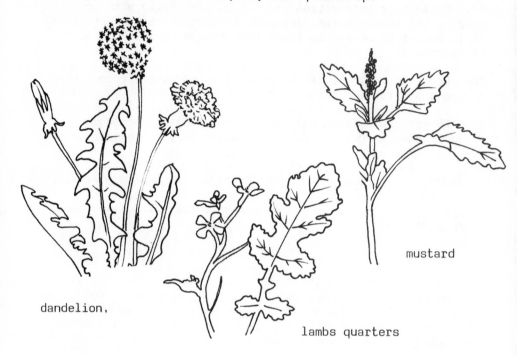

dandelion,

lambs quarters

mustard

MILKWEED - The young shoots of milkweed also may be boiled, although older stems are too acid and milky for use. Young pods are excellent when cooked.

MUSTARD - These greens are excellent cooked. They will aid your digestion. The roots can be ground as a garnish for meat.

PINE NUTS - The cone of the pinon pine yields a small nut inside a thin shell. They are harvested by Indian people in Nevada, California, New Mexico and other places. They are usually roasted and eaten hot, although they can be eaten raw or in a soup.

WILD FRUIT AND BERRIES - Many wild berries are edible. Many are eaten raw. Many, along with other wild fruits are good dried or even canned for later use.

WILD OATS - This grain is roasted or singed over a fire to get rid of the sharp beards. Then it can be ground into a meal and used for flour or soup thickening.

Why use herbs for healing? An understanding of their true nature will help answer that question. Herbs have a definite relationship to all other aspects of nature, including humans. The way herbs interact with people, when introduced in the form of tea, powder, or when smoked, is a result of the nature of the specific herb. All herbs differ in the way that they affect us, and we all react differently to them. Basically, I see an herb as a "command" -- a "command" from God or the Great Spirit. An herb is an embodiment of light and the will of the Creator. When an herb is introduced to the body, the body reacts to the Creator's will, or command.

An important aspect of using herbs for healing is respect. If one can see that an herb is an aspect of God's will, and is knowable -- would one knowingly violate the will of the Creator? Herbs must be used as what they are -- living, sensitive creatures. If they are thought of as inert, dead substances, such as the pills one buys at a drug store, they have less to give to you -- because you have not given them respect.

Humans and herbs belong together. Herbs are a gentle medicine, however, and reflect this aspect of our Creator's love for us. Please be gentle with herbs, and they will fill you with the love of the Creator.

As with other wild plants, herbs deserve your love and respect, especially when you're picking them. Herbs should be picked when their properties are strongest: when leaves are grown and green, when flowers are fully flowered, when roots are grown but not old and woody. If you are not sure of the time, ask the herb.

Herbs dry best in shade. When dry they should be stored in a dark place in airtight containers so that they retain their properties.

If possible we like to use herbs that grow nearby, especially for medicine. However, this isn't always practical as we sometimes need herbs that don't grow locally.

There are so many useful herbs, that we can't list many here, but we've chosen a few that we find helpful. For more information we again refer you to the many excellent books now available on the subject.

ALFALFA is high in vitamins and minerals, stops internal bleed-ing, and aids in treatment of arthritis.

BURDOCK ROOT is a blood purifier, a tonic, and an aid in lung congestion.

CATNIP is soothing to the nerves, especially for infants, and also reduces fevers and helps to cure colds and relieve intestinal spasm.

CAYENNE pepper is a seasoning which also is used to dilate constricted blood vessels, and help to cure colds.

CHAMOMILE is soothing to the nerves, and good for toothhaches, earaches, and indigestion.  It is also a tonic and tissue strengthener.

COMFREY LEAVES soothe the stomach, purify the blood, stop in-ternal bleeding, help gallstones, headaches, cuts and burns. Externally, they make a good poultice.

COMFREY ROOT is a blood purifier, and also helps rheumatism, flu, gland disorders, coughs, colds and stomach ulcers.

ECHINACEA was used by some tribes as a blood purifier, and to heal ulcers, infections, insect bites, abcesses, sores and wounds.

EPHEDRA (Mormon, Squaw or Indian tea) is a stimulant which can help relieve congestion and arthritis.

GOLDEN SEAL ROOT is soothing to the mucus membranes, good for flu, skin eruptions, nose bleeds and sore throats.  It is a tonic and antiseptic.

HOPS is a sedative, and blood cleanser. It can be used to expel poison and kill worms, and to cure headaches.

HOREHOUND breaks up congestion, helps cure coughs, lung and throat ailments, ulcers, and is an antidote for poisons and venomous bites, and a laxative.

JUNIPER BERRIES help to heal indigestion, coughs, skin diseases. They are also a diuretic.

MATE is a South American Native tea which is a stimulant and purgative.

MULLEIN helps get rid of colds and congestions, coughs, sore throats and skin irritations.

OREGON GRAPE ROOT is a blood purifier and tonic, improves digestion and skin.

PEPPERMINT aids in stomach disorders, with heartburn, gas and flu.

PLANTAIN stops external bleeding, makes a poultice for infections, rashes, bee-stings.

RASPBERRY LEAF is used for colds, canker sores, stomach complaints, female problems and wounds.

ROSE HIPS are high in natural vitamin C.

SAGE helps cure colds, skin disorders, and is used for purification.

SASSAFRAS is a flavoring which purifies the blood, helps toothaches and skin problems.

SPEARMINT is a flavoring which soothes the nerves and stomach.

SLIPPERY ELM is used for ulcers, internal bleeding, burns and inflamed mucus membranes.

UVA URSI (Bearberry, kinnikinnick) is a tonic and diuretic.

YARROW is used for colds, external and internal bleeding, flu and fevers.

YELLOW DOCK (Curly dock) helps with boils and other skin eruptions and rheumatism.

YERBA SANTA is used for chest congestion, asthma, and, externally, for poison oak.

BEAR TRIBE HERBAL TOBACCO is our own kinnikinnick mixture of good herbs.  It aids people who wish to stop smoking tobacco, and has none of the tobacco's poisons.

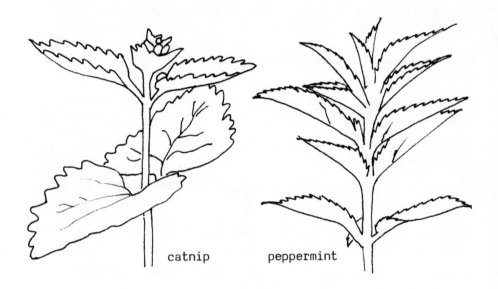

catnip          peppermint

When we get sick we often use herbs and other natural medicines to heal ourselves.

Even with Good Medicine, it's hard to keep perfectly healthy these days.  Living in an industrial country we are constant targets of chemical warfare and nuclear radiation. Hardly a day goes by that you don't see a news story about the "newly discovered" harmful effects of some food, drink, wrapping or drug that the Food and Drug Administration has previously blessed.  All the while the defense business continues to create new forms of germs and viruses for future warfare. Some of these, it seems by reports of flu and other epidemics, sometimes slip past their protective defenses.  So, if you don't live in a situation where you can grow your own food, drink only pure mountain water, breathe only fresh air, and not be exposed to people who do otherwise, it's pretty inevitable that some time during each year you'll be sick, with at least a cold or the flu.

The Bear Tribe has the same attitude toward doctors as we do toward auto mechanics. If you know just about what is wrong, what you need to get it fixed, and you can't do it yourself, then take your body to a doctor or your car to a mechanic. But if you can fix either on your own, you run a lot less risk.

We believe that doctors are good for mechanical problems -- taking preventive tests, giving innoculations, setting broken bones, prescribing antibiotics for serious infections, delivering babies if home delivery seems inadvisable -- but we feel that, like other mechanics, they don't have as many answers as they think they do, and they often overcharge for their advice and labor.

Consequently, we're always trying to find ways to keep our bodies functioning well, and to do minor repairs ourselves.

None of us are expert nutritionists or herbalists, but we do read what we can on the subject, and talk with people who are willing to share their expertise with us. Nor do we believe that herbs are the only good method of treatment. Like homeopaths (like cures like) we feel that small quantities of any drug or substance that gets your natural defenses working is good. There have been times when we've felt our own defenses were weak enough that we've used normal quantities of antibiotics or decongestants. But the side effects of such drugs have proven bad enough that we avoid doing so if at all possible.

Here we'd like to hsare with you some of the cures that we've actually used for colds, flus, and minor infections with good results. We can't promise these cures will give you the same results, but they're worth a try. If you are pregnant, dealing with a small child, or seriously ill, you should, of course, see a body mechanic.

The cold is one common and annoying sickness that responds well to home care. If you are getting slight sniffles and take 250 mgs. of vitamin C (preferably organic) four times a day, that is sometimes enough. If it isn't, the best cure we've discovered is <u>chewing</u> (don't just swallow) one large clove of organic garlic in the morning, and one at night. If you chew some parsley afterwards, it gets rid of the taste. If you still can't stand the taste, try cutting a small garlic clove into tiny pieces, putting it in a cup and mashing it. Add the juice of ¼ small lemon. Brew a cup of herb tea -- mint is good -- and add the garlic, lemon and some honey. Let it sit three minutes. Drink a cup three times a day until the cold is gone. We've cured bad colds that have gone to the throat or ears in four days using this method. Sun Bear's favorite cold remedy is hot apple cider vinegar and honey tea, which is made by adding a cup of boiling water to 2-3 tablespoons of vinegar and as much honey as you need to make it drinkable. Some of us substitute lemon juice for vinegar in this recipe.

Another herbal cure we've used for colds, flus and other infections caught in the early stages is our herbal infection mixture, consisting of one part golden seal powder, to two parts each of myrrh and echinacea powder. This really tastes bad so we put it in large sized capsules and take 3 or 4 each day. If you can rest as soon as you feel a cold or flu coming on, that helps a lot. So does a long, tepid, soaking bath. Also be conscious of not exposing other people to your mucus.

Teas that we've found to help cure colds and flu are yarrow, comfrey leaf, and chamomile mixed together. We usually put a tablespoon of each in about a quart of boiling water, and let steep for 20 minutes. If this is all you'll be using for a home cure, make it medicine strength, which is one tablespoon of the mixture to one cup of water. We have also used ephedra (squaw) tea to relieve masal congestion.

If we have a fever with a flu we sometimes take large capsules filled with cayenne pepper (capsicum). The cayenne helps us to sweat more profusely which gets rid of the toxins in our body so the fever can break. We also take a cayenne capsule followed by some lemon juice before we take our sweats, as this causes us to sweat more and get rid of more toxic matter. Cayenne does speed up your heart and circulation so be cautious if you have any heart problems. Some tribal medicine people use sweats to make a fever run its course quicker. We don't recommend that a lay person use this method. Instead, use cold baths or alcohol rubs given every 15 to 30 minutes until the fever is down, or sponge the person off with cool cloths. In between coolings, be sure the person is covered well so they don't chill.

For teas to combat a fever, take peppermint and elder flower (or yarrow) tea made by adding 2 cups of boiling water to ¼ ounce of elder flowers (or yarrow). Drink, then go to bed. The tea works by opening the pores so the toxins can come out. This is okay for children. Medicine strength sage tea is also good. If the fever is 104 degrees F. or higher it is <u>dangerous</u>, and you'd better get to a doctor fast.

For stomach flu (or food poisoning) the quickest cure we've found is taking large capsules of golden seal powder, along with Vitamin C. We've taken them every hour or two for up to eight hours, and been rid of all the flu symptoms by then. When we have stomach flu, we don't try to eat until we feel like it, and we usually start off with citrus fruit. Peppermint, chamomille, and comfrey tea, separately or together seem to settle the stomach. You can also try vinegar and honey tea for stomach pain or flu.

Remember that often what we consider colds or other illnesses are really the body cleansing itself of the toxins (poisons) it can't handle. Heavy medication will suppress the symptoms without really helping effect a cure. When your body is trying to clean itself out the best thing you can do is help it by fasting or eating only lightly, taking an enema if you know how to properly, drinking herb teas to cleanse the kidneys, sweating, bathing in hot then cold water, and using dry body massage with a rough cloth or luffa to cleanse the skin. Sleeping is good as the body can often work better if we're not disturbing it. Don't do any of the things we've suggested unless they feel right to you and your body. Remember, more natural methods of healing often take longer than chemicals. Be patient and listen to your body. Respect it and consider it worthy of healing. Pray for whatever healing is supposed to come to you. Picture yourself as healthy again.

In an emergency situation, a visualization technique can help. In a reassuring, positive tone of voice, let the victim know that you are there to help him, then direct him to close his eyes. Place your fingers or palm very lightly on the injured spot and tell the victim to focus his attention on the touch of your hand. Change the position of where you are touching him and repeat this instruction. For best results, apply your touch to areas which are further from his head than the pain area.

Speak positively but not excessively. As you touch him briefly, spot after spot, direct him to put his attention on the feeling of your touch. If there is any trembling or pain experienced, keep up the treatments for several minutes up to an hour, if necessary, until most of the pain has been relieved. At this time the victim may be directed to apply his own touch to these areas and may thereby aid himself.

Normally there is pain and slow recovery with injuries, sprains, burns, headaches, and colds as the victim is avoiding the "hurt" area with his vital energy. Although it may seem

otherwise, it is not the power from your finger which aids him;
it is his own vital force that he generates by focusing on the
touch of your hand on his body.  All you are doing is placing
him in communication with the injury, which allows him to send
his own vital force to the spot in order to promote healing,
and stop the pain.  Needless to say, if there is any first aid
equipment available, it is to be used accordingly.

In cases where you are alone, this technique is just as
effective.  Instead of talking to the victim, talk to yourself and apply the touching system on your own body.  Allow
yourself the realization that the vital healing force is there;
all you have to do is to direct it by focusing on the right
spot.  Normally, this force flows naturally to all parts of the
body, thus keeping one in good health.  However, in the case of
a sudden injury, pain may create fear, panic and shock which
results in the mental blockage of this force.

"Our old food we used to eat was good.  The meat from the
buffalo and game was good.  It made us strong.  These cows are
good to eat, soft, tender, but they are not like that meat.  Our
people used to live a long time.  Today we eat white man's food,
we cannot live so long -- maybe seventy, maybe eighty years, not
a hundred.  Sweet Medicine told us that.  He said his food would
be sweet, and after we taste that food, we want it, and forget
our own foods.  Chokecherries and plums and wild turnips and
honey from the wild bees, that was our food.  This other food
is too sweet.  We eat it and forget ... It's all coming true,
what he said." Fred Last Bull, Keeper of the Sacred Arrows of
the Cheyenne Tribe told that to an audience in Busby, Montana
in  1967.

We feel that Sweet Medicine's words of prophecy are true,
and that more people every day are becoming aware of the
possibility that the food they are eating to sustain them may,
in reality, be killing them.

Each day we see the Food and Drug Administration raise new
issues about the safety and purity of the food we eat.  First
it was breakfast cereals, then cyclamates, now red dye #2,
which is used in just about everything.  And just because the
FDA decertified red dye #2 doesn't mean it's off the shelves.
Manufacturers have to stop producing it, but they are allowed
to sell the inventories they have that contain it.  Now red dye
#40, which is being used to replace #2 is also suspected of
causing cancer.  Preservatives  are also exceptionally harmful
in food.  Sodium nitrate and sodium nitrite, used, again, in
just about everything, produce changes in cell structure and
may cause cancer.  BHA and BHT, petroleum products used to
preserve many other foods, cause a reduced growth weight, liver
problems and fetal abnormalities.  Stilbestrol, a hormone
popular for fattening cattle up, causes the meat to be mostly
water fat, not protein, and can cause breast cancer and fibroid
tumors in women, sterility and impotence in men and arrested
growth in children.  In late 1970, the FDA doubled the amount
of stilbestrol allowed in cattle feed.  We could go on, but you
probably get the idea.

What can we do?  We all have to eat, and most of us can't afford to buy only health food products and game.  What we have done is try to balance our budget with the knowledge we have about nutrition, and about the things that are particularly harmful, with no redeeming qualities.

White flour and white sugar, from all reputable reports, seem to be of no value to our bodies.  So we try to substitute wheat flour and honey whenever possible.  If someone gives us a bag of white flour we don't throw it away, but we use it in combination with wheat.

We try to grow as much of our fruits and vegetables as possible.  We recycle things we can't eat for compost, we don't use organic sprays, and we put a lot of love into our garden.  In return we get natural foods, safe from pesticides and hormones.  As we've said in the past, it is feasible for most everyone to have a garden these days, to help your budget as well as your body.  Even in the city, you can find vacant lots or backyards where you can plant a small garden.  To preserve our fruits and vegetables for the months when they can't grow, we dry or can them.  Remember to check out abandoned orchards, or orchards where you can pick things yourself, and ask the grower whether or not he uses pesticides.  Organic fruit is better, but so hard to get these days that we use other fruit, but peel it or wash it well.

Sprouts are a good year-round way of getting Vitamin C and minerals.  They are easily made with alfalfa seeds, lentils, wheat and other grains and seeds.  Start with organic seeds, put them in a jar, let them stand in water for about eight hours, drain, wash and rinse them with water three or four times a day for the next three days.  By the fourth day they should be fairly sprouted.  Rinse them, then put them in the sun for a day so their chlorophyll will come out, bag them and refrigerate them until you use them in salads, eggs, soups, stews; almost anything.

To get unadulterated meats we not only raise our own animals but also make our own feed.  If you buy commercial chicken feed, for instance, you get just about all the hormones that commercial chicken farmers do.  If you raise your own chickens, using feed you've made, you're also fairly certain of getting good, fresh eggs.

For those of you who can't raise your own meat, we suggest looking into small animal raising operations in your area.  In some places you can get organic chicken or rabbit meat if you ask around. It's also possible to buy beef directly from a rancher before the cow has been sent to the feed lots for its hormone-fattening diet. Some butchers do sell wild game, and buffalo or venison are a great beef substitute when available.

We often substitute vegetarian dishes for meat, and this alternative is available to anyone, wherever they live. When you make vegetarian dishes, it is important to get a complete protein which is done by the correct combination of grains, cheese, beans, legumes, etc.

We meet our dairy needs with a cow. For those of you not fortunate enough to be able to have one, we suggest checking small dairies, or health food stores for raw milk. From it you can make your own butter, yogurt, and cottage cheese fairly easily at home. If you prefer the prices of nonfat skim milk, find out how it is produced. The spray drying method does not destroy food value while the roller drying method, which requires high heating, causes destruction of protein and vitamins.

We usually check out natural food co-ops, or go directly to farmers, preferably organic, for our wheat, rice, lentils, etc. If you can get together with some friends, and buy in bulk quantities, you can get much better prices on these items, as well as fruits and vegetables.

What you eat can drastically affect how you feel, think and look. We feel that taking the extra time to get and cook foods that will help to keep us in good condition, is one of the best investments we can make.

To eat well, it is essential that food is prepared, served, and eaten with prayers and love. People in negative states should not cook, as their attitudes can poison the food. People on "food trips", be they vegetarians, macrobiotic, fruitarian, meat only, or whatever, often get angry if their particular demands are not being met. Such people should be kept out of the kitchen until they learn to respect other people's feelings on food. We have found that people who make diet their religion have a difficult time living in groups that don't agree with them. However, we now have people of all food persuasions living together harmoniously. The secret? Love, respect, patience, and the ability to close one's mouth.

In the kitchen, it is also helpful to practice self reliance. Experiment. Don't become dependent on recipe books. If you're not exactly sure how to make something, use your intuition. As long as there is love in your heart, you'll do fine.

# Finances

We feel sad and frustrated each time we see people forced to give up their plans to build a home in the country. Usually they have to return to town and look for a job. To us, it means that those people have ended up paying into an economic system without gaining the reward they sought. Somebody else profited from their mistake. In addition, the people who were caught in that trap will probably become discouraged and find it more difficult to try again. A little more financial planning could have saved their home, their plans, and their dreams. It is important to have a realistic idea of what to expect, and be prepared for it.

Rising costs are not just a city problem. Everything you will need will cost something in terms of cash, transportation, time or labor. Gasoline alone will cost a substantial amount, and whether you now believe it or not, there will be unexpected but necessary trips to town with a vehicle.

The throw-away society we have grown up in has made it too much a habit to be wasteful. We seem to have lost many of the old skills of economizing. Our grandparents who lived through the Great Depression were magicians at recycling, re-using, saving, and just plain using less in the first place. Chicken bones were saved for the broth, and it was unnecessary to buy instant soups. Little chips of left-over soap were collected to be used again in a drawstring bag made of two wash cloths. Socks were darned. (See if you can find anyone who knows how to darn.) Fabric scraps were saved for quilts and patches. The amount and variety of stuff that was saved and used again was impressive. The amount of stuff that was just saved was impressive too, and whatever is still around is still valuable, provided it's in reasonable condition.

The breakneck pace of living in the 80's makes it attractive to do many things the expedient way. There is room for conveniences, and it is important to count human energy too when we figure cost. For a family trying to make a start in a self-reliant lifestyle, but still having to keep a job, it is brutal to insist that they must wash their own clothes by hand because a laundramat is too wasteful. The time and energy they save by using machines in that instance, can be better spent winterizing a house or salvaging lumber.  The point is to be conscious of the cost of everything, so your choices will serve you better.

Learn to expect the unexpected.  There will be flat tires, broken down equipment from time to time, injured livestock in need of veterinary attention, incidental expenses in building, and personal needs.  When your vehicle needs attention, it behooves you to repair it as soon as possible, on a priority basis.  You will find that being without it slows down or stops your work.  You may be able to get by without it later, but while you are learning to be self reliant, you will need it for materials, feed, food, firewood, trash, fertilizer, road maintenance, people and critters.

Budgeting can be a pain in the neck. However, our attitude is that your budget is your friend.  There is little way of planning your spending and when it will occur unless you take this step.  It is therefore impossible to plan your income.  Budgeting is also a way of seeing what you can afford, and when, and how much the alternatives will cost.  If you have a car but need a truck, write down your alternatives.  Your car is paid for.  But to move enough 2 x 4's to frame your house will take 30 trips to town in your car.  How much does that cost?  You could rent a truck for two days.  How much does that cost?  Is there anything else you can use the truck for at the same time?  How much will you save later by doing that?  How much is your car worth?  Is there a market for it?  How much would it cost to buy a truck?  Then keep it running?  And how much does it cost to run either one?  Is a truck useful for all your needs, or would you be constantly adding gas to an empty truck that only gets 15 miles to the gallon?  These questions can be answered only when you have taken the time to realistically budget it out.  Keep your work sheets.  Write down your conclusions.  This information will be available when you need it later.

Here is an example of a very fictional budget.  <u>You will have to check local prices and availability each year</u>.

### HOME INSULATION

| | | |
|---|---|---|
| Insulate to R38 with fiberglas | $1000.00 | (depending on the size of the house) |
| Insulate to R19 with less fiberglas | $650.00 | |
| You have "saved" | $350.00 | |

BUT NOW YOU HAVE TO GET YOUR FIREWOOD.

Firewood for a home with R38   (4 cords of pine x $60.00) - $240.00

Firewood for a home with R19 (10 cords of pine x $60.00) - $600.00

By using the cheaper way of insulating you saved $350.00, but you have had to spend an additional $360.00 for wood, in one year only. You could have "paid for" the extra insulation in just one season by using less wood.  You are probably still cold, and need another woodshed which will cost another $40.00 to build, if you're very careful.

## FIREWOOD FOR HEATING

This is another fictional budget.

Pine            $60.00 per cord, no delivery
                   8.00 to drive your own vehicle to pick up the wood,
                        one cord at a time
                 $68.00 for three weeks of heat.  This equals $23.00
                        per week.
$23.00 x 25 (the number of weeks you must heat) = $575.00 per year.


Birch           $90.00 per cord, delivered
                no cost for pickup
                 $90.00 for six weeks of heat.  This equals $15.00
                        per week.
$15.00 x 25 (the number of weeks you must heat) = $375.00 per year.

Cost of heating for one year with pine        $575.00
Cost of heating for one year with birch        $375.00
Savings from getting the "expensive" wood      $200.00


## GETTING YOUR OWN FIREWOOD

First check to see if you need a permit to allow you to cut wood on government land.  In most cases this is a fire regulation because of the increased potential for fire when chainsaws and vehicles are brought into a wooded area.  If you need a permit, it will cost about $10.00 which is not much.

Now let's be idealistic and say you have a truck, a pickup with relatively decent mileage.  And you must go 50 miles to cut wood.

50 miles in an empty truck ÷ 17 miles per gallon of gasoline
= 2.94 gallons.  At $1.00 a gallon,

| | |
|---|---|
| cost of gasoline for empty truck | $2.94 |
| motor oil and wear and tear | $3.00 |
| gasoline for a full truck (12 mi./gal.) | 4.17 |
| permit | 10.00 |
| cost of driving only | $20.11 |

| | |
|---|---|
| cost of a reconditioned chainsaw, hypothetically | $295.00 |
| cost of a new chainsaw with a guarantee | $359.99 |

| | |
|---|---|
| cost of chainsaw oil ($1.79/qt. x 2 qts.) | $3.58 |
| five gallons of gasoline for the chainsaw | 5.00 |
| | $8.58 |

Let's say you bought the new chainsaw with the guarantee to save on repairs, and you are able to use it to cut 15 cords of wood, replacing only a $35.00 chain.

| | |
|---|---|
| Cost of chainsaw | $359.99 |
| Chain replacement | 30.00 |
| | $389.99 |
| | ÷ 15 cords |
| | $26.00 cost of chainsaw per cord |

So far, here are the costs:

| | |
|---|---|
| Cost of driving | $ 20.11 |
| chainsaw per cord | 26.00 first cord |
| | 26.00 second cord |
| | $ 72.11 for the trip |
| | ÷ 2 cords of pine |
| | $ 36.05 per cord for pine |

You have spent two hours driving and six hours cutting and loading wood.  You have saved $47.90, and it took eight hours.  Was it worth it?

Such financial hypothesizing can help you to determine real costs, which often vary greatly from apparent costs.

## INSURANCE

Insurance is a good idea too. We lost our poultry in a fire one year, and our insurance was very helpful when we re-built our flock. It would have been difficult otherwise to recoup our losses. But take a good look at insurance, and weigh the likelihood of your needing it. Insurance is extremely costly, and if you don't need it, it can really drain your finances. But medical emergencies can be even more costly. Find out what medical care costs. Find out what insurance costs. And be sure you know what coverage you're buying. It is a bitter disappointment to have spent thousands of dollars to buy insurance, only to find that it does not cover your loss, or that the deductible is so large that you, in essence, are paying the whole bill yourself, or that the company will pay your claim and cancel your insurance. Self insurance, which means religiously setting aside a certain amount of your money in a savings account you don't touch unless there is a real medical emergency, has proven to be an effective insurance method for some people and groups.

## OTHER FINANCIAL REALITIES

You will need to pay for your supplies, be they for building or for generating income. Lumber, nails, roofing, insulation, concrete footings, wiring for electricity are all becoming more expensive. Seed for crops, feed for livestock, veterinary supplies can all take big bites out of your budget.

Unless you have vast financial resources readily available, you will need a reliable source of income. Get at least part of that happening before you move to the country, and be sure it works. Do not depend on anything that hasn't yet become reality.

In the fairly recent past, there have been some attempts on the part of federal and local government to provide services to people feeling the financial pinch. These attempts have not borne much fruit, as far as we have seen, though they were good ideas all. We found that the weatherization programs were so short of money that they had to be limited to the very elderly. The SBA (Small Business Administration) provides a great deal of common sense advice, but no specific information, and very little funding. You'd be better off to write a grant for a research project. Local food banks can only give what they have. If all they have is 14 cases of saltines, that's what they give out. Food stamps are more or less expensive, depending on your eligibility, but undermine your self reliance. If you honestly qualify, do use them while you must, but know that their value is limited compared to what you can do for yourself. Likewise, unemployment can be a large expenditure of time and energy. If you need the income, it is better to stay employed as long as you need the income, or change your occupation to one you can do while you're building your self reliant home base.

We recommend you take a close look at what it costs to do the things you want to do. Financing is complicated, compared to the old days when a person paid his money and took the goods. When you look carefully at loans and financing, you find that the interest, no matter how low, is the real money-maker for banks. Ask specific questions, such as "When I make my first payment of $300.00, how much of that money pays interest, and how much pays principle?" The answer could be shocking.

If you must borrow money, go in with your eyes wide open. What happens if your payment is late? What if interest rates go down? Can you re-finance? Is there an early pay-off figure? If you are ahead in making your payments, do you still have to pay every month, or can you skip the one month? You might find you'd be better off to save the money and pay it when it's due.

All this means that you will have to find income which doesn't cut too badly into the time you must spend getting your shelter together before winter. If you are very lucky, you will have money coming in from something you did in the past, like writing a best-seller or buying an oil well. But for most of us, this is not the case, and we have to develop an industry to keep us in the chips.

Spending should be done carefully. If you have cash, you are in a better position to bargain for what you buy. Still, be sure you are getting a good deal. Scout out second-hand items. Carefully check out things that need repair. It might get you in deeper than you meant to be. Sometimes you will have to buy something new. Wait for a sale, if you can.

Do not count on trading for everything. Trading is only now becoming popular, and it still takes some looking sometimes to find a taker for your goods who has anything you are interested in. Trading can take up a lot of your time, although trade organizations help to make it more feasable.

If you have a phone, keep the bill paid. Keep up your land payment, if you have one. Delinquency charges set people back far enough so they frequently fail to recover. Interest charges on accounts are astounding. Best to always pay cash. But someday you might need credit, and you will want to be considered a good credit risk.  Pay your taxes so the county won't auction off your tax delinquent land.

Some of the things which can be done to generate income are cutting and delivering firewood (which requires an investment of time and money in chainsaws, gas and incidentals and is pretty seasonal), selling produce (which again is seasonal, and you need a whole lot of it), and selling eggs.  Selling milk will come under the jurisdiction of the state department of agriculture.  Selling most food items comes under many rules and regulations from health department inspectors and FDA. This kind of industry should be successfully operating fully before you move it to the country.  Remember that more of your time will be spent in getting back and forth once you're on the land.  Keeping bees and selling honey; raising and selling earthworms; harvesting and selling herbs; baking and selling pies and cakes; making candy; making sprouts are all ways to bring in some income.  But, unless you'll be doing any of these on a large scale you'll need some other kind of cottage industry to support you.

# Home Industries

Home industries are a boon to self reliance, but you have to work at them as regularly and conscientiously as you would at any other job. This should not be difficult, for after all, you are working toward your own gain, and not someone else's. You should try to have some organized space just for the industries you develop, and certain time in the week just for working on these.

You should be producing goods for which there is a demand. You should try to produce a quality item at a minimum of expense both in money and in labor. Your time will be valuable, so do not spend too many hours on items which sell slowly. Remember that most people must economize, and you will have to keep your cost as reasonable as possible, but do not sell your time too cheaply.

Marketing is important. Unless you have friends with an outlet for selling your products fairly rapidly, you will have to do a little leg work yourself. You will have to find out what people buy best, and try to make your products appealing to them. Some items sell best in boutiques, some at fairs, and some through mail order. Try all these possibilities.

Keep good records of your business. Keep caught up. Nothing is worse than botched up bookkeeping and filing. If you owe money, pay it. If someone else owes you, collect it. But you can do these things well, only if you follow good, ethical business practices.

Sewing is a creative industry, but find out what items are popular. Usually, people will not buy what they think they can do themselves. That reduces your chances of making it on potholders and quilts and toys. In some places, denim clothing is popular, and articles made from "worn" denim can be remade according to current styles. Materials can be bought at thrift stores for long skirts, chair seats, hats, bags, baby slings, jackets, tool aprons, and other things.

Outdoor articles are more in demand than they were 10 years ago, and money can be made from custom making sleeping bags, tipis, day packs, and containers and covers for various items. It is best to fill orders, so that your materials are not all sewn up in things that aren't being sold. This means you may have to advertise in a couple of classified sections.

Also consider leather work such as making moccasins, purses, shirts, pants, jackets. These are all good, useful products that will help others as well as your finances. If you have access to hides, tanning them and selling them is another way of making money.

Another creative, sometimes lucrative industry is furniture making -- and you can make any number of things. Chairs, tables, bureaus, desks, lofts, redwood tubs can all be made and sold. If you prefer to work on a smaller scale, you can construct childrens furniture, doll furniture or even toys. We've met people who make their money doing all of these things.

Jewelry making is another way of getting finances together. You can make beaded items or silver, metal, copper or gold ones. You can also make pillows, pillow furniture, stuffed toys, quilts, stonewear and ceramics.

When you're planning a cottage industry your imagination, your craftwork inclinations, what will sell, and how you'll sell it, are the things you must consider.

# Trading

Who needs money?

The old-timers lived happily without it for many thousands of years. They built their own shelters, grew or hunted for their food, made their clothes and weapons, and traded for whatever goods they could not produce, or services they couldn't perform.

With cities and middlemen came the need for money, checkbooks, credit and all of the other civilized abstractions that keep us from remembering the true value of both goods and services. Today many people are trying to turn away from money and conduct their business by barter. This concept has become popular enough that there are barter companies in several large cities that arrange trades for their big-money clients who recognize, aside from other considerations, the tax advantages of trading.

We've been trading, whenever possible, for the past few years. We believe that learning to trade is an important first step in creating a viable economic alternative to the system while it exists, and that trading will replace money after the cleansing. We've traded turquoise jewelry for beadwork, beads, blankets, baskets, feathers, pottery, pictures and leatherwork; then we've turned around and traded some or all of those items for turquoise. Which way we traded depended upon what we had more of at one time, and what we needed. We've also traded arts and crafts for dental work, medical help, foodstuffs and herbs. We've traded our labor picking fruit for part of the fruit we've picked. We've had people pay back money loans by working on our magazine. We partially paid people working on our mailing list with a wool blanket. We've taken soy beans and beads in trade for subscriptions.

If you watch children trading baseball cards or water pistols you'll see that trading can, and should, be a lot of fun and more satisfying than dealing in pictures of dead presidents. Probably half of our trade deals so far have been for the pure joy of the give and take of a trade. The other half enabled us to get items we needed with no cash outlay. We've made some terrific trade deals at pow wows and shows largely because of our willingness to trade. There are some rules we try to follow to make all of our trades happy ones, and we pass them on to you.

(1) Never agree to a trade unless you are completely happy with it. There should be no thoughts of exchanges or refunds in a trade.

(2) Don't ever let anyone push you into a trade. As trading grows, so does the possibility of con-people who'll try to get rid of their junk through trading.

(3) Conversely, don't ever try to push someone else into a trade. Some people just aren't financially able to trade at this time. For instance, many Indian silversmiths can't afford to trade their goods because the people who sell them raw materials demand cold cash for these materials.

(4) If you think the other person is making a bad trade, through ignorance of the items being traded, tell him. If he still wants to go ahead, that's his business.

(5) For a trade to make both parties happy, they both have to feel that they are the one who has done just a bit better. Always be willing to throw in that last little item to make the other person feel that they have the edge. One happy trade between two people will usually lead to others.

A problem that we still encounter in trades is having to assign a dollar value to items in order to judge whether the trade is fair. For instance, when we traded with our dentist, he billed us full charge for his services then he picked out the items he wanted and we billed him for those. We are so conditioned to think of value in terms of money that it is hard to break the habit, but if we were stuck for a while in the country with a toothache, and a dentist came along and said he'd fix it if we gave him a squash blossom necklace, we bet we wouldn't think too much about what that necklace has cost us. When we have to trade for need as well as fun, then we will begin to attach real value to things again. To a starving man, a loaf of bread will be worth a brick of gold.

The best, probably only, way to learn to trade is by trad-ing. To get in some practice go to a pow wow, Indian, antique or collectors show, a flea market or counter-cultural fair and see how you do. Once you feel comfortable at trading, try it wherever you think there's any possibility it might work. If

it doesn't, you haven't lost anything.  If it does you've converted another person to taking it out in trade.

      Trade organizations are a good way to introduce people to
trading, and to expand the scope of trades you can make.  The
trade organization we belong to works like this.  We pay a
monthly cash fee to cover their postage, phone bills, etc.
If we need printing done, we find out if a member printer can
do our job.  If he does, he gives us an invoice for the regular
cost.  Our account shows we owe credits for printing.  Then
someone may call us for turquoise, firewood, an ad in Wildfire,
and we bill them and get credit for what we sold.  The advantages are that we don't have to find a direct trade, and that
we have access to materials we couldn't trade for directly.

# *Harmony*

One of the blessings of leaving the city and getting a rural home is that many hassles cease to be.  Your energy can be directed to real building and real achievement for your own gain. The newness of life style may lead some people to think that all controls may be dropped, but we have found that attitude to be naive and unwise.  It ultimately saves time, worry, and even money to "keep it together" with the law and the neighbors.

## MOTOR VEHICLES

Keep all your vehicles in legal shape.  Keep them in safe operating condition.  Headlights should work, and so should windshield wipers, muffler, horn, etc.  Some state laws require certain tires or chains during the winter.  Know what they are. If your car is stopped, you will be given a notice to repair anything that doesn't work.  You may also get fined.
Make sure that only licensed drivers operate your vehicle. Insurance is a good idea, even if it isn't mandatory.  A vehicle can be an asset or a pain in the neck.  Keep it together.

## BUILDING CODES

Counties can interfere if you seem to be building without a permit.  They can issue a stop-work order.  If you violate an order, the legal consequences will be very serious and will cripple anything else you try to do.  It is easier to just buy the permit.  The same goes for electric and septic permits.

## USE OF FIREARMS

Do not hunt under any circumstances if you don't need to. If you have other things under control, you probably won't need to.  But if you do, get the license, even though you might feel negative about it.  If you poach and get caught, it will be a sorry day indeed.

Some ordinances prohibit the discharge of firearms within certain zones and within certain distances of dwellings.  If you have firearms, become familiar with local laws pertaining to them, and carefully observe them.

## SCHOOL AGE CHILDREN

If you have school age children and you object to sending them to public school, be equipped to provide a decent alternative. School authorities can come and test the children at any time, to be sure they are learning a standard amount and type of matter. If you keep children out of school without providing an adequate education (private tutoring, homebound studies, or whatever the local law requires) there is a risk of the children being removed from the "unfit" home.

## DRUGS

Don't use them. While the legal hassles they cause are nasty, the other things they do to people are even worse.

## ZONING

If you are moving into a new area for you, scout around and find out whether outhouses are forbidden by law. Also find out whether or not you will be free to raise livestock. If you live in an irrigation district, learn the regulations. If you don't learn them, not only will the law be on your tail, but so will all your neighbors.

## CAMPFIRES, FISHING

Don't ask for trouble. If you don't KNOW it's alright, don't do it. It is never good to flaunt the law. If you're sure it's alright to fish, take only what you need, and be prepared to show your license to any fish and game personnel who might check on you. Most campfires need a permit, and they are usually free, so it is stupid not to get one if it is required.

## CRITTERS

A little awareness and consideration will keep most people out of trouble with the wildlife. Do not try to approach animals or capture them. Friends can be made of them without domestication. Go to extra measures to avoid their homes and areas during mating and baby animal seasons. Avoid rabies-carrying species at all times. Do not touch or handle dead animals. Remove their bodies with a shovel, and bury them away from children and your own pets.

# FOLKS

If you move to the country, you might have neighbors in the area. They will probably resent your being there, since they probably moved to be away from people, the same as you. They were there first, so you will have to be on your best behavior to keep from alienating them further. They will appreciate it if you keep to yourself and mind your own business. Avoid asking favors and borrowing things. Keep your noise level down. Keep your area clean and free of eyesores. At first, your neighbors will wish you would go away, and some will even try to drive you away. Don't give them the excuse they are looking for. A good relationship can always develop. Don't be too eager to be there to help, but be ready to combat fire or share road maintenance. This is a real part of your responsibility anyway. Keep your animals out of the neighbor's garden. Don't trepass or let your guests trespass because they don't know where the property lines are. Respect the water supply. Keep your business to yourself.

# POETRY and LEGENDS

O Great Spirit,
Sun, Moon, Sky and Sea;
You are inside,
And all around me.

Your Breath comes so gently,
It sweeps across the land.
It blows with such power,
To heal our fellow man.

Your eyes are upon us,
From ourselves we cannot hide.
We must move with our changes,
As with the changing tide.

Thank you for your beauty.
Thank you for this life.
Teach us to follow
The path of your Light.

O Great Spirit,
We greet you with our love,
We yearn for your wisdom,
The blessings of your love.
Lend us your guiding love.

O Great Spirit,
Sun, Moon, Sky and Sea;
You are inside,
And all around me.

Thanks to Antahkarana
for this song

Sometimes
I long
to shout --
"Stop! Stop
the slaughter
of our Mother
and of the good
and bountiful
beauty upon Her!"

this longing,
this voice --
within was given
to me by the Great Spirit.
It is the voice
of love.

Be silent.
Listen.
From the silence
within yourself
you will
hear it too.

It is a roar.
It is a whisper.
And it is ever
present --
waiting to guide
you, if only
you will listen.

The Voice
will reveal
to you
to respect
your little brothers,
the beauty creatures,
and to preserve
the plant and water
nations.

From it,
you will learn
the friendliness
of trees
and not to curse
the rain.

## Listen . . .

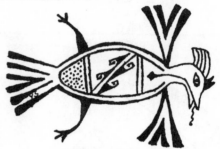

Walk in the rain
and be thankful
for its goodness.

Give thanks,
when our Mother
turns Her colours --
season to season;
they are beautiful
each in their own
way and we
also turn and change
spinning out part
in the cycle.

You will learn
that you
do not need
so many things
and gadgets
that you are killing
yourselves and your
Mother to obtain.

Everything you need
has been provided.
It is here --
the Voice
will tell
you --
if only you will
listen --

Wi i ni napa

## *The Runner*

When the old shaman dies
the chosen one receives his
gift through a vision
from his animal.

To learn of this spirit
the young shaman
must go to the forest
must wait
hungry for knowledge.

He runs in the dark wood
following the mule deer's
narrow trail
wearing a necklace of white bones
and a magic bag at his throat

He runs to meet his pain
he runs to meet his power
fasting, enduring, chanting,
invoking sacred names.

He runs
forward into the forest,
until the light catches him,
holds him.

There his wild animal
leaps upon him,
throws him to the ground
granting him the power
forging in him strength.

The runner becomes shaman
all white bones and magic.

Gloria Hulk

# *The Corn Woman*

My son comes in
from a land of clouds
which yesterday
was last summer's garden.

I had watched him
at the edge of the field
where an old woman was standing.

She bent over his shoulder,
her thin hair blowing,
bare feet hidden
beneath the blanket.

All her sisters gone,
she has been waiting
to touch the season
when her children
will sing in the wind.

Her fingers rattled
on his arm and I knew
that he was listening

although only his eyes
tell me of that voice
which spoke of rivers
and the good sleeping soil

Joseph Bruchac

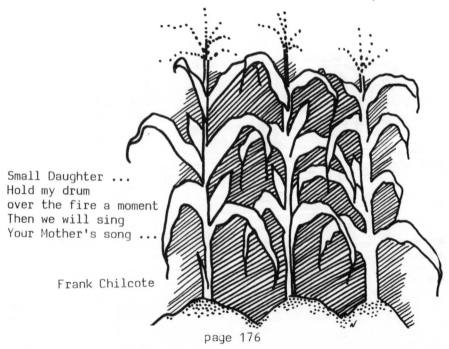

Small Daughter ...
Hold my drum
over the fire a moment
Then we will sing
Your Mother's song ...

Frank Chilcote

# Circles of Life

Child of Mine, let us sit together
    in a Circle of Two 'round the Fire.
Grandmother Moon peeks at us
    rising up from the Wilderness,
    gliding 'round beyond the Mountains.

It is a Good Night, the Loon Wails.

We shall talk of the Womb, Little Sister,
    it is Time you should know
    how it Comes and Goes, rising and emptying
    for the Little Ones yet to be Born.

    Small as your fist: circular, small tight sphere,
    glistening in the deep dark
    never yet prepared for Landings,
    nor shed itself in the Absence of them.
Yours is empty and quiet as yet.

    For a few days a Nest is my Womb,
    of Red, dear, not White like our Relative;
Mine lies full, like Grandma up there.

Yours too will fill with vast nourishments
    to empty Life's Bright Red River
    trickling toward the Light of Sun.

Then the quiet time, while other Growings carry on,
    when Roots grow Strong and
    the egg grows silently and
    Moon goes Invisibly on her path.

Smoke with me, Child, there is more to come.

What stops this great Silent Rhythm?
How does it Cease, then to Resume?

Circles, Child, two Circles
    becoming One Circle to Grow
        to two, alike yet so unlike
            to grow to four and eight and on and on,
                to Fill the Nest.
        Nine Moons filling the Great Circle
        Then to Push on Out, Another of Life's Rivers
        Meeting the glare of Sun and growing
                    on the Air and Soil of Mother Earth.

The Red River trickles on, cleansing the now-stretched sphere;
    again, and again, and again.

Forever you ask?

Be Still, Child, the Moon comes, the Loon Calls.

You are soon to have your Beginnings:
    the End of your Childhood of Freedom.

I am soon to have my Ending,
    the Beginning of my Final Freedoms ...

Circles, Child of Mine, Circles 'round the Fire.

                                        Morning Star

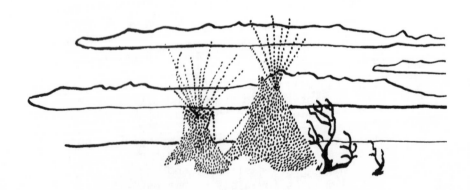

# The Legend of Siwash Rock

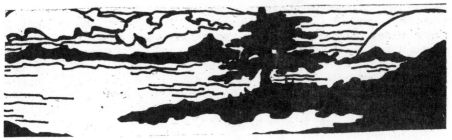

In the days before the whiteman came, a woman of the Northern Squamish people came to her husband and said, "Come.. It is almost time."

Taking him by the hand, she led him out of the village through giant cedar, fir, spruce and balsam groves until they came to the shore. After a short time of following the curling beach line they came to a jutting peninsula, and it was at the furthest tip of this that she said, "Here," and turned to make her way into the heavy bushes marking the borderline between beach and forest. He watched her figure, clumsy with child, disappearing, and smiled to himself.

"Will it be a boy or a girl?" he wondered softly, then, turning, he waded into the sea and lifted his arms to the sky.

"Great Spirit," he prayed, "cleanse my soul as I swim, as the sea shall cleanse my body. Grant that I may greet this new spirit entering the world totally cleansed in spirit and body so that I will not jeopardize his or her future life in this place. O Great Spirit, strengthen my arms as I swim, that they may keep me afloat in my Sister Ocean until the arrival of the young one. O Source of All Life, grant that I may avoid the shame of Unclean Fatherhood. From me the young one will learn of man ... Great Spirit, help me now to show him a clean, pure spirit, so that he, too, will live his life in a clean way, praising you. Or if it is a girl, let her know the strengths of man so she will live a life of honor, knowing a pure man when she sees one. O Great Spirit, this child's life depends on you, came from you and will return to you in the end. Help me now to greet him or her in a manner befitting one who has just recently come from your presence."

And so saying, he plunged into the sea.

Hours passed as the woman on shore and the man in the water each strove in their own way to greet the child's entrance into this world.  In the bushes, the woman was riding another kind of sea, the waves of the sea of life sweeping over and through her body, while out in the channel, the man never ceased his tireless strokes against the ocean tide.  As the time moved past him, he imagined he could hear faraway drums beating ... almost like listening to the pounding hearts of the mountains ringing closely round the land by the water.  Slowing his pace somewhat, he lifted his head yet higher above the water.  Yes, he could hear it now!  Not drumbeats, but a faraway distant chanting, almost indistinguishable against the sound of the ocean tirelessly lashing the beach, almost seeming a part of the mountains and forest and sea.

Looking towards shore, he heard a small cry from his woman. The time was near indeed!  Praying to himself now, he resumed cleaving the waters.

As he swam, the distant chant drew nearer, and became clearer to his ears.  Eventually the ringing song filled the land and echoed from the sky and mountains.

"We are the messengers of the Great Spirit!" he heard. "Let all who hear hide their eyes, for to look on us is death! We are the messengers of the Great Spirit!  Let the waters part before us ... let all in the sea flee from our path.  To touch us or the water we have touched is death!"

His heart sank within him.  He had heard, from his grandmother, of the three men, giant spirit-people, sent by the Great Spirit on their unknown mission, and their great canoe who had passed this way twice before, long ago.  There had once been a youth in the water who had refused to leave their path.  He died.

He glanced at the shore again.  If he left the water now, his child would be greeted by an unclean father, and in the very beginning of its life, the most important time of all, it would encounter the limitations of disease, those of the body and also those of the spirit, which will manifest as greed, lethargy, thoughtlessness, carelessness ... all the associates of an unclean spirit.  No, he would not burden his child with these. It would be better to die here in the water than to crawl on the shore at the behest of the three gigantic men in their canoe, and jeopardize his child's whole life.

By this time the canoe had come close enough for the men in it to see him as he resolutely swam onward.

"Ho!" cried the nearest, in the prow.

"Ho, mortal! Are you deaf, that you did not hear us warning the people away as we approached? Why are you still in the water?"

He licked his lips and drank a little salt water to moisten his throat, and pointed to the shore.

"My wife lies in the bushes with our first young one," he answered, and even as he pointed, the distant wail of a newborn child floated across the water. "I would not greet my first child unclean," he said. "I would rather die."

As he waited in the water for his death, his mind travelled back over his recent life. How good she had been to him! And his parents and neighbors. They would throw a huge potlatch in his honor, and give away all their possessions. A time of mourning would follow, after which the neighbors would "mysteriously" replace the necessary tools for living in their section of the longhouse. He knew they would miss him, but accept his loss ...

He was brought out of his reverie by the steersman rising from the stern of the canoe to point his paddle at him.

"Mortal," he said, not unkindly, "you have shown great bravery in daring our wrath for the sake of your new daughter, for she is indeed a girl-child. With your bravery you have won immortality, for whenever your tribesmen pass you by, they shall see, and recall the virtues of clean fatherhood. You shall pass the ages as a large rock, standing here in the waters where you have defied us, but you shall not be barren, as is one who is forsaken by the Spirit. No, you shall bear three trees, one for each of your loves ... your wife, your child, and your people."

And extending his paddle, he reached out over the water and lightly touched the man of the Squamish people on the shoulder.

Today Siwash Rock still stands, and the story of the man who defied the spirits for the sake of his wife and child is still told.

Indeed, the Indians say that if you go to Vancouver, British Columbia, and follow the shore to the furthest tip of Stanley Park where you can see the bold beautiful rock holding its hardy trees aloft, you can turn into the underbrush at that point, and, if you are lucky, you will find a fairly large rock, about the size of a woman, half-sitting, half-curled on the ground.

Next to it they say, will be another small rock, in shape
vaguely similar to a young newborn baby ... a lasting tribute
to one man's bravery, and forever a reminder to the Squamish
peoples to greet their children into this world clean in heart,
mind, and body, and so to provide them with a foundation of
rock-like strength on which to build their lives.

retold by Yarrow

Sometimes the birds
change their songs.
those who know this
can read the messages
an oriole weaves
into the swing of its nest.

Like the songs
of hump-backed whales
which last for hours
and are new each year
something is said
in the songs of the birds.

They changed
when the first cities
formed from the mud
of an ancient plain.

Some people remember,
but like Dewey Beard,
the old Oglala warrior
who was the last survivor
from the Custer Fight
and Wounded Knee,
they forget when
the wrong people
ask them questions.

When the new songs begin,
will you hear them?

Joseph Bruchac

## OTHER BOOKS AVAILABLE FROM THE BEAR TRIBE

**SUN BEAR: THE PATH OF POWER,** by Sun Bear.  In this book, Sun Bear continues to interpret ancient philosophies for today's readers. In **SUN BEAR: THE PATH OF POWER,** you will learn:
- how to find and follow your own path of power
- how to seek and find vision in your life
- how you can find sacredness in everything, in the dramatic and the daily hum-drum
- how you can hear the earth when she speaks to you
- how you can accomplish your goals, and grow stronger in you path of power every day.

272 pages.  Illustrated paperback.  $9.95.


**THE MEDICINE WHEEL: EARTH ASTROLOGY,** by Sun Bear and Wabun.  This book came about as the result of a vision Sun Bear had.  It is a system of earth astrology to help people in their daily living and in determining their life path.  This book has helped over 150,000 people world-wide to live in harmony with themselves and the Earth Mother.  210 pages, illustrated paperback.  $5.95.

**THE MEDICINE WHEEL,** by the Bear Tribe.  The Medicine Wheel Circle is a beautiful 12-inch color circle which visually presents the entire Medicine Wheel according to Sun Bear's vision.  Printed on heavy paper.  $4.00.

**BUFFALO HEARTS,** by Sun Bear.  This book expresses the traditions and history of the first Americans as seen through the eyes of a contemporary Native American, Sun Bear.  **BUFFALO HEARTS** gives the history of the struggle of famous Indian leaders against the invasion of European cultures and gives some brief biographies of some famous Native leaders.  It also informs about Native religion and culture.  128 pages, illustrated paperback.  $5.95.

**SNOWY EARTH COMES GLIDING,** by Evelyn Eaton.  This book recounts some Native American traditions and ways as seen through the eyes of an extraordinary woman, the late Evelyn Eaton.  In addition to being a writer, she was also a Pipe Woman, a healer and a true bridge between the heart and the mind.  108 pages.  Illustrated paperback.  $5.95.

**AT HOME IN THE WILDERNESS,** by Sun Bear.  For those who want to
live in the wild, there is no better teacher than the author
of this book.  As a Native American born and raised in Minnesota, he learned the ancient survival techniques of his people,
the Chippewa Indians, and is an excellent teacher to make you
feel "at home in the wilderness."  The book includes instructions for both short-term and long-term survival in near and
remote wilderness.  90 pages.  Illustrated paperback.  $5.95.

**THE BOOK OF THE VISION QUEST: Personal Transformation in the
Wilderness,** by Steven Foster and Meredith Little.  In this new
edition, the authors have compassion and encouragement for the
many of us who seek vision to give meaning to our lives.  They
have prepared and guided many hundreds who sought their help.
162 pages.  Illustrated paperback.  $8.95.

**WILDFIRE: the Medicine Wheel Network Magazine,** is concerned
with earth awareness, environment, health and healing, bridg-
ing cultures, male and female energy, children, work and
money, spiritual focus, and many other topics.  $5.00 per year
for two double issues.


ORDER FROM

**THE BEAR TRIBE MEDICINE SOCIETY**
P.O. Box 9167, Spokane, Washington 99209


Add $1.50 postage and handling for the first item,
and 60¢ for each additional item.

# RVs & Campers

# Campers

A Wiley Brand

# RVs & Campers

## by Christopher Hodapp and Alice Von Kannon

# RVs & Campers For Dummies®

Published by: **John Wiley & Sons, Inc.,** 111 River Street, Hoboken, NJ 07030-5774, www.wiley.com

Copyright © 2021 by John Wiley & Sons, Inc., Hoboken, New Jersey

Published simultaneously in Canada

For general information on our other products and services, please contact our Customer Care Department within the U.S. at 877-762-2974, outside the U.S. at 317-572-3993, or fax 317-572-4002. For technical support, please visit https://hub.wiley.com/community/support/dummies.

Wiley publishes in a variety of print and electronic formats and by print-on-demand. Some material included with standard print versions of this book may not be included in e-books or in print-on-demand. If this book refers to media such as a CD or DVD that is not included in the version you purchased, you may download this material at http://booksupport.wiley.com. For more information about Wiley products, visit www.wiley.com.

Library of Congress Control Number: 2021938286

ISBN 978-1-119-79034-1 (pbk); ISBN 978-1-119-79035-8 (ebk); ISBN 978-1-119-79030-3 (ebk)

Manufactured in the United States of America

SKY10027279_052521

# Contents at a Glance

# Table of Contents

# Introduction

One afternoon in late summer of 2020, our friend and neighbor Lora knocked on our door to tell us out of the clear blue sky that she was selling her house and everything in it and hitting the road in an RV. Her teenage daughter had gone off to college earlier in the year. Their huge five-bedroom house was way too big, way too expensive, and way too empty for a woman living all by herself to maintain. So, she sold it in the midst of the real estate boom of COVID-19, and she held a huge garage sale to get rid of her unneeded furniture and a lifetime of assorted accumulated stuff.

It all happened so fast that we couldn't quite believe it. Later that week, she pulled into our driveway with the used Class C motorhome she'd bought and christened "Big Betty." She was headed first for Salem, Massachusetts, a place she'd always wanted to see, with her two giant sheepdogs, her small auxiliary dog, and a cat. A small party formed in the rain in our driveway, friends and neighbors seeing her off. Lora is a pretty, upscale sort of lady, gregarious and caring, and she'd seen many of us through some major crises. The entire neighborhood hated seeing her go.

There was no route she intended to follow, no trail leading her to some destination, no deadline to get anywhere by some specific date. The five of them — Lora and her four furry companions — were going out to see the country; meet new people; discover new cities, villages, and landscapes; and go wherever her whims and Big Betty carried her. With no more mortgage payment, property taxes, insurance, homeowner's association fees, utility payments, lawn care, or other assorted home maintenance to pay for, suddenly being on the road meant she could afford this lifestyle almost indefinitely. "I'll try it for a couple of months and see if I like it," she cheerily said as she left town. As of this writing, Lora has been gone almost eight months, and she's still traveling.

When history books get written about the 21st century, we suspect there will be a big fat asterisk at the natural demarcation point of the year 2020 — before COVID and after COVID. It would be difficult, if not impossible, to come up with a single event, industry, or activity that wasn't dramatically altered by the national and global shutdowns that accompanied the COVID-19 pandemic. That included the world of recreational vehicles (RVs). The RV business had already been enjoying an uptick in sales and interest for several years, but when every other form of vacation travel shut down because of pandemic restrictions, RV dealerships sold out of nearly everything on their lots in record time, and parks and campgrounds in all 50 states were packed solid. And in 2021, the RV industry anticipated manufacturing well over half a million new trailers, motorhomes, and campers — the highest annual number in recorded history.

We may know our friend as Lora, but her name is Legion, to paraphrase a famous parable, and she is many. More than 11 million American households own an RV today, and over a million Americans are living in an RV full-time. It's for Lora and all those other new, first-time RVers like her that we decided to write this book.

With so many millions of people of all ages setting out on their first RV vacation each year, our goal is to give you enough knowledge that you won't feel overwhelmed by the vocabulary, the equipment, and the written and unwritten rules of the road. Whether you're planning to take the occasional weekend adventure, or you've got itchy feet to go and keep right on going, owning an RV should be a fun experience. But to keep it fun, there is a lot to be aware of before you even set foot on a dealership's parking lot and even more when you take your first trip. All the things we learned the hard way are in this book, in the hope that you'll never panic and just keep on rolling.

# About This Book

Shopping for and camping in an RV is supposed to be fun, so we want you to feel informed and confident from the first time you enter a dealership to the time you leave on your inaugural camping trip. In this book, we acquaint you with the types and sizes of every RV imaginable — what they're called and what makes them ideal or unsuitable for your situation. We help you decide whether your rig should tow or be towed, and we even tell you what a *toad* is. We arm you with RV driving tips and explain the mystic forces of weight distribution. You get the lowdown on your RV's systems for power, gas, heating, and air conditioning, and we even give you the straight scoop about water and poop.

By the time you finish this book, you'll be able to hitch up, hit the road without it hitting back, and set up camp like you've been doing it for years. Most important, we help you decide whether the RV lifestyle is for you — whether you intend on camping for a few weeks a year, living on the road full time, or something in between.

Because of the way this book is laid out for beginners, seasoned RVers may think there's nothing here for them. But there's a use for it you may not have considered: Perhaps you're the captain of your rig, the master of all you survey from the throne of your driver's seat. But if you're traveling with a spouse, a friend, a partner, or perhaps your teenage kids who don't know how your RV operates, we hope you'll pass this book to them before your next big trip. Life on the road is so much easier when you have a helping hand or two to keep things running smoothly. If you don't have the time, patience, or opportunity to teach your traveling companions how to operate or troubleshoot your RV and its systems, let us do it for you!

There's a practical side to sharing this book with your traveling companion, too: Unexpected accidents can happen on the road. RVers and campers frequently seek out the perfect spot in the wilderness, far from civilization. But no one is indestructible or entirely bulletproof. If something were to happen to you as the principal driver and your traveling partner had to take over the steering wheel suddenly, they would need to know the basics of how everything in your rig works.

Within this book, you may note that some web addresses break across two lines of text. If you're reading this book in print and want to visit one of these web pages, simply key in the web address exactly as it's noted in the text, pretending as though the line break doesn't exist. If you're reading this as an e-book, you've got it easy — just click the web address to be taken directly to the web page.

# Foolish Assumptions

*RVs & Campers For Dummies* starts from scratch, as though you know almost nothing about RVs, so we make a couple of presumptuous assumptions:

>> We assume you're toying with the notion of having an RV of your own, or at least renting one to see if you like it.

>> We assume you've at least owned your own automobile and know how to drive, but we don't assume you've ever towed anything in your life.

>> We don't assume you know your Class B from your fifth wheel or your fresh water from your black water (and trust us, you don't want to mix them up).

>> We don't assume you're mechanically inclined or that you know which end of the hammer gets used for installing screws.

# Icons Used in This Book

Throughout this book, you'll find *icons* (little pictures in the margin) that will help you spot material of special interest. Here's a guide to what the icons mean:

TIP

Anything marked with the Tip icon is a bit of advice that's handy or helpful to know, like a shortcut or a practical suggestion to save you time, effort, money, or a headache. Owning your rig makes you part of the rolling confraternity of fellow RVers, and we all like to share our hard-won tips and experiences "for those who may follow."

TECHNICAL STUFF

The Technical Stuff icon points out interesting information but not essential to understanding the subject at hand. If you're in a hurry, you can skip anything marked with this icon.

REMEMBER

The Remember icon marks stuff you probably should commit to memory or at least write on the back of your hand.

WARNING

Anything marked with the Warning icon is important enough to warrant either a "Don't do this!" or "Be sure to. . . ." We probably learned it the hard way, so you're the lucky beneficiary of our bungling.

# Beyond the Book

In addition to the material in the print or e-book you're reading right now, this product also comes with some access-anywhere goodies on the web. Check out the free Cheat Sheet for a quick rundown of the different types of RVs and campers, tips on renting an RV, advice on what you can and can't do in rest areas, and information on where to come for free. To access the Cheat Sheet, go to www.dummies.com and type **RVs & Campers For Dummies Cheat Sheet** in the Search box.

Visit our Facebook page at www.facebook.com/rvsfordummies for updates, videos, tips, tricks, and more.

# Where to Go from Here

Like all *For Dummies* books, ours is designed so you can read it from cover to cover. (We always advise everyone to buy one copy for every bathroom.) Or you can head straight for the topics you're most interested in — use the table of contents and index to find what you need.

If you're looking at motorhomes, you won't need to read Chapter 7 on tow vehicles. If you're already familiar with the various types of RVs that are available, Chapter 2 may bore you to smithereens. If you climb into your rig, turn on the power, and nothing happens, sit down at the picnic table and thumb your way to Chapter 14 about electrical systems. It's your book now, so use it as you see fit! There's a lot of information stuffed into these pages.

Finally, before we jump in, a word of caution about this or any other book about RV ownership: Never make a potentially expensive purchase based solely on something you read in a book or online. Depending on your personal circumstances, investing in an expensive RV may very well be the biggest purchase you'll ever make, with the possible exception of a house. We know everybody has their moments of weakness and susceptibility to pretty looks and a smooth line of patter, and your first RV can be a lot like your first teenage romantic crush: The heart wants what it wants. But throughout this book, we repeatedly urge you to avoid impulse buying and do lots of research before you hand over your hard-earned cash. You'll be glad you did. Happy travels!

# 1

# Getting Started with RVs and Campers

Discover the world of recreational vehicles (RVs) and life on the road.

Learn the difference between a trailer, a motorhome, a fifth wheel, and more.

Choose the rig that's right for you, factoring in size, shape, arrangement, and price.

# Chapter 1

# Joining the Cavalcade of Rolling Nomads

They've been known by different names over the last hundred years: campers, caravans, tin cans, trailers, Winnebagos, motorhomes, and RVs. There are teardrops and minis, pop-ups and tagalongs, fifth wheels and toy haulers, and motorhomes as small as vans and as big as buses.

When we were growing up, *camper* was the word for a shell on a pickup truck, while *recreational vehicle* (RV) was strictly something with its own engine, like a motorhome, and no single word fit everything you could camp in. Nowadays, both words are used more loosely. We had to pick one, and in this book, we chose to use *RV* as the best overall term for anything with wheels that you can eat and sleep and have fun in, including motorhomes, trailers, fifth wheels, and truck campers.

So, what sort of people have an RV? People just like you — and almost anybody else. Identifying a cross-section of RVers in order to define some "average" owner is as futile as trying to nail Jell-O to a wall. RVs are owned by campers and glampers, nomads and full-timers, homeschoolers and gig workers, loners and families, retirees and newlyweds, weekend warriors and tailgaters. Super-rich, middle-class, and flat-broke campers park side-by-side in campgrounds every day and then sit around each other's campfires and share in the fellowship of RV life.

All the other chapters in this book are the how-to's of RVing, from buying to boondocking to plumbing. But this first chapter is an overview of who's RVing, why they're doing it, and what effect it's having on the culture. Friends and family, even acquaintances, ask us all the time, "What kind of people go RVing?" And, more commonly, "Why would you even *consider* living full time in an RV?" In this chapter, we try to answer both.

RVing is wrapped up with the romance of the open road. Sooner or later, the majority of RVers you encounter will say that they hit the highway because they wanted to actually see and explore the country around them. So, we talk about how and why those highways came about, why Route 66 is such a big deal to RVers, and why the United States, in particular, really is the land of the RV.

# Everybody's Doing It

Perhaps life on the road as a modern nomad sounds like an exciting adventure you'd like to attempt. Or maybe you want to take your kids on one last great adventure as a family before your oldest goes off to college. Or if you're older, maybe you want to bond with your grandkids by exploring the country together. Maybe you just saw a magazine photo of a couple gazing out the back window of their RV at the morning sunrise over a bucolic brook and started wishing it was you instead of them.

Despite a commonplace media image of RVers as either a vast platoon of elderly retirees or out-of-work, flinty nomads chasing day-labor jobs like the Oakies in the 1930s, the truth is that RVers come from every age, income, education level, and socioeconomic status.

Whether they intend to use an RV only for a couple of getaway weekends a year, live in one year-round, or anything in between, everybody has their own very personal reason for buying a trailer or motorhome. Over the years, we've heard these reasons most often:

>> You fondly recall a wonderful summer trip to the Grand Canyon as a child, when your family borrowed your uncle's motorhome.

>> You're getting close to retirement age and suddenly that three-bedroom house seems like way too much expense and responsibility to hang onto anymore.

>> You despise the four months of cold weather and shoveling 10 inches of partly cloudy off your front stoop every time it snows, but you otherwise love your sticks-and-bricks home the rest of the year.

>> You realized during the COVID-19 pandemic that you really can work from anywhere with a Wi-Fi connection, and you'd like to see the rest of the country.

>> The idea of waking up to a new and different view outside your window every morning seems too romantic for your soul to pass up.

In short, there as many reasons as there are people, and there are literally millions of RV owners on the road today, chasing their dreams and loving the lifestyle.

**TECHNICAL STUFF**

If statistics are your thing, chew on these: A recent study found that RV ownership has increased over 62 percent since the year 2001, and the record 11.2 million RV-owning households are split almost evenly between those *over* and *under* the age of 55. The biggest increase was among 18- to 34-year-olds, who now make up almost a quarter of the market. An incredible 9.6 million *more* households intend to buy an RV within the next five years. And among existing owners, 84 percent of 18- to 34-year-olds said they intend to buy *another* RV in the next five years, while 78 percent of them would prefer to buy a new model instead of used.

In the following sections, we walk you through the main groups of people who are RVing these days. Don't see yourself in one of these categories? See yourself in more than one? You're not alone!

## Weekenders and vacationers

The biggest group of RVers you'll find on the road are the weekenders and vacationers. The industry says that the majority of RV owners are these types of campers. Most are still working for a living, and loads of them have families. They live in traditional houses, condos, or apartments year-round, but they use their RVs to get away for short breaks.

Because of that, the traditional travel trailer is generally designed and constructed for occasional use, and that's partially why you see such a wide range of options and prices for them. Because of that wide financial spread, you should probably look upon a weekend travel trailer and a well-equipped one for full-time living with two very different levels of expectation in price, quality, features, and longevity. What you choose should be dictated by how you intend to use it. (We give you lots of information about picking and choosing a rig to best suit your needs in Chapters 3, 4, and 5.)

# Snowbirds and retirees

There's no denying that a substantial number of RVers on the road are seniors 55 and up. They make up about half of all RV owners in the United States. Like migrating birds, seniors have been fleeing from wintertime weather since the dawn of time, or at least since the founding of Miami Beach and the invention of the umbrella drink. These *snowbirds,* as they're commonly called, flee their chilly, snowy, northern states to Florida, Alabama, Texas, and the other Gulf states east of the Rockies, or Arizona, New Mexico, and Nevada in the West. In fact, a big swath of Canadian snowbirds cross the border every year in their RVs to head for the very same places. That's why you hear a lot of *eh*s in Tucson every January.

The explosive sales of RVs has helped make warm-weather chasing a truly mass, mobile movement. But unlike the snowbirds of old who bought timeshares or vacation homes, RVs give them the ability to go wherever they like. Retirees like waking up to a new view out the front door every day, too, and RVs represent freedom of mobility and travel that airplanes and timeshare contracts can't offer. And retirement generally means there's more discretionary time and money than an average family has.

TIP

Throughout the warm-weather states, there has been a growing clamor for elaborate and huge luxury RV resorts. They often have hundreds of RV parking spaces to accommodate the largest motorhomes, fifth wheels, and other rigs, with full hookups. The best ones have pools, shops, restaurants, social rooms, laundry facilities, and much more. Prices are high, but most offer monthly rates for extended stays. And if you get sick of being in your RV after a while, many also offer small one-bedroom cabins or villas for rent or purchase.

# Full-timers

The number of RV owners who choose to live on the road 365 days a year is growing dramatically. According to the RV Industry Association (RVIA), 450,000 people were living in RVs in 2010; as of 2021, that figure is over a million. RV manufacturers have responded by offering models with as much living space as possible, using slide-outs that expand when you're parked. More and more rigs are equipped with residential-grade appliances like refrigerators, dishwashers, and washer/dryer units — items that would have only been found in the most expensive units until recently. The largest fifth-wheel trailers and motorhomes feel more like a house than an RV.

On the other hand are "minimalist" full-timers in vans and Class Bs, with variations in between. Our parents once wisely cautioned us against being owned by our possessions. Singles and empty-nesters alike can feel overwhelmed by the costs, daily care, and maintenance of a house. Yet, a 25- to 40-foot-long home on wheels can be kept neat and orderly with a minimum of effort and expense. It can be incredibly liberating.

**WARNING**

Living perpetually on the road is a big commitment to change. It comes with its own challenges, and much of that stems from the problem of establishing a legal *domicile* (a permanent mailing address for everything from health insurance to filing taxes and voting). RV-friendly states like Florida, South Dakota, and Texas make it simpler to establish a legal domicile, but in most cases, you have to visit your home base at least once a year to stay legal.

**TIP**

Escapees RV Club (www.escapees.com) is a major provider of services for full-timers, like mail forwarding and roadside assistance. Their Xcapers group within the club is geared to helping full-timers. They even have their own annual gathering each year, called Convergence.

## Traveling workers and the gig economy

Internet connectivity and a smartphone in everybody's pocket has nurtured the gig economy. If you can work from home, it doesn't matter where home is, and the COVID-19 shutdowns brought that sharply into focus. Home can just as easily be a place on wheels wherever the Wi-Fi works.

There's no sense in denying that living and working in an RV can be a very attractive choice for economic reasons, regardless of someone's age. On the road, we've met plenty of twentysomethings who wanted out of Mom and Dad's house, and an RV was the only way they could afford it. We've encountered several folks who inherited an RV, and living in it seemed more attractive than paying for an overpriced apartment. But whatever the reason they started, these RVers eventually decided they loved it and had no intention of "escaping" the road and returning to an anchored life.

## Women on the road

The original RV full-timers were people following a mobile job. But the newest full-timers in the RV landscape are the growing number of women. We've talked with women RVing alone, single women, as well as widows and divorcees who are either childless or empty-nesters. The lure of the adventure of the open road is common, and the ongoing development of lighter, towable trailers and smaller, easier-to-maneuver motorhomes has made it far less daunting for anyone to indulge their dream.

Sometimes the women we talked to had been unhappy, trapped in a little apartment and an unfulfilling 9-to-5. But more than a few we've met found themselves trying to care for a 3,000-square-foot house with a big yard, and couldn't figure out why they were doing it. A 30-foot universe is a universe that can be handled. A condo or even a retirement community is an option, but it can seem like a retreat from life, with more potential for loneliness.

This was the situation with Lora, our friend and neighbor, the first person we personally knew who told us, with no warning, that she was selling her large suburban house and most of the stuff in it to hit the road in an RV. Lora is a bright, happy woman with all sorts of choices. She wasn't destitute or desperate when she made this one. And this is the ultimate point — most of us are out here RVing because we *want* to be. We want to see the world and experience life on a higher plane. We're living a fun life that's much cheaper than the old-style suburban house, car, and 9-to-5 job. We're here, out on the road, because we're nomads by nature. And when we pull up stakes to move on, we don't ever say "goodbye," we say, "See you down the road!"

# Workampers

The sudden about-face in the economy in 2020, compelled millions of Americans to change their lifestyle dramatically almost overnight. Sales of RVs to people no longer able to afford their homes, or who have become work nomads pursuing jobs in the gig economy, are also at an all-time high. For a big group of retirees, day-to-day living on a paltry Social Security check is nearly impossible. As full-time RVers, they can subsidize their retirement by seeking part-time jobs and traveling to wherever the work is. Many RVers pick up jobs as campground hosts, Amazon workers, seasonal tourist attraction or resort employees, and sugar beet harvesters in Nebraska and North Dakota (or other agricultural jobs).

For many years, Amazon has employed thousands of transient workers (many of them retirees) living in trailers, who chase seasonal warehouse jobs across the country. The Amazon CamperForce program arranges for campground sites so these temporary workers have a place to park their rigs while working for several months at a time. Wages are low, hours are long, and the work itself can be tedious and exhausting, but Amazon's appetite for workers is inexhaustible. It's entirely possible that the box that arrived this morning with your favorite tea, a bargain box of soap bars, and a Frisbee for the dog was packed by a CamperForce RVer.

More and more companies are beginning to realize the benefits of these types of mobile employees. Some openly prefer older workers, who tend to be more dependable. Workers on Wheels (www.work-for-rvers-and-campers.com) and Workamper News (https://workamper.com) are two websites for connecting RVers and employers. They let you subscribe to a free daily email newsletter with job listings and opportunities.

# Road scholars

The nationwide closing of schools for the COVID-19 pandemic dramatically increased the number of families who decided to "road-school" their children in the family RV. Children no longer tethered to classrooms, are learning about their country and the world in national parks and national historic sites. Zoos, parks, museums, monuments, nature centers, even shopping for groceries, all become learning experiences and teachable moments.

Fulltime Families (`www.fulltimefamilies.com`) is an online community that provides guidance, information, and resources for parents and children, including recommendations for road-schooling. While many states have reporting requirements for homeschooled children, many RV families make Florida or Texas their legal state of residence because they have beneficial homeschooling laws and are welcoming of full-time RVers.

# Going green and living off the grid

We talk about *boondocking* in Chapter 20, but since the very earliest trailers were designed, the goal has been to last as long as possible without external electric and water connections. If the desire to live "off the grid" with the smallest possible carbon footprint keeps you awake nights, an RV may be the answer. The green movement and the tiny house movement are natural bedfellows with the RV world. Innovations that cram more features and conveniences into cramped spaces have been the trademark of trailers and motorhomes since the 1920s.

As solar and battery technologies continue to improve, more and more people look upon RVs as the ultimate "green machines." RV builders today are offering solar-ready trailers and motorhomes, and conversion of older units to accommodate solar panels and lithium batteries is becoming the most common request for RV dealers and service centers. Look for a "solar ready" sticker on RVs when you go shopping. It means the rig is prewired for easily adding solar panels. (Be sure to check both Chapter 14 about electrical systems and Chapter 20 on boondocking.)

The RV industry has its own environmental certification program for vehicles. To earn a Certified Green sticker, RVs have to meet or exceed specified energy- and water-efficient requirements, by using LED lighting, stronger composite construction materials, sustainable materials in interior design elements, and energy-efficient appliances.

Meanwhile, electric cars and trucks aren't quite up to towing RVs of any substantial weight for an extended length of time or distance. Not yet, anyway. (We talk about the anticipated electric truck market in Chapter 7.) And there are currently no electric motorhomes on the market. But they will doubtless be available very soon. Unfortunately, what can't be depended on is the ready availability of electric charging stations. Until there are a sufficient number of quick-charging stations at rest areas, truck stops, shopping centers, and other convenience points, electric vehicles won't be practical for any kind of long-range road trips, much less as tow vehicles.

## Glampers

At the opposite end of the spectrum from boondockers are the *glampers* (a mash up of *glamorous* and *camper*). If you're a certain age, you may remember comedian Billy Crystal's Fernando Lamas character exclaiming, "You look MAH-velous!" It could be the unofficial motto of glampers.

Glampers celebrate the good life with all the comforts and conveniences of home, but in an elaborate tent or a dazzling (usually vintage) trailer. If boondockers want minimalism, glampers want maximism. That means beautifully decked-out classic trailers, with lots of retro decor, mood lighting, gourmet food, and a big dose of cuteness. Glamper trailers are designed by their owners to make you go, "Aw, that's so *cute!*"

Sticking with a particular theme (like '30s Western dude ranch, Paris boudoir, '50s living room, or '60s "atomic modern") is a major plus. If a 1950s wall lamp looks coolly retro, wrapping it in a string of phony pearls ratchets it up to glamper level. In fact, a proper glamper is dressed to match her rig, and regards a string of pearls as a proper accessory while whipping up lobster thermidor and truffles over the campfire. If this kind of thing is up your personal alley, get inspired by picking up MaryJane Butters's *Glamping with MaryJane* (Gibbs Smith). Girl Camper (https://girlcamper.com) is an online community and resource specifically for women on the road, with a strong emphasis on glamping. And for those who can't afford to jump in and start such an undertaking themselves, a growing number of high-end campgrounds offer glamper accommodations in vintage trailers.

## International tourists

*"I will live in Montana. And I will marry a round American woman and raise rabbits, and she will cook them for me. And I will have a pickup truck . . . maybe even a 'recreational vehicle.' And drive from state to state. Do they let you do that?"*

—*Soviet Captain Vasili Borodin, in* The Hunt for Red October

## THE GYPSY IN THE SOUL

In the 2021 film *Nomadland,* van-lifer Fern, on a visit with her family, has her lifestyle defended by her embarrassed sister, who says she's like one of the pioneers. It's not a terrible comparison, especially when you're looking for a road to a Bureau of Land Management (BLM) campground out West, and you feel like a befuddled trail guide who got the whole wagon train lost in Donner Party country. But the far better metaphor is the Rom.

In the 19th century, the *Rom* were the remarkable Romany people, commonly called "gypsies." Their roots are uncertain — a mysterious people without a country of their own, almost perpetually on the move. Typically, they hunkered down in winter. They lived in wagons called *vardos,* famed for their interior woodwork, and if you've peeked into one in a museum, the comparison with an RV is too obvious to miss.

One of the best books about them is *The Gypsies* by Jan Yoors (Waveland Press), a Belgian who ran away to live with the gypsies when he was 12. His academic parents permitted it, and it went on for years, while he came home often enough to keep them from renting out his room. Yoors wrote about the deep family ties of the Rom, but the other building block of life was the *kumpania,* the people they traveled with. A great prejudice existed against the gypsies, and so, to live on the road, they developed a complex set of signs for one another, to tell their *kumpania* who followed whether the town they were coming to was safe and what resources they would find when they got there.

But RVers today have the Romany code beat all hollow, with incredible amounts of information and mutual aid, in the form of resources like YouTube and the Internet. You don't have to be Daniel Boone anymore, chopping down trees with your bare teeth and whittling snow tires out of deposits of snow. The refinement of the Internet and the invention of Wi-Fi has made it possible for improbable people to strike out for parts unknown, with the comfort of their own *kumpania,* a group of like-minded people who will help and support them.

If you're walking through a campground as the sun goes down, it's getting more and more commonplace to hear couples and families speaking a foreign language — Russian, Portuguese, Japanese, Romanian, Chinese, German. These international travelers visit the United States to actually see and experience it at ground level. The rise in popularity of renting RVs over the last decade has made it easy for anyone in the world to plan their own uniquely American RV vacation. The American landscape is every bit as alluring to other people around the world, and the romance of Route 66 and the endless highway has been exported nearly everywhere by our pop culture.

# The Song of the Open Road

More than anything else, mobility defines the RV lifestyle. RVs are the ideal symbol for so many Americans because they call to mind distant horizons, exploring the unknown, and the eternal, impatient wanderlust to see what lies beyond the next turn in the road. Roads are important to RVers for the same reason planes are important to pilots. But they don't just carry us where we want to go. Roads define us, and so the famous ones become something tons of RVers want to experience.

## "Intrepid autoists"

In 1903, Horatio Nelson Jackson and his co-driver, Sewell Crocker, were the first people to drive an automobile across the United States. It took just over two months. Jackson did it on a bet to prove cars were more than a passing fad, and it made headlines. Their feat made it all too clear that American roads were just plain lousy. They didn't have it much better than a Conestoga wagon on the Oregon Trail.

In the two decades that followed, cars became an ordinary part of American life, but anyone driving one farther than church on Sunday was considered an "intrepid autoist." The few highways built were privately funded by consortiums of businessmen, and they were called *auto trails*. The quality was miserable by our standards, often *macadam* (a gravel surface) or just plain dirt. A few small, expensive sections were brick.

Those early highways covered some ambitious stretches: the Atlantic Highway, down the eastern seaboard from Maine to Miami; the Lee Highway, from Washington, D.C., to San Diego; and the National Old Trails Road, from Baltimore to San Francisco. The most famous one was the Lincoln Highway, from New York's Times Square to Lincoln Park in San Francisco. The promoters who financed them loved romantic or memorable names, like the Dixie Highway, the Yellowstone Trail, and El Camino Real. And those names stuck to those routes, even to the present. But taking a trip on one, particularly the whole way, was a little like climbing Mount Everest.

The big change came in 1919, in the wake of one embarrassing, high-profile trip. The U.S. Army sent out a highly-publicized expedition on the Lincoln Highway to see how long it would take for a convoy of military vehicles to cross the country by road, if the time ever came to defend the West Coast. The answer was a dismal 62 days, just one day shorter than Jackson and Crocker had taken 16 years before. By the end of the journey, none of the men on the convoy had been killed, but there were an almost unimaginable 230 road accidents and many injuries.

So, the federal government decided to get in the road-building business. A young officer on the trip, Dwight Eisenhower, never forgot his battle to cross "Darkest America." Later, as a famed general during World War II, he saw first-hand the Autostrade in Italy and the Autobahn in Germany, the great European "superhighways," and he wanted something similar for the United States.

## Getting scientific

Between 1926 and 1956, the United States went on a 30-year road-building binge, creating the *United States Numbered Highway System* (sometimes referred to as Federal Highways or U.S. Routes). By the end of it, the infamous two months it had taken to cross the country fell to just two weeks.

**TECHNICAL STUFF**

In 1926, to reflect the new, scientific age, it was decided highways would now be numbered, in a grid pattern, and the numbers would tell you something about the road you're on. Odd numbers were north–south highways; even numbers ran east–west. The lower numbers began in the east and went up as you moved west; a three-digit number was reserved for breakaway spur routes. Most of the two-digit numbers ending in zero ran across the country. Lots of exceptions were made over the years, so you can't count on it absolutely, but the basic numbering system of U.S. routes is still there, and it still works to give you an idea of the road you're on.

You'd think people would appreciate all that work. But the American Association of State Highway and Transportation Officials (AASHTO), the agency of state highway engineers who cooked up the system, was flooded with complaints. Newspapers began weighing in, grousing that numbered highways sounded cold and indifferent and didn't have the charm or easy shorthand of names like the Dixie Highway. Over the years, people clung to calling them by the old names. Highway 80 remained the Dixie Highway, and U.S. 30 was still and forever the Lincoln Highway.

But there was one road from the period that didn't need a name. It had nicknames like the Mother Road or the Main Street of America, but you didn't hear them much at the time. It managed to create a mystique with two numbers on a plain black-and-white sign (see the nearby sidebar).

## GET YOUR KICKS ON ROUTE 66

In October 1960, the TV show *Route 66* premiered on CBS, a loose anthology about two Beat Generation guys on the road to find out about Life. Its jazzy instrumental theme by Nelson Riddle, and its ride, a Corvette convertible, made it the definition of cool. It was shot on location across the country, unusual for its time, and dealt with all the hot-button social issues of the day, with a good deal of violence thrown in, guaranteeing a hit.

Route 66 ran from Chicago, Illinois, to Santa Monica, California, cobbled together out of three of the old auto trails. In the '40s and '50s, it became a major artery moving people from the East to the sunshine and economic opportunity of the Golden West. By 1960, Route 66 was already a legend, and it already had its own catchy tune, "Get Your Kicks on Route 66." CBS didn't want to pony up to actor and jazz pianist Bobby Troup to use his popular song in the show. But Nelson Riddle's tune became one of the first TV-show themes to hit the *Billboard* charts, while sales of Corvettes zoomed to more than 10,000. It's ironic that, from the day of the premier, the road they were on, Route 66, was already on its way out, and its days were numbered.

Today, the so-called Historic Route 66 is an RVer's Holy Grail, and it's still the mother lode of roadside attractions. But seeing it can be sort of catch as catch can. After the famed highway was decertified in 1985, efforts began to save the unique cultural heritage of Route 66. Eventually, Congress passed a bill to match funds for historical preservation projects. Restored, neon-lit motels, cafes, and gas stations began popping up or reopening all across the old route.

## President Eisenhower and the Interstate Highway System

*"Eight lanes of shimmering cement running from here to Pasadena. Traffic jams will be a thing of the past. . . . I see a place where people get on and off the freeway. On and off, off and on, all day, all night. Soon, where Toontown once stood will be a string of gas stations, inexpensive motels, restaurants that serve rapidly prepared food. Tire salons, automobile dealerships, and wonderful, wonderful billboards reaching as far as the eye can see. My God, it'll be beautiful!"*

*—Judge Doom, Who Framed Roger Rabbit?*

This was Judge Doom, the bad guy 'toon of *Who Framed Roger Rabbit?*, with his evil plot to kill the Los Angeles Red Car streetcar line in favor of highways and automobiles. This was the vision of the men who built the Interstate Highway System, the massive, federally funded project started in 1956, and finally declared complete in 1992. It was a remarkable achievement, and it was vitally needed. But there's no question it changed the nation in ways we're still trying to understand.

The most important thing to understand about all the old U.S. highway systems, including Route 66, is that these were essentially stretches of highway linking towns in a chain, going *through* the towns. In fact, the highway usually ran right down Main Street.

By contrast, the newfangled engineering idea with the Eisenhower Interstate Highway System was "controlled access," with no intersections, no way on or off the road apart from strategically placed exit ramps miles apart. Depending on where you go, the interstate was called a *freeway,* an *expressway,* or a *throughway.*

Eisenhower's planners designed a system that bypassed all major cities, to keep traffic moving. But he eventually caved on this under pressure, and we ended up with something nonsensical: a highway that bypassed the little towns, yet plowed right through the heart of all the major cities with an asphalt assault and, ironically, made traffic in cities even more congested from the start. In rural areas, that word, *bypassed* was the death knell for little towns when the interstate passed them by for the sake of efficiency.

Battles went on for years, with "freeway revolts" fighting the system. One of the most famous was in Tucumcari, New Mexico, a town Route 66 had put on the map. We drove across I-40 in the late '70s, when the eternally unfinished interstate abruptly ended and detoured you off through the town on the old Route 66. But in July 1981, the new bypass was finally dedicated. When the interstate routes were completed, motels and cafes in the town started closing soon after, just as they had in so many other towns.

This is the reason for the nostalgia around Route 66, with its fun vibe of America in its prime. As little towns folded their tents, decaying from the economic blow, the interstate became a symbol of progress rolling over the small, mom-and-pop businesses, and the relentless sameness of the chain hotels and restaurants.

# The Road Less Taken

There's an unofficial motto of RVers: "What's your hurry?" That's why so many of us like stargazing, because we like to be where we can still *see* the night sky and then take the time to do it. The interstate is great, but RVers love to take the scenic route. If you ask about it around the campfire, someone will have done Route 66, at least part of it. Sooner or later, you'll probably be tempted to do some of it yourself.

I-40, from North Carolina to Barstow, California, is the modern interstate covering the most miles of old Route 66, the ones west of the Mississippi. But don't confuse it with U.S. Route 40, the old National Road, which has its own fans. Like 66, it's also called the Main Street of America for the number of cities and towns it passes through, particularly across the Midwest. But U.S. 40 is farther north than the I-40 that covers much of Route 66. Confused yet?

It's an acquired skill, finding the old roads, especially if you're doing Route 66, because it was decommissioned as a highway. You can't stay on it all the way from Chicago to Los Angeles, and sometimes, just finding a particular stretch of it can be tough. To try to save part of it, states stepped in and recommissioned selected stretches as "Historic Route 66," with special signs. But driving some parts can be dicey for a big RV. For example, one famous stretch is called the Oatman Highway, up to the mining ghost town of Oatman, Arizona. With its 48 miles of incessant, hairpin, switchback turns, on a two-way road with opposing traffic and no shoulder, it's a road restricted to vehicles under 40 feet. In the old days, this section was called "Bloody 66." Lots of RVers have done it, but you need to approach with caution.

It takes planning to do any of the Mother Road. Planning it is the fun part. There are smartphone apps out there, like the Route 66 Ultimate Guide, and there's also the lovingly written and regularly updated *Route 66: EZ66 Guide for Travelers*, by Jerry McClanahan (National Historic Route 66 Federation). Sources like these will help you follow the choppy and broken route that can get you so quickly and frustratingly lost.

RVers love all these slower, scenic routes, and they talk about them a lot. Unlike Route 66, most of them are still commissioned U.S. highways, and they make for great trips. You can follow the Lewis & Clark National Historic Trail or the Great River Road, steering the course of the Mississippi River through ten states. There are apps for both trips and websites of people who've done it.

Here are just a few of the major old U.S. highways, apart from Route 66 and Route 40, that you'll also hear about around the campfire:

» **U.S. 30 and U.S. 20:** These roads run parallel to one another, and both are parallel to I-90, running across the northern United States from east to west. They still call U.S. 30 the Lincoln Highway, and it still runs from New Jersey to Oregon, while U.S. 20, the longest highway in America, is still the old Yellowstone Trail. Both are famed for their incredible scenery.

» **Highway 101, the King's Highway, or old El Camino Real:** The great north–south West Coast highway. It's famed for its remarkable scenic drives and hairpin mountain curves. It runs from Los Angeles to Mount Olympus in Washington State. The Pacific Coast Highway, also incredibly popular for RVs, is a state road, California State Route 1.

>> **U.S. 1:** The major north–south East Coast highway is the old Atlantic Highway, running from the Canadian border to Key West in Florida, through just about every major East Coast town.

>> **Dixie Overland Highway:** Not to be confused with the Dixie Highway, the Overland runs east–west. It's the old auto route between Savannah, Georgia, and California, across the South. Much of it is the old Route 80, a haven, like Route 66, for nostalgia, Southern-style, with some very pretty towns.

**TIP**

There are scenic highway websites, like the very good www.myscenicdrives.com. But in the planning stage of any trip, you just can't beat the *National Geographic Guide to Scenic Highways and Byways* (National Geographic). Every region of the country is here, all 50 states, with 300 suggested drives on the old U.S. routes, as well as the state and county roads. Each drive offers a few brief but detailed paragraphs on the condition of the roads, sights to see, even suggested times of year, and the majority of them can be easily done in a day.

## BEHIND THE DOORS IN TRAILERDOM'S MECCA: ELKHART, INDIANA

Every RVer should try to make a trip to Elkhart, Indiana. It's like going on a pilgrimage. If you own an RV, your whole rig, or at least a lot of what's inside of it, was likely built in Elkhart. More than 80 percent of the RVs in the United States are made in this part of northern Indiana, so the opportunities for factory tours are a major draw. But for a town of 50,000 people, Elkhart has a lot of attractions and museums; the Wellfield Botanic Garden, the Museum of American Art, the New York Central Railroad Museum, historic homes like the Ruthmere mansion, even the Hall of Heroes Superhero Museum.

But one of the best things to do in Elkhart is to visit the RV/MH Hall of Fame (www. rvmhhalloffame.org). This museum dedicated to RVs and mobile homes is beautifully laid out, with interior exhibits parked along a curving road. People started renovating cars into RVs about a week after they were invented, and you'll get to see things from this early period, like the 1915 Model T Ford with a "Telescoping Apartment" custom addition. Other exhibits include a 1913 Earl Travel Trailer, movie star Mae West's personal motorhome while working at Paramount Pictures, a gem of a 1974 GMC motorhome from when General Motors briefly entered the RV business, and a 1958 Wally Byam prototype mini Airstream trailer. If you love RVs, you'll have a blast! It might even inspire you to modify your own rig.

# Chapter **2**

# Surveying the Wide World of RVs and Campers

Any RV is like a small vacation home that happens to have wheels and a license plate. Like vacation homes, RVs can be as simple as a tent, as cozy as a cabin, or as spacious as a penthouse suite. But unlike a house, you can pack up and move it to a different location when you get bored with the surroundings, irritated with your neighbors, or numbed by the weather. Try that with a timeshare condo.

The term *recreational vehicle* (RV) is an all-purpose tote bag crammed full of types of vehicles to choose from. (Arguably, a bike is a recreational vehicle, but we won't get into semantics.) The RV world has its own vocabulary that can baffle a beginner. But all the different types of RVs and campers can be divided into three basic categories:

» **Travel trailers or towables:** These don't have their own engines, so you have to pull them behind something else, called a *tow vehicle*.

» **Motorhomes or coaches:** These are self-contained, drivable RVs with built-in engines. No tow vehicle is required.

>> **Truck campers (sometimes called truck caps or camper shells):** These actually have to ride piggyback on another vehicle — usually a pickup truck.

You can find all kinds of variations within these categories, more every day it seems, but these are the basics you'll encounter when the love of your life suddenly elbows you at 7 a.m. on a Saturday and says, "Let's go to the RV show!"

The type of RV or camper you ultimately pick will depend on how you plan to use it — your needs and wants. But you can't (or at least *shouldn't*) make that decision without knowing what's available. So, that's what we cover in this chapter. If you don't have an RV or camper yet but you're looking to get one, this is the chapter for you!

# Motorhomes

You've seen them on the highway: giant motorhomes the length of a Greyhound bus with a sparkling paint job, the driver sitting up high in a big, comfy, padded chair behind a giant picture-window windshield. These are the Class As, and the moniker is easy to remember. But this is only one classification of motorhome. Motorhomes actually come in all kinds of sizes and configurations.

Motorhomes (sometimes called *motor coaches*) are extremely popular, partly because you don't need a separate vehicle to tow them with. The simplest way to think of a motorhome is an engine and transmission mounted on a chassis, with a complete trailer plopped on top. Motorhomes can be powered by gasoline or diesel engines, and both engine types have their cheerleaders and detractors (see the nearby sidebar). (Some manufacturers are working on electric coaches, but they're in the infant phase of development.)

**TECHNICAL STUFF**

Motorhome manufacturers don't actually build the engines for their vehicles, and few build the steel chassis they sit on. Instead, they buy parts from established consumer truck builders like Ford, Chevrolet/GMC, RAM, and Mercedes. Parts for larger and diesel units come from the makers of commercial trucks and buses, like Cummins, Freightliner, and Spartan.

One of the attractions of a motorhome is that passengers can get to everything easily while the vehicle is on the road. Safety experts agree that everybody should remain seated and belted in at all times when tooting down the highway, but the reality is that everybody (except the driver) can get up, move around, go to the bathroom, walk back and lie down in bed, raid the fridge, or watch a movie, all without stopping. That's not the case with a towable trailer.

# GASOLINE VERSUS DIESEL

In the RV world, the question of whether to buy a gasoline-powered motorhome or towing vehicle versus a diesel-powered one can sometimes enflame the sort of religious passions unseen since the Spanish Inquisition. Online discussions can quickly turn into battling revival meetings competing to save the souls of the undecided.

Most Class A rigs are powered by diesel, but some models have gasoline engines. With Class B and C, you have more choice. The same is true when you go shopping for a tow vehicle. Ford, Chevrolet/GMC, and RAM all offer a diesel option for their heavier-duty 0.75-ton and 1-ton consumer pickup trucks. We talk all about choosing towing vehicles in Chapter 7.

The pro-gasoline side has immediate economic savings in their favor. Gas-powered trucks and motorhomes are usually less expensive than diesels, often by a lot. And the price-per-gallon of gasoline is cheaper than diesel, too (at least as of this writing), and these beasts are mighty thirsty. Diesel fuel can be formulated differently, depending on the time of year and where you are in the country, because it's a thicker, oilier type of fluid than gasoline. Get stuck with the wrong kind of diesel fuel when the temperature gets bitter cold, and it can turn into a gel, making it difficult to even start the engine. Many sources also recommend adding diesel exhaust fluid (DEF) every time you fill the tank to keep smoke from belching out of your exhaust pipe — so there's another expense.

Diesel fuel also stinks worse than gasoline, and it seems to get all over everything sooner or later. That sounds like a whiny complaint, but there are folks who regard it as a deal breaker. You'll undoubtedly step in a puddle of diesel fuel or get it on your clothes when you fill up. And you can't always be positive that every gas station you come to has diesel. It's less common when you get off the highway and take the scenic route. So motorhome RVers like to stick to truck stops, where diesel is always available (and where they have the room to maneuver their long rigs).

The biggest Class A motorhome diesel engines are usually on par with those found in commercial trucks. That means they're much more expensive to maintain than gasoline engines. That quick-lube place on the corner isn't going to give you its $19.95 oil change special for your Class A. The engine will have to be fixed and maintained by an RV dealer or a commercial truck service center. Because of the way diesel pushers are built, working on one often means the mechanics need to access the engine by going into your bedroom, bathroom, or closet and opening up the floor to reach components inaccessible from the outside. That adds time and expense. And no matter how long the shop needs to fix your RV, remember that you've just lost both your house and transportation until it's fixed.

Now that we've talked you out of it, diesel has lots of advantages over gasoline, which is why most Class A motorhomes have diesel engines. Big Class As weigh a lot, even when

*(continued)*

*(continued)*

they're empty. And diesel engines generate more horsepower and torque, which means they can pull more weight more efficiently, especially when it comes to climbing hills. High-end Class As are packed full of heavy appliances, real porcelain toilets, granite countertops, custom wood cabinetry, and other weighty materials, even before you throw in your family and all their stuff and fill all the water tanks. A diesel engine is better at handling that massive load. (These same issues come into play when choosing a diesel truck for towing a heavy, loaded fifth-wheel trailer.)

Diesel also gets slightly better mileage per gallon than gasoline. With a big Class A coach, expect about 9 to 11 miles per gallon with a diesel engine, and closer to 7 to 9 miles per gallon with gasoline. Diesel engines cost more to buy, but they last much, much longer than their gas-powered counterparts. Diesel engines are designed for the long-distance, weight-hauling chores of commercial trucks.

Another consideration is that diesel Class A motorhomes often ride quieter on the inside because most are *diesel pushers,* with the engine mounted all the way in the back of the coach. Gasoline engines are usually up front, under the cockpit floor between the front seats.

Bottom line: If you intend on keeping your motorhome or tow vehicle for a long time and putting more than 100,000 miles on it, a diesel engine is the hands-down favorite. It also wins if you're driving a heavier motorhome that's towing a car or boat. But if you suspect you'll only use your RV a few weeks a year and you plan on putting less than 10,000 miles on it annually, you can lean toward the savings of a gasoline engine.

**WARNING**

It's actually illegal in many states for people to bounce around inside of a moving trailer that's being towed, with a long list of really good reasons. And don't think of leaving your pet back there. By contrast, in a motorhome, everybody is supposed to remain in their seats when it's moving, and many of the couches, chairs, and even dinette seats are equipped with seat belts. Children should be belted in at all times. It's a lot like being in a plane when the captain turns off the seatbelt sign. Even on the smoothest road, it can be a bumpy experience. And you can turn into a human cannonball if the driver suddenly hits the brakes.

When you pull out of your driveway in a motorhome, it carries everything, even electricity (most motorhomes have onboard electrical generators). When you compare sizes and prices with towable RVs, the sticker shock of motorhomes takes some getting used to, but remember, you're self-propelled. You don't have the additional expense of buying a $30,000 to $70,000 truck to haul it with. You also don't have to tow anything behind you, although plenty of people do add a hitch to the back end to drag a car or even a boat. (You can find more about towing a car in Chapter 19.)

There are three basic classifications of motorhomes, and naturally, they don't follow a logical order. Class A is the biggest, Class B is the smallest, and Class C is somewhere in between. To further confuse the matter, some manufacturers have tried to straddle those categories and blur the lines between them, particularly with the new categories of B+ and C+.

## Class A motorhomes

Class A motorhomes (like the one shown in Figure 2-1) are the most common type of motorized RV you'll find on the road. One way you can spot a Class A and tell it from other types is that the front end is usually flat, without a hood and with a big picture window for the windshield. Driver and passenger seats are right up in the front, like sitting in the front row of a movie theater without anyone blocking the view.

**FIGURE 2-1:**
Class A motorhomes are the big dogs of the RV world.

*Photograph courtesy of Christopher Hodapp*

Class As generally range from 25 to 45 feet in length (more than three times as long as your average midsize car these days). They're typically roomy enough on the inside to comfortably accommodate 8 to 12 people as you roll down the road or turn in for the night. They can also be some of the biggest and most luxurious RVs around.

Class As tend to be wider than the average towable, which means more space inside. Class As are most likely to have the latest features and gizmos, the most automated accessories, the most interior decor choices, and even the kind of full-size appliances you've got at home. It's common to find Class As catering to the market of full-time RVers, with a king-size bed, lots of closet space, multiple and roomier bathrooms, big living and dining room areas, washers and dryers, and sometimes even dishwashers. Some have outdoor flat-screen TVs and stereo systems so you can sit around the campfire and still watch the football game. Some have exterior kitchenettes with a sink, fridge, and maybe even a microwave or gas stovetop, in case you prefer cooking outdoors. And some even have a large *toy hauler* (a garage compartment in back), so you can bring your Harleys, all-terrain vehicles (ATVs) or even a small car with you.

Class As usually have gobs of storage inside and out because of the way they're designed. In most cases, the indoor living space sits high off the ground, with tons of "basement" storage compartments down below that are accessible from hatches on the outside. And as if their bus-size bodies weren't ginormous enough, many Class As built after 2000 have between one and four *slides* (slide-out extensions that expand the indoor living space dramatically when you're setting up camp; see Figure 2-2) — it's sort of like driving your own personal Transformer robot that turns into a condominium. Class As are the hands-down favorite choice for people who want to live full-time on the road and feel like they're in a house, yet mobile enough to easily move day after day.

**FIGURE 2-2:**
A typical Class A motorhome with its slides extended.

*Photograph courtesy of Christopher Hodapp*

## SAFETY SYSTEMS

Class As may be the most expensive, most luxurious, most option-packed motorhomes on the road, but they typically don't have air bags and are not required to be crash-tested by the National Highway Traffic Safety Administration (NHTSA). Other types of motorhomes (Class Bs and Cs, described later in this chapter) are built around an existing truck cab that comes from the auto manufacturer with airbags and other safety systems you're accustomed to in a modern car. They also come equipped with in-dash entertainment packages, and heating and air-conditioning systems that keep the driver and passenger in the cab comfortable. Those systems were engineered into the vehicle by the original truck manufacturer and crash-tested by the NHTSA.

*None* of that is the case with the typical Class A motorhome cab, which is custom built by the RV maker. In addition to few or no airbags, Class As rarely have any kind of anti-collision warning or avoidance system at all. If you're driving a diesel-pusher, you don't even have a big, heavy engine block out in front of you to at least absorb some head-on collision impact.

If the lack of these types of safety systems is a deal breaker for you, you may want to compromise a little and look at a large Class C motorhome or a fifth-wheel trailer instead.

## Getting used to driving

Even though they're big-rig trucks or buses under the floor, these monsters of the RV world really are remarkably easy to drive. These massive rigs generally have air suspensions and air brakes for a smoother ride and greater safety, so you won't feel like you're hauling a load of railroad ties to Poughkeepsie. They've got automatic transmissions, cruise control, power steering and brakes, everything you're used to in your Subaru, just a lot more of it. The driver and passenger seats can feel a lot like a La-Z-Boy recliner. And the most recent models are bristling with video cameras and a big video monitor to help you see everything around you before you change lanes or back up.

TIP

Unlike drivers of commercial trucks, most states don't require motorhome drivers to have a commercial driver's license (CDL) to drive a Class A motorhome, even if it's the size of a Walmart semitruck. If you're considering buying a Class A (or an extremely large fifth-wheel trailer), check with the bureau of motor vehicles in your state about their RV driver's license requirements. Some may have weight and length restrictions that will require you to pass a CDL test, which can be daunting. Fear not — we talk lots more about piloting your RV in Chapter 11.

**WARNING**

Just because somebody handed you the keys and you don't need a special license to drive one, doesn't mean it will be as simple as getting used to the quirks of an unfamiliar rental car. As easy to drive as Class A builders try to make them, you can't just hop in and drive away from the dealer without some basic lessons and practice. Their sheer size, weight, and design make these giants extremely dangerous to you, your passengers, other drivers, pedestrians, and surrounding objects if you don't know what you're doing. Fortunately, a few large dealers are starting to come around, offering a driving confidence course. All of them should do so.

**REMEMBER**

Any avid watcher of Wile E. Coyote cartoons can tell you that accidents and emergencies can happen at any time. If you're traveling with a spouse, partner, or friend on a regular basis, they need to get behind the wheel and get comfortable driving your rig, too. Your copilot should know the basics and peculiarities of driving your motorhome and feel confident doing so if need be. If you're the kind of person who insists on doing all the driving and never relinquishing the driver's seat under any circumstances, that won't help anyone if you break your leg or an anvil falls on your head.

## Considering the pros and cons

Class As excel at being self-contained, with large water and fuel tanks and electric generators. You can pull over anywhere and boondock. They're quick to set up when you stop and quick to be ready to leave. And they're among the most spacious RVs available.

But these massive Class As have their drawbacks. Class As give up their benefits when you have to run an errand or take short day trips. They're designed for the highway, not downtown city streets or rough terrain. They don't come in 4-wheel drive models, so you won't be going mud bogging in a Class A. And if you get stuck trying, you'll be calling for a giant, very expensive tow truck.

The biggest issue is where to park such a rolling whale, both when you're on the road and when you're not. Because it's not only your vacation home but your vehicle, too, running to the grocery for that forgotten quart of milk means closing down your entire campsite, pulling up stakes, and taking the whole family to the Piggly Wiggly where you pray there's a big stretch of empty asphalt to park it in.

A Class A motorhome won't fit in your two-car garage at home or the underground parking lot at Grandma's condo. And forget parallel parking at a space downtown. That's why you see so many Class A motorhomes towing a car behind them on the road. Fortunately, Class As are designed with towing a second vehicle in mind, because it's so common.

RVers refer to their towed cars as a *toad* or *dinghy*. We talk all about towing your toad in Chapter 19.

There is an enormous price spread when it comes to shopping for a new Class A motorhome. Class As have a reputation for costing in excess of $200,000 for a high-quality, well-appointed rig. But in recent years, Class A builders have developed lower-priced rigs to appeal to a wider group of shoppers. Depending on market conditions, options, and manufacturers, you'll encounter prices from as low as $65,000 to over a million dollars. But the overwhelming majority of new Class As range from $80,000 to $150,000.

## BUS CONVERSIONS

Full-size, commercial, cross-country passenger buses (the kind with the Greyhound logo painted on the side) are made by specialty manufacturers like Prevost. These are also the starting place for the most expensive, top-end, rock-'n-roll-band tour buses, and other million-dollar dream machine motorhomes.

If you wonder how the billionaire tech moguls at Burning Man manage to cope with the deprivation of desert life far from civilization for a week every year, this is it. Quite literally anything that can fit into 45 feet of metal and fiberglass can be had, if money is no object. Typically, bus conversions have massive water holding tanks, high-wattage electrical generators, and 100+-gallon fuel tanks to power every conceivable appliance for extended periods of time. The latest in onboard electronics and communication technology stays constantly connected to the world. These rigs have custom everything — waterbeds, Jacuzzis, gourmet kitchens, TV screens in every conceivable location, rooftop party decks, giant aquarium tanks. . . . You name it — anything's available for a price.

When you get into this sky-high price range, these are not assembly-line, mass-market vehicles. It's not uncommon for a custom, luxury RV builder to make only a handful of units every year. And it's likely that fewer than a hundred of these top-end RVs are made in any given year by all the customizers combined.

For the *not-quite* billionaires out there in search of a price deal, some of the larger customizing companies do make a few off-the-shelf, non-customized models that still have the most requested top-end features. And because personal fortunes can rise and fall overnight, along with the bored desire to have something new and shiny every year, there's a fairly good-size used market for these royal barges. Just be aware of the problems you'll be taking on, with specialty service and a killer cost of upkeep. Maintenance will be anything but routine.

If you buy one of the larger diesel-pusher Class As, you're literally driving what is a giant commercial truck or bus under the floorboards. Consequently, they're among the most expensive RVs on the road to operate, maintain, and have repaired. Just changing a flat tire on one of the larger rigs is a major undertaking, and you can't do it yourself. One single tire on the biggest Class A motorhome can cost you more than a set of four tires plus a spare for your Toyota. Class As must be serviced at RV dealerships or commercial truck centers.

**WARNING**

In Chapter 5, we talk about doing your homework before you buy. If you're seriously talking yourself into buying a low-priced Class A motorhome — new or used — make sure you read reviews from other owners and ask questions on Internet RV forums before plunking down your money. Cheap motorhomes can turn into hair-pulling, spouse-blaming, buses full of headaches and repair costs. They're cheap for a reason, and they won't have anything approaching the level of quality, workmanship, and reliability found in a more expensive unit.

# Class B motorhomes

Class B motorhomes (like the one in Figure 2-3) are the opposite of the big Class As in size — they're the smallest self-contained coaches on the road. Some people still use the '70s term *van conversions* to refer to these, because Class Bs are basically heavily modified delivery or passenger vans.

Manufacturers typically buy Ford Transit (gas or diesel), Chevy Express (gas), RAM ProMaster (gas), or Mercedes Sprinter (diesel) vehicles to build them, and they range in size from about 17 to 28 feet in length. Because of their limited size, Class Bs are best suited for a single person or a couple. Some claim to have sleeping space for up to four people, but that's really only practical if the other two passengers are young children.

## Big features, small packages

On the inside, Class Bs manage to cram lots of living amenities into a tiny space. They have a kitchen with a stovetop and microwave, a TV, a bed that folds away (usually into a couch) when it's not needed, heating and air conditioning, and a little bit of storage space for clothes. They also have a small bathroom with a toilet, shower, and onboard water tanks so you never have to use a porta-potty at an outdoor fair again. And they have a built-in generator to create your own electricity when you want to stay in the great outdoors, far from the closest electrical hookup.

*Photograph courtesy of Christopher Hodapp*

But make no mistake: Unless you're a minimalist loner or an experienced champion of the tiny-house movement, a Class B motorhome really isn't suitable for full-time living. Class Bs are great for the weekend camper and the impromptu trip. They're popular for tailgating parties, as well as corporate owners. We've also met lots of Class B camper couples who were newlyweds and honeymooners, if you know what we mean.

Class Bs are so versatile that they can double as a second family car. A Class B will usually fit into an ordinary parking space, with a great go-anywhere style. Some even come equipped with four-wheel-drive options. And, depending on the design, if you have a grim, unyielding homeowners' association (HOA) governing your neighborhood that forbids parking RVs in driveways, most Class Bs look like a regular van on the outside. (Just be aware that they're too tall to fit in an average garage.)

## Yays and boos

Because of their smaller size and lighter weight, Class Bs get far better mileage than any other motorhome. They're easier to drive and maneuver, and their engines and vehicle systems can all be serviced at your local car dealership or service center. Like their bigger motorhome cousins, the back-end living space is accessible from the front seats, even when you're on the road. Just don't come looking for lots of excess space. If you're trying to camp, you're going to run out of room for gear fast, but you can easily tow a storage trailer for longer trips.

Some standard Class Bs may have a lower ceiling than a bigger motorhome or trailer, so if you're tall, make sure you can deal with it. Before you buy, tour as many as you can find, walk around inside and make sure you won't whack your head on a low-hanging air-conditioner or constantly trip over a recessed floor in the bathroom.

## SUPER BS

In recent years, manufacturers have pushed the limits of Class B sizes to make them bigger and add more amenities. These *Super Bs* or *B+* motorhomes are still regular vans underneath, but they're taller and longer, with more room — typically, they're 30 to 32 feet in length. Unlike a standard Class B, the manufacturers cut away everything but the van's front cab and add their own fiberglass body behind it. The biggest ones can sleep as many as four very friendly people, as long as you all keep the word *snug* in mind.

Super Bs often have a slide-out section to get even roomier inside, and the rooflines on these bigger Bs can be higher, too. Most Class Bs have a pretty low ceiling, but Super Bs either start out as a taller cargo van or add a raised fiberglass roof. A high-end Class B+ like a Coach House has a singular appearance, much more like a streamlined Class C motorhome than a van, with a remarkable level of amenities for the size. A Super B like the Thor Compass may just as well be called a Class C, the boundary is so fuzzy.

*Photograph courtesy of Christopher Hodapp*

Speaking of bathrooms, Class Bs and some small travel trailers feature a *wet bath* to keep from having a separate space-hogging shower stall. A wet bath has a drain in the floor and a handheld shower head so that the entire bathroom becomes your shower stall. Although it saves lots of space, it means that all your *People* magazines, your toiletries bag, and anything else in the bathroom will get soaked. Depending on the arrangement, you may be standing right up against the toilet while you shower or even sitting on the toilet lid as you attempt to shave your legs.

The price range of Class Bs can be frustrating. Even though they're much smaller than their Class A competition, they aren't priced that way. Square foot for square foot, Class Bs are the most expensive of all RV types on the road. They commonly start at $90,000 and can go upwards of $200,000. Even used Class Bs tend to retain high resale value.

# Class C motorhomes

Class C motorhomes are the midsize option of motorized RVs: smaller than a Class A, but bigger than a Class B. They're generally built on a truck frame from Chevrolet/ GMC, Ford, or RAM, and the front ends commonly look like a medium-size delivery truck. Some of the biggest Super Cs (see the nearby sidebar) are built on a Ford F-550 or F-650 truck, or a Freightliner truck with a Cummins diesel engine.

Despite all the variations in size, the usual dead giveaway that you're looking at a Class C is that there is an extended storage or sleeping area hump sprouting out over the top of the truck cab, while the rest of the body can be boxy (see Figure 2-4). The living area also often sits lower to the ground than it does in a big Class A, so you have no steep stairway to climb up when you go in and out the main door. Class Cs generally run between 21 and 45 feet long.

From a distance, Class Cs look like a big box of living space hung on the back end of an existing truck cab. In the business, this is called a *cutaway frame,* because it uses a truck or van front end, and cuts away the rest of the truck to add the RV box on the back. This setup permits the vehicle to utilize all the airbags, in-dash climate controls, and other safety systems built in by its original manufacturer. The front seats are fully open to the rest of the motorhome, so like the other types of motorhomes, passengers can get up and move around while you're on the move.

Like the As and Bs, Class Cs are self-contained, with at least one bathroom, kitchen, dining area, and living space; they typically have a private bedroom with a queen-size bed as well. Class Cs are a good compromise when it comes to price, size, living space, and versatility. Many companies use slides to expand the interior living areas — usually widening the living and dining areas, and quite often enlarging the bedroom. Many smaller Cs only use a bedroom slide. As for storage, you'll find plenty of both, inside and out.

**FIGURE 2-4:**
Class C motorhomes have a distinctive hump over the truck cab.

*Photograph courtesy of Christopher Hodapp*

The common "cab-over" hump area in a Class C can make for some interesting spaces from one model to the next (see Figure 2-5). Some people use it as a sleeping nook, giving it a special sort of "upper bunk" or "tree fort" feel favored by kids, and most manufacturers provide a removable ladder to access it. Bigger, less-agile adults may find the cramped space to be a little too hard to crawl up into and way too claustrophobic to sleep in. Other campers use it as a raised, out-of-the-way storage shelf, often protected with a cargo net or doors to keep things from falling off when bouncing down the road. The area can be quite large, depending on the model, and it's great for big, bulky items that don't easily fit into storage cabinets. A few other models mount a large flat-screen TV and entertainment center over the opening, with access doors to get to the big empty space behind it.

You find a lot of variety in Class Cs. They may have outdoor bonuses like an exterior TV and speakers, or an outdoor cooking area with its own sink, fridge, stovetop, or microwave. Murphy beds that fold out of the wall are the new thing in the last few years, and both Class B and C motorhomes take full advantage of them. Because of their "big box on the back" design, some models convert the back end into a *toy hauler* (a sort of traveling garage with a ramp), which lets you bring motorcycles, ATVs, bikes for the whole family, canoes, kayaks, mobility chairs, or anything else you can pile in. Some of these let you reconfigure that backdoor ramp when you pull your toys out and make it a raised patio, with its own safety rails to keep the kids and the family dogs from falling off the back end. Some even have a second bathroom in the "garage," so campers can use it without parading through your living room to get to the bigger family bathroom inside.

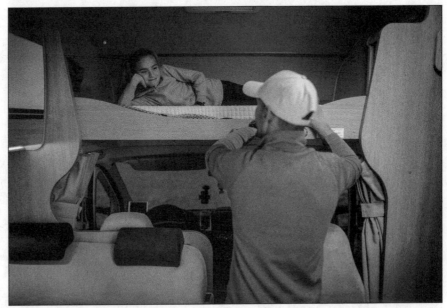

**FIGURE 2-5:** Kids love the upper bunk sleeping area in a Class C. It can also be used to store bulky items on the road.

*Virrage Images/Shutterstock*

Because they're the middle children in the motorhome family, they usually cost a bit less to maintain than the giant Class A buses, and the smaller gasoline-powered ones don't require an expensive commercial truck or RV dealership to maintain their engines and drive trains.

Class C motorhomes can be a better buy than either their bigger Class A or smaller Class B motorhome cousins, though you should always look at resale value for every rig and be prepared to take a bigger hit in that regard. The cheapest are priced new as low as $50,000, while some of the most option-packed Super Cs or C+ units (see the nearby sidebar) come in at just under $300,000, or so. But there's a big bunch of sizes and models that hang around the $60,000 to $125,000 range.

## SUPER CS OR C+

Like the Super Bs, manufacturers of Class C motorhomes have stretched the definition of that label to include giant "almost-Class-A" versions. The biggest (like the one shown in the nearby figure) are usually built on a Freightliner chassis with Cummins diesel engines and Allison transmissions. But despite their size and features, they still retain the distinctive front-engine truck cab with a hump overhead design. In their outline, they look very much like some sort of luxury semitruck.

Because of raised customer expectations demanding more and more high-end options, some of the top Class A makers have started to offer the biggest and most feature-laden Super Cs on the market. So, if you're looking at Class As, it's worth peeking into some of the high-end Super Cs, too.

*Photograph courtesy of Christopher Hodapp*

# Towables

A towable RV is just what it sounds like: an RV with wheels under it that has to be pulled around by a separate tow vehicle. Most people simply refer to them as *trailers* or *travel trailers*. Towables are usually described by their total length, along with a few specialty designs or functions: *travel trailer, fifth wheel, toy hauler, pop-up,* and *teardrop*. (We cover those specialties in the following sections.)

The travel trailer (see Figure 2-6) is the classic American RV, and they've been around for almost a hundred years (or longer, if you stretch the definition). Trailers are the modern-day equivalent of a wagon pulled by horses. Emperor Napoleon famously had a carriage he took on campaign with many of the luxuries we think of today in an RV. After his final defeat at Waterloo, it was displayed all over England for years and wowed the locals.

TECHNICAL STUFF

In the RV universe, trailers are the most common vehicles you'll encounter and unquestionably the most economical. When you stroll through your first RV show or wander onto a dealer's lot, the sheer number of trailers you'll encounter can be overwhelming, like an endless all-you-can-eat Las Vegas smorgasbord. There are more sizes, shapes, models, variations, options, and prices of trailers than you can chuck a badly aimed stick at. Travel trailers can be as short as 8 feet or as long as 45 feet. They can be 4 feet tall or more than 13 feet tall. They can come with no slides or as many as six. They can sleep one person or a dozen.

TECHNICAL STUFF

Trailers are usually designated by their overall length. According to the Recreational Vehicle Industry Association, (RVIA), the length stated in ads and catalogs, on websites, and on an RV's factory sticker is supposed to be the complete length of the trailer, from the very front edge of the hitch coupler in front all the way back to farthest tip of the rear bumper.

TIP

When you go shopping, one of the biggest discoveries you'll make is that a 30-foot trailer has more indoor living space than a 30-foot motorhome. The reason is what's up front, or what isn't. A motorhome gobbles up really important indoor real estate with its cockpit (where the driver and a passenger sit and the steering and driving controls are located). A trailer doesn't need any of that, which means more usable room for you to spread out at the campsite.

TECHNICAL STUFF

You probably already noticed that some trailers have more wheels under them than others. Shorter, lighter trailers (usually 23 feet or less) will only have one axle and set of wheels under them. Anything longer than 23 feet will probably have two axles and four tires. Only the heavyweight giants of the trailer world (like fifth wheels) have three axles and six tires. All those extra wheels spread the weight around to keep a heavy trailer from bending its axles and prevent the tires from wearing down prematurely when it's fully packed.

Photographs courtesy of Christopher Hodapp

**FIGURE 2-6:**
Travel trailers can be short or long or anywhere in between.

# TRAVEL TRAILERS, PARK TRAILERS, AND DESTINATION TRAILERS

Occasionally, you'll encounter the terms *park trailer* and *destination trailer*. These terms have very real distinctions when it comes to the trailer business.

An RV type of trailer is a *travel trailer*, which means it's meant to be moved around — it has wheels, it's fairly self-contained, and its utilities like water, power, and sewer hook-ups are meant to be temporary. In other words, you can travel with a travel trailer. Duh.

A *park trailer* (also known as a *park model*), on the other hand, is a different sort of beast. The RVIA pretty narrowly defines a park model as a trailer meant to be hauled some-place and then have its wheels and hitch taken off and parked pretty much perma-nently. Hence, the name *park model*. Although a park trailer may have slides to increase the interior room, it can't be any bigger than 400 square feet on the inside. Lots of park models have big "cathedral" picture windows, high ceilings, sliding-glass doors, ceiling fans, fireplaces, extra bedrooms, and other amenities and comforts of a house. But park trailers don't have generators or freshwater, blackwater, and graywater tanks, because they aren't needed. All utilities like electrical, water, and sewer lines have to be hooked up securely, as they would in a normal house. When you see a park model, it usually has a covering around the base, called a *skirt*, that covers up the pipes, heating ducts, drains, and other stuff that would normally dangle down in a house's basement or crawlspace. They often have a deck built on and a semipermanent stairway leading up to the door. Even a semi-attached carport is a pretty common addition.

For all intents and purposes, a park model is designed to be a small house that stays put. *Can* it be moved if necessary? Yes. But it's a major undertaking to do it when your park model is, er, parked. Even if you get wanderlust and decide to disconnect every-thing, jack it up, and reattach wheels and a hitch, park models are often wider than RVs, which are limited to just 8½ feet. That makes them an oversize load as far as the U.S. Department of Transportation is concerned, which means that a commercial truck has to move it into place or haul it anywhere else. You won't be moving it yourself with your Ford F-150 pickup.

A *destination trailer* occupies a fuzzy space between the travel and park trailers. Like a park model, destination trailers are big, with lots of square footage inside. But a destina-tion trailer is designed so that you can tow it (or have it towed) to your favorite vacation or retirement spot, and still have the option of easily changing your mind when some-body abruptly builds a warehouse overnight, blocking your view of the mountains or your path to the trout stream. The wheels and the tow hitch stay on a destination trailer,

*(continued)*

*(continued)*

they're under the 8½-foot width limit, and the temporary campground utility hookups all work just like an RV.

Travel trailers are designed to be at least marginally aerodynamic so that they're easy to tow without driving like a cinder block on a windy day. Not so with a destination model — they're meant to be moved, just not every other day. Like park models, they can have giant windows and sliding-glass doors, ceiling fans, high ceilings, and lots of space. But a destination trailer still adheres to the 8½-foot width limit, so if you have a truck that's robust enough to move it, you can go find a new happy trout-filled place far from that warehouse without a lot of problems.

In the following sections, we walk you through some of the specialty kinds of travel trailers you may want to consider.

## Toy haulers or sport utility trailers

If you ever thought wistfully about owning an RV but just couldn't bear the notion of going anywhere without your motorcycles, bikes, trikes, ATVs, snowmobiles, canoes, golf carts, or race car, the toy hauler is for you. These trailers have the usual RV amenities of a kitchen, dinette, couch, bedroom(s), and bathroom, as well as an additional empty space in the rear with a fold-down ramp. Drop the ramp, push all your big stuff in, lash it all down, and hit the road. Some versions even let you reconfigure the ramp as a raised, outdoor patio deck after you're done unloading.

The goal of most RV designs is never to waste valuable space, and many toy haulers are set up to do multiple duties. The garage area may have a TV, flip-up bunk beds, or fold-out couches you can open up after you park and pull out the Harley. Some have a second bathroom, so that campers outside can use the facilities in the "garage" without traipsing through your living room. More compact ones may convert the garage area into the main bedroom with a fold-down Murphy bed or one that lowers from the ceiling, figuring that you won't need to sleep until after you've dragged all your stuff out at the campsite. Others make use of the garage area to set up a home office. There's tremendous variety in these types of trailers, with more introduced every year.

**TIP**

In addition to the options that the manufacturers build into them, toy haulers are also a favorite of disabled campers or those with limited mobility. You can use the drop-down rear ramp as your way into and out of the trailer.

Toy haulers come in many sizes. There are toy haulers as short as 19 feet that have enough room for a motorcycle, an ATV, or a couple of mountain bikes. The biggest ones are fifth-wheel trailers, which give you the ultimate combination of indoor living space *and* a big garage. Just be aware that a fifth-wheel trailer requires a beefy truck to haul it. (More about fifth wheels later in this chapter.) And there are also several toy hauler motorhomes on the market. Instead of towing a small car behind, we've seen these motorhomes with a golf cart, Mini Cooper, Fiat, or Smart Car tucked into their onboard garages.

**WARNING**

One word of caution with toy haulers: Be sure you know the total weight of your motorcycles, ATVs, or any other major items you want to put onboard before you go shopping. Just because you *can* fit everything into the back of your rolling garage, doesn't mean you *should*. Don't ever exceed the weight limits of your trailer or your tow vehicle. Doing so can do serious damage to your RV, but more important, can cause extremely dangerous driving problems. We talk lots more about weight and packing in Chapter 8.

## Lightweights

One result of typical cars getting smaller every year has been that the RV business has had to get creative when it comes to building and marketing trailers that can still be towed without a pickup truck or hefty SUV. Back in the days of yesteryear, when dinosaurs ruled the Earth, the average American car was a colossal, steel behemoth, with a V8 engine and a transmission capable of powering an M1 tank. You could haul around a 40-foot aluminum trailer with an average fully-packed family sedan or station wagon, and still have plenty of horsepower left to drive it up to the top of Pikes Peak without breaking a sweat. But that hasn't been true for several decades now. In the demand for smaller, lighter, more fuel-efficient vehicles, the auto manufacturers have split their efforts between making littler (and seemingly identical) cars, while building massive and increasingly luxurious pickup trucks. The average "full-size" SUV in the 2020s is a pale imitation of the ones that dominated the market in the 1990s and early 2000s.

We talk lots more about tow vehicles in Chapter 7. The point is that not everyone wants to buy or own a pickup truck. If the only thing you have to haul a trailer with is a two-door, midsize car with a 4-cylinder engine and little more towing capacity than the average riding lawn mower, there are still towable options to consider if you lower your expectations a bit and keep the word *cozy* in mind.

Most so-called *lightweight* or *featherweight* trailers tend to tip the scales at 4,000 pounds or less. But be aware that adjectives like these are about as informative as seeing the word *FRESH!* on a bottle of dishwasher detergent. They're advertising claims and not any sort of official industry designation. There are still several trailers that weigh no more than 2,500 pounds and still have enough amenities in them to please a single camper or a really friendly couple.

Lightweights are smaller and built of lighter or thinner material than their bigger trailer brothers. When Airstreams first hit the market in the 1930s, built with aluminum, they were considered "lightweight" trailers — and they *were*, at that time. Although average travel trailers are built on steel frames and have real wood framing, floors, cabinets, and more on the inside, lightweights often use aluminum underneath and thinner, lightweight material for walls and other panels. In recent years, more companies have attempted to fill this niche. But some manufacturers have been specializing in lightweights for some time and continue to innovate: Little Guy, nüCamp, and KZ Sportsmen are frequently cited as the top makers of these tiny trailers.

**TECHNICAL STUFF**

One way lightweight trailers can save on size and weight is by ditching the usual blackwater holding tank needed for toilet waste and using a cassette toilet instead. A *cassette toilet* is essentially a small, portable holding tank that slides underneath the toilet. When it's full and time to dump, the cassette is pulled out and taken to the campground dumpsite or poured out into a public toilet. Cassette toilets have been popular in RVs in Europe for many years, and they're also being used in camper vans, truck campers, and pop-ups.

## Teardrop trailers

The teardrop trailer design has been around since at least the 1930s, and it continues to be popular, especially as more single campers have been taking to the road. The very first ones were often home-built units, and magazines like *Mechanix Illustrated* would publish trailer plans so the intrepid do-it-yourselfer could knock together his very own teardrop or mini trailer out in the garage workshop. Everything old seems to be new again, and today you can find modern plans online to build your own.

A teardrop trailer usually looks exactly like what it's called, with a big, rounded nose in the front, tapering down to an aerodynamic point in the back (see Figure 2-7) — sort of like a comma turned on its side. The tiniest teardrops have little in them besides a bed for one or two *very* friendly people, some lights, and maybe a TV. In the back end, they often have a tiny kitchen area hidden under a flip-up hatch. Most have an onboard 12-volt battery system that can power a few essentials and can be recharged by plugging into a 120-volt electrical outlet, a generator, or solar panels, or by hooking up the trailer's electrical hitch connector to your car and starting your engine.

Typically, these tiny titans are no more than 5 feet tall from the pavement to the roof, and between 4 and 6 feet wide. At just 8 feet long and less than 1,000 pounds, the smaller teardrops are lightweight enough to push by hand and store in your garage. Best of all, the smallest SUVs can tow them.

Photograph courtesy of Christopher Hodapp

**FIGURE 2-7:**
This tiny TAG teardrop by nüCamp can be towed by almost any car.

Teardrops are very high on the cuteness scale and often elicit *ooh*s and *aah*s from passersby. The term *glamping* (a combination of *glamour* and *camping*) comes up often when looking into retro-styled teardrop trailers. You can find more on this subject in Chapter 3, where we cover the fun of glamping in a teardrop or vintage trailer.

**REMEMBER**

Not all teardrop trailers are super tiny. There are teardrops big enough to stand up in. Large or small, the design is an eye catcher, and some manufacturers make them spacious enough for two people to comfortably camp in for longer than just a weekend. These have a bed (often tucked under the sloping roofline in the rear), a kitchen, a small bathroom (often a space-saving wet bath), and even a little storage. Depending on their loaded weight, they can still be towed by a smaller SUV.

## Off-road trailers

If "cute" is not really your image, you'll be happy to learn that a growing number of smaller trailers — described as *outback* or *boondocking trailers* — are offered with more rugged, off-road designs and accessories. These trailers usually ride higher off the ground than most small trailers, with more aggressive off-road tires and stronger suspensions, rooftops bristling with solar panels, communication antennae, accessory racks, and even robust steel fenders and rock guards to ward off damage from debris as you drive down rock-strewn dirt roads or dusty trails.

The makers of many of these rigs have radically rethought the standard trailer designs of the past. You'll find lots of off-road RVs that look like odd construction equipment, military surplus, or the sort of vehicle *Star Wars* characters might vacation in. They tend to be fairly lightweight so they can be pulled by a crossover or small SUV. Some feature slide-out exterior galleys, wildly shaped awnings, flip-up doors, pop-up canvas roofs, and other ingenious design innovations. Intrepid wilderness explorers, survivalists, or dedicated loners getting in touch with nature can all find a rig to love with these units. Combined with a four-wheel drive towing vehicle, these rigs can venture where motorhomes and fifth wheels dare not tread.

Other variations of this theme may be referred to as *adventure trailers* or *zombie apocalypse RVs*. In many cases, these aren't trailers but more like a mash up of motorhome and truck camper styles that are designed to survive any global calamities, real or imaginary. They look like military-grade vehicles, with a dash of Hollywood thrown in. If the *Mad Max* or *A-Team* vibe is what you're looking for, top manufacturers of these include Action Mobil, EarthRoamer, EcoRoamer, and UNICAT.

## Pop-up trailers

A running gag in old cartoons from the '40s and '50s was the prefabricated house that came in a box. The cartoon character would push a big, shiny red button on top of the box. Then the parcel would shake and bulge, quickly unflap and unfold, and — *voilà!* — suddenly, there was the fully furnished, full-size house, with a white picket fence, a car in the driveway, and a full-fledged flower garden. Pop-up trailers (like the one shown in Figure 2-8) are sort of the camping equivalent of that.

Loads of first-time RVers start out with a pop-up trailer, just to find out if they'll enjoy camping or how often they'll really use it. If you've experienced camping in a tent before, a pop-up will seem like stepping into the cushy lap of luxury.

A pop-up is a sort of mashup RV, with the bottom half of a tiny travel trailer, combined with a canvas or vinyl tent that unfolds out of the top. They're called by many descriptive names: *expandables, folding campers, pop-ups, crank-ups, fold-ups, fold-outs, tent trailers,* and sometimes just plain old *campers*. Depending on the options, the lower hard-sided trailer portion can contain beds, a sitting/dining area, a rudimentary kitchen with a sink, a small refrigerator and a stovetop, a compact toilet, a propane furnace, sometimes even an ingenious shower, and more. The upper tent half of the trailer expands to give you a roof over your head and create what is essentially an elaborate screened-in porch on wheels. For privacy, curtain flaps can be rolled down over the screens. And depending on the model, you can sleep anywhere from two to six people in these deceptively roomy and compact trailers.

**FIGURE 2-8:** Pop-ups are a great, inexpensive way to get your introduction to RV life.

Pop-ups have been around for decades and remain popular for many reasons, but here are two of the main ones:

>> **They can be some of the least expensive RVs on the market.** Many can be had brand-new for as little as $4,000, and used units can cost as little as $1,500 if you aren't afraid of a little cleaning and repair. Even the biggest, most luxury-laden brand-new models with all the options are generally priced under $20,000.

>> **They're lightweight — usually under 2,000 pounds — and ultra-compact when folded down.** That makes them easier to store and easier on your gas mileage, compared to a larger trailer. Nearly any midsize car can haul one, and even the very biggest pop-ups generally weigh under 3,500 pounds.

As RVing has gotten more popular with younger campers, companies have offered lots of variations of pop-ups to attract first-time buyers and tent camp-ers in search of a more comfortable experience. On the other hand, new designs of "off-road" pop-ups have a nearly military look, great for fishermen and hunters. The least-expensive units use a mechanical crank to make the magic unfolding operation happen, and the final setup of the tent portion requires an arrangement of poles and straps. More expensive models motorize the process or use a hydraulic lift to simplify the deployment of the tent into a push-button operation. A few even combine an air compressor with a nylon tent that actually inflates in a matter of a minute or so. And as Figure 2-9 shows, not all pop-ups are soft-sided tents — A-liner, Chalet, and Forest River's Rockwood line all feature an unusual hard-sided, pop-up design that ditches the tent completely. When fully opened, they resemble tiny A-frame cabins on wheels.

*Photographs courtesy of Christopher Hodapp*

**FIGURE 2-9:**
A hard-sided A-frame pop-up trailer by Aliner.

All of these reasons make a pop-up trailer an ideal way to get started with RVing. In fact, more than a few families pass them down from one generation to the next. Even if the canvas tent portion gets tattered and torn after a couple of decades, a pop-up of any vintage can usually be re-canvassed for around $1,500 or less.

# Fifth wheels

Although technically a towable, RV people give fifth-wheel trailers (see Figure 2-10) their own category because they have specific requirements and features over and above the typical travel trailer. Fifth-wheel trailers (sometimes nicknamed *fivers*) are the giants at the top of the towable beanstalk. If you want an RV that you can tow and park with your own separate tow vehicle, and still have the most interior floor space and onboard features possible, this is your answer.

FIGURE 2-10:
The distinctive overhanging design of a fifth-wheel trailer requires a special kind of hitch mounted in the bed of a pickup truck or other utility truck.

*Photograph courtesy of Christopher Hodapp*

What puts a trailer into the fifth-wheel category is its unusual shape and towing method. Instead of the usual trailer chassis and frame that hooks on a hitch at the back end of your car, SUV, or truck, the front end of a fifth wheel stretches its neck out and hangs over the top of a truck bed. And instead of the usual trailer hitch with a ball on it mounted below the rear bumper that most trailers use, a fifth-wheel utilizes a *king pin hitch*, a large metal bracket mounted in the middle of the truck bed itself, to more evenly spread the weight of the trailer into the center of the truck. What this means is, you must pull a fifth wheel with a pickup truck, and usually a heavy-duty one.

Of course, if you decide to buy a different truck a few years down the line, your dream trailer goes right on being your home on the road. That's not the case with a motorhome, where your RV *is* your truck, and vice versa.

A different option is available for fifth-wheel RVers if a pickup truck seems too limiting for your taste. Freightliner, International, Peterbilt, and others make 2-ton diesel towing trucks that resemble a small semi. These unusual trucks have a low deck in the back made just for towing fifth wheels (or horse and livestock trailers with gooseneck hitches). Companies like SportChassis and Utility Body Werks take these trucks and further customize them inside and out. Depending on how far into the deep end you wade with options, these are the luxury Cadillacs of the tow vehicle world, often costing well over $100,000 and frequently closer to $150,000. But you'll have a truly one-of-a-kind towing vehicle and an impressive rig. We talk a whole lot more about tow vehicles and options in Chapter 7.

In return for being forced to buy a special truck just to haul a fifth wheel, what you get are the largest possible travel trailers on the market. Manufacturers stress wide-open spaces in fifth-wheel trailers. The large living spaces, better insulation, residential-grade appliances, and other luxury amenities of a fifth wheel make them the top choice for full-timers. If you travel with lots of family and friends or you're expecting lots of houseguests, a fifth wheel is probably your best choice. They can typically sleep 8 to 12 people.

The largest fifth wheels are 45 feet long and as tall as the tallest motorhomes. Even though they have a head start in the square footage department, most fifth wheels also have multiple slides that dramatically increase the living spaces even more when they're fully opened at the campsite — having five slides on a fifth wheel is not uncommon.

The raised, gooseneck portion of the interior is reached by a short staircase inside and is commonly a large master bedroom suite with loads of closet space, or a spacious split-level living room area.

Fifth wheels are available with countless options and decors. Depending on your needs and wants, you can get full-size appliances, washers and dryers, electric fireplaces, home theater seating, big-screen TVs, multiple bedrooms, plenty of sleeping options, and lots more. The area inside the unique overhanging upper deck up front is reached by a short set of stairs and is generally used for a roomy master bedroom suite with loads of closet space or a spacious split-level living room area. And because your towing vehicle is not built-in as it is with a motorhome, your RV money is spent on the trailer itself.

Unlike with a motorhome, passengers can't ride inside a moving trailer. That means if you have a large family or a gaggle of fellow vacationers with you, passengers are limited to how many can fit inside your towing vehicle, or they have to follow in a separate car.

For safety-conscious owners, it's a comfort that modern trucks are engineered with the latest air bags and anti-collision warning systems, whereas a comparably sized Class A motorhome probably won't have any of these.

Of course, the RV world being the RV world, someone out there built a very different sort of fiver, the Scamp fifth wheel, tiny and adorable, which can be towed by just about any truck. If nothing else, it proved that a fiver can still give you all sorts of options.

# Truck Campers

If you already own a pickup truck or like the all-in-one convenience of a motorhome but you don't like the price tags, a *truck camper* (sometimes called a *truck cap* or a *camper shell*) may be just the right solution. Once the favorite weekend solution for hunters and fishermen, truck campers are getting more popular as entry-level units for new or single campers.

Essentially, a truck camper is an RV shell that is plopped into the back end of an existing pickup truck bed and rides piggyback (see Figure 2-11). They're extremely versatile because they can be easily removed and left behind when your camping trip is over, returning your truck to its normal, daily uses.

**FIGURE 2-11:** A truck camper or camper shell slides on and off of your pickup truck, and may be just the entry-level RV for you.

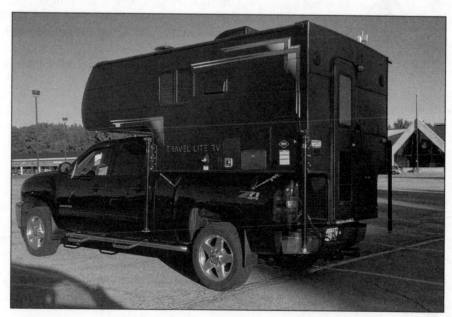

*Photograph courtesy of Christopher Hodapp*

The better camper units have hydraulic lift jacks that flip down and extend to the ground; these jacks raise and lower the shell to install or remove it from the back of the truck. Push the button, and the shell is lifted high enough to clear the tail-gate end of the truck. After the shell is on the back of the truck, tie-down straps, brackets, and turnbuckles are used to secure the shell from falling out on the road or bouncing around. Less-expensive models use a manual cranking system to do the lifting and lowering.

You can buy a new truck camper for as little as $6,000, but they can run well over $50,000 depending on the options and features you want. The biggest ones extend over the top of the truck's cab like a Class C's cab-over hump, and these days some even have a slide to increase the usable interior space after you're parked. An interesting variation is made by Northstar Campers (www.northstarcampers. com) — its truck camper incorporates a pop-up roof.

The most useful truck campers have a kitchenette with a sink, refrigerator, cook-top and microwave, dinette table, and enough seats for everybody; a toilet with at least a privacy curtain; and even a shower. You get many of the same amenities you'd find in any other trailer, including a furnace and a water heater powered by propane (technically, liquefied petroleum gas, or LPG), as well as an air condi-tioner. Typically designed for two people, some truck campers' convertible places allow you to sleep as many as four. (A handful of designs claim to sleep six, but that's unlikely unless at least four of them are under the age of 10.)

**WARNING**

Pay close attention to the total loaded weight of any camper shell you're interested in, along with the maximum loaded capacity of your truck. The heaviest campers combined with four people and their belongings piled into the truck itself may be more than your average light-duty quarter-ton pickup can handle. You may have to step up to a half-ton pickup to safely haul the truck camper of your dreams.

# Chapter **3**

# Decisions, Decisions: Knowing What You Need

C hapter 2 gives you an outline of what's available in the RV world, which is pretty much any size or price you can imagine. But which one is right for you?

In Part 2, we discuss the nuts and bolts of researching a brand, choosing a dealer, checking a warranty, and finding the resale value. But in this chapter, we're more general, helping you narrow down the class and type of RV to suit your needs. We cover some issues regarding pulling or being pulled, in terms of motorhomes versus towable trailers. We help you consider how much space you need and which amenities you can't live without.

When you've made decisions about the subjects in this chapter, you'll have narrowed the field quite a bit, enabling you to feel less overwhelmed by the number of companies and models out there to choose from.

# To Pull or Be Pulled, That Is the Question

The first big question you have to answer when you're in the market for an RV is: Do you want to tow a separate vehicle, or do you want to use your vehicle to tow your RV? (Or are you going to try to go it without a separate vehicle altogether? Before you go that route, check out the nearby sidebar, "RVing without a separate vehicle.")

## CAMPING TOAD-FREE

In the beginning, RVing in a motorhome can look very attractive, and you may think you can get by without a car. Maybe you think you can try to structure your travels in such a way that, for example, you always stop at the grocery on the way to the campground. Okay, fair enough.

We've seen lots of people in smaller Class C and B+ motorhomes camping without a car. On rare occasions, we've seen them have to pull up stakes from a full hookup because they had to go somewhere, and on the whole, they seem to take it in stride.

The thing is, you just can't foresee everything that may happen when you're on the road, including the truly oddball stuff, like when our dog, Sophie the Power Poodle, got dreadfully sick and we had to find an emergency animal hospital in the wilds of Montana.

You also can't anticipate the fun things, like finding out the pretty little town you're in is having a wine festival that you really want to visit. Of course, the pleasure of a Class B or small Class C is that you *can* more easily find a place to park it when you head out for that festival. But if you're planning on a Class A and you're thinking you'll be able to find a place to park it in that pretty little town, well, we don't envy you.

These are the scenarios you need to play out in your mind. Yes, when you're driving a coach, other options for transportation are usually available: Maybe you can take the occasional Uber or Lyft, and you can always rent a car for the duration of your stay, which is very easy to do in popular camping areas (on the other hand, it can have its annoyances — Enterprise won't deliver a car to you in the middle of Yellowstone).

The fact is, Americans are very used to absolute freedom of mobility. This country is very spread out, the popular camping states are even *more* spread out, and it's difficult to function without access to a car, particularly on a long journey. Be honest with yourself about your priorities and how much hassle you're willing to put up with in order to leave your vehicle at home.

Before we started RVing, we knew that some people in motorhomes towed a car. Both Class A and Class C motorhomes can tow a car, which they often call a *toad* (towed, get it?), although RV magazines often use the term *dinghy.* What we didn't know until we started RVing was how *many* people in motorhomes tow a car. We've never seen any reliable stats on this, but in the summer months, in hot camping areas like South Dakota and Wyoming, we were seeing about three-quarters of the large Class As towing a car. On more than a few occasions, we've seen Class As towing *both* a car *and* a very large pleasure boat behind that, just like the Southern Pacific Railroad.

We've met people driving Class As who were totally on top of this issue of towing a toad from the moment they bought. Lots of these guys have chosen rigs like a Dynamax Super C with a Cummins engine specifically for its remarkable ease of towing heavy loads. But from personal experience, just talking to other campers, we've gathered that an amazing number of people don't really think through this issue at the buying stage. If that sounds familiar, this section is for you.

## Go big or go home: Opting for a motorhome or fifth wheel

Motorhomes and fifth wheels tend to win on sheer size. These two categories are the rigs of choice for full-timers. As a rule, you just won't get that kind of space in a standard travel trailer. Some trailers mimic the feel of a fifth wheel, but we had trouble finding them.

We well remember our first trip to a gigantic Lazydays dealership. Just in trying to understand all our options, we kept pleading, "Okay, we've seen the huge, luxury fifth wheel and motorhome. Now show us the trailer you've got that's just as luxurious on the inside." The saleslady said it would be easy, and she *did* try, but we just didn't find it sitting on the lot. Trailers offer an incredibly wide range of sizes and amenities, but you have to look a little bit harder to find one that looks as luxurious as a Class A inside. And so, on the whole, we'll hand over the victory laurels on size to a Class A or fifth wheel.

Motorhomes also win hands-down on boondocking, because almost all of them have their own electrical generator. Trailer people usually have to haul a heavy "portable" generator along with them and, worse, find a place to stow it. If you tow with a truck, the truck bed is the obvious place, but that means you just lost a great deal of storage space.

**WARNING**

Again and again, we've heard stories about generators being stolen out of the back of a truck — one guy we know actually chained his down. Having had some similar items stolen from an open pickup, including a riding mower, we understand the issue.

You can have a generator installed in a trailer. A closet is the favorite place, but there are other, more imaginative options. (We saw one guy boondocking with an ultralight who had the entire trunk of his tow car filled with big, heavy golf cart batteries.) But the fact remains that motorhomes are great for a pull-off-anywhere boondocking situation — spending the night wherever you like without ponying up for a campground.

**REMEMBER**

If you're planning to boondock on a distant piece of Bureau of Land Management (BLM) government land, it may be very difficult to get a bloated Class A down some of those rugged roads. Class A motorhomes simply are *not* all-terrain vehicles. More than a few have been driven down into a steep gully, only to get wedged at both ends and suspended with the wheels off the ground.

There's no question that the Class A motorhome can feel like the royalty of the RV park. The poor little trailer, parent to it all, can seem to fade in the face of all this glamour. Or does it? Because, when you get to the park and set up camp, the advantage goes to the guy pulling a trailer. Take less than five minutes to slip the bonds of your ball hitch, and you can go anywhere you please, in the full-size tow vehicle that can take you wherever you want.

**REMEMBER**

Towing a car is just plain more problematic than towing a trailer. (We may get some flak over saying so, from a few of the Tiffin faithful, but we stand by it.) If you've never towed a car before, read Chapter 19 while you're still in the planning stage. It's an in-depth explanation of your options for towing, as well as the problems and expenses involved. You'll have a much clearer idea about whether towing a car is something you can embrace.

Another aspect that may be a win for a towable trailer instead of a motorhome is budget. Let's say you're just starting out with a yen to go RVing, and there's no way you can afford a large motorhome, nor can you afford a major tow vehicle, a truck, or a large SUV. A small trailer could be your best option, because you may be able to tow it with the vehicle you already drive.

For years, we owned a Honda Odyssey, a very popular family minivan. The 2020 Odyssey has a respectable tow rating of 3,500 pounds. You can find lots of great small trailers out there with a dry weight that's less than 3,000 pounds. In our own Airstream family, you don't even have to go with an ultra-light Basecamp — the 16-foot Bambi with the classic silver-bullet shape comes in with a dry weight under 3,000 pounds. Just search the web for "trailers with dry weight under 3,000 pounds" or whatever weight your car can tow. Your options and choices are much bigger than you think.

# DISCOVERING VINTAGE STYLES OF THE '40S AND '50S

Recent bursts of imagination in the RV business have brought back so much that was good in America in the middle of the last century. *Canned ham* trailers have made a comeback, and major manufacturers are getting into the vintage game, like Gulf Stream with the Vintage Cruiser and the Riverside Retro by Riverside RV. And the return of the teardrop trailer has opened up a great option for first-time RVers, with their lower cost and ease of towing.

Teardrop trailers were a product of the earliest years of towable campers, in the 1930s, and they have a very '30s outline. The buzzword of the period was *streamlined,* with sleek, aerodynamic designs that said a new age had arrived. For the glampers we talk about in the first chapter, canned hams and teardrops are the rig of choice, with their glamorous retro appeal.

At their most basic level, a teardrop is a towable bed. You may have seen very simple ones in a camping store like Cabela's or Gander Outdoors. The first teardrops were built around a standard piece of 4-x-8-foot plywood, with another sheet bent to create a rounded roof. Like the first Airstreams designed by Wally Byam, many were home-built, from kits or simple instructions published in magazines of the day, such as *Popular Mechanics.* When the '50s arrived, bigger was better. Cars could tow more weight, highways were more dependable, and Americans wanted more space. By the early '60s, teardrops died out.

The return of the teardrop came in the late '90s. We saw one of the first ones in Europe, and if we hadn't been on a busy highway in the south of France, we would've turned around and followed, just to get a better look. We were thrilled when we began to see them in the United States, where the designers were attempting to give the essentials of the design a bit more space and a few more amenities, such as a kitchen and a toilet or even a small *wet bath* (a combined shower stall and toilet). Most had a fun outdoor kitchen at the rear, with a lift of a clamshell hatch, though others had small kitchens inside, in the wide-end front. In the next decade, designs began plumping up even more, like the Tab Outback 400, part of their popular Outback line, and the Little Guy Max. Both kept the vintage charm and teardrop outline while including a much larger kitchen and a queen-size tuck-away bed, with built-in TV and stereo. These trailers offer easy towing and the freedom of easier access to the backcountry.

Whatever the size, teardrops have cute nailed down at all four corners. If you have a teardrop, people will often stop you and ask about it. One of the biggest advantages is that just about any family car or van can tow a tiny teardrop. (Always check the stats on your own vehicle to make sure.) A classic bed/teardrop can even be pulled by a motorcycle. Many teardrops actually have handles — they're so lightweight, you can push one into your garage.

# Space Odyssey: How Much Do You Need?

The second key question you need to answer has to do with interior space: How much do you really need?

Our first travel trailer was an Airstream 23FB (those initials stand for "front bedroom"). It had an amazing floor plan, one of the best uses we've ever seen of a mere 23 feet from stem to stern with no slides. And if we'd been camping in the thing — and *only* camping in the thing — we'd probably still own it.

But we weren't. Our first major road trip had us out for well over two months, visiting family in California, six states away from home. California in the winter, a winter that was breaking all records for rain. And the 23FB, despite its nifty floor plan, had no space whatsoever for a living room. Apart from the bathroom and the galley, it contained only a dinette and a bed. It had a very large shower stall, but not large enough for a pair of recliners. Lying in bed just to watch TV is depressing — you feel like you've got the flu. The best of dinettes aren't made for long-term sitting comfort, and many a dreary hour was spent standing up and staring out the door at the incessant downpour, thinking what we really needed was an ark. We won't deny the snappishness that began to affect our domestic bliss. In the end, we weren't halfway home before we got on the phone to our dealer to find out what would be involved in trading up to a larger unit.

In our rambles through the campgrounds of America, we've seen lots of people who just can't *stand* not being outdoors. They're out in any and all weather, even if they have to wear snowshoes. They're often the ones with the most elaborate campsites, lighted awnings and cooking tables, and comfy chairs, with an assortment of killer decorations. This sort of camper will often look for an "outside kitchen," available in many RVs, where, with the lift of a hatch, all the essentials of meal preparation can be had without ever going back inside your rig. You may be this sort of person yourself, in which case interior space isn't your biggest worry. But this attitude just isn't universal. Your RV is your home on wheels, and if you'd like a few of the comforts of home, you have nothing to be ashamed of.

**TIP**

The biggest question to answer is: How long at one stretch are you liable to be in your RV? Are you a weekender? A two-week-a-year vacationer? A snowbird? Or is full-timing even remotely in your fantasies? The length of time you'll be living in your RV will dictate how much size you need.

In the following sections, we walk you through some other major considerations when you're deciding how much space you need.

# SQUIGGLY LINES AND LABELED SQUARES: MAKING SENSE OF FLOOR PLANS

Some people are very good at reading floor plans, tossing around terms like *traffic flow* and *direct access.* The rest of us need a little help.

In the exploration stage of considering an RV, you'll see lots of videos and photos of the insides of people's rigs. But you also need to understand a little about floor plans. Why bother? Well, start checking out the websites of RV manufacturers. An amazing number of them will only give you a picture of the exterior, accompanied by a series of floor plans labeled with a model name or number. When new models are being debuted, these floor plans may be all you've got to judge by.

Often, people look at floor plans because getting to see inside an RV you're interested in, the one that may be your heart's desire, takes time, effort, and perhaps a long drive. The better you get at judging from a floor plan whether a particular RV may be right for you, the less likely it is you'll drive to another state to get a look inside a unit that wasn't at all what you thought it would be.

Take full advantage of the wonderful resource of YouTube. Just about every trailer, fifth wheel, and motorhome out there, including the tiniest teardrop, has some dealer or owner, somewhere, who does a walk-through of that specific trailer on video. Print out that floor plan if you don't have a company brochure, and refer to it as you watch. Very quickly, you'll get a sense of paper versus reality. Not everyone is Steven Spielberg, but some of the dealers who've been doing this for years produce videos on YouTube that are far beyond merely helpful — some people actually buy based only on these videos, hopefully because they're an old hand or they're already very familiar with the company. Many manufacturers have brief videos with a lovingly art-directed fly-by through the interior, but a 40-minute video walk-through with someone like the knowledgeable T.J. at Princess Craft in Texas will give you a very good idea of whether this particular model is worth tracking down.

There's no question that we recommend walking through *any* vehicle before you commit to buying it. But in the RV universe, particularly now, when manufacturers are overwhelmed and dealers are asking for a down payment to hold the particular rig you want, that may not be possible. The fact is, if the RV you've ordered is very similar to the one you've seen (for example, an older model), you'll probably be very happy with your RV-on-demand. Of course, make absolutely certain what the dealer's policy is, in case you don't like it.

*(continued)*

*(continued)*

If you're trying to make the best of looking at a floor plan, here are a couple tips.

- **If the floor plan you're interested in is, say, a 25-foot trailer, try to get into** *any* **25-foot trailer, more than one of them, just to get an idea of the feel of 25 feet and what can and can't be done with it.** We're not saying there's a lack of imagination in the business, but RVs within their class and size tend to fall into certain recognized patterns when it comes to the placement of the major amenities. Get to know it, and that floor plan will probably look more familiar.

- **Familiarize yourself with as many units as you can that are made by that manufacturer, to get a feel for their product.** A square line drawing from above of a corner bed tucked between the bathroom and side wall will seem clearer to you if you see how it was done in another of the units they've built.

## SLIDES AND WHY YOU NEED TO THINK ABOUT THEM

The RV industry has gone slide bonkers, with not just one or two in a unit, but sometimes four or five of them. The single *full-wall slide* is also fairly common now — at the push of a button, one entire side of your motorhome expands, like Moses parting the Red Sea. It's darn near miraculous.

The advantage of slides is, obviously, the added indoor space. The disadvantages are, to be honest, numerous. First, slides add a whole lot of weight — as much as 1,550 pounds apiece — which affects your gas mileage, tires, and more. Second, you don't have to be an engineer to understand that a slide is a major compromise to the structural integrity of an RV, and there are consequences to installing one. Many common maintenance issues in an RV are an easy fix, but when something goes wrong with a slide, it can have far more devastating consequences. And where slides are concerned, the fact is that, sooner or later, something is going to go wrong. Here are just some of the possibilities:

- **Water leaks:** Leaks caused by slides can be insidious and can go on for some time before they're detected. If you find that the floor around the slide is soft, don't shrug it off — it probably means that water is coming in and damaging your subfloor.

- **Drafts:** Along with water, slides also allow in drafts, and this affects your air-conditioning and your heating. People who cold-weather camp complain of the slide-related drafts.

- **Debris in the mechanism:** To prevent this, many slides now have *slide toppers* (clever awnings that roll out automatically with the slide, to keep debris from falling in and causing problems). But doing your lubricant treatments, which are necessary to keep your seals in good condition, can be a bit more difficult if you have a slide topper. Give your floor a quick sweep before you engage your slide, for the same reason, possible debris.

- **Pests:** Pests of all sorts will have easier access to your RV interior. Enough said.

If you're caring for them properly, the slide problem you face may be an easy fix, but they're usually on the expensive side. Just be sure to check the warranty of any RV you're considering, and ask specifically about slides. (More on warranties in Chapter 6.)

If you decide to get an RV with a slide, you'll need to take more care making and breaking camp. You truly need to inspect your space before you go pushing that button — one tree branch you didn't notice can cause serious damage.

A big RV with lots of slides can also cause an etiquette problem at your campsite. You pull in the size of a school bus, pop the hydraulic switch, and blow up to the size of a 747. Don't be surprised if your neighbor is a bit grumpy over it. Always try to be polite and smooth things over. (RVers are, in general, the nicest people on earth, so it shouldn't be a huge problem.) Always ask for a large pull-through space, one that's designed for a rig of your length *and* width (most campgrounds only ask about length). The older the park, the narrower the spaces, so just keep that in mind when deciding where to stay.

Speaking very generally, people who spend a lot of time parked in an RV love slides for the added living space, while people who enjoy being constantly on the move find them an annoyance and often not worth the bother or added expense.

At an RV show, you'll nearly always find the slides already open when you step inside. Never, *ever* be embarrassed to ask a salesperson to close those slides, so you can see what the unit looks like without them. You'll also get a chance to see if they operate smoothly or if they shudder and sound like a couple of bricks thrown into a clothes dryer.

Can you still function in a trailer without opening the slides? The answer: No, you probably can't. In fact, in the first trailer we looked at, as the slides slowly closed, we had to step away, toward the door. And after they were shut, the dinette was snugged up against the kitchen cabinets, and there was no access whatsoever to the bedroom or bathroom. The smiling salesperson informed us that this was the reason they'd put in a second entrance door in the new models, so you could still reach the bedroom when they were shut.

Worse, whenever we asked if they had anything *without* a slide, salespeople tended to look at us as though we'd slipped a cog. In the end, this was one of the many reasons we chose Airstream, because its trailers are slide-free. (Airstream only uses slides in its Atlas touring coach.) We decided that slides were against the laws of physics, and just weren't for us.

# Traveling with kids

When it comes to space, there isn't a more important issue at the decision-making stage than whether you're traveling with kids.

There's a big difference between a pair of retirees with wanderlust and a family of five living on the road, even for a short time or on a seasonal trip. You may think that someone trying to live long-term in a travel trailer with three kids and a dog not only is attempting the impossible but may be in need of psychiatric help.

But it can be done, like most things in life, with planning and effort. Good parenting on the road is something we've watched with awe and admiration. We've seen homeschooling going on around the picnic table, and history and science lessons being taught in the national parks and at national historic sites. In fact, we're beginning to think kids on the road have it better, because they're learning so many life lessons while they're seeing the country — and learning to be flexible to boot.

TIP

RVs have always been a family affair, and the industry has historically been skewed toward this market. In the last few years, even rock-star motorhomes are commonly offered in a model with bunks for the kids. But for the family of five, there's no doubt that the ride of choice is a fifth wheel. The upside of a fifth wheel is that it's the best bang for your buck on space. The downside is that you'll need a very specific tow vehicle, with the tow power and the proper coupling hitch. A Class A motorhome is loaded with space, but it has a loaded price tag to match.

Kids are happier on the road when they have a space, no matter how small, that they can call their own. In fact, kids *love* having a small space — they'll set up their personal camp in the upper bunk or on the platform bed above the driver's seat without complaint. It's like building a snow fort in the backyard!

TIP

This is a major question: To bunk or not to bunk? You'll see models that claim to be able to sleep eight or even ten people. Check them out and think it through. Quite often, this added sleeping space is achieved by making the dinette and sofa into a bed. There's nothing wrong with that, and many weekend camping families have been doing it happily for years. It's also a great solution for grandparents who host the grandkids on occasion. But if you're going to be on the road for a long time, it can get dreary and tedious, dismantling the dining room table and reconfiguring the couch cushions to make that bed every night, and remaking it all in the morning, folding and stowing pillows and blankets, all before anyone can sit down to breakfast. Bunks that are built in, or that close up and flip open like in a Pullman railroad car, are more convenient.

Top of the convenience ladder is the bunkhouse model, with a little room just for the kids. And you don't *have* to go with a giant fifth wheel to get family space.

Many toy haulers have a bunkhouse room, and trailers do as well. For example, take a look at the Grand Design Reflection, the bunkhouse model, with a generous bunkhouse room for the kids at the opposite side of the kitchen and living room to the parents' bedroom, very much an echo of a fifth wheel. You'll see there are trailers out there with a very doable floor plan for a family.

**WARNING**

However, safety can be an issue in bunkhouse style, especially for the kid who wants the upper berth. If your little ones are quite little, or if they have any problems with night terrors, sleepwalking, or seizures, you're going to want to install some sort of cargo netting for safety. Again, turn to YouTube, which has tons of great videos on bunkhouse safety.

Speaking of safety, another thing you're going to want to look for is a *step well cover*. In our trailer, two little steps get us to the ground, but a Class A has a lot of basement storage, which means that at living level, you're pretty high off the ground. Depending on the rig's design, when the door is shut, you may be looking at a stairwell — an open space with several steps — and kids can easily take a fall into them. Even pets can take a tumble, especially older ones not made of rubber anymore. Websites like DoItYourselfRV (www.doityourselfrv.com) have instructions for making one yourself, but nowadays many rigs come with some sort of covering for the well, including an easy push-button type.

## Traveling with pets

People love having their pets with them on the road. Apart from just dogs and cats, you'll see literally every other kind of pet imaginable in RVs: birds, ferrets, hamsters, rabbits, even the occasional potbellied pig. Of course, pets don't require as much preplanning when shopping for an RV as kids do. No one homeschools their Schnauzer. But when you're shopping, you may want to stop to consider potential pet issues.

In the last decade, the United States has become far more welcoming of dogs, and an amazing number of places don't mind if you bring Bowzer along on his leash. More than 50 percent of RVers travel with a dog, and it's the rare RV park that won't allow you to have one. Many of them have fenced-in dog runs and bark parks, which even pop up here and there in truck and rest stops. KOA puts dog playgrounds or runs in all of its campgrounds. But every campground insists that you keep your dog on a leash when not in a fenced-in area. And you must always clean up after your dog. Often, you'll find a plastic bag dispenser already there for you, if you forget to grab one before your walk.

Many people on the road are only looking for space for a Chihuahua, and a lap will do. But you'll see plenty of folks with multiple pets. And if you're trying to travel with two Golden Retrievers and a Great Dane, space in your RV for them should be something you think about when you're shopping. Most vets and trainers say that dogs, like children, feel more comfortable if a small area belongs to them, and they should have a dog bed there. If yours is crate trained and loves being in it, be sure you've got somewhere in your rig where the crate will conveniently fit without crowding the spaces you need to get to regularly. You should also consider your tow vehicle if you're using one, and where your pet will ride.

Maybe our dogs have just been odd, but we've traveled over the years with several different breeds, and they all want to be in the recliner or the bed along with us, while the dog bed sits empty. Our present dog, Sophie the Power Poodle, a difficult handful at home, is a dream on the road, maybe because we started traveling with her when she was a puppy. Our SUV tow vehicle has one rear seat designated hers, with a generous platform dog bed that gives her a safety line while letting her look out the window — a great idea, and she loves it! The dog previous to her, Wiley, was more difficult, and because of various health problems, he was happier on travel days with a mild tranquilizer. But before you resort to pharmaceuticals, give nature a chance: A typical dog loves being in the car and looks at a road trip as an adventure.

You don't have to buy a trailer at Camping World to use their very large RV stores. You'll find lots of options there for your pets, including all sorts of outdoor beds and containment systems. There's such a thing as handy portable dog fencing, and you can set up a little area as part of your normal campsite, like a large playpen. We saw one guy who went whole hog, setting up enough of the fencing that it took in the entirety of his campsite, so when he opened the door, his dog could jump out without coming to grief and wander at will. As we watched, it only took him 10 or 15 minutes to set up, so it's not quite as labor-intensive as it sounds, though you'll need a space for storing it.

Loads of campers travel with their cats, too. This seems a tall order to us, especially because cats tend to attach to places. The cats we've owned didn't travel well, even to the vet, though of course they weren't used to it. However, it can be done, and we've seen it. Besides, if you live on the road, your RV becomes the place your cat attaches to. Just be aware that you'll need space for the litter box where you won't trip over it (the bathroom of an RV, in this case, is perhaps not the best choice). The classic kitty litter open tray isn't the best idea for RVing, either. Go to YouTube, search for "RV with cats," and stand back — the RV community has tons of online advice for making trips with your cats easier.

WARNING

Also, be aware that, according to our vet and several veterinary websites, cats in a tow vehicle should be transported in a carrier. We knew a guy whose cat always rode on the back dash, but we don't recommend it. One slam on the brakes could cause an injury.

# Working from the road

On the issue of home office space in RVs, manufacturers are *way* behind the times. Once, on a company tour, Chris asked one of the designers why it was so difficult to find an RV with a built-in desk. The clearly annoyed designer shrugged it off and groused that everybody was going to have their little wants: "Everyone thinks they know better how to design an RV."

Sorry fella, but in this case, they *do* know better. Over 40 million Americans regularly go RVing, with 25 million on the road in any given year, and more people now work from home than ever before. With the COVID-19 pandemic, the number of at-home workers skyrocketed higher than ever before. You don't have to be Einstein to figure out that millions of Americans would like to be able to work from the road.

For a decade, RVers who fall into this category have been pleading for models skewed toward them, with a small desk area, a proper charging station to keep needed devices organized, and a reasonable Wi-Fi connection solution. This wouldn't be a difficult design change, but so far, the RV industry has turned a deaf ear. Many an RV built for two is inflicted with a positively *enormous* dinette area, far beyond what's needed, while some of that valuable space could easily have been used for at least a tiny desk.

A dealer will tell you he can accommodate you. He'll direct you to the bunkhouse, which can be "easily reconfigured," or worse, to the dinette. "Hey, you guys like to work together! Won't it be great, sharing a workspace across from each other?" No, it won't.

**TIP**

So, now's the time to examine those scary words *custom job,* the ones that sound so expensive. Many companies specialize in custom work for RVs, more of them every day. But the truth is, if your workstation is simple, you really can do much of it yourself. Office furniture from specialty RV furniture makers is usually expensive. The majority of great offices in RVs we've seen were done by the owners. You can find tons of videos on YouTube telling you how to yank out a too-big dining area and redo it for a desk, often something residential, picked up someplace like IKEA. A much smaller eating area can be done at the same time, or you can use recliners with tray tables that can be raised and then folded down again. There are all sorts of ideas for redoing an area of an RV with a vanity or a dresser. Actually, a bunkhouse can make a terrific office, if you don't need the space for the kids. It all depends on how much space you need for what you do.

**REMEMBER**

If you know you'll need an office, think about it during the shopping process. And never underestimate the power of YouTube. Search for the name of the model you're looking at, and see if anyone has already done it.

# Honestly Assessing Amenities

Do you really need a washer, dryer, dishwasher, and fireplace in an RV? In the higher-end RVs, these amenities can dazzle a first-time buyer, and it's understandable. Seeing what can be done in an RV is cool! You may decide that, for your style, these appliances are absolute necessities, but give it a think.

We don't mean to go all psychological here, but there's a tendency to think that if you're going to be on the road for a long time, you must have all the conveniences you have at home and that you'll be unhappy without them. The RV industry nowadays certainly plays into these fears, with amenities available to campers that our parents couldn't have imagined.

In the following sections, we cover the main ones to consider.

## Fireplace

The electric fireplaces in many big RVs tend to get smirks from some people, who wonder why you don't just start a campfire. But they're cute, casting a pretty light at night, and more important, serving as an electric space heater. When you're camping, you often come in wet and chilled. Heating your sitting area with an electric fireplace is very comfortable.

Of course, RVs have heating systems, but these fireplaces make a nice little addendum to it, particularly if you're hooked up to shore power in a park. Firewood and furnace propane both cost you money, but an electric fireplace uses the campground's electricity. So, if nothing else, they have a slight economic benefit.

## Washer and dryer

Full-timers on the road or snowbirds who live in an RV for months are the ones who want washers and dryers the most, and it's understandable. They're becoming increasingly common in large rigs, including fifth wheels, Class As, Super Cs, and certainly in "destination" trailers built for long-term use.

TIP

The overwhelming majority of campgrounds have washers and dryers (you pay with coins or sometimes credit cards), as do most of the larger truck stops. Let's be frank here: Many people find the thought of hauling tons of laundry in and out dreary and weary, and they may find the thought of using a public laundry distasteful, imagining the worst. We're not exactly wealthy, but we hadn't used a public laundry, or even a private apartment one, since we were in our early twenties. Having our own washer and dryer was a convenience we were used to, and this makes the idea of having your own built-in washer/dryer very appealing on the road.

But RV washer/dryer units are generally small, and there are lots of things they can't handle, like bedspreads and heavy loads of bath towels or bathrobes, even jeans in some cases, which means you may find yourself having to use the occasional campground laundry anyway, as well as having to hang-dry some items. Ventless dryer systems, for those who don't want to cut a hole in the side of the trailer for an installation, take a good deal longer to dry clothes.

Leaks in RV washing machines are fairly common. Remember, the plumbing lines for that machine are being subjected to the stresses of bouncing down the road, and it's hard not to have any problems eventually. You need to be alert to them. However, it's arguable that, even including a service call, the money it costs you will be well spent, because you're not pumping cash into a public laundry.

Using a public laundry has its advantages. The job goes far more quickly than you'd think, because you'll probably have access to multiple machines at once, if it's not crowded. We pack enough clothing that we can get by at least two weeks without having to cope with the laundry, and we also keep a small collapsible laundry tub, where it's just as easy to hand-launder little things and clip-hang them to dry. For us, investing two or three hours every two or three weeks isn't a trial. Pack your special little laundry kit, with detergent pods and Woolite, bleach wipes, hanger clips, and collapsible clothes bags — it's kind of fun! Be sure to check the campground's store for small, convenient sizes of laundry detergent and dryer sheets so you don't have to haul around the 2-gallon super-saver sizes on the road. When you get the hang of it, it's not much more of a pain than laundry day at home.

Believe it or not, there are portable washing machines available that are no larger than a kitchen wastebasket. A couple of them use old-fashioned foot power to agitate your clothes, but others have an electric motor. Typically, even the better ones have few features beyond agitating and spinning, and they can't handle much more than a couple of bath towels at a time. We tried one for a while, but it just wasn't worth the space it took up in the back of our tow vehicle, as well as all the folderol of setting it up and taking it down. But if you have enough space to keep one in your RV, they could be an inexpensive compromise, as long as you only want to wash a few things at once, no more than you can find space to hang-dry.

# Dishwasher

The arrival of RV dishwashers, we admit, has left us scratching our heads. Yes, you've got one at home. But home plumbing can cope with a dishwasher and garbage disposal, while an RV usually can't. You'll only see built-in dishwashers in the high-end luxury RVs, and they help to drive up the price. If you're determined to have one, you can get it as an after-market add-on, but they're a bit pricey, and you'll lose precious cabinet space. A drawer dishwasher can make a nice substitute fit for an oven, if you prefer a convection microwave. We've also seen them installed in the kitchen island section of a fifth wheel.

Like floor space, a dishwasher in an RV does seem to be an issue tied to whether you travel with kids. Cooking for a family or a large group requires more effort and makes more dirty dishes.

**WARNING**

Even dishwashers designed for RV use are subject to the rough treatment of bouncing down the road. Manufacturers that install residential appliances in RVs are tempting fate because they aren't designed for mobile use and need to be fixed by household repair services. Yet most appliance factory-authorized repair services won't touch a residential unit in a trailer or motorhome because mobile use violates the manufacturer's warranty.

**REMEMBER**

RVs are designed to use as little water as possible to extend your time away from civilization. We tell you more than you'll ever want to know about plumbing in Chapter 15, but be aware that RV plumbing systems were never intended to accommodate the level of water use that dishwashers and washing machines demand. If you intend to park at a campsite with full hookups to provide continuous fresh water and a wastewater drain connection to get rid of what you use, you're in clover. Wash all the dishes and clothes you like. But the minute you go boondocking, you'll need to close up the water-gulping appliances and wait for a return to civilization.

Also, you should get all grease and food bits off before running an RV dishwasher. Even in full hookup, graywater tanks can't handle lots of grease and food.

**TIP**

If you're on a budget, you can find lots of mini, countertop dishwashers on Amazon at very reasonable prices (between $200 and $400). They operate essentially like many of those in the '50s and '60s did, by attaching a water and drain hose to the sink. Some of these appliances get surprisingly decent reviews, but the complaints are as expected: annoying hoses, leaks, an inability to handle truly dirty plates and pots. With an RV, the biggest negative is going to be the counter space you give up and/or finding a place to stow it.

# RVs ON TV

If you're trying to get an idea of which RV you may want, TV can be a great place to start. One of our favorite shows is *Going RV,* on both the Travel Channel and the Great American Country channel. You follow a buyer through the process of shopping for an RV. Even if that particular buyer isn't a reflection of you and your needs, you'll learn a lot, and you'll start picking up the lingo of RV shopping. Retail prices are also bannered rather than coyly hidden, another plus for your learning curve.

All of which is great, so long as you remember one thing: Nobody, at least nobody with a brain, buys an RV this way. In the course of 30 minutes, the shopper is shown three RVs, and by the end of the show, with a roll of the drums, they choose the one they want. Arguably, this is good showmanship, but it's a lousy way to buy a trailer. Shopping is a long process. It's also one of the most pleasurable parts of choosing an RV, and you shouldn't let anyone spoil it for you. We've walked into dealerships where there's a general feeling in the air, put there by the salesperson and their manager, that we're expected to buy an RV before we leave. Why did you bother us otherwise? It's surprisingly easy for intelligent people to fall for these tactics, when the salesperson hauls you into their office with the old line, "What will it take to put you into that Thor Hurricane today?" Usually the correct answer is, "More than you've got." If you haven't decided yet, don't let them railroad you.

# 2

# Buying Your RV

» Cracking the code of an RV loan

» Preparing for sneaky unexpected costs

# Chapter 4

# Fitting an RV into Your Budget

When you think about it, everyone has to live within a budget. Even Jeff Bezos tries to make purchases that are wise and fit in his monthly budget. We hear Switzerland is going for a bargain price.

For those of us who aren't billionaires, the restrictions of budget are a little more important, and the effects of bad decisions can be lasting. So, in this chapter, we talk about buying decisions, like whether you should go new or used. We also explain some realities of RV loans, while clueing you in to some of the terminology and tactics that can cost you a lot more than you need to pay. Finally, we cover some costs you may not have considered and offer advice on how to cope with them.

## New or Used: The Wide World of RVs

A little shopping for an RV online will tell you that the price range is very, *very* wide. A luxury Class A motorhome can easily cost $1 million, while a pop-up can be had for less than $10,000, and that adorable retro canned ham can be yours new for $18,488 MSRP (manufacturer's suggested retail price). And no one pays the MSRP.

From this standpoint alone, there's an RV for every budget. But there's no question that buying used is one of the first things that comes to mind, whenever any shopper is considering how to get the best bang for their buck. So, let's start with a discussion of the advantages and disadvantages of both new and used.

TIP

Whether you're buying new or used, you're going to need the best information you can get on the resale value of the rig you're buying. Get online and feed in the older versions of the model you want to buy, on RV Trader (www.rvtrader.com) and NADA guides (www.nadaguides.com). Get a solid idea of what your used RV is worth.

## Buying used

The biggest argument for buying used is depreciation, because an RV does a *lot* of it (as much as 40 percent in the worst cases) within four years. The experts say an RV will drop in value 30 percent from its MSRP the moment you drive it off the lot. Of course, no one pays the MSRP. But the hit in the first year of another 10 percent, and 6 percent each year after that can seem like a grim statistic. At six years, it's probably worth about half what you paid for it.

REMEMBER

These numbers aren't carved in stone — they're averages, and there are many exceptions. We bought our last three RVs with a wary eye on their resale values. Our last two have been Airstreams, in large part because of their remarkable resale value. Airstreams are admittedly in some rarified air, but they're not alone in having a low rate of depreciation. The same was true of our Pleasureway Class B motorhome.

Pundits of the RV park have been counseling people to buy used for decades. If you find that perfect used rig that buyers dream of, late model and gently used by a loving owner, you'll save the depreciation from the first two years out of pocket. Plus, the owner has probably done some upgrades, as well as ironing out any of the typical new-RV maintenance issues.

WARNING

Have a realistic understanding of your own budget and its restrictions. A major disadvantage of buying used is one we've seen many times: When someone on a budget who dreams of owning a luxury Class A motorhome decides to buy one used, all too often they're unaware of the upkeep costs on a rig that expensive. Just like owning a thoroughbred racehorse, a big rig can eat a lot of hay (or cash, as the case may be). And when a set of new tires for a Tiffin or other huge diesel pusher can easily cost more than $5,000 (no, that's not a misprint) the cost of upkeep is an issue you need to look at before diving into a used luxury rig, particularly the rock-star luxury of something like a Newmar or Prevost.

# Buying new

Many of the advantages of buying new are obvious: No one owned it before, so you're not buying someone else's mistakes. You'll have the factory warranty, whether you purchase an additional warranty or not. You'll have the latest bells and whistles of design. And you'll have the pride and fun of something shiny new.

Theoretically, you'll also have the enjoyment of that RV's best years, before things begin to fade and go wrong, though obviously this isn't always the case. And an RV isn't a car, so there will be little maintenance issues to iron out at the least (see Chapter 5). You can head off a lot of grief by doing your brand homework.

There are many ways for a first-timer on a limited budget to have the pleasure of buying new and to experience camping, just to see if you like it. Pop-ups and tear-drops and the various casita styles are great entry-level rigs. As an added plus, they quite often have solid resale value. If nothing else, if your money is tight, simply come up with a mental number — the ideal you'd like to pay — and search the web for "great RVs under $10,000" (or whatever the amount is). You'll have lots and lots of choices.

**TIP**

Because of its classification as a second home (or a first home), the interest on an RV loan is tax deductible, which is another plus on the "buy new" side.

There are some other advantages to buying new. In some respects, you'll have more support from both dealer and manufacturer, because they're pushing that model right now. It's outrageous how often owners are told that a part they need for a unit five years old, or even less, is no longer available, an appalling lack of support. At that point, you're now "rehabbing" rather than servicing the unit, and you may need to find someone imaginative who can install or jury-rig a similar part.

But there's one more advantage to buying new, one you should consider: In many respects, the issue of depreciation is overplayed a bit where RVs are concerned. There are a lot of crepe hangers on the web or around the campfire, where you'll hear that "only a *moron* would buy a new RV." But take a look at the typical rate of depreciation on a car — those stats are just as bad as or worse than an RV. According to Black Book, a source on used car values, the average car will depreciate 20 percent to 30 percent in the first year, and a staggering 15 percent to 18 percent every year after that. In five years, a car will lose 60 percent *or more* of its original value. None of this stops people from buying new cars.

**REMEMBER**

In Chapter 5, we say that buying an RV is *not* like buying a car, in terms of maintenance and warranty reliability. But in this respect, depreciation, many RVs have an edge over cars. Just like every buyer is unique, so is every purchase, and resale value is a moving target.

# Taking Out a Loan

Talking about loans for an RV tends to bring a new RV purchase to mind, but you can get financing for a used one, from an online lender, bank, or credit union, or a dealer if the RV is sitting on their lot. So, the issues of RV loans and their effect on your finances is pretty universal to both new and used.

Most people budget things on a monthly basis. In fact, people can become so fixated on monthly budget figures that they don't look at anything else. This is why you'll see predatory loans being advertised with a picture of the RV and bannered across the top, "Only $149 a month!" But with the depreciation that occurs on almost any RV, a loan, especially a long-term one, is how people end up being *upside-down* (owning more than the purchase is worth) on an RV loan. (See the nearby sidebar, "Underwater exploration," for more on this subject.)

No, we're not anti-loan. We just want you to have the facts. There's no question how much RVing has changed, and one of those facts is that if you're living full-time in your RV, or part of the year as a snowbird, taking out an RV loan is a justifiable and logical expense. But there are still some loan issues you should be aware of before you make final budgetary choices.

**TIP**

Look at what number crunchers call "the cost of servicing the loan," meaning in simple terms, the interest. That's what the annual percentage rate (APR) means in the title of your loan, and those two little words, *compounded annually*, are incredibly expensive. Generally, RV loans have a higher rate of interest than cars (as high as 18 percent in some cases). Einstein said that compounded interest was one of the most powerful forces on Earth. When your lender describes it as a "simple" loan, what they mean is that you won't be paying interest on the interest, just the principal.

Here are some sobering figures, from Credit Karma (www.creditkarma.com): You buy a $50,000 RV, after making a good, solid $10,000 down payment. You pay off the loan over ten years at a pretty common and not scary-sounding rate of 6.5 percent. Your total cost in interest would be $14,503. And if you take out a 20-year mortgage, that number becomes a crushing $31,574 in interest! In other words, you paid nearly as much in interest as the amount of the loan.

Ever wonder how anyone can make any money lending money? This is how.

# UNDERWATER EXPLORATION

Okay, so maybe you *are* upside-down on a loan. Does it really matter? This RV is what you want, for yourself and your family, what you've dreamed of, and grousing about interest on loans seems like a petty point. Well, look at a typical case of being underwater on a loan, what's sometimes called *negative equity*.

Ted and Marie are in their late fifties, and they've decided they can afford to take an early retirement, to enjoy life while they're young and healthy enough to do it. After a lifetime of saving, they treat themselves to a Class A motorhome with a $250,000 price tag, which isn't unusual at all in the Class A universe. After all, they're planning on being in it for months at a time. They're even planning on doing Alaska.

Four years later, Ted suffers a devastating stroke and passes away. Marie is left alone. She's never really handled their money matters, and she no longer has any interest in camping or seeing Alaska. Her life has changed completely, in a single day. She wants to simply sell the RV and pay off the loan. This is when she discovers, to her horror, that she still owes $195,000 on a vehicle that is now worth only $140,000. She can keep on with the steep payments while the RV rots in costly storage, or she can sell it before the situation gets any worse and dip into their life savings to the tune of $55,000.

This dark scenario has happened to people. Yes, it's the worst-case scenario, but it *can* happen. Another possibility is an RV that's stolen or totaled (or both), and you get the typical kiss-off check from your insurance company. You could end up owing more than they gave you on a long-term loan for an RV you no longer even have. (This difference in value is what GAP insurance covers; if you have an expensive RV, you should check it out.) This is why it's not wise to ever be upside-down on any loan, particularly a long-term loan, where it can happen more easily. And this is the reason that resale value is so important when looking at any rig. Ask yourself what will happen if, somewhere along the way, you're forced to sell.

# SOME COMFORTING NUMBERS

According to stats from the RV Industry Association (RVIA), less than half of the RVs purchased in the United States in 2020 were financed, and these tended to be more expensive units, with an average cost of over $45,000. In other words, a remarkable number of people do *not* finance this purchase. Many are using their savings, and many are buying less-expensive rigs. And of course, many of those who buy used are doing so because they won't have to carry a loan. (This is probably the biggest advantage to buying used.)

*(continued)*

*(continued)*

When someone presents you with the attractive figures on a 20-year loan, your first question should be, "What'll it cost me per month to go to ten years?" Again, people assume something that isn't true. They assume that the $149 monthly payment will double to $298 on a ten-year loan. It won't. Yes, the payment will be more, but typically it won't be anywhere *near* double. ***Remember:*** Always take out the shortest loan possible.

Another good idea, if you're lucky enough to have a little windfall here and there, is to make monthly payments that are larger than the billed amount. The game is to pay off that loan as quickly as possible. Be sure to ask if there is any penalty for paying off your loan early. Commonly on loans, anything you pay over the minimum payment goes directly toward the principal, because you've paid your interest fee for that month (but be sure to ask about this before you sign on the dotted line — not all lenders accept *principal-only* payments). ***Remember:*** As you pay down the principal, you're cutting down on interest owed.

All these decisions are personal, but one piece of advice is solid: Don't take out a 20-year loan on anything that depreciates. These long-term loans were meant for houses, where value typically goes up, or at least remains stable. But consider making your last payment on a Class C motorhome when your newborn is in his sophomore year of college. (Of course, if you can talk him into living in the thing to save on a dorm room, you could come out ahead.)

# Expecting the Unexpected

With an RV, there are always unexpected costs you didn't budget for, especially if you're a first-time buyer. We don't just mean unforeseen maintenance costs down the road either. In this section, we cover some of the biggest surprises you'll be hit with that you may not have thought of.

## The tax man cometh

Some of the worst unexpected costs are state sales and vehicle taxes. Often, people go outside their home state to buy an RV because a local dealer may not have the RV they're looking for. But there are people who try to dodge the sales tax on an RV purchase by buying in one of the handful of states with no sales taxes. Depending on the state and the price of your RV, that sales tax can be enormous. (A 5 percent tax bill adds another $5,000 to a $100,000 RV purchase.)

One of the pluses of buying an RV from a dealer (new or used) is that, if you're financing the purchase, that big tax bill can be included in the total amount of the loan. Instead of writing a huge check to your state revenue department, the dealer will fold the cost in. But if you're an out-of-state buyer, you need to ask some questions.

Federal law prohibits two states from taxing the same purchase. So, many states have a reciprocal tax collection agreement with each other. On your contract, you may see sales tax added to the cost of your rig and assume it's a required tax payment to the state you're buying in. But you need to ask about it before you sign. The dealer may be collecting your state and local taxes, and they'll handle passing that along to your state revenuers. Or the dealer may make a mistake and collect the tax for their own state. And some won't collect any sales tax at all if you're out of state.

If they don't collect tax for your state, when you arrive back home and you go to get your RV license plates, you can be slapped with that whopping sales tax bill at the Department of Motor Vehicles (DMV). And you have to pay it out of pocket before those nice folks will give you your plates. So, be sure to discuss the tax issue with the dealer's finance people, and be sure that you take all your purchase and loan contracts with you to the DMV so you can document what you paid.

## Insurance

RV insurance can get short-sheeted in the excitement of shopping. Lots of first-time buyers just go home and call their existing auto policy companies to add the new RV to their coverage, but that's not necessarily the best or most flexible RV coverage. RV insurance rates are all over the place, depending on issues like the value and type of rig, whether you're a full-timer or part-timer, your driving record, and your credit rating.

**TIP**

Shop online for the best rate, and have an eye on this issue before you buy. Some rigs cost a lot more to insure than others, so find out what it will cost to insure that Dynamax Super C before you buy it, particularly if there's any chance at all that it will strain your budget.

A couple of other important things to know:

> **>> Before you leave home to go pick up your new rig, find out how the insurer handles covering that fuzzy period of time between leaving the dealer's lot and your arrival at home, especially if you're not buying in your home state.** You don't want to damage your brand-new rig on the drive home, only to be told you didn't arrange for insurance coverage soon enough.

>> **Ask how the insurance company handles coverage when you're pulling a trailer behind a separately insured tow vehicle, or if your separately insured toad is being pulled behind your motorhome.** You don't necessarily want to pay for double coverage.

>> **Ask about coverage of your RV's contents, especially if you're hauling your motorcycle in a toy hauler.**

We've been very happy with Good Sam's RV policies (currently managed through National General Insurance). A recent claim was handled quickly and cleanly, with an incredible amount of speed, patience, and politeness, despite the fact that the accident was our fault. But American Family, Geico, Hartford, Progressive, and USAA all offer specialized RV insurance as well. Some even offer special policies for vintage and classic RV owners.

**TIP**

Our Good Sam policy offers a *storage option,* which means we pay a very reduced premium whenever the rig is in storage, where the odds against damage are much lower, unless there's a 9.0 earthquake or it's hit by a meteor. If we were camping in the rig all the time, we'd be paying about $2,600 a year for coverage for our trailer, but the storage option shaves at least half off our annual premiums. If you go this route, you have to let the insurance company know when the rig comes out of storage and when it goes back in again. If you forget, you run the risk of an accident not being covered. If you want to save money with this sort of coverage, you have to be a bit neurotic and come up with some sort of bulletproof reminder to call the insurance company before you travel.

## Storage

Consider yourself fortunate if you own a large piece of property and the option of keeping your RV parked at home. Roughly a third of Americans, over 70 million of them, live in communities with a homeowner's association (HOA). We'd be willing to bet that the vast majority of them won't let you keep an RV in your own driveway. Our HOA allows us to park our rig on our own property no more than five days a year. HOAs tend to have hired-gun "community management" firms that drive through your neighborhood, incessantly looking for trash can, mailbox, and other violations. Buying an RV is like waving a red flag in front of a bull.

This is one of the biggest advantages of buying a Class B motorhome. Many HOAs regard them as vans, not RVs, so you can avoid storage costs. If this is the major reason you're choosing a Class B, make sure you won't get stung after the fact, by some vacillating bureaucrat who changes their tune and decides that any high-top van is an RV after all. If you can get it in your garage, you're generally okay. But chat with your neighbors ahead of time and nail down this issue with your own HOA, instead of buying first and getting hit later.

Storage facilities often have trouble getting zoning and may end up far outside of town, leaving you with a long drive to your RV. That's why it's always fun driving through states like South Dakota, where it seems like every house, no matter the price range, is incomplete without the decorative touch of an RV parked alongside. You get the feeling neighbors judge one another's RVs far more than their houses.

In recent years, with the upsurge in RV sales, finding affordable storage in urban and suburban areas has been a serious challenge, so investigate before you buy. Prices vary widely, depending on the size of the rig and whether you need indoor or outdoor space, and security can be iffy. In 2021, we paid $127 a month for a 40-foot parking space in a gated self-storage facility with onsite security, unfortunately exposed to the weather. Interior storage in the same establishment was going for $320 a month, until the owner converted those buildings into smaller, individual warehouses.

Luxury, indoor high-end RV storage facilities with all sorts of amenities are slowly becoming more common around the country, but it's expensive. If you can afford the eye-watering rent, some of these places offer private garage stalls, 30- and 50-amp electrical hookups, and pre-trip preparation services, making sure your RV is always ready to go on a moment's notice. But these aren't the typical storage options you'll find, and they're costly.

# Chapter 5

# Doing Your Homework

In Chapters 2 and 3, we concentrate on the various types of RVs and on helping you make some key decisions.

Here, we go into the trenches to choose a company and a model. This process will be a lot easier if you know whether you want a trailer or a motorhome. Because even if you know what *kind* of RV you want, you'll face a dizzying array of makes and models.

In this chapter, we fill you in on the companies that make RVs, what to expect, what to look out for, and why buying an RV isn't quite like buying anything else.

## Working on Your Short List

What you're working toward in this section is a personal *short list,* a list of companies and models that seem right for you. The list will be constantly changing, expanding when you discover new models that seem promising and shrinking as others on the list are discarded. Doing some deeper research will be easier when you've come up with a manageable short list and begun to zero in on the perfect RV for you.

## Getting to know the major players

If you've never been camping before, many of the names of RV manufacturers will be foreign to you, even the famous ones. So, to begin working toward your short list, start by visiting one of several websites that list all the RV manufacturers and all the models. Yes, the lists are long, but it doesn't have to be intimidating. Here are some places to start:

» **RVT** (www.rvt.com): RVT is an RV sales site. If you scroll to the bottom of the home page, you'll find not only *all* the manufacturers and models, but another list of the top manufacturers — 32 of them — in alphabetical order, from Airstream to Winnebago. Click the links for each manufacturer, and you'll find everything on the website that's for sale.

» **Wikipedia** (https://en.wikipedia.org/wiki/List_of_recreational_vehicle_manufacturers): Wikipedia's list of recreational vehicle manufacturers is "nonexhaustive," but it's a good list of more than 50 majors, with links to the Wikipedia page for each company.

» **RV Insider** (www.rvinsider.com): RV Insider has lists at the bottom of the home page, with links to reviews of the companies and their models.

» **National Automobile Dealers Association (NADA;** https://www.nadaguides.com/RVs/Manufacturers): NADA is a great site you'll be going to often.

Start getting to know the names of manufacturers and clicking those links for more information. If you see something you like, jot it down on your short list. Many manufacturers make only one kind of RV, which is particularly common with motorhomes. Others build a wide variety — you'll see names like Keystone and Heartland again and again. You'll be surprised, over the course of a few days, how quickly these names become familiar to you.

## Considering smaller RV makers

TIP

Do you long to buy from a small, independent or family-owned company? Those companies do have a higher rate of customer satisfaction, and they're out there. A surprising number of RV manufacturers have remained stubbornly independent, and there are many small, family-owned companies running the gamut in price and size. Here are some examples:

» **Coach House** (www.coachhouserv.com): Coach House is a family-owned manufacturer of luxury Class B and B+ motorhomes in Venice, Florida, and its rigs get high marks for quality. Similar quality Class Bs are made by the independent Canadian companies Pleasure-Way (https://pleasureway.com) and Leisure Travel Vans (https://leisurevans.com).

# JUST THE FACTS, MA'AM: THE RV INDUSTRY

The RV industry is very American, and at its best, it's imaginative and innovative. But briefly, we need to address some general facts about the business that aren't always positive.

RVs were once made by smallish companies, most of them in northern Indiana, started by people excited to build campers, often employing craftsmen from the local Amish population. As the RV industry grew, it weathered many storms, but the worst came with the financial crisis of 2007 and the brutal recession that followed. Credit got scarce, sales were down, and businesses were closing so fast that little Elkhart, Indiana, became a standard stop for every presidential candidate, there to deliver their economic plan over the industry's bleached bones.

A decade of frenzied acquisitions followed, with big companies swallowing up smaller ones, anything that looked appetizing. Thor Industries is now the biggest manufacturer of RVs in the world, because of its last two acquisitions (of the large manufacturer Jayco and then Hymer, the biggest producer of RVs in Europe). Thor may now be Godzilla, but the biggest mega-competitor nipping at its heels is Forest River, which was acquired by Warren Buffett's company, Berkshire Hathaway; soon Forest River began snapping up other companies, including the makers of anything that moves, from cargo trailers to buses to pontoon boats. Two other companies are attempting to conglomerate themselves into competition, dominating the remaining 20 percent of the market. The iconic Winnebago company is expanding; they recently bought both Newmar luxury coaches and the popular Grand Design company, as well as Chris-Craft Boats. Meanwhile the REV Group, manufacturers of ambulances and fire trucks, has acquired Monaco, Holiday Rambler, and, most recently, Lance Campers.

What this means is that most of the RVs made in the United States are coming from two corporations, making them a near monopoly, no matter how many company names you see. Businesses run by monopolies tend to be lousy for consumers. They're not innovative, nor are they flexible. Instead, they're utterly and completely profit driven.

>> **EarthRoamer** (https://earthroamer.com): EarthRoamer is a Colorado-based company that's the undisputed king of the "zombie apocalypse" style of luxury off-road RVs, built on Ford Super Duty truck chassis. This expensive RV has spawned several imitators, though the company also sells late-model reconditioned RVs for a more reasonable price. If what matters most to you, apart from quality, is the gasp you'll elicit in envious campers boondocking in the Grand Tetons, go for it, because this thing will take you anywhere.

>> **Casita Travel Trailers** (https://casitatraveltrailers.com): A star of the "tiny trailer" movement is little Casita Travel Trailers in Rice, Texas, with their cute, and very small, towable trailers that get high ratings for quality at a reasonable price.

>> **Oliver Travel Trailers** (https://olivertraveltrailers.com): The more expensive Oliver is a luxury version of a trailer similar to Casita, and it's still made by the Oliver family in Hohenwald, Tennessee. These molded fiberglass designs — two halves sealed along the middle — leave far less chance of leaks. They also have good resale value.

Interested in a teardrop? This is an easy short list to put together, and the majority of them are American made by independent or family-owned companies:

>> **Timberleaf Trailers** (https://timberleaftrailers.com) in Colorado

>> **Vistabule** (https://vistabule.com) in Minnesota

>> **Camp-Inn Teardrop Travel Trailers** (www.tinycamper.com) in Wisconsin

Even the larger companies, where it will be easier to track down a dealer, still belong on the list of independents:

>> **nüCamp** (https://nucamprv.com): nüCamp may seem bigger, but it's a boutique company in Sugarcreek, Ohio, maker of a popular line of teardrops and the stylish new Avia trailer.

>> **Little Guy Trailers** (https://golittleguy.com): An equally stylish competitor, Little Guy Trailers, also in Ohio, is the builder of several models, including the adorable Little Guy Max, an attention-grabbing beauty with tons of room, despite its teardrop shape.

**REMEMBER**

A fun aspect of teardrops is their tight support groups, with gatherings and events throughout the year. Another is the new breed of tough-guy off-road teardrops, with a *Star Wars* vibe. Even if you want more room in the future, a tiny trailer can be a great, economical way to get started in the RV life. And if you're determined to have something absolutely sprawling in size, be careful watching YouTube videos about teardrops — the charm is hard to resist.

**TIP**

Finding the products from these guys isn't as simple as hopping in the car and driving to the nearest Camping World on a Saturday morning. Most of these smaller manufacturers have relationships with a limited number of dealers. Geography can affect this — we liked Lance trailers and put it on our short list, but it's a California company, and east of the Mississippi it was tough to find a Lance dealer with a good selection. Like the previously mentioned Casita, some manufacturers like to deal directly with the public and have no dealerships at all. New Horizons RV (https://horizonsrv.com) in Junction City, Kansas, for example, specializes in large fifth wheels and toy haulers that take a custom approach, working with a buyer through the build phase to give them exactly what they want, and their reviews reflect this quality. Luxe Luxury Fifth Wheels (`https://luxefifthwheel.com`) is another custom house out of Elkhart, Indiana, with showrooms for products in Southern California and Texas. They produce high-end, quality products that are ideal for the full-timer, with responsive management that will build you your dream.

## AN RV IS NOT A CAR

Bob Wheeler is the president and CEO of Airstream and a powerhouse in the RV business. Speaking in 2020 for the industry as a whole, he said, "The fact is that 50 percent of our buyers are first-time RV owners. Just about every one of these people thinks he's buying a car, and their expectations are extremely high."

The 1970s were the decade of the Crappy American Car, and the lack of dependability was legendary. But in the decades since, cars have become remarkably dependable, with solid warranties. They require little investment of care or thought. And this is why the high expectations of confusing an RV purchase with buying a car are so dangerous.

First, no RV, even a well-built RV, will *ever* be as trouble-free as a car.

RVs aren't built the way cars are, with precision robotics on an assembly line and electronic diagnostics. They're built by hand, with lots of employees. This makes them expensive to build, and manufacturers cut various corners to keep the price from inflating to levels that could put them out of business.

But the sad fact is that too many RVs are manufactured too quickly, by crews working too many hours for too little money and sometimes with too little training, and shoddy workmanship is the result. These units are passed on to dealers to cope with, and when they come back like a boomerang, with a long list of issues, the dealer can't cope. In many cases the RV in question sits in the dealer's repair bay for weeks, if not months, while warranty work isn't done, with endless debates over whether it qualifies. Dealers often can't get the parts they need from the manufacturer, while many dealer techs aren't properly trained (though the industry is trying to do something about this). But there's an unacceptably high number of "fixes" that occur that aren't fixes at all. You get it back, and the problem is still there. Customers are routinely bounced back and forth, between manufacturer and dealer, with no clear notion of who can be held accountable.

There are ways to protect yourself from an RV purchase that ends this way. The two most important are thorough research and a thorough pre-buy inspection.

On the bright side, far more people are happy than unhappy with their RV purchase. According to the Recreational Vehicle Industry Association (RVIA), a 2019 study found that 88 percent of owners were happy, so the odds are in your favor. Make those odds a surefire win, by doing your homework!

The Class B market is carpeted with small custom houses. A handful of new companies, including Relic Trailer (https://www.relictrailers.com) and Old School Trailers (www.theoldschooltrailer.com), are making adorable custom vintage trailers. These RVs are going to be harder to see into and harder to lay hands on. Call these companies, and they'll try to help you. The Casita website, for example, will send you the location of a happy Casita owner who doesn't mind if you look at their trailer, an imaginative approach to the problem.

We hesitate to mention companies like Foretravel (www.foretravel.com) in Texas, because, though family owned and well built, they're also custom motorhomes that have a startling price tag, heading toward a Newell or a Prevost. If you're lucky enough to be able to push toward a million bucks for an RV, go for it. But most of us play in a ballpark with considerably cheaper seats.

## Zeroing in on the RVs you're interested in

You'll read a lot of dreck online about RV shopping that sounds more like voodoo. For example, don't buy a trailer that was built on a Friday. We've got a better one: Don't buy a trailer that had 23 online reviews saying the roof leaked.

Maybe it's not quite that simple, but there are all sorts of ways to gauge the quality of any RV you've got your eye on. If you've found a company that looks good to you, start by going to the company's website and heading to the About page. Yes, the company wrote it, but it's still revealing. It should be one of your first research steps.

Next, look at the real-world resale value of that model, easily done on RV Trader (www.rvtrader.com). You can get more precise numbers on the website of the National Automobile Dealers Association (www.nadaguides.com). Enter the model name and info, and take a look at what a two-year-old one is worth today. The constantly-shifting model names in large companies will make this harder, of course. It's meant to. If the RV you're looking at has no model history at all, be wary.

# Finding Resources You Can Trust

As you plow into the information below, keep one thing in mind: There's no such thing as too much research! In looking through the wreckage on review sites, where people bemoan a disastrous RV purchase, the most common remark seen is "I guess we should've done a little more homework." And the flip side is there, with owners saying in 4- and 5-star reviews that they're glad they *did* do so much research, because they got the right RV for them.

# YOUR FIRST HOMEWORK ASSIGNMENT: WATCH *THE LONG, LONG TRAILER*

There are surprisingly few movies out there about the RV life. Albert Brooks's 1985 film *Lost in America* is worth seeing, if only because it's so relevant — it's about a pair of yuppies who take off to live in a Winnebago and see the real America. *RV,* with Robin Williams, plays for lowbrow comedy while indulging some truly grotesque stereotypes about the sort of people you'll supposedly meet on the road. But without doubt, the film that the RV universe loves most is the 1954 Lucille Ball and Desi Arnaz comedy *The Long, Long Trailer.* And brother, is it long. Director Vincente Minnelli had a ball poking fun at the gigantic travel trailers that were becoming popular in the '50s, choosing one of the largest at that time — a 36-foot New Moon by Redman. Redman, now called Champion Homes, was one of the first companies to make a splash selling "manufactured housing," which it still does. But back in 1953, the year it was founded, they built the New Moon, a monster trailer designed to be a home on wheels.

This movie was never one of our favorites until we actually bought a trailer. The reason it's such great homework is because Lucy and Desi make every mistake in the book, and the seasoned owner cringes, seeing all of them coming. They go to their first RV show clutching a brochure with a floor plan that looked so *big* on paper, but it walks so small. Dejected, they fall in love with the first thing they see. They're dazzled by fluff, like the musical doorbell and the window into the tiny oven. They convince themselves an RV will actually *save* them money when the cheerful salesperson tells them about the low, low monthly payment. They know nothing about tow vehicles and don't realize they're also going to have to buy a brand-new car. And have a custom hitch welded on. And install trailer brakes. So much for the budget. Neither of them has ever camped or towed a big load, and they start at the top, making it all harder.

Some scenes have fallen into campground legend, like the scary drive through the Sierra Nevada mountains, with Lucy hiding an overload of boulders for a rock garden. We'd like to believe no one would attempt to fix dinner in a moving trailer, a situation mined for major laughs. But in another scene, they take a wrong turn, stick with it instead of backing out at once, and end up miles down a miserable and unused logging road where they can't even turn around, a thing Google Maps hasn't put a finish to. "I meant turn left right here!"

And the look on Desi Arnaz's face as he's learning to drive the "40 feet of train" is a joke that hasn't faded in seven decades. It will hit every first-time buyer of a 40-foot motorhome who never drove anything bigger than a Honda Civic right between the eyes.

Watch it, have a good laugh, and hold on to one takeaway when things go wrong: "Trailer brakes first!"

Doing the research is easier than it sounds. In fact, if you love RVs, doing the research can be a *fun* part of the process. Read on for our tips on where to start.

# The Internet

Your most valuable tool when you're researching the RVs you're interested in is the Internet. In this section, we walk you through the myriad resources at your disposal from the comfort of your own home.

## Review websites

Cruising the web looking for reviews of a particular RV can be a terrifying experience. The main reason is that the Internet becomes the shadowy world of catastrophe, the related tale, true or not, of "my disaster with a 30-foot Schmuck trailer." You'll see stories of roofs peeling off while driving through the Rockies, flooded basement storage, slides that fell out, and one poor guy who got his door kicked in by a moose in heat.

**REMEMBER**

As you read reviews of the RVs you're interested in, just remember that you're on the dark side here, seeing the worst of the worst. Perhaps one in ten happy customers will leave a glowing 5-star review, of anything. On the other hand, angry customers are three or four times as likely to leave a negative review. You don't have to be Pythagoras to figure out that all review sites are weighted toward the negative. And it takes a *lot* of 4- and 5-star reviews to undo the damage done by a single negative review. Some angry owner may very well post the same negative review and horror story on dozens of websites just to make sure everybody sees it.

Most people tend to take negative reviews more to heart, feeling that they're the ones that are more trustworthy. Other people wonder if *any* reviews are trustworthy. In the end, read all reviews carefully, to see if they sound authentic. Consult as many review sites as possible, not just one. Companies have been accused of posting phony, bought-and-paid-for positive reviews and, conversely, of sinking positive ones, and there's little regulation of the power of the web.

Take a handful of negative reviews with a grain of salt, and use your own common sense to evaluate them. The greatest rig on earth will have a couple of sullen, badly spelled, 1-star reviews. This is where the common sense comes in. One review, even a devastating one, doesn't necessarily rate dumping an RV from your short list. The far more disturbing (and more trustworthy) factor here is if you keep seeing the same problems, over and over, attached to the same product.

When you're on a review site, be aware of the dates they were posted. You may discover that a popular fifth wheel has taken a distinct downturn in the last year or two, while a fifth wheel with a fairly crummy reputation a decade ago has had an uptick, with a company that's trying to clean up its act. In the changeable world of RVs, reviews have more value if you see them set in a time frame.

Probably the biggest problem with review sites overall is that, if you've chosen an RV that's a bit more unusual (like the Little Guy Max, for example), you're not going to find the 147 reviews you get under Keystone Montana. But stick with it, keep searching, and remember that a small number of reviews can still be reflective of a general attitude on the part of owners.

When you're going online, beware the self-appointed expert. For example, Airstream was one of the companies on our short list. People in several forums confidently stated that Thor had "just bought" Airstream, and it would now go downhill. It sounded true, but it wasn't. Airstream was in trouble in the '70s, until two entrepreneurs founded Thor and acquired the company in 1980, quickly making it profitable again. In other words, Airstream was the *foundation* on which Thor was built 40 years ago. Professors call this *circular citing*, with people just quoting other people who don't know. Always look for other sources for facts that affect your choices.

Here are some review websites you should be sure to check:

>> **RV Insider** (www.rvinsider.com): There aren't tons of review sites out there that are strictly for RVs. You'll find far more review sites for campgrounds. Various forums will discuss brands, but the only RV-specific review site that charges no membership fee is RV Insider. It may have little competition, but it's a great resource. The website is very well organized, with tons of information. And there's a tone to the reviews on RV Insider, a feeling that they're a bit more serious, real RV owners trying to be fair and honest.

On RV Insider, it's easy to cast a wider net than just one trailer. Enter a company name, like Starcraft or Aliner, and you'll get all sorts of information, starting with the overall rating score of that company. Below that, you'll see all the Starcraft or Aliner models that appear on the site, with the number of reviews beside each one, and again, the average number of stars. This gives you an excellent notion of whether the company, as a whole, deserves to keep its place on your short list.

>> **Pissed Consumer** (www.pissedconsumer.com): Pissed Consumer is an interesting site, but it can be an upsetting one. By its very name, you can tell you're seeing the dark side, which doesn't mean you shouldn't take careful note of reviews posted here and fold them in with what you've found elsewhere. Pissed Consumer covers any and all products, but you'll find a lot of RV and dealer reviews here.

## Facebook

If we were asked to choose which resource was the number-one most helpful to us, it would be Facebook groups. RV companies and most specific brands have Facebook support groups for owners.

There are two types of Facebook groups: private and extra super-secret private (meaning outsiders can't even peek in to see what's being said). Most RV groups are just private. If you ask to join because you're considering buying that specific model, most of them won't turn you away, which will enable you to ask questions of your own. Nowhere will you find more people being more honest about the specific rig you're interested in.

And while you're hanging out on Facebook, don't forget to tell friends and relations, many of whom you may not be aware of owning an RV. Post photos of a model you're considering and ask for their input. You may be surprised what you can find out with very little effort.

## YouTube

YouTube is a terrific place for a first-time RV buyer, and for an old hand. You'll find two types of videos about RVs — the ones posted by dealers or occasionally manufacturers and the ones owners of the brand have done. Both are equally valuable.

You'll also find YouTube network shows, put together by RVers who've made selling the lifestyle their day job. We started by following a show that's been around awhile, Long Long Honeymoon (www.youtube.com/c/LongLongHoneymoon), branching out to Less Junk, More Journey (www.youtube.com/c/LessJunkMoreJourney), Embracing Detours (www.youtube.com/channel/UCa3A0eTpagC3D532A-39i0A), Gone With the Wynns (www.youtube.com/user/gonewiththewynns), and many more in the busy RV world of YouTube. They're filled with good advice, and you can follow the people you like best through their adventures, learning from their experiences. On occasion they'll go live, and you can ask them questions.

We've never come across anyone trying to sell you anything on these YouTube network shows, apart from some Amazon links to recommended products. They get a tiny percentage of the sale, so it's a nice way to say thank you for all their help.

# Books and magazines

*Trailer Life* magazine, published by Good Sam, has been a go-to source of information and support for campers since the 1930s. But as of January 2021, *Trailer Life* and its sister publication, *Motorhome* magazine, have been terminated, and a new publication, *RV Magazine,* has taken their place. *RV Magazine* has a slick format and a positive tone, in a convenient single publication, but as of this writing, it's not the source of solid information on models and accessories the others were. Though there has been no formal announcement, it looks as if the other Good Sam institution, the annual buyer's guides for both RVs and tow vehicles, has also gone the way of the dinosaurs, though there may be an online version.

*RV Lifestyle* (https://rvlifemag.com) is an excellent magazine published in Canada. It offers an annual buyer's guide edition, online back issues, and electronic subscriptions.

You'll find very few books out there on the topic of RV reviews. Author Randall Eaton (www.rvreviews.net), under the company name JR Consumer Resources, is selling four of them:

>> *Motorhome Comparison Guide*

>> *Travel Trailer/Fifth Wheel Comparison Guide*

>> *Lightweight Travel Trailer Comparison Guide*

>> *Truck Camper Comparison Guide*

Eaton is also selling *How to Buy an RV and Save* and *Top 100 RV Dealers.* There's a link at the top of the page to another download, RV Extended Warranties.

There is good information in these books. But on the whole, whether you get what you paid for them is debatable. If you come across the first three books on Amazon, as we did, you're going to pay around $70 apiece for them. On the website, you'll be offered various price breaks and bundling packages, as well as less-expensive e-books as downloadable PDFs, which are not available on Amazon.

You'll pay an additional fee for just about everything. Eaton offers reviews of individual models, at $25 apiece. Although the information in them is expanded, much of it is company information taken from the books. A pre-buy checklist is another $25.

Randall Eaton is very knowledgeable about RVs, and it's clear no companies were given any sort of preference. His download on extended warranties is more reasonably priced and up to date, with some good advice. But much of the info in the comparison guides is dated and can be found for free on Wikipedia or on the manufacturer's own website. The meat you're looking for comes at the end, in a brief "Comments" section for each company, and it's pretty general, including a list of recalls. This list, too, can be found for free on the Internet. But if money isn't an issue for you, and if you feel deeply comforted by having books rather than websites, Eaton's books may be a way to go.

If you've zeroed in on one model, and you want as much information as possible on it, you can order that single review of, say, a Minnie from Winnebago — a far more economical way to go.

## RV shows

We'll say it upfront: We love RV shows! Even now, when we're very happy with our trailer and our tow vehicle, we love going to them. There's a persistent notion that you can pick up an RV with a fantastic, last-minute markdown price at a show from a dealer who'd rather sell at a loss than haul it back home. Many an Internet pundit will tell you this is no longer the case, but we've seen some examples, with our own eyes, of at least a pretty darn good price on a show RV.

But the truth is, what we love about RV shows doesn't have anything to do with bargain hunting. If you're just starting your search, and you're truly lost about what you want, you can find out more in three hours at a decent RV show than in weeks on the Internet. More important, you won't find out in isolation — you'll be surrounded by other RVers. Even if you're not good at striking up conversations with strangers, you'll be surrounded by the chatter, and you'll find out all sorts of interesting things. At a big show, like the ones in Tampa, Florida, or Hershey, Pennsylvania, you'll also be surrounded by industry professionals. You can ask them questions, too. Plus, all the sellers that glom on to a show, with everything from solar panels to outdoor furniture, are not only fun, but a convenience.

The COVID-19 pandemic shutdowns resulted in the cancellation of RV shows all around the country. This was a devastating loss for people shopping for RVs, because shows are such a great place to see many of them at once. "Virtual" shows just don't cut it. There are too many things about an RV that you need all your senses to assess. Does that "ultra-lite" feel like a Cracker Jack box when you cross the floor? Do the cabinet doors feel disastrously cheap and badly installed, with wood-colored paper already bubbling on the surface? Does it just not seem as spacious as you thought? Can you actually stand up in the shower stall? Does the bed feel like it was carved from sandstone? These are the questions answered quickly at a show, sometimes in moments, as soon as you walk inside.

## Campgrounds

Campgrounds are a great place to research RVs, but so few people think of them. Take some time and just drive through RV campgrounds, looking at the rigs there. Even better, walk through the park. We've never been hassled over it by a campground manager. If you happen to see a rig that's a brand you're considering, see if the owner is out front or has the door open. RVers are nice people, and there's nothing they like to talk about more than their rigs. With one weird exception (an odd and grumpy gentleman), we've never been refused. Ditto for truck stops, gas stations, and the like — if you see a rig you're interested in, ask about it.

**REMEMBER**

We *don't* ask to go inside someone's RV, and neither should you. But you'd be surprised how often you'll be invited to have a peek, if you're polite.

## Factory tours

We're big cheerleaders for taking a company tour for any model you're looking at. Over 80 percent of RVs are made in northern Indiana, so this may not be practical for you, but check where the model you're interested in is made. Factory tours are a tradition in RVs, an old-fashioned and relatively inexpensive way to do customer outreach. You'll learn a lot about the brand you're looking at and the business as a whole. If a tour guide boasts about how quickly their RVs are built, an alarm should be making a noisy clanging sound in your head. But if they point out a special facility that dumps water on their rigs to test for water leaks or highlight other quality control capabilities, your confidence should increase.

**TECHNICAL STUFF**

If you're ordering a brand-new RV instead of buying one off a dealer's lot, top manufacturers may let you visit their factory when your unit is being built. The dealer can provide you with a *build number,* and the factory may alert you when your RV enters the production line, giving you the opportunity to see it being assembled.

Chapter **6**

# Dealing with Dealers

S hopping for an RV is fun — or at least it should be. But even if you've done your homework, coping with certain issues can be a little scary. Warranties, for example, can bring on hives.

Coping with your first RV dealer can be nerve-wracking, too. It's like car buying in some ways — you're beset by pushy salespeople, haggling over price, getting waylaid by a professional sales closer who could talk you into buying a rat-skin bumbershoot, and signing a 6-foot-long purchase contract that reads like a tech company's terms of agreement.

In this chapter, we make it a little easier for you, especially if you're a newbie, by explaining some things you may not know, confessing mistakes we've made, and offering a few warnings regarding both dealers and warranties.

## Getting the Lay of the Land

When you're shopping for an RV, there's one thing that makes it similar to car shopping: If you've done any homework at all, you'll follow the brand, not the dealer. And unless you're shopping used, you won't find a Chevy in a Ford lot. Dealers have relationships with various manufacturers, or in rare cases, with only one manufacturer (this practice is common with Airstream dealers). But even the biggest mega-dealer won't have every brand you want to see.

**WARNING**

On your first shopping trip, it may seem easier to settle on something you like on the lot you're in. An amazing number of people buy something after their first trip to Camping World. *Don't buy an RV this way.* Here's why:

>> **You really haven't begun to see what's out there.** Just because you saw what one dealership had, even if it's a mega-dealership, that doesn't mean you've seen everything.

>> **You haven't come close to researching this model or the price it's being sold for elsewhere.** You may have done no research at all, including resale value. The dealer may offer you "easy" financing, but you can't know whether that's a disaster brewing until you know something about this model's resale value. (You don't want to end up being upside-down on an RV loan — see Chapter 4.) Often the salesperson who helped you will get you to focus on one RV, and then address the issue of price by calling in someone from management who is, in reality, a "sales closer."

The closer's tactics can get downright theatrical. When a closer gets hold of you, convincing you that this whole RV thing can be tidily handled in one day because you're getting an absolutely criminal discount, you've lost control of the situation. *Get out of there.* Go home, and do some simple searches on the computer before you even think of buying what you saw that day.

**TIP**

Within the confines of carrying what you're interested in, you need to look for the *best* dealer. Not all RVs cost more than cars and trucks, but loads of them do. Which means this could be the biggest single purchase of your life, second only to your house. Getting the dealer right is nearly as important as getting the RV right.

**WARNING**

We don't recommend buying an RV online. The COVID-19 pandemic has made both travel and shopping difficult, and the Better Business Bureau has reported an uptick in scams involving online brokers on sites like Craigslist, eBay, and Facebook Marketplace. Often, these RVs aren't merely junk — they don't even exist. Know the typical price of the unit offered — if the deal sounds too good to be true, it probably isn't. It's tough for people shopping for unusual or specific vintage rigs, because sites like eBay are a resource for them. But one complaint we hear often is that a vintage rig on offer has suffered water damage, the kind of thing you can only judge with your own eyes (and nose). So, contact the seller, and start a conversation. Make a good-faith offer if you desperately want it. But the best way to protect yourself from scams is to never put down money on an RV that you haven't seen and inspected in person.

More than 3,000 RV dealers exist in the United States. There are lots of good ones out there, so try to find one. When you buy an RV, you'll have an ongoing relationship with your dealer, perhaps more than you realize at the outset. For one thing, your dealer will be handling your service work. When you come back from your shakedown with any problems, it's the dealer you'll be going to.

## DEALING THE OLD-FASHIONED WAY

Pundits of the RV park will tell you there's no money in selling RVs and that the real money is in warranties and financing. Well, it's half-true anyway. There *is* money to be made the old-fashioned way, by selling the unit. The dealer may claim they're giving you a rig at cost or near cost, but this figure probably isn't reflective of what they paid for it. In fact, they may not have "paid" for it all — instead, they may be merely servicing a line of credit, in a system called a *floor plan*. The dealer probably didn't sit down and write a check for those ten new Jaycos that came in — instead, they pay for the unit when you buy it. Profit on the unit sale is especially large with the Class As and luxury rigs. In general, it's reasonable to expect a dealer to take 20 percent off the manufacturer's suggested retail price (MSRP), even 30 percent in some cases. Understand that a dealer has more wiggle room on a $200,000 Tiffin than they do on a $20,000 Aliner. But don't believe the dealer when they tell you they're giving it away.

According to online RV expert Sondra Rochelle, if a big dealership can sell 70 units a month, they may be looking at a profit of $2 million a year on finance charges alone. So, yes, the big money is in warranties and financing, and the days of giving you a better deal on a cash purchase are long gone. Many dealers will cut you a great deal up front, and then collect big upcharges, some of them sneaky, on financing, warranty, and various long-term maintenance plans. This is one reason sticker price shouldn't be your only consideration when shopping.

**REMEMBER**

One complaint is common among RV owners: The dealer may treat you differently when you show up with a problem than they did when you were buying. Almost no one thinks to ask these questions when they're in the breezy, friendly shopping phase, and the salesperson is showing you pictures of their kids: "Do you have hassles with this brand getting warranty work parts? How long does it usually take to get repairs done?" These aren't questions that will thrill a dealer, especially the second question, because too often the answer is, "Four or five weeks, at least." But you may get an honest answer, even a discussion of the problems they're having finding qualified service techs.

# Choosing an RV Dealer: Giant and Nationwide or Small and Local

The biggest network of dealerships in America, by far, is Camping World (www.campingworld.com). Lazydays RV (www.lazydays.com), famous thanks to the Travel Channel, has at present only 11 dealerships in comparison to Camping

World's 120. For the big guys, the largest part of their customer base is first-time buyers. For a local dealer, their bread and butter is the return customer, upgrading or bringing in friends and family members. For this reason, it's far more important to the local dealer that you're happy and you don't regret your purchase.

We're not going to tell you that a local dealership, one that's been in that town for a long time, is *always* a better way to go — different people have different priorities. But local dealerships *are* far more dependent on the goodwill of the locals who've bought from them over the years than very large, multi-store, or national RV dealers are. The big guys can afford to make you angry. Local dealerships can't afford to do that. A mega-dealer may be able to give you a better sticker price but in the end, you'll probably be a lot happier having a relationship with a local independent dealership.

If a dealer tells you they won't service an RV they didn't sell, avoid them. By the rules of the game, if a dealer carries a company brand, they're obligated to service that brand, same as with a car.

Research your potential dealer, the same way you research your potential RV. You can use all the standard online sources we discuss in Chapter 5, but be sure to check the good old Better Business Bureau (www.bbb.org). Read the complaints, and look at the bottom to see what attempt was made at a resolution. Not all complaints are fair — some people like to gripe, and others are just plain nutty. There's probably no such thing as an RV dealer who's *never* had a BBB complaint. But we did many side-by-side searches — feeding in, for example, the name of a local dealership in Indiana we'd heard well of and comparing it to a similarly sized dealership that was part of a West Coast chain — and the results were stark, even considering that several locations of the chain dealer were being bundled. The chain dealership had more than 40 complaints in three years, whereas the long-time local dealership had only 1. This was not an issue of Friendly Midwest versus the Big Bad Coast either. We got very similar results feeding in local California dealerships. Quite often, complaints regarding the locals read more like misunderstandings or a single inept salesperson rather than predatory behavior.

Predatory behavior is what you're looking out for. These methods will probably hit you in the gut when they happen, but read about them first, to see them coming, and to avoid them. Complaints include the following:

>> A dealer who presses you to finance your purchase, when you came in wanting to buy outright.

>> A dealer who claims two different prices — a higher one for a cash sale and a lower one for a financed sale.

>> A dealer who presses you, hard, to buy the extended warranty from their own company or one they have ties with. Always remember, warranties are a profit bonanza for dealers — they can upcharge as much as 100 percent. (We cover warranties in greater detail later in this chapter.)

>> A dealer who strains for any excuse to mine your credit card number, telling you they need it in order to hold an RV you want to look at, even for the time it may take you to drive there.

>> Dealers who practice bait-and-switch tactics, in which the RV you find on arrival is not the same one, at the same price, you discussed on the phone.

>> Dealers who haven't submitted the required tax, title, and licensing paperwork to the state, months after the purchase.

>> Vehicle identification numbers (VINs) that don't match, which the buyer may hear about from the license branch.

>> Upgrades and dealer prep that were promised and never done.

>> Upgrades and services you didn't want or ask for that got slipped into the avalanche of closing paperwork.

>> Warranty work that takes months to do, with no ongoing contact or explanation from the dealer.

>> Never returning the buyer's phone calls after the purchase is complete.

These are some of the behaviors you're looking for in complaints, to decide whether to buy from a dealership.

A good dealer will spend a lot of time with you after a purchase, particularly in the walk-through, teaching you how systems work. This is something to look for in reviews, dealers who threw buyers to the dogs on the big day instead of making sure you understand all systems.

We've heard people argue that large chain dealerships have more clout and can do better than local ones when making a plea on a warranty claim that was refused. Maybe so, but it does seem that the real power here is on the manufacturer's side, particularly the large ones, who can make all sorts of demands on their dealers that seem fairly outrageous. We're back to the power of the mega-corporations again. The dealer cares more about their relationship with the manufacturer than they do about their relationship with you.

# Following the Rules of the Road: Tips for Working with RV Dealers

We saw a relevant story on one of our favorite RV sites about a couple who did a lot of research on the toy hauler they wanted, and then went into the dealership and asked for it. But *asking* for an Acme Super Viper isn't the same thing as *getting* it. You can only see what's there to be seen, and when the dealer tells you they have something similar, you're *going* to look. And so they looked and found one they liked even more than the one they came in asking for. Happy and excited, they put down a large deposit to buy.

The problem here is that all their research just flew out the window. When they went home that night, they discovered that the toy hauler they had bought was much heavier and their vehicle couldn't tow it. (You really shouldn't blindly trust what a salesperson says on this subject — they're trying to make a sale. Find out your tow rating from the vehicle manufacturer before you buy *anything.*) Worse, they'd plunked down a personal check in a state that didn't have a "cooling-off period" for any signed contract.

They were now officially in the stew. And that's why working with a dealer that has a good reputation is so important.

Here are some rules of the road for shopping that'll prevent you from ending up where this poor couple did:

>> **Make room in your schedule and budget for one night in a hotel near the dealer that stocks the model of RV you're interested in.** You may have to drive quite a distance to get to the dealer that carries the RV you want. You may even decide to fly. This is quite an investment of time, money, and high hopes. Don't rush it.

>> **If the dealer shows you something you love, and you decide you want it, don't put down the binder money there and then.** The chances of someone else strolling in and buying it right after you leave are fairly minuscule. But it's still better to lose the RV than to walk into a bad deal. Take that evening to do some due diligence. Search the web for that model of RV and the dealer if you haven't done so already. Check and double-check as many facts as you can before you go back in the morning.

>> **Remember that the salesperson in a dealership is probably not an expert on RVs, though they may sort of present themselves that way.** There are exceptions to this rule, of course, but don't be surprised if you've

done a little research on one particular brand you're interested in and you know more about it than the salesperson does. Their expertise is probably sales, not camping.

>> **If a salesperson tells you that you'll get a better price if you buy today, don't listen.** This is nonsense. Walk in a week from now, and they'll say the same thing.

>> **That moment when you lay down the check but you haven't yet accepted delivery of your RV is your most powerful one in the exchange between you and the dealer.** So many people get excited and focus on other things, while feeling some information overload. This is your time for a thorough inspection and for determining dealer prep that hasn't been done. This is the time when nobody can say that *anything* wrong with that RV is your fault. This is the time for your product delivery inspection (PDI). We did the PDI ourselves, which was probably dumb — you should be a *part* of the PDI, but especially considering the price of the unit, you should probably hire an expert to help. The last time we bought, neither of us was in any shape to crawl under the thing, and you really should see the underbelly of your RV before you buy it, and the roof as well.

## LAWYERING UP

Many RV blog experts suggest you hire a lawyer to look over the sales contract before you sign it. This is an option, of course, but not one we can heartily recommend, especially if you're working with a stable, reputable dealer. Your dealer won't think you're strange if you want a lawyer to look over the contract — according to our own dealer, faxing the contract to a lawyer before the buyer signs has become fairly common. But if your lawyer gives you a heads-up about a particular clause, the dealer isn't going to change their standard contract for you. And if you walk away from the deal, there's a very high probability that when you walk into another dealership, the very same contract clause will be waiting there for you. Our dealer said that his customers who are attorneys themselves are the ones who just sign the contract, merely scanning over it, if that — they know it's standard boilerplate.

The cost to hire a lawyer to look over a sales contract is typically around $300, but if a lawyer offers to attempt a negotiation, the price will go much higher. If you're spending a quarter of a million dollars, this is a minor expense. But if money's tighter, we suggest you at least read some online articles about RV sales contracts yourself. Find out about common clauses that work against you, like so-called *forced arbitration clauses,* in which you agree not to sue anyone but to go to arbitration instead. Acquaint yourself with some of the terms you'll see, and then read the document before you sign it. *Always.* If you're not a lawyer, at least you'll know what you're signing.

**REMEMBER**

An RV being sold as "new" may have been through a lot of abuse, from a rough delivery to a winter sitting on the lot, even being at a show. Don't legally accept an RV until the work you need has been done. In a time when factory warranty repairs can take months, you'll be astonished how quickly these problems will be fixed if the sale is hanging on their being done.

Don't happily haul your RV home, only to find out all the problems in the days to come. At that point, you've lost your power.

# Worrying Over Warranties

Warranties may be the most contentious issue of RV ownership, bringing out opinions like cannon fire. And nowhere are the decisions more personal, based on the value of your rig, the number of potential expensive problems in its features, your personal finances, and several others issues, including your own temperament in dealing with major hassles.

Many RV owners refuse to carry any sort of warranty or service contract. They use a system that requires both self-discipline and arguably a bit of risk, a form of self-insuring — setting aside enough money to cover anything that might happen — after an assessment of the most expensive possibilities. This, along with insurance for calamities like fire and accident, is all they carry. They certainly have one excellent point: Getting work done on your RV is usually a breeze if you're simply paying for it, with no warranty hassles, because a manufacturer or warranty company can find endless reasons to deny your claim. But around the RV park, we've also heard people praising their warranty for picking up the tab for a repair they couldn't have afforded otherwise. In the end, if the possibility of the air-conditioning and the slide breaking down in the same week would keep you up nights, self-insuring probably isn't for you. Even if the needed part is relatively inexpensive, the labor costs can run between $100 and $300 an hour.

Of course, when you're buying from a dealer, the purchase of a warranty may be seen as a given, and if you refuse, you'll get the hard sell. The warranty hard sell can take on a vague sort of threat, implying it would be irresponsible to hit the road without one: "What's going to happen to you in the middle of the desert when it breaks down? Think of your family! Think of your children, stranded by the side of the road with no food and water!"

And, unfortunately, because it's so easy to roll the cost of the warranty into the financing of the rig, many people go with the extended warranty offered by the dealer, and they're not even *close* to the best price they could get if they shopped around online. *Remember:* Even if your dealer is giving you a choice, the choice they're giving is a handful of warranties *they* favor. We didn't get a great warranty deal this way, and we'd bet you won't, either.

We're not great believers in warranties, and we don't usually buy them, especially for things like TVs and appliances, but we *do* carry one on our RV. The idea of not having a warranty just made us too nervous. In the end, on the last RV we bought, it probably wasn't the right decision, at least in our first three years of ownership. Our Airstream trailer has had few problems, and the company has always honored its own three-year factory warranty without question. But nobody has a crystal ball.

The reason Airstream's behavior surprised us is that factory warranties tend to be a joke, and getting work done can be tough. Many RV factory warranties are only one year, hardly a sign of confidence in their product. Companies that, with great fanfare, offer a two-year warranty are usually making trailers, where disastrous repair costs are less likely than they are with a motorhome. Compare this to even an inexpensive car, where a typical factory warranty is now five years or 60,000 miles (up from three years in the past), with an amazing *ten*-year powertrain warranty. This is what people are used to, so the weedy, one-year, 12,000-mile limited warranty on an expensive Class A motorhome comes as a shock.

**TIP**

Extended warranties on motorhomes are very expensive. One thing you might look into, to save money, is a *limited warranty,* which is like catastrophic health insurance — it's there to cover disasters, rather than every little thing. For a motorhome, this is often a *powertrain warranty,* covering the engine and transmission, where the cost of a failure can be heart-stopping.

One bright spot is that, with the explosion of RV buying, as well as online warranties and online wholesale bundlers, lots of new faces are getting in the game, and competition always makes things better.

Even the terminology of warranties can be confusing. An *extended warranty* simply means one that carries you beyond what the company offered just because you bought it (a *factory warranty*). An extended warranty is the same thing as a service contract, an attempt to insure yourself against an expensive breakdown. These are sometimes called *named component warranties,* or confusingly, *comprehensive warranties,* in that they list what's covered, which of course isn't "comprehensive," because if it's not listed, it's not covered. Warranties can be complex, and little words like *cosmetic* can cause you a problem.

*Exclusionary warranties* are more expensive and less confusing, because they simply cover everything, period. They give you a much easier-to-understand list of what's *not* covered by the warranty.

TIP

We've heard complaints about warranties that limit where you can have your covered service done. Some policies state you can only have service at your own dealership, while others are vague, implying coverage is greater than it is. But an RV is very likely to develop a problem far from home. Make sure you know for certain whether you have the right to use the *nearest* licensed service bay, as well as convenient mobile RV service. Even if they're in 50 states, a single option for service in a state the size of Texas or California may still leave you hours from repairs.

Many warranties offer various come-ons that are essentially comfort food, like roadside assistance, picking up hotel and travel expenses in case of breakdown, and even lock-out services.

Yes, you can buy a service contract for a used trailer — Good Sam will cover rigs as old as 15 years — but it'll cost you more. People who rehab vintage trailers, as a rule, either have a bit of cash or are *very* handy. In a rehab, you'll have warranties on various appliances and upgrades, but a service contract is harder. It's difficult enough to get insurance, because determining the agreed value of a vintage rig is a challenge.

TIP

As a rule, you shouldn't fold your warranty coverage into your finance agreement. If you do, you're paying interest on a service agreement. Plus, you're probably paying more for that agreement than you would if you simply contacted the warranty company yourself. This is true even if the dealership is owned by the same people — you'll get a better online price from Good Sam directly than you will if you buy the same service agreement through Camping World.

TIP

If the warranty you're looking at runs into the thousands of dollars, we recommend running it past a specialized RV attorney. Unlike a sales contract, it's easy to pass up a bad warranty and buy a better one. An attorney can alert you to vague and loaded terminology that is problematic.

This may sound silly, but the most important thing you can do to protect yourself is to *read the warranty before you buy it.* Most people will admit they didn't read the fine print. Collect all your paperwork, and document everything. Know where your paperwork is. Look for phrases in a warranty that just sound like a trap. If it says it won't cover anything due to damage from shaking, in an RV, you've got the wrong company.

# LEMON LAWS AND RVs

The fact is, lemon laws are for cars and trucks. Somehow, the RV industry has been able to keep them, in most states, from being passed when it comes to trailers and motorhomes. California, Louisiana, and Texas are the exceptions, though you should always check for the most recent info. This makes RV shopping something of a Wild West. Basically, a *lemon law* states that if a new car can't be repaired within a certain number of days (often 30 days), it must be bought back from the consumer who's stuck with it. Of course, it's more complex than this, and even in the three states listed, aspects aren't covered by the law. You need a lawyer to walk you through it.

Too many owners of new RVs have endured absurdly long waits to get work done under factory warranty, waits that wreck the camping season for them. They're still paying their finance payments and maybe paying for storage, but they have no RV. We think lemon laws would be good for the industry in the long run. We get it — manufacturers can go under if their product has problems and their warranty promises were too generous, but they need to see the big picture of consumer confidence. Of course, this isn't likely right now, with sales so high that manufacturers can't keep up with orders.

When people online talk about resorting to a lawyer and the lemon laws over an RV, they often mean the Magnuson–Moss Warranty Act, which is a federal law meant to protect consumers from misleading warranties.

You can find many attorneys online offering detailed discussions of these laws, and it's really beyond our purview here. Suffice it to say, our hope is that you never end up needing these laws. But if you do, Google "RV lemon laws" and your state, and see the many explanations of your rights under federal and state law.

# Chapter **7**

# Adding a Tow Vehicle to Your Trailer

I f you're buying or already own a motorhome, your rolling vacation home already has its own built-in motive power, so you can skip this chapter. But if you've got your eyes set on a trailer, a fifth wheel, or a truck-mounted camper, you're going to need a towing vehicle capable of hauling whatever you ultimately buy.

Most first-time RV shoppers fall in love with a dream rig without giving much, if any, thought to how they're going to pull it. If you're dealing with a truly responsible RV salesperson or private owner who wants you to be happy with your purchase, they may bring up the topic early in your discussions just to make sure you understand the limitations imposed by a tow vehicle's capability. But in reality, RV dealerships are selling a dream, and they want to sell you as much trailer as they possibly can. They aren't going to let a little thing like your inappropriate tow vehicle get in the way of a big sale. So, we'll be the bad guys and tell you the hard truth: No, your Chevy Volt won't be able to haul that 33-foot monster trailer with its five slides and 100-gallon water tank.

Tried-and-true American full-size pickup trucks are, without question, the top choices for tow vehicles in the RV world. But if you're going to tow a traditional travel trailer and you're willing to stick to smaller, lighter ones, SUVs, crossovers, and minivans can also safely be used as tow vehicles, as long as you don't exceed their towing limits.

In this chapter, we give you the lowdown on your choices for towing your prize trailer and what those baffling terms like *curb weight* and *GVWR* actually mean. In Chapter 8, we explain the nuts and bolts of hitches, along with how to figure out what your specific rig weighs on your first visit to a truck stop's CAT scale. Because these subjects are directly related, we absolutely recommend reading *both* of these chapters before you decide to buy a tow vehicle or stick with the one you already own.

# Choosing Wisely

No one wants to fall in love with the trailer of their dreams, only to be told they also have to drop a fat wad of Simoleans on a new tow vehicle — especially if the tow vehicle turns out to cost more than the trailer!

If you already own the vehicle you intend to tow a trailer with and you have no intention of buying something more robust in the near future, you should still research your vehicle's towing limits and payload capacity, and buy a trailer or camper that doesn't exceed those safe limitations.

We've owned two trailers that could be pulled by our existing 2017 Chevrolet Suburban full-size SUV (affectionately nicknamed "The Red Scare."). We needed the Suburban's secure and climate-controlled cargo space inside, which can't be had with a pickup truck's open bed. Plus, the cargo in a pickup is almost impossible to reach without climbing up into the truck bed. Because we also use the Suburban as our only daily passenger vehicle, our decision was an easy one, and it has worked out well for us — but it did dramatically limit the RVs we could buy.

Another thing to consider is how much you'll actually use your trailer in an average year. Do you think you'll hit the road for weeks or months at a time? Or will you just drag it out on Labor Day weekend and take it to the state park 20 miles away? Will your rig spend the majority of its time parked in storage? If you're new to camping and unsure about how much you'll really like it, it's arguably foolish to run out and buy a new $68,000 pickup truck on top of what you paid for your RV. Fortunately, there are loads of trucks and SUVs available in the used market.

Of course, if you're dragging a long, heavy, traditional travel trailer or a fifth wheel, there aren't many alternatives to pickups. And if you're eyeing a truck-bed-mounted camper unit, you obviously have *no* other choices. So, start deciding what color you want your pickup truck to be. But depending on the RV you want to tow, you may not need a pickup truck to pull a traditional trailer — as long as you confine yourself to smaller, lighter trailers.

**REMEMBER**

Towing a trailer of any size is serious business, so you really must do some investigative work to determine the towing limitations of your vehicle. These ratings don't appear on the new vehicle window sticker, and even the owner's manual doesn't always give you the accurate information. This is partially why lots of RVers take the attitude that there's no such thing as having "too much truck" instead of towing with a vehicle that's just on the cusp of being overloaded by a too-heavy trailer.

**TIP**

The simplest way to find out the exact towing capacity of any vehicle (not just a pickup truck) is to contact the manufacturer directly (just go to the website and look for a Contact page). When you give them the *vehicle identification number* (VIN), they'll be able to tell you the towing limits of your specific truck or car. They can lay hands on your truck's or car's statistics much quicker and more reliably than you can determine them from the owner's manual. For more on weights and capacities, check out the nearby sidebar.

## WHAT HAPPENED TO THE FAMILY STATION WAGON?

Back in the days when family sedans and station wagons were massive bulge-mobiles powered by enormous V8 engines, pickup trucks and SUVs made up a tiny sliver of the consumer automotive market. Four-door sedans comfortably sat six adults on their wide bench seats that were more like a living room sofa than a car seat. They commonly featured massive trunks that you could smuggle several teenagers in for a night at the drive-in movie theater and still have room left over for two sets of golf clubs, a spare tire, and a case of beer. And the longest station wagons could shoehorn up to ten people in them, along with roof racks for piling up luggage. Pickup trucks were things that farmers, carpenters, and plumbers drove, and you didn't often see them parked in a suburban driveway. SUVs were few and far between, favored by resorts for picking up piles of luggage and passengers at airports, occasional off-road sportsmen, and hunters. But all that changed dramatically starting a half-century ago.

Up until the 1970s, when gasoline was cheap and plentiful and nobody gave a hang about gas mileage, RVers just bought the biggest, most robust car on the lot, had a heavy trailer hitch welded to the chassis, piled Grandma and the kids into the back seat, and hooked up the trailer, and away they went. But over the last 50 years, the average family car has shrunk in size, weight, engine power, and payload capacity to comply with federal gas mileage, emission, and safety standards. Meanwhile, big families got smaller, as fewer couples decided to have children. So "family cars" no longer needed to be big enough to have their own zip code.

*(continued)*

*(continued)*

In the early 1970s, a combination of a decline in American petroleum production, Middle Eastern politics, a revolution in oil-rich Iran, and other world events caused fuel prices in the United States to skyrocket almost overnight. In 1973, the oil-producing cartel OPEC (short for Organization of the Petroleum Exporting Countries) suddenly put in place an oil embargo on the United States, which led to the great energy crisis of the '70s. Gasoline was rationed, and long lines at gas pumps became an everyday fact of life. Almost instantly, everyone started to care very much about a car's gas mileage.

In 1975, Congress enacted the first Corporate Average Fuel Economy (CAFE) standards in response to the oil embargo. CAFE standards established an average vehicle fuel economy that each car manufacturer's entire fleet had to achieve. The goal was to double the typical gas mileage of every American car manufacturer's *combined* output of cars within ten years. In 2007, the Clean Air Act set even higher CAFE standards. And subsequent worries over climate change have led to even more regulations nationally, especially in California (which has enacted even more stringent requirements in an effort to phase out all fossil-fuel-powered vehicles by 2035).

In the face of all these regulations, carmakers created a loophole for themselves: Medium- and heavy-duty trucks were treated very differently when it came to mileage requirements. If an auto company could come up with enough tiny, lightweight, high-efficiency cars to offset its overall fleet's mileage, it could still make and sell plenty of lower-mileage-achieving trucks. It was like buying indulgences from the church in the Middle Ages so you could sin for 70 years and still get into heaven. So, minivans and SUVs were reclassified as "trucks" instead of "passenger cars," and pickup trucks, vans, and SUVs became more luxurious to appeal to suburban buyers. That's why today's pickups and SUVs can be more deluxe on the inside (and a lot more expensive) than most passenger cars are.

# Finding Your Vehicle's Tow Ratings

Unfortunately, the answer to "How much weight can my tow vehicle handle?" is not a straightforward one. We wish it were, but your truck or car won't easily give up those secrets.

Every car, truck, van, or SUV is supposed to have a sticker, or *data plate*, that lists some of the information that will help determine how much weight it can haul. You'll usually find it down low inside the front driver's side door on the frame, but it can also be inside the glove compartment, stuck on the end of the dashboard, and even inside the fuel door. The data plate is also one of several places on your vehicle where its VIN is printed.

But the car or truck data plate doesn't tell you all you need to know. Most only list the total gross vehicle weight rating (GVWR) and how much of that weight each of your car or truck's two individual axles can handle, known as the *gross axle weight rating* (GAWR). Check out the "Knowing your weights from your capacities" sidebar for more on these terms.

## KNOWING YOUR WEIGHTS FROM YOUR CAPACITIES

When you go hunting for information about tow vehicles and their trailer hauling capacity, right off the bat you'll be assaulted with a list of terms and abbreviations that probably never entered your mind before. Here's a guide to those terms:

- **Curb weight:** The total weight of your empty tow vehicle loaded with a full tank of gas, plus all its weighty options like roof racks, beefy running boards, and that massive heavy-duty, off-road front grill you paid extra for.

- **Gross combined weight rating (GCWR):** The maximum combined weight of both the loaded trailer and the loaded tow vehicle, including all the people and cargo in both, plus the filled fuel, water, and waste tanks. (Don't leave this out — all that water in a trailer weighs a lot.) Also known as the gross trailer weight rating.

- **Gross vehicle weight rating (GVWR):** The maximum amount your fully packed tow vehicle can weigh, including you and your passengers, all its fluids and options, all the cargo inside, *plus* the tongue weight of the trailer you're hauling.

- **Manufactured weight (or ship weight):** What your trailer weighed totally empty when it rolled off the factory's assembly line. Be aware that this is a base figure and may not include optional extras added by your dealer (or by the previous owner, if you bought it used).

- **Payload capacity:** The *total* amount of weight the vehicle can safely carry, including people and all other stuff crammed into the vehicle. To calculate the payload capacity, subtract the vehicle's curb weight from the GVWR.

- **Tongue weight:** The downward pressure the trailer puts on the tow vehicle's trailer hitch. That weight can vary a whole lot, depending on the trailer's design and how you distribute its load. If you pack everything in the front end of the trailer (in front of its axle), the tongue weight will be heavier than if your belongings are more evenly distributed. If your water tanks are all behind the trailer's axle, the water weight when they're filled will try to drag the back end of the trailer down (like a seesaw) and help take more weight off the tongue in the front.

- **Tow capacity:** The estimated weight that the vehicle can tow. To figure out the vehicle's tow capacity, subtract the GCWR from the vehicle's curb weight.

Meanwhile, your trailer has its own data plate (as do motorhomes). Along with your RV's VIN, the data plate shows the trailer's total manufactured, unloaded weight; its total GVWR; the number of axles it has; and the GAVR, how much of its total weight should be distributed onto each axle. (When we talk about physically weighing your rig later in this chapter, you see why they want you to weigh each of your axles separately when your whole rig is completely packed.)

**TIP**

You'll find another sticker near your vehicle's data plate that tells you the proper air pressure for your tires, so you don't have to stand on your head with a flashlight and magnifying glass trying to find it on the tire itself. Some data plates even tell you the size of your tires.

**WARNING**

Underestimating the weight limits for your RV or thinking that "close counts" can be dangerous or even deadly by causing handling problems, especially at highway speeds. It can also be grounds for an insurance company to deny coverage to you if it can be determined that exceeding recommended weight limits caused a wreck. Never, ever, *ever* try to fudge on the weight calculations and capacity of your tow vehicle and its hitch. The manufacturers aren't just casually suggesting estimates or guidelines on their data plates — these are the firm, top-end limits that must not be ignored.

# Shopping for a Tow Vehicle

If you go to online discussion groups for RVers and search the topic of *tow vehicles* (sometimes abbreviated as TVs), be prepared to witness zealotry, antagonism, and persecution as great as any religious war of the last two millennia. Hell hath no fury like an Internet scold lecturing on the evils of underpowered tow vehicles. Innocently asking, "What kind of tow vehicle should I buy?" or "Can my Chevy Tahoe tow a 28-foot trailer?" unleashes thunderbolts of fire and brimstone, because everyone who has ever hauled a trailer has their own opinion, personal anecdote, or horror story to relate. Overwhelmingly, the answer that dominates these discussions is "Don't ask stupid questions. Buy a heavy-duty pickup. Preferably a Ford F-series, or be damned for all eternity."

There's a reason for that kind of fanatical devotion. The first Ford F-150 went on the market in 1943 and is currently in its 14th generation. Ford F-series pickup trucks (F-150, F-250, F-350, and F-450) are the number-one class of passenger vehicles in the United States, and the F-150 alone is America's best-selling vehicle. Put another way, if Ford were to spin off its F-series trucks as a stand-alone company, it would be rated in the top 50 of the Fortune 500. With that kind of popularity, there's no wonder there are so many F-150 evangelists looking for new converts.

## "YOU CAN TOW THAT 28-FOOT TRAILER WITH A JAGUAR!"

One aspect that gets left out of tow vehicle conversations is that towing capacity and pulling power aren't all you need to consider. An underpowered truck or SUV may be perfectly capable of towing a heavy trailer down a flat road under normal conditions. As one salesman put it to us, "You just won't necessarily be the first guy to reach the top of the hill." Even massive semis on the interstate that have power to spare still struggle going up steep grades if they're hauling a heavy load. But just as important are stability and stopping power, and they can't really be quantified or assigned a mathematical measurement.

A handful of experts in the RV community modify the frame and suspension of tow vehicles to exceed the manufacturers' towing limits. To show off their engineering skills, they turn up at RV shows hauling massive trailers with small two-door coupes, demonstrating that tow capacity has as much to do with load distribution as engine size. The important issue they leave out is stopping power.

It's just a plain and simple fact that a heavy-duty truck is engineered as much to stop safely with its load as it is to pull that load. As you and your trailer come roaring down a 5 percent grade (and yes, those are common in mountainous areas), a heavier truck that is specifically designed for towing will handle the rolling inertia of all that trailer weight that's trying to shove you to the bottom of the hill.

But Ford isn't the only name in the game. Perfectly suitable tow vehicles are sold by Chevrolet, GMC, Jeep, Nissan, RAM (formerly Dodge), and Toyota. Even when you're confined to pickup trucks, there's no lack of variety.

In the following sections, we walk you through truck sizes, cab and bed configurations, and more. But for an up-to-date, side-by-side comparison guide, check out Good Sam's annual *Guide To Towing* (https://webcontent.goodsam.com/trailerlife.com/digital_editions/TrailerLifeTowGuide2020.pdf).

## Understanding truck sizes

There are four official pickup truck categories in the U.S. market, and the size and weight of your RV will directly affect the size of the truck you'll need to haul it with.

### Midsize (or compact)

These small trucks and SUVs are popular with drivers who need to use them as their personal vehicle on a daily basis. Towing capacities range between 5,000 and 7,700 pounds, which is fine for towing lightweight boats, motorcycles, or utility trailers; hauling bags of mulch; or moving the occasional refrigerator or couch. These days, many RV manufacturers are offering lightweight travel trailers that can be safely pulled by these smaller trucks, so you aren't necessarily restricted to teardrops and other tiny trailers.

Examples include the following:

>> Chevrolet Colorado

>> GMC Acadia

>> Honda Ridgeline

>> Jeep Gladiator

>> Nissan Frontier

>> Range Rover

>> Toyota Tacoma

## Full-size (or half-ton)

These trucks are the most popular and best-selling ones in the United States. They can carry a respectable payload and can safely haul most traditional travel trailers. In fact, most (if not all) of these are available with factory towing packages. Typically, full-size trucks have a maximum towing capacity from 9,740 to 13,200 pounds. Because of their enormous popularity in the last two decades, manufacturers offer countless options and amenities in these full-size trucks that used to be found only in luxury cars. You won't need to give up comfort when you drive a pickup or big SUV these days.

Examples include the following:

>> Chevrolet Silverado 1500

>> Ford F-150

>> GMC Sierra 1500

>> Nissan Titan

>> RAM 1500

>> Toyota Tundra

Full-size SUVs — like Chevrolet Suburban, Chevrolet Tahoe, Ford Expedition, and GMC Yukon — also fall into this category.

If you're in love with a fifth-wheel trailer, you're going to have to bite the bullet and step up to at least a three-quarter-ton pickup (see the next section). The design of the towing hitch system on a fifth wheel requires an open pickup truck bed (or a flatbed truck) to mount it. In an effort to convince consumers that any ol' pickup truck will do, some RV manufacturers are marketing lines of so-called "lightweight" or "ultralight" fifth wheels. They're trying to persuade RVers that the less expensive half-ton pickup trucks that you typically find in suburban garages will work just fine. But no matter what your RV maker may claim, a typical half-ton pickup is just not capable of safely handling the weight and size of a fifth-wheel trailer, fully loaded with water and belongings, plus the weight of the heavy hitch itself and a truck cab full of passengers.

## Heavy-duty (or three-quarter-ton)

These larger pickups have beefier engines and transmissions in both gasoline and diesel models, with tremendous load and pulling capacities. If you're going to pull a fifth wheel or an extremely long and heavy traditional travel trailer, these trucks are ideally suited for the job. Typically, they have a towing capacity from 10,000 to 19,000 pounds and have optional towing packages. A specialized fifth wheel hitch is mounted directly in the truck bed and centered over the rear axle, which gives it better stability and pulling power. These trucks are also heavier than their full-size cousins, which makes for safer towing and helps reduce trailer sway.

Examples include the following:

>> Chevrolet Silverado 2500

>> Ford Super-Duty F-250

>> GMC Sierra 2500

>> Nissan Titan XD

>> RAM 2500

## Ultra-duty (or one-ton)

For hauling the very biggest and heaviest fifth-wheel trailers, ultra-duty pickup trucks are the clear choice, with towing capacity from 20,000 to 35,000 pounds. These heavy, rugged vehicles are usually aimed more at pulling power and towing capacity than luxury, which means they lack the softer, more carlike ride of lighter trucks — although, the Ford King Ranch line of trucks is a noteworthy exception when it comes to luxurious interiors. Ultra-duty trucks come in gasoline or diesel models. Optional dual rear wheels (DRW), also known as dualies, dramatically increase their towing capacity to as high as 35,000 pounds.

## A DIFFERENT OPTION FOR FIFTH-WHEEL HAULING

A different option is available for fifth-wheel RVers if a pickup truck seems too limiting or pedestrian for your taste. Dodge, Ford, Freightliner, and GM make more muscular, medium-duty towing trucks, and companies like SportChassis (http://sportchassis.com) and Utility Bodywerks (www.utilitybodywerks.com) customize these trucks inside and out. These unusual trucks (like the Freightliner M2 SportChassis in the nearby figure) have a low, flat deck in the back, perfect for towing fifth wheels or horse and livestock trailers with gooseneck hitches. With a GVWR of a whopping 66,000 pounds, they're obviously powerful enough to haul the heaviest fifth-wheel trailer on the market.

*Photograph courtesy of SportChassis, LLC*

Depending on how far into the deep end you go with options, these are the luxury Cadillacs of the tow-vehicle world, often costing well over $100,000 (and frequently closer to $150,000). But you'll have a truly one-of-a-kind towing vehicle and an impressive rig — along with indulging in the experience of being your own big-rig truck driver.

Because of their increased size, stiff ride, more expensive maintenance, and thirst for fuel, most of these trucks aren't really suited for everyday passenger travel, but they *are* unsurpassed when it comes to hauling the very biggest trailers. Just be aware that, depending on engine size, transmission, rear-end gear ratios, and other optional features, there can be as much as 10,000 pounds difference in these trucks' towing capacities from one model to another. So, do yourself a favor and carefully research the vehicles you're interested in. These trucks naturally sit higher than smaller trucks and ride rougher. So, take a test drive before you throw down a down payment, to make sure you and all your family members can climb in and out easily and that the suspension doesn't shake the fillings out of your teeth.

Examples include the following:

>> Chevrolet Silverado 3500

>> Ford Super Duty F-350

>> GMC Sierra 3500

>> RAM 3500

# Cab and bed configurations

Traditional pickups were built with a single bench seat for the driver and up to two passengers. But as the popularity of pickup trucks grew, manufacturers began to offer a wide variety of cab and bed configurations.

## More seating

These days, two doors with twin bucket front seats and a center console in between them are the industry standard for a *regular cab.*

*Extended cabs* have front- and back-seat rows, with two regular-size doors in front and sometimes two narrow doors to access the back seats. (Others have flip-down front seats instead of back doors to let passengers squeeze into the back).

*Double cabs* (or *quad cabs*) have two seating rows and four regular-size doors. The back seats in extended and double cabs are smaller than the front seats and don't have much legroom for adults, but they do also fold down or flip up to turn the back row into cargo space or a bed for your family Labradoodle.

*Crew cabs* (see Figure 7-1) are the largest pickup cabs on the market, with two full rows of regular-size seats and four full-size doors. Think of an SUV that has an open truck bed in the back. Crew cabs can comfortably seat five adults, or the back seats can fold down for more indoor cargo space.

**FIGURE 7-1:**
Ford F-150 crew
cab with two rows
of seats and four
full-size doors.
Crew cabs have
the most interior
space and can
seat up to five
adults.

## Bed length

The standard length and width of pickup beds were traditionally designed to carry a 4-x-8-foot piece of plywood. Today, pickup truck beds come in several different lengths — as short as 5 and as long as 9 feet.

## Bed covers

Truck beds are normally open to the elements, but car builders and aftermarket accessory companies offer a huge range of truck-bed covers, lids, and hard shells to protect cargo from the elements and discourage thieves with sticky fingers.

WARNING

One downside is that covers can't be used with fifth-wheel hitches, which require an open bed. In fact, any kind of side rail added to the top edge of a pickup truck bed is in danger of being torn off by a fifth wheel the first time you make a sharp turn.

## Tailgates

Manufacturers have become creative with their tailgates and side panels in recent years. RAM pickup trucks offer recessed cabinets built into the side panels, called *RAM boxes* that are perfect for stowing tools and accessories in an easy-to-reach area. Ford, Chevrolet, and GMC offer tailgates that include a foldout ladder to make it easier to climb into the truck bed. Split tailgates are also available — they open from the side like a standard car door instead of flipping down.

# Considering optional features

Just like buying a car, trucks have a wide range of available options to make towing your RV simpler and safer. Because truck makers are aware of the vast RV towing market, they offer optional equipment and features specifically with towing in mind.

## Factory tow packages

The cheapest and simplest time to outfit a truck or SUV with special towing capability is on the factory floor when the thing's being assembled. Factory towing packages are designed by your truck builder to work with your RV without modifications or added headaches. Plus, unlike aftermarket products and devices that are usually "one size fits all," your factory warranty will cover all these components, and insurance companies won't give you a hard time if it's a factory-installed option that caused an accident.

Factory towing packages can include some or all of the following:

>> Built-in trailer hitch receiver and six-way electrical connector for your trailer lights, brakes, and electrical power

>> Extended towing rearview mirrors to see around wide trailers

>> Multiple navigation cameras (important these days because pickup trucks and large SUVs frequently have miserable visibility and loads of blind spots)

>> Hitch-assist graphics on the dash-mounted backup camera screen to help visually line up the truck's hitch ball with your trailer's tongue

>> Built-in trailer braking controls that work in tandem with your truck's own braking system

>> Engine braking that automatically downshifts on steep grades to avoid overheated brakes

>> Incline brake assist that prevents your vehicle from rolling backward on hills when you're stopped and take your foot off the brake (it releases again when you push on the accelerator)

>> Larger radiator and transmission cooling system to prevent overheating

>> Stronger rear suspension to help prevent sagging when your trailer is attached

## Optional diesel engines

Diesel engines have more pulling power and torque and longer lifespans than gasoline engines do. Diesels are also generally paired with a heavier-duty transmission and get better fuel economy. Resale value is usually higher for diesel trucks, even with high miles on them. But diesels cost more to buy — stepping up to a diesel engine in a new pickup can add anywhere from $3,500 to $7,000 to the price. Their maintenance is more expensive and they weigh more, which can decrease a truck's total payload capacity. Plus, diesel fuel is more expensive than gasoline and not as widely available. And you may also need to add an anti-gel fluid to your fuel in winter.

TIP

Turn to Chapter 2 for more on the subject of gasoline versus diesel engines.

## Four-wheel drive

If you live or travel in snowy parts of the country, four-wheel drive (4WD) is a great option to have. And if you plan to tow a trailer off-road in rugged country, it can be indispensable. But four-wheel drive adds weight to your truck and cuts down your fuel economy, even if you're using it in two-wheel-drive mode 99 percent of the time. It can also lower the towing capacity of the truck. Then again, at least you can get one of those snazzy 4x4 decals to stick on the side of your truck bed.

## Cosmetics

If mileage and payload capacity are most important to you, beware of after-market custom options that can add hundreds of pounds of weight. Heavy-duty running boards, massive front grills, steel bumpers, and other add-ons all increase the weight of a truck, which lowers the payload capacity. Those imposing, heavy steel aftermarket front grills that make your ride look like an apocalyptic battle bus outfitted for the zombie wars are designed for off-road ruggedness, not highway economy.

# ELECTRIC TOW VEHICLES?

It's taken longer for electric vehicles (EVs) to become popular in the United States than their dedicated cheerleaders had hoped. When we were writing this book in early 2021, there were no full-size electric or hybrid SUVs or pickup trucks on the market suitable for towing anything but the very lightest trailers. Nevertheless, more and more people are asking if they can haul a trailer with an electric car or truck for anything beyond short distances. The answer: Not quite, but maybe soon.

Bowlus, a trailer company that makes a lightweight aerodynamic aluminum trailer based on a distinctive bullet-shaped design from the 1930s, has tested its 25-foot, 4,000-pound Road Chief trailer behind a Tesla X. Bowlus claims a full charge gives you a range of 200 miles. Other trailers of similar size and weight are likely to have similar range. Of course, the Bowlus costs almost $200,000, plus the price of the Tesla, so for the moment, hauling trailers with EVs is still expensive and rare. Despite rosy promises and predictions of EV trucks with 10,000 or more pounds of towing capacity and a range of hundreds of miles, nothing on the market just yet can live up to such lofty goals — but they're being promised.

Battery technology still has to improve a lot before consumer-market electric trucks will be able to reliably tow medium to heavy trailers over long distances.

Just before the COVID-19 pandemic led to nationwide shutdowns, the following electric towing vehicles were projected to be entering the marketplace by 2022:

- **Bollinger B1 (an electric SUV) or B2 (an electric pickup):** These are expected to have a 7,500-pound towing capacity with a 200-mile range.

- **Ford F-150 Electric:** An all-electric version of America's top-selling pickup truck.

- **GMC Hummer EV:** Available as an electric SUV or pickup. Projected to have a 350-mile range. One innovative feature is that all four wheels will be able to turn to a 90-degree angle, so the truck can crab-walk its way into a parking space without parallel parking.

- **Lordstown Endurance:** More of a light-duty pickup, it'll feature a 6,000-pound towing capacity with a driving range of 250 miles.

- **Rivian R1T:** This truck is sized between a midsize pickup and a full-size pickup. It features all-wheel drive, the ability to tow up to 11,000 pounds, an adjustable air suspension, and self-driving capabilities, with a top range of 400 miles.

*(continued)*

*(continued)*

- **Tesla Cybertruck:** Projected to have 7,500-pound capacity with an adjustable air suspension that can provide up to 16 inches of ground clearance. The cab will seat six people, and the truck bed will be 6½ feet long. Unlike any other truck on the market, the visually striking angular body is shaped like a stealth fighter (or Doc Brown's DeLorean in *Back to the Future*) and made from stainless steel (see the nearby figure). Tesla anticipates a driving range of up to 500 miles on a full charge. If it lives up to its prerelease hype, this one will be the hands-down leader in the EV truck race.

Mike Mareen/Shutterstock.com

# Chapter **8**

# Getting Hitched and the Alchemy of Weight

Between your RV and your tow vehicle, there's one vital bit of hardware you'll need: a trailer hitch. It's not overstating things to say that the hitch you install on your vehicle is the most vital part of towing, yet new owners probably give it the least amount of thought. If you've never owned an RV before, you may think all you need is one of those chrome-plated balls bolted to your bumper, and you'll be in business.

No one expects you to learn all there is to know about hitches and sway controls and weight distribution systems. If you're buying from an RV dealer, they'll probably want to include the price and installation of the proper hitch on your vehicle as part of the deal. They know the specs and details of their rigs, and they usually have a stock of different hitches on hand for new installations. But if you're buying used from someone, or you decide you can just pick one up at Pep Boys and install your own hitch cheaper than a dealer, you need to know at least the basics.

**TIP**

If you haven't read Chapter 7 yet, go back and read it first. Understanding weight ratings and capacities is important, and a tow vehicle can't tow anything until it's matched with a hitch. In Chapter 7, we cover towing capability; in this chapter, we explain how to figure out just how much weight you're pulling around.

# Getting to Know Your Trailer Hitch

Standing athwart the tow vehicle and the trailer is the lowly, unassuming trailer hitch. It's the chunk of hardware that connects the two. A hitch has to be robust enough to drag several thousand pounds around the countryside without bending or breaking, yet allow the two vehicles to move back and forth and up and down independently of each other.

**TECHNICAL STUFF**

## FIFTH-WHEEL HITCHES

Fifth wheel trailers use a very different hitch than traditional trailers. The front end of a *fiver* is specially designed to extend farther forward and hang over a truck bed. Towing a fifth wheel feels more stable than towing a traditional trailer because the tongue weight pushes down in the center of the truck frame instead of weighing down the tow vehicle's back end. Consequently, fifth-wheel hitches aren't part of the same hitch classification system mentioned in this chapter.

Instead of an A-frame, fifth wheels have a bar with a large kingpin hanging down in front. The hitch is bolted into the truck bed and has a large, horseshoe-shaped plate, looking like an open set of jaws. It's remarkably similar to the kind of mount you see on semitruck rigs when their trailer is disconnected. When hitching up, you back up your truck under the trailer's kingpin, and the slot in the hitch guides the pin into the proper position, where you then lock it down.

Fifth-wheel hitches are identified by the amount of weight they can manage comfortably, as well as by differences in their locking design. There are a few different mechanical ways in which locking is accomplished: a *sliding bar*, a *single jaw*, and a *double jaw*. Sliding bar hitches are less expensive, but they have more slop in them than the other types, permitting the trailer's kingpin to shift around. That means they'll clank a bit when you accelerate or hit the brakes. And it's important to know that a slightly different mounting style of hitch is needed if your truck bed is 6 feet in length or shorter.

The base plates on top of fifth-wheel hitches pivot forward and backward to let your trailer rock up and down on inclines without binding. If they were rigid, you'd ruin yours the first time you pulled into a steep driveway and the truck tilted up. The plate would bend and the kingpin would twist off. But more expensive hitches have what's called a *four-way pivot head* that also lets the trailer rock from side to side without damaging the hitch. That's important if you're going to pull your fifth wheel over rough, uneven terrain with lots of ruts and gullies.

A fifth-wheel hitch usually sits up on four legs, which need to be firmly attached to the truck. To make the job simpler, along with allowing front and back location adjustments, the hitch sits on a pair of rails that get bolted through the truck bed and into the frame. Special mounting brackets let you remove the hitch and rails completely, in case you need to use the truck bed for cargo without any obstructions in the way — although, bear in mind that these traditional fifth-wheel hitches usually weigh several hundred pounds.

A relatively new kind of fifth-wheel hitch, called the Ultimate Connection, is made by Andersen Hitches (https://andersenhitches.com). Its lightweight (less than 50 pounds) tubular aluminum frame attaches to a standard set of truck-bed mounting rails and can also be used in a short-bed truck. Instead of a large hitch plate, a special low-friction coupling device is installed on the fifth wheel's kingpin and slips over a ball mount on the top of the hitch frame. In spite of its aluminum construction and seemingly bare-bones design, this deceptively sturdy hitch can support a trailer tongue weight of 4,600 pounds. Best of all, it can easily be installed and removed by one person in less than one minute.

# The hitch receiver

If you've got a factory-equipped trailer hitch receiver on your tow vehicle (it's a square tube under the rear bumper), that means you can look up the towing capacity and tongue weight limits the manufacturer designates for your vehicle, buy the proper tow hitch to fit it, and away you go!

Some small SUVs, minivans, and crossovers come from the factory with a 1¼-inch Class I or Class II receiver to accept accessories like a hitch-mounted bicycle rack, kayak carrier, or mobility scooter lift.

Pickup trucks and larger SUVs with factory tow packages are almost uniformly equipped with a 2-inch receiver and set up for a Class III hitch. They're extremely versatile and can handle hauling an average midsize travel trailer. In addition to their stated towing weight, Class III hitches can be combined with a *weight-distribution hitch* to increase their towing capacity to as high as 12,000 pounds. (More about weight-distribution hitches in the "Weight-carrying and weight-distribution hitches" section, later in this chapter.)

If your vehicle didn't come factory equipped with a hitch receiver, an RV dealer or specialized hitch dealer can mount a receiver to the underside of your car or truck's frame. There are also less robust bumper-mounted receivers available.

**TIP**

Hitch receivers aren't just found on the rear end of cars and trucks. Most motorhomes come with a hitch receiver to attach a tow bar or trailer and haul a toad behind them. A receiver can be attached to the front of your car or truck to mount a bike carrier. Other folks install one on the back end of their trailer to haul bikes, hitch-mounted barbecue grills, a cargo box, or even a flip-down shelf to lash down everything from lawn chairs to giant beer coolers. Don't go hog wild and pack too much on one of these hitches — most traditional travel trailers aren't designed to hang hundreds of pounds off their back bumpers, like the folks in Figure 8-1 did.

**FIGURE 8-1:**
Just because it fits doesn't make it safe. Most weight-carrying receivers on the backs of trailers aren't designed to safely support more than 200 to 300 pounds.

*Photograph courtesy of Christopher Hodapp*

## What's what on the trailer hitch

At the bare minimum, several parts make up a trailer hitch:

>> **Receiver tube:** A square tube on your tow vehicle that your hitch assembly slides into. There are usually a pair of steel rings or hoops on either side of the tube for attaching safety chains.

>> **Ball hitch:** The main body of the hitch itself. It slides into the receiver. The business end has a mounting hole for bolting on a hitch ball.

>> **Hitch pin and pin clip:** A metal rod with a slight bend in one end that slips into a hole in the receiver and the hitch to lock it into place. The bend keeps the pin from moving, and a big cotter pin (or hair pin) secures the other end. If you're the nervous type, you'll be relieved to know there are hitch pins available with a keyed lock to prevent someone from disconnecting it.

>> **Hitch ball:** The magical part that actually connects your tow vehicle to the trailer and lets it move left and right, up and down. Hitch balls are usually chrome and come in several different sizes. The diameter of the one you need should be stamped by the manufacturer on top of the hitch coupler on your trailer.

In addition to the hitch parts, there are several parts on the trailer end of things up around the A-frame of your rig:

>> **Coupler:** The metal cap at the pointy end of your trailer frame that slips over the top of the hitch ball. Always make sure that the hitch ball matches the stamped-on size of the coupler.

>> **Hitch lock:** A locking lever that closes a metal flange over the bottom of the ball. Located on top of the coupler, this is the part that allows side-to-side motion yet still keeps the trailer firmly locked onto the ball. The lever has a hole in it for a pin or a padlock to keep it from accidentally popping open.

>> **Wiring harness:** An electrical cable that plugs into the back of the tow vehicle; lets the trailer's marker lights, turn signals, and brake lights work; applies the trailer brakes; and keeps your trailer's batteries charged when you're driving.

The RV world today generally uses a thick, round seven-pin (or seven-blade) plug to connect a trailer and tow vehicle. Some trailers and older trucks are equipped with a similar-looking six-way plug, which lacks a pin for powering backup (reverse) tail lights on the trailer. That's not usually a problem, because most travel trailers don't have backup tail lights, but these six-way connectors are getting less common. And just because you may encounter them, the boat trailer and U-Haul worlds usually use a smaller, rectangular four-pin plug. Because these different plugs aren't interchangeable, there are cables and plugs available to let you easily adapt and connect mismatched plugs.

A trailer has a couple of simple safety systems built into it that you need to hook up whenever you hit the road.

>> **Safety chains:** A pair of heavy chains that loosely connect the trailer to the tow vehicle just in case the tow hitch fails or wasn't properly connected. If your trailer suddenly lurches off its ball hitch, the chains prevent the trailer from completely falling off in the middle of the highway and causing a crash.

Be sure to cross the chains, one over the other, underneath the hitch coupler when you hook up. Twist the chains to shorten their length if they're dangling onto the ground, but be sure you leave enough of a loop to handle your truck making a sharp turn without stretching them apart.

Crossing the chains lets you use shorter chains, which helps prevent uncontrolled swaying, and they act as a cradle for the coupler if the trailer becomes uncoupled from the tow vehicle. More important, in the event of a decoupling incident, the crossed chains will attempt to drag the trailer in a straight line behind your truck, whereas straight chains will let it swing wildly from side to side. Also, allowing chains to drag on the asphalt as you drive down the interstate will often create a shower of sparks you can't see from the driver's seat, which is the last thing you want to have happen when driving through parts of the country where wildfires are commonplace.

>> **Emergency breakaway trailer brake cable:** A thin cable that hooks onto the back of your tow vehicle. This is the last chance to stop a runaway trailer if it pops off the hitch. If the cable gets yanked, a long pin will get pulled out of its housing (like a hand grenade — without the explosion part), and the trailer's electric brakes will instantly be applied with every bit of force they can muster to stop the trailer.

## Trailer hitch sizes

Hitches come in several sizes and classifications, depending on how much weight they're going to be lugging around and how they're attached to the tow vehicle (see Table 8-1).

WARNING

No hitch can increase the towing capacity of your tow vehicle beyond its manufactured limits. Towing a trailer or toad is only as strong as the weakest link in the system.

REMEMBER

The actual towing capability of your truck, SUV, or car and the towing capacity of your hitch are a joint effort: The world's biggest, brawniest trailer hitch cannot magically make your Prius macho enough to drag a 9,800-pound trailer up a 7 percent mountain grade, nor can a hitch that's too scrawny safely haul that same heavy trailer up that same steep hill, even if you're pulling it with a Ford F-350 heavy-duty pickup.

**TABLE 8-1**     **Trailer Hitch Sizes**

| Classification | Gross Trailer Weight (GTW) | Tongue Weight (TW) | Receiver Tube Size | Suggested Applications |
|---|---|---|---|---|
| Class I (weight carrying) | 2,000 pounds or less | 200 pounds or less | 1¼ inches | Hitch-mounted cargo carriers, small bike racks, mobility scooters, the smallest teardrop trailers |
| Class II (weight carrying) | 3,500 pounds or less | 525 ponds or less | 1¼ inches | Smaller trailers and pop-up trailers, small boats, large bike carriers |
| Class III (weight distributing) | 8,500 pounds or less | 850 pounds or less | 2 inches | Medium to large travel and utility trailers, horse trailers |
| Class IV (weight distributing) | 12,000 pounds or less | 1,200 pounds or less | 2 inches | Large travel and utility trailers, large horse trailers, toy haulers, big boats |
| Class V (weight distributing) | 20,000 pounds or less | 2,000 pounds or less | 2½ inches | Largest toy haulers, equipment carriers |

# Weight-carrying and weight-distributing hitches

In Table 8-1, Class I and Class II hitches are considered *weight-carrying* types, while Class III through Class V are *weight-distributing hitches*. Here's the difference:

» **Weight-carrying hitches** are generally attached under the rear bumper of the tow vehicle, and the bumper has to support the weight of anything that gets connected. That's partially why they have a much smaller weight capacity.

» **Weight-distributing (also called *load-equalizing*) hitches** are mounted to the vehicle's frame and distribute the weight across both axles. This helps prevent a sagging rear end on your truck or SUV and spreads the load throughout the whole vehicle. It also helps to cut down on trailer sway.

A weight-distributing hitch equipped with load equalizing bars looks odd at first. In addition to the hitch coupler on the trailer's A-frame, two steel bars or rods mounted on hinges are connected at one end to the ball hitch body. The other ends of the rods swing out parallel along the A-frame and are secured either by chains or by a removable bracket. When the trailer's weight is lowered onto the hitch, the bars try to gently bend and transfer weight through the hitch and its receiver onto the tow vehicle's chassis. Although the weight is more evenly distributed, the mechanical friction of all that trailer weight pushing against the rods and their mounting brackets also acts as an anti-sway mechanism by making the trailer work slightly harder to turn abruptly. (With a setup like this, your rig can make a small symphony of groans as the bars try to resist unwanted turns.)

# Weighing Your RV

Finding out the detailed weight of your RV is something you need to do. You shouldn't just look up your trailer, motorhome, or tow vehicle's specs from the manufacturer. In order to get the most useful data, you'll need to make a trip to the truck scales at least twice — once when it's empty, and again when it's fully packed.

Fortunately, truck scales are fairly easy to come by if you live anywhere near an interstate. Larger truck stops are commonly part of the CAT network of professional truck scales and can be easily spotted by their yellow-and-black signs featuring their logo, a silhouette of a cat's head. As of this writing, more than 1,800 CAT scales are spread across 47 states, and they're usually found in the truck stop parking lot behind or beside the building. A single reading usually costs less than $15, and multiple readings are a few dollars more.

Lots of new RV owners can feel intimidated the first few times they pull up to the scale — being the only RV in a lot full of 50 or 60 idling semis can give you an inferiority complex. Don't get freaked out by the experience or feel like you're holding up the pros with your trailer.

TIP

You always want to know the worst-case scenario with your RV weight, so fill your truck's gas tank and your rig's water tank before you go to the scale.

The scale will have three separate platforms. Which wheels go on which platform depends on what type of rig you're weighing and just what information you need to have. Pull forward onto the CAT scale until you get to the intercom box. Then push the call button and tell the attendant what you want to weigh. If at some point you need to disconnect from your trailer for multiple readings, alert the attendant that you'll be a few minutes. They do this all day long so they can talk you through the various steps.

Here's a guide to how to weigh various setups:

>> **Truck or SUV towing a trailer (see Figure 8-2):** When weighing your truck and trailer, both vehicles must be completely on the scale with the front wheels of the truck on platform 1 and the drive, or rear, axle of the truck on platform 2. The trailer's axle should be parked on platform 3.

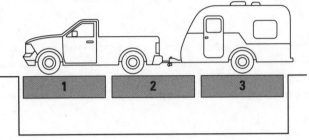

**FIGURE 8-2:**
Weighing a truck or SUV towing a trailer.

© John Wiley & Sons, Inc.

>> **Motorhome or truck camper (see Figure 8-3):** When weighing a motorhome or a pickup truck with a slide-in camper, park the front wheels on platform 1 and the rear wheels on platform 2. Platform 3 should be empty.

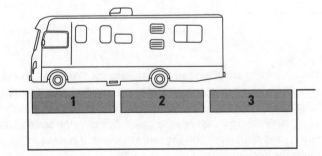

**FIGURE 8-3:**
Weighing a motorhome or truck camper.

© John Wiley & Sons, Inc.

>> **Motorhome towing a car (see Figure 8-4):** When weighing your motorhome and toad, the motorhome must be completely on the scale with the front wheels on platform 1 and the rear wheels of the motorhome on platform 2. The tow car should be on platform 3.

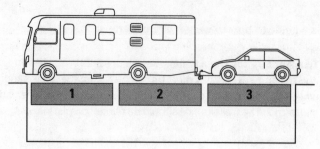

**FIGURE 8-4:**
Weighing a
motorhome
towing a car.

>> **Truck and fifth wheel (see Figure 8-5):** When weighing your truck and fifth-wheel trailer, the whole rig must be completely on the scale, with the front wheels of the truck on platform 1 and its rear wheels on platform 2. Park the trailer's wheels on platform 3.

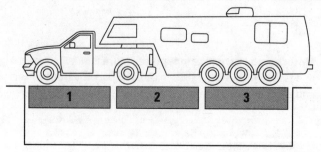

**FIGURE 8-5:**
Weighing a truck
and fifth wheel.

Other useful information can be had using the CAT scale. You can (and should) find out the total weight of a travel trailer when it's empty (curb weight) and when it's fully packed (usually referred to as gross vehicle weight rating [GVWR]). To weigh just the trailer, pull onto the scale so the trailer's wheels and hitch jack fit on the same platform, if possible. Chock the wheels, lower the hitch jack, disconnect your hitch, and make sure your tow vehicle is sitting on a different platform or pulled off the scale completely. You want to weigh the trailer all by itself on one platform.

You can also determine the tongue weight of your trailer (the amount of weight your trailer is heaping onto the hitch on your truck or SUV). That's important to know because the strength of a hitch is rated based on that weight. Pull your trailer's wheels onto Platform 3, but park the hitch jack over Platform 2. Chock the wheels, lower the hitch jack, unhook your tow vehicle, and pull it forward enough that its wheels are off Platform 2 or off the scale completely. Platform 2's measurement will be the tongue weight.

**REMEMBER**

When you're finished, tell the attendant. Don't leave your rig on the scale — pull off so the next truck can use it. Park and go in to pay, and get a printed copy of your various weight readings. CAT also has a phone app that helps to speed up this process, but we prefer talking to the attendant because the app has limitations and can't handle multiple readings.

# 3 Taking Your First Camping Trip

# Chapter 9

# Stocking Up on Accessories: What Your RV Didn't Come With

Your new RV came with a handful of specialized accessories and a small suitcase crammed full of manuals, warranty cards, and information packets. But it probably didn't come with *everything* you're going to need. So, this chapter lets you know what you do and don't really need and what you must have for your first overnight excursion.

We start off with the essentials, and we end with some helpful items to make the life of a road warrior easier or just plain fun. After all, without any toys, what's the point?

# BEFORE HITTING THE RV CAMPING MEGASTORE

You're driving along, and suddenly you spot every new RVer's Valhalla: your first RV camping megastore! You saunter in with the firm conviction that all you really want is a goofy welcome mat, maybe some plastic dinner plates. And maybe a set of novelty salt and pepper shakers shaped like little trailers, and two throw pillows with wacky camping sayings on them. Oh, and a little pine-tree air freshener and a plastic hula girl for the dashboard. Yet, despite the best intentions to control your passions, somehow you manage to walk out with a thousand smackers worth of hoses, cables, adapters, blocks, wedges, rugs, yard art, outdoor furniture, tools you've never seen before in your life, and a handful of little plastic and metal clips, fittings, fiddelyboos and doodads that you've already forgotten what they're for.

It happens to the best of us.

There's an old admonition that says, "Never go grocery shopping when you're hungry." Looking up RV accessories on Amazon or going to the RV camping megastore is kind of like that. Save yourself both cash and grief by driving your rig home from the dealer and fully exploring it before buying things you may already have onboard.

If your RV manufacturer and/or dealer is responsible (or at least charitable), throughout the vehicle's nooks, crannies, cubbies, and closets, you'll probably find at least the following:

- A thick power cable to hook up electricity
- A slinky sewer hose and plastic elbow hookup connector
- Hand cranks that fit the stabilizers, slide mechanisms, and hitch jack
- Perhaps another long crank to manually reel in your awning
- A swollen suitcase stuffed full of manuals, instruction sheets, legal warnings, warranty cards, schematics, and other assorted ephemera

Any or all of these items are not necessarily standard (except the last one), and we're not kidding when we say look *everywhere* — RV builders can manage to conceal the most useful items in the zaniest places. So, look in the corners of closets and under seats and couches (take off the cushions and see if there are trap doors). Peer into the depths of all outdoor "basement" storage compartments. Look under your bed, which may be on hinges so you can flip it up and access the space underneath. (If you bought a used unit, you may really luck out if the seller included more helpful accessories.)

After you've determined what you already have, you can confidently enter that RV camping megastore ready to shop!

# The Bare Necessities

Before you venture out on your shakedown trip or a longer road excursion, you need some basics. This section has you covered.

**TIP**

Don't limit your shopping to Amazon or the giant RV accessory stores like Camping World. Walmart usually has one or two aisles between the automotive and sporting sections dedicated to RV accessories. And always take a slow stroll through the trucker accessory areas in larger truck stops — you never know what handy or clever item you'll come across.

## Wheel chocks

Anything with wheels is designed to roll around. But when your RV is parked, it needs to stay put. If you have a motorhome, you probably figure that all you have to do is pull in, put the gearshift in Park, and start camping. If you have a trailer, maybe you figure that after you uncouple, your hitch jack sitting on the ground is all it takes to keep your rig from developing a case of the creeps. Not so!

The solution is a set of *wheel chocks* (otherwise known as *wheel blocks* or *wedges*). The majority of these are plastic, and they come in a variety of sizes and styles. Most are bright yellow, orange, or red, so you're more likely to see them on the ground when you break camp. Push them snugly up against the front and back of at least one tire on both sides of your rig. Typically, you only need a total of four chocks to keep your rig from rolling off your campsite. (Yes, it happens.)

Some RVers with *tandem* (dual) axles prefer a mechanical, crank-out set of wheel locks. These metal contraptions expand and press against the inside surfaces of two tires. Whatever you use, make sure it's snug against the tires, because you don't want your RV to roll away after you're disconnected. We speak from experience, and no, we don't want to talk about it.

## Leveling blocks

When you go to park your RV and start setting up camp, you'll quickly discover that not every campsite is perfectly flat and level (see Chapter 13). It's important to be level because certain accessories onboard won't work properly if you're leaning to one side. So, invest in a stack or two of plastic *leveling blocks.* Like wheel chocks, leveling blocks are usually made of brightly colored plastic for visibility. The most useful types stack and connect to each other like big, flat LEGO blocks. Most are an inch thick, and a set may come with a carrying bag.

TIP

Some people cut their own leveling blocks out of boards, but we like the plastic sets because they grip securely to each other instead of sliding when they're stacked. Plus, they're handy for several other purposes. Besides leveling, you can use them as pads underneath the stabilizer jacks and hitch jack and even, in a pinch, to help support a sewer hose that's sagging. Manufacturers make different styles in plastic and rubber for all these different purposes, but the simple, multiuse leveling blocks are economical, versatile, and practical.

## Water hoses

We talk all about your water system and hoses in both Chapters 13 and 15, but the first time you go to the RV store, you should walk out with at least the following kinds of hoses:

>> **Drinking water hose:** Drinking water hoses differ from the green plastic garden hoses that are probably piled in a tangled mess in your garage. Usually white or blue in color, drinking water hoses are free from unusual chemicals in the plastic and the fittings. You may see some specifically labeled as "food-grade" hoses.

REMEMBER

Every drop of water that you use inside your rig to cook, wash, or shower with will pass through the drinking water hose first, which means that it needs to stay as sanitary on the inside as possible. The distinctive color of the hose helps you to remember never to use it for anything else.

TIP

A 25-foot-long drinking water hose should be more than long enough to reach most campsite hookups, but we carry two in case we come upon a distant water source — it's easier to deal with two 25-foot hoses than having one 50-foot line all the time.

TIP

If you use an inline water filter cartridge, also have a couple of short hoses, 4 to 6 feet long, to give you flexibility in placing the filter. Campground water spigots can be buried in a little pit or up high on a pipe or even mounted within a pedestal. That's why you need flexibility in setting up.

>> **Utility hose:** At least one standard garden hose should also be onboard for all your water needs besides drinking. You need it for washing the rig or the dog, rinsing off the area around your wastewater dump, hosing down the in-laws to break up a fight, and other general uses. When you're boondocking, you can connect it to a special adapter cap on your wastewater line to drain off and direct graywater away from your campsite.

# Sewer drain hoses and accessories

Your rig may have come with a flexible slinky sewer drain hose from the factory or dealer. But it's generally a good idea to have one or two backup hoses and plastic sewer connector elbows with you. (We talk about draining your wastewater tanks in Chapter 15.)

When you set up your sewer hose at a campsite, you need to have gravity on your side so wastewater runs downhill from your rig to the drain pipe. You want to use the shortest possible hose because excess length snaking around on the ground or sagging in low spots makes it harder to keep that downward slope.

Sewer drains are rarely located on a campsite exactly where you need them. The good news is that 3-inch RV sewer hoses and their twist-lock fittings are universal and connectable. If one hose is too short to reach, add a second one to it. In our rig, we determined that having a 15-foot, 10-foot, and 5-foot hose onboard will handle every connection situation we may encounter. Depending on the length of your rig and the location of its wastewater drain valve, yours may need a much longer reach — we've seen fifth-wheel and motorhome owners carrying as much as 45 feet of drain hose!

Plastic sewer drain hoses come in two general types: super-flexible and a more rigid, accordion style. Both types have their fans. The more flexible ones collapse more easily, which take up less space in storage, while the stiffer accordion-style ones take more abuse and won't crush if you step on them, though they take more room to pack away. Drain hoses come individually or in kits with various connector elbows and adapters. Because the hoses can crack without warning over time (and at the most inopportune moments), you'll find them sold at most onsite campground stores.

**WARNING**

When stowing your hoses, never let your drinking water hose come into contact with your sewer drain hoses and fittings! The last thing you want to do is contaminate your freshwater supply with bacteria from sewage. Store all your sewer drain hoses and connectors in their own plastic tote, or permanently reserve a storage compartment on your rig just for them.

**TIP**

Some larger rigs that have more than one toilet may be equipped with two black-water waste tanks, one under each bathroom. This means two different wastewater drain valves at opposite ends of the vehicle. Instead of connecting them one at a time when you drain them, pick up two more sewer hoses and a sewer line Y adapter (or wye fitting). That will allow you to connect the two drains together and then attach them to a third hose that goes to the campsite dump.

You'll also need the following sewer-related accessories:

- >> **Drain hose support:** You should have an *expandable sewer hose support* (also known as a *sewer hose tree*). This odd-looking, collapsible contraption comes in several lengths, from 10 to 30 feet, and can be plastic or aluminum. It's used to hold up your sewer drain hose and keep a downward angle from your drain valve to the dump connection.

- >> **Blackwater tank flush hose:** If your RV has a blackwater tank flush inlet (see Chapter 15), you may consider a dedicated garden hose in a completely different outlandish color to be used only for flushing out your sewer tanks. Like your sewer drain hose, store it in its own separate bin or vinyl bag to prevent any possibility of contamination of your drinking water hoses. Keep it in the same tote or cabinet with all your sewer drain accessories.

- >> **Blackwater tank deodorizing treatment:** You need a package of RV toilet/ blackwater tank enzyme or deodorant chemicals. The handiest come in small water-soluble packets (sort of like laundry detergent pods), but others are solid tablets or bottles of liquid chemicals.

## Electrical cables and accessories

In this section, we fill you in on the electrical cables and accessories you need.

TIP

The manufacturer, dealer, or previous owner of your RV should have provided a main power cable with your RV. In most cases, you shouldn't need to buy a longer or shorter one because most campgrounds try to put their power pedestals in the center of the campsite.

### Shore power cables and extensions

A long power cable is one of the heaviest and most ungainly items you'll have to wrestle with in your rig on a regular basis. Especially on a 240-volt/50-amp rig, a heavy duty, 50-foot power cable can weigh upwards of 45 pounds. But if you routinely find that your factory-supplied main power cable is much too long for your normal use, consider a shorter (and lighter) replacement, and an extension cable, like a home extension cord, to drag out only when needed.

TECHNICAL
STUFF

If you have a fifth wheel or motorhome, your power cable may be permanently mounted on a retractable reel in one of the basement storage cabinets. That makes it easy to deploy and roll up again without tangling. These cables are usually hard-wired to your rig and not easily detachable.

Your main power cable will have straight brass prongs on the male end and a twist-lock connector on the female end (which is the end that hooks into your rig). The female end may also have a plastic, screw-on ring that helps keep the cable from accidentally coming unplugged. But a 30- or 50-amp extension cable won't have that twist-lock feature, locking ring, or even the same connector. It'll merely have a female end that mates with the straight prong male plug.

## Household extension cords

You should have a couple of heavy-duty household three-prong extension cords onboard for those unforeseen circumstances when you want to plug in outdoor lights or appliances. Most rigs come with at least one external 120-volt electrical outlet because campers often need to have household current handy outside. But if yours doesn't have one, bring at least one extension cord long enough to conveniently reach from the *shore side* (the driver's side, where your utility hookups are located) power pedestal to the other side, where you'll be sitting or working. If you think you'll need more than one or two outlets, throw in a cheap power strip, too.

Indoor outlets are never where you really need them to be. For use inside, grab a couple of 6-foot household extension cords, too.

## Surge protector/power analyzer

You probably have surge protectors on various electronics in your house to keep expensive devices from getting zapped by lightning strikes or power spikes. Heavy-duty, whole-house surge protectors do exist, but they aren't very common. The RV world is another matter.

Like your computer, TV, or music system at home, your RV itself is one massive electrical device that plugs into a big electrical socket. After decades of staying at hundreds of campgrounds, we can honestly say that we've encountered calamitous electrical problems once in a blue moon. But they can and do happen, often enough that you should protect yourself and your rig.

Damage to wiring, switches, receptacles, and electrical boxes may be visible on a campsite power pedestal, but usually it isn't. A previous camper may have whacked the pedestal with the back end of their RV and uprooted it. There may be a short circuit, or the receptacle may have been hastily installed with some of its wires crossed one night in the dark by a tired, overworked campground manager. Or a buried cable may have been gouged when the campground's backhoe dug up a dead tree. And if your rig gets zapped by a major electrical problem, it can cause a chain reaction to all the electronic devices you've plugged into it inside.

TIP

Later in this chapter, we suggest that you include a handheld voltage meter as part of your basic tool kit. But an informative surge protector/power analyzer can tell you lots more information in a single glance than a volt meter can. (We talk more about diagnosing electrical problems in Chapter 14.)

The most common RV surge protectors are portable ones (see Figure 9-1). You plug a portable surge protector into the 30- or 50-amp receptacle on the power pedestal, and then you plug your RV's power cable into the protector itself. In other words, it's between the incoming electricity and your rig so it can detect and stop a problem before it gets inside your vehicle.

FIGURE 9-1:
Portable RV surge
protectors.

*Photograph courtesy of Christopher Hodapp*

WARNING

Make sure you buy one that fits your rig's power requirement: 30-amp and 50-amp surge protectors are *not* interchangeable.

Permanent surge protectors can be wired inside your rig, but the portable ones are simple, are visible outside where you want to see them, and can be easily moved. If you trade up next year to a different RV, as long as it matches the power requirements of your new unit (30- or 50-amp), you can take a portable surge protector with you.

RV surge protectors can be simple or complex, depending on how much you want to spend. The most useful ones don't just shut off the electricity when they detect a problem. Some have nothing but a couple of LED lights that show whether they're working properly. Some have a series of indicators that give you more detailed information (the wrong voltage, an improperly wired outlet, a missing ground connection, flipped polarity, and so on). Others have a numerical meter that displays different codes depending on the problem detected. A few connect via Bluetooth to send a message to your smartphone and keep you informed as to its status.

TIP

Just make sure any portable unit you buy says it's weatherproof and has some sort of warranty. That doesn't mean you can submerge it under water, but it does mean it won't hurt if it gets rained or snowed on.

These units can be expensive, and they come in a wide range of models and prices, depending on how many features you want. They can be as cheap as $99 or cost several hundred dollars for the best ones.

WARNING

Because these units can work on most RVs without any modifications, in a dark and crowded campground, an expensive surge protector can be stolen. Most are made so you can close the cover on the power pedestal box, which helps prevent the plug from getting yanked out easily. If you're worried about theft, carry a cheap padlock or cable lock to either lock the power box cover down or wrap through the protector's handle and around the pedestal pole. In fact, a couple of surge protector manufacturers make locks specifically to secure their units from thieves. Or you can have a permanent protector installed in your RV if you're that nervous about it. After all our time on the road, we've never had one ripped off, but it can happen.

## Gozintas, gozontas, and dog bones

The origin of the words are obscured by the mists of time, but Jethro Bodine of the 1960s TV show *The Beverly Hillbillies* first coined the engineering term *gozinta* (as in "this *goes into* that") to describe an adapter that lets a wrong-shaped thing go into a different shaped thing. If you've ever had to plug a three-prong computer power cord into a two-prong outlet without angrily prying off the third prong with a pair of pliers, you hopefully bought a two-prong gozinta. A variation is, of course, the *gozonta* (as in "goes on to").

Let's say your rig is a big 36-foot fifth-wheel with every available option and two big air conditioners up on the roof that require a 240-volt/50-amp power hookup. You pull into your campsite at the state park. You drag out your power cable to plug in. But, alas, the power pedestal only has 30-amp service. Your 50-amp plug won't fit. Vacation over? Not if you have your trusty dog bone, the most useful gozinta in your arsenal.

A *dog bone* (or *pigtail*) is a short cable with big fat plugs on either end, and it's called that by campers because of its dog-bone-like shape (think of a Golden Retriever holding a long gym sock with knots on both ends in their mouth). Dog bones come in a wide range of variations (see Figure 9-2), all designed to let you plug your rig's power cable into a different style power outlet.

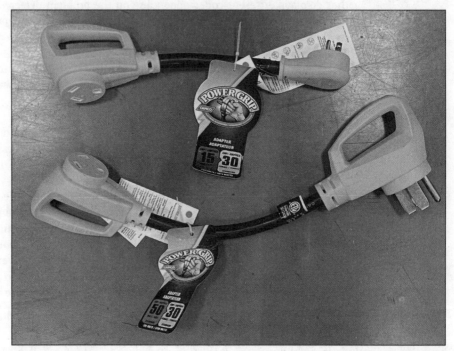

Photograph courtesy of Christopher Hodapp

**FIGURE 9-2:**
Some of the most common dog-bone adapters let you plug your 30- or 50-amp rig into a different type of outlet.

TIP

The first dog bone you'll probably want to own will let you connect your 30- or 50-amp rig to your household wall outlet while it's sitting in your driveway. You need one that has a 15-amp male plug on one end and a 30- or 50-amp female plug on the other end. (Alternatively, there are smaller one-piece plastic 15- to 30-amp adapter plugs that do the same thing.) In addition, if you have a 30-amp RV, buy a dog bone that lets you plug into a 50-amp receptacle. If you have a 50-amp unit, get one that lets you use a 30-amp connection.

WARNING

Electricity and power systems are never any stronger or more powerful than their weakest links. Plugging your 30- or 50- amp RV into a 15- or 20-amp household receptacle using a dog bone or adapter plug will not magically give you any more than 15 or 20 amps of power. It only lets one kind of plug fit into a different kind of outlet. You can use a dog bone at home to charge your rig's batteries; run the lights, TV, and stereo; and maybe turn on the vent fans. But try to flip on the air conditioner, and your home circuit breaker will shut you down for tempting fate. (We talk more about power requirements in Chapter 14.)

TIP

You may need one other gozinta if you have an older tow vehicle or trailer. Most current RVs and tow vehicles plug into each other using a round, seven-pin (or seven-blade) connector to power a trailer's or toad's running lights, turn signals, trailer brakes, and brake lights. But older vehicles may have a similar-looking six-way (or six-pin) connector that lacks a circuit for reverse lights when you back up. If your towable and your truck or motorhome have mismatched multipin connectors, there are gozinta cables and plugs that let you adapt between the two and connect them together.

## Basic tools

If you're the handy-homeowner type of person or a dedicated shade-tree mechanic, you may have a garage full of gleaming, rolling tool cases like the Penske racing team has in their garage, packed full of every kind of wrench, screwdriver, hammer, pliers, socket, saw blade, and power tool on Earth. But on the road, packing up every possible tool is impractical. There are tools you absolutely shouldn't do without, and then there are the ones you'll use once every five years that you could either buy on the road when you need it or borrow from another camper if you're in a jam.

TIP

We prefer using a single medium-size tool box as our RV tool kit because it helps fight the urge to bring too much, "just in case." Keep your RV tool kit separate from your home tools and stored onboard your rig at all times so you won't be tempted to raid it for a job around the house.

At the very least, you should have the following in either your rig or tow vehicle:

>> **At least two pairs of work gloves:** This way, you can lose at least one pair.

>> **A combined SAE/metric socket wrench ratchet set.** (See the sidebar below.)

>> **A multi-bit screwdriver:** The simplest multi-bit screwdriver has an easily reversed shank with a flat head and a Phillips head on either end; more complex ones have several different types of heads stored in the handle.

>> **Leatherman-style multi-tool:** Various versions have between 8 and 21 different tools in one handy package, including needle-nose pliers, screwdrivers, knife blades, can and bottle openers, saws, scissors, and more. It's hard to beat a multi-tool when you're trying to accomplish a small repair job quickly. We keep one in our trailer and one in our truck.

# SAE VERSUS METRIC?

SAE tools are named for the Society of Automotive Engineers, the original organization that standardized old English (or imperial) measurements of feet, inches, and fractions for tools, nuts, and bolts in the auto industry.

By contrast, the metric system was originally developed in France and uses decimal points and measurements divided into tenths. Metric tools are marked in millimeters, and the tools from one standard don't exactly fit the fasteners of the other (*close*, but not quite).

Imperial measurements were adopted as the official weights and measures in the United States before and after the American Revolution. We got them from England. Even Thomas Jefferson, lover of all things French, couldn't bring himself to convert the new United States over to the metric system when he became president, saying it was "too French" even for his taste.

In the early 1910s, when the U.S. auto industry began to take off, scores of American car companies and mechanical engineers began to realize that some standardization of part and tool sizes and terminology was needed to avoid total chaos any time you needed to have the spark plugs changed or a headlight replaced. The SAE was officially formed around the time of World War I, and it fought for uniform measurement standards and terminology in the auto, boating, tractor, and aircraft industries. (In addition to tool and part sizes and measurements, it also defined the term *horsepower* as a method of uniformly stating the pulling power of an engine.)

Until the 1970s, average Americans didn't need or have metric tools for working on their autos since the bulk of trucks and cars in the country were made in the United States. Unless you owned or worked on an imported car, there was no reason to have them. But the rest of the industrial world went with metric standards, which make a whole lot more logical sense. (Who the heck remembers anything about fractions after the ninth grade?)

Beginning in the '70s, more imported cars began to enter the American market than ever before — Datsun (now Nissan), Mazda, Toyota, and Volkswagen began opening their own American auto manufacturing plants using metric standards. And U.S. car companies also began to use metric parts made in other countries. Great Britain, where the imperial measurements of inches and fractions originated, gave up its old ways and went metric in the '70s to gain access to global trade markets, leaving the United States as the lone developed industrialized nation clinging to the old standards.

In 1975, Congress adopted the Metric Conversion Act and established a commission to compel Americans to ditch inches and fractions from hardware and containers and accept metrics in their daily lives. But almost immediately, the argument became a point of national pride ("We didn't need metric tools to get to the Moon, you know!"). The law and its commission were pretty much ridiculed by the public — note that even though our wine bottles may be marked in milliliters today, our milk still comes in quarts and gallons.

Fifty years later, both SAE parts and metric parts can still be found in new U.S.-made cars and trucks. It turned out it was easier and cheaper for everybody to just buy a second set of wrenches and sockets instead of completely retooling the American industrial market.

» **Hammer:** Because you never know when something will need a damn good whacking.

» **Channellock pliers:** The jaws on these pliers are extremely adjustable and can help you turn large nuts and bolts, wide plumbing connections, stiff valve handles, and lots more.

» **Needle-nose pliers.**

» **Lineman pliers:** These are heavy-duty, straight-nose pliers with strong wire-cutting blades.

» **Vice grips:** Have at least one set of these locking pliers onboard.

» **A set of precision/jeweler's screwdrivers:** These fit tiny adjustment set screws and screws found on many electronics. (They'll tighten the frames of your eyeglasses and sunglasses, too!) Try to get a set with both flat and Phillips heads.

» **A set of SAE/metric hex wrenches:** Hex wrenches are those L-shaped little wrenches IKEA gives you to build furniture with. Hex screws show up in the darndest places.

» **An adjustable crescent wrench:** It's a good idea to have a medium-size crescent wrench for tightening and loosening plumbing, gas, and hydraulic fittings; battery terminal connectors; and more.

» **Wire stripper/crimping tool:** You never know when you will have to do a quick electrical repair.

» **Razor/utility knife and blades:** The disposable plastic ones are convenient but not as strong as the old-fashioned metal-handled type.

>> **Plastic 8-inch torpedo bubble level:** For checking the level of your rig when setting up. Some come with a magnet, but you don't need an expensive one — they're extremely easy to lose at a campsite, especially in the dark, so we always carry a couple of them.

>> **Electrical multi-meter (volt meter):** For testing campsite power pedestal voltage, indoor voltage, RV batteries, fuses, faulty electrical connections, and more. It doesn't need to be expensive.

>> **Tire pressure gauge:** Some of the most common RV accidents are caused by tire problems. Many motorhomes come equipped with built-in tire pressure monitors, and there are also third-party monitoring kits you can add to any vehicle. But the cheapest solution is using a $10 mechanical pressure gauge and checking your tires regularly and faithfully. If you have a Class A motorhome, make sure your tire gauge can read up to 150 psi — gauges made for car, bike, and motorcycle tires usually don't go higher than 100 psi.

>> **Inexpensive LED flashlights:** Put them around the inside of your RV, in glove compartments or the center console of your tow vehicle, and everywhere else they may come in handy. We bought a box of a dozen for $20. What they lack in brightness they make up for in convenience. It's a good idea to have a well-made, hands-free work light, but any flashlight is a godsend when you need it, so the more the better.

# Expendables

We used to be in the film business, where stuff like tape, lubricants, and other "throwaway" supplies were called *expendables*. It's a good idea to have the following handy:

>> **3M Command hooks and accessories:** Nearly everything you can think of can be stuck to the walls of your RV with this incredible line of self-adhesive hooks, tapes, brackets, and accessories. Make a mistake, and they can be easily removed without leaving marks or glue goo on the wall. Every RVer should have lots on hand.

>> **QuakeHold! museum putty:** This stuff is heaven-sent in an RV. Any sort of dish, tray, lamp, vase, or accessory (even heavy-duty stuff) can be temporarily held in place on a countertop with a wad of this reusable putty. For example, we use it to hold our toaster oven in place on the kitchen cabinet. An essential.

>> **A small kit of spare mini auto fuses:** Because you never know when you might blow an onboard fuse.

- **»** **Black and yellow rolls of electrical tape:** Black is for most electrical repairs. Electricians use yellow for high-voltage wiring, but we also use it as high-visibility marking when needed. For instance, stick a piece on the nose of your trailer's hitch coupler to make it easier to see on a backup camera.

- **»** **Duct tape:** Like the Force in *Star Wars,* it has a light side and a dark side, and it binds the universe together.

- **»** **A roll of Velcro.**

- **»** **White and yellow Teflon pipe thread tape:** White for water, yellow for propane connections.

- **»** **Flex Tape:** Products from the Flex Seal brand are a true miracle of modern science. Flex Tape can instantly seal a crack on almost any surface, is super-adhesive, and comes in white, black, and clear.

- **»** **A tube of clear silicone caulk/sealant.**

- **»** **WD-40 spray lubricant:** Because the front door of your rig will start squeaking sooner or later.

- **»** **A silicone lubricant spray:** For keeping window gaskets and door weather seals flexible.

- **»** **Assorted zip ties:** You'll have a bazillion uses for these.

- **»** **A box of disposable latex or nitrile gloves:** For jobs involving your toilet and blackwater tank. Also great for smearing fresh grease on your hitch mechanisms and stabilizer parts.

Not everybody will need or want these items, especially if you're just a weekend camper. But if you're going to spend any length of time on the road, consider making room for these:

- **»** **A cordless drill:** If your rig has manually cranked stabilizers instead of powered ones, an 18-volt cordless drill with a ¾-inch socket on it can raise or lower you scissor jacks in a matter of seconds. Having one with you is worthwhile just for that.

  Get the kind that has variable speed and torque adjustment. A high-speed one can bend, warp, or overtighten a fitting in seconds before you even realize it.

- **»** **Box-end wrenches:** Depending on your rig, you may or may not have a hand crank to manually retract a stuck slide. Some require the use of a ⅝- or ¾-inch wrench, so it's worthwhile to buy a set of long, "jumbo" box wrenches that can fit your hitch ball, wheel lug nuts, and the slide's driveshaft. Jumbo wrenches

**TIP**

are tougher to store, but they'll give you better leverage when trying to turn a big, stubborn bolt, which can be especially helpful when you're crawled up under your motorhome cussing at the jerk who engineered this mess. You may never have to use them. But if you suddenly do need them, they're not always easy to borrow from a neighbor. So, stow them in an out-of-the-way place.

# Fun Extras

Now that you know the basic stuff you need to have onboard, the sky's the limit on everything else you find in the RV toy store. The desirability of many accessories relates to your own tastes and the level of amenities in your RV. For example, if you're a coffee hound, and you're camping in a tiny teardrop, a French-press coffee maker would be a great gadget, allowing you to make brewed coffee without a microwave or a coffee maker.

An added bonus to RVing is that the Great Outdoors can be your porch, living room, dining room, and front yard. And loads of RVers love decorating the outside as much as the inside (see Figure 9-3).

**FIGURE 9-3:**
Some RVers go hog wild with their outside campsite decor.

*TerryKelly/Getty Images*

With this individuality in mind, here's a brief idea list of some items you may want to consider.

>> **Lawn chairs:** Spend some time deciding on these because you may be spending lots of time sitting in your lawn chairs, day and night.

>> **A collapsible outdoor work table.**

>> **A portable propane grill.**

>> **Outdoor lighting:** LEDs and plastic-covered bulbs are far less fragile than glass ones. If you intend on clipping lights to your awning edge, don't forget to pick up clips. A less expensive alternative is a packet of name-badge clips from an office-supply store.

>> **Campsite all-weather rugs:** Really useful in sandy or potentially muddy areas.

**WARNING**

Be aware that some campgrounds forbid these rugs because they can kill the grass underneath over time.

>> **A tabletop ice maker:** For margarita lovers. Much cheaper than having one installed in an RV freezer.

>> **Collapsible buckets.**

>> **An Instant Pot:** An Instant Pot is a great way to cook on the road. Check out *Instant Pot Cookbook For Dummies* by Wendy Jo Peterson and Elizabeth Shaw (Wiley) for loads of recipes. (One of the authors is an RVer herself.)

>> **Battery-powered stick-up puck lights for unlit closets and more.**

>> **An electric space heater:** For those times when you want to save propane and only want to warm up a small area like your bedroom. (See Chapter 17 for more about space heaters.)

# Chapter **10**

# Packing for the Road

I n Chapter 9, we cover the things you should have with you for the RV itself, the levelers and tools and adapters. Now it's time to pack everything else, all the stuff for you!

Standing in your RV for the first time, beginning to decide what to take and where to put it, is a memorable moment. A lot depends on the length of your stay in the RV and the sort of trip you'll be taking. Will it be a weekend getaway or a cross-country months-long adventure? The systems you're accustomed to in your house or apartment can't really be used in this new environment. Your RV requires a new way of thinking.

When space is extremely limited, clever organization is an absolute necessity. Clutter is a major enemy to you in an RV, whether you're by nature a slob or not. Neither a Felix Unger nor an Oscar Madison can cope with clutter in an RV, and you'll start losing your things pretty quickly as you paw through closet bottoms and high shelves crammed with crap. There are some simple ways to avoid this problem, even if you're not a neat freak by nature. In this chapter, we've got you covered.

# Following Some Basic Packing Tips

Organization guru Marie Kondo is hardly the first person to suggest that purging your life of junk will make you feel freer and happier. RVing is remarkable for the fact that it's a chance to start all over again with a clean slate. So, don't drag the junk weighing down your life along with you when you hit the road.

Old dogs can learn new tricks, and there's nothing like an RV for teaching you. An astonishing number of organizational tricks that we picked up RVing have seeped into our sticks-'n'-bricks home, making life better there.

**TIP**

So, what do you take and how do you make room for it? Packing is easy to divide into kitchen, bathroom, and bedroom, but first, a couple general tips:

>> **When you're packing your RV for the first time, think about probability.** In other words, try to stow the things you'll access nearly every day in the prime storage that's easy to get to, and put those dress shoes you *might* need if you meet those friends for dinner in Phoenix somewhere less accessible, like the storage cubbies you'll usually find under an RV bed.

>> **Use *all* your storage space, without any waste.** Often that means up-and-down space, perhaps a high shelf. You need to come up with systems to store all your belongings and to find them when you need them.

>> **Rely on plastic tote boxes.** When you keep a home and regularly go RVing, it can be a bit of a wrench trying to think of every little thing you may need, every time you go. And when your rig is in storage, there are all sorts of things you don't want to leave inside of it. We've found it effective to keep several plastic tote boxes packed all the time, stowed together and out of sight at home, so they're out from underfoot. The things in the boxes have been road-tested. They're the things we know we'll want or need, from Worcestershire sauce to instant cocoa, and even if we use them at home, too, we don't raid the containers for our house. Then, when it's time to pack up, we just grab the containers and haul them out to the RV, so we know we've got the essential items, without thinking too much about it. Getting ready for a cross-country trip is busy enough.

>> **Don't try to buy in bulk.** Bulk buying doesn't work when you're RVing, and neither do huge, economy-size bottles, so Sam's Club and Costco giant-size supplies aren't really ideal. There's just nowhere to store them. Unfortunately, they're so popular that it can be tough to find the smallest size of things, from laundry detergent to ketchup. Camp stores often stock them, as do convenience stores (where they're overpriced). You can refill the small bottles from your large size at home, but be aware that, particularly with constant vibration and temperature changes, these won't last forever. Items like bleach can seep from old containers.

>> **Don't forget your important paperwork.** It's not the fun kind of packing, but your paperwork should always be with you. Keep copies at home whenever possible. We keep the registration for our trailer in our glove compartment, alongside the tow vehicle registration and the proof of the poodle's vaccinations. But we also have a small strongbox in the SUV, like truckers use for paperwork — they're available at most truck stops. It's the perfect place to keep a copy of the service contract, as well as maintenance records and receipts. Sitting on the shoulder of the busy highway when your electrical system has failed isn't the time to wonder if you're covered for it. It's a time for seeking your zen moment of calm control, knowing all will be well. You've got this handled.

# Packing a First-Aid Kit

All the RV websites tell you to pack a first-aid kit. Store-bought first-aid kits have a reputation for being old finger bandages and dried out alcohol swabs, crammed in a little box with a red cross on it that gathers dust over the years because you never touch it. We decided to put together our own kit, and it has worked well. We bought a medium-size clear plastic container made for food storage, so it has an anti-moisture seal and it's sturdy, with a convenient handle.

To aid you in putting yours together, here are the items we stow in it. We've used nearly all of these items at one time or another:

>> **Thermometer:** You never know when you'll need it. And pack an extra battery, along with the instructions that came with it, unless it's the one you use at home and you're familiar with it.

>> **Sunscreen:** Also bring burn gel with aloe vera and lidocaine in case you forget to put on the sunscreen.

>> **Alcohol:** Not the kind you drink around the campfire, but the kind you use to clean wounds. Also bring ointment for cuts or scrapes, like Neosporin.

>> **Skin moisturizer:** You may find that the air is drier in your RV than it is at home, and patchy dry skin can be annoying. Ditto for talc.

>> **Imodium:** For the most common ailment of the world traveler.

>> **Benadryl:** A great over-the-counter medication for colds and sinus problems you may have in a climate that's very different from what you're used to. But that's not all Benadryl is good for. If you're suddenly afflicted with an allergic skin reaction to some odd plant life, try two Benadryl. Ditto in case of a bee, wasp, or other insect sting or bite — it almost immediately reduces the

swelling and itching. Benadryl has even worked for our dogs after they stuck their muzzles into some angry bug's business (just be sure to check with a vet about how much to use based on your dog's weight).

>> **Zicam:** Zinc will help to both prevent and minimize an oncoming cold or flu infection that can wreck a trip. In our experience, colds are shorter and far less miserable when we start taking zinc at the onset of symptoms. Doctors think it works by preventing viruses from replicating. It's something of a miracle cure, and you should have some on hand.

>> **Bandages, gauze, and tape:** Something else that's handy is a bottle of New-Skin or LiquidSkin, for keeping annoying small cuts clean and letting you get your hands wet. It comes off easily with a bit of alcohol, or just peel it off.

While we're on the subject, take time to go over all your prescription medications — the older you are, the more likely it is you're on more than one. Have the original bottles with you, and always tuck a list of them away with your onboard important documents. Be aware that, in the age in which we live, tons of medications are considered extremely stealable. If something happens to your meds on the road, you'll be dealing with increasingly numerous, confusing, and draconian prescription drug laws that vary from state to state. For something like your blood pressure medication, you may be able to arrange for your family doctor to send another prescription to a local pharmacy. If it was a pain medication or any other controlled substance, you're probably out of luck. Keep your meds in a secure place.

# Finding Fun Storage Hacks

Camping stores are fun, but if you've never been RVing before, make some trips to IKEA, The Container Store, Michaels, Jo-Ann, Dollar Tree, and anyplace with storage boxes and home/kitchen stuff. These things, as a rule, aren't very expensive. All these stores feature most or all of the following handy items.

## Plastic storage totes

Covered storage tubs and collapsible plastic crates make the RV world a simpler, saner place. If your rig is blessed with several basement storage compartments, prepare to rejoice. Storage tubs are unsurpassed for storing and organizing all your cables and hoses, and for keeping bulky items together or apart. They also protect the items inside, in case your storage area isn't perfectly weatherproof.

Some of the items to store in tubs include the following:

>> **Leveling blocks and wheel chocks.**

>> **Freshwater hoses, filters, and faucet connectors.**

>> **Sewer hoses and connectors:** If you've got a dedicated blackwater tank washout hose, put it in the tub with this stuff. (Don't forget — never let freshwater hoses and sewage-tainted ones come into contact with each other. Give them their own separate homes.)

>> **Electrical cables.**

>> **Surge protector and dog-bone/gozinta plug adapters.** Maybe toss in the TV cable as well.

>> **Grilling tools and supplies:** Include fire starters; small, disposable propane canisters; a long-nose lighter; and propane extension hoses and adapters to connect your gas grill to the RV's propane supply.

>> **Campsite décor:** Awning lights and your favorite yard art can be stowed in here.

Push deep into the compartment anything you don't have to access often. Label the tubs on the tops and sides, and stack more commonly used stuff on top of them.

## Hooks and Command strips

You'll probably become a hook junkie and an absolute evangelist for stuff that hangs from 3M's line of Command strips. Their removable wall hooks and shelves hold a surprising amount of weight, and they go up *anywhere*. Most RVers have wall hooks right by the door, for flashlights and caps and keys, and Command hooks are perfect for this.

You can buy small plastic storage containers and mount them on the wall with Command strips, too. They work well for tools like spatulas and barbeque tongs that won't fit in tiny RV kitchen drawers. TV and stereo remotes were driving us nuts, until we hung a couple of Command open caddies, one in the living area and one by the bed, where we now tuck up all remotes for that area.

If you're into magnets and you have an expanse of steel in your rig that they'll stick to, have a look at the Perch magnetic wall system. (We Airstreamers are out of luck because aluminum won't take magnets. So we just attach with Command strips over the magnets.) If you're willing to start drilling holes in the wall, IKEA features several storage systems with a mounted rail and various hooks and containers that hang from it, which is handy in a kitchen or bathroom.

## Shelf and drawer caddies

Buy a ton of these things — you're going to need them. These caddies are designed as drawer organizers for everything from pencils to silverware, so you'll find them in office and kitchen departments of places like The Container Store and IKEA. We've even found them tucked into larger plastic storage boxes for arts-and-crafts projects. Amazingly, they don't have to be particularly tall — an inch or two will act as a stabilizer, keeping your stuff from flying all over the place.

We make it a rule not to store any bottles of liquid in a cabinet or on a shelf unless it's in a plastic caddy or tray, as shown in Figure 10-1. Everything from alcohol to dishwashing detergent gets bounced around when you drive, and caps, lids, and squeeze tops easily open up if a bottle falls over. We've had two small bleach bottles in a row that ruptured along the bottom seams and began leaking. (It helps to mark the date on all bottles with a Sharpie, and keep an eye out for blisters in the plastic.) A caddy or tray underneath your bottles will help contain leakage disasters.

**FIGURE 10-1:**
Tray caddies will stabilize your bottles.

*Photograph courtesy of Christopher Hodapp*

# Tension bars

You'll see them in camp stores, most from a company called Camco, and wonder what they are. Just buy a couple, and have them on hand. They're essentially spring-loaded sticks you can quickly screw and unscrew to tighten or loosen, and you can use them to brace just about anything, like soft drinks in the fridge. You can block a cabinet closed, like a sliding door that's slipping open on the road. With their rubber ends, they can also give you extra reach to get to fan switches over your head. We even use one to prevent the Poodle from knocking her squeaker balls under an opening in the kitchen cabinets. Useful and versatile.

# Stackable cabinet organizers

These organizers are wire platforms with long legs, so another layer can be stored underneath and easily seen. They come in many styles and sizes, and they're perfect for RV cabinets where wasted pantry space is often up-and-down rather than side-to-side. Look for adjustable-length wire shelves and vertical plate and cookware racks.

Containers designed for offices can go on the wall for utensils that are too big for tiny RV kitchen drawers (see Figure 10-2).

**FIGURE 10-2:** Wall space can turn to storage space for larger items.

*Photograph courtesy of Christopher Hodapp*

We've seen tortuous methods for storing plastic grocery bags, but the easiest is a simple canvas tube bag on a doorknob or C-clip. It's great for travel with a dog — before a walk, pop out a bag, like a Kleenex, and pocket it for possible cleanups.

**TIP**

This one will save you lots of grief and money: Get a tiny notebook, one that's a keeper with decent binding, and take some time in your new RV to get measurements, including the width, height, and depth of all cabinets, drawers, and closets. Then, when you're standing in The Container Store, you won't have to wonder if that cute wire basket will fit under the sink. This tactic has come in so handy that we've added our home measurements and we keep the notebook in the glove compartment. When you're spelunking through an antique store in Montana and stumble on a treasure, it helps to know if it's too big for the credenza in the hall.

# Packing Your Tuxedo

Internet pundits like to chide RVers for overpacking, telling you to toss out half the clothes you've packed — you won't wear them. This advice is good, but the truth is, some trips are harder than others. In our 30-foot rig, we generally have room to spare, even on a weeks-long trip. But our two-month, cross-country Christmas with the family is tough. We're packing warm clothes for the Midwest and lightweight ones for California. Our family *loves* to eat out in nicer places, so pile in some nicer clothes. Chris will probably have at least one Masonic speaking engagement, so he has to pack a suit, if not a tuxedo! And don't forget all the Christmas presents. You see the picture that's forming, bulging at the seams.

At the start, packing for an RV trip may seem easier than packing a suitcase. If your rig is fairly large, you may be thinking, "This is great! Never had this much room when I was flying!" But you'll be amazed how quickly it evaporates.

REMEMBER

Be stingy packing clothes, but always take one outfit for the opposite weather of the sort you're expecting. This is especially true for RVers, because you're not flying over the country, you're driving through it and experiencing it. Midwesterners can forget that any rise in elevation will drop the temperature, while the desert can get cold at night; in winter months, the temps can drop 40 or 50 degrees after the sun goes down. Fleece is great for this, lightweight and warm, good for layering. Also, for heavier-duty cold, several companies make packable puffer jackets that are tiny and lightweight when folded into their pouch.

Look for new ways to pack and store your clothes, too. Even in the most ginormous Class A or fifth wheel, closet space is at a minimum, as are drawers. Our 30-foot trailer has no drawers at all, apart from one in the kitchen, which isn't *that* unusual.

Shoe storage is always a problem, and solutions range wide, depending on your type of RV. A popular one is a length of canvas shoe bag mounted along the side of the base of the bed, though in some RVs, the bed structure won't accommodate it. Shoe packing bags can be helpful, too — they keep each pair together, rather than piled loose in the bottom of a tiny, dark closet. You can color-code them, which gives you a fighting chance of finding what you're after. And the bags can be hung on hooks.

Of course, minimalism is the key, and the less junk you take, the better. Don't pack three jackets when one will do, no matter how cute they are. For a potential night out, take one nice jacket and some simple black pants. No one in Albuquerque will notice that you wore the same thing in Flagstaff.

REMEMBER

You can always wash your clothes and wear them again, even if you don't feel like a big laundry day. Orvis, L.L.Bean, REI, Back Country, Cabela/Bass Pro Shops, and others sell lightweight camping and hiking pants that can be washed out in a sink and will hang dry quickly.

Shoot for a care-free RV lifestyle, where less belongings equals a better trip. But when fate hands you something tougher, do your best to cling to basic storage and organization principles. And take a deep cleansing breath.

TIP

At the end of your first trip, take stock of what you never wore, and don't drag those items along a second time.

## CUBIST ART

Zippered packing cubes, invented to keep the inside of a suitcase organized, are terrific for RVs. Most have a carrying handle for hauling back and forth, and the bags can take advantage of vertical or confused space. They also save you a lot of effort when you're doing the laundry. When packing at home, we color-code, each having their own color, and with different-size bags for socks, underwear, T-shirts, sweaters, and so on. The charm of this system is that, when you return with clothes that were never used, you can just unpack them from the bag, still neat and clean, and pop them back in your dresser or closet.

A good addition is oversize Ziploc-style bags. They're not always available in the grocery, but you can find them at Target or Walmart, as well as on Amazon. The Hefty 2.5-gallon jumbo bags are ideal for sweaters and such, and they last for many uses. Plus, they're cheaper than heavy-duty vacuum storage bags. Pack the extra clothes, burp the air out, and things stay clean and accessible, while the clear bags enable you to see what you're after. Label them with a Sharpie.

# Kitchen Aid: Packing Food and Utensils

There's tons of online advice out there about assembling your RV kitchen, but you may not feel it all to be helpful. Kitchen advice can be very personal, based on your rig, your needs, and your preferences.

Some RVers in big rigs are setting up full kitchens for families, and others want nothing more than a campfire and a cast-iron frying pan. Some people love to cook in any and all situations, and for them, RVing just represents new toys and new outdoorsy recipes. For others, cooking is one of the dreary jobs they're camping to get away from. Either way, you're going to have some new kitchen challenges, and changes will seep into the way you do things. You may drag along several heavy electric kitchen appliances and find they're only in the way. RVing tends to bring back grandma's tools — hand-crank mixers, non-electric can openers, and so on. They're handy and lightweight, and they stay off of your limited counter space.

A major aid to RVers is all the new-style collapsible kitchen stuff. Our bucket, spaghetti strainer, dish tub, and hand-wash tub are all made of accordion-style silicone that makes finding a place to store them so much easier.

We tried bringing our own pots and pans from home, but there was just so little room for them. The solution was a set of nesting pots, with detachable handles. The most popular sets are from Magma, and ours have performed well. One little 10-inch area now holds three pots, a frying pan, and a Dutch oven and lids, all stacked inside of each other. Our cast-iron Lodge skillet is still under the bed, though, just in case.

In the following sections, we help you plan to grill out and cover issues of food safety and storage.

## King of the roast

A weekend camper can do meal prep at home, using the compartmentalized trays available in home stores to freeze dinners and then popping them in the microwave for great home cooking easily done. But the ultimate RV cooking convenience is grilling. It's great for people who want hamburgers and brats, or the gourmands who want to whip up some dill salmon with honey garlic dipping sauce.

RVers love to grill, and it makes sense — it's an easy and communal way to cook outdoors, you probably already know how to do it, and it's fun! Plus, it helps to cut down on interior kitchen clutter and is more consistent than a campfire. You can cook just about anything on a grill, including your vegetables, so you'll need fewer pots and pans.

Lots of parks and RV campgrounds have large, communal grills; you'll just need to have your own charcoal. Some even have an outdoor kitchen sink for washing pots, pans, and dishes. That way you won't have clean up from the family reunion cookout in your rig's tiny kitchen sink.

If you want, take as much grill as you have room for, but there are tiny mini-grills out there for every budget, for propane, charcoal, and even electric — and we haven't even mentioned hibachis. You should still take a folding prep table, though, because campgrounds don't want you grilling on the picnic table.

For the ultimate space saver without much of an investment, you can even find super-cheap, single-use, disposable grills, which look like a Jiffy Pop popcorn aluminum tray, prefilled with self-starting charcoal, a thin wire grate, a fold-out wire handle, and some flimsy support feet.

**TIP**

A new game-changer for grilling is silicone grill mats. They're inexpensive and easy to clean, and they can even out the heat on a tabletop grill. They help keep your grill clean, and make it easier to use a large, communal grill.

**TIP**

You can also cook over a campfire, and it isn't as hard as you may think. Get yourself a campfire grill grate, an iron skillet, a metal (un-meltable) spatula and tongs, and you're in business. And the food tastes heavenly, even if you singe it a bit. You'd think that every self-respecting campground would have a fire pit for campfires at every space, but a large number of them don't. We carry a collapsible metal fire pit for those situations, as long as fires are permitted on the property.

# Food safety and storage

When you're RVing, it's often hard to get to a supermarket or restaurant, and not just because you're camping in the middle of nowhere. If you're constantly on the move, trying to cover distance, arriving at camp each night and leaving each morning, it's tiring. At times you may have access only to a convenience store filled with junk food. So, you need to be able to feed yourself, simply, with what's onboard. We keep at least a week's worth of meals in the pantry at all times — canned food like chili and beef stew, tuna, canned soups and baked beans, and stuff for five-minute meals like rice, pasta, and instant potatoes. You've got a fridge, so we keep cheese, packaged lunchmeat, and eggs onboard, along with frozen chicken and prepacked hamburgers. And don't forget the powdered milk! This isn't your grandmother's instant milk. Our favorite brand, Milkman, tastes great, and it's so handy to have milk anytime you want it. It also works in recipes as a milk substitute.

WARNING

Spoilage does become an issue with food on hand. Try to use all leftovers in three days, four at the outside. Be aware that long-term storage in an RV, with extremes of heat and cold, can put pressure on those use-by dates. Campers tend to push that date anyway because it's a hassle to get to a market. Keeping food fresh is tricky enough with packaged food, but even canned goods and dried foods, like rice and noodles, won't keep till the End of Days and should be checked, especially if they're left in your rig all the time. RVers tend to haul enough canned goods for a nuclear bomb shelter. Look for deep dents that may have harmed the seal, and if you see a bulging or leaking can, toss it out. And try not to overpack these heavy items in the first place.

REMEMBER

All experts agree that your eyes, and especially your nose, are always the best test. If food is discolored or if it has picked up a dicey smell, toss it out. Very often people on the road will think they've picked up the flu when what's really hit them is good old-fashioned food poisoning, brought on by foodborne pathogens. The same awareness you have at home has to be followed on the road.

TIP

Use an airtight plastic bread box, available online for around $15. You'll be amazed how much longer your bread will last, without the hassle of freezing it and taking up limited freezer space. We're nuts about OXO clear plastic vacuum containers (www.oxo.com), and we use them at home now, as well. They're easy to keep clean, you can see what's in them, and your cereal, dog food, granola, and other dry food will all stay crisp and fresh a whole lot longer.

Pests can appear anywhere, but you're more prone to them in an RV, so keeping your food sealed up is a top priority. Everything that didn't come from the store well sealed *must* be put in some sort of airtight, sealed container or Ziploc bag. Otherwise, you're putting out an invitation to the local bug and rodent community. (We have lots more on pest prevention in Chapter 18.)

# THE 300-POUND FANTASY

In an RV, packing is not just an issue of finding a place for something. It's an issue of having to haul around all of that something. We talk about issues of weight and its distribution in Chapters 7 and 8. Your gross combined weight rating (GCWR) is the weight of the whole shebang — the RV itself, as well as any cargo, fluid in tanks, souvenirs, cats, dogs, and people. Some manufacturers play it pretty close to the bone — for example, we saw one estimating that your personal belongings will come in at around a modest 300 per person. Right.

Fifteen-hundred pounds is a far more common figure you'll see tossed around for the probable weight of personal stuff, but it's still a guess with a wide target. It's always a good idea to have lots of room to play with in between the tow rating of your vehicle and the probable gross vehicle weight rating (GVWR) of your rig, its weight when loaded down with everything including water. And water weight is a *big* hit. If you're boondocking or winter RVing and you need to travel with full water tanks, at over 8 pounds per gallon, that's potentially *hundreds* of pounds of extra weight.

At the start, it's not a bad idea to weigh a few of the boxes you're hauling out to the RV on a bathroom scale, just to get a notion of what stuff really weighs. Hopefully, you did as we suggest in Chapter 8 and had your brand-new, empty RV weighed at a truck stop's CAT scale, along with your tow vehicle. The first time you're fully packed for an average trip, go back to the CAT scale again. The difference will probably shock you. If the tanks are full, subtract those numbers, as well as any weighty upgrades you've done to the rig, and then accept that all the rest of that weight is the crap you brought onboard. This experience can be soul-crushing. But it's important not to play guessing games about what all those extra clothes, books, lawn chairs, photo equipment, bikes, bathrobes, and fuzzy slippers did to your load.

Even if you didn't weigh your rig when you bought it, find out your fully loaded weight, and compare it to your manufacturer's recommended load limit. The manufacturer will tell you there's no wiggle room for this limit, so you've got to solve your weight problem if you're over what the RV chassis and tow vehicle can safely carry. Limitless basement storage space doesn't mean restraints are off — motorhomes have weight limits, too, and that space invites overloading.

For a more in-depth treatment of these issues, read Chapter 8. For now, try to remember to pack with an even distribution of weight, with heavier items to the front. Don't pile too much into the back of a trailer and risk causing sway. Actually, don't pile too much *anywhere*.

# Chapter **11**

# Driving, Parking, and the Dread of Backing Up

You've finally signed all the papers, finished your pre-delivery inspection, and the service manager has done a lightning-fast explanation of the rig's systems. Finally, your salesperson meets you at the showroom door, gives you one final handshake, hands over the keys, and says, in the most casual voice possible, "There's an empty parking lot down the street. You might pull it in there and practice a bit before you head home. Happy campin'!"

And here you thought no one would be dumb enough to sell you 30 feet and 9,000 pounds of rolling vacation home without offering up a little instruction on how to safely drive the thing.

In their exuberant haste to sell you an RV, the salesperson may have confidently assured you that "these big babies drive just like your car" or "you'll never even know this trailer's behind you!" But the reality is, they *don't* drive like a car, and yes, you *will* know.

If you've never hauled a trailer before or been behind the wheel of anything bigger than a Ford Fiesta, it can be intimidating to suddenly confront piloting a ginormous rig that is quite literally the size of a crosstown bus. So, let's begin RV driving school with patience and positivity because we'd hate to think of anyone *not* RVing because they're scared to drive the thing.

# Preparing to Pilot Your Own Private Battleship

There's an old gag about RVs. A shopper shows up at a dealer's lot one day and asks, "What do I need to know to drive one of these big motorhomes?" The salesman thinks for a moment and answers, "How to write the check."

Fortunately, there are dealerships across the country who feel a duty to provide driving lessons for their customers, especially when they're buying motorhomes. Unfortunately, those dealers are rare. Towing a trailer — *any* trailer — or driving a motorhome isn't difficult, it's just different. It does take practice and some acquired skills, along with a lot of patience. Like being invited to a formal dinner with your future in-laws at your town's most expensive restaurant, if you start by doing everything in slow motion and pay careful attention to everything around you, you won't make the driving equivalent of dropping the soup course in your lap.

The vast majority of states don't require any special driver's license for RVs weighing less than 26,000 pounds or for towed vehicles weighing less than 10,000 pounds. But that doesn't mean you can leap behind the wheel without learning some new driving skills. Depending on the RV, you're potentially driving a massive rig every bit as big as a semi. But even with a small trailer being hauled by a midsize car, most of the same rules apply.

In this section, we get you started nice and easy with some tips to make you comfortable.

## Drafting a copilot

If at all possible, have a copilot. RVers are lucky because, like barn owls and shingleback lizards, they tend to travel in pairs. You may be a loner, but having someone in the passenger seat instantly doubles your awareness of what's around you, *especially when you're learning.* Your copilot is your navigator. When you're driving, they should be looking at your GPS, in-dash navigation, or road atlas and calling out upcoming lane changes and exit instructions, because you'll be busy watching the road and the signage.

**TIP**

Especially in case of cellphone failure, it's a good idea for your navigator to have a copy of *Rand McNally Motor Carriers' Road Atlas* (get the one that's spiral bound with laminated pages — it survives road trips and abuse better), which lists hazards like steep road elevations, low overpasses, narrow bridges, and other potential trouble spots for RVs to avoid.

**REMEMBER**

One of the dicey moments for a newbie is gassing up. You can pull in and realize you're trapped in a station with tight corners and parked cars you can't navigate. No, you don't *have* to use truck stops, but you're really better off doing so, especially at the start, because of the higher navigability.

Arm your co pilot with an "exits" phone app, or one of the truckers' bibles, *The Next Exit* or the smaller and quicker *Pocket Truck Stop Guide.* Even some so-called truck stops have very small areas for gas pumps, like any convenience market. The *Pocket Truck Stop Guide* lists all truck stops with an L, M, or S (for large, medium, or small). The more detailed *Next Exit* even tells you if the truck stop is RV-friendly, with dedicated pumps. When in doubt, slow down while your navigator looks over the lot before you pull in to see if you can get out of it again.

Next, have your copilot outside spotting for the rig to avoid hitting the pumps, the canopy, or other obstructions like concrete pillars, and do it again when you leave. You'll do the same thing setting up camp, with your copilot outside making sure you're aligned to your hookups, without whacking a tree or neighboring RV. And when you tackle your first back-in campsite, your copilot needs to be outside guiding you in. This is why you need walkie-talkies or a pair of cellphones (we prefer walkie-talkies because of spotty cell service in the wilds).

**REMEMBER**

Never be afraid to say these words: "Hey, could you get out and look at that?" But if you aren't traveling with anyone, follow the first instruction given to all first-time truck drivers: G.O.A.L. *Get. Out. And. Look.*

## BACK TO SCHOOL

There's no shame in admitting that driving a motorhome or hauling a towable unnerves and overwhelms you. But a frightened driver can wind up being a danger to themselves and others on the road. If, after some practice trips, you just plain feel like you've made a terrible mistake and gotten in over your head, RV Basic Training (www.rvbasictraining.com) is a good place to turn. They offer one-on-one training in your own vehicle. They have a team of instructors around the country, and prices start at $450 for a full day of instruction, as long as you go to them (they'll charge travel expenses to come to you). They also publish an excellent instruction manual on RV driving and qualifying for a Class B commercial driver's license, which may be required for the very biggest and heaviest rigs.

Another personalized RV school is RV Driving School (www.rvschool.com). They've partnered with the Family Motor Coach Association (FMCA), which offers discounts steered specifically to motorhome owners.

# Practicing until you can't practice any more

Your salesperson's advice to pull your rig into an empty parking lot and practice before you head home is good advice. Be ready for this before you leave your house to go pick up your new rig. You can buy orange cones online to practice with — they're handy, but you don't need them. Throw some cardboard boxes and plastic water jugs in the car to act as soft obstacles during your first practice session. Bring another adult with you — spouse or buddy — on pickup day. Choose a vast expanse of asphalt free from curbs, landscaping, and other cars, and start the learning process.

Set the boxes or jugs out to represent sharp corners, gas pumps, parked cars, or narrow parking spaces. As you master each one, keep thinking of other potential circumstances you may encounter on the road. Practice until you feel comfortable maneuvering, and you don't hit the boxes anymore.

TIP

Here are some essential tips for piloting your towable or motorhome and the key issues you'll encounter doing them. When you're out in that big empty parking lot, practicing your heart out, set up scenarios for each of these situations so you'll be ready to face them when the time comes:

>> **Walk around your vehicle before you do anything else.** Like breaking camp, anytime you move your RV, first take a walk all the way around your RV and tow vehicle before you get in. Check to make sure that stabilizers are up and the hitch is properly connected, and make sure there are no obstructions.

>> **Adjust your mirrors and cameras.** A huge number of RV accidents are caused by improperly adjusted mirrors, and a driver who couldn't see what was around the rig. All the cameras in the world won't replace your mirrors. If you don't have extended towing mirrors, get some. They're large, convex (fisheye) mirrors that will give you a much wider view of the lane next to you. Be sure to tilt the convex mirrors down so you can see as much of the lane next to you as possible and spot any car that is directly beside you.

If you have one (or more) cameras on your rig, familiarize yourself with how to change views on the camera monitor so you're not fumbling and swerving on the road while trying to figure out the controls. Have your copilot walk around your rig as you switch cameras so you can determine for yourself what each one can and cannot see.

>> **Get used to the feeling of stopping.** There's a saying, "I'm not afraid of being able to drive an RV; I'm afraid of being able to stop one". Stopping your rig will feel very different from stopping a car or a pickup truck, and it takes a *lot* more room to accomplish. At highway speeds, all that weight you're hauling means it could take you *eight times* the distance to stop as it does in your car. We talk a lot more about brakes later in this chapter (see "Coming to a stop: Trailer brakes first!").

>> **Make sure to signal your turns and stops.** Always use turn signals before making a maneuver. Begin signaling before you actually turn or change lanes, and keep the signal on until you've completed your move. The brake and turn signal lights on trailers in particular, are often not as noticeable as they are on cars. Billboard your intent.

>> **Identify your blind spots.** You're going to have plenty of 'em. We'll warn you right off the bat that any time you turn your rig, neither you nor your copilot will be able to see anything down along the blind side of your trailer until you straighten out again. Identify the worst blind spots and what you can and can't see in your mirrors or over your shoulder as you maneuver. If you're driving a motorhome hauling a toad, you'll never see your car back there in your mirrors. You must rely on a camera.

Tall and wide towing mirrors can actually create their own dangerous blind spots. We see this most often in shopping center parking lots and at intersections. A high curb, a pedestrian, a bicycle, or even a small car approaching you from the right or left side can be completely obscured by the body of the big mirror and the windshield corner post. The issue is worse at night, because people and objects on your sides aren't lit up by your headlights. Under the wrong set of circumstances, you may not even know they're there. Taking it easy, especially in pedestrian-filled parking lots, is your only defense.

>> **Watch out for concrete curbs.** A low-lying concrete curb hit or scraped at just the right angle can bend a wheel rim and deflate a tire. This is by far the most common damage sustained on RVs. It's easy enough to do this in your normal passenger car as you negotiate your way out of a tight fast-food drive-thru lane or a drive-up ATM, but it's even easier to do with a motorhome or trailer.

>> **Get acquainted with tail swing.** Tail swing is one of the top causes of damage to motorhomes and towables. The big concrete-filled or steel bumper posts that surround things like gas pumps and dump stations are the greatest threat to the body of your rig because of tail swing. And when your fiberglass or aluminum trailer meets with steel or concrete, it always loses.

Think of your towable or motorhome like a playground teeter-totter lying on its side, with each end swinging left or right instead of up and down. When you make a turn, your rig pivots on its wheels — everything in front of them follows your lead, but everything behind the back axle begins to swing in the *opposite* direction. It's also called *off-tracking,* and it's at its worst in a Class A motorhome. The longer the RV and the more distance you've got between the rear wheels and the back bumper, the more side-to-side room it takes as your back end pivots while you turn, going where you never intended. *Remember:* All vehicles off-track, including your car. You just don't notice it with a short wheelbase. Unless, of course, you manage to run your rear wheel over the curb.

The average trailer rear end swings out from as little as 15 inches to as much as 4 feet in a sharp turn. Knowing that distance (and judging it from the driver's seat) is the only way you'll keep from taking out a gas pump, bumper post, or campground power pole when you pull away and turn sharply. The general rule is to pull straight forward until the rig's back wheels are past the object you're trying not to hit, and *then* make your turn. But the only truly safe way to avoid hitting a big immovable object is to have a buddy outside talking you past it.

## HELPFUL DRIVING VIDEOS

Many issues of driving an RV are universal, but motorhomes, fifth wheels, and towable trailers all have their own quirks. Watching some YouTube videos before you begin to practice will help build your confidence. We've screened untold hours of them and can recommend some of the best:

- **Lazydays RV Driver Confidence Course:** If you're driving a large motorhome, this video from Lazydays is for you. This 40-minute online class is an excellent overview of motorhome issues. Find it at https://youtu.be/4CeThR_A4VI.

- **"Towing in the Mountains" by Jaunt Junkies:** For standard trailer towing, this video is an excellent introduction to a nervous topic. You can find it at https://youtu.be/UiQXKLpQ1UQ.

- **Long Long Honeymoon:** Sean and Kristy have several good videos on their YouTube channel, Long Long Honeymoon, including "The Scoop" (https://youtu.be/RLtfrBWzNCw) and "For Beginners: How to Back Up a Travel Trailer" (https://youtu.be/1zlOfBGr1i4).

- **Changing Lanes:** For the world of fifth wheels, the YouTube channel Changing Lanes has some great videos. "Towing a Large 5th Wheel RV" is a detailed presentation on topics from towing power to the details of your first parking lot practice session. It deserves the well over a million views it's gotten. Find it at https://youtu.be/87runDszXLQ.

- **"How to Back in a 5th Wheel" by Sunset Seekers:** This video has some excellent advice, too. Find it at https://youtu.be/x7k2dMSvJoU.

Watch these videos in the stress-free atmosphere of home. Then watch again on pickup day. It will help you when you hit that parking lot.

>> **Pull straight, turn late.** You've seen signs on semis that say "Warning: This vehicle makes wide right turns." Well, you're one of them now. Making a right turn in a motorhome or hauling a trailer is filled with potential obstacles. If you get to an intersection and just turn right immediately, you can set yourself up for a twofer: Not only will you curb the tires on your right (potentially causing a bent wheel and a blowout) and maybe even take out a stop sign, but you'll possibly clip a car in the lane to your left with your swinging tail end.

The solution is to pull straight ahead and make your right turn as late as possible — preferably after the last wheels on your rig are past the curb.

**WARNING**

Because of a lot of factors, including your physical distance from the tail end, many RVers don't hear the sounds of the side or top of their rig getting scratched, bent, or torn open by an obstruction. Loads of folks climb out of their rig at a rest stop or gas station and discover, to their horror, that the side of their pride and joy has been damaged, without any idea how it happened or when.

# What's Your Clearance, Clarence? Knowing How Big You Are Before You Hit the Road

Before you hit the highway, you need to know the size, or *clearance*, of your motorhome or towable. Never take the word of your salesperson or even the specs from the manufacturer. Hitch up your rig, grab a ladder and tape measure, and find out for yourself. Write all the measurements on a notepad and post it on your visor or dashboard, because you never know when you'll need them.

Here's what you need to measure:

>> **Length:** Measure the total real length of your rig, and the length with any tow vehicle (or *toad*) attached. This information will be the first question a campground asks when you make a reservation. They're trying to assign you a space that will fit your rig. What you need to know as a driver is the complete tip-to-tail length, from hitch ball or front bumper to rear bumper and anything else sticking off the back end, like a bike rack.

>> **Height:** Most states mandate a maximum legal vehicle height of 13½ feet. The tallest fifth wheels and motorhomes are often right at that limit, but don't just take the manufacturer's word for it. Measure yours, from the street to the top of your tallest rooftop-mounted equipment (like air conditioners, antennas, roof fan housings, and any cargo lashed to the roof). Do it when your rig is hooked up for towing, because the height might be different from its parked, unhitched position.

When you're on the interstate highway, you shouldn't have issues with the height of your rig. But after you exit the interstate, those height warning signs you never noticed before, everywhere from charming covered bridges to ATM drive-thrus, are vital. You don't want to peel your RV's roof open and have to pick up your AC unit off the street. That's no way to make a sunroof.

» **Width:** Measure the widest possible points of your full rig, and keep in mind that your towing mirrors may be the widest thing you've got. It may be that your towing vehicle is actually wider than your trailer, especially if you have a truck with *dualies* (two sets of tires on the rear axle). Lane width isn't something that comes up often, but you may run into construction zones with narrow, restricted lanes.

Starting in 1952, motor vehicles and trailers permitted on public roads could be no wider than 8 feet. But since 1976, vehicle width has been increased on federal highways to 8½ feet. Consequently, lots of RV manufacturers build their rigs right up to that 8½-foot width (with slides closed). But all roads are *not* created equal.

Normal traffic lanes in the United States can be anywhere from 9 to 15 feet wide. Over the years, as cities have become more and more choked with traffic, highway engineers have attempted to shoehorn more lanes onto existing roadways by reducing or eliminating shoulders and medians and making lanes narrower. This situation is often most noticeable in major cities with high-density highways. Creating carpool lanes made the lane width problem even worse. When high-speed traffic lanes get reduced to 9 feet wide, that means your 8½-foot-wide RV has only 3 inches of maneuvering room on either side before you hang over into another lane. Worse, in some road construction areas, highway departments may temporarily reduce lane widths to the very same 8½ feet your RV may measure, leaving you zero room for error.

High speeds and rush-hour traffic on narrow, shifting highway lanes, like the ones around Los Angeles and Orange County, mean you'll be having a harrowing drive most of the time. When faced with this scenario, experienced RVers try to arrange their schedule to pass through these areas very early in the morning or avoid city driving altogether.

Incidentally, highway tollbooth lanes are some of the narrowest passages you'll have to negotiate. Go through them at a dead creep.

TIP

Northeastern states have some of the oldest roadways in the country, and their height restrictions can cause RVers some real headaches. One of the worst drives of our lives was on I-495 snaking across Long Island in New York. New York City's huge metropolitan area is crisscrossed by its scenic parkway system, which was built for autos in the 1920s. Trucks and RVs are forbidden to drive on them because they have bridges and overpasses as low as 6'10" — lower even than many covered parking garage ceilings! Even the cab of a standard pickup truck comes dangerously close to scraping its roof.

Driving our Class B and pulling a small utility trailer through New York City had been harrowing enough for one day — no RVs with propane tanks are allowed through the city's tunnels, which meant miles of detours out of our way. But we made it to I-495, only to be stopped by a three-hour traffic jam with our gas tank running on vapors. As we crawled our way east with our 9½-foot-tall rig, we discovered to our horror that every exit we approached hoping to pull off for gas had a height restriction of just 7'10"! At one point, Chris asked how much we really liked our rooftop air-conditioner. Desperate people fleetingly entertain desperate measures.

# Backup Plan: Backing Up Like a Pro

There's no denying it: Some RVers fear backing up more than anything else. There's a reason back-in campsites cost less. We've seen RV driving manuals and videos that just cop out and say to avoid backing up whenever possible. But life's not like that. Motorhome drivers pulling a car with a tow bar or two-wheel towing dolly are forced to do this, because they *can't* back up, at least not without unhitching. Having been in this situation, we sympathize; the whole structure of your road trip may be built around this issue. (We talk about towing a toad in Chapter 19.) But the truth is that, for the rest of us, sooner or later, you're going to have to back up, and it's best to get comfortable with it.

Planning ahead will keep you out of most situations. There are areas you'll learn to avoid. As newbies, we stopped in Salt Lake City and ended up in a university rabbit warren of narrow, one-way streets and little, inaccessible strip malls, choked with traffic. We had to stop in the middle of the street and execute a series of backups and dicey turns, with Alice walking the outside and waving off traffic. Google Maps or GPS can keep you from some of these situations, while you look for easy-in, easy-out strip centers near the highway, but it won't solve all problems. This isn't just an issue of old, downtown areas. Even many new shopping zones have put up *bollards* (metal or wood posts) and deliberately constructed height restriction bars specifically to keep trucks and RVs out of their parking lots; we saw this a lot in California.

**REMEMBER**

When you approach any parking lot or driveway, look around for your escape route before you enter. If you can, pull over, get out, and walk the area. Make sure the driveway doesn't have an inclined entrance or curb steep enough to cause your trailer to *bottom out* (scrape the pavement) in the back.

# Getting from Point A to Point B Stress-Free

Describing real-life driving scenarios probably won't teach you nearly as much as the first long driving trip you take in your personal rig. We can't hope to prepare you for every possible situation, but safe RV piloting is mostly about being an attentive driver and developing a few specialized habits about speed, steering, keeping safe distances, planning ahead, and most of all, braking.

## Paying attention to your speed

RV experts overwhelmingly agree: Never drive your motorhome, trailer, or fifth wheel faster than 65 miles per hour. It's a matter of opinion, but it's probably in a fifth wheel that you'll *feel* safest and smoothest at higher speeds, so you'll need to exercise more caution if you've got a lead foot. Many RVers themselves suggest staying around 60 miles per hour, and some states have a lower speed limit (often 55 miles per hour) for mobile homes or anyone towing. They do this for a reason.

**WARNING**

The faster you drive, the greater the danger of losing control. As your speed increases, so does the distance it takes to react and to stop. Turbulence from trucks and windy conditions get exponentially worse as your speed goes up, which can have a drastic effect on your steering *with no warning*, and a downhill incline will always be more dangerous. The slower you're driving, the greater your chances of being able to stay in control of your rig. Having a tire blowout on a trailer at any speed is a terrifying experience, as the trailer swerves and bucks out of control. At higher speeds, that-out of-control trailer can drag you anywhere it wants to go.

So, where's the fire? These aren't the idle concerns of a couple of worrywarts and nervous Nellies. Unstable campers and motorhomes can, *and do*, roll over, and trailers take the tow vehicle with them. They can also take out other nearby drivers. So, back off the accelerator. It's not a Ferrari.

# GONE WITH THE WIND

One of the biggest shocks for a newbie RVer is the effect wind can have on your rig. Everyone is cautious when driving on icy roads, but RVs are susceptible to being buffeted by winds other drivers aren't even noticing. Recently, an Airstreamer we know was rolled over into a field while towing. Thankfully, no one was badly hurt, but we've heard about this kind of accident too many times. The winds weren't particularly bad, but when a fast-moving truck blew past him, he lost control in the gusty wake. It's a witch's brew of your speed, the truck's speed, and the wind speed, as well as direction. The one element you *can* control is your own speed, and the slower you're going, the higher the probability that you'll keep control of your rig.

You need to become wind aware. If there's any concern, get wind reports online before you leave in the morning, and double-check your sway bars. If you see a warning sign such as "Dangerous crosswinds," believe it. Slow down, and if you're hit by a crosswind, don't panic, but gently steer against it. Winds can rise suddenly. For example, passing over the Mississippi River, a seemingly windless day can start knocking you around like a kite. It helps to know if an area is problematic, so talk to other RVers about your route — Facebook groups are great for this. We were run aground two years running attempting to cross New Mexico in January, where high winds are common and wind events go on for days. The second time, we monitored hourly wind speeds online, then drove two nights in a row when they rightly forecast that it would die down after 6 p.m. Staying on the move finally carried us safely out of Wind Alley.

So, how bad is bad? You'll feel a 15-mph wind, especially if it's hitting you broadside. Realize that in a 30-mph wind, it's difficult to walk. Any wind is easier if you're driving into it rather than being hit in the side. But it's nearly impossible to have one-size-fits-all wind advice, and even scientists don't try. So many factors, including the weight you're pulling and the expanse of your RV's surface, can affect your safety. But by the time wind gets to 20 miles per hour, the effect on your rig will dramatically increase and passing trucks can cause shifting turbulence in their wake. With 30 mph winds, you may not be safe. You'll start to get a feel for how much wind your RV can take, but let caution rule. Those white knuckles on the steering wheel are a warning.

When in doubt, get off the interstate. You may be able to shift to a state or county road, a frontage road, even the business route. You'll keep on eating miles, but you won't be at highway speed, and you'll often have trees and buildings to shelter you. But you may have to pull off and just call it quits. Probably the most important thing is to be flexible, willing to change your plans if the weather rears its head, instead of stubbornly hanging on to them. It's not melodramatic to say we're talking about your life here.

For more on high winds and tornado awareness, see Chapter 12.

REMEMBER

Always believe the posted speed limit signs, especially on a highway exit. Slow down more than a car would for all exits — you may not see the sign for the curve or suggested speed limit until you're in the middle of it. RVs are top-heavy — their center of gravity is much higher than a car's. When you steer into a turn at high speed, the inertia of that weight up high combines with centrifugal force, which makes the rig want to lean out and over as it turns. Tires can lose their grip on the pavement. The problem is compounded if you realize too late that the turn is too sharp for your speed and try to correct it by steering more sharply. It's much safer to begin slowing down long before you get to the exit ramp, and keep your speed below the exit's posted limit.

REMEMBER

Slowing down *off* the highway is just as important. In western states, where they have flash floods, there may be concrete drainage ditches built in the pavement at intersections, and they can be impossible to see. The first time we drove across one at 30 miles per hour with a rooftop cargo carrier on our car, the carrier lurched so violently it punched in our roof. Drive across one in an RV, even at the posted speed limit, and you'll feel like you drove over a land mine. And speed bumps are the bane of every RVer's existence. Slowing down will always reduce the chances of tearing up your rig.

## SHORTER DAYS AND MORE BREAKS

Back in the Paleolithic Era when we were in college together, we drove every summer between California, Texas, and Indiana. It wasn't uncommon for us to drive ten hours a day. Our goal, as a rule, was 450 to 500 miles per day, and we drove as long, as far, and as fast as possible without time-consuming stops. We were 20, and we thought we were invincible.

Four decades later, RVing finally taught us to take our time, enjoy the scenery, and make new discoveries. Typically, we drive no more than four or five hours a day. Instead of long hours behind the wheel with almost no breaks, we try to have a nice, hour-long lunch stop, as well as breaks just to get out and walk around. During a grueling drive in traffic or on twisting mountain roads, we pull off and just relax for a while in our rig. We're dragging around a bedroom, bathroom, living room, and kitchen, so we take advantage of it.

We're lucky because we can work on the road and aren't anchored to a set number of vacation days. But even if you are, you can cover more ground this way than you think, perhaps 250 miles in a day. In this model, the driving days themselves are an enjoyable part of any trip. When the weather's good, we make time for local sights (see Chapter 23). Driving fewer hours helps at the end of the day; you're not exhausted setting up camp, and there's still some daylight left. We can enjoy the sunset, in a camp chair with a cold drink. Try not to let the destination be everything. Let the journey be rewarding, too.

There's an added bonus to slowing down: Dropping your cruising speed by just 10 miles per hour will dramatically improve your fuel economy.

## Keeping your distance

Keep plenty of distance between you and the vehicle in front of you. At highway speed, it can be catastrophic if you're right on somebody's tail. Pick a spot on the road ahead, like a milepost. When the vehicle in front of you passes it, start counting seconds (or one-Mississippis) until you reach the same spot. The rule of thumb is to leave one Mississippi between you and the vehicle in front of you for every 10 miles per hour. At 50 miles per hour, that's 5 Mississippis.

## Steering you right

Motorhomes don't have as much problem backing up, when they're not towing. They steer just like a car, forwards and backwards. But when a trailer gets brought into the situation, everything changes.

You normally steer a car or truck with your hands on the top half of your steering wheel, in the ten o'clock and two o'clock positions. But backing up with a trailer or fifth wheel attached forces you to change that habit every time you put the gearshift in reverse:

1. **Put your dominant steering hand on the bottom of the steering wheel, in the six o'clock position.**

2. **As you slowly back up, push your steering hand to the *left,* which rotates the wheel *clockwise,* and the back end of the trailer will magically begin to turn to the left, too (short trailers react faster than long ones).**

3. **Pull forward and straighten the truck and trailer out again.**

4. **Shift into reverse and put your hand back at the bottom of the wheel again.**

5. **Now push your steering wheel to the *right, counter-clockwise,* and the trailer goes *right.***

Yes, it really is just that simple. Every time you put your rig into reverse, grip the *bottom* of the steering wheel and steer left and right from there. Have a look at Figure 11-1 and you'll see what we're talking about. Burn that into your brain, and you won't get confused ever again.

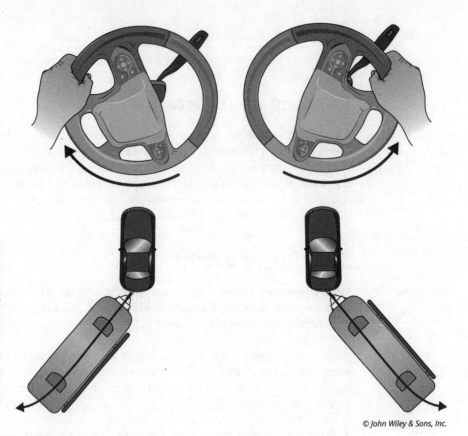

**FIGURE 11-1:**
When backing up a trailer, put one hand at the six o'clock position of the steering wheel — the direction your hand turns the wheel is the direction your trailer's back end will go.

© John Wiley & Sons, Inc.

TIP

The empty parking lot is the time to work with your partner on signals and terminology. Some drivers rely on hand signals, but we strongly advocate actually talking to each other. Use a cellphone or walkie-talkie, but have the driver's window down so you can hear any frantic yelling.

Make sure you both agree on directions. It does no good to have someone behind, with an incredibly clear view, but your words to one another are unclear — "I said left! The *other* left!" Every driver's preferred terms are different. "Stop" is easy, but you must agree on what "left" means. Some use "passenger side" and "driver side," but when backing up, we just use "go right, go left," because, when backing up, this is exactly what the driver's doing with the underhand method. Left means the driver's side, and right is the passenger side. There'll be testy arguments aplenty, but when you get in the groove with one another, backing into a campsite goes smoothly. Eventually.

REMEMBER

If you're RVing without a buddy, ask for help from the campground host — someone will be happy to talk you through. It's harder with a stranger, but better than creaming a power pole.

## JACKKNIFING

Remember your brother tormenting you as a kid with his game of "Stop hitting yourself, stop hitting yourself!" It's possible — and very easy — to back up and turn so sharply (called *jackknifing*) that you can crunch your tow vehicle's back bumper or rear quarter panel with your very own RV. So, yes, you just hit yourself. And no, we don't want to talk about it.

If you're backing up and you have to make an extremely tight turn, do it very slowly and keep checking that your trailer corner isn't going to contact your truck's bumper, tail lights, or back end. By the time you hear anything suspicious, the damage will be done. You should know that one of the most common mishaps for a fifth wheel is busting out your pickup truck's back window with the front corner of the trailer section while making a too-sharp turn.

If it's not perfect, pull forward to regroup and get the trailer straight in line behind your tow vehicle; then back in again. Think of it like rebooting your smartphone or taking a mulligan in golf. And stop worrying that someone watching may be laughing at your attempts. Everybody has to learn somehow.

## Coming to a stop: "Trailer brakes first!"

In the film *The Long, Long Trailer,* RV newbie Desi Arnaz's nightmares are haunted by the screams of his trailer mechanic. "It's like 40 feet of train. So remember, *trailer brakes first!*" Any towable bigger than a small utility trailer should have its own braking system that's remotely controlled from the tow vehicle. If you're towing a toad behind your motorhome, it should have its own remote-controlled brakes, too.

A car or trailer being towed down the road builds up inertia the faster you drive. If there were no separate brakes on it and you applied your truck's brakes, the vehicle being towed would still try to keep rolling along at highway speed and shove against the hitch, making the whole rig unstable. In other words, you're not pulling it — it's pushing you. When you're driving, a free-rolling trailer without brakes has nothing to prevent it from bobbing around on the hitch ball, especially when going down a steep hill. It wants to keep rolling at 60 miles per hour, and you're in its way. Even if you were just driving at 30 miles per hour and trying to stop at a stop sign, the weight of the rolling vehicle in tow behind you could potentially shove you out into the intersection until your truck's brakes finally managed to stop you both.

If you ever owned a bicycle with hand brakes instead of coaster brakes, you already know why it's important for the trailer to slow down first. You applied the rear brakes first, and *then* the front brakes to come to a stop. If you did the opposite, the front wheel would try to stop, while you and the back wheel kept on going, hurtling you over the handlebars.

We don't want to lecture you about your tow vehicle, but if you're towing a trailer of any size, you're going to be happier with a truck or SUV that has a factory tow package. A factory-installed towing system includes more than just a trailer hitch receiver under the back bumper, and there are many things it will do automatically. The dash-mounted panel has a manual control so you can apply the trailer's brakes separate from your truck's, if need be, and adjust the braking intensity (see Figure 11-2). And the system will include a trailer (or *tow haul*) setting for the transmission that selects gears to help climb hills or slow down when descending (see Figure 11-3).

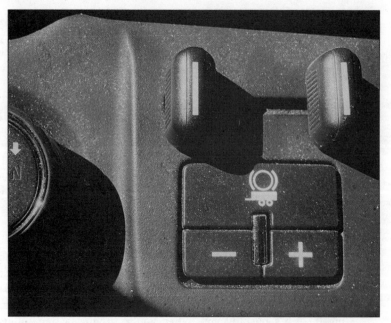

Photograph courtesy of Christopher Hodapp

**FIGURE 11-2:**
The brake controls for a factory-installed towing package.

Your trailer brakes are very important to you now. On a nervous downhill drive, your instinct, if you've never towed before, will be to keep hitting your brake pedal and ignore your trailer brakes — a bad idea. With an integrated tow package, when you hit your truck's brake pedal, the onboard computer applies the trailer brakes slightly *before* your truck's brakes kick in. It constantly shortens or lengthens that delay based on how fast you're driving. The controller gradually adds more braking power the longer you hold the brake pedal down. That's partially why factory tow packages are so useful. After-market trailer brake controllers are also widely available for vehicles that weren't equipped at the factory, but they aren't able to monitor your speed and compensate like a factory one can.

**FIGURE 11-3:** The tow-haul button for a factory-installed towing package.

**REMEMBER**

The brake controller also has a manual control for the situations when you want *only* the trailer brakes to be applied. Any trailer can start to sway under the right road conditions: descending a steep hill, bouncing on a rough washboard road, or in windy situations. At the first sign of a sway beginning (and believe us, you'll know when it does — the back end of your tow vehicle will start to jerk left or right), take your foot off the gas, and *gently* apply the trailer's brakes first without tapping your truck's brake pedal. Don't try to correct things with the steering wheel — keep steering straight ahead. Pump the trailer brakes by squeezing and releasing the controller rather than just slamming on the brakes. The drag of the trailer trying to slow down while the tow vehicle keeps going straight is normally all it takes to calm the situation and bring the trailer back into line.

**TECHNICAL STUFF**

The brake controller should have an adjustable braking intensity control on it. Before you hit the road, pull onto a side street and apply the trailer brakes only. You need to adjust the intensity so the trailer's brakes work gradually instead of trying to skid to a sudden stop. Then apply your vehicle brakes normally and judge the effectiveness of the trailer's brakes working in conjunction with your truck. You'll probably have to do this multiple times. Be aware that this setting may react differently at highway speeds versus on a downtown city street, so it may take some fiddling to finally get it adjusted properly.

## Handling hills

Road steepness is calculated by how far it rises or descends over a certain length of highway, and it requires both geometry and trigonometry to determine. Don't worry, no one will ask you to figure it out on your own — highway departments do that for you. On major and most secondary roads, a dangerously steep hill (up or down) will have a sign telling you the steepness of the grade and how many miles it goes on. The signs are there especially for big-rig truckers and you in your RV, so pay attention to them!

When the interstate highway system was envisioned in the 1950s, one of the design requirements was to keep steep hills at a minimum — generally no steeper than a 6 percent grade. Exceptions were made for passing over the most mountainous areas, but grades steeper than 7 percent are not permitted on interstates and federal highways. But if you get off those roads, the limitations go out the window and roads as steep as 10 percent to 15 percent or more exist around the country. They can be breathtakingly scenic but extremely challenging for an RV, if not downright impassable.

Because you asked, the steepest public street in the United States is in Pittsburgh, Pennsylvania. Canton Avenue is just 650 feet long and is a 37 percent grade. That's not a misprint. Just for comparison, a 45-degree angle would be a 100 percent grade. Fortunately, you won't be climbing anything like that in an RV.

### Going up . . .

Pulling a heavy load up a long, steep grade will push your engine and transmission to their limits. If you're using cruise control, deactivate it and accept that your speed is going to drop, a lot — you don't get extra points for getting to the top in record time. Get into the right lane with the big-rig semis, and turn on your hazard lights if you drop below 45 miles per hour. As the hill gets steeper, your engine may begin to bog down from the strain. Eventually, the automatic transmission may downshift into a lower gear to give you more pulling power, or you may do it manually yourself.

This is partially where a factory tow package really helps, because your vehicle should have a *tow haul* setting built in. When you activate it, it modifies the shifting of your transmission and other features as the road conditions change.

Because of the load and the higher revolutions per minute (RPMs) from the lower gear setting, your temperature gauge will begin to rise as the engine heats up. If it's extremely hot outside and the gauge creeps into the red danger zone, pull off as soon as possible, keep the engine running, and turn on your vehicle's heater — you and the family will bake, but it will help lower the excess engine heat.

## . . . and going down

**WARNING**

Driving your rig down a long, steep grade is potentially the most dangerous situation you'll find yourself in with an RV, and unless you live in a mountainous area of the country, you won't get to practice this beforehand. There's no such thing as driving down a mountainous road too slowly. You can't just rely on your motorhome's, tow vehicle's, or trailer's brakes to prevent you from going too fast. If you just sail down the hill at highway velocity and then jam on the brakes whenever your speed gets alarmingly fast, you risk burning up your brakes *and* completely losing control of your rig.

The sign for a steep downgrade likely has the warning, "Trucks use lower gear." That means you, too. Before the road begins to drop, you need to slow *way* down and get in the right lane. Your speed needs to be determined by your own sense of caution, not by the other traffic around you. Whether you have a built-in tow haul setting or not, drop your transmission into a low gear and keep slowing down until the engine's RPMs sound close to normal. You need to use the low gears and resistance from the engine to prevent you from using the brakes too much (called, appropriately, *engine braking*). Diesel motorhomes usually have an engine (or exhaust) braking setting built in.

Truckers and experienced RVers often say that if you pump your brakes and the vehicle doesn't slow down by 5 miles per hour in less than three or four seconds, you're going too fast to be in control. The transmission and engine braking in a typical pickup or SUV probably can't keep you from speeding up entirely by themselves. You will need to pump the brakes — don't just hold down the brake pedal all the way down the hill. If you apply the brakes for longer than about 15 to 20 seconds at a time, you're in danger of literally burning them up. You may even see (or smell) a semi descending with smoke billowing out of its axles, or that smell may be coming from your own brakes.

**WARNING**

A runaway truck ramp is something you hopefully will never have to use. In mountainous areas, these are occasionally installed in case a truck or RV's brakes fail and it comes roaring down the hill, unable to stop. The concept is simple, if slightly terrifying — it's a short exit ramp that ends abruptly in a pit filled with sand. When a vehicle careening out of control pulls into it, the sand pit swallows up the speeding tires, the rig sinks into it, and it instantly stops. It's like the highway version of an emergency parachute.

# Chapter **12**

# The Shakedown: Your Maiden Voyage

This is the big day! This is what you've worked toward ever since you watched your first episode of *Going RV*.

The shakedown trip is an RV tradition, and it should be fun. But it's kind of like having a new baby in the house: You're nervous, and you don't want your kid to grow up with all sorts of neurotic tics because of what you failed to do on that very first day. But rest easy — in this chapter, we walk you through your maiden voyage.

**TECHNICAL STUFF**

A lot of the terminology of RVing comes out of the early trailer days of the 1930s, when the guys who built them used boat fixtures so they used those same words for the same places in a trailer — *galley* for kitchen, *head* for toilet, and *aft* for the back end, for example. *Shakedown* is an old bit of American naval slang, when the "shakedown cruise" was taken onboard a vessel fresh out of the naval yards to look for and iron out all the inevitable little problems.

**WARNING**

If you're completely new to RVing, you need to be armed with some basic knowledge and tips before heading for the campground. Read Chapter 13 so you can confidently get situated and properly connected to the park's facilities. And also read all of Part 4 to wrap your mind around how your rig functions before you attempt your first trip.

**REMEMBER**

Some of the things we talk about in this chapter will seem familiar if you've already done your pre-delivery inspection (PDI). That's because, even if you had a great PDI before accepting your rig, little issues will come up. It's difficult, sitting on a dealer's lot, to operate every single system the way it will run in a park. You do the best you can, but the shakedown is when you look for problems in battle conditions.

# Taking Your Shakedown Cruise

There are two purposes to a shakedown trip:

>> To familiarize yourself with a new rig's systems

>> To make sure those systems are functioning properly

For this reason, a shakedown is just as important to an experienced RVer, though it's a more nerve-wracking experience for the first-timer.

In this section, we tell you what to expect from your shakedown, as well as what to look for.

## Whither do we wander? Deciding where to go

We once saw a guy on Facebook announce that he was taking the family on a shakedown of his brand-new fifth wheel, driving from Ohio to Mount Rushmore. *Mount Rushmore?* That's over 1,300 miles from Ohio, not an ideal shakedown trip.

Of course, some people with a case of nerves may cling *too* close to home, like the driveway. You need genuine travel conditions. The ideal shakedown is less than four hours from home — far enough away to be a real trip, close enough to be able to get back easily if you need to.

**REMEMBER**

A shakedown to check your systems for *boondocking* (dry camping without any hookups) really should be a separate thing. You should know your rig well before you boondock. The shakedown should be a trial run for all your systems, so a place with full hookups is best.

One more point: You should be someplace on your shakedown that has clear cell-phone service and Wi-Fi. The isolated electronic wilderness of places like Yellowstone isn't ideal. Don't be too far away from civilization in general. You may need a hardware store.

How long should it take? We've heard people say a shakedown should be a week, but you may not have that luxury. The truth is, you can test all your RV's systems in a single weekend. But if things are going great, stay out another day or two!

TIP

They used to say it was good luck if it rained on your wedding day, but we think the same may be true for a shakedown. We faced a sudden, blinding downpour and hailstorm the first time we towed a big trailer, and it was scary. Yes, we'd checked the weather, but in the Midwest in springtime there's *always* a 50 percent chance of a thunderstorm. All in all, it probably gave us confidence that we could handle whatever the road dished out.

## Getting set to set up camp

If you've never been RVing before, the shakedown will be your first experience of setting up and breaking camp. Now's the time to pick up good habits. RVers tend to travel in pairs, like swans and barn owls and shingleback lizards. Working in support of one another is quick and efficient, and now's the time to practice these new jobs.

Throughout this book, we mention the videos you should make of your dealer's specialist explaining the most difficult or confusing systems in your rig. Your shakedown is when you'll be glad you did that. We had never used the style of weight-distributing towing system found in our RV (and it had been years since we'd used one at all), but the video we took of our dealer's hitch specialist going through the steps was invaluable the first few times we did it alone.

REMEMBER

Your personal videos are great because they're the *right* videos for your rig. General online advice is good, but nothing beats a video of your own system, partly because every manufacturer uses its own preferred suppliers. We were having a major hassle setting up our old-fashioned, reliable, nonmotorized Zip Dee awning, red-faced, heave-hoeing all over the place, pretty certain it was broken. We should've filmed our salesman operating it, but it seemed pretty easy at the time, so we didn't. Two online videos left us even more confused. When our dealer sent us a link to a more obscure online video for our model that added one little step, it was like a miracle. No more huffing and puffing and heave-hoeing! That's the power of the right video.

## FRANKENSTEIN'S MONSTER

Every RV is a Frankenstein's monster, cobbled together out of different companies' products. One of the issues we hear about a lot is the high-saturation technology that's becoming so common in RVs, especially Class A motorhomes. It's a given that all humans over age 50 are destined to yell at technology. But you don't have to be over 50 to find high-tech controls confusing. After all, complex home entertainment systems have been annoying people for years.

Unfortunately, it's not uncommon to get handed a bushel basket of remotes, one for each TV, the stereo, the DVD player, the HD antenna, outside speakers, and so on. The manuals can make the situation even worse. There's a reason for the gag line, "It reads like stereo instructions." We had a friend who went camping alone on a shakedown and didn't realize late on a chilly night with the windows shut that when she was watching TV, she was bothering her neighbors, because the Battle of Midway was also blasting out of her outside speakers at high decibels.

Now, on your shakedown, is the time to get acquainted with all this confusion of devices and remotes, with no stress and no one looking over your shoulder.

## Knowing what to check

What should you check? Everything. Check every appliance, every hose, every switch, every tank system. Flick every switch, plug into every outlet, open and close every cabinet. Everything.

REMEMBER

If you haven't discovered it yet, most of the electrical, water, and heating, ventilation, and air-conditioning (HVAC) systems are designed to work in two ways:

>> Hooked up to the campground's shore power and water

>> Self-contained using only propane, your 12-volt coach batteries, and a stored water supply

So, remember to use each appliance on *both* systems — the campground's electricity, as well as the 12-volt battery. Unplug the shore power, and get a feel for what gets fussy running on battery power and what can't run on it at all, even if you never plan on boondocking.

TIP

What else do you check? Here's a short list in no particular order:

>> **Refrigerator:** If your refrigerator can run on both electricity and propane, make sure it does.

>> **Stovetop/range:** Light each of your propane range's burners and the oven. Or if you have an electric range or induction burners, check them all.

>> **Water heater:** If yours can run on both electricity and propane gas, test both. Take a shower and see how long the water stays hot.

>> **"City" water:** Your water pressure may seem low, especially if you're not used to RV water systems.

**REMEMBER**

When hooked up to the "city" water supply, your pressure is dictated by the park's pressure making its way into your freshwater hose.

>> **Water pump:** Disconnect your city water hose, fill your freshwater tank, and turn on the water pump. Note that the water pressure from your pump may be different from the city connection, partially because the campground's water pressure may be higher or lower than your onboard pump. If you hear a rumble under the floor every time you turn on a water faucet or flush the toilet, don't fret — that's your water pump doing its job, and they're notoriously noisy.

>> **Faucets and plumbing:** Run every faucet in your rig one at a time, and look under every sink for dripping water. Flush the toilet and look around its base to see if there are any leaks in the pipe or hose it's connected to or in the foot pedal. Don't forget your washing machine or dishwasher if you have these amenities. Run them their whole cycle; then check for leaks.

**WARNING**

Even tiny leaks can lead to major problems and damage over time. And bouncing down the road can put lots of stress on flexible plastic plumbing pipes and hoses.

>> **Electrical outlets:** Check every electrical outlet and every USB port. Our dealer gave us a courtesy electrical outlet tester — they're handy because they check things beyond simply whether you're getting power. There are also USB port testers out there, but they aren't a necessity — just plug a device into each one and make sure it shows that it's getting power.

>> **Awning:** Fully set up your awning and check for smooth operation. If you're new to awnings, remember that it should be retracted if there's any chance of winds over 15 miles per hour. Retracting the awning sounds like one more annoying thing you have to do, but it'll become second nature to you. A high wind can twist your heavy awning right off your RV where it will proceed to beat up your rig. You really shouldn't take off for the day and leave an awning open if there's any chance at all of a storm or high winds.

**TIP**

Don't let rain build up, either. In campgrounds, you'll see awnings lowered a bit on one corner — that's so rainwater can drain off.

>> **Slides:** Check every single slide, and then check them all again. Before you hit the switch, do a walkaround outside and be sure none of the slides will hit a tree, a power pole, a water faucet, or an adjacent RV. Don't let anyone walk into or sit in a slide room until it's fully opened. Open and close them more than once, and look for issues like shuddering or binding. Also be conscious of things that need to be closed up before rooms can be closed. Cabinet doors, interior passage doors, even outside compartment doors are sometimes held up by clips and can be ripped off when slide rooms are opened. (Fear not — we talk more about slides in Chapter 18.)

Now that they belong to you, you should learn a bit about which kind of slides you have. Know if they're electric or hydraulic and who makes them. An annual checkup at your dealer is highly recommended, but on a routine basis, look for problems yourself. Watch for dry or twisted seals, as well as debris. There are little rules for slides, like don't leave your flip-flop sandals under a couch or bed where they can get sucked into the system and wreak havoc on it. A lot of this may have been thrown at you at the dealer, and maybe it overwhelmed you a little. Now's the time to get comfortable with it.

>> **TVs, antennae, and cable connections:** Your RV may have a roof-mounted TV antenna for receiving an HD-TV signal, and there may also be an antenna booster switch on the wall where the cable connects. Your rig may have a DVD player or a streaming device (or at least somewhere to plug them in). Make sure all these things function.

You'll need to let your TV program itself for over-the-air or cable stations every single time you move camp, but if you're relatively near civilization, you should be able to pick something up. If you've been on cable for the last 20 years, be aware that if an HD antenna can't get a perfect picture, it won't give you *any* picture, but you'll see it trying. (Modern TV systems can be devilishly complex, so be sure to consult any manuals or instructions your dealer provided in order to determine how your particular setup works.)

>> **Wastewater system:** Wait until your wastewater tank or separate graywater and blackwater tanks are at least 40 percent full, and then do your first wastewater dump. It would be a lie not to admit that this is a nervous moment for a newbie. Get out your manual, and also check out Chapter 15 of this book. Then maybe watch a YouTube video (you may find one specific to your rig). When we'd done it the first time, we climbed back into the SUV and ecstatically called a friend to say, "We did it! We dumped the sewer tank! And it was *easy!*" Yes, she thought we were nuts. It's the little things in life that make it worth living.

>> **Climate control:** Some things will be easier to check than others. Sailing against the wind on your HVAC system may be tough, depending on how complex your thermostat controls are. If it's the dead of summer with the hot sun baking down on your roof, you'll have to fool the furnace into coming on.

Start by setting the air conditioner fairly low so the RV eventually gets chilly inside. If you have ducted air throughout the rig, check to be sure air is blowing out of every single duct. Then switch over to the heat pump setting (if you have one), and turn the temperature up enough to get the heat working. Finally, turn off the air conditioner/heat pump and switch over to the furnace setting. Crank up the temperature enough to activate the furnace.

The propane furnace is a separate unit from your rooftop air conditioner/heat pump, and it's usually mounted near the floor with its own floor-level ducts. Its fan will start running first, and after about 30 seconds or so, the propane burner will ignite. When it does, check all the furnace's ducts throughout your rig and be sure they're all blowing warm air.

>> **Generator power:** If you're in a motorhome or a fifth wheel equipped with its own generator, disconnect the comforting shore power from the park and run your systems for a while just on your generator. Make sure that the major power-hungry appliances like the air conditioner and microwave oven function on generator power.

Try to be noise-aware, if your generator is loud (not to mention stinky — it's a running motor after all). Because of the noise and exhaust, be aware that many RV campgrounds completely prohibit the use of generators on their property, while others adhere to "quiet time" rules. So, you may need to do this part of your testing in your driveway at home or in a Walmart parking lot. If all else fails, tell your neighbors what you're doing, so they won't think it's going to go on all night.

>> **Wi-Fi:** As RVs become more dependent on Wi-Fi and Bluetooth devices, Internet service on the road is becoming a serious necessity. More and more rigs are built with systems that must connect to the Internet in order to properly function. That's fine in some utopian Wi-Fi paradise, but Internet and cellular service often doesn't exist in the serene, isolated places RVers want to camp. Many of the huge national parks and other wilderness areas simply don't have Wi-Fi or cellular phone service at all. Campgrounds may tout "high-speed Internet access," but even in this day and age, campground Wi-Fi tends to be lousy, and many campgrounds give you grief if you want to stream videos, transfer large files, or back up your hard drive to the cloud.

RV manufacturers are slowly trying to address consumer demand for Internet connectivity by installing mobile routers that connect to cellular networks and broadcast a Wi-Fi signal in and around the RV. Depending on their level of sophistication, these routers can often be used to boost a campground's Wi-Fi signal as well.

We talk more about Internet on the road in Chapter 13. But the weak link in the chain (or at least the expensive one) is the service provider. Your RV isn't going to come from the factory with a system that you can just flip on and instantly access the web. AT&T, T-Mobile, and Verizon are the big dogs in the cellular network business, and if a Wi-Fi router in your rig depends on cell service for its data connection, you'll have to sign up for an account and pay for some kind of data plan first. Although an onboard Wi-Fi system sounds terrific, you may find that using your existing smartphone (or investing in a separate cheap one) and making it a data hotspot is far more economical than hassling with a built-in system. In fact, many campers buy smartphones from multiple providers in order to have service in as many locations as possible. If AT&T doesn't adequately cover your favorite camping area, it's possible that T-Mobile or Verizon does. Multiple phones can solve that.

## HOW SOON WE FORGET

Your shakedown is the time to begin forming good habits. For example, it's really, really important to be aware of your graywater and blackwater tank capacity and to know what the level is. If you're stationary for weeks on end, it's not something you're going to worry about — you'll be in full hookups all the time. But when you pick up and move, or if you're on the move more often, you need to develop the habit of glancing at the tank monitor panel at least two or three times a day, depending on how many people are in your party and on your personal activities. You'll quickly get a feel for just how much ordinary living it takes to fill those tanks. Pick up the habit of checking, and it won't creep up on you, *literally,* when a wastewater tank of soapy water comes up your shower drain because it has nowhere else to go.

There are tricks you can use to remember things: Our trailer came with a whiteboard mounted near the door — the perfect spot for a don't-forget list, as well as for your camp-setup list, the key things you mustn't forget when arriving and leaving. Our list isn't absurdly long, and it's not *everything* we have to do. But it includes the things that are either annoying or dangerous to forget, and they're easily neglected when you're tired or distracted or when the campground is scolding you over its checkout time. When you're leaving camp, make glancing at the whiteboard the last thing you do before you close and lock the door.

Unless you live in your rig full time, weeks or months may go by between camping trips, so you may forget what some switches are for, what the perfect thermostat setting is, or what steps to follow to activate an appliance. We own a label maker, and it's been great in the RV. Labels make life in the RV easier, particularly if you haven't been in it for months. As you learn things on your shakedown, you'll quickly discover that manufacturers don't always clearly label wall switches or appliance control panels (like for your water heater or furnace). Print out a small label, and adhere it by the switch. While you're at it, if you've got multiple TVs, mark the back of each remote for the TV, DVD, or stereo it belongs to.

# Finding a Campground

Choosing a campground is a lot like choosing a hotel. There's a big difference between a Best Western on I-70 and a Sandals resort in Jamaica, but each one is trying to supply what the customer wants. Different things will be important to you if you're looking for a place just off the highway for a single night or a resort campground that would do your family for a weeklong vacation.

Most of the chain campgrounds have amenities like a small camp store, showers and bathrooms on-site, as well as a laundry and a central wastewater dump station. From these basics, they'll climb the price ladder, with things like patios, grills, cable TV, playgrounds and petting zoos for the kids, daily activities, a pool, and even food service of various sorts. With individual campgrounds, amenities are harder to predict. They run the gamut from pricey "resort" RV parks to isolated wilderness campgrounds to small campgrounds catering to overnighters. For example, in rural areas, it's fairly common to find a standard mobile home park that offers a few spaces to RVs that need a place to stop for the night.

## "I THOUGHT CAMPING WAS SUPPOSED TO BE CHEAP!"

In the United States, it's getting harder to find a good campground at a low price, particularly on holidays and weekends in the busy summer season. Many forces are driving up the cost. The last decade has seen many campgrounds doubling in price overnight, from around $25 or $30 a night to $50 or $60. Often, in these situations, the campground was bought by an investor, something called a real estate investment trust (REIT). REITs go around gobbling up any sort of real estate that generates income, including apartments, hotels, and RV campgrounds. It doesn't help when these REITs drive a change that's becoming common: setting aside a larger number of prime spaces for long-term campers and snowbirds. When campgrounds remove camping sites in order to install cabins and *park models* (stationary trailers), it's good for them (because it guarantees steady income), but bad for the campers (because they now have fewer spaces). Meanwhile, state and federal authorities have made it difficult and financially burdensome to build new campgrounds, so the loss of so many spaces is problematic for those who don't want to use a "campground" as a home half the year.

The $30 campgrounds are still out there, but they're a lot harder to find. This is what makes boondocking so appealing. You can save lots of money on a cross-country trip, even if you only boondock every other night.

In the following sections, we give you the skinny on finding a campground. We tell you who the major companies are, how to get a good price, and tips on booking your reservations and checking in.

## Knowing your options

When you're looking for a place to camp, there's a wide world of options. Getting to know the names of the major chains and clubs will come pretty quickly, and this section will help. Many privately owned campgrounds belong to some sort of association, chain, or network, and quite often, a membership club (with a yearly fee) is the best way to access them.

**TIP**

If you're intimidated about where to start looking for a campground, we strongly recommend the AllStays Camp and RV iPhone app or their website (www. allstays.com). It lists almost every campground in the United States, along with myriad RV services like dump stations, truck stops, Camping World locations, RV mechanics, overnight parking places (like Costco, Walmart, and Cracker Barrel), propane dealers, low bridges, and other helpful services too numerous to mention.

### The big names in campgrounds

Here are the major players in campgrounds:

>> **Kampgrounds of America (KOA;** https://koa.com**):** This is the big kid on the block, a chain of more than 500 campgrounds in the United States and Canada. When we started out as roadies, we really liked KOA and rarely wandered off the farm. KOA is very convenient for a newbie. It publishes a directory, available in every campground office. The directory is logically laid out, with a full-page map of each state and the KOA locations, followed by the pertinent info on each campground. KOA's website and phone app are also convenient and easy to use. If you pay $33 a year, you'll get a membership number that will make check-in easier and allow you to rack up reward points for future discounts and free nights.

Each KOA campground is privately owned, but KOA has strict standards and a quality level you can generally count on. KOA helpfully classifies its properties, too. Each campground is rated as Journey, Holiday, or Resort, with rising cost and amenities from basic overnight stopovers to fun-filled destination resorts. There's usually a KOA near every major city and noteworthy attraction. And they're usually very well marked on interstate exit signs, which makes them easier to find, especially after dark.

» **Good Sam Club** (www.goodsam.com): Good Sam is the granddaddy of RV clubs, going back to the 1930s. It's the largest organization of mutual aid for RV owners, with more than two million members. As of this writing, it costs $29 a year to join. The club doesn't own Good Sam campgrounds, and they don't dictate standards and quality level to campground owners the way KOA does. Good Sam isn't a franchise, but more like a seal of approval. Good Sam offers loads of other services like road assistance, RV insurance, and extended warranties. It also has a very large and informative website and phone app.

The massive, annual *Good Sam Campground & Coupon Guide* lists more than 12,000 RV parks and campgrounds, and of these, 2,300 of them that are rated and offer a discount (usually 10 percent) to Good Sam members. The guide is available to members at Gander Outdoors, as well as Camping World, which is owned by the same parent company. For members, the price is $10, and you should be able to recoup the cost pretty quickly with the discounts and coupons contained in this very hefty volume. There's a staggering amount of information for RVers, before you even get to the campground directories organized by state. Even the ads are a great source of information for things to see and do in the place you're headed.

» **Yogi Bear's Jellystone Park Camp-Resorts** (www.campjellystone.com): If you're traveling with younger children, Jellystone Parks are a great option. Jellystone has about 75 campgrounds designed around the classic Hanna-Barbera cartoon characters Yogi Bear and Boo-Boo Bear. It's a very kid-friendly place. Yogi and his friends make an appearance daily in the high season, in full costume, and there are various camp activities, too.

» **Passport America** (https://passportamerica.com): Unlike Good Sam, with its many services included in the membership, Passport America focuses on offering campground discounts, and they're big — as much as 50 percent. For someone on the move, the 1,800 listed locations, with a $44 yearly membership fee as of this writing, make it worth looking into.

» **Escapees** (www.escapees.com): Escapees is another campground discount club with more than 800 campgrounds. It costs $40 annually at the time of this writing and offers many other benefits to members.

**REMEMBER**

As in all clubs, the participating campgrounds may not grant you the full discount on a heavily trafficked holiday like the Fourth of July weekend.

## National and state parks

America's national parks are the gold standard of the camping experience. People come not just from the United States and Canada, but from all over the world to see the wonders of Yellowstone, Yosemite, Arches, Glacier National Park, and the

Great Smoky Mountains. The prices are reasonable because the government foots most of the bill. Often, the biggest downside is getting in for the nights you want to stay. Parks like Yellowstone are incredibly crowded, particularly in the high season.

REMEMBER

There are 59 national parks, but don't forget the lesser-known and numerous state parks. The *National Geographic Guide to State Parks of the United States* lists nearly a thousand, and it's far from inclusive. Again, these are state-supported, and prices are reasonable. The majority of states charge a small entrance fee, and activities like horseback riding and boat rentals require additional fees. Many state parks offer a singular experience, reflecting that state's history or geography. Famous or not, they're incredibly popular, with about 750,000 visitors each year. Search the web for the state you're going to, and pull up the state's information website to check it out.

WARNING

Some federal and state parks may not be able to accommodate a rig over 30 or 35 feet, and yes, that includes the tow vehicle! This isn't always true, but you need to ask. Some parks may have a limited number of spaces that can accommodate something longer, and you'll need to reserve months (even up to a year) in advance. Because they aren't a business, government parks aren't very responsive to the changes in RVing in the last two or three decades. Fortunately, privately-owned campgrounds have sprung up to welcome bigger rigs near the most popular national parks and landmarks.

## Resort and membership parks

In the last few years, there has been an explosion of luxury RV resorts. *Resort* is a word that gets tossed around a lot — some resorts are merely RV parks with a few extra amenities, while others are so high-tone they only allow Class A motorhomes. The chains that exist aren't large — for example, Sunland Resorts has only nine properties (in California and Florida). Along with resorts, membership RV parks are becoming a major player, where you'll be expected to pay a yearly fee to access the campgrounds. Lots of them are also in snowbird magnet locations, like Florida and Arizona, and they're often also called "resorts" rather than boring old "campgrounds." Most also have cottages available, which are popular with snowbirds.

Some of the resort campgrounds are downright dazzling in the amenities offered, everything from pickleball to samba lessons. Kids love having a pool, and for some RVers, access to a golf course is appealing. Ideally, you should avoid paying for amenities you don't use just to get a little sunshine, but when you love the property and its location, it may be worth the cost.

RVers staying only one or two nights can feel downright ghettoized at these resort properties, because many are completely geared toward long-term residents. A couple times we've tried to stay in one (that was listed in the Good Sam campground guide) and the person on the phone didn't seem certain a one-night stay in an ordinary trailer was even allowed, and they had to go fetch a higher authority. You may also get a space that isn't the greatest, but if it's all that's available where you're stopping for the night, go with it.

Here are some of the popular RV members-only resorts and clubs:

>> **Thousand Trails** (https://thousandtrails.com)**:** Thousand Trails is the major player in the private campground business. It owns 81 properties outright, and these properties cling to the coasts: California and the Northwest, the Great Lakes, the Northeast, Florida, and South Texas. Thousand Trails also has amity relationships with two other campground chains; various membership upgrades will gain you low-priced access to these parks as well. The rates run to the expensive, particularly if you buy an Elite pass, which gives you total access instead of having to move every 14 days with a regular camping pass. An Elite pass runs into thousands of dollars, and companies have sprung up that trade in used ones, sort of like a timeshare.

We're not saying Thousand Trails is a rip-off. We're just saying it's a *very* complicated system, and you'll have to do your homework. Various passes confine you to one of the five regions in the system, which may not be best for you. Also, spaces have a tendency to be reserved in advance, and the system isn't geared toward last-minute decisions. If you camp a great deal, or if you're a full-timer, there's money to be saved here. But know what you're getting into before you shell out any cash. Watch some YouTube videos by people who are happy and unhappy with their membership and who explain the reasons why.

>> **Harvest Hosts** (https://harvesthosts.com)**:** With a yearly fee of $79 as of this writing, Harvest Hosts connects you with nearly 1,500 small agricultural businesses — wineries, dairy farms, breweries, local museums, and various attractions — that are willing to let you boondock for the night on their property. These opportunities are what makes it so desirable to be able to dry camp comfortably for at least one night.

These sites are not in campgrounds. You may need to cope with a less-than-ideal or less-than-level site. Plus, these locations may be quite a bit off the highway. But they're a lot of fun! And you may just find your new favorite wine or ice cream — and the business where you're staying will find a new customer!

>> **Boondockers Welcome** (www.boondockerswelcome.com)**:** For $30 a year (as of this writing), this club helps you find places to boondock. Most of the setups through Boondockers Welcome are one to three nights. But despite the fact that people who boondock a lot get very good at finding places, this is a club that may appeal.

TIP

An amazing number of places offer free camping. We discuss this subject in Chapter 20.

## Making reservations

Through the week, you shouldn't have much trouble finding a space, but you're better off making reservations. We try not to leave a campground until we know where we're going next.

When you're making a reservation, the campground will need to know the full length of your rig and tow vehicle, as well as your power needs (30 or 50 amps). If you've got a big rig, be sure to tell them if you want an easier pull-through site and full hookups. Some of the prettiest sites we've ever had were back-in sites — many older parks are loaded with them, from the days when the average trailer was a lot smaller. But if you have a huge rig, a back-in may be tough to cope with. And if you're in a motorhome towing a car (commonly referred to as a *dinghy* or a *toad*), backing up may be impossible unless you unhitch your tow bar first.

REMEMBER

The majority of campgrounds are seasonal. Parks that close in winter outnumber the four-season parks. If you're on the road from late fall through early spring, make sure the campground you're heading for really is open. But if you're in a bind and you can't find a place to stay the night on a cold-weather trip, try calling a park that's technically closed. They may let you plug in to electrical for the night at least. Any campground in winter may ask you to fill your freshwater tank instead of staying connected all night to their "city" water faucet to prevent their plumbing from freezing.

When making reservations, a campground will probably ask some basic questions, like the number of people in your group and whether you have a pet. So far, we've never been charged for our dog, but some campgrounds do charge an additional fee per child. This hits a sour note with us — after all, camping is supposed to be the ultimate family vacation.

If you have a vintage rig, tell them so. Some campgrounds won't allow a rig more than ten years old. You can't blame them for the policy — it really is a negative to drive into a campground, particularly one with a lot of long-termers, and find broken-down, old trailers surrounded by the rusting clutter of months or years.

But like most bureaucratic rules, a blanket policy starting at a particular year just begs to be abused. It's always a comic moment when they ask us, because it's tough for anyone but a rabid fan to tell the difference between an Airstream trailer made in 1980 and one made in 2020. And it's downright offensive to spend $30,000 to rehab a classic 1955 Spartan, only to be told that it's too old to occupy a space in the park. Recently, we reserved space in Orange County, California, and were told that if the rig was more than ten years old, they needed a picture of it, which seemed like a fair compromise.

## Checking in

Like hotels, campgrounds need to check you in. If you've made a reservation, the process will go more quickly. Be sure to note the campground's checkout time. Noon has been the standard forever, but many are now 11 a.m. and a few are as early as 10 a.m. If events have made the checkout time a major hassle for you on a certain day, ask the office — many campgrounds offer a late departure, possibly for an additional charge.

**TIP**

Campground offices aren't manned 24 hours a day, so when you make your reservation, always ask how late the office is open. All sorts of things can hold you up on the road. If you find yourself in need of a campground after hours, most of them post the available spaces on a bulletin board or in a night box somewhere outside the office door. You can pick a site, fill out the paperwork, and pay in the method requested on the form. Some smaller and older campgrounds won't accept credit cards after the office closes (and a few won't accept them at all), so be sure you have enough cash on hand to tuck into the envelope before you pull in for the night, or bring your checkbook (if you have such a thing these days). Also, take note of the after-hours phone number — most campgrounds have someone living on-site at all times to handle any problems, day or night.

# Chapter **13**

# Setting Up Your Campsite

ost RVers want to get away from the annoyances of urban civilization. But the majority of them also like to take a bit of it with them in the form of conveniences like electricity, water, a sewer hookup, and a reliable Wi-Fi connection.

Setting up your campsite is as easy a routine as anything you do at home, but it can seem daunting when you've never done it before. In this chapter, we explain the basics of getting settled into a campground site, including how to hook up the connections you'll find there.

**REMEMBER**

There are so many RVs with so many systems that it would be impossible to give you a precise checklist for your specific rig. But in terms of their essentials, these systems are the same, because their function is the same: to supply you with the comforts of home in the great outdoors.

## Pulling into the Campground and Finding Your Campsite

All systems are go, and you're pulling into camp. To a complete newbie (and we've been there), some of this may sound depressingly time-consuming, but it's not. When you get into the routine of setting up a campsite, you should be able to do it in about 15 minutes, 20 at most.

TIP

In addition to reading this chapter, watch a couple YouTube videos to get a visual of how easy it is when you know how. Our favorite is the Long Long Honeymoon video at `https://youtu.be/SYH7Ka7ZGmEj`.

**REMEMBER**

On your first arrival, remember to drive slowly, particularly after dark. Camps are loaded with kids, as well as joggers, dog walkers, and bikers, and you're new to seeing everything around you. (Turn to Chapter 12 for more on some of the issues and peculiarities of campgrounds.)

Ask for a pull-through site your first time out of the gate, but recognize that you may not be able to get it. Most campgrounds offer both *back-in* and *pull-through* campsites, and they're exactly what they sound like:

>> **Pull-through campsites** are the hands-down favorite for most RVers because they're so easy: Just point the nose of your vehicle and pull on through. They're great if you're only staying one night.

>> **Back-in campsites** are less popular and tend to be a remnant of the past, when trailers were much smaller. They also tend to be narrow. Staying in a very old park in Newport Beach, where spaces ran up to $200 a night, it was downright painful to watch a 46-foot Class A motorhome try to squeeze into one of the back-in sites. It took over an hour.

Some campgrounds have a staff member lead you to your site and help you get lined up with your various utilities. But even if it looks like they're getting impatient, it's a good idea to get out of the driver's seat and lay eyes on everything yourself. After all, it's not their rig, it's yours, and you can't always get a perfect view of potential obstructions from behind the wheel.

**WARNING**

No matter how excited you are to kick back with a beer after a long drive, don't assume that a campsite will accommodate your rig because they gave it to you. Even if you're lucky enough to have an RV that's bristling with video cameras (and most aren't), no set of cameras can see everything. Look for low-hanging tree branches directly over your rooftop air conditioner. If your rig has slide-out rooms, be sure trees, utility poles, lampposts, power pedestals, and even the RV in the adjacent campsite don't interfere when you deploy. The same goes for your awning.

**TIP**

At the risk of repeating ourselves, parking in a dicey place is easier with a buddy and a cheap pair of "family band" walkie-talkies. Or, if your tow vehicle is equipped with a hands-free smartphone connection, just call each other on your phones so the driver doesn't have to juggle anything while maneuvering. If you're alone, and you don't have eight cameras, you may have to get out a few times during this process and see for yourself where all your hookups are to make sure you can reach everything.

# On the Level: Leveling Your RV

After you've parked in your site, the first order of business is to make sure your rig is level.

It's a fact of life that most campsites aren't perfectly level from side to side. They can be concrete, asphalt, gravel, dirt, grass, or sand, but even the solid-surface ones have low spots from the hundreds of rigs before you. If it rained recently, on pea gravel or sand, your rig may even sink a bit as it settles.

Being level isn't just a question of your personal feng shui. Things in your RV don't always work right unless it's level. Also, RVs and their chassis are flexible, and a severely unlevel rig can subtly flex the frame. In an unlevel rig, the doors and cabinets can swing open or closed on their own (which is spooky), and some types of RV refrigerators don't want to run properly. Worse, slide-outs can actually buckle and do damage to their mechanisms if the RV isn't perfectly flat when you deploy or retract them.

**TECHNICAL STUFF**

In recent years, some high-end motorhomes and fifth wheels come standard with automatic self-leveling jacks. Push a button, and the rig rumbles and shudders as the jacks lower and adjust themselves over even the lumpiest campsite. But the rest of us poor shlubs have to level the old-fashioned way.

**WARNING**

As eager as everyone is to pile into the RV, don't let anyone inside while you're still leveling and getting unhitched. A sudden jolt from decoupling can cause a lurch bad enough to knock someone off their feet.

**TIP**

One of your first tool investments needs to be a $5 bubble level (sometimes called a *spirit level* or *torpedo level*). The 8-inch plastic ones work just fine. Some RVs come with a bubble level on top of the hitch jack, but they aren't always reliable. (We've yet to find one that is.) Others may have a curved bubble level mounted on the front of the trailer's body that lets you quickly see your side-to-side level with just a glance. The benefit of having a separate level is that you can move it around anywhere to double-check.

If you don't have a bubble level, smartphones these days often come with a built-in level app. Lay the phone flat on the A-frame or the floor inside, and it will show your status at a glance by changing color when you're perfect. If you deleted the app (or you can't find it), lots of free or cheap apps are available that do the same thing. But beware: Your RV's floor inside may be slightly bowed. Experience will tell you the best place to make the final determination about your level.

## Leveling side to side

The first step in leveling your RV is determining that your rig is sitting level from side-to-side. Put the bubble level on your rig's A-frame turned left to right, and see if you lucked out and are in the sweet spot. Like miracles, it has been known to happen.

If one side is lower, it's time for the creative engineering. This is when you'll need plastic *leveling blocks* (see Chapter 9). They're about the size of a big bathroom floor tile. Start by putting one or two of these blocks in front of or behind the wheels on the low side. Then pull the rig up onto them. If you're alone, inching up onto the blocks and *just far enough* to balance on top of them without driving off the other side can be frustrating, so a helper makes it easier ("Up, up, up, back, back, back, STOP!").

After you've done it a few times, you'll get a feel for how many leveling blocks you need — for us, it's one block per off-center bubble space. Very scientific.

When the low side is up on the blocks, check your side-to-side level. You may have to drive off and try again. It's an imprecise science — one may be not quite high enough, two may be a smidgen too high, so close counts.

When you're satisfied, put down *wheel blocks* (also known as *chocks* or *wheel wedges*) in front of and behind at least one set of tires on both sides of your rig to keep it from rolling away. Some RVers with dual axles prefer a crank-out set of wheel locks that go between tires, purpose-built for tandem axles.

You're still not done with leveling, but you'll probably have to unhook from your tow vehicle before you tackle the next step.

## Unhitching your trailer from your tow vehicle

**REMEMBER**

Before you start to lift your trailer off your hitch ball, make sure your tow vehicle is in Park and your trailer's wheels are chocked. If the ground feels at all soft or muddy, you can place a stack of your leveling blocks under the jack's foot before you start lowering it.

**WARNING**

The instructions here are skewed to the most common hitch, from tow vehicle to trailer. In a fifth wheel, all the same issues are occurring, but the system is a bit different due to the coupling system being mounted in the bed of the tow truck. A fifth wheel also has a turning radius unique to the system that can make parking it a bear for the uninitiated. Again, if you're a newbie, learn that system thoroughly, and take a video of your dealer walking you through it. Practice in your own driveway — a lot — before you take on the campground.

# "CAN'T I JUST STAY HITCHED?"

If you're just trying to eat up the miles by spending the night and moving on the next morning, you may not bother to unhitch. But you may have trouble getting level front to back. If the front end of the trailer is sitting lower than the back end, raising it up while still hitched is pretty simple with your hitch jack. But if the trailer's nose is up too high when you pull into your campsite, you'll have to unhitch and get your tow vehicle's hitch ball out from under the A-frame so you can lower the trailer enough to get level.

If you stay hitched, be sure to unplug your RV's multipin electrical cable from your tow vehicle prior to connecting to the site's power pedestal. This keeps stray power from your rig from frying your car or truck's electrical system. (We talk lots more about RV electrical systems in Chapter 14.)

Hitch jacks can be manually cranked or blessedly motorized. Either way, follow these steps:

1. **Depending on your equipment and the way it's installed, you first need to remove any anti-sway or weight distribution bars attached to your A-frame and hitch.**

   All the ones we've used recommend keeping everything connected together and raising the hitch jack just high enough to take the tension off the bars. This puts the most strain on your jack because you're also lifting the back end of your truck or tow vehicle. So, expect it to groan and complain a bit in protest.

2. **As you raise the jack, yank on the stabilizer bars until they swing free from their A-frame brackets.**

3. **Unfasten their locking pins and chains, pull out the bars, and set them aside.**

   Put them underneath the trailer's front end, in the back end of the tow vehicle, or put them back loosely on their trailer brackets, anywhere you won't forget them when it's time to re-hitch.

4. **Lower the hitch jack back down until the weight is off of its pedestal foot again.**

5. **Unhook the safety chains and the breakaway brake cable, unplug the multipin electrical connector from your tow vehicle, and remove the locking pin or padlock from the flip-down hitch latch (or *locking lever*).**

6. **Take one last look and make sure nothing is left connecting your trailer to your tow vehicle except the hitch coupler itself.**

7. **Flip up the latch to release the internal mechanism gripping around the ball.**

**8. Now you can raise the jack up again.**

Keep raising it until it's high enough for the ball to clear the underside of the hitch coupler.

TIP

If the latch is stubborn and raising the jack only drags the back end of your tow vehicle up in the air even after you flipped up the latch lever, lower the jack again by a few inches. Get into your truck and push the brake pedal down as you put the gearshift in Forward or Reverse. Then quickly pump the brake a single time so you move forward or backward by *just a fraction of an inch*. All you're trying to do is break free from the stuck latch mechanism by releasing any strain on it. If you keep the driver's side window open, you'll hear the latch loudly click as it releases. Put the vehicle back in Park and raise the jack again until the coupler clears the hitch ball.

**9. Slowly pull your tow vehicle forward and park it.**

## Leveling front to back

You're in the home stretch now. Grab your trusty bubble level again, and this time turn it lengthwise on your A-frame so it's measuring the trailer's level from front to back.

Lower the hitch jack until the bubble shows you're level. Now, go up into your RV and check the floor level in a couple of places. You're looking for the best compromise in a long RV, to avoid feeling like you're leaning uphill or downhill inside. Keep adjusting until it feels right to you.

When you've done all this, you want to make sure your rig stays that way until you hit the road again. If you have motorized stabilizer jacks, it's as simple as pushing a button. But most smaller rigs have manual scissors or hydraulic jacks. Yours may be permanently attached to your trailer's frame, but if they're freestanding, they need to be placed under all four corners of your RV in flat, sturdy locations on the metal frame.

TIP

Manual stabilizer jacks come with a long hand crank. Keep it in your RVs storage cabinet, in case you need it. But hand cranking is both time consuming and tough on your wrist after a while. Using a cordless 18-volt electric drill fitted with a ¾-inch or 19mm socket adapter is a lot simpler and much faster. You can find the socket for less than $10 at Amazon and most RV camping stores.

WARNING

If your drill has the ability to adjust its speed and torque, use the slowest setting — high-speed settings can overtighten the jack so hard and fast that it can wrench the drill out of your hands and twist the crankshaft or strip its threads.

# Connecting Your Utilities

When your rig is level and secured in place, your next task is to connect your power, water, and sewer lines, along with turning on your propane gas supply. We talk much more about electricity in Chapter 14, water and sewer in Chapter 15, and propane gas in Chapter 16. Be sure to read those chapters before you embark on your first trip. But this section offers the essential steps to take when connecting your utilities.

## Electricity

We cover your RV's electrical system in Chapter 14, but this section offers a primer on getting everything connected at the campsite.

Start by opening the hinged cover on the campsite's power pedestal. Inside, you'll see several circuit breakers, and at least two, and probably three, kinds of electrical outlets (see Figure 13-1):

>> Two 15- or 20-amp, 120-volt household-style outlets

>> One three-prong, 30-amp, 120-volt outlet

>> Probably one four-prong, 50-amp, 240-volt outlet

**TIP**

RV advice columns will tell you to always use a voltmeter to check the outlet on the power pedestal before you plug into it. We recommend the use of a good surge protector when connecting to shore power, and not just to prevent power surges that can devastate your electrical system. The best surge protectors have a visual LED warning display that alerts you if the electrical connection isn't wired correctly, has the wrong polarity or voltage, or isn't properly grounded, and they'll shut down the power to your rig if they detect something wrong. RV surge protectors can be expensive, but in our experience, they're worth the money.

To connect your power, follow these steps:

**1.** **Make sure the power pedestal circuit breakers are all in the off position.**

**2.** **Plug the female end (without prongs) of your rig's big, thick power cable into your RV's power inlet.**

It may have a flip-up cover over it and should be marked as *shore power* or *120V/30 amp* or *240V/50 amp*.

Some motorhomes and bigger trailers have their power cable hard-wired directly into the rig and frequently mounted on a self-winding reel inside of an exterior storage compartment.

**FIGURE 13-1:**
The power panel
of the campsite's
pedestal should
look similar
to this.

*Photograph courtesy of Christopher Hodapp*

3. **Plug the male end (with the brass prongs) of your power cable into its appropriate outlet in the box: three prongs for 30 amps, four prongs for 50 amps.**

TIP

If you have a surge protector for your shore power, plug it in to the outlet first. Then plug your cable into the surge protector's outlet.

4. **Turn on the circuit breakers in the pedestal box.**

5. **Go inside and turn on the shore power switch that powers up your systems.**

6. **Make sure your refrigerator is set on Auto or Electric.**

TIP

It's very easy to drive off without your surge protector — you may want to put this on your whiteboard or to-do list. And remember, expensive surge protectors are one of the most stealable items in the park (second only to portable generators), so consider a padlock.

# Water

We explain all about your rig's water and sewer systems in Chapter 15, where we cover the difference between hooking up to a continuous supply or filling up your holding tanks. But when you arrive at camp, here are the basic steps:

1. **Locate the campsite's water supply.**

   Near the power pedestal, you'll find a pipe sticking out of the ground, usually with a good old-fashioned garden-hose spigot. Think of it as your own personal spring.

2. **Turn it on and let it run for a moment to blow out any rust or sediment that may be in the pipe.**

TIP

   Many RVers screw on an inline pressure regulator to prevent a high-pressure blast from the park's water supply from possibly blowing apart their plumbing connections. But before you do that, look at your rig's city water inlet and see if your manufacturer has already installed one at the factory; it will be stamped there. A double-dose of regulators can bring your pressure way down.

3. **Connect your white or blue drinking water hose to the campground's spigot.**

   If you want to use an inline water filter, you'll need to use a short section of hose to screw the filter into and then attach your longer hose to the other end of the filter.

TIP

   If the filter is brand new, turn on the water again at the spigot and let it run for a minute to blow the excess activated charcoal out of the filter.

4. **If you're going to use the campground's water connection as a continuous supply, screw your hose into the *city water* (or *freshwater*) inlet valve on your RV.**

   Turn on the campsite spigot, and you're all set! Move on to Step 6.

   ***Note:*** If you're going to use your freshwater holding tank and water pump for your water needs, skip this step and move on to the next one.

5. **Use the hose to fill up your freshwater tank.**

   On many rigs, that inlet may be hiding behind a small locked hatch on your RV. Other rigs may put all water connections inside of a compartment door on the shore side. There may be no screw-on valve, just an open pipe with a cap on it. Shove the hose into the pipe, turn on the camp spigot, and let it run. When the tank is filled, water will come streaming out of the pipe into the ground, so go shut it off before it turns your campsite into a mud bog. (Other types of rigs use a single inlet connection for city water and filling the tank, with a valve to switch between the two.)

6. **Go inside and let the RV's sink faucets and shower run for a minute as the incoming water blows air out of the pipes.**

REMEMBER

If you're using your holding tank, you'll need to turn on the water pump.

7. **When the faucets stop sputtering and the water runs in a steady stream, turn them off.**

## Sewer

The campground sewer connection is normally a round 3-inch plastic pipe set in the ground. Some have caps or lids, but there's no uniformity. Some may have nothing more covering them than a rock.

In Chapter 15, we tell you more than you'll ever want to know about connecting your sewer lines, so skip to that chapter for the full details.

WARNING

You can already see that the shore side of your rig, around the power pedestal and water supply, is getting busy. Adding the sewer line's slinky hose makes it even more crowded, like a convention of drunken snakes. After dark, it's easy to trip over this no-man's land of shore connections. Be careful!

TIP

If you're only staying overnight, you're probably okay with not bothering to hook up your sewer hose. Again, learn to keep an eye on your inside graywater and blackwater tank gauges. But if you're parked for any longer, or you anticipate showers and other activities that create lots of wastewater, go ahead and set up your sewer hose so you can conveniently drain off graywater as needed.

REMEMBER

Save up enough graywater to help wash out the slinky hose when it comes time to drain the blackwater tank.

## Propane

When you've got water in the system, you can turn on the propane (technically known as liquefied petroleum gas, or LPG). (We tell you all about propane in Chapter 16.) Go to your propane tanks and open up the gas valve on at least one of them. If you have a crossover valve, set it for your preference — to pull gas equally out of multiple tanks, or just one at a time.

Like the water, gas lines get air in them. Propane or dual-fuel appliances like water heaters, refrigerators, and furnaces have built-in ignition systems. When they first try to come on but there's still air filling the lines, you'll hear them clicking until gas arrives and their burners finally light. Your stovetop and oven likely have manual ignition controls.

# Making Life Comfortable

With everything unhitched and the utilities all properly connected, you can now concentrate on spreading out and getting comfy. You're ready to deploy your slides, hook up your TV and Wi-Fi (if you really want them), and get down to some serious loafing by the campfire.

## Opening your slides

If your rig has slide-out rooms, you can open them up after you've got all your utilities up and running. Start by making sure there aren't any objects or obstacles inside or outside the slides. Take an inspection walk around the outside of your rig. Be sure to look up, to check for tree branches or other low-hanging obstructions.

TIP

If there are at least two of you, have one person outside as a spotter while the other one stays indoors pushing buttons. Make sure you can hear one another as you open the slides.

If your slides have locking bars to prevent them from opening on the highway, unlock or remove them. When the slides are all opened up, reinstall any slide locking bars that may have come with your rig.

WARNING

On many RVs, the deployed slides sit at the ideal skull-whacking height, with a sharp metal corner. The universal go-to answer is to buy several foam swimming pool flotation noodles and cut them to the proper lengths. They come in an assortment of bright colors, which helps you see them, and if you use a different color for each slide, you can always tell which one goes where. Just cut a slice lengthwise and wrap it around the slide's bottom edge.

## Getting TV service

Cable TV seems almost quaint in these days of streaming video. You may have cut the cable at home years ago, and now you're parked in an outdoor paradise to be one with nature. So, there's no way on Earth you'd ever want to watch TV when you're camping. Except the playoffs are on Sunday. We get it. Most RVs these days come with at least one TV, and bigger rigs have more than one, so you're covered.

TECHNICAL
STUFF

Before the switch in the United States from analog to digital (HD) TV transmission two decades ago, over-the-air reception was always a static-filled crapshoot when it came to tuning in a decent picture, unless you were near an urban area. Over the years, campgrounds reacted to RVers demanding TV reception in isolated areas by installing a basic cable TV package in their campsites. The switch to HDTV changed that a bit. Local TV stations were given multiple side-band stations, doubling and tripling the number of stations and networks viewers could tune in without cable, satellite, or streaming. But many campgrounds still have cable TV hookups on their properties.

## Connecting to cable TV

You'll often find an unmarked coaxial TV cable mounted on or near the power pedestal, in a metal box of its own, or screwed to a wooden post. They can be almost anywhere — at some campsites, it just sticks out of the ground. There should be a coaxial TV connection marked on the shore side of your rig, sometimes behind a flip-up cover. Depending on how yours is wired, you may have two coaxial connectors, marked *CABLE* or *SAT* (for satellite). Hook up the camp's cable connector to your rig's with a long coaxial TV cable, and you should be able to tune in cable stations and networks.

TIP

The campground's map usually has a list of over-the-air and cable stations available. There may be a charge for the service. Some goofy cable TV companies require the campground to hand you a full-blown digital converter box with its own remote control in order to unscramble stations.

REMEMBER

Don't discount the usefulness of being able to tune in local TV stations. Local events, weather warnings, sports programming, and other timely information can be useful and help you find out about the community you're near in ways your phone apps can't.

## Programming your TV

When RV makers install a TV, they're usually kind enough to also attach it to an external antenna on the roof (not always, but we'll pretend they did on yours). Like your digital set at home, the TV will have multiple ways to program stations, depending on whether you're using an antenna, cable, or another source. Check your TV menus.

The TV can't decide on its own whether to use your antenna or cable, so your RV may have a separate switch on the wall to flip between over-the-air and cable signals feeding into the TV. It may look mysterious, with an indicator light — the light on means it's switched to the antenna, perhaps with an amplified signal booster as well. It should be turned off to use cable.

When you have the antenna turned on, use your TV's manual to see the particulars of tuning in. Your set needs to memorize the available stations. After it's done programming, if you want cable, turn off the antenna, switch the TV's input setting from AIR to CABLE, and program those stations as well.

Just remember when you're channel flipping that you have two sets of choices — cable or on air — that require you to switch the antenna off or on.

Programming your TV in each new park is confusing at first. Make a video of your dealer tech showing you the system, and consult it until you get the hang of it.

### Tuning in to satellite TV

RVers who demand more dependable TV wherever they go can opt for a portable satellite dish. DISH Network has led the industry with its RV packages; it offers a small, self-contained satellite dish contraption that looks remarkably like a 1950s hair dryer helmet. It can either be mounted to the roof of your rig, or just plopped on the ground anywhere it can have a clear view of the southern sky. It connects with a coaxial cable to your rig's external cable connector — some have a specific one marked *SAT*. Indoors, you need a receiver box.

The service does require a monthly subscription, and the dish and receiver can be a little pricey. But they work even in the middle of the Mojave desert, when there's no other reception of any kind.

### Streaming TV

You can use a TV streaming device like Apple TV, Amazon Fire TV, Roku, Chromecast, and more on the road. But they all depend on a robust Internet connection to work, which isn't always easy or even doable everywhere. (More on that in the next section.)

## Communicating with the outside world

You escaped to the distant solitude of the Great Outdoors to get away from the hustle and bustle of daily wage-slave drudgery. And the second question the kids ask after "When do we eat?" is "Why doesn't my phone work?" The RV industry — both manufacturers and campgrounds — have been slow to adopt the most recent technology when it comes to remaining in constant, high-speed communication. But, to be fair, there is no single, one-size-fits-all solution for accessing the Internet and cell service when you're on the road.

RVers have to be creative and flexible in order to stay in communication. You need to be prepared to use free Wi-Fi hotspots, shared campground Wi-Fi systems, cellular data plans, and if you're *really* in the wilderness, even satellite services. If your work relies on a constant Internet connection, your solution will be very different from casual, social users.

Eventually, the national adoption of 5G cellular systems will make almost every-thing we say in this section obsolete. But like everything else, campgrounds far from major cities and towns will likely be the last places to get the newest technology.

The best go-to website for up-to-date researching of Internet connectivity and RVing is www.rvmobileinternet.com. It provides detailed reviews, methods, and buying guides for nearly every type of situation.

In the following sections, we walk you through your options for getting online.

## Wi-Fi hotspots

The world is full of free and subscription-based Wi-Fi hotspots, from hotels, res-taurants, and coffee shops, to truck stops, libraries, public parks, and even some interstate rest areas.

If you pay for a home subscription to Xfinity Internet services, you have access to tens of thousands of its hotspots around the country that you can take advantage of if you're armed with your login and password info from home.

Public hotspots are much slower than you're probably used to at home. They also don't broadcast a strong signal, so you have to be as close as possible to their transmitting router. If you'll be relying a lot on hotspots, you may want to invest in a quality Wi-Fi antenna and signal booster to help improve the signal strength.

## Campground Wi-Fi

Plenty of campgrounds claim to offer "free high-speed Internet access," but like other advertising slogans, it's a meaningless phrase. The better campgrounds have usually invested in a system with multiple transmission masts dotted around their property, and they'll give you the login and password when you check in (it's usually printed on their site map). But many campgrounds may try to limit your streaming, particularly in the high season.

Few campground "shared" Wi-Fi systems were designed to handle the explosion of Internet data at high speeds required for video streaming and high-res, live gaming that's erupted in the 2020s. Wi-Fi signals aren't strong, so covering lots of acreage with a decent signal and passable bandwidth is an expensive proposi-tion that needs constant upgrading — all to accomplish something that customers take for granted and don't want to pay for.

Depending on its system, the campground may warn specifically against video streaming and may throttle your use (or shut you down completely) if you bog down their system. It's sort of like everyone simultaneously flushing their toilets at half-time during the Super Bowl. You're sharing the connection with lots of other campers. So, if you're checking your stock portfolio when everybody logs on at 9 p.m. to binge all 23 seasons of *Ancient Aliens* or livestream the Minecraft championships, nobody will be happy. Plus, campground owners and staffers are rarely skilled IT experts capable of fixing router problems.

## Cellular data

For several years, we used our cellphones to create our own hotspots when we were on the road. That's usually a matter of changing a setting in your smartphone's preferences or control panel to let a laptop, tablet, or other device log in to your phone's private hotspot. As long as you can pick up a decent cell signal, you can use it to access your email, work on the web, and even stream videos — as long as you're willing to pay for it.

**TIP**

Data plans on cellphones vary a *lot* and they're constantly changing, so keep an eye out for deals on so-called "unlimited" data plans. Otherwise, your first bill after a two-week road trip could be a shock, especially if your laptop decides to download a software upgrade and back up its entire contents to the cloud without your knowing it.

Another option is less convenient, but works if you can deal with the limitations. Plenty of cars, trucks, and SUVs have onboard cellular data plans, like GM's OnStar system, which is provided through AT&T for a monthly subscription fee. Turn on the ignition, and devices in and around your car can log on to the car's Wi-Fi signal. The obvious downside is that it only works when the car is running.

## Onboard RV mobile routers

Similar to the OnStar system, some RV manufacturers are beginning to offer mobile routers in their rigs, connected to a cellular data system. These devices connect to a cell signal, and then broadcast a Wi-Fi signal throughout your trailer, motorhome, or campsite. Airstream was one of the first RV makers to start installing these units and offering monthly or annual data plans (through AT&T) that could handle multiple devices and entertainment streaming. More companies have followed suit.

**TIP**

If your rig doesn't have one, Winegard (https://winegard.com), Togo (https://togorv.com), and other companies are making combination Wi-Fi extender/cellular router systems that use cellphone data plans. Research these products carefully before you buy anything, because the equipment alone can be expensive, and then you have to pay for the data plan. Because installation may involve drilling holes in your RV roof, professional installation is probably a good idea.

# CAMPGROUND ETIQUETTE

Campgrounds are unique places. Campers come from all over the country and even the world. They're young and old, kids and retirees, working folks and trust-fund babies, loners, couples, and extended families. If you stay in the same place for a while, you may have all new neighbors every evening. So, the number-one rule of RVers is: *Don't be rude.* Here are a few more rules of common-sense etiquette. Overwhelmingly, our campground experiences have been positive, in hundreds of parks, and most campers follow these rules almost instinctively.

- **Try to keep the noise down.** RV parks often have group events, and various holidays may be lively, so try to join in. People in RV parks often have movie nights outside in summer. Outdoor entertainment systems have been a mixed blessing at best. It's tough to enjoy the Great Outdoors and marvel at the twitter of the mountain meadowlarks when the guy 15 feet away from you insists on blasting out the roaring football crowd or Bruce Springsteen's *Greatest Hits* on his rig's outdoor speakers. Smile and let your neighbors enjoy the Big Game, but they shouldn't inflict three games in a row on you. A very common park annoyance we've seen is people who don't seem to even know their outside speakers are on, for hours on end.

  After sunset you'll see campsite lights come on and fires start. Conversations drift along on the breeze, and last into the wee hours. Just be aware that the campground may post distinct "quiet time" hours (usually 10 p.m. to 6 a.m.), during which everyone is expected to avoid yodeling contests, rebel yells, and karaoke competitions.

- **Don't walk through someone else's campsite.** It's like cutting across someone's front porch. Similarly, your rig's backyard where all your shore connections reside is also the next site's *front* yard. Don't junk it up, and for heaven's sake, don't get careless when dumping your wastewater. No one wants their picnic area festooned with shredded toilet paper from your sewer hose mishap.

- **Pick up your trash.** Don't let the disposable dinner dishes get strewn all over the campsite and blown down the road. Bag up trash as soon as you generate it. And never leave trash, bagged or otherwise, outside overnight. It attracts the local rodentry and other wildlife. Keep it inside your rig or walk it to the dumpster.

- **Don't burn plastic cups, bags, knives and forks, or Styrofoam plates in your campfire.** It stinks. And bottles and aluminum cans don't burn at all. Besides, after you leave, the campground staff will have to shovel out your campfire trash. Just because you have a campfire going doesn't mean you can throw everything in it.

- **Avoid using a generator.** Electrical generators are the bane of campgrounds. They're noisy, stinky, and most important, not needed if sites have electricity. Many developed campgrounds forbid or limit their use, so save it for the boondocks. Similarly, if you have a diesel motorhome, be aware that firing up your engine and letting it run at the crack of dawn has the same effect, even if you can't hear it over the AC inside.

- **Keep your dog on a leash when not in your RV or the dog park.** Don't tie up your pooch and leave them unattended. Always pick up your dog's land mines and dispose of them. Nobody likes stepping in dog poop, especially in their own campsite.

- **Don't light up your RV and campsite bright enough at night to look like the face of the sun.** Loads of campers and stargazers around you want the solitude and serenity of a darkened sky. So after 10 p.m., cut back on the illumination level.

# 4

# Understanding How Your RV Works

Figure out the basics of RV electrical systems.

Understand the ins and outs of your rig's water and sewer systems.

Learn about propane's many uses and safe handling.

Keep comfortable with your heating, ventilation, and air-conditioning system.

# Chapter **14**

# Electrical Systems

Our very favorite RV salesperson lives by a simple motto: "If a new RVer understands their water, power, and poop, they're ready to go camping!" We agree with that perceptive, if piquant, observation.

When you drive through an RV campground, take a look at the driver's side of the rigs. You'll see a fat electrical cord — it looks like a garden hose — and a thick, twisty snakelike tube about the size of a kid's Slinky toy, both sprouting from the side of nearly every rig you pass. The other ends are plugged, screwed, or wedged into various connections near the ground. All that stuff is about water, power, and poop.

**REMEMBER**

Unlike in your house, you need to stay aware of everything you consume in your RV, because on the road, no resource is truly unlimited.

We start this part of the book with electricity because it's probably the first thing you want to turn on after you park your rig. In your house, you don't worry about where electricity comes from and everything it operates until there's a power failure. But an RV is very different because it's been designed to be as self-sufficient as possible. You can pull into a campground and plug into the campground's electricity, but you don't necessarily *have* to, as long as you understand your RV's limitations.

Discussions of electricity can easily become eye-glazing when words like *volts*, *amps*, *current*, or *wattage* appear, especially if you've never had to learn this stuff before. So, we keep this chapter as simple as possible. If you *really* want to know much more about electricity and electronics, snatch up a copy of Doug Lowe's *Electronics All-in-One For Dummies* (Wiley).

# One RV, Two Kinds of Power

Whether you know it or not, your home is wired for both 120 and 240 volts (V) of *alternating current* (AC), in which the electrons running through the wire are constantly flowing back and forth in alternating directions. If you look at the labels on electrical appliances, light bulbs, and phone chargers that you normally never look at, you'll usually see that they're rated for 120V of AC. If you have an electric clothes dryer, an electric heating and air-conditioning system, or an electric stove, it needs even more energy in order to work, so it requires 240 volts of AC.

Your car or truck is very different. Your vehicle's engine has an *alternator* under the hood that generates 12 volts of *direct current* (DC), in which the electrons run through the wires in one direction only. What that means in practice is that you can't take the blender from your kitchen out to the car and plug it in to the dashboard to mix up a smoothie. Unless you're driving a Tesla, your vehicle has a 12V storage battery in it. That battery's main job is to store up enough 12V energy to start the car again the next time you turn the key. The battery has a limited amount of energy stored in it, which is why your battery dies when you accidentally leave the headlights on all night — the battery had no running engine to keep supplying it power.

An RV combines *both* kinds of power — AC and DC. There are two distinct electrical systems inside to make use of *both* 12 volts DC *and* 120 volts AC (abbreviated as 12VDC and 120VAC), depending on what's available:

>> **House or coach power:** This is 12VDC electricity that lights up the living areas of your rig. If you're not plugged into external power, you can operate some devices and appliances *for a limited time* on 12V storage battery power alone.

>> **Shore power:** Plug your big, fat power cord into an external AC power supply at a campground, and you'll have nonstop power for your appliances and accessories, just like at home. At the same time, 120 volts are sent into an onboard *power converter* in your rig that converts it down to 12VDC to run all your 12V accessories and keep your house batteries recharged.

# UNDERSTANDING WHAT'S WATT

**TECHNICAL STUFF**

When it comes to talking about electricity, people who aren't licensed electricians or who don't work in hardware stores often bandy about a bunch of different terms interchangeably. We don't want to nuke you with too many at once, but these are the essentials.

*Voltage* (measured in *volts*) is a specific amount of energy that's waiting patiently to start moving down a wire when you flip on a switch. But voltage can't go anywhere by itself. In order to start moving through a wire, electricity needs to be able to flow in a big circle, called a *circuit*. Think of it looking like a dog frantically chasing their tail in circles — it has to start somewhere and eventually meet back up with itself in order to complete the circuit. A battery has *plus* and *minus terminals,* or *positive* and *negative* sides, while the AC voltage in your house has a *hot* side and a *neutral* side. The electricity is able to move from one side to the other in a complete circuit. A switch interrupts that flow when it's turned off.

When a circuit is completed (like turning on that light switch in the bathroom), the movement of electrons through the wire is called *current*. And the higher the voltage, the more current will start flowing. For instance, your household wall plug's 120V pumps out much more current than your Ford's 12V car battery, which has more current than your 1.5V AA flashlight battery. That flowing current of excited electrons is measured in *amperes* or *amps* (A).

The combination of voltage with current is called electrical *power*. The higher the voltage *and* the greater the current, the more electrical power you have. That electrical power gets expressed as *watts* (W). You multiply volts times the current to calculate wattage:

Watts = Volts × Amps

For example, when you go shopping for electrical generators, manufacturers advertise the amount of electrical power their units are able to generate in watts. It's usually at that moment when you come to the sickening realization that you shouldn't have slept through four years of high school math classes.

Wattage also helps you figure out how much electrical power you can safely push through an electrical circuit without overloading, overheating, or otherwise endangering the wiring. Fuses and circuit breakers are identified by how much *amperage* (current) they can safely conduct without any damage or danger. If you exceed their intended amperage, they protect you by shutting off the power. Amps equals watts divided by volts:

Amps = Watts ÷ Volts

*(continued)*

*(continued)*

Say you have a 1,000W microwave oven plugged into a 120V circuit. If you divide the microwave's watts by voltage, that gives you the amount of amps it's trying to use in the circuit, which is 8.3. As a comparison, a single 100W light bulb draws just 0.8A.

Back when we were in film school together, Ol' Doc Timmons told us a simple shortcut to determine amperage and keep an added margin of safety when calculating power requirements: If you use 100V in the equation instead of the more correct 120 just for sake of round numbers, a 1,000W toaster works out to 10 amps. In reality, it draws less, but *overestimating* power consumption is always better than *underestimating*. And you can do it in your head a lot easier. This is the magical math boondockers are in search of so that they can calculate whether each appliance can run on their generator. (We go into this subject in more detail in Chapter 20.)

**TECHNICAL STUFF**

Your RV isn't made for sailing trips, but the term *shore power* actually comes from the nautical world. When they tie up at a dock, boats and ships have the same problem RVs have: Unless they run their engines to generate electricity the whole time they're in port, they need to hook up to external electricity and pump in fresh water from onshore. Over the years, as the trailer world and campgrounds all settled into some sense of agreement when it came to utility hookups, the driver's side of the rig came to be called the *shore side* and the 120V AC power hookup got nicknamed *shore power*.

# What Runs What

Because you've got lots of different devices powered by lots of different sources at different voltages and sometimes at different times, it's important to know just what system runs what in your RV.

## Engine or chassis system

When you start up your pickup truck, SUV, or the engine of your motorhome, its 12VDC battery and spinning alternator send electricity to the cockpit devices involved with the "driving" part of your rig. These include the ignition, headlights, turn signals, dashboard radio or entertainment system, dashboard heating and air conditioning, windshield wipers, horn, power seats, windows and door locks, plus anything plugged into the cigarette lighter or USB power ports around the driver and passenger seats (like your phone, backup cameras, and GPS units). It also sends power to operate the towing brakes and your rig's marker and brake lights. And, as an added bonus, it sends electricity to your RV's house batteries to keep them charged while you're driving.

## The 12VDC house power system

The 12VDC house battery or batteries in your rig are what let you run much of your living-space devices and accessories when you have no other outside source of electricity. These include interior and exterior lights, vent fans, propane furnace fan, water pump, slide-out motors, power awning, electric or hydraulic leveling jacks, power hitch jack, 12V TVs (if you have them), plus your monitoring panels, safety alarms and detectors, and the all-important 12VDC-to-120VAC power *inverter* (more about this magical device later in this chapter).

Because RVs prioritize the mission of keeping their own house batteries charged, they're designed to snatch electricity wherever they can get it. Plug into a 120VAC campground power pedestal, and your RV converts it to 12VDC and charges your batteries. If you connect your trailer to a tow vehicle with a multipronged seven-way hitch plug or start your motorhome's engine, some of that electricity will flow into your house batteries from your engine's 12V alternator. The same is true if you have solar panels. If the sun is shining, the solar panels send a trickle charge to your batteries. (This is why your trailer shouldn't be plugged into both shore power and your tow vehicle at the same time — it may cause an overload and fry your tow vehicle's electrical system.)

Your RV will have one or more large house (or coach) batteries that are the heart of its 12VDC electrical system. Most RV batteries are called *deep-cycle batteries,* and although they may look just like the battery under the hood in your car, they're actually quite different. Batteries in your car are made to be steadily charged all the time by your running engine and to provide a big, fast burst of energy to crank the electric starter when you turn on the ignition. But if you routinely leave your headlights on long enough to run down the power in your car battery and constantly have to jump-start it, every time that happens, its storage capacity is weakened until it can no longer keep a charge.

TIP

Deep-cycle batteries in your rig are *made* to be drained and recharged over and over (although you shouldn't let them drain below 50 percent). They don't need to pump out a powerful blast of high current the way your car does. Instead, they're made to provide a nice, slow, steady current over a much longer period of time. In order to have more storage capacity, RVs often have two 12V batteries wired together (referred to as *in parallel*). For more information, check out the nearby sidebar, "Stalking the perfect battery."

# STALKING THE PERFECT BATTERY

RVers who like to boondock are always in search of more and more battery capacity so they can remain unplugged as long as possible. Here's a guide to your options:

- **Lead-acid deep-cycle batteries:** Most rigs come from the factory with one or two 12V lead-acid deep-cycle batteries (sometimes called *wet cell batteries*), and they're the types favored by the industry. They're also the least expensive, usually costing less than $100 apiece. If you find yourself on a trip and need an immediate battery replacement to get rolling again, these are the most commonly stocked and available types of RV batteries you'll find. Even Costco and Walmart stock them.

  Lead-acid batteries are easy to spot — they have removable plastic caps. Carefully pop off the caps, and you can see clear electrolyte fluid that should be covering the lead plates inside. They do need to be checked regularly, though. When the fluid level of electrolytes (or what you probably think of as "battery acid") gets low enough that the metal fins are exposed on top, carefully add distilled water to the battery. And don't forget to wear rubber gloves and eye protection while you're doing this.

  Alternatively, some rigs are designed (or modified) to combine two very high-capacity 6VDC golf-cart-style, deep-cycle batteries wired separately (referred to as *in series*) to add up to 12 volts. You're really making a big 12V battery out of two smaller 6V ones.

- **Absorbed glass mat (AGM) batteries:** These batteries are designed to provide far more power more consistently for a longer period of time than lead-acid types. Sometimes called *dual-purpose batteries*, they provide a big burst of power when you ask for it, just like a standard car battery does, but they also discharge more slowly than lead-acid ones (on the other hand, they charge faster). AGMs are sealed shut, so there's no fluid level to check regularly. They're more expensive than lead-acid ones — anywhere from $120 to $200 apiece — but they're the best all-around battery available for RVers. And they can be used with most standard RV wiring and charging circuits without needing modification. Check with your RV dealer or manufacturer to make sure your onboard convertor is AGM compatible.

- **Lithium batteries:** In recent years, lithium battery technology has made great strides as rechargeable power sources for the laptop, smartphone, and electric car industries. The ones for RVs are called *lithium-iron-phosphate*. (The chemical symbols are Li, Fe, and P, so the batteries are called LFP, or LiFePo batteries.) LFPs charge and recharge faster than any other battery types, and they discharge their power more slowly and evenly. Plus, they can hold a charge for a lot longer, which means you can store your rig for as long as six months and still have electricity in them. Not so with a lead-acid type that gradually loses its charge.

  LFP batteries have lots of pros, cons, challenges, and limitations (starting with being *very* expensive). They weigh about half as much as a comparable lead-acid battery and are a quarter of the size. Depending on the type and claims of the manufacturers, an LFP RV battery can be recharged anywhere from 2,000 to 8,000 times before you need to replace it — they can last as long as ten years. In comparison, the typical lifespan for a standard lead-acid type is three to five years, depending on how you take care of it. Just consider that two standard 12V lead-acid deep-cycle batteries cost less than $200, while a single LFP battery can be in excess of $1,000.

In addition, LFPs require a very different type of charging system than your rig probably came with. You can't just yank out your existing lead-acid batteries and plop in an LFP replacement. LFPs can be very finicky when it comes to recharging because they don't usually like the fluctuating voltage that can come from solar panels or your tow vehicle's engine. And they don't like charging in cold weather — better ones have an internal heater to warm them up before charging. So, you'll also have to invest in some different onboard electronics and wiring to overcome these issues if you use an LFP. Having a conversion of your existing electrical system done professionally can run as high as $5,000.

Some RV manufacturers are starting to install LFPs as an option, even pairing them with onboard solar panels and power management systems that smooth out their fluctuating voltage. More and more people are asking for them. LFP batteries will eventually wind up as the favorite for RVs as they become more commonplace, and more companies solve some of the complexities of charging and maintaining them. But at the time of this writing, they're still considered pretty rare, with no real consensus about onboard charging and power management systems.

By contrast, lead-acid and AGM batteries have both been around for decades, are available nearly everywhere, and are comparatively inexpensive. Nine out of ten RVs have them and do just fine with the old technology. We know that sounds like the grumpy curmudgeon's excuse to be a cheapskate, but for now, it's still the industry standard. Equally important, RV service techs fully understand their charging systems, and replacement parts are pretty easy to come by. So, if you're interested in converting your batteries to LFPs, do lots of homework before diving in.

## Shore power

Shore power comes from an external power source. Your rig's big, thick power cable is connected to a campground's power pedestal or some other outlet and plugged into your RV. (At the risk of being called a couple of nags, we'll remind you again to use a surge protector — see the nearby sidebar "Why you should use a surge protector" for more information.)

Shore power provides electricity to the voltage- and wattage-gulping appliances in your RV. These include the air conditioner or heat pump, the microwave oven, bigger TV sets, the electric water heater, refrigerator (unless it operates on multiple power sources), electric heaters, electric fireplace, washer and dryer, and just about anything else that has to be plugged into a household wall socket. That includes your laptop computer and phone chargers, too. In almost every case, if an appliance creates heat when it's turned on (like coffee makers, toasters, space heaters, and hair dryers), you'll need to be hooked to shore power to use it. The only exception is if you have a built-in or portable generator to fill in when you can't hook up to external electricity.

## THE CAMPGROUND POWER PEDESTAL AND WHY THAT PLUG WON'T FIT

Depending on your RV and its requirements, the connection is usually rated for 30A/120V or, for larger rigs, 50A/240V. (Having more than one AC unit on the roof means it's 50A.) 30A and 50A have distinct types of plugs, so you can easily tell the difference when it's time to plug in.

Most campgrounds these days offer 50A/240V service at some or most of their sites, but some older campgrounds haven't been wired to provide 50A power for larger rigs. (State parks are notorious for this.) Always ask when you make reservations. But in case you have a power cable that won't match what the campsite has to offer, adapter plugs and cables (known to RVers as *dog bones*) will let you plug into the "wrong" kind of outlet. Just remember that, on 30A, you can only run *one* of your AC/heat pump systems at a time (see Chapter 9).

Just be aware that a dog bone adapter only lets you use a different *plug* — it doesn't give you more electrical power than the outlet's circuitry has to offer. For instance, a 50A cable adapted and plugged into a 15A household outlet will still only give you 15A of power. You may have successfully gotten plugged into some electricity, but turn on a high-amperage appliance like the air conditioner and — *pop!* — the circuit breaker will trip because you had the unmitigated audacity to ask it for so much power.

We keep referring to 120V shore power, but a 50A hookup is actually labeled as providing 240V. So, what gives? In reality, the 240V receptacle on the campsite's power pedestal is providing *two* 120V circuits side-by-side to your shore power connection cable. If you look at the pedestal's 50A circuit breaker, you can see that it's two circuit breakers side by side sharing a single handle that has "50" stamped on it. When the current gets into your trailer, the wiring is separated into two different *legs* of 120 volts that are wired to different devices or outlets. If the outdoor breakers detect a short or overload in either leg, the shared handle connecting them will shut off both legs. If you have two air-conditioner units, they don't require 240 volts to operate — each one is wired into its own separate 120V leg. That's why you can run a single air-conditioning unit on a single-legged 30A/120V circuit if need be.

# WHY YOU SHOULD USE A SURGE PROTECTOR

Before you plug your RV into a shore power outlet, you should use a multimeter or volt meter to double check the voltage, just in case there's an internal electrical problem at the pedestal. But to be truly cautious, use an informative model of surge protector that can diagnose a wiring or voltage problem and protect you against system damage. We talk about the different types of surge protectors and analyzers in Chapter 13, but we want you to know why we're so insistent on this.

Every time you pull up to a campground power pedestal, you're plugging into a potential for electrical problems. You're susceptible to fried electrical systems if the park's power pedestal isn't wired properly or has been damaged — and that can happen more often than you think. Most power receptacles and circuit breaker switches used in these pedestals are fairly rugged, but they weren't really designed to be constantly flipped on and off or plugged and unplugged hundreds of times. Circuit breaker switches can wear out over time. (Always be suspicious if you see burn or scorch marks around the outlets — that indicates a previous problem.)

The wiring in a campground isn't always as neat and orderly as it is behind the walls in your house. Much of the wiring that feeds electricity to the campground's dozens, scores, or even hundreds of power pedestals is buried underground. That alone can invite damage from water in the ground, being dug up accidentally by lawn crews, being gnawed on by rodents, or from RV owners carelessly whacking their rigs into the pedestal and even tearing it out of the ground — and that's just off the tops of our heads.

Electricians and campground staff can also make mistakes. Because of daily use, power pedestals can take lots of abuse, and replacing broken circuit breakers and outlets can be a daily chore, especially at giant campgrounds. For instance, a three-prong, 30A RV receptacle is supposed to be wired for 120V. But to a careless or harried electrician who's been used to household wiring, that outlet can look deceptively like a household 240V dryer plug. If they don't look carefully at the receptacle's voltage rating, these 30A outlets can be easily wired incorrectly as 240V instead of 120V. Plug your 30A power cord into that, and your rig's electrical system can be fried in a matter of seconds because it was jolted by twice as much voltage as it expected.

Surge protectors can be expensive, but diagnosing and repairing an internal electrical problem in an RV can be a whole lot more costly. As in a car, when your electrical system is fried, it may never function again the way it once did. Don't take chances. Bite the bullet, and invest in a decent surge protector.

We talk about hooking up to the power pedestal back in Chapter 13. But when the electricity gets into your RV, it's helpful to know what it does when it gets there. All your electrical appliances and accessories inside instantly heave a massive sigh of relief because your rig was designed to work best with shore power. The fridge cools faster, the heating and air-conditioning system becomes fully functional, the microwave oven will actually cook your soup, and all your 120V wall outlets will have full power coursing through their veins. It's just like being at home.

# Convertible Electricity

Because RVs are made to adapt to different electrical conditions, there are two helpful, built-in devices that let you convert voltage back and forth:

>> **120VAC to 12VDC converter:** Wired into your shore power system is a 120VAC-to-12VDC *power converter,* and it does exactly what it sounds like. The converter takes the 120VAC electrical current when you're hooked up to shore power and converts it to 12VDC in order to power all your onboard 12V appliances and devices. So, all your lights will burn brightly without flickering every time the water pump comes on. And, as an added bonus, the converter will fully recharge your house batteries.

>> **12VDC to 120VAC inverter:** Many RVs also have a device that does just the opposite when you're not connected to shore power. A *power inverter* takes the 12VDC electricity from your house batteries and boosts it to a limited amount of 120VAC. And by limited, we mean limited.

You're asking that original 12V of battery power to carry a big load, so your rig probably has very few outlets actually wired into the inverter. RV manufacturers will often label these special outlets with a sticker. They're usually reserved for operating your TVs and DVD player and charging your phones, laptops, and other very low-wattage items. But if you try to plug in anything remotely robust (like a toaster, coffee maker, water kettle, or electric heater), the inverter's internal circuit breaker will reward your arrogance by shutting it down. And you can forget running the air conditioner.

As the saying goes, there's no such thing as a free lunch. Transforming 12V into 120V is costly, both in dollars and in energy use. Inverters are rated in the number of watts they're able to summon up, and the more wattage you want, the more expensive they are. The other consideration with using an inverter is that it will drain your house batteries very quickly. Check your manual or look around in your RV for a power inverter on/off switch. They don't just come on automatically.

If your rig doesn't have one and you think you really need one, portable inverters can be bought separately and used in both your RV and your tow vehicle. The upside of using it in your truck or car is that you can leave the engine running, which prevents the battery from being drained. You can find them for sale online, in camping stores, and in larger truck stops.

Power inverters come in two varieties: *pure sine wave* and *modified sine wave* (which is the cheaper of the two). The difference is how smoothly the 120V are regulated. If you intend to use an inverter to power any delicate sort of electronic devices, rechargers, or even just a digital clock, you need a pure sine wave inverter. A modified sine wave unit can only be used for things like light bulbs, power tools, compressors, or small heaters. They can damage and even destroy electronics.

# The Fuse Panel

Although your RV has two electrical systems, most RVs are designed with a single panel of fuses and circuit breakers to protect your onboard devices from short circuits and overloads. When a single electrical device in your rig suddenly refuses to run, move, light up, or make a telltale noise you're used to hearing, your next step (after cussing up a blue streak) is to head for the fuse panel.

You're probably more likely to have to chase down a blown fuse or tripped circuit in your RV than in your home. To simplify tracking down the problem, each fuse and breaker will be labeled in some way with a short description of what it's protecting. In some cases, they may be simply numbered with a corresponding list mounted on the inside of the panel door or just listed in your owner's manual.

Before you start trying to troubleshoot a dead electrical device or circuit in your RV, first check the obvious thing: Go outside to be sure the power pedestal's circuit breaker switch is still on *and* the power cable is still connected. It sounds stupid, but humor us. Others before you have torn their hair out hunting an electrical problem all afternoon, only to discover that their shore power cable had simply come unplugged.

## 12V fuses

A *fuse*, in its most basic form, is a thin piece of wire or metal that is designed to literally burn up when too much current tries to gallop through it. (That's what it means when somebody says they "blew a fuse.") The purpose is to burn up the 50¢ fuse before the power zap can go on to burn up your more expensive device.

Your RV fuses are plastic, automotive-style, plug-in types with two distinctive metal blades, and they protect the circuits in your 12VDC house power system. They come in different colors stamped with the amperage they can handle coursing through their internal fuse wire before burning apart. The most common fuse amperage found in RVs is 15A, and it's a good idea to have several extra ones onboard with you.

TIP

Trying to remove one of these fuses from a crowded panel can be tough to do with adult fingers. Auto part stores, Walmart, and truck stops often sell a small selection of fuses in a kit with a special plastic tool to make fuse removal easier. Lacking that, you can carefully use a pair of needle-nose pliers to get hold of the fuse and gently rock it out of its socket.

The downside of these fuses is that you really can't tell just by looking at the fuse panel whether one has blown. You have to pull them out and look closely at the side to see if the internal wire has a gap in it. Never replace a fuse with a larger fuse rated for more amperage. Doing so risks damaging the very item it's supposed to be protecting.

TECHNICAL
STUFF

Various items in your rig have very different types of fuses. Some are thin glass tubes with a visible wire inside. These are usually wired in-line with a specific device and hide inside of a twist-apart plastic sleeve about the diameter of a pen. These are commonly found connected to powered hitch jacks and in some overhead ventilating fans like Fan-Tastic Vents (www.fantasticvent.net). Another very different type is a *fusible link* or *terminal fuse*. These are usually wired very close to the positive (red) terminal of your house batteries, and they're a thin piece of metal or wire designed to burn in half in the event of a catastrophic short circuit. Accidentally cause a major short circuit by touching a wrench or screwdriver to both battery posts or between the positive post and the rig's metal chassis, and you'll get zapped with a spectacular electrical arc caused by the short circuit. The terminal fuse is supposed to sacrifice itself before the short causes major electrical damage to your battery or your rig (or welds your wrench to your battery terminal).

## 120V circuit breakers

Circuit breakers are different from fuses because they don't actually burn up inside when they get overloaded. Instead, they're an on/off switch equipped with a middle, *tripped* position. When too much amperage tries to overload the circuit, an internal band of metal inside the switch heats up, expands, and shoves the switch from its on position to an off-center tripped setting.

**TIP**

If you look in your fuse panel at the breakers, you should see all the switches in the same on position except the problematic one. As with fuses, if you trip the circuit breaker, you first need to track down the source of the overload and turn it off, unplug it, or find the cause of the problem before turning the breaker back on. To reset the breaker, push the switch all the way to the full off position, and then flip it back to the on position. If it refuses to stay on, you still have a short somewhere.

# Generators

Not everybody wants to stay in a campground all the time, and there may be situations when the weather or road conditions prevent you from doing so even if you want to. If you don't have the option of plugging into 120VAC power, but you still want to use all (or at least some) of your high-wattage appliances, there's another option available: Use a generator. A *generator* is your very own mobile power plant, with a self-contained motor. Generators come in diesel, gasoline, and propane-powered models, and in all sizes weighing as little as 30 pounds and as much as several hundred pounds. The bigger they are, the bigger their power output is. Versatile dual-fuel generators are set up to run on either gasoline or propane.

It's rare to find any size of traditional travel trailer that's factory-equipped with a built-in generator, although they're out there (usually on a fifth wheel or toy hauler). Mostly it's because of weight considerations. But if you have a motorhome with one, you're a rolling volts-wagon! You really can be completely free to stop and set up camp anywhere that's legal. Even if you're driving down the highway, an onboard generator can still let you generate 120VAC to fire up the microwave or cool down the bedroom with the overhead air conditioner.

**TIP**

In a motorhome, generators usually get their gas or diesel supply from the vehicle's fuel tank. Manufacturers are usually thoughtful enough to shut down the generator's motor when your fuel tank dips below a quarter of a tank so you won't run it dry in the middle of the desert. The bigger onboard units can crank out as much as 12,000W, which should be more than enough for average campers.

The best portable generators for RVers are designed to be quieter than those made for industrial or commercial use. Consequently, they're more expensive. They generally have both standard household outlets and 30A/120VAC receptacles to make it easy to connect your rig's power cable.

**TIP**

Before you buy a generator, add up the combined wattage requirements of the major items in your rig that you intend to operate *at the same time.* You should probably just leave the 1,500W hair dryer at home. Either that, or lower your expectations and only turn on items one at a time as you need them.

## Power output

Generators come with a potentially baffling list of various outputs and capacities they're able to handle. They're rated with two sets of operating wattages: *starting watts* and *running watts.* Anything with a motor will require more watts to get started than it does to operate steadily. For example, a coffee maker may need 1,000W whenever it's turned on. Same with a microwave oven. Even a lowly phone charger can draw 11W when it's plugged in. But although a big 15,000–BTU air conditioner may operate just fine at 1,600W, when its fan motor and compressor first start up, it can draw several thousand watts of power. When you're running the generator and plug in or turn on a big appliance, you'll hear the generator bog down at first as it struggles to supply enough electricity to handle starting up the device. After it catches its breath, it settles down into a steady speed again to supply the device's lower running watts.

## BREAK THE RULES WITH A SOFT STARTER

As a rule, if you're packing up in your driveway on a hot day, you can't turn your air conditioner/heat pump on unless you have at least a 30A circuit installed close by. But there is a way to break that rule: An aftermarket device quickly gaining in popularity is called the EasyStart soft starter, made by Micro-Air (www.microair.net/collections/easystart-soft-starters). Dometic, which is one of the largest RV appliance makers in the United States, offers its own version, called the SmartStart (www.dometic.com). What this ingenious bit of electrical hocus-pocus does is absorb the jolt of that first rush of power needed to start an air conditioner/heat pump compressor motor. It slowly starts and increases the compressor speed gradually so that the system requires a whopping 75 percent less start-up current. And what *that* means is that a rig rated for 30A or 50A may be able to run its air conditioner on just 20A or less.

The device must be added to your rooftop air conditioner/heat pump units, and unless you're very experienced with wiring, we recommend having a professional do it. You could easily mis-wire and fry your air conditioner's internal wiring.

If you intend on installing it yourself anyway, be aware that adding a soft starter may void your air conditioner's warranty. Just be mindful of the issue, and do your homework before having one installed.

# Weight

The biggest issues with portable generators are usually size and weight. It's a bad idea to buy one you can't possibly lift if you regularly travel alone or with a fellow camper who can't really help you. Units that can generate less than 4,000W typically weigh less than 50 pounds and are about the size of a medium to large cooler. When you get above 4,000W, they begin to get unwieldy, especially for one person to move alone.

A 9,000W generator can tip the scales at 200 pounds and is technically "portable" only from the standpoint that it's got a handle and wheels. So obviously, you need a pickup truck or van for it to ride in, unless it fits in your rig's exterior storage compartments.

To get around the weight problem, there are smaller RV-friendly generators that can be plugged into each other to double their wattage output, just like having two house batteries hooked in parallel to have greater capacity. Two smaller generators are easier to lift than one massive one.

# Fuel

Another consideration is the fuel the generator runs on. If it's a propane unit (and many are sold as dual-fuel compatible), you can tap off your trailer's external propane (technically, liquefied petroleum gas, or LPG) tanks. But generators don't crank out as much wattage when running on propane as they do with gasoline. If it's a gasoline-powered unit, you'll also have to haul around a big can of gas in your tow vehicle, which can be unpleasant and messy inside an enclosed SUV or van.

Generators are notoriously inefficient. If you're counting on running one all night in the late fall to keep an electric space heater or electric blanket going, you'll probably have to run outside every four or five hours and refill the tank. If you're using your onboard propane to run a generator instead, keep careful watch on your propane tank levels or you'll suddenly find yourself empty.

**WARNING**

Like all combustion engines, generators pump out deadly carbon monoxide when they're running. Always keep your generator away from open windows or vents on your rig.

# Noise

If you're boondocking off-grid and parked in the wilderness or a Walmart parking lot, no one will care if you run your generator. But if you're in any sort of developed camping site with neighboring campers around, the quickest way to become the scourge of the park is to crank up your noisy, stinky generator. Most full-service campgrounds and RV parks either forbid them outright or ask you to limit their use. If the campground has electrical hookups, you shouldn't need to run one anyway — plug into a power pedestal and turn on all the stuff you need. But if it doesn't and you've got other trailers or tents close by, running a generator for more than a few minutes is considered rude.

## Maintenance

Generators are like spouses, kids, and dogs: They don't like being neglected. If you keep fuel in the tank so it's always ready to start, that fuel needs to be replenished, replaced, or drained on a regular basis. It's also recommended that you not only fire up your generator at least once a month but also hook it up to your rig and run it under a full load of the most power-hogging thing you have. Just plugging in something small like a phone charger doesn't give the generator's internal mechanisms and electronics enough of a workout.

### LITHIUM "GENERATORS"

Poke around online and you may find articles touting so-called "lithium generators," proclaiming that they require no fuel and have no fumes to deal with. Just be aware that these are *not* generators at all — they're actually portable banks (or stacks) of rechargeable lithium batteries. They have to be plugged in and recharged by 120VAC household current, a 12VDC cigarette lighter outlet in your car or truck, or a solar panel.

Technology changes fast, especially in the world of batteries these days. But the current state of the art for these portable units only lets them provide a limited amount of wattage. At the time of this writing, we haven't encountered any equipped with a large RV-style 30A/120VAC outlet to hook your rig into, which is just as well because they don't have enough power to operate your high-wattage, shore-powered appliances for very long. But they *can* act as an additional battery backup supplement to your house batteries. They're generally equipped with a built-in inverter that transforms 12VDC to 120VAC. Most of them have one or two household 120VAC outlets, a 12VDC cigarette lighter outlet, and several USB ports for charging phones and smaller devices.

By their nature, lithium batteries are expensive, and if you want more power from these units, you'll pay dearly for it. At current prices, a portable 2,000W lithium unit costs $2,000 or more. Some of these allow you to buy more battery packs and stack them for more reserve capacity. It's up to you whether the cost is worth it.

Even though it sounds odd, some generators do come with their own onboard batteries, for the sole purpose of letting you just push a button to start the engine. If you've ever owned a self-starting snow blower, you know that its battery needs to be kept on a trickle charger for most of the year or replaced every year because of neglect. You usually figure this out in the middle of the biggest snowstorm of the season when you need it most. Self-starting generators are the same way. Less expensive or smaller generators have a pull-start, like an old-fashioned lawnmower or chainsaw — you yank on a spring-loaded rope a few times and, with any luck, it starts.

## Security

Despite their weight and size, there is literally nothing more expensive and valuable (and, therefore, potentially stealable) than a generator sitting on the ground or in the open bed of a pickup truck. Crawl around on the Internet, and you'll see story after story of RVers with sorrowful tales about their expensive generator disappearing in the night. Even the big, heavy ones. And even in the middle of nowhere. Part of the issue is that even RVers don't want the noise and the exhaust too close to their rig's open windows, so they stage their generator some distance away. Their noise attracts the attention of passing thieves, and so does their often brightly painted visibility. Consider using a stout chain and beefy padlock to secure your generator to something large and immovable, even if you never take it out of your truck.

# Chapter **15**

# Water World: The Wonders of Plumbing

I n Chapter 14, we tell you that our favorite RV salesperson's motto is, "If a new RVer understands water, power, and poop, they're ready to go camping!" We cover power in Chapter 14. We cover the other two parts of that equation — water and poop— in this chapter. And these two parts are inextricably tied together, like bacon and eggs, peanut butter and jelly, Minneapolis and St. Paul.

Like electricity, water is one of those basics of life that most people don't think much about these days. Turn on the faucet and, as long as you remembered to pay the water bill, water flows out of the tap from someplace, somehow. And then when it gurgles down the drain, it just goes someplace else — most people don't really think about where it goes.

The trouble with living in an RV is that you suddenly have to pay *lots* of attention to where your water comes from and where it goes. Every drop of clean water in your RV has to come from a water tap and a hose connected to your rig. And when that water gets used for anything and either runs down a drain or gets flushed down the toilet, it all goes into tanks in the bowels of your RV and eventually has to be gotten rid of in a sanitary (and legal) manner — every last bit of it.

Worry not. In this chapter, we fill you in on both of these subjects, and we make it as hygienic and trouble-free as possible.

REMEMBER

Dumping your RV's wastewater system is the great socioeconomic leveler of RVing. Rich or poor, high or low, young or old, we all have to do it.

# Understanding How Water Works in an RV

Underneath your trailer or motorhome are several large tanks that look like big boxes with pipes connected to them. In all but the very simplest and smallest RVs, there are two basic water systems that function separately from each other:

>> **Freshwater system:** The freshwater system is exactly what it sounds like — nice, clean, fresh water flows into your RV through a hose connected on the outside. If you're in a campground and hooked up to the campground's water supply with a hose, you've got all the water you'll ever want, on demand. But if you can't stay tied down to a campsite hose connection, then more drastic measures are called for. You use that hose to fill up an onboard *freshwater holding tank*. After it's filled and you disconnect the hose, that tank is all the water you have at your disposal until the next opportunity you have to fill it up again.

>> **Wastewater system:** The wastewater system is where the water goes after you use it to shower, cook, wash dishes, brush your teeth, or flush the toilet. To make it slightly more complicated, most RVs are set up with two wastewater tanks, depending on what kind of stuff is floating around in that used water:

 • *Graywater* is water mixed with nothing more unpleasant than soap and maybe the food rinsed off of your dinner plates. Graywater usually drains from the kitchen sink, the shower stall, and perhaps the bathroom sink. Pour out the coffee pot or rinse the dog's bowl, and it all goes in the graywater tank. So does the soap and shampoo from your morning shower.

 • *Blackwater* is the water and everything else that gets flushed down the toilet (and in some rigs, stuff that drains from the bathroom sink, too).

Somewhere in the mountain of manuals and spec sheets that came with your trailer or motorhome, there should be a list of the capacities of your onboard *holding tanks*. What holding tanks actually hold is water. Your specs will tell you how many gallons of fresh water you can stuff into its tank, and how much wastewater can go down your drains into those tanks before you have to empty them.

If you mostly stay hooked up to the utilities and connections at campgrounds, the size of your holding tanks may never matter to you — you have a continuous supply of fresh water, and it all runs into the campground's sewer or septic system when you've "used" it. But if you're a *boondocker* (camping off the grid instead of in an RV campground) or you get into situations in which you can't stay hooked up to water and sewer connections, the sizes of your holding tanks will become very important to you very quickly.

## THE FIRST RULE OF WATER

If you remember nothing else about pipes, tanks, and drains and what goes on inside of them, let it be this: Water will not flow uphill by itself. If left to its own devices, water will always be dragged by gravity downhill. It's true in your house or apartment, and it's true in your RV. That's why your holding tanks are lower than your sinks and toilet. It's why your sewer drain and tank drains are lower than anything else on your RV. It's also why your "slinky" sewer drain hose must run downhill from your RV's drain connection to the campground's hole in the ground.

In old black-and-white science-fiction movies, when a scientist discovered a horrible super-powered ray or potion that would eventually turn a common household pest into a gigantic building-destroying monster, there was always some cautionary buttinsky expert played by Whit Bissell visiting the lab before all hell broke loose, who said, "Doctor, be careful! Properly harnessed, this discovery might help mankind, but it can also kill!" Then at the end when the monster had been vanquished, the same Professor Know-It-All would puff on his pipe, stroke his beard, and say, "We meddled with the forces of nature. . . ."

Water in an RV is a lot like that. Properly kept where it's supposed to be, water makes life wonderful, especially when it comes to cooking, washing, showering, flushing the toilet, or rinsing mud off your Schnauzer. But let it loose, and it will become an uncontrollable creature that will wreak havoc on your RV quicker than you can say, "Attack of the Giant Creeping Water Monster." In theory, water is supposed to remain in tanks, pipes, and hoses, or at the very least outside. But tiny water leaks don't stay tiny or harmless for very long, and because most RVs have plywood flooring under the carpet or vinyl, and either wood or particleboard walls, water takes to them like a big expensive rolling sponge. A tiny leak that lets the rain in around windows, doors, and slides, or that silently drips under your toilet or sinks, can result in buckled floors, a bountiful crop of colorful mold, and worse. Every RV shakes and rattles on the road, and RV plumbing is usually plastic. Connections can vibrate loose even in the best of rigs. So, always be on the lookout for water where it doesn't belong, or — perish the thought! — solid floors that feel soft.

In a relatively small trailer, tanks may hold 10 to 15 gallons apiece, whereas a massive motorhome or fifth wheel may have holding tanks of 100 gallons or more. It's mostly a function of how much room you have under the floorboards, and the tank capacity directly affects how long you can stay and play without refilling or dumping them.

TIP

Manufacturers usually figure the average camper will create more graywater from washing and cooking than blackwater from flushing, so don't be surprised to discover that the wastewater tanks are smaller than your freshwater tank and that the graywater and blackwater tanks are different sizes.

# Using the Freshwater System

At home, fresh water is fed directly from a pipe in the ground or the street into your household plumbing system. It's a pretty simple arrangement. But because your RV is made to work regardless of whether it's connected to a continuous water supply, it has a few more components than your house.

In this section, we explain how you get fresh water in the first place, how to store it if you're going to be away from civilization for a while, and how to make sure you have enough water pressure and hot water to rinse the shampoo out of your hair.

## Getting fresh water

RVs usually have two ways of getting fresh water into them, and the one you choose depends on whether you're sitting in a campsite with its own water supply or not.

### From a campsite

If you're at a campsite with a water supply, connect a drinking water hose from the spigot coming out of the ground at your campsite to the freshwater inlet valve on the side of your rig (see Figure 15-1). Turn on the spigot, and the water flows into your RV's plumbing system, where it waits patiently until you turn on a faucet or flush the toilet. The water pressure in your rig is entirely dependent on how strong the campground's water supply is. So, if everybody in the whole campground decides to take their showers at 8 a.m., your own shower may not be as robust as you'd like. But the good news is that the water supply will be continuous and endless.

**FIGURE 15-1:**
The freshwater
inlet valve.

*Photograph courtesy of Christopher Hodapp*

**TIP**

The freshwater inlet valve is usually on the *shore side* (driver's side) of the RV. On many rigs, it's called a *city water hookup.* The inlet has a female hose fitting so you can't hook it up backward. The female end of the hose attaches to the campground spigot, and the male end screws into the RV's inlet valve.

**WARNING**

Never use a standard garden hose or expandable "pocket hose" to fill your water tank or connect to the city inlet. Use only a hose designed for drinking water (sometimes labeled as *food grade*). These hoses are usually white or blue, and they come in many lengths, from 4 to 50 feet. All camping stores carry them, but you may not always be able to find one at your big-box hardware center. To prevent it from being contaminated, never use your freshwater hose for anything else.

**TECHNICAL
STUFF**

Because the water pressure can vary a lot from place to place, modern RVs generally have a regulator valve built into the city water connection to prevent super-high water pressure from blowing up all the plumbing pipes buried inside your walls. Camping stores also sell small brass pressure regulator valves for less than $10 — you can screw one onto the hose in case your rig doesn't have a regular built in. (If it is built in, words to that effect will be engraved around the valve along with the pressure it's rated for.)

## CAN YOU DRINK WATER FROM YOUR RV FAUCET?

If you've lived in the same community all your life, you're probably used to water tasting, smelling, and feeling the same. You may not have ever thought about it before. But when you're on the road, you'll soon find out that water is different depending on where it comes from and how it's treated before it gets to you. Fortunately, water in campgrounds has to be tested regularly and is perfectly safe to drink or wash with, even if it smells odd or tastes different. It's the water you shower and brush your teeth with, and there's nothing to be afraid of. That said, most RVers prefer bottled water for drinking.

As long as you're getting your fresh water from a home, a reputable business, or a campground, there is a reasonable expectation that any water safe enough for the local population is safe enough for you. But the actual taste of water can vary a lot from place to place. As a regular practice, you should use a water filter on your incoming supply, and that helps with the taste. It also helps to sanitize your fresh tank to keep microbes from growing and thriving. We talk more about this subject in the sidebar "Keeping fresh water fresh," later in this chapter.

## When you're on your own

Maybe you're not in a campground with a continuous water supply on hand. You're in a Walmart parking lot or boondocking out in the wilderness. If that's the case, you have to preplan by filling up your freshwater holding tank before you leave civilization behind, and conserving as much as possible until you can fill up again.

### FILL 'ER UP

Filling the freshwater tank uses a different connection than city water. On most RVs, the freshwater holding tank inlet (see Figure 15-2) is hiding behind its own small, lockable door and a screw-on plastic cap. It can be on either side of your rig. On most trailers, there is no hose connection — it's simply a pipe you push the end of your hose into, turn on the spigot, and let it run until it's filled. There's nothing technical about it — when the tank is full, water will come pouring out of the pipe and splash on the ground, so you'll know when to say "When!" and shut it off.

On many motorhomes and higher-end fifth wheels, all your water connections may be clustered together on a panel inside an exterior compartment (called a *wet bay*) on the driver's side. Unlike the open-tube inlets on most trailers, there may be a single connection for your water and a switch-over valve (called an *Anderson valve*). That lets you choose to fill your freshwater tank or operate on city water with the simple turn of a valve instead of moving the hose.

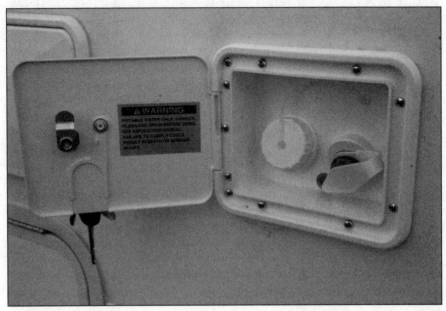

**FIGURE 15-2:**
The freshwater holding tank inlet.

**WARNING**

Fortunately, water faucets are pretty easy to come by, starting in your own driveway at home. But if you're filling your freshwater holding tank from an unfamiliar source, pay close attention to any warning signs with the words *nonpotable water*. That doesn't mean you can't carry it around with a handle — it means "Don't drink it!" You'll almost always find these notices around public wastewater dump stations. Well water can get contaminated easily when it's too close to an underground septic system, and you don't want that anywhere *near* your freshwater tank. Hoses located at RV dump stations are strictly for the purpose of hosing off spilled junk from around the dump connection or out of your drain hose.

## MAN THE PUMPS!

The city water hookup gets its pressure from the source it's connected to. Because your onboard water tank has no pressure of its own, it requires a 12-volt electric water pump to push water from the tank up to your showerhead. The pump works off of your batteries, so you don't need to be plugged into external electrical power for it to work.

Somewhere in your RV, there is a water pump switch that you have to be turned on before the water will flow. Sometimes this switch is combined with the panel that tells you the water levels in all your holding tanks. It usually has a tiny indicator light to tell you it's on.

**REMEMBER**

The first time you turn the pump on, deep from within the bowels of your rig, you'll probably hear a low rumble as it spins to life and pressurizes the plumbing. When enough pressure is achieved throughout all your pipes, the pump will slow to a stop. After that, every time you turn on a faucet or flush the toilet, the pump will feel the pressure drop and rumble back to life again until it re-pressurizes everything. This noise can be a little disconcerting the first time you flush at 3 a.m., but it's totally normal.

Over time, you'll get to know the sounds of your water pump. One thing to keep an ear out for is if you pump all the available water out of your fresh tank. When the tank is dry, the pump will run and run and moan continuously until you turn it off manually. If the tank *isn't* dry, but the pump won't stop running, either a faucet is running somewhere in your rig, or you have a leak. Start looking!

**TIP**

If you're in a campground hooked to the city inlet, but the park's water pressure seems too low, in most RVs, you can boost the pressure by turning on your water pump as long as you also have water in your freshwater tank. That combines both your freshwater holding tank and the city water to plump up the pressure to a higher level.

**WARNING**

If you're boondocking and conserving all possible battery power, flip off the water pump switch until you really need to use the water again. Otherwise, it'll continue to use power as it monitors and adjusts the water pressure. Late at night, it's common to occasionally hear the water pump thump on and off as it adjusts the pressure. Another reason to turn off the water pump switch when the water pump isn't in use is to prevent floods. Accidents happen, and a faucet in a moving RV may shake open enough for water to start flowing. When you stop driving five hours later and open the trailer, a little trickle of water fed by a constantly running pump can drain all your fresh water and send it to places you don't want it.

## DEALING WITH TROUBLE

Water pumps are sometimes finicky little monsters, and they're arguably the source of more complaints than any other single device in RVs. Most of the time, water pumps are trouble free. But not always.

Sometimes air gets caught in the system and causes the water pump to start banging or pulsating every time you turn on a faucet. The pump normally makes sound anyway, but the banging can seem catastrophic when you hear it the first time. Most frustrating is that the sound may not happen consistently. Air in the system may be causing the pipes or the pump to vibrate when it runs, in which case their mounting screws and brackets may just need tightening. In some cases, the pump's pressure switch (which detects changes in water pressure when you turn faucets on or off) may need adjusting or has gone bad. Some do-it-yourselfers will add a pressure balancing expansion tank (called an *accumulator*) to alleviate the noise; others try to muffle it by remounting the pump on a rubber pad instead of the wooden floor.

## KEEPING FRESHWATER FRESH

The tastes and qualities of water can vary a lot. In bigger cities and towns, municipal water gets treated with a variety of chemicals in between where it originates (like a river, stream, lake, watershed, or underground well) and where it blasts out of your faucet. Chlorine is commonly added to purify water, but the amount varies from place to place and even from one season to the next. If there's a lot of chlorine in the water, it may smell a bit like a swimming pool.

If the water source percolated through or over rock (like limestone), the water company may add softening chemicals to this hard water to prevent pipes from clogging with lime deposits. But soft water can sometimes make your skin feel slick, as though you can't get all the soap washed off.

If you're out in the country, and the water supply comes straight out of the ground from a spring or a well, there may be nothing added at all. But iron can occur naturally in water, which can leave an orange residue on your shower floor over time (that's why rust is, well, rust-colored). Those of us who have lived in the country know that iron in the water can eventually turn white clothes orange if they're washed in some well water enough times. Other well water might have a rotten egg smell from sulfur that occurs naturally.

Fortunately, RVers have an inexpensive method to keep some of the odder sights, smells, and tastes of unfamiliar water to a minimum. Camping stores sell simple, inexpensive, disposable water filters that screw onto your hose (see the nearby figure). Pick up a spare 4- or 6-foot white hose to connect to the campground spigot, screw on the filter, and then attach your usual drinking water hose to the other end of the filter. Use that setup whether you're hooked up to the city water connection or filling up your holding tank, and throw away the used filter at the end of the camping season. If you have a large rig and several family members onboard using lots of water on a daily basis, or you're staying in one location for an extended period of time, you can also install a much larger whole-house type of filtration system with replaceable cartridge filters in your rig or in the hose line.

*(continued)*

*(continued)*

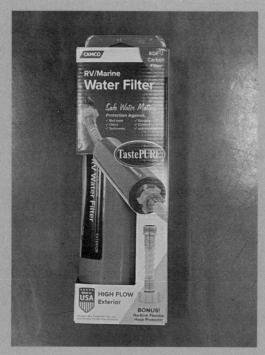

*Photograph courtesy of Christopher Hodapp*

Sanitizing your water system every spring before your first trip is a good idea. Before you start, be sure that your wastewater tanks have been fully drained, either before you parked for the winter or before you start getting ready for the first trip of the year. Then follow these steps:

1.  **Check your specs and find out how many gallons your freshwater tank holds.**

2.  **For every 8 gallons, mix up 2 tablespoons of plain old chlorine bleach (don't use the scented stuff).**

    That works out to ¼ cup of bleach for a 16-gallon tank or ¼ cup plus 1 tablespoon of bleach for a 20-gallon tank.

3.  **Turn on your water pump, and turn on every water faucet in the rig, even the shower.**

4.  **Let the bleach water run through the system for a few minutes, and then turn everything off and let it all sit overnight.**

5. The next morning, run all the faucets again and drain out the freshwater tank.

6. Refill the holding tank with fresh water (no bleach), and run it all through again to get the last of the chlorine smell out.

You'll probably fill up the graywater tank pretty quickly. If you're hooked up to a campground sewer drain, this isn't even an issue. Open up the graywater drain valve, and let it flow out. But if you're at home in your driveway, make sure to open *only* the graywater drain valve and let it drain. As long as that tank was empty when you started this process, you'll just be letting heavily diluted, sanitized water out on the ground, which is harmless.

Another potential problem: Your RV is plumbed to switch between city water pressure and your onboard pump. An internal valve flips one direction or the other, depending on which source it's coming from. If the valve gets stuck while you're hooked up to the city inlet, water will backfill into the holding tank and start gushing out the side of your rig.

The good news is that replacing a water pump in an RV is a relatively inexpensive job in most cases. Fortunately, water pumps have enough common problems that most manufacturers mount them in a place under the floor or behind a cabinet where they are accessed easily. Plus, it's pretty old technology, so virtually all RV mechanics are very familiar with their most common issues.

## Getting to know your water heater

The very scientific and technical term for lovers of cold showers is *lunatics*. The rest of us know that bathing in an icy stream only looks good in travel photos and gauzy romantic movies. Fortunately, most RVs have their own water heaters, just like home. *Unfortunately*, the majority of RV water heaters are *not* like home.

Your house or apartment likely has a water heater that holds anywhere from 20 to 60 gallons of piping-hot water ready to supply your long soak in the tub. But because the number of RVs with full-size bathtubs is miniscule at best, manufacturers see no need to have a giant tank of hot water onboard. The vast majority of RV water heaters have a holding tank that holds just 6 to 10 gallons. So, if you're the kind of person who likes to take 25-minute showers while belting out a complete medley of Broadway show tunes before emerging, you're going to have to compromise. And if you've got a whole family, all of whom need to shower before they go to dinner, it's apt to be a cold experience for the last ones in line.

In the following sections, we introduce you to the two types of water heaters found in RVs.

## Standard propane/electric water heaters

In your home, water heaters are either gas- or electric-powered, depending on the utilities your crib is connected to. In an RV, most water heaters (like the one shown in Figure 15-3) work on *both* propane gas *and* electricity, and you get to decide which one to use. If you're in a campground connected to external electrical power, flip on the electrical switch, and a metal heating element inside the tank starts cooking your water. If you're boondocking and not connected to outside electricity, flip on the propane gas switch, and you'll hear some clicking, followed by the *whoosh* of a gas burner igniting down in the water heater. The good thing about a 6-gallon tank is that it's decently hot in less than 30 minutes.

*Photograph courtesy of Christopher Hodapp*

**FIGURE 15-3:**
A typical Apco propane/electric water heater with a 6-gallon tank.

TIP

Like fifth wheels and motorhomes, the largest RVs have bigger water heaters to handle the load for more expected campers onboard. As more long-term RV owners have demanded more residential-type accessories like washing machines, RV builders have installed water heaters as big as 16-gallon units. A combination propane and electric water heater will make hot water slowest on electrical power, faster on propane, and fastest of all if both electrical and propane burners are turned on.

Never turn on your water heater unless you're hooked up to a city water connection or you have a tank full of fresh water with the water pump running first. The most destructive thing you can do is activate the gas burner or electric heating element in an empty water heater.

A water heater has a pressure relief valve that opens if the internal pressure gets dangerously high. The simplest way to quickly make sure you have water in your water heater before you turn it on is to go outside, open up the compartment where it's located, and pull on the pressure relief valve lever. If the tank is full, water will steadily flow out of the open end of the valve until you release it. If water flows out, you're safe to turn on the water heater. If water doesn't flow out, double check to make sure the wintertime water heater bypass valve is in the open position and the heater's drain plug is installed.

In Chapter 18, we talk about winterizing your RV, and water heaters get special mention because it's easy to forget that they hold onto water unless you specifically drain them manually. Water freezing in your water heater can cause serious and expensive problems.

## Tankless/on-demand water heaters

In recent years, more and more homes have been equipped with tankless, on-demand hot water systems. Instead of a big tank of percolating water in a closet, the garage, or your basement, these systems use a super-heated gas or electric burner and forced airflow that cooks up hot water instantly as it passes through the system on its way to your shower. Turn on the water in the bathroom, and the burner springs into action immediately. Turn off the taps, and it shuts off. Homeowners like these systems because they're extremely energy efficient and compact, and they create a limitless supply of hot water.

RV manufacturers have been slow to adopt these tankless water heaters, but they're becoming more and more common every year. The downside is that replacing a standard propane/electric RV water heater with a tankless one can be expensive: New units run between $500 and $1,000, plus the cost of installation. So, our advice is to go through at least one camping season with your factory-installed unit and consider upgrading only if it doesn't live up to your normal use.

The majority of these "portable" or RV tankless units use propane only and don't have an electric-powered capability the way the standard heaters do. So, before you choose to install one as an upgrade, be aware that it will be using your propane. In the wintertime with the furnace on, your propane water heater will cause you to use up your finite propane supply faster, forcing you to refill your propane tanks more often.

# Dealing with the Wastewater System

Everybody goes, and so we come to the subject most dreaded and feared by first-time RV owners. If your introduction to this subject was the scene in the Robin Williams movie *RV* that involved an exploding geyser of liquefied poop or the scene from *National Lampoon's Christmas Vacation* in which Cousin Eddie empties his Winnebago's sewage into a storm drain in the street that later explodes, allow us to calm these waters, so to speak. There's really nothing to dread, as long as you pay attention to what you're doing. In fact, properly done, it shouldn't even be unpleasant.

Earlier in this chapter, we let you know that your RV likely has both a graywater tank for soapy water from your sinks and shower and a blackwater tank for the stuff from your toilet. The reason to keep them separate will make sense to you when you understand how it all gets dumped when the tanks fill up. (There are a couple of exceptions, and we address them later in this chapter.)

## Getting down and dirty with your RV toilet

To quote the eminent 20th-century philosopher Tom Lehrer, "Life is like a sewer: What you get out of it depends on what you put into it." For example, sooner or later in life, everyone learns the painful lesson not to flush heaping wads of toilet paper or any other foreign objects down the can. So it is on the road.

Unlike your house, RV toilets don't have flush handles mounted to a big porcelain tank of water on the back. Instead, they have a foot pedal you step on or a lever you push on the side of the bowl. Most RV toilets have a two-part action: Push down partway, and water pours into the bowl; push down all the way, and a blade slides aside in the bottom of the bowl to let everything fall through the hole by gravity and plop down into the blackwater tank. Hold the pedal down and let the running water sweep away as much junk from the bowl as it can. Let it go, and the blade slides shut again, leaving about an inch of fresh water to cover the very bottom. The water prevents odors from rising out of the tank and also keeps a rubber seal or gasket around the blade from drying out. Some RV toilets are also designed with a handheld sprayer to help wash away stains and debris.

**TECHNICAL STUFF**

The best RV toilets are porcelain, just like your home toilet. But some manufacturers install less expensive plastic toilet bowls to save money. If your RV is a keeper and you love it, replacing a plastic one with porcelain is a very common, inexpensive upgrade.

# DEFYING THE FIRST RULE OF WATER: MACERATING PUMPS

Wastewater systems rely a lot on gravity, but that's not always an easy thing to accomplish. Not all campsites are created equal. You will inevitably encounter situations in which the campsite sewer connection pipe is sticking up so high out of the ground that your wastewater drain can't possibly rely on gravity to work. Or you may be in a situation where the closest dump connection is too far from where you're parked for your slinky hose to do anything but fill up and just sit there. The solution is a macerator. And here you probably thought the macerator was a 1990s Spanish dance craze at wedding receptions.

A macerating pump is like a garbage disposal for sewage. (If you're eating, put down your sandwich before you continue reading.) It takes the black tank's solids, grinds them up, adds water to the mess to make a slurry, and then pumps the freshly ground and puréed sewage out your drain hose to the dump — even uphill.

The pump can dramatically help to speed up your dumping procedure, which is a godsend with giant fifth-wheel and motorhome tanks. In fact, some big rig makers install these pumps onto their drains as a feature. Campers report that a good pump can empty a 30-gallon tank in less than three minutes.

In larger camping stores and online, several manufacturers sell macerator pumps as complete portable kits for RVers, and loads of campers swear by them. Some, but not all, portable pumps do require 120-volt AC power to work, so pack an extension cord. Other 12-volt pump kits come with a long cord and alligator clamps to clamp on to your battery when you need it.

When you're looking to buy an RV, be sure to ask if the toilet has a macerator pump. They're rare, but they do show up. Factory-installed macerating pumps are more common when toilets can't always be physically located directly over holding tanks. If you have a rig with more than one toilet, one may be perfectly placed over your blackwater tank to plop its stuff straight down. But the other toilet may be clear at the other end of the rig, and the waste has to run down a horizontal pipe under the floor to get to the blackwater tank eventually. That situation has all kinds of potential clogging problems when poop and paper are involved. The solution is a macerating toilet.

The downside is that a toilet pump requires electricity to work, which can be an annoyance if you've pulled off the road to use the can and your battery is dead.

The one must-have toilet accessory all savvy RVers keep close by is a toilet brush. RV toilets don't traditionally fill up with a self-rinsing, deep pool of standing water like the ones at home, so teach yourself and your fellow travelers to clean up before vacating the bathroom. One positive of using an RV toilet is that you don't need a traditional plunger, because it won't work.

Like it or not, your blackwater tank will have solids accumulate in it from the toilet. Poop will break down eventually, given enough time and enough water. So will toilet paper, as long as it isn't wrapped up too tightly. Feminine hygiene products, baby wipes, toy cars, rubber balls, and half-eaten apples won't. And when it's time to get rid of everything, it all has to travel through your RV's pipes and valves, wending its way through that flexible hose on its way to the campground sewer.

## Checking your holding tank monitor

Water systems in RVs are designed to help you conserve water, for obvious reasons. When you get the hang of life in your rig, you'll develop new habits. Most RV showerheads, for instance, have a shutoff switch built into them. Instead of wasting water and needlessly filling up your graywater tank by letting it run while you're lathering up, flip the switch off until you're ready to rinse again.

Of course, if you're in a campground with city water and a sewer hookup, none of this is a problem. But when you're boondocking and not connected to an external water source, what you have is all you've got until you can get more. The same is true of wastewater when it runs down your drains. If you get careless and forget to drain your wastewater holding tanks, eventually they'll fill up, and that water will find somewhere else to go when the tanks overflow — like gurgling up through the shower drain, for instance. So, make it a habit to check your holding tank monitor panel frequently.

Depending on the manufacturer, your holding tank monitor panel (see Figure 15-4) will show you approximate levels in gallons, percentages, or fractions. You'll probably have to push a button to activate it — the panels usually don't stay on all the time. Your water pump switch may also be located on the same panel. Get in the habit of checking the panel whenever you walk past it, so eventually, you do it without thinking.

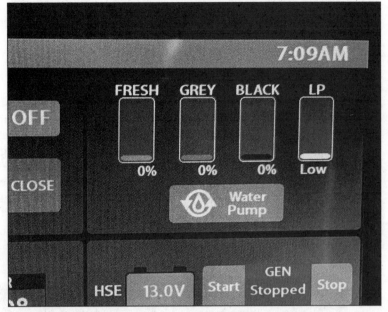

7:09AM

FRESH  GREY  BLACK  LP

OFF

0%    0%    0%    Low

CLOSE

Water Pump

**FIGURE 15-4:**
Your holding tank
monitor panel
may look
different from
this one, but they
all do essentially
the same thing.

HSE  13.0V  Start  GEN Stopped  Stop

*Photograph courtesy of Christopher Hodapp*

# Emptying your wastewater tanks

As your graywater and blackwater tanks fill up, you'll need to start thinking about how you'll get rid of all that wastewater. You've got two choices, depending on whether you're parked in a campground or boondocking without any hookups. In a campground with a full set of hookups at your campsite, you'll be connected to the site's sewer drain. If you're not in a campground, sooner or later, your tanks will fill, and you'll have to find an RV dump station.

## At a campsite

In Chapter 12, we offer the basics of hooking up and unhooking when you're at a typical campground. But the connection we're concerned with when it comes to wastewater is the sewer drain, which needs more detail.

**WARNING**

Any time you're handling a sewer connection, you run the risk of contaminating your hands with bacteria from raw sewage. And you really don't want that to happen, especially if you have a cut or an open sore on your hands. Whenever you're connecting or disconnecting your sewer drain or using a dump station, always wear a pair of rubber gloves. Some campers dedicate a pair of rubber work gloves to the job, but the most sanitary solution is to keep a box of disposable latex or nitrile exam-type gloves handy.

In the following sections, we walk you through how to connect your sewer line and how to manage your tank dumps.

## CONNECTING YOUR SEWER LINE

When you arrive at the campground, there will be a large round pipe (usually white or green plastic) sticking up slightly out of the ground on the shore side of your campsite, somewhere near the power pole. It'll have some kind of cap over the top that screws in or just lifts off — we've even seen nothing more than a flat rock covering the end of the pipe. The important part is the pipe, not the cover. If there isn't one of these pipes in the ground, make sure the campground knows you need a full-hookup site.

After you find the pipe at the campsite, follow these steps to connect to the campsite's sewer (see Figure 15-5):

**FIGURE 15-5:**
A "slinky" hose properly connected to a campsite sewer.

*Photograph courtesy of Christopher Hodapp*

1. **Look under your RV on the shore side for a 3-inch diameter pipe with a plastic cap on the end.**

   In most cases, there will be two plastic pull-handles next to it, one gray and one black (see Figure 15-6). This is your sewer drain.

FIGURE 15-6:
A typical sewer (wastewater) drain valve has a 3-inch pipe where your waste drains out, a graywater handle, and a blackwater handle.

*Photograph courtesy of Christopher Hodapp*

2. **Push both handles in to make sure they are both *fully closed* before you do anything else.**

3. **Connect the female end of a flexible, twisty, "slinky" sewer hose to the end of your RV's sewer drain.**

   These hoses have male and female ends on them. The male end is smooth with two little plastic lugs or pegs on it; the female end has two elongated J-shaped hooks coming out of it. The female hooks twist on and lock the hose to your RV's pipe.

TIP

   It's a good idea to have at least two, or even three different lengths of slinky sewer hoses onboard because sewer hookups are never in the same place twice. We carry 5-, 10-, and 15-foot hoses, and each length can be attached to another for longer reach.

   Another helpful item to have on hand is a *sewer hose tree,* an expandable plastic trestle device that supports the slinky hose off the ground and provides a gradual descent from the trailer down to the sewer drain hole. Don't forget: Water cannot run uphill. Do all you can to be sure your RV sewer drain is *higher* than the sewer hole in the ground and that the hose has no sharp rises in it. You may actually need to drive your RV up onto some extra leveling blocks to achieve enough height, although it only has to be a couple of inches. Otherwise, your sewer water won't want to leave your RV!

**4.** **Twist a solid plastic elbow nozzle onto the male end of the hose, which is the end that drops into the campsite sewer pipe.**

There are 90-degree right-angle elbows, often with a rubber collar or seal around them, and optional 45-degree angled elbows in case the sewer pipe is crooked or unusually mounted (we've almost never used a 45-degree one). Make sure you get a clear elbow, so you can keep an eye on the flowing sewage as it drains. It sounds disgusting to actually watch your personal waste burble down the drain, but it's for a good cause: You need to see whether there's stuff in your wastewater at various points in the operation.

Don't open those drain valves just yet! Now that your sewer line is connected to a drain, take a minute to consider wastewater management (see the next section).

## PREPLANNING YOUR TANK DUMPS

You'll usually generate more graywater than blackwater, and for that reason, most RVers open up their graywater drain valve after they're hooked up to a campsite sewer so the graywater tank doesn't fill up after a couple of showers. That's certainly the most convenient way to manage graywater, especially if you're at a campsite for more than just an overnight stay. But any time you go RVing, you need to plan ahead for certain situations.

TIP

You actually need to keep the blackwater tank drain *closed* as long as it is practical. If it doesn't fill up with enough liquid, or you just leave the drain open the whole time you're parked at the campground. In that case, the solid waste and toilet paper sludge won't break down enough or have enough volume to slowly make its way toward the sewer drain and leave when you really do need to dump everything. The average RV toilet flush, to be graphic, doesn't have enough oomph behind it to prevent toilet stuff from just lazily laying in your slinky hose. In fact, before you actually do dump your blackwater tank, go into the bathroom and step on the flush pedal for a few minutes to run more water down the bowl because the more liquid you have, the merrier your dump will be.

TIP

If you're parked at a campsite for a while with a sewer hookup, you still *want* both wastewater tanks to fill as much as you can before you pull the handles and dump the blackwater tank. So, how do you manage that? Let's say you're staying in the same spot for four days. Go ahead and keep your graywater drain valve open most of the time when you're connected to a campsite sewer. As long as it's open, all that shower and sink water drains straight into the graywater tank and right down the slinky hose into the campground sewer outside. But don't open the blackwater tank valve. The night before you leave, go out and close up the graywater drain valve so it stops draining out. You want to store up enough of that great soapy water to clean out the blackwater from your slinky hose when you're done dumping. You're trying to accumulate at least 5 gallons in your graywater tank. Do the breakfast dishes, wash your hands, and do any other last-minute cleanup jobs that puts water down the drain.

## DUMPING YOUR WASTE

You're finally ready to dump the last of your wastewater tanks and hit the road! Now is when all this tap dancing with your tanks pays off. If you do this properly, you won't even get your hands dirty or get gunk on your shoes. But put on your rubber gloves again, at least until you've comfortably done this a few times. With your gloves on, follow these steps:

1.  **Assuming your sewer hose is hooked up (see the preceding section, "Connecting your sewer line"), pull the handle on the blackwater tank first and let 'er rip.**

    As long as your sewer hose runs downhill from your trailer into the sewer pipe in the ground, the junk in the blackwater tank will gurgle out. If you have a clear plastic elbow on the end of your hose, you can watch the contents and its progress as it flows. (Surprise fun fact: Blackwater is actually sludge brown. You're welcome.)

    Depending on the size of your tank, how much liquid you're dumping, and how steep the incline is from your RV's drain to the hole in the ground, fully draining it may take more than a few minutes, especially if you have a motorhome or fifth wheel with massive tank capacity. When you're satisfied that everything's flowing, there's no need to babysit it — go finish packing up your campsite as it runs. And whatever you do, don't trip over the hose.

    Eventually, the blackwater will slow to a trickle and then pretty much stop entirely. Now's the time for the big switchover.

2.  **Push the blackwater drain valve closed on your RV, and then open the graywater valve.**

    Now you'll see why they say it's gray — soap in that water gives it a sort of cloudy appearance. No need to babysit this process either. The reason you wanted to have a fair supply of graywater held in reserve (see "Preplanning your tank dumps," earlier) is to wash out any remaining toilet waste residue from your flexible drain hose.

3.  **When the graywater stops running, close its drain handle and give the blackwater one a push again to make sure they're both tight.**

4.  **Now comes the moment of truth: Slowly twist off the slinky hose connection at the trailer valve, and lift that end of the hose up in the air.**

    What you're doing is letting gravity drain the last of anything left in the hose toward the sewer end of things and down the pipe, instead of all over you.

5. Work your way down to the other end of the hose as you keep lifting until you finally reach the plastic nozzle.

6. Lift the hose nozzle out of the hole, put away the hose, and put the cap back on your RV's drain pipe and the sewer hole cover.

7. As a final bit of business, go inside and run a gallon or so of water into the toilet so that it covers the bottom of the blackwater tank, and drop in your favorite RV toilet deodorizer chemical.

You can proudly proclaim that you've successfully made your first sewer dump. It's like the RV version of a bar mitzvah. Today you are a real road warrior.

WARNING

When you're done with your slinky hose and its plastic nozzles, store them completely separate from your freshwater drinking hose. The majority of RVs come with at least one small area to store a sewer hose. In motorhomes, that may be in the same compartment with the drain connections. Other rigs have a hollow space inside the rear bumper to slide your hose into. Some have a 4-inch plastic tube slung under the RV frame with a twist-on cover. But if you have no convenient place built-in, or it's too small for any extra hose sections you buy, consider storing them in a plastic tote box with a lid so you can stack other items safely on top. However you store yours, keep them away from anything else in your storage areas. Bacteria can easily contaminate items and transfer to your hands without your even knowing it.

## At a freestanding dump site

Some campgrounds don't have full hookups with individual sewer connections at every campsite, and many state and national parks don't have them at all. However, nearly every RV campground will at least have a freestanding sewer dumpsite (like the one shown in Figure 15-7), usually near the office or front gate. You'll see a sewer pipe with a foot-actuated lid and a concrete apron around it, as well as a water supply strictly for rinsing out your drain hose and cleaning up any spills or messes. Some may have a credit-card-activated lock on the pipe cover.

Some of the larger truck stops along the interstate highway system also have RV dumpsites that you can use for a small fee. Pilot Flying J Travel Centers (https://pilotflyingj.com) are noteworthy for specifically catering to RVers — they typically have an RV dump, a propane refill station, and fuel pump islands designed to conveniently accommodate the largest motorhomes and trailers.

Many of the more than 50 Cabela's (www.cabelas.com) stores across the country welcome overnight RV parking, and more than a few of them offer a dumpsite that you can use for a small fee. This isn't the case at every Cabela's, so check with the location near you before counting on it. (Cabela's and Bass Pro Shops have merged, but unfortunately the Bass Pro Shops locations usually do *not* provide for RV over-nighters or dumping.)

**FIGURE 15-7:**
A public wastewater dumpsite.

You may also find a local RV dealership that offers a dumpsite. Smartphone apps or websites and apps like Allstays (www.allstays.com/apps) and RVshare (https://rvshare.com/dumpstations) are invaluable when your tanks are full to the brim and you need to find a dump station.

The good news is that the procedures outlined earlier (in the "At a campsite" section) are essentially the same at a dump station.

**REMEMBER**

Be a conscientious and courteous RVer. Always hose down and wash off any spillage or messes you make around the dump station. Confronting your own waste is unpleasant enough; confronting somebody else's is just plain gross.

## Other ways of dumping wastewater

In some circumstances, you can't easily connect your RV to a sewer drain, and you need to rely on some different methods to get rid of your wastewater. For example, you may have a complex campsite that you've spent hours getting set up just right. You've rigged lights on the awning and hooked the grill to the trailer's propane supply; a crowd has assembled to watch the big game on your outdoor TV. Having to disconnect everything and discombobulate your site just to go dump your holding tanks up by the front gate, only to come right back again, seems like a major wrench. In these situations, you have a couple options.

### CALLING THE MOBILE PUMPER TRUCK

Keep an eye out for notices in some parks that a mobile "honey wagon" wastewater pump-out service may be available. These mobile trucks can sometimes be found serving parks that don't have on-site sewer hookups.

Like a residential septic tank service, this is a truck or trailer with a big waste storage tank and a pump onboard. We said water can't travel uphill without help. Well, that's what the honey wagon's pump is for. A hose is connected to your rig's wastewater pipe, the pump is started, your valves are opened, and — *voilà!* — your wastewater is vacuumed out of your RV tanks and up into the honey wagon's tank. Pay the driver, and your holding tank contents are driven off into the sunset.

**WARNING**

## NO, YOU CAN'T LET IT ALL HANG OUT

In the olden days, toilets in passenger trains had signs in them saying "Do not flush in station." That's because they just dropped their contents onto the ground below, and no one wanted to contemplate a pile of human waste as they stood on a station platform waiting for the 12:30 train to Cleveland. As the train rolled along, you pushed a foot pedal to flush, the bottom of the toilet bowl opened up, and the stuff just plopped out onto the tracks, which is why wild strawberries and blueberries by the railroad tracks were so plentiful and tasty — it was all that fertilizer.

Likewise, in the earlier days of trailer camping, there were no agencies like the Environmental Protection Agency (EPA) passing rules about where you could dump your holding tanks. But those days are long gone.

Graywater that has soap *but no grease or food floating in it* is considered "wash water" by most state and federal authorities. As long as you don't discharge it on the ground somewhere where it may run down into an aquifer or some other body of water like a lake or stream, you can open up your graywater dump valve and let it drain in the great outdoors. That means that you need to scrape your dishes and wipe off the food and grease before you plunge them into your soapy sink water. That way, your graywater stays unadulterated and isn't classified as *sewage.*

Blackwater is a different matter. What's in there *is* raw sewage. You can't legally dump blackwater anywhere but an officially sanctioned dump site or sewer hookup. Get caught doing it on public land, and you'll be heavily fined.

## USING YOUR OWN PORTABLE HONEY WAGON

They're called by lots of pet names — portable poop wagons, honey wagons, tote-along waste tanks. . . . Whatever they're called, they're low-slung, plastic tanks on wheels with a handle like a kid's wagon (see Figure 15-8), designed for you to be able to dump part or all of your wastewater into and then haul it by hand to a nearby dump site. They come in a variety of sizes — the biggest we've seen is 42 gallons (weighing more than 300 pounds when it's full), which is a whole lot of liquid. Some extremely small or ultra-light trailers use these wagons instead of onboard blackwater and graywater waste tanks.

**FIGURE 15-8:**
A portable waste tank wagon.

*Photograph courtesy of Christopher Hodapp*

In practice, the wagon is connected by a short flexible hose to an RV's wastewater drain and filled to capacity. You then (slowly and carefully!) pull the wagon to a nearby dump station. The hose is reconnected to a lower drain on the tank, and the other end goes into the dump station pipe. Open the wagon's drain valve, and away it goes, down the sewer. Tip the wagon on its end to drain the last of the load, rinse it out, and you're done.

**WARNING**

In reality, there are plenty of opportunities for this process to turn into a serious mess. Even the how-to videos designed to show how easy they are to use can't hide the many ways of overflowing or spilling or sloshing or improperly holding the hose that will result in an unpleasant experience. Before you purchase one of these trailers, be sure you understand the details of this kind of regular wastewater dumping.

An even more miniaturized variation is the *cassette toilet,* which has a removable tank you can slide out, carry, and dump into a regular toilet. Because they require no plumbing, these types of small, self-contained toilet systems are common-place in van conversions, camper vans, some truck campers, and a few pop-ups.

Some RVers carry portable waste wagons for emergencies when they can't easily connect and dump their big onboard waste tanks. Several models are made to store on the rear ladder of a trailer or motorhome, or a separate bracket can be added to store it on the rear bumper of your rig.

## Washing out your blackwater tank

Like speed limits, gravity isn't just an annoyance to be ignored — it's the law. Human waste reacts to gravity just like everything else. If it drops from your toilet down into the blackwater tank and it hits a dry spot that doesn't get much water splashed on it or isn't quickly submerged, it'll dry out. So will paper and the *next* camper's personal load. And so on, and so on. You get the picture.

TIP

Use your common sense. Flush often during your morning constitutional. Flush lots of water. Never flush paper towels, baby wipes, feminine hygiene products, or any foreign objects. And don't ever flush tightly wound, heaping wads of paper (it'll have a tough time getting past the RV toilet's narrow drain hole anyway).

Fortunately, because blackwater tanks can get a buildup of junk in them, some (not all) manufacturers have installed a way to wash them out. Even if yours didn't, there are three ways to do it:

>> You can use your RV's built-in tank washout hookup, if it has one.

>> You can use ice and water softener or detergent.

>> You can do it manually.

We cover these three methods in the following sections.

### Using your RV's built-in tank washout hookup

On the side of your RV, there's an inlet for a city water hookup that you screw a hose into. If yours is equipped with it, there may be a second, similar-looking hose connection nearby (see Figure 15-9) that's labeled quite differently (and for the love of all that's sacred, don't mix them up) — it may say "Sewage Tank

Rinse," "Black Tank Flush," "No Fuss Flush," "Quickie Flush," or other words to that effect — it does *not* say "Freshwater Inlet" or "City Water"! On the *inside* of your black tank, the other end of this hose connection is actually a high-pressure sprinkler head designed to spray clean water all over the tank's insides to wash it down and hopefully break up any tough residue.

**FIGURE 15-9:**
Your rig may have a blackwater tank rinse-out flush valve. Don't get it confused with your city water inlet!

**WARNING**

Never, ever walk away from your RV while the blackwater tank washout process is going on. Never! You *will* lose track of time, get sidetracked, talk to a neighbor, fight with your partner, chase the dog — *something* will get your attention as the tank fills. If it overfills, sewage water can erupt from the vent on the roof of your rig in a spectacular aerial display or come up through your toilet and potentially flood the inside of your RV before you know it. This happens to scores of RV owners every year, and in the worst cases, the vehicle is a total loss because of it. We cannot emphasize this point enough.

Now that we've scared the crap out of you, here's what you do to clean your black-water tank:

**WARNING**

1. **After you've dumped your blackwater tank, and before you empty the graywater tank, connect one end of a garden hose to the tank rinse-out inlet and the other end to the campsite water spigot.**

   Do *not* use your drinking water hose for this! In fact, many RVers buy a special orange or yellow hose for the sole purpose of performing this job because it can potentially contaminate the hose or its connections. (Lots of folks buy a brass Y-connector so they can attach two hoses at the same time to the campsite faucet).

2. **Turn on the water to the hose.**

   You'll hear it start to splash on the inside of your black tank.

3. **Let the water run for about two minutes, and then open the black tank drain valve again while it's still running.**

   This is why you want that clear elbow on your slinky hose. Watch the water as it drains, and you'll see more crud flowing out from the bottom of the blackwater tank that was left behind when you just dumped it.

   Unless you have a remarkably clean tank now, you're still not done.

4. **Close the blackwater tank valve again, and let the water keep running.**

   Now, you have to get very attentive.

5. **Go inside your RV and start monitoring your blackwater level meter.**

   Keep pushing the monitor button every few minutes as the tank gradually fills with water. You can't check often enough. When it reaches three-quarters full, monitor even more obsessively.

6. **As soon as the tank monitor says it's almost 100 percent full, go back outside and turn off the water hose.**

7. **Open the blackwater tank drain valve again, and watch the wastewater again as it flows out.**

8. **If the water continues to have junk tumbling out as it gets close to empty, close the blackwater valve and do the whole thing again until the blackwater finally runs clear.**

9. **Open the graywater valve and let that soapy wash water clean out your slinky hose.**

10. **When you're finished, run 1 or 2 gallons of water into the toilet, and put in a dose of deodorizing chemical.**

If your rig is not equipped from the factory with one of these clean-out fittings, they can be added to existing tanks. Several companies make them.

RV repair techs sometimes call these blackwater tank flush systems a "use it or lose it" device. That means if you ignore it and never bother to use it regularly until your tank develops a serious internal buildup problem, the fitting inside the tank may be so covered with caked-on, petrified gunk that it won't let the clean water blast into the tank — meaning, it can be useless. So, that's a good argument for doing this process regularly as part of your dumping ritual.

## Using ice and water softener or detergent

If you don't have a built-in tank washout hookup, there's a simple and inexpensive alternative for scrubbing the interior of your blackwater tank:

1. **When you're ready to leave your campsite and hit the road, go pick up four or five 10-pound bags of ice.**

2. **Slowly dump all the ice cubes down your toilet drain.**

3. **Pour ½ cup of Calgon liquid water softener or ½ cup of powdered (not liquid) dishwasher detergent down the toilet drain.**

4. **Run a few gallons of water in, and then drive your RV to your next destination.**

   Driving on bumpy, curvy, twisty roads is a help. The ice will slosh and scrub the junk in the tank.

5. **Get set up again at the next campsite, and let it sit overnight.**

6. **The next morning, run enough water into the tank to fill it up again (keep checking your blackwater tank monitor).**

7. **Drain the blackwater tank normally.**

Veteran RVers disagree on this one — some say it works great, while others say it's almost totally ineffective. Try it for yourself.

## Doing it manually

Because holding tanks are pretty inaccessible, other alternatives are available for washing out the blackwater tanks, and they all have their fans and detractors. Here are two options:

>> **Using a tank-cleaning wand:** A *tank-cleaning wand* is a long device that screws onto a garden hose, passed through a window or door into the RV, and pushed down through your toilet drain opening. Swirling and moving the

wand around in the hole sprays water around the inside of the tank. It helps to have a helper outside to turn on and off the water and watch the clear sewer elbow to report when the water runs clear.

>> **Using an external drain flush valve:** RhinoFLEX, Flush King, and other makers of slinky hoses and sewer connectors make various fittings and hose collars that attach to your RV's wastewater drain pipe with a garden hose connection for rinsing your blackwater tank. This operation is tricky because it shoots water back up the drain pipe into the bottom of the blackwater tank, only for it to come back down the drain pipe and hose. The hose connection has a backflow prevention valve in it to keep sewage water from backing into your garden hose. Read all instructions carefully, and follow them to the letter, or you'll have a real mess on more than just your hands. While you're at it, watch video demonstrations of these kinds of valves on YouTube if possible before you tackle the job.

## Caring for and feeding your blackwater tank

Even though you're driving around with your own portable toilet and sewer tank onboard, if you properly maintain the system, it won't smell like a porta-potty inside your RV.

**TECHNICAL STUFF**

Some rigs have a vent pipe on the roof over the bathroom through which smells rise from the blackwater tank and drift away.

You can take a couple steps when it comes to the care and feeding of your blackwater tank and toilet to keep them smelling like a spring day (or at least as free of stink as possible).

### Deodorizing the tank

The first preventive step is something you should do every time you finish emptying your waste tank: deodorizing the tank.

Pick up a package of RV toilet enzyme or deodorant chemicals — Walmart and most campground stores carry these, so they're pretty easy to find. The handiest come in small water-soluble packets (sort of like those laundry detergent pods), but others are solid tablets or bottles of liquid chemicals. Many come in citrus scents and they're sold under lots of brand names.

The only warning everyone has when it comes to deodorizers is to be sure you never buy a toilet chemical that contains formaldehyde. We've never seen a single product that has formaldehyde in it, but everybody warns you anyway, so we will too. Formaldehyde is banned in water systems by the U.S. Environmental Protection Agency (EPA).

REMEMBER

All these chemicals need some water in the tank to be activated.

## Choosing the right toilet paper

When you visit a camping store, you'll encounter special RV toilet paper. The theory is that you must only flush extra-thin, extra-flimsy, extra-expensive RV toilet paper down your trailer or motorhome's drain. It's specially made to break apart faster and easier in your holding tank than the usual five-ply, soft-as-an-angel's-butt toilet paper you use at home. Online arguments rage about this subject (RVers have a lot of time on their hands), and because people are naturally risk-averse to potential toilet and blackwater tank calamities and misadventures, it can take on an extra level of panic in some folks.

The truth is that all toilet paper will dissolve, given enough time and water. That's what makes it suitable for flushing down toilets, unlike phone books, catalogs, and corn cobs. Even the fluffiest, thickest, cushiest stuff on the market dissolves. If you don't believe it, fill up a mason jar with water, drop a few pieces of toilet paper in, close the lid, and shake it up. Let it sit for ten minutes, shake it again, and it'll look like a souvenir holiday snow globe scene, minus the little figurine of Santa and his sleigh.

It's not the toilet paper itself that's problematic — it's the amount involved, in proportion to how much liquid is in your holding tank to break it down, plus how long it all sits there and percolates. Without enough liquid and enough time, wads of undissolved toilet paper can pile up on the tank bottom or collect around its internal drain pipe, dry out, and make stalagmites that are much harder to get rid of. Another problem with gobs of toilet paper in an RV is that it can shred and stick to the tank's insides, where it can cover up and interfere with your all-important tank monitor sensors. That means when you check the water level in the blackwater tank, you won't get an accurate reading.

TIP

Everyone develops different habits and phobias on the road, and we're no exception. In all our trailers and motorhomes, we've always abided by the motto followed by many boat owners who deal with marine toilets and similar issues: *Never flush anything down the toilet that hasn't passed through your body first.* We put a plastic garbage bag in the bathroom and try to put as much "used" toilet paper in that as we can, instead of risking blackwater tank blockages. But plenty of other RVers don't go to that kind of trouble and report their tanks do just fine.

## WHAT ABOUT WINTER AND WATER?

We'll leave you with this science-class reminder: Water freezes in weather below 32 degrees. Even if you have an RV that heats all its holding tanks (and those are not all that common), your rig can't possibly leave the heat running without fail, 24 hours a day for very long if you're traveling or boondocking. Even if you could, there aren't many RVs that also keep heat flowing around their exterior wastewater drain valves. Under the wrong weather conditions, more than a few campers who risk camping in freezing weather with their tanks even partially filled can tell horror stories of frozen drain valves and hose connections, ice-filled slinky hoses, and the dreaded "poopsicles." If your tanks don't have a source of heat, you can wind up with slush in them in a startlingly short time.

With those cheery images of the yuletide season in mind, we refer you to Chapter 18, in which we cover winterizing your rig and the challenges of cold-weather RVing.

# Chapter **16**

# The Propane Gas System

The standard propane gag goes like this: This guy is flying a private plane, his first time soloing when the engine suddenly bursts into flames. The plane goes into a nosedive, and the pilot panics. He grabs the emergency parachute, kicks the door open, and bails out. As he's hurtling toward the ground, he's struggling into the chute harness and madly trying to figure out where the ripcord is. Suddenly, he looks down, and to his shock, sees another guy below him. But instead of falling, this guy is shooting straight up from the ground. As they pass, the frantic pilot screams, "Hey! Do you know anything about parachutes?" And the guy yells back, "No! Do you know anything about propane heaters?"

The third "utility" used in an RV, after electricity and water, is gas. More properly, we're talking about a particular kind of gas called *propane* (or, more correctly, liquefied petroleum gas, or LPG). Plenty of people new to RVing purchase their first rig in spring or summer and figure they'll never need propane because they don't plan to turn on their heat.

Nay, nay.

The truth is that, when you start camping, propane can be more vital than electricity. It can keep you warm, cook your food, keep the dishes clean, provide a hot shower, and, believe it or not, keep your refrigerator cold. In fact, if you're living off the grid or boondocking, you can even run some electrical generators with propane. In this chapter, we explain just what propane is, how to use and store it safely, and where to get more when you run out.

Considering how many millions of RVs equipped with propane appliances are on the road every year, and how many tens of millions of propane barbecue grills are used year-round, propane accidents are very rare. But the fact is, nothing in your RV could be more dangerous under the wrong set of circumstances. You can't get lazy about propane safety.

# Understanding the Basics of Propane

If you've ever owned a gas barbecue grill, you probably already have a little experience with propane, or more properly, *liquefied petroleum gas* (LPG). This wondrous fuel has unique and magical properties that make it ideal for life in an RV.

Gasoline, kerosene, and diesel fuel are all flammable, liquid fossil fuels, and they're refined from crude oil, which comes out of underground wells. Propane is refined from oil and natural gas the same way.

Propane is a gas when it's allowed to float around in the air because it actually boils into vapor — at 44 degrees *below zero!* But if you squeeze lots of propane gas into a tank, and then keep on squeezing and compressing it so you can cram more and more gas into that same tank, it settles down and turns into a liquid. *Magic!* (See the nearby sidebar for more on propane's liquid-versus-gas properties.)

What makes propane magical is that a small amount of liquid turns into a whole lot of useful gas. When you open a valve and let some escape, that newly freed puff of pressurized liquid heaves a big sigh of relief, hits the warm air, and instantly vaporizes into a gas. What this really means, in practical terms, is that a gallon of compressed, liquefied propane will last a whole lot longer and provide a whole lot more usable heat and energy than a gallon of gasoline or kerosene because it expands into so much gas when it gets outside of its tank and "un-compresses." Propane doesn't burn as hot as gasoline or diesel, but it burns a whole lot cleaner. (Imagine how gross your barbecue ribs would taste if they were roasted over a diesel fuel fire.)

**REMEMBER**

Because propane contracts when it gets cold and expands when it gets warm, don't be surprised that your propane refill station will only put 80 percent of the tank's total capacity into it. They do that so the gas inside has room to swell on a hot day.

In the following sections, we fill you in on which appliances in your RV run on propane and help you get to know your propane tank.

## Knowing what it runs

In an RV, propane is used for a variety of purposes, mostly involving heating things up. Electricity is great for heating things too, but only if you have plenty of it. In an RV, that's not always going to be the case. As we said in Chapter 13, life is all Skittles and beer if you can plug into a continuous source of electricity. But because RVs are designed so you can exist on battery power if you're careful, the first thing that has to go when you're off the grid are the electric appliances that generate heat. Turn on a toaster with nothing but 12-volt (V) battery power and an inverter, and you'll be lucky to get the bread warmed up enough to melt butter.

Propane to the rescue! Your RV's propane supply is used to heat your rig, cook your food, give you a hot shower, and, believe it or not, keep your refrigerator cold. We told you propane was a miracle.

TIP

Before any of your propane appliances will work, you need to open one or all of the gas valves on your refillable propane storage tanks (depending on whether or not you have multiple tanks with a crossover valve) and purge the air out of the gas lines. To do that, follow these steps:

1.  **If you have more than a single LPG tank on your RV, set the crossover valve properly.**

    You can manually switch between tanks as they empty or let the valve do it for you.

    Opening the valves lets propane run out of the tanks and into the gas lines that lead to your RV's appliances.

2. **Go into your rig and light one of the burners on your stovetop.**

   It may take a while for the burner to light because the propane gas has a long way to travel down a skinny length of pipe, pushing air ahead of it before it finally arrives at your stove.

3. **Make sure that the burner's igniter is actually making a spark.**

   If it isn't, light the burner with a long-nosed butane lighter.

4. **When the burner lights, turn off the burner.**

In the following sections, we walk you through the appliances in your RV that rely on propane.

## Furnace

In your home, you're probably used to having a furnace that rumbles to life, after which a gentle waft of warm air moseys its way to your living room. RV furnaces are way too impatient for all that "gentle waft" stuff. The majority of RV heaters are forced-air furnaces. That means a powerful 12V fan starts spinning, the gas burner ignites, and the fan blows the heat from the burner out into your living space. Meanwhile, the carbon monoxide exhaust from the burned propane blows out of a vent on the backside of the furnace outside of your rig. That outdoor exhaust vent gets mighty hot mighty fast when it's running. So, don't push an outdoor lawn chair up against it.

**REMEMBER**

A propane furnace is an entirely different device than an electric heat pump that may be a part of your air-conditioning system on the roof. RV furnaces are generally mounted very close to the floor in most rigs because heat rises. Also, a heat pump actually stops making any heat if the outside temperature drops into the low 40s. A propane furnace works in any conditions. (We talk all about your whole heating, ventilation, and air conditioning [HVAC] system in more detail in Chapter 17.)

## Stovetops and ovens

The most visible use of propane in your rig are the burners on your stovetop (some people call it a *hob*).

In the olden days (up until the Woodstock years), gas appliances in a house usually required a constantly burning pilot light that acted like a tiny candle that never went out. The pilot light would wait patiently until you turned on a knob, or a thermostat clicked on, and a healthy stream of gas would start to flow in. The pilot light would ignite the gas, the burner or other appliance would go *whoosh!*, and the flames would get to work heating. Ten minutes later, you had hot soup.

Today, gas appliances in homes use an electronic igniter and no pilot light. You turn a knob, the igniter makes a snapping sound as it makes a spark, the gas starts to flow, the spark ignites the gas, and away you go. The more luxurious and expensive RVs on the market use this type of electronic ignition on their appliances, so they work just like home.

But the majority of RV stovetops are like a backyard barbecue gas grill. They use a *piezo igniter* to create the ignition spark. You turn the burner's knob with one hand, and with the other hand, you keep punching an igniter button or twisting an ignition knob until it successfully ignites the flowing gas. The piezo igniter is always the first thing that breaks or clogs up on our backyard grill, and it's not always dependable in our RV, either. Consequently, we always keep a long-nosed butane lighter close to our trailer's stove to light a stubborn burner.

When it comes to the oven, expensive RVs may have sophisticated ones, but the majority use a time-tested design that has changed little over decades. Less expensive RV propane ovens don't use a pilot light or a piezo igniter for reasons known only to the RV gods of Elkhart, Indiana. As primitive as it may sound, you open the oven door, stand on your head so you can see the long gas burner inside, flick your long-nosed butane lighter, and reach it back along the burner until you see the little gas pipe inlet. With your other hand, you twist the oven temperature knob to the ignite setting while keeping the lighter flame over the gas pipe and attempting to not fall on your face. Finally, the propane arrives at the oven and goes *whoosh!* lighting up the entire length of the oven burner. No, we're not kidding.

**REMEMBER**

When you're cooking in your rig with propane, always open a kitchen vent, turn on a vent fan, or crack open a window close by. Propane is very clean-burning, but it still creates some carbon monoxide.

## Water heaters

The water heater (covered in more detail in Chapter 15) may be one of the primary propane appliances in your rig. If you have a traditional, combination propane/electric unit, there will be an internal switch in your rig that allows you to choose between running it on electricity (if you're connected to a campground's power pole) or propane (if you're boondocking) or both (if you want to heat up your water as fast as possible). When you flip on the propane switch, you may hear the electronic igniter clicking as it sparks until the burner ignites.

## Refrigerators

"What?," we hear you whatting. "What does propane have to do with my refrigerator?"

# HOW DOES A PROPANE REFRIGERATOR WORK?

Your household refrigerator has a mechanical compressor and uses electric fans to blow cold air into the fridge. The process is called *compressor refrigeration*, and an air conditioner essentially works the same way. They add cold air to cool things off.

RV fridges don't have compressors. Instead, they use a totally different method to keep your food cold that doesn't involve any moving parts. It's called *absorption refrigeration* because it uses chemical reactions and physics to absorb or suck out heat from the refrigerator literally. The process of cooling things takes longer than it does with compressor units, but it works on the principle that *removing* heat makes things colder.

On the backside of the fridge is a small boiler. A propane or electric burner heats up a mixture of ammonia, hydrogen, and water. As they boil, the three elements split apart and rise up through pipes in the fridge. Different interactions between the three elements at various stages expand and contract the ammonia, absorbing heat from inside the refrigerator.

*Two-way* RV refrigerators can be powered by plugging your rig into 120VAC or by switching over to propane. When you're plugged into shore power, the electricity is what heats up the boiler. But when you're not, your propane gas takes over. The only electricity the refrigerator uses while running on propane is to periodically ignite the burner (powered by your rig's 12VDC battery system), and you'll hear the igniter clicking away occasionally as it cycles on.

The latest and greatest RV fridges are three-way units, meaning they can operate on 120VAC, 12VDC, and propane, making them great for all situations. You can turn off the propane, and as long as your 12V system is charged, working, and getting recharged by your tow vehicle's or motorhome's electrical system, it will keep running and stay cold as you drive even on the hottest days.

If you're boondocking, just be aware that running the typical RV fridge off of nothing but 12VDC may drain your average batteries below 50 percent in less than six hours. By contrast, running your fridge off of propane gas will use up about 1½ gallons in a day. Be especially aware of that in extremely cold weather when you may also be running your furnace continuously.

Look at your RV fridge to see if it has to be told manually whether to run off of 120VAC, 12VDC, or propane gas or if it has an automatic setting to handle it for you.

Folks new to RVs are usually dumbfounded that the same stuff that burns your dinner on the stove and keeps you from freezing in cold weather can also keep your food cold and even make ice cubes. That's what makes propane such magical stuff for RVers.

The top RV refrigerator manufacturers are Dometic and Norcold. Compared to the refrigerator you have at home or in your dorm room, RV fridges are made with sturdier material on the inside and few moving parts to survive years' worth of bumps in the road and constant temperature changes.

The refrigerator in your home is a serious energy hog because it *can* be. Household electricity is always available, so the motors and compressor pump in your big home fridge have plenty of power. But RV refrigerators don't always have that luxury. The ones in most RVs are designed specifically to operate in all kinds of circumstances. After all, no one wants to have $200 worth of groceries spoil when it's 90 degrees outside, and the campsite power plug gets accidentally kicked out of its socket.

The most common RV refrigerators are two-way or three-way units. That means they can keep your food cold by operating on 120VAC electricity or with propane and 12VDC. See the nearby sidebar to find out how these fridges work.

## Outdoor accessories

Many RVs come equipped with one or two handy outdoor gas connections (see Figure 16-1) that allow you to easily tap into your onboard propane tanks. They can supply a barbecue grill, auxiliary burners or cooktops, patio heater, gas camp-fire, or other propane accessories — depending on how elaborate you want to make your campsite. Invest in an extension hose or two because these outlets aren't always located close to where you want to use them.

Unfortunately, there are a wide variety of propane fittings, hoses, and adaptors in circulation, so not every accessory will easily plug into your rig straight out of the box. Online suppliers, including Amazon, don't always do a good job describing the various fittings and connections they offer. Fortunately, the larger RV camping stores, like Camping World, carry a big range of extension hoses and adapters to solve these connection problems.

Photograph courtesy of Christopher Hodapp

# Getting to know your propane tank

Because propane tanks are pressurized with a potentially explosive substance inside, they require more attention than just simply refilling them whenever they run out of gas. Depending on the RV you have and how you'll be using them, there are several types and sizes available.

## Types of propane tanks

Two different types of propane tanks are found in RVs: the type approved by the American Society of Mechanical Engineers (ASME) and the type approved by the Department of Transportation (DOT). Here's the difference between the two:

» **ASME:** ASME-approved tanks (see Figure 16-2) are permanently mounted to your RV's frame and are usually found in motorhomes. If you have an ASME-approved tank, you have to drive your RV to the propane refueling station.

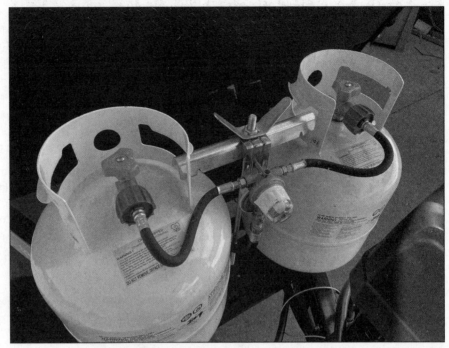

**FIGURE 16-2:**
Portable,
refillable propane
tanks on a trailer
are typically
mounted
vertically up front
on the trailer's
A-frame.

ASME tanks are located down near the frame, underneath the rig. You can generally access these tanks by opening a hatch or compartment that reveals the refilling connection and a gauge to tell you how much you have left in the tank.

**WARNING**

In addition to the way they're mounted, propane tanks are specially designed to be used only in one position: standing up vertically or on their side horizontally. The difference is on the inside. A tube inside the top of the tank where the gas comes out has to be upright when it's being used. Liquid propane always sits in the bottom of the tank, and the gas rises to the top. If you turned a propane tank upside down and hooked it to your barbecue grill, raw, liquid propane might pour in and shoot enough flame skyward to look like a SpaceX rocket launch. So, always make sure the gas cylinder is mounted so that the valves are on the *top* of the tank.

ASME tanks in a motorhome aren't portable and can't be removed or exchanged. So, plan ahead before you set up your rig for a long, extended stay somewhere. (Having to break camp and drive your motorhome somewhere just to refill the propane tank can be frustrating.)

» **DOT:** DOT-approved tanks *aren't* permanently attached to your RV and are portable. These are the same style of tanks used for your backyard propane grill. You can leave them on your rig and pull up to the refill station, or you can dismount them, put them in your car or truck, and go into town to refill them.

DOT tanks are typically stored vertically in the front of the rig, close to or on top of the A-frame tongue (see Figure 16-3). Propane tanks are installed upfront because they can be weighty when filled, so they help balance out the cargo weight of a fully packed trailer. Some may have a plastic cover over them to prevent them from getting dirty. Or they may be inside of a compartment or even in a drawer all their own. Still others are out in the open air.

**FIGURE 16-3:**
Propane tanks on large trailers and fifth wheels may sometimes be inside a cabinet or pull-out drawer.

*Photograph courtesy of Christopher Hodapp*

# DISPOSABLE TANKS

In the camping world, you'll encounter there is a third type of propane tank. These are small, dark-green, disposable, 1-pound propane cylinders, commonly used for small camp stoves, propane lanterns, and personal heaters (see the figure). These handy tanks are generally sold by Coleman and Bernzomatic and designed to be used once and thrown away, not refilled. (Some companies sell special fittings designed to refill these small tanks using a standard 20-pound portable propane tank, but the DOT does *not* authorize this practice, so do so at your own risk.)

Photograph courtesy of Christopher Hodapp

## The mystery of tank sizes

The most common DOT type of propane tank sizes used on trailers are 20-, 30-, and 40-pound tanks. The 20-pound size is also known as a 5-gallon tank, and they're the ones commonly used with gas barbecue grills.

As long as yours are in good shape without rust or dents, you can easily exchange empty 20-pound tanks for full ones at retailers like groceries, travel stops, convenience stores, and gas stations. A common provider of these exchange stations is Blue Rhino, and you can usually spot the large, white, outdoor rack displays.

Exchanging tanks is the most expensive way to buy propane. Refilling your tanks is much more economical.

The larger tanks are taller and subsequently heavier when filled with the liquefied gas. They aren't normally sold by retailers. Tanks bigger than the 20-pound size generally need to be refilled instead of exchanged, although some dealers do offer an exchange program.

Those pound ratings are actually the theoretical weight of the tanks when empty, but even those can fluctuate:

>> When filled, a 20-pound tank holds about 4.7 gallons and weighs around 36 pounds.

>> A filled 30-pounder holds 7 gallons and weighs about 50 pounds.

>> A filled 40-pounder holds 9.4 gallons and can weight anywhere from 58 to 71 pounds.

## Tank inspection requirements

A refill station can reject any tank they deem to be damaged. With the bigger tanks, RVers tend to keep theirs for years and rarely exchange or replace them. But to keep tanks in service for a long time, they need to be properly cared for. Don't get caught by surprise with an un-refillable propane tank. Tanks can be rejected for being too rusty, too dented, or too old, or for having obsolete valves and fittings.

All propane tanks have a manufacturing date stamped into the metal, usually near the collar. Permanently mounted ASME tanks don't need to be officially re-inspected and periodically certified by a trained technician, but portable DOT tanks do. For decades, a DOT tank was required to be inspected after their first 12 years of life. But DOT regulations changed in 2017. The current requirement is that portable tanks must be inspected and recertified by a qualified technician ten years after their manufacture date, and the new inspection date must be stamped on it. After that, these tanks must be re-inspected and recertified every five years. If the date is unreadable, that can be grounds for not refilling it, so don't get mad at the technician.

## Tank anatomy

A portable DOT propane tank has a valve with a small handle or knob on it and a metal sleeve (or *collar*) at the top that sticks up a couple of inches. The collar is slotted so you can grab hold of the tank and carry it. But the collar also protects the tank's valve and hose connection from getting banged around.

The collar has a wealth of information stamped into it (see Figure 16-4). It shows the date and name of the manufacturer, the tank's maximum pressure capacity, its last inspection date (if it has been inspected since it was first made), a serial number, and more.

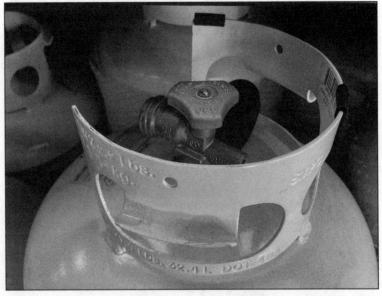

**FIGURE 16-4:**
The collar of a portable, refillable DOT propane tank contains lots of information.

*Photograph courtesy of Christopher Hodapp*

At the base of the tank is a shorter collar that suspends the cylinder body itself off the ground. That's so moisture underneath the tank won't easily rust it out. And that bottom collar provides a flat surface under the rounded tank so it won't fall over.

Refillable tanks today are required to have what's called an *overfill protection device* (OPD) attached to their valves. When the tank is being refilled, the OPD reacts to the pressure inside the tank and pops open when the tank is filled to its proper level. A puff of icy cold propane gas escapes from the OPD to tell the technician that it's full, and it prevents any more from being pumped in.

## Tank mounting stuff

Trailers can come equipped with one, two, or three propane tanks. On your rig, there should be a removable tank holder bracket that screws down and grabs the tank collars to prevent them from bouncing around or falling over. The tank bases also sit in a pan to give them a solid, flat surface.

Short hoses screw into the valves on the top of the tanks using a large plastic knob and quick-release fitting. They are then usually attached to a crossover valve and a pressure regulator (refer to Figure 16-5). Some crossover valves have a mechanical indicator that shows when gas is flowing out of one or both tanks and when it's empty. The crossover valve can be manually switched from one tank to the other or set to draw propane from both tanks at the same time.

**FIGURE 16-5:**
A pressure regulator and crossover valve on a typical dual tank system.

**TECHNICAL STUFF**

Modern propane tanks must use a QCC1/Type 1 brass quick connector to hook up a hose. Hoses have a large plastic, knurled knob, and they easily twist on and off the fitting without much effort. Very old tanks don't have this type of connector and are no longer approved for use.

**REMEMBER**

The crossover valve lets you easily switch from one empty tank to another full one, or use the propane out of all tanks simultaneously. Depending on your system, this can be done manually or automatically. A regulator may or may not be built into the crossover valve. It does what it sounds like — regulates the gas pressure coming out of the tank so a too-strong blast of propane won't blow open your hoses and fittings.

**TIP**

The short rubber hoses that connect the tank to the crossover valve or regulator can wear out or crack over time. It's a good idea to buy one or two spares along with a roll of yellow gas-approved Teflon tape in case you have to replace one in the middle of nowhere or while you're freezing in a snowstorm.

# Keeping Your Tanks Full

In your car, you get used to glancing at your fuel gauge periodically to make sure you don't run out of gas. To prevent you from getting stranded by the side of the road, cars even have a warning light and a gentle alarm to tell you when you're getting dangerously low. You'd think something so useful and so common in the automobile world would be equally common on most RVs for propane. But no.

## Determining how much propane you have left

ASME propane tanks on motorhomes have a gauge mounted on the tank itself, usually near the refill valve in the back of your rig (see Figure 16-6). Because they're permanently mounted, the tank has a *float sensor* inside, same as your car's gas tank. The sensor floats on top of the liquid gas in the tank and drops lower as you use up your propane. In addition to the gauge on the tank, better motorhomes also have an indicator on the dashboard or on a separate panel inside the coach.

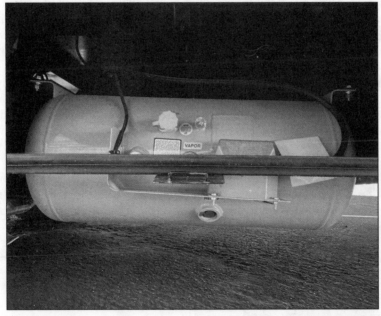

**FIGURE 16-6:**
A permanently mounted ASME motorhome propane tank contains an inlet valve and a built-in mechanical float gauge.

*Photograph courtesy of Christopher Hodapp*

But the removable tanks on towable RVs are a different matter. Some rigs come with a factory-installed propane monitoring system, but they're in a tiny minority. The problem is that portable DOT tanks don't have built-in gauges or float sensors inside of them, so there's no easy, consistent, or even accurate way to hook up an indoor propane monitor to them.

An Internet search for "RV propane gauge" will swamp you with all kinds of products, from simple to complex to ridiculous, things to screw on, tape on, or stick on your tanks in an effort to simply measure your propane levels. Some of these gadgets rely on reading the temperature changes outside of the propane tank to figure out how much liquid is left inside. Some try to measure the weight of the tank. And some only work with 20-gallon tanks because they're the most commonly used size. Not many of these devices are reasonably reliable, and after you buy a few in desperation, you'll find most aren't especially accurate.

The Holy Grail many RVers want is a system that will allow them to monitor the tanks from their smartphone, but, alas, we have yet to find one that actually works properly or consistently. In our case, we use a removable brass in-line pressure gauge between the tank valve and crossover hose, but even that isn't perfect and has to be taken off before we roll because our tank cover is too cramped to leave it on.

TIP

A home remedy for checking propane tank levels is to pour a cup of hot water down the side of the tank, and then slide your hand down until you feel a temperature change. The heat warms the metal tank, but it can't warm up the cold propane inside, so you can feel the difference when you hit the liquid level.

TIP

All this propane measuring folderol is partially why your rig may have more than one tank. If you set your crossover valve manually to use one tank at a time, the next one will stay full until you switch it over. When your propane appliances stop working, go out front and switch over to the full one. And then start looking for somewhere to refill the empty one and top off your current one in use.

REMEMBER

An added benefit of this method is that it helps you keep tabs on just how long a single tank of propane will last you. If you use your rig only a few times a year, always in warm weather, never use the furnace, only use electricity for the refrigerator and water heater, and you rarely turn on the oven or stove, a single tank of propane may easily last you a year or two. If it's freezing outside and your furnace runs constantly, you may only get a day and a half (or less) out of a full tank.

## Filling up your propane tanks

Depending on where you live, you may never have been to a full-service gas station before, where a smiling attendant comes up to your window, asks what kind of gas you want, fills your tank for you, and takes your money. Self-service gas stations have been the rule in most places since the 1970s. That's not the case with filling your propane tanks. Self-serve propane stations do exist, but they're rare. Unless you've been properly taught how to handle this process and you're confident about it, let the station or store technician handle the job.

You may not have noticed propane refill stations if you never owned an RV before, but they're actually quite plentiful, if you know where to look (see Figure 16-7):

>> **Campgrounds:** Most decent-size campgrounds offer propane tank refilling. Large RV resorts also sometimes offer a mobile propane refill service that will come to your campsite.

>> **Truck stops:** Many truck stops and travel centers are able to refill propane tanks. Keep an eye out for Pilot Flying J Travel Centers, in particular. They provide services for RVers like propane refilling, wastewater dump stations, and dedicated RV lanes with special fuel islands designed to accommodate long rigs.

**FIGURE 16-7:** When you're hunting for a propane fill-up, look for a big horizontal tank shaped like a giant Tylenol capsule with some pump equipment at one end.

*Photograph courtesy of Christopher Hodapp*

>> **Local propane dealers:** Many towns have local propane dealers because RVers aren't the only ones who use propane. Industrial customers often use propane to power forklifts and other motorized machinery. Farmers use it for drying grain and other crops, among other things. And residential customers use propane to heat their homes in areas where natural gas service isn't available. So, use your smartphone to look for the closest propane dealer.

>> **Farm supply stores:** Many farm supply stores and hardware stores refill propane tanks.

>> **U-Haul:** Another common source for propane is larger, full-service U-Haul truck rental locations.

TIP

If you find yourself close to empty without any other prospects, call the closest RV dealership and ask.

There are some basic rules to follow at the propane station.

REMEMBER

>> Shut off your engine, and don't ever smoke or have an open flame anywhere near the propane refill equipment.

>> Be sure all gas appliances inside your RV are shut off. Don't forget the refrigerator.

>> Remove your tank cover if you have one, or open your propane compartment or drawer.

>> Close the valves on the tops of your propane tanks, and close the cross-over valve.

>> Some places offer to fill your tanks while they're mounted on the rig, but if you can, it's safer to remove them and let the technician bring the tank to where they're working. They may want to weigh the tank when it's empty and again when it's filled.

>> Have everyone get out of the vehicle in case of a propane leak and to keep anyone from trying to restart an appliance or start the engine.

>> When the tanks are full, put them back on the tank holder, line up the hose connections, reattach them, and then screw down the tank retaining bracket. Put the tank cover back on and go camping!

Obviously, in a motorhome you won't be removing the tanks. The tech will plug their hose nozzle directly into the propane fill connection on your internal tank. The tank's built-in gauge will tell them when it's full, along with a pressure relief valve that spews a puff of gas when it reaches 80 percent capacity.

# Locating Leaks

All modern RVs are equipped with propane detector sensors and alarms, usually mounted close to the floor (see Figure 16-8). Many of these alarms are combination carbon monoxide and propane detectors. Propane is heavier than air, which means if it leaks inside a home or an RV, it wants to sink down and hug the floor.

**FIGURE 16-8:**
A combination carbon monoxide and propane leak detector alarm.

*Photograph courtesy of Christopher Hodapp*

**WARNING**

If the alarm goes off or you smell gas in your RV longer than just a few seconds when you light a stove burner or the oven, get outside fast and leave the door open to ventilate it. Do *not* stop to turn on light switches or do anything else that can cause a spark. Then go immediately out to your propane tanks and shut them off until you can have your propane system checked for leaks.

**REMEMBER**

If you crawl down on the floor and look with a flashlight, you'll see that your propane detector has a date printed or stamped on it. Test its alarm periodically, and keep track of the date printed on it. Alarms need to be replaced every seven years because they lose their sensitivity over time. A replacement propane detector alarm costs less than $60 and is very easy to install yourself. It's usually four screws and two wires. Be sure to see what brand yours is and measure the size. Most are fairly standard, so you won't have to cut a new hole or enlarge the existing one.

## "PHEW! WHAT'S THAT STENCH?"

All by itself, propane is colorless and odorless. "Hey!," we hear you heying. "No it isn't! Propane stinks like a skunk eating bad egg salad left in a hot car for a week in August!" That's because people found out the hard way in the 1800s that if you can't see or smell gas, you don't know it's there when you light a match, and it'll blow up when it gets angry. With a reputation like that, it was a pretty hard sell to get people to let the gas company install reading lamps with open flames in their houses and charge them money for it.

So, the gas industry helpfully adds a very distinctive stink scent to propane and natural gas specifically so you'll suddenly exclaim, "Phew! What's that stench?" if there's a leak. Don't blame the dog or your cousin Charlie.

When you're igniting your stove burners or oven for the first time after turning on your propane system, it's natural to get a slight whiff of propane just before the gas is ignited. But if that telltale propane smell continues after things are properly ignited or when your furnace or water heater are turned on, you may have a leak somewhere. Get outside, quick.

**WARNING**

Some people advocate looking for propane leaks with a lit match or lighter. These people are technically known as *imbeciles* and informally known as *dangerous imbeciles*. *Never do this.* The only safe, quick, no-cost way to hunt for a propane leak is to use your nose to get close to the source, and then spray the suspicious pipe, hose, fitting, or valve with soapy water and see if it bubbles from the escaping pressurized gas.

The better way is with a portable leak detector (see Figure 16-9). Handheld gas and propane leak detectors are available from Amazon and other sources for less than $35. It's worth buying one and keeping it onboard. They have a flexible "sniffer," a beeping alarm, and an LED meter that shows any level of gas that it detects as you move it around your appliances, tanks, hoses or pipes.

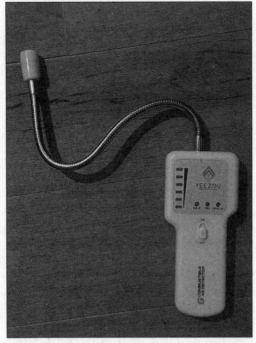

**FIGURE 16-9:**
A handheld leak detector is a safe, dependable way to check pipes, hoses, and appliances for a propane leak.

*Photograph courtesy of Christopher Hodapp*

## THE ETERNAL DILEMMA: LEAVE IT ON OR TURN IT OFF?

One of the very first questions new RVers ask is, "Do I turn off the propane whenever I'm driving?" When you ask this question, that's when somebody usually pipes up with the parachute joke we started with. And after almost a full century of combined years between us both of camping and driving and being around propane, we can answer with a resounding reply, "Yes, you probably should turn it off. But loads of RVers don't."

Your manuals will tell you always to turn the propane off when you drive. RV companies will tell you the same thing. So will repair techs. So will RV magazines, websites, and YouTubers. So will corporate attorneys. "Never drive with the propane turned on," they'll sternly intone. And then they'll sheepishly admit, privately over a beer, that the real answer is, "It depends."

The first consideration is your refrigerator. An enormous number of RVers report that they regularly keep the propane gas on, so their refrigerators keep everything cold when they're on the road. If you have only a two-way refrigerator onboard that needs either 120V or propane to operate, it's a tougher call. As long as everything in the fridge

(continued)

is already cold, and as long as nobody opens the door after you disconnect from shore power, the refrigerator *should* stay plenty cold for a minimum of six hours and probably longer, depending on the weather outside. Frozen food will generally also stay frozen, although ice cream probably won't survive very well. But that's when the "it depends" answer kicks in.

The other concern that many RVers have is the topic of freezing water lines and holding tanks in the wintertime. An unheated trailer headed down the road gets very cold very fast when the weather drops below freezing. That means water lines and tanks below the floor level and under the trailer's chassis can start to freeze very quickly when combined with the wind chill of highway speeds. Because the vast majority of RVers are fair-weather campers, most don't take their rigs into bitter cold weather unless they're quickly headed south for warmer climes. And those who do tough it out in freezing temps try not to put water into their systems at all until they hit warmer weather.

We talk about winterizing and wintertime camping in Chapter 18. But where the "It depends" answer comes into play on this subject has to do with trailers that are designed to blow heat from the propane gas furnace into the holding tank areas and around plumbing pipes. Every company, brand, and model does things differently, but certain trailers and motorhomes do heat these areas just enough to prevent freezing the water system, as long as the propane remains on.

So, the scoffers set their thermostats in the low 40s as they drive, just enough to keep the slush out of the tanks and ice out of the pipes. It's not really sufficient for long-term stays in subzero weather, but it is enough to get you through a couple of days of travel through a wintertime cold spot.

The official answer that you should turn off the propane tank valves before you roll is to prevent the extremely rare possibility of a propane fire or explosion as you drive. The reasoning goes like this: If your rig crashes and a propane hose or pipe gets split, propane may start flowing out of it and be ignited by a spark or the flame of an appliance in the RV. Scoffers at this say that modern propane systems are equipped with a valve that detects a sudden runaway flow of gas that may come from a severed line and shuts off the flow automatically. And so, the controversy and equivocation continues apace. . ..

The one thing everybody agrees on is that you should turn off all propane appliances before you pull up to a fuel island in a gas station or truck stop. RV refrigerators tend to be mounted on the driver's (shore) side of rigs. Propane furnaces and water heaters are often on that side, too, which can be right next to a gas pump as you pull up to a fuel island. And someone may climb into your rig to grab a bite of lunch and turn on a propane device. The fear is that gasoline vapors during refueling may be ignited when an onboard propane appliance's burner ignites at just the wrong moment. The safest thing to do is stop before you pull up to the pumps and close your propane valves.

# Chapter 17

# Heating, Ventilation, and Air Conditioning

We may all believe that camping in the Great Outdoors is such a soothing experience with limitless bounties to be had that pesky stuff like cold, rainy weather or blistering desert heat won't matter when compared to the majesty of Nature's glories. But that's utter piffle.

Let's get real. What's the fun of hauling a second home on wheels into the far-flung wilderness with a great kitchen, a leather sofa, a big TV, a comfy bed, and the other amenities of home if you're going to sweat to death in it? Likewise, when you're sopping wet from the pouring rain and the temperature suddenly plunges to 38 degrees, a smoldering campfire of wet logs is no real substitute for central heating.

Fortunately, your rig's heating and air conditioning systems let you scoff and sneer at all but the most extreme temperatures. And when the weather really is perfect, RVs have features that let you make the most of it, inside and out.

# Starting with the Basics

Parking under a big shady tree to keep the sun from beating down on your camp-site isn't always possible or practical. When a trailer or motorhome sits out in the sun all day with all its systems turned off, it can get unbearably hot inside in a very short time. To naturally keep things as cool as possible *without* using elec-tricity requires a combination of shade, old-fashioned ventilation, and common sense.

Your RV's rooftop is probably covered with a white rubberized material that reflects the sun's rays and doesn't absorb the sun's heat as fast as a dark color would. You probably have a screen door on the entrance and at least a couple of windows with screens so they can be opened without letting every fly, mosquito, or stinkbug in a three-state area descend on your living space. But there are a couple of other low-tech features in your rig that can help keep things cool — or at least less hot — besides just opening the windows.

## Awnings

You probably think that the big awning on most RVs is just for keeping the rain off your campsite or giving you some shade to sit under on a hot day. It also helps to keep your whole rig cooler by casting a huge shadow along the camp side of the trailer. Some RV companies also install smaller sun awnings on the shore sides and back ends of their rigs to shade as many windows as possible. It's remarkable just how effectively awnings cut down on interior heat, while still letting you enjoy the view.

**WARNING**

A giant awning flapping in the breeze *can* unexpectedly take on the characteristics of a sailboat, and not in a good way. It's okay to keep awnings deployed the whole time you're at campsite, as long as you're diligent about checking the weather forecast for both rain and high winds. But because weather can change quickly, be sure to reel in your awnings if you plan to go sightseeing or be away from your campsite for more than a few hours. Sustained winds over about 15 miles per hour with occasionally stronger gusts can damage awnings, tear them up, and even rip them right off their mountings completely.

**TIP**

Some RV makers offer motorized awnings with wind sensors that will automati-cally roll them up when the breezes blow too intensely to prevent your RV from trying to sail off into the Bermuda sunset.

# Rooftop fans

Your RV may be equipped with at least one ventilating fan mounted in the ceiling (see Figure 17-1). Fans are great for quickly removing hot, stale air (or stinky smells) from a rig that's been closed up for a long time. They're also gangbusters for clearing out the humidity in the rig when you take a hot shower.

*Photograph courtesy of Christopher Hodapp*

If you open a couple of windows at the farthest end of the RV and turn on the ventilating fan, it instantly creates a steady breeze throughout the rig, sucking in cooler air from outside and blowing the hot air out of the roof. As an added bonus, the rooftop fan is the fastest way to clear kitchen smoke from the RV after you burn your toaster strudel or overcook your grilled cheese sandwich, and the smoke detector won't shut up.

Vent fans are rated by how many cubic feet of air they can potentially move per minute (abbreviated as *CFM*, short for *cubic feet per minute*). Designed to work on 12 volts of DC power, most fans have a plastic clamshell lid on the roof that either opens automatically when the fan is turned on, or needs to be cranked open manually. The better ones have a speed control and a thermostat to keep them from running all the time; some even have a rain and wind sensor that will automatically close the rooftop lid. The most common ones are Dometic's Fan-Tastic (www.dometic.com/en-us/climate-and-comfort/ventilation-solutions/rv-roof-vents) and Maxxair's Maxxfan (www.airxcel.com/rv/maxxair/products/fans).

**TIP**

One of the best things about these fans is they're usually a whole lot quieter than your rooftop air conditioner/heat pump, which can be a real issue when you're trying to sleep. Fans are quiet enough to leave them running most of the time, even when you're sleeping. And because they run off of your 12-volt house batteries, they're perfect for boondocking.

# Depending on Your HVAC System

When the weather outside is either too hot or too cold to rely on just opening windows and turning on a fan, you may need to bring out the heavy artillery. RVs aren't usually very well insulated, so they tend not to handle extremes of hot and cold without using their built-in heating, ventilation, and air conditioning (HVAC) systems.

As a rule, warming up a cold trailer is easier than cooling down a hot one, at least from an energy-use standpoint. Your RV likely has two completely separate systems: a propane furnace or heater and an electric air conditioner or heat pump. The furnace uses propane (technically, liquefied petroleum gas, or LPG) and a 12-volt circulating fan, but an air conditioner or heat pump requires lots of electricity.

## Air conditioners and heat pumps

If you stand outside your rig and look up at the roof, the big lump that's probably taller and fatter than anything else up there is an air conditioner or heat pump. In a house, your central air conditioner is split into two big units: a noisy compressor that sits outside and a blower inside that sends air into the ducts all over your house. In an RV, these two are combined under one self-contained housing on the roof. If you have a larger RV, you may have two or even three of them up there.

The simplest installations literally consist of cutting a big square hole in the RV's roof and bolting the air conditioner over it. It's sort of like a window air conditioner that's been mounted face down. These will have small adjustable vents (like the ones on the dashboard of your car) mounted on the underside of the air conditioner where it hangs down into your ceiling, along with fan speed and temperature controls. Other RVs have ductwork in the ceiling to spread the air more evenly throughout the rig's interior, and the temperature controls are mounted in a wall panel thermostat. Ducted air systems also cut down on the amount of interior noise caused by the unit's blower fan.

REMEMBER Your air conditioner is the single biggest electricity hog on your rig. If you don't run the air conditioner, you can often get away with plugging in your RV to a household 120VAC outlet in your in-laws' driveway (sometimes referred to as *moochdocking*) and have enough power to run almost anything else onboard. But turn on one air conditioner, and you'll need a 120V/30A connection. Turn on *two* air conditioners at one time, and you'll need a 240V/50A connection.

TIP Because your RV's fattest energy drain comes when the air conditioner's compressor comes on, a recent development is a device known as *soft starter*. It slowly ramps the compressor up to speed and eliminates the traditional power surge that air conditioners cause (see Chapter 14 for more information).

TIP If your RV's air conditioner gradually seems to stop cooling over time (or just suddenly won't cool at all), don't necessarily expect the worst immediately. RV air conditioner/heat pump units require little in the way routine maintenance, but they do need to be cleaned regularly. They have interior filters that you should wash or replace every year, or more often if you hang out in dusty climates. When you've removed the filters, take the opportunity to carefully vacuum out dust from the condenser coil as well. Just be careful not to damage the coil itself.

Just like the big outdoor compressor at your home, the rooftop unit has a metal evaporator coil under its plastic cover that can get clogged with dirt, dust, and other assorted flotsam. For instance, cottonwood trees in early summer shed so much of their white, floating seed fluff that in record time, it can totally seal up a rooftop air conditioner. If you camp in a pine forest in the spring, you'll notice that pine trees heave out huge clouds of yellow pollen that can cover everything in a matter of minutes. And the heavy winds in the Southwest can blow colossal dust clouds that can clog your rooftop unit's coil. So, opening up and cleaning the dust and dirt out of the exterior units on at least an annual basis is a good idea.

REMEMBER Cleaning the units on the roof can be tricky or even dangerous if you're not comfortable with heights and ladders. And there's nothing quite like attempting to skate across the slick rubber roof of a big rig with a fresh layer of morning dew on it. Some RV manufacturers discourage you from climbing on the roof at all. Read your rig's manuals for cleaning recommendations and judge your own skills and comfort level before you attack this job yourself.

# HEAT PUMPS VERSUS AIR CONDITIONERS: WHAT'S THE DIFFERENCE?

The simplest way to understand a heat pump is to think of it as a cooling air conditioner that can also heat in reverse. An air conditioner doesn't technically *make* cold air — it's actually sucking heat *out* of the interior air. It does this by using a heat-absorbing refrigerant chemical that circulates through the system. (*Freon* used to be the most commonly known name brand of refrigerant before it was phased out in the early 2000s as an ozone-damaging greenhouse gas. Most modern RV heat pumps these days use more eco-friendly R-410A refrigerant. But to this day, loads of people still use the term *freon* as a generic name for the stuff.)

When refrigerant is cold, it's liquid. It gets pumped through an indoor coil where it absorbs heat from the surrounding air inside your RV. But as it warms up, the liquid "boils" and turns into a vapor. The hot refrigerant vapor then passes through a compressor, which sends it to another coil outside, where it releases that heat, cools off, and turns back into a cold liquid again. Rinse and repeat. When the compressor turns on, it needs a big jolt of electricity, and you can hear it as it cycles on and off.

The big benefit of a heat pump is that the same unit cools when it's hot outside and heats when it's chilly. When you need it to heat instead of cool, the heat pump essentially reverses the whole process. The refrigerant absorbs heat from the outdoor air, turns the liquid into to a hot vapor, and pumps it through the compressor to the indoor coil. A fan blows air across the coil and sends the warm air into your living room. The refrigerant cools off, liquefies, and heads back to the outdoor coil to go find more heat to suck in.

Unfortunately, you can't count on a heat pump in the dead of winter because when the outdoor air drops much below about 40 degrees, there's less and less warmth out there to be absorbed. When the temperature falls into the 30s, heat pumps are as useless as a boat anchor, which is why you need to use your RV's propane furnace instead.

If you're a typical RV owner, you'll probably call it quits for the camping season in the autumn at just about the time of year that nighttime temperatures start falling below freezing. It's also the time of year that many campgrounds close down for the winter. If your rig has a heat pump and you stick to the pleasant seasonal weather, you may never turn on your propane furnace the whole time you own your rig. But if you're the more intrepid type of camper (or a full-timer) who intends to enjoy also RVing in the cold winter months, be sure to check out our winterizing and winter camping sections of Chapter 18.

Besides cleaning, the pressurized pipes and coils that contain the unit's refrigerant can get banged around a lot at highway speed or when you're bouncing across the desert, and they can spring a leak occasionally. If you've cleaned the coils and filters, and the air conditioner still spews nothing but warm air, have a dealer recharge the system with new refrigerant and check for leaks. If it's a tiny leak (or if it can be repaired), recharging the system every year is usually a whole lot less expensive than replacing an entire unit.

**TIP**

RVers should always be on the lookout for water leaks, both from your rig's plumbing system and from rain outside getting inside. If you see dripping water forming a small puddle next to your rig, your first inclination may be to fear the worst and believe your plumbing has sprung a leak. But before you call your dealer in a blind panic, try turning off your air conditioner for a while and see if the drip stops. When they're operating, air conditioners generate an enormous amount of water from ice-cold refrigerant reacting with the warm, moist air outside. That condensation water has to go somewhere, and your RV may have a small pipe or tube that safely drains the water from the rooftop unit, down through the rig to drip harmlessly onto the ground.

## Propane furnace

All but the tiniest, most basic RVs these days come equipped with a forced-air LPG furnace (see Chapter 16). The furnace burns propane gas to create heat and circulate the air with a powerful 12-volt motor, so it will work without your RV being plugged into shore power. The furnace is vented to the outside to get rid of carbon monoxide and moisture as it burns.

The propane furnace has a specific cycle it goes through when it operates, and it makes distinctive sounds you'll quickly become familiar with. When you turn it on, the furnace activates its 12-volt blower fan to create a draft through its system and blow any debris out of its exterior vent. Next, you'll hear the clicking of its electronic ignition attempting to light the internal propane burner. Propane begins to flow through the burner, and a spark from the igniter sets fire to the gas with a characteristic *whoomp.* When the RV warms up to the desired temperature, the furnace's internal gas valve closes again. You'll hear the roar of the burner stop, but the fan will continue to run for a minute or so to ensure that any remaining propane or carbon monoxide exhaust are all safely blown out of the system into the outdoors.

What may surprise you is just how fast the propane-fired furnace can heat up your living space — even in a big motorhome or massive fifth-wheel trailer. Smaller rigs may have one or two furnace ducts or registers, while bigger units can have several of them in various locations around the rig. They're usually mounted near the floor because warm air naturally rises (so try not to block them with shoes, totes, or dog food bowls). One downside is that the blower fan can be noisy, especially if the furnace is located near your bed.

**TIP**

If your furnace's fan runs without any heat coming out and won't shut off, it's a pretty good bet that you've run out of propane. If you have two or more LPG tanks on your rig, make sure the tank valves are open, the crossover valve is set properly, and that you've still got gas left. (Try igniting one of the gas burners on your stove just to make sure gas is still flowing throughout your system.) In really cold weather, we stubbornly prefer running outside and manually switching between propane tanks when one empties, so that we can keep track of how fast we're using up our gas. It helps us remember to have the empty tank refilled as soon as possible. But for reasons known only to the Fates, we'll sheepishly admit that this almost always happens at 4 a.m. while we're sound asleep on a 20-degree night and icicles have started forming on the poodle's nose.

**REMEMBER**

If you're boondocking and only using your 12-volt house batteries for electricity, a propane furnace motor can run your batteries down pretty quickly if you let it run all night. Every electric device that creates heat — from toasters and coffee pots, to hair dryers and space heaters — gobbles up electricity that you can't provide without a generator or a campground power hookup. So, if you're camping for any length of time in continuously cold weather, stock up on sweaters and consider down-filled camping quilts or sleeping bags instead of trying to keep the whole RV a nice toasty 72 degrees all the time. Or, give up boondocking when it's bitter cold, and be sure you can access shore power.

One other item to think about is that some RVs use the propane furnace to divert a bit of heat into your water tanks under the floor to prevent freezing. The gas furnace isn't affected by subfreezing outdoor temperatures like the heat pump. So, if you're camping in cold weather with water in your tanks and plumbing system, you need to set your thermostat to about 40 degrees or so, and run the furnace continuously to prevent a freezing pipe catastrophe — even when you're driving.

**WARNING**

The propane furnace doesn't have any moving parts besides its fan, and it doesn't take much maintenance. But because the furnace doesn't get used much in the summertime, the exterior exhaust opening can look just like a welcome mat to wasps, especially of the mud dauber variety. If your rig is in storage a lot, you may never see any of them swarming around as they build their new dream home inside your furnace vent. Their mud huts can easily block up the exhaust port, which can prevent the furnace from operating. And wasps aren't the only pesky squatters who see your furnace exhaust opening as a potentially cozy homestead: Birds, mice, spiders, even the occasional frog may try to take up residence in it. So, the opening needs to be checked regularly for debris and unwanted houseguests. Better yet, there are screen kits available for RV furnaces that can easily clip onto the exhaust vent and repel foreign invaders.

# Hydronic heating

Because bigger trailers and motorhomes have so much indoor square footage to heat, some rigs come with a very different sort of heating system. Instead of a propane furnace with ducts in various places, a *hydronic heating system* may consist of pipes that wrap all around the circumference of the rig along the floor or are installed underneath the floor in a snakelike pattern. Instead of burning propane and running noisy fans, the RV uses the water supply and a special continuous, onboard water heater. Hydronic water heating units can be powered by electricity or propane.

Hydronic heaters are similar to old-fashioned steam heat radiators or hot water baseboard heating with a boiler in the basement. The system pumps hot water through the piping and is controlled by a thermostat. The hot water circulates continuously, so the heat is evenly distributed throughout your living space. And because the heat simply radiates out of the piping around or underneath the floor, there is no fan noise and no blowing air in the rig. To save energy, some systems installed in motorhomes also direct heat from your engine while you're driving to help heat the water.

**TIP**

A bonus is that you also have a larger, continuous supply of hot water available at all times for your showers. Another bonus for diesel motorhome owners is that a hydronic system can be installed with an engine preheating option that circulates the engine's coolant (antifreeze) through the heating unit to warm up your rig's engine without starting it and letting it idle.

Hydronic systems are often featured in the most luxurious, top-end Class A motorhomes and fifth wheels. But hydronic systems remain pretty rare in smaller motorhomes and traditional travel trailers (the top-end Airstream Classic is one noteworthy exception).

The most common brands of hydronic heaters are Alde, Aqua-Hot, and Hydro-Hot, but you may see articles or used RV ads that use Alde as a generic description.

For all you'd ever want to know about hydronic heating systems and installing them in an RV, visit John Carrillo's Heat My RV website (https://heatmyrv.com).

# Trying Alternative Heating Methods

The built-in heating systems we discuss in this chapter are the most common ways to keep warm in an RV. But that nether region between 40 degrees (when heat pumps stop working) and 32 degrees (when pipes can begin to freeze if you don't run the propane furnace) sometimes can be handled, or at least supplemented by, a couple of alternatives.

Instead of wasting their propane heating an entire rig all night long, many campers prefer to turn the furnace down to a minimal temperature to prevent frozen pipes and then sleep with an electric blanket. If you're trying to conserve propane or you just want to heat a small area in your RV, space heaters can be a good choice. They can also be useful if your rig has annoying cold spots in your living area that the furnace or heat pump stubbornly fail to get warm enough. If nothing else, using alternative heating devices can be good for marriages and relationships on the road when it comes to the age-old "I'm freezing!/Well, I'm burning up!" thermostat feuds.

## Electric space heaters

There are loads of different electric space heaters on the market — infrared radiant (with long, glowing coils like a big toaster), oil-filled radiators, ceramic convection, and more. Some have circulating fans or blowers, but not all do. And in an RV, size is always a critical factor. In recent years, electric heaters masquerading as artificial fireplaces have been popping up in RVs to add both heat and a homier ambience.

We use an oscillating ceramic heater to send heat out in a wide area when we're eating or to watch TV, as well as an upright, oil-filled electric radiator (shaped like an old-fashioned steam pipe radiator) for keeping the bedroom comfortable at night. The radiator-style heater is slower to heat an area, but it's completely silent, which is perfect for bedrooms.

The most important thing to remember is never to use a heater that exceeds the capacity of the 120-volt circuit breakers in your rig (which are usually rated at 15 amps). Like hair dryers, electric heaters are rated in watts. If the heater's highest wattage is too close to the limit of your rig's electrical outlets, it can easily trip your circuit breaker, especially if another appliance is also plugged into the same circuit. So, stay at 1,500 watts or less.

**WARNING**

Never plug an electric space heater into a standard household 16- or 14-gauge extension cord. These heaters have short power cords on them for a reason: Their high wattage will encounter more resistance the thinner and longer the wire gets, and a too-thin extension cord can quickly get dangerously hot.

We can tell you that leaving any space heater turned on while you sleep is always potentially dangerous, but some people just have to learn by doing. As a teenager, Chris once plugged an electric space heater into a thin, 12-foot-long, 16-gauge household extension cord and let the unit run all night. He was startled out of a deep sleep a few hours later to discover that all 12 feet of the too-wimpy extension cord had melted and burst into sparking flames, without tripping the household circuit breaker. While the mental image of a screaming teenage boy jumping up and down in his underwear desperately hunting a fire extinguisher may seem briefly comical, it wasn't a bit funny at the time. If you must use an extension cord, be sure to use the shortest and thickest one possible (10 or 12 gauge).

# Propane space heaters

Auxiliary propane space heaters are extremely efficient and will give you the most heat for your money. In fact, they're actually *more* efficient than your RV furnace, which gulps down the propane much faster and vents so much heat to the outside.

Fortunately, you can find many propane-powered space heaters on the market made for indoor use that can be safely used inside an RV and require little or no electrical power. Some are portable and can be moved anywhere, while others are wall-mounted units.

Here are the most commonly used propane space heaters:

>> **Ceramic and catalytic infrared radiant heaters:** A large ceramic pad or brick inside of the unit is uniformly heated by the burning gas and works by warming up the *objects* in a room like standing in a shaft of sunlight. These don't have thermostats, just HI and LOW heat settings.

>> **Blue flame convection heaters:** Cool air is drawn through vents at the bottom of the unit, gets heated by the gas flame, and the hot air rises out the top. These work by heating the air like your furnace at home does and are thermostatically controlled. And in case you wondered, they really do have a pretty blue flame that burns, shielded from inquisitive fingers or paws by a glass window.

A favorite among RVers is the Mr. Heater Buddy series (www.mrheater.com/product/heaters/buddy-series.html) of indoor-safe ceramic radiant heaters. Powered by handy, green, disposable 1-pound propane tanks, they crank out between 4,000 and 9,000 BTUs of heat. They can quickly warm up a 225-square-foot area and have several important safety features that will shut them down if they're tipped over or if the pilot light fails. The Mr. Heater Big Buddy portable heater can handle up to 450 square feet for larger spaces, and has the same safety features. Both can also be hooked up to a larger 20-pound propane tank or your onboard tanks with a hose in case you need to run them for an extended time. Camco's Wave series (www.camco.net/heaters) of ceramic heaters are also very popular.

**WARNING**

There are plenty of other suitable propane units on the market, but be sure they're described as *vent-free*. Vent-free heaters burn the gas more efficiently than those with an open flame and produce as little exhaust as possible. But don't be misled! All burning propane gas gives off deadly carbon monoxide, and people die every year from improperly operating portable propane heaters inside their RVs. Propane heaters need fresh oxygen *and* a way for that carbon dioxide to get out of your living space. So, be sure to operate your propane space heater near an open window and a vent fan.

# 5

# Tackling Some Advanced RV Topics

# Chapter **18**

# Storage and Old Man Winter

**M**ost RVer have to store their rigs at some time or another. According to industry statistics, a typical owner uses their RV in summer and stores it in winter. Lots of owners build specialty garages, but for people who can't park it at home due to homeowner's association (HOA) or local restrictions, putting it away in winter storage is the only option. And because indoor storage in heated facilities costs an arm and a leg, outdoor storage is the most common answer.

RV parks that close in winter have a very practical reason: Water pipes freeze. If you've never seen the sort of ice sculpture that a ruptured, frozen water pipe can turn itself into, just take our word for it — it's spectacular. So, if your rig is in storage, particularly where it's going to be exposed to harsh winters, there are specific steps you need to take to protect it. Otherwise, your RV's plumbing is perfectly capable of creating a magnificent ice sculpture of its own.

A surprising number of people (including us) do winter camping. Some people even like it. Cold-weather camping in an RV is not necessarily out of the question when the mercury drops below freezing. But there are some things you need to think about before setting out to mush across the frozen tundra with your rig.

## FINDING A PLACE TO STABLE YOUR RV

We mention some storage issues and options in Chapter 4 because new buyers often forget about storage fees when considering an RV. If you can park in your own driveway, garage, or other storage area, unloading and regularly checking on your RV is much simpler. But plenty of RVers don't have that option. If you live in an apartment, your landlord probably won't let you park it there, and most HOAs forbid RV parking in your own driveway or on the street for more than a few days a year. Most cities and towns also ban long-term on-street RV parking.

Lots of self-storage warehouse facilities offer outdoor parking areas for storing boats and RVs. Specialized RV storage lots with private garages are expensive and hard to find — especially with the huge increase in RV ownership in recent years. Storage lots haven't kept pace with trailer and motorhome sales. Supply and demand means RV storage prices have risen considerably in the last decade.

If a neighbor has an RV or boat, don't be afraid to ask them where they store it. And don't ignore the private campgrounds near your home. You may have never checked out the campgrounds in your neck of the woods, but they could be great options for storage. Lots of campgrounds provide a parking area for storage, especially during winter months when they're closed. Income from storing is a nice little influx of money for campgrounds during otherwise lean months.

# Winterizing and Storing Your RV

The worst thing for an RV is to sit unused, regardless of the time of year or the temperature outside. Systems can break down; bugs and rodents can move in; tires can deteriorate; dust and dirt can get into every crevice; and the sun can attack paint, plastic, and fiberglass. So, *winterizing* is a generic term for prepping your rig for any long-term storage, whether or not it's cold outside.

**WARNING**

Read over this section carefully. If you're storing an RV in a part of the country that never deals with freezing weather, you can skip some of the steps dealing with coldproofing your plumbing. But just because unexpected flukes can strike without warning (hence, the term *unexpected*), we'll remind you that parts of normally warm-all-the-time south Texas froze solid for a week in February 2021, along with much of the rest of the country.

Freezing winter temperatures aren't just a nuisance. To an RV parked in storage, subfreezing temps can wreak havoc on both plumbing and batteries. Even if you intend to use your trailer or motorhome throughout the winter, it may sit for a time unheated and unoccupied. All it takes is *one single night* of bitter cold to do serious damage. So, you need to prepare your rig.

Winterizing your RV isn't especially hard or time-consuming, but you do need to be conscientious about it. Freezing weather tends to sneak up on you, so don't wait too long into the season to winterize. RV dealers frequently offer winterizing specials in fall. If you're nervous about doing it yourself, don't wait until the day after an ice storm to make an appointment.

TIP

Anything you do only once a year is vulnerable to being forgotten. Scientists who study such things use the term *brain farts.* The first season that you winterize your RV, it makes good sense to take photos or videos to document what you're doing. That way, you can retrace your steps when it comes time to do it again or when you pull your RV out of storage in the spring. Your own photos and videos help a lot when you're trying to remember where drain valves or shutoff valves are located, or when you're trying to recall the order in which you need to do things.

## "ICEBERGS, DEAD AHEAD!"

The biggest potential for damage in winter is always water — both the water in your plumbing system and the water from rain and melting snow leaking into your rig. When water freezes, it expands. When water is trapped inside a pipe, the ice swells, and the pipe can burst. If the water is stuck inside a valve, ice can break seals or split apart connections. Outside, if water gets into a crack or seal on your roof, like around rooftop air conditioners or fans, it can push the seal apart when it freezes. And when temperatures turn the ice back to water, it can leak into your RV. If you live in the Sun Belt, "where the skies are not cloudy all day," the sun's relentless ultraviolet rays can quickly dry out and degrade rooftop seals. That's why you or a dealer need to check your roof occasionally and squirt new caulk along seals that are developing cracks.

In recent years, the RV world has been using PEX plumbing for its water lines. PEX water lines are like a combination of rigid pipes and flexible plastic hoses or tubing, making them perfect for trailers and motorhomes. When bouncing down the road, they flex instead of breaking. When temperatures drop down into the twenties and lower, they resist bursting even when full of ice. But remember that *resist* is not the same as *prevent.* The only surefire way to protect your plumbing in winter is to get all the water out or replace it with antifreeze.

# Step 1: Housecleaning and more

To start, give your rig a thorough cleaning, inside and out. Wash off any road grime, bird droppings, insect splats, or dead leaves. Then dive in prepping for long-term storage. The side benefit is that when you come back in the spring to go camping again, your rig won't require much sprucing up.

Here's a list of things to do:

>> Shut off the supply valves from your propane tanks.

>> Extend the awning and hose it down to clean off any grime or debris. To prevent mildew, let it dry *fully* before rolling it back in.

>> Extend your slides and get rid of any junk that may have collected on their roofs, like sticks or leaves. Lubricate any rails and guides that you can manage to reach.

>> Check all your tires for proper inflation.

>> Protect and rejuvenate all rubber window and door gaskets with silicone spray.

>> Put grease on your hitch jack stand, stabilizer mechanisms, and the underside of the hitch latch assembly on the end of your A-frame. It will help ward off the formation of rust when the raw, unpainted metal gets exposed to months of moisture.

**REMEMBER**

Water isn't the only freezable thing in winter. Check under sinks and in storage cabinets and remove bottles of any liquid you have left at the end of the season, like window cleaner, shampoo, or dishwashing detergent. A full bottle of just about *anything* can swell up and burst during a hard freeze.

## Fighting humidity

If you live in a high-humidity part of the country, an enclosed RV that's subjected to major temperature changes without any ventilation is a perfect place for mildew and mold to grow. Boat owners have to deal with the same issue because they're *always* around 100 percent humidity.

A preventive product favored by RVers is DampRid moisture absorber (https://damprid.com), which comes in a small, disposable plastic bucket. Strategically place several of these buckets around the interior of your RV, and the stuff inside absorbs moisture, filling the bucket. In warmer weather these buckets can fill pretty quickly and are easy to spill or knock over. Check and replace them often.

Another product that passively absorbs moisture out of the air are bamboo charcoal bags.

A less practical but more robust solution is to use an electric dehumidifier, but they have to be plugged in and dumped often — sometimes as often as once a day.

The underside of a mattress is especially susceptible to mildew. Your body heat and moisture contribute to the problem every time you sleep in it. Most RV beds are built on a wooden platform over a storage compartment, so the underside of the mattress gets no air circulation. And if the mattress is warmer than the platform, that hot/cold combination creates condensation that further soaks into the fabric. The wooden platform itself can also mildew, and even rot, pretty quickly.

The simplest way to prevent mold and mildew is to remove the mattress from the platform in storage and store it at home or stand it against a wall. You can slide some 1-inch wooden slats or foam swimming noodles split in half lengthwise between the mattress and the platform. We went with a popular solution and installed a Froli system (www.froli.com), a German invention for boat berths. Its interlinked plastic springs are screwed to the platform, leaving air between it and the mattress. Claims that the system increases comfort are probably overstated, but it works great to prevent mildew and is easy to install. The only downside has been the tendency of our mattress to slide when we're driving, so we use bungee cords to keep it in place. Other RVers advocate a layer of mesh material laid between the platform and mattress; common brands include HyperVent (www.hyperventonline.com), Sailrite (www.sailrite.com), and Ravenwolf Marine (www.ravenwolfmarine.com), along with generics.

## Getting the food out

Remove all food, right down to the crumbs. Pay special attention to the refrigerator and freezer — wipe the insides down and block open the doors to prevent any moisture inside from turning into mold or mildew.

Make sure you didn't leave a stray box of cookies or loaf of bread stored in the oven or the back of a drawer. A quiet RV means the coast looks clear to bugs and the local rodent population, and pests can make their way inside in a dozen different places. The smell of food makes them go crazy looking for it.

## Keeping the critters out

Speaking of pests, your RV has more than a couple of openings that let walking, crawling, and flying critters outside sneak in. It helps to keep food out of a stored RV, but not all pests are drawn by food — some just want to retire to a quiet vacation home and raise a family. One of the worst infestations we ever dealt with was a recent arrival to American shores: stink bugs, so named because they stink when you squash them. Hundreds of them swamped the outside of our rig one autumn morning, a time when they're very active, looking for a nice place to overwinter and lay eggs.

Bees and wasps are drawn to refrigerator, furnace, and water heater vents, and they'll quickly build hives there if left alone. Mud daubers especially love the nooks and crannies inside propane furnace vents. The best preventive is installing wire mesh over all open vents. Common sizes are available at camping stores.

Mice can be a major problem with RVs because they're tiny enough to squeeze through small openings under your rig, and they chew *anything.* Constantly. Normally, bigger animals can't get into your coach, but mice can do it easily. Their bodies have very soft cartilage, and a determined young mouse with ambitious dreams can jump as high as a foot or more and squeeze through an opening as small as ¼ inch! Adult mice can get through a hole the size of a dime, and rats can crawl through a space the size of a quarter.

Our Class B van sat unused in our own driveway once for a couple months, without a spec of food in it. But mice found a way in, ripping up an armrest and shredding the foam inside, along with toilet paper and Kleenex — it looked like a ticker-tape parade had run through our rig. Plus, there were poop pellets all over. Mice are always on the lookout for anything to make a comfy nest. That same winter, we had a squirrel move into the engine compartment, where it began gnawing on wires.

We spoke with a couple on the road who stored their Class A all winter without checking inside. In the spring, they discovered, to their horror, that a raccoon somehow had gotten inside and couldn't find its way out again. They found its body under the bed. It likely snuck in through a basement compartment door that was left open the night before they put it in storage, and it got trapped inside the coach when they closed and locked everything the next morning. Wire, cushions, and upholstery got ripped to shreds as the frantic animal tried to find food or escape. The repairs cost them thousands, and raccoons forever lost their cuteness factor in their eyes.

**TIP**

So, if at all possible, do routine checks on your RV while it's in storage. Also, do a careful search underneath and inside your RV looking for any possible entry points. Anywhere you see holes where wiring, pipes, or hoses run through the floor or walls, stuff steel wool into them — mice won't try to chew through it. You can also use spray-on expanding foam filler, as long as it doesn't interfere with pipes or wires you may need to access in the future. Cover large gaping openings like those under some slide-out areas with screen material or metal hardware cloth, being careful not to block the moving mechanisms. Inside, consider putting down glue traps for both bugs and mice. And for heaven's sake, don't believe the Internet RVers' home remedies of putting out dryer sheets and Irish Spring soap bars to repel boarders. They make fine air fresheners, but they don't repel nibbling rodents.

# Step 2: Away goes trouble down the drains

After your cleaning is done and you're finished running water, drain the freshwater tank and the plumbing. Consult your manufacturer's information to locate the freshwater drain valve, which is probably outside underneath its tank. You may have to crawl underneath your rig to find it.

**TECHNICAL STUFF**

Some kind RV companies make winterizing easier by locating all water and sewer hookups, along with drain valves, inside one convenient wet bay cabinet. These cabinets are pretty common on Class A motorhomes and big fifth wheels. But other manufacturers make it a pain in the neck by hiding plumbing system drain valves under closet floors or dinette seats, behind bathroom cabinets, or underneath the rig outside.

Your RV should have a pair of hot- and cold-water *low-point drain valves.* Water wants to run downhill, and gravity drags it to the lowest spots. The valves are installed as low as possible in your plumbing system, so water left in the pipes can make its way to those low points. The valves may be inside somewhere near the floor or outside.

When they're open and draining, go inside and open all your faucets to the center position (halfway between hot and cold). This lets air into the pipes, which helps push the water out of the low points. Flush the toilet three or four times to get rid of the water in its supply lines. And if your shower has a handheld head, open the shower valve halfway between hot and cold, take the head off the wall, lay it on the shower floor, and stretch out its hose so it can completely drain. Otherwise, a 3-foot-long hose full of freezing water can damage the seals in the faucet.

If your rig has its own dedicated water filter system, you need to bypass that unit or disconnect it completely until spring. And if your refrigerator has its own water filter (like many residential ones do, for ice and drinking water), remove that filter as well. Letting filters freeze while soaked with water will likely crack their plastic housings.

**REMEMBER**

If your RV is equipped with an ice maker, washing machine, or dishwasher, consult your manuals for details about draining these appliances. Water left in them to freeze in the winter can cause expensive damage.

**WARNING**

When the freshwater tank drain stops running, flip on your water pump for a few seconds to purge water out of its internal reservoirs and valves, but don't let it run any longer than that. Running a water pump dry can damage it!

# Step 3: Dealing with the water heater

Your water heater tank is probably full of water, and the rig's low point valves can't drain it. Water heaters with tanks have a plastic drain plug near the bottom. There is also a pressure/temperature relief valve near the top. Prop open that valve's test lever — water will probably begin to dribble out. Now remove the heater's drain plug to completely drain its tank. Don't forget to store the plug inside the heater's cabinet for the season or in your toolbox so you can put it back in the spring.

TIP

It's a good idea to buy one or two extra water heater drain plugs and keep them in your RV toolbox. The nylon plastic ones are easily torn up by wrenches or ruined by cross-threading them, and they're easy to lose. When it's time to reinstall the plug in the spring, you'll need to wrap the threads with white Teflon plumber's tape to prevent leaking.

TIP

Before you go to the next steps, check your manuals to find out how to isolate your water heater from the rest of your water system. There may be one or two valves on or near the water heater that you close to keep any more water from going into the heater's tank. If they're on the back side of the heater, you may have to access them from inside your RV (under a seat cushion, behind a bathroom cabinet, at the bottom of a closet, inside their own compartment, under a removable hatch near the floor — they're in there somewhere).

# Step 4: Dumping your wastewater tanks

Make a final dump site visit to empty your black and gray wastewater tanks for the season. If you have a black tank cleanout connection or toilet wand, give it a serious washout (see Chapter 15 for information about dumping your wastewater system and tanks). Otherwise, any solids left inside the tank for the winter can work up a serious stink in the spring when water and heat reactivates their stench-making abilities.

# Step 5: Evicting the last of the water

Even though all your tanks are empty and your drain valves are open, enough water can still be loitering in your plumbing system to freeze and cause damage. Getting rid of the last of it can be done two ways. Some RVers will even combine the two methods.

## Using compressed air

If you have your own electric air compressor or air pump, this method is the simplest way to get rid of the last bit of water from your pipes.

RV stores sell an ingenious device for just this purpose — it's a small plastic fitting called a *blowout plug* that screws into the city freshwater connection on the shore side of your rig. One end is a male garden hose connection, and the other end is a stem valve like you have on your tires. Simply screw the fitting on the city water inlet and connect your compressor's air hose to it like you're filling up a flat tire. Be sure you set the compressor's air pressure up to 35 pounds per square inch (psi) or higher so it's strong enough to blast out any remaining water. A 2-or 3-gallon compressor works great — you don't need a giant one. But even a small, 12-volt air pump used for filling tires generally has enough strength to do the job.

TIP

We generally stick with the compressed air method instead of filling our plumbing with antifreeze (see the next section). The reason is that we continue to take road trips in the winter, and it's a pain in the neck to purge the pink stuff out of our pipes every time we want to hit the road in freezing weather.

## Pumping in RV antifreeze

The other option is to pump antifreeze into all your RV's pipes and faucets. Unlike the poisonous antifreeze your car or truck engine has in its radiator, special *recreational vehicle/marine antifreeze* is non-toxic and made with propylene glycol. It's designed for use in freshwater systems and comes in a gallon jug. It's easy to spot — it's a distinctive hot pink or orangish color (RVers often just call it "the pink stuff"). Unlike automotive antifreeze, the pink stuff is fairly cheap, so pick up three or four gallons the first time you do this so you won't run out in the middle of the job.

The simplest method is to use an antifreeze hand pump, which looks like a plastic version of an old-fashioned bicycle pump with an extra hose. The outlet hose screws into the city freshwater connection, and the contraption's inlet hose goes down into an open jug of antifreeze. A helper makes this process quicker. (If you have a bored teenager around the house, working the pump is the perfect job to Tom Sawyer/Karate Kid them into doing.)

Before you start, make sure you isolate the water heater from the rest of the plumbing by closing its input and output valves. (It requires no antifreeze because you already drained it.) Then go inside your rig and shut off *all but one faucet*, starting with the one farthest from your water connection. Turn on only the cold side of that faucet, go outside, and start working your hand pump. When pink-colored foam starts to dribble out of the faucet, shut it off and do the same with all the rest of your rig's faucets, one at a time. When all the cold-water lines have fluid in them, switch to the hot-water side, again, going one at a time, and keep pumping fluid until all your faucets are completed.

The toilet's water inlet needs antifreeze, too. Push the foot pedal down as your helper keeps pumping until pink foam starts to run into the bowl. And if you have an exterior, handheld shower or an outdoor kitchen sink, it needs to have antifreeze, too. (It's a good idea to completely remove the handheld shower head and its hose from its connection to the faucet.)

If all that hand pumping seems like too much work, there are winterizing pump convertor kits available to modify your RV's existing onboard water pump with a siphon hose and valve. You'll need to have access to your RV's water pump (some of them can be hard to get to). After it's installed, you simply stick the siphon hose into a jug of antifreeze. Flip on the pump, and go open up your faucets one at a time. That way, the rig's water pump does all the hard work for you.

## Step 6: Dosing your drains

Pour 2 cups of RV antifreeze into all sink drains and the shower floor drain. This will push the standing water out of their curved drain pipes (called *p-traps*) and fill them with the pink stuff. Also, pour a cup or two into the toilet bowl without flushing. The antifreeze will keep the rubber toilet gasket from drying out, and it will prevent any smells from the blackwater tank from drifting up into the RV when warm weather arrives.

## Step 7: Beware the phantom menace

When you park your RV, the last thing you probably do before locking the door is turn off the master power switch (sometimes called a *battery* or *house power disconnect switch*). But most RVs have a couple of electrical devices that *never* turn off — some stereo receivers, Wi-Fi boosters, TVs, powered antennas, carbon monoxide or smoke detectors, and commonly, the propane detector alarm that sniffs for gas leaks. They're known as *power vampires* or *phantom loads*. These devices may only use a few milliamps (a thousandth of an amp), but even a tiny load can, given enough time, drain your batteries stone dead — even when the main disconnect is turned off.

The voltage from lead-acid, deep-cycle batteries should never be allowed to drop more than 50 percent, or they'll quickly lose the ability to recharge at full capacity. If your RV's house batteries are lead-acid or absorbed glass mat (AGM), the safest way to protect them from losing their charge or freezing is to remove them to your garage and plug them into a 12VDC trickle charger overnight every couple weeks. At the very least, if you leave them onboard, disconnect the black (negative) wire from the terminal posts. (We tell you everything you need to know about batteries in Chapter 14.)

# MOTORHOMES: DON'T FORGET THE "MOTOR" PART

All the winterizing steps in this chapter apply to trailers, campers, and motorhomes, but don't forget the part of your coach or tow vehicle that drives. Before you park any car, van, truck, or bus for months at a time in the dead of winter, you need to take steps to ensure it'll start up again next spring. Schedule any regular maintenance in the fall, like changing the oil and transmission fluid, checking tires for excessive wear and proper inflation, and having any mechanical issues repaired while you're thinking of it at the end of camping season. You don't want to take a quick, spontaneous weekend getaway on the first warm weekend of the year, only to be haunted by an annoying mechanical problem you put off fixing back in the fall. Plus, you'll probably find out the hard way that your dealer has a hundred other rigs in line ahead of you every spring.

Gasoline and diesel fuel don't keep their potency when stored for a long time, and if you have diesel fuel in the tank left from summer, it can gel in cold weather. For lack of a better term, fuel goes stale. Fuel stabilizing chemical additives made by STA-BIL, Opti-Lube, and others prevent your gas or diesel fuel from breaking down over the winter. Put about 10 gallons of fuel in the tank, and pour in the stabilizer (check the instructions for the right amount). Start the engine, and let it idle for ten minutes to circulate the treated fuel into the engine's fuel lines, carburetor, and fuel injectors. You shouldn't have problems the next time you start it up.

Finally, depending on your storage situation, hook the engine's battery to a trickle charger overnight several times a month, or start the engine once a week and let it run for a few minutes. Some owners prefer to remove the engine battery altogether, like their RV's house batteries, to prevent freezing. A trickle charger should still be used regularly to keep the battery in top shape all winter.

**WARNING**

Before you store lead-acid batteries, open their plastic caps and make sure the sulfuric acid electrolyte is fully covering the lead plates inside. If it isn't, refill them with distilled water. Be careful around open battery cell caps. Wear rubber gloves and eye protection — the acid is extremely corrosive.

**TIP**

If you're lucky enough to store your rig on your property or have access to electricity, you won't necessarily have to remove your batteries. Plug your rig into shore power every couple of weeks and let the RV's internal convertor and charging system keep your batteries at full capacity. Just don't leave them plugged in longer than an eight hours or so. Overcharging lead-acid batteries without actually using their stored electricity can result in the charger cooking the battery cells and boiling off the electrolyte.

# Step 8: Taking care of odds and ends

How much more you do with your rig is up to you and your storage situation. Obviously, an enclosed indoor storage area is the best because, apart from cold, the sun can cause damage to fiberglass, paint, caulking, and plastic fittings, especially those massive, swoopy decals RV manufacturers love to cover their rigs with. The UV rays in sunlight can degrade an RV exterior regardless of how hot or cold the temperature may be, so don't think you're immune from sun damage when the weather drops below zero. (After all — people who go skiing in frigid weather get sunburned all the time.)

If you can't keep your rig indoors, the next best alternative is a canopy overhead (like a carport). It also protects your RV against ice or hailstorms. That said, plenty of RVers keep their rigs parked out in the open all year.

**TIP**

Here are a few odds and ends to consider before you abandon your baby for the season:

>> Be sure all tires are properly inflated when cold. (Tire pressure increases when they warm up on the road and decreases when they're cold.)

>> Chock your wheels so your rig can't easily roll away.

>> Lower your trailer's hitch jack to make it harder for anyone else to hook it up and make off with your RV. And slip a padlock onto the closed hitch latch lever. It won't stop a serious thief, but it may deter a casual one.

>> Close all window shades and curtains.

>> Lock all outdoor compartments.

>> If you have hydraulic stabilizers, don't extend them to raise up your rig while in storage. If they develop mechanical problems, you may wind up with a major job trying to retract them just to get to the dealer.

>> Don't forget to lock the front door when you leave.

Some owners buy a cover to shield their rigs from the elements, winter and summer. You need one that closely fits your RV and is made of breathable fabric. Avoid cheap covers, and never use plastic ones — a blue or black plastic tarp will trap moisture and encourage mold and mildew. The best covers have reinforced corners to resist tearing, plenty of tie-down straps, and even a zippered section that lets you access your side door without totally removing the cover. Manufacturers will list some of the more popular RVs their covers fit. And online RV-owner communities specific to your rig can often steer you in the right direction when hunting for the perfect fit.

**REMEMBER**

Tires don't just wear out from lots of driving. Old age can kill them, too. If you know your RV isn't going anywhere for an extended period of time, consider a set of tire covers. The sun baking down on rubber tires can dry them out and age them prematurely. Also, don't let tires sit for extended periods in water, snow, or mud.

# Pulling Your RV out of Storage

When the freezing weather blessedly comes to an end in the spring, you'll need to retrace your steps to de-winterize everything:

» Recharge and reinstall (or reconnect) your batteries, and turn on the main power switch.

» Refill, reinstall, and turn on the propane tanks. Make sure all your appliances are working again.

» Close the drain valve on the freshwater tank and the hot and cold low point valves. (Don't worry — if you forget, they'll remind you by leaking all over the driveway as soon as you start putting water in.)

» If you isolated the water heater using its bypass valves, switch those back over to the summertime setting. Replace the water heater's drain plug, remembering to wrap its threads with a turn or two of white plumber's tape. Be sure the pressure/temperature relief valve lever is closed.

» Connect a drinking-water hose to the city water inlet and turn it on.

» If you used the compressed air method to purge the water lines in the fall, open up all faucets and turn on the shower. Lots of air will sputter out until it gets purged out of the plumbing pipes and the faucets all run smoothly.

» If you used the "pink stuff" antifreeze method, follow the same steps. But you need to run each faucet until the pink foam stops and clear water is flowing. That can take longer than you think. Don't forget to keep an eye on the graywater and blackwater tank levels so they don't overflow from all those faucets running.

» When that water runs clear and stops sputtering, move the hose from the city hookup valve and fill your freshwater holding tank to at least 20 percent.

» Turn on your water pump with the faucets still running to get rid of any remaining pink stuff and to purge any last air from the pipes. When the water's all clear and stops sputtering, turn off all the faucets and give the pump a few minutes to recharge the water pressure. It'll shut itself off when the water pressure equalizes. If it doesn't, you have a leak somewhere.

# Wintertime RVing

If you've read this far, you've got a pretty good idea why camping in subfreezing weather can be challenging. But despite the tribulations, plenty of people continue to use their RVs in winter and love it. We usually take a couple of long road trips in winter ourselves. Depending on how long you intend to be on the road in the cold, and whether you're staying in a freezing cold region, or just passing through on the way somewhere warmer, there are steps to make camping possible in freezing weather. If your rig isn't built for the cold, and it's extremely cold outside, you may have to stick to bottled water for drinking, cooking, and washing, give up showering and using the toilet in your rig, and use alternative heaters to supplement your propane furnace. But you can still go cold-weather camping in just about any RV.

## Keeping you and your RV warm

The number-one consideration with wintertime camping is to how stay warm. Unfortunately, the vast majority of RVs aren't especially well insulated. And a combined air-conditioner/heat pump on your roof is useless when the temperature outside nears freezing. If it comes on at all, you'll only get cold air out of it. The typical RV's propane furnace can blast enough heat to chase you out, but all that glorious warmth is quickly undone by thin walls, ceilings, and drafts around windows and doors.

TIP

So, here are some basic keep-warm ideas:

>> **Clothes:** The simplest solutions are often the most effective. So, pack sweaters, sweatpants, thick socks, and the warmest blankets you can find, especially down. You may want to give up going barefoot for the duration of the season and bring your fluffiest slippers.

## FOUR SEASON RVs

Some manufacturers offer specific features in their rigs that make cold-weather camping more pleasant. Forest River/Northwood's line of Arctic Fox trailers and truck campers are especially designed for all-year camping. Keystone's Montana fifth-wheel trailer is an extremely popular all-weather choice for those wanting a more spacious rig. But Jayco, Keystone, Airstream, Heartland, Lance, and many others also make better-insulated, four-season trailers and motorhomes. Check online and ask owners questions to find the best winter rig for you.

» **Blankets:** Don't forget about bedtime. Down-filled sleeping bags and camp blankets can collapse into small bundles for storage when not needed, but they're extremely warm. And two people under one blanket stay warmer than one. So, share your body heat with a buddy. Just sayin'.

» **Rugs:** One of the coldest things in your RV in the winter is the floor. Consider putting down area rugs and runners to cover your laminate or vinyl floors. Try to use rugs with rubberized backing or use double-stick tape to keep them from becoming slip-and-fall hazards.

» **Windows:** If you're not blessed with thermal, double-pane windows (not many rigs are), cover your windows inside with at least a layer of clear plastic. If you can deal with not looking out, buy a roll of Reflectix, which looks like aluminum-foil bubble wrap. Cut covers from it to tape over your windows.

» **Vents and fans:** Rooftop fans are especially drafty because they're usually separated from the outside by nothing more than a thin plastic lid. Puffy insulation "cushions" are available from RV stores; they're designed to stuff into the recessed fan opening or sunroof frame inside your RV, but you can easily cut your own from foam material.

» **Exterior skirting:** If you intend to stay in one spot for more than a few days, consider buying custom skirting to enclose the base of your whole rig or make your own temporary version. Rigid foam insulation board is available from home improvement stores in 1- and 2-inch thicknesses in 4-x-8-foot sheets. They can be cut easily with an electric jigsaw fitted with a smooth knife blade. Tape the sections together with duct tape or FLEX TAPE to keep them from falling over or blowing away. As an alternative, some RVers simply surround the rig's chassis with hay bales to block the wind and cold. Be sure you enclose the area around your wastewater dump valves and drain pipe to help prevent them from freezing.

» **Electric blankets and space heaters:** Instead of heating up the whole RV, use an electric space heater to help keep *you* warmer wherever you happen to be. If you like to curl up on your couch to watch TV or read, wrap yourself up in an electric blanket or a smaller electric throw. That will help you conserve your propane gas supply.

We discuss some additional heating units in Chapter 17. But we'll warn you right now: Subfreezing temperatures and boondocking make a bad combination unless you have a substantial generator. Any heat-making devices that rely on electricity — like your built-in furnace, electric space heaters, or propane heaters with a powered circulating fan — can deplete your house battery power in a matter of hours. If you're in a motorhome or fifth wheel with an onboard generator, you're self-contained (at least until you run through all your gas or diesel fuel). But the best way to conveniently stay warm in the majority of trailers and campers is to plug into shore power at a campsite.

# AVOID CARBON MONOXIDE POISONING!

No matter how clean burning it is, propane still generates carbon monoxide, which is odorless, colorless, and deadly. Your onboard propane furnace is designed with a vent outside so its exhaust doesn't get into your living space. A gas cooktop and oven should have a ventilation hood and fan to direct their exhaust outside, too. But portable propane-burning space heaters and other accessories simply release their exhaust into the air around them. Without any ventilation to let fresh air in and bad air out of a confined space like an RV, carbon monoxide can make you pass out before you know what hit you, and kill you in your sleep. Yes, it's that serious.

Practice these safety tips when using extra heaters to keep your rig warm in winter:

- Regularly test your propane, smoke, and carbon monoxide alarms all season long to make sure they're functioning. Make it a habit to install fresh alarm batteries every spring.

- Never use your propane cooktop burners or open oven as a quick heat source in a cold RV. Open flames pose a huge danger in a closed rig.

- Any time you're operating a propane heater of any kind in an enclosed area, you need to crack open a window or a roof fan lid or run the stovetop vent fan to prevent the buildup of carbon monoxide in the air. We know that sounds crazy when it's 20 degrees outside, and the wind is blowing, but better some heat loss than a life lost.

## Keeping water from freezing

If you could deal with traveling without fresh water for the trip and never needing the toilet, cold-weather camping would be a cinch.

Check your RV's manuals or contact the manufacturer to find out whether your rig has features to prevent freshwater and wastewater tanks from freezing. The tanks may be enclosed in a heated area under the floor, with warm air circulated from the forced-air propane furnace. If that's the case, set your furnace's thermostat to 45 degrees or above and let it run all the time, even when you're driving.

Yes, we know that "everybody" says turn off your propane and never run your propane furnace when you're driving. But any risk of a propane fire while you're driving is minuscule, whereas turning your 50-gallon freshwater tank into a 400-pound ice block is a certainty in continuous, subfreezing temperatures. Some RV manufacturers actually put this contradiction in their manuals, admonishing you to *always* turn off the gas when you're moving but *always* leave it on in subfreezing weather to prevent water from icing up. You know what they say about consistency being the hobgoblin of little minds.

# Using helpful cold weather accessories

You'll want to consider some aftermarket accessories or additions if you expect to do much subfreezing RVing:

>> **Water tank heating blankets:** These are electric blankets that get taped, glued, or strapped to your freshwater and wastewater tanks. If your rig doesn't have a furnace that warms them, you'll need some of these.

>> **Heated water hose:** Camco and RV supply companies sell these in different lengths. They're essentially a drinking-water hose wrapped with electric heating tape and insulation. A 120VAC plug is provided to plug into power.

**REMEMBER**

Only use a heated hose continuously if the campsite faucet itself is heated or otherwise protected by some kind of housing. (We've seen campground water faucets covered with a plastic bucket and an electric light bulb inside to keep the spigot just warm enough not to freeze.) Bear in mind that a heated hose won't freeze, but the little bit of water in the exposed metal hose connections where it screws into your RV might. Best use is to only connect when you need to shower or wash dishes; then disconnect the rest of the time.

>> **Electric heat wrapping tape:** Use it to protect pipes, especially the wastewater dump valves and drain pipe. You can also use it to wrap a water hose and make your own heated supply hose.

>> **Coiled food-grade hoses:** These are lightweight and much more compact than a traditional garden-style hose. They're clear and they come in multiple colors, although they're usually considerably thinner in diameter than you're used to: Filling a water tank with them can take three or four times as long. When you're finished, you can easily hold one end up in the air and watch all the water drain out so it won't freeze.

>> **Handheld hair dryer:** Keep one onboard along with an extra-long 120V outdoor extension cord. They work great for gently thawing out frozen pipes and connections without melting the plastic. Professional-grade heat guns normally used for burning off paint put out way too much heat and can melt expensive plastic fittings, valves, and housings.

## SNOW CHAINS REQUIRED

Mountain states like Oregon, Washington, California, Colorado, and Montana may require a tow vehicle or motorhome always to carry tire chains or other traction devices, even when they're not needed. If you've ever watched *Ice Road Truckers,* you probably know why. Mountain roads are always susceptible to unpredictable weather, especially from Halloween until April.

When mandated, tire chains have to be attached to a vehicle's powered drive wheels to provide traction, and they come in single-tire or dual-tire configurations (in case you've got "dualies" on your truck or rig). *Drag chains* are an additional set of chains that are used on at least one axle of a trailer if it's equipped with its own brakes, so it can grip the road while it's being towed.

*Traction devices* can come as a heavy set of actual metal tire chains or made of thinner metal cables (lightweight, less storage space, and a little easier to put on and remove). A relatively new product in the United States comes out of Norway: *snow socks,* which look like a set of wheel covers. But traction device laws are different for every state, and chains are the only type accepted by all of them. It doesn't happen that often, but police can ticket and fine you if you're not carrying a set in your rig or using them when required. Police can detain you until you put them on. And if you don't have any at all, they can order you to park until you can get a set.

Never drive faster than 25 miles per hour with tire chains attached. They should only be used when there is snow or ice on the road and removed as soon as possible. That's because when the asphalt is dry, they can tear up the road, destroy your tires, and rip up the chains themselves.

You may never in a million years ever, ever, *ever* need to use these, but practice putting them on and taking them off in your own driveway anytime you're headed for a mountain state.

# Chapter 19

# Tow, Tow, Tow Your Toad: Towing Your Car Behind Your Motorhome

You've probably seen a big motorhome rolling down the road towing a car behind it. Maybe you just figured it was a deranged tailgater with a lead foot, but it's actually a seasoned RVer who planned ahead. There's no getting around the fact that, if you've got a huge motorhome, you're driving around your own personal parking problem that doesn't lend itself to quick stops in tight quarters. Nobody wants to spend an hour getting settled into the perfect campsite and suddenly realizing the only way to run an errand, explore the town, or hit the drive-through is by pulling up stakes.

RVers call the car they pull behind them a *lifeboat*, a *dinghy*, or most often, a *toad* (not as in frog, but as in "towed"). Towing a car or truck behind your rig comes with its own set of issues, not the least of which is cost — you can't just wrap a bungee around the front bumper of the family car, lash it to your motorhome, and take off for the Grand Canyon.

In this chapter, we explain the different towing methods and help you decide which one may be best for you. We also explain why you can't easily tow just any car you like.

# Considering Your Towing Options

Your campsite is all set up and you're finally ready to attempt making margaritas with a Pringles can because you left the blender at home. And then it hits you: There's no ice, and the closest convenience store is back in town. If you're towing a trailer or fifth wheel, disconnecting your tow vehicle and heading for the closest ice machine is simple, but if you're driving a motorhome, it's more complicated. Towing a toad makes motorhome life almost as convenient as life with one of the smaller RVs.

Apart from pulling a small car into the cargo bay of a toy hauler, there are three ways to connect a toad to your RV:

>> **Flat towing:** All four wheels of the toad are on the ground.

>> **Tow dolly:** The toad is pulled up onto a two-wheel tow dolly.

>> **Car trailer:** The toad is loaded onto a flat car trailer all its own.

Each method has its pros and cons. But bringing a toad requires a not-insignificant investment in extra equipment, regardless of which solution you choose.

In the following sections, we walk you through each option in detail, but if you're short on time and you just want to know what's easiest, here's the answer: Despite the extra equipment, modifications, and other factors, most motorhome owners who regularly tow a toad say they prefer flat towing to any other method. Connecting and disconnecting a toad from a set of tow bars takes just five minutes and beats the heck out of dealing with an extra trailer or tow dolly.

If this entire section turns you off hauling a toad behind your RV, there is another alternative many campers consider, especially if they're staying in or near a populated city: Rent a car. Enterprise (www.enterprise.com) will deliver one to you wherever you are (within reason). Or just get a ride with Lyft or Uber.

## Flat towing

*Flat towing* (also known as *four down towing*) means all four wheels of your toad are rolling on the ground behind your motorhome. Attaching a car to the back of an RV with a tow bar, putting the toad's gearshift in neutral, and heading down the road can sound like the simplest method, at least at first. But there are challenges and expenses you need to be aware of. Tow bars can cost as little as a few hundred bucks, but the added systems and modifications to your toad can run into several thousand dollars.

In the following sections, we walk you through what to expect.

## First things first: The tow bar

In order to attach your toad to your motorhome, you need a tow bar. There are several different styles of tow bars on the market, but the most popular are from Blue Ox (`www.blueox.com`), Demco (`www.demco-products.com`), Husky Towing Products (`www.huskytow.com`), Reese Towpower (`www.reesetowpower.com`), and Roadmaster (`www.roadmasterinc.com`).

There are two basic designs for tow bars, and they both have different weight limits:

>> The first is shaped like a Y or a wishbone. The single end (the *drawbar*) mounts to a hitch receiver on your motorhome, and the two extended arms mount to the front of the toad using a special base plate. Some units also attach a cross member between the two arms to keep them from spreading apart. When you disconnect from the toad, the arms stay attached to the RV and fold up relatively flat against the back bumper.

>> The other type is a rigid, inverted Y and mounts on hinges to the front of your toad. Disconnect from the RV, and the tow bar swings up and fastens against the front grill of the toad with the short drawbar end sticking straight up.

Both types require a custom-mounted *base plate*, which is a metal plate attached below your toad's front grill that the tow bar securely fastens onto.

A professional RV mechanic should install the base plate — don't try this at home.

## Required safety systems

In addition to the tow bar, some safety systems need to be attached to your toad when you're flat towing.

### SAFETY CABLES

Safety cables keep the toad attached to the RV in case the bars come loose or are improperly fastened. Like safety chains on a trailer, the cables need to be crossed under the tow bars so they can act as a cradle to keep the drawbar from falling and digging into the ground if it comes loose, which would do major damage to your toad's front end.

### TAIL LIGHTS

Your toad needs to have Department of Transportation (DOT)–approved tail lights that mimic the lights on your RV. Turn on the turn signal or hit the brakes, and lights on your toad communicate that to the drivers behind you.

An umbilical cord with a seven-way electrical connector can be hard-wired into your toad to plug into your motorhome. Properly wired, the cable actuates the tail lights, the license plate light, and some types of supplemental brakes, along with sending 12-volt power from your motorhome's charging system to your toad's battery.

**TIP**

If hard wiring is beyond your budget, you can get magnetic tail lights that can be temporarily mounted on your toad and plugged into the RV without hard wiring or modifying anything.

## SUPPLEMENTAL BRAKES

All states require auxiliary brakes on any trailer or vehicle being towed over a certain weight limit (laws vary from state to state), so your toad will need its own remote-controlled braking system installed. These units are most commonly a shoebox-size device that gets strapped into the toad's driver's seat or on the floor with an *actuator* (sort of a robot foot that quite literally jams on the brake pedal when it gets a signal).

Here are the different kinds of supplemental braking systems available:

» **Preset systems:** Preset systems belt into the toad's front seat and connect to the motorhome with a wiring harness. Whenever the motorhome's brake lights illuminate, the controller stomps on the toad's brake pedal with a preset amount of force. The unit is easy to swap from one vehicle to another, which is important if you use different cars or buy a new one.

» **Proportional systems:** Sometimes called *inertia* or *surge brakes,* proportional systems use similar control units, but instead of being wired to the motorhome, they have an internal inertia-sensing device, like the accelerometer that senses movement in your smartphone. The unit detects changes in speed and inclines from the behavior of your RV: You slow down, and it applies the brakes. You slow down very fast; it does too. You drive down a hill; it applies the toad's brakes to match what you're doing up front. These units also strap into the toad's driver seat and are the most popular choice of RVers. They're also easy to move to different vehicles.

» **Direct systems:** Direct systems require a hydraulic or air hose connection from your motorhome's brakes to the toad's supplemental brake control box. Step on the brakes up in the cab, and the toad's brakes are applied in the very same proportion at the same time. This type of system is mechanically complex and should only be undertaken by an experienced mechanic.

>> **Vacuum assist system:** In a vacuum-assist system, the control box is connected to the motorhome with an umbilical cord. It activates the toad's internal braking system by triggering an auxiliary vacuum pump and applying the toad's power brakes without its engine running. Proponents say this system gives more precise control and is easier on the toad's braking components because it needs to push the brake pedal with much less force.

There are dramatic differences between manufacturers, models, and types of braking systems in terms of complexity and features. Many, but not all, have a radio-controlled monitor and adjustment control that mounts on your motorhome's dashboard to tell you whether the toad's brakes are working properly. Most of these brake control units require 12-volt power from your toad's cigarette lighter plug or another source. Unless you have an umbilical connection that keeps the car battery charged from the motorhome's engine system, it's easy to run down the toad's battery with these units, especially on a long day of descending steep hills and continuous braking.

## FORWARD! ALWAYS FORWARD!

As a teenager in the late 1930s, Chris's dad had a 25-year-old Model T Ford that he bought for $20. It was his very first car, and it had a broken steering mechanism, so it couldn't turn left. That meant Dad had to get to wherever he was going by executing a series of right turns. He went around the block a lot. Hauling a toad with a tow bar is a little like that.

As long as you go forward, the toad dutifully trails behind you without many issues. But you can't back up your rig if you're towing with a tow bar — it will cause damage to both the tow bar itself and the front end of your car (and possibly even the back end of your motorhome). In practice, what this means is that if you pull into a gas station or truck stop and find yourself hemmed into a parking mess, you'll have to climb out, completely disconnect your toad, shove the brake equipment out of the front seat, start the car, and park it somewhere out of the way before you can begin to back up your RV. The good news is that connecting and disconnecting a tow bar is pretty simple and only takes a couple of minutes. But it's a major annoyance that can arise at the most inconvenient moments. Urban or suburban shopping areas are a veritable minefield of narrow streets, tight parking lots, one-way roads, and other obstacles that demand backing up.

It's not always possible, but try never to pull into a place before you figure out how you'll get out.

Another issue is whether a braking unit has a breakaway braking feature in case your toad becomes disconnected from your RV. Consult your dealer and look for online discussions about toad braking systems before deciding what to buy. Also, ask fellow motorhome drivers at campgrounds or gas stations what system they're using.

## Tow dolly

If the limitations of flat towing seem too daunting, another option is to use a *tow dolly*, a two-wheeled contraption that sort of resembles a really low Roman chariot with rubber tires. The front end of the tow dolly connects to your RV with a ball hitch like a normal trailer. Over the axle are a pair of flat ramps that tilt down to the ground for loading. You carefully pull your toad's front wheels up onto the ramps, securely lash down the toad with ratchet straps, and head into the sunrise. The front wheels ride up on the dolly, and the back wheels roll freely on the road.

Make sure your toad will fit properly on the dolly's platform ramps, and that it has enough weight capacity to safely haul your car.

The tow dolly has its own set of trailer brakes and DOT tail lights built in, so you don't need to modify or rewire the toad itself — the umbilical cord from the rear of the RV takes care of everything.

New tow dollies can cost anywhere from less than $1,000 to $4,000, depending on features. If you want to try before investing in one, U-Haul rents car-towing dollies for $40 to $60 a day.

One ongoing expense of tow dollies is that many states require them to be separately titled and registered with their own license plates. That's usually a relatively minor expense compared to the rest of the auto world, but money is money.

When you arrive at a campground, you'll need to figure out a place to store the dolly — that can be challenging on a tight campsite, although some campgrounds have a small parking area set aside for just such purposes. Some dollies are designed to fold in half when not in use to make storage less of a hassle.

## Car trailer

The simplest solution with the least potential wear and tear on your toad is to just pull it onto a trailer of its own and lash it down. You can use an open flatbed auto carrier trailer or a covered utility one. Auto carrier trailers usually have a set of short ramps in the back that fold up or detach after loading, or a fold-down door that acts as a ramp. They have their own DOT-approved lighting and their own set of electric trailer brakes. When you shop, be armed with the length and width measurements of your toad, as well as its gross manufactured weight — you don't want to overload the trailer's capacity.

A new enclosed car hauling trailer can go for between $5,000 and $10,000, while a new open-deck, flatbed auto hauler runs between $3,600 and $9,500. But you can find lots of used ones on the market, and U-Haul rents auto carrier trailers, too.

**REMEMBER**

If you're considering an enclosed trailer, make sure your toad is able to squeeze inside, and that you can climb out of the car when it's in there! Chances are, you won't be able to open the car door, which means you either need to climb out the driver's side window or crawl through the car to a rear tailgate. For this reason, you may want to consider a convertible or something like a Jeep with a removable top as your toad.

Whatever you do, make sure the toad is in Park, the emergency brake is on, and it's secured to the trailer with ratchet straps before you take off driving.

The biggest issue with a separate toad trailer is getting rid of it when you're actually camping. If you can get a pull-through campsite long enough to accommodate your motorhome, the transport trailer, *and* your unloaded family car all together, that's terrific. But most RVers really want to ditch the trailer somewhere out of the way until they leave. Check with the campground when you reserve a spot and ask if they have a trailer storage area.

**REMEMBER**

Many states require car trailers to be separately titled and registered with their own license plates, just like tow dollies.

# Considering the Vehicle You're Towing

You may think that a big Class A or Class C motorhome with a whopping diesel engine can haul anything you throw into it or hang off its bumper. But all motorhomes have towing limitations just like any other tow vehicle. Most of them are able to safely tow a car or average pickup truck without weight issues, but beware of your own worst impulses. Lots of campers look on their toad as a vast, untapped wealth of extra storage space just waiting to be packed to the gills with extra stuff. Be sure your motorhome can handle the weight you want to pull!

As people smarter than us have often said, the most affordable car you can have is one you already own. If you own a car or truck you intend to tow flat behind your rig, that's a big expense you've avoided. But not every car or truck on the market can be towed this way. In fact, remarkably few can.

Any car with a manual transmission can be flat towed — push in the clutch, take it out of gear, and tow away. Not so with automatic transmissions — even when your car's in Neutral, the drive wheels spin the axles, which spins the driveshaft, which spins the transmission as you roll. Without its own engine running, oil can't circulate throughout your car's transmission, and you can do extensive and expensive trip-ending damage in a startlingly short time. And in case you wondered, electric car owners are currently out of luck when it comes to flat towing. Their drive motors are directly connected to the car's wheels and can't be disengaged.

**WARNING**

Some RV advice sites will confidently tell you that an unmodified car or truck can be safely flat-towed in Neutral as far as 200 miles before risking any damage to the transmission. We're not advising you to do anything of the sort, and we frankly wouldn't gamble our car's transmission on such a claim.

**WARNING**

There's a reason why the most commonly towed toads on the road are Jeeps. Many of their vehicles are engineered specifically for recreational towing and can mechanically uncouple their driveshaft without having to remove it. Some (but not all) 4-wheel-drive pickup trucks, full-size SUVs, and crossovers from Ford, Chevy, GM, and RAM have this ability, as do several Fiat, Honda, Kia, and Toyota cars. Until it was discontinued in the United States in 2018, the tiny SmartCar was enormously popular as an RV toad. But research this subject carefully before you buy anything — specs can vary widely from model to model and year to year. Several RV websites provide a list of towable vehicles every year, but even they will caution you to get assurances from an auto dealership or manufacturer that the specific individual model you've homed in on is flat-towable.

**REMEMBER**

Towing with all four wheels on the ground means your toad racks up wear and tear on tires, suspension, and more. A 5,800-mile round trip from New York to Seattle and back puts those same 5,800 miles on your toad's odometer, tires, and other mechanical systems.

If you're hell-bent on flat towing your favorite car despite its mechanical unsuitability, you can have a driveshaft de-coupler and/or an auxiliary electric transmission oil lubrication pump installed — RV dealers usually install these, not car dealers. But if you make those kinds of custom modifications, all that money goes down the drain if you buy a new car in a year or two.

If you're using a tow dolly, front-wheel drive cars work best, because their drive wheels are raised off the road and don't spin. But if you don't have a front-wheel-drive vehicle, you're back to needing a toad with a manual transmission or one that can decouple its driveshaft just as you need if you're using a tow bar.

**WARNING**

Because the toad's nose rides up at an angle on the dolly, you can easily end up dragging its rear end on high curbs and inclines. That's one reason lots of campers prefer Jeeps as toads — they tend to have higher ground clearance than the average coupe or sedan.

On the plus side, you'll save a bundle of boodle with a tow dolly because your toad won't need anything done to it. If its odometer is connected to the front wheels up on the dolly, your 5,800-mile trip won't be recorded as mileage. And you'll only put extra wear on the rear tires. On the downside, a two-wheel car dolly is susceptible to fishtailing at highway speeds, although there are anti-sway devices that can help counteract this problem.

REMEMBER

Just like with a tow-bar setup, you can't back up with a tow dolly. Don't forget to order and install a rock deflector for it (see the nearby sidebar).

## GUARD YOUR NOSE

As you drive, your toad is rolling just a few feet behind your motorhome's rear wheels. Rocks, gravel, and other road junk can get kicked up by the RV's tires and do major damage to the car's body and windshield. A short trip down a gravel road can leave your car looking like you got caught in a three-day meteor shower. There's no uniformity to the situation — some RVers never have the problem, while others discover their car's a paint-chipped wreck after just a single incident. Solutions include the following:

- A rock shield that mounts on the tow bar between the RV and the toad's front grill or directly on the front of the car itself, to deflect road projectiles.

- A screen-like mesh that mounts across the tow bar, parallel to the road surface, that lets wind and water through but blocks rocks and dirt.

- A removable nose cover called a *bra* that fits over the toad's grill and a portion of the hood. Some larger variations actually stretch up over the whole hood and windshield and include covers for the side-view mirrors, too.

- Rubber mud flaps mounted behind the motorhome's back tires.

- A brush-like curtain (nicknamed a *hula skirt*) or solid rubber rock guard that hangs under the full width of the back end of the motorhome to prevent dirt and rocks from hurling out.

Many of these devices are brand- or vehicle-specific, so make sure the one you want actually fits the tow bar arrangement and the toad you own.

Finally, don't be tempted to put a full cover on your toad until you get to your destination — a flapping cover beating against the car at highway speed can do more harm than good by trapping grit and grinding it into the paint.

# Chapter **20**

# Boondocking and Living off the Grid

**B**oondocking (camping free of any campground hookups) has taken the RV world by storm. Considering that the price of an ordinary KOA campsite has soared to $60 or more per night, you can save a *lot* of money boondocking. But if you ask truly passionate boondockers, you'll find more than people who economize. (No one who ponies up $2,000 for a new set of lithium trailer batteries is completely motivated by cost.) For some people, boondocking is beyond a hobby and more of a passion — they love trying to extend the number of days they can camp with available water and power they generate themselves. When you've set up camp in complete isolation (or near to it), you'll find a pioneer sort of feeling that you'll never get in a parking space of a KOA.

As long as people have gone camping (at least a couple centuries, in terms of recreational camping), there have been boondockers. In fact, before the invention of the RV, *everyone* boondocked — this was the definition of *camping out.* But as RVs grew more comfortable, more luxurious, more homelike, a reaction set in. Because, to achieve all that homey comfort, you had to be chained to the RV park.

Also called *dry camping,* boondocking enables you to have much more freedom. The problems are obvious — going without water and power, or generating power for yourself. Though you can do it in the nearest parking lot, boondocking is often tied to free camping on government land.

This chapter probably won't give you every tip and every trick of dry camping, a subject that could fill a couple books by itself. But it's an introduction — a handy guide for getting your feet wet "adventure camping."

TIP

Check out the Boondocker's Bible (www.boondockersbible.com) for loads more no-nonsense advice for dry camping.

# This Land Is Your Land, This Land Is My Land: Finding a Place to Boondock

The federal government owns a staggering amount of land in the United States — 650 million acres of it, roughly one-third of the nation, and most of it is available for camping. In fact, these recreational programs are mandated by the federal government. You can hike or bike the trails; go rock climbing, canoeing, or kayaking; go hunting or fishing; ride dirt bikes and all-terrain vehicles (ATVs); and backpack or RV your way across some spectacular places, with a remarkable amount of freedom. For example, people who love ATVs have very limited places to run them, but on Bureau of Land Management (BLM) land, there's enough space to give the other guy a little bit of elbow room. Just go to the BLM website (www.blm.gov), and you can find the best places to go to pursue your individual passion.

Legally, on most federal land, you're allowed to stay 14 days; some national forests allow you to stay as long as 21 days. After that, you have to break camp and move a certain number of miles away before you set up another. The exact numbers are a moving target, based on the agency and the field office. The government just wants to discourage people from living on this land permanently, though of course, there are people who do (but they have to be mobile enough to pull it off).

Online, people often refer to all federal land as "BLM land," but not all of it is BLM, and there are differences in the types of federal land. Camping rules are different for the different agencies, which is why you need a bit of awareness of who's the boss of the land you're on. You can find out who's in charge with the smartphone apps FreeRoam (https://freeroam.app) and US Public Lands (https://apps.apple.com/us/app/us-public-lands/id723185418).

These are the major federal agencies that administer public land:

>> **Bureau of Land Management (BLM):** This is the big kid on the block, with 245 million acres, much of it considered "cast-off" land, places no one wanted to homestead. Along with opportunities to boondock, there are free and

low-cost campgrounds, but the BLM's idea of a campground and yours may be two different things. In some of these "developed recreation areas," there may be as little as a boat launch, a vault toilet, some fire rings, and a sign. You've left the KOA far behind. Sometimes you can see why this is orphan land that the National Park Service didn't want, but much of this land has its own rugged, natural beauty.

Some BLM areas are simply public lands, while others are wilderness areas, conservation areas, or even national monuments. Check with the local field office if you have questions.

>> **U.S. Forest Service (USFS):** The USFS is BLM's nearest competitor in size, with 193 million acres contained in 154 national forests located in 40 states. It can be confusing, but remember that a national forest isn't a national park, and it's not a state forest, either. In a national forest, you'll find campgrounds run by the USFS, which oversees these lands; they charge like any other, but the prices are kept reasonable.

Free camping for a limit of 14 or 21 days is also the rule for boondocking in national forests, and their beauty makes them some of the best camping locations to be had. You can also get information online at the USFS website, including links to specialty maps, like the Motor Vehicle Use Map (`www.fs.fed.us/recreation/programs/ohv/ohv_maps.shtml`), which is helpful if you're an RVer looking for camping space. The rangers for the park you're visiting are the best people to contact for updated information.

National forests are, well, forests. They're loaded with trees, which makes them gorgeous, but a bit trickier to navigate.

>> **Fish and Wildlife Service (FWS):** FWS has a big chunk of public land, 89 million acres (76 million of which is in Alaska), but it doesn't really do camping. FWS offers "recreation opportunities," mostly related to hunting and fishing within the system of wildlife refuges it administers.

>> **National Park Service (NPS):** Everyone wants into the national parks — they're the gold standard of camping. But getting into one can be difficult, especially in the high season. Plus, opportunities for boondocking in national parks are limited or nonexistent. These places are already so popular, they don't want to cope with a sea of boondockers pushing out the caribou.

But national parks can be a great place to begin your search for places to boondock. BLM and USFS land often borders national parks. So, if you're just starting out adventure camping, begin in an NPS campground, or a pay campground nearby, and then find a nearby promising piece of public land and go for it. If you can detach or you have a toad, consider searching out places to park before you drive your whole rig out there.

TIP

If you're 62 or older, consider buying an America the Beautiful Senior Pass. The cost is $80 for a lifetime membership, or you can buy an annual pass for $20. All federal recreation projects will honor the pass, and give you either free access or a discount for campgrounds and other amenities, like guided tours. Check it out at www.nps.gov/planyourvisit/passes.htm.

>> **Bureau of Reclamation (BOR):** The BOR is mostly in the West, and its mandate is water management — the bureau manages 7.8 million acres and has an impressive number of campgrounds, 590 of them, with a total of 5,700 sites with RV hookups.

>> **Army Corps of Engineers (ACE):** The ACE is the largest federal provider of outdoor recreation services and one of the best-kept secrets in camping. Some 90 percent of its recreation sites are within 50 miles of a major metropolitan area, making them easily accessible. There are more than 450 of them nationwide, and the ACE has leases on many more. But they're not in every state — they tend to be where the ACE's projects have been and where the ACE continues to manage bridges, harbors, and large-scale engineering projects, which means you're often in an area of historical interest as well (a nice plus). ACE parks aren't free, but they're cheap, clean, and well run.

TIP

ACE campgrounds were shut down during the COVID-19 pandemic, whereas BLM campgrounds for the most part stayed open, highlighting the fact that you need an awareness of individual agencies and their policies. Sudden shutdowns are ongoing, often due to flooding, and you should always check reservations on agency websites before departing for a trip.

REMEMBER

Technically, federal land belongs to all of us. But the government has the final rights here. For example, the government may lease the land out to local ranchers, miners, or energy producers, and their rights will come before yours. Though it varies from state to state, vast tracts of government land are a western phenomenon. For example, a mere 0.3 percent of Connecticut is federal land, but over 80 percent of Nevada is. Still, when you're east of the Rockies, Google the state you're in, and you should find some sort of public-land camping. For example, there is no BLM or ACE land in Indiana, but Blackwell Horse Camp in the Hoosier National Forest, near Indiana University in beautiful Bloomington, is a free campground and horse training area with great trails. Most states have an opportunity — you just have to dig to find it.

There are two kinds of camping on public lands – camping in developed campgrounds, which are either free or charge a small fee, or *dispersed camping*. Both employ dry camping, because many "developed" campgrounds have no, or limited hookups. In dispersed camping, you simply go off the road and stake out your space like a pioneer on a wagon train. Finding good sites for dispersed camping is more of a challenge. The agency field office managing the land you're on will usually help you find great areas to camp, and you should talk to them in person or by phone.

TIP

When you're looking for good dispersed sites, finding sites others have used makes life easier, and it's better for the land itself. Follow signs to designated primitive camping or pull over to use one of your apps like FreeRoam, and use Google satellite images to see the area from above. Searching for a site to camp can feel a little like being a CIA analyst, but it's not that hard to find signs that other people have camped there before. You'll get good at looking for the typical signs from above, like an unnamed dirt road off a marked and traveled one, with a roundabout circle at its end where RVs have come and gone. Online reviews will be a huge help, too.

Another tip is to look for a trailhead. As you drive into national forest areas or state parks, you'll see a rustic sign pointing up an equally rustic road, and it'll say something like "Bear Whiz Trail." Follow it. This takes you to the trailhead, where hikers and bikers begin their journey. You'll often find all sorts of things at the trailhead — a map and historical marker, sometimes even restrooms. The trailhead is a good place to look around for a campsite, because so many RVers camp here to use the trail.

REMEMBER

When you find a viable spot, you're in the boonies, and people are camping out here for a reason. Drop your city ways, and don't park too close to another camper.

If you set up camp someplace you shouldn't, never fear — the kindly forest ranger will knock on your door and give you about ten minutes to clear out. Rangers are typically very nice people doing a vital job. But if you find a crabby or officious one, for heaven's sake, *don't argue with them.* Do as you're told, and blog about it later to get it off your chest.

Even if you're in the right place, an officer finding you on government land may ask you all sorts of questions about things like the expected length of your stay. Some of these questions you may find a bit invasive, like whether the RV is your permanent home. Full-timers sometimes get the feeling they're getting knocked with all sorts of assumptions that they're dark characters who need to be watched. It's okay. Be polite, and go on with your stay. Attitudes can change, and you can help by giving them a positive experience with a happy and polite full-timer.

REMEMBER

Be sure to read the individual agency rules for any public land you're camping on. There *are* rules for these places — even BLM campgrounds are not a free-for-all. Most of them are the common-sense rules campers already know (leash your dog, obey posted signage, camp at least 200 feet from the road and from the water).

## TRAMPING DOWN THE ROAD LESS TAKEN

A Land Rover Defender towing a Bruder off-road trailer can go *anywhere*. But for most of us, there are limitations. If your trailer or motorhome is a bit larger, you're probably going to have trouble getting down gully-ridden roads, across dry creek beds, or setting up camp without any level ground at all. If you see a sign warning that the road is only for "high-clearance vehicles," and you're towing 30 low-slung feet, you may have problems. If you're in a big Class A motorhome, you may not have made it as far as the sign.

Hikers and tent campers can better handle the service roads leading to these areas. For RVs, anything bigger than a Class B could be an issue. Often, a prime boondocking area you're after is several miles down a dicey road. If you're pulling a trailer with a truck or full-size SUV, find a place to pull off and unhitch. Go on *without* towing in order to scope out the road ahead. An online reviewer may have said the road "isn't too bad," but scouting ahead in person can save you a whole lot of grief.

Give yourself plenty of daylight hours to find your campsite! In fact, considering the wilderness nature of so much of this land, if you get held up while searching out a particular place, and the sun begins to set, you're better off spending the night right where you are rather than attempting to go farther in the dark.

## NOT ALL WHO WANDER ARE LOST

Then again, a whole bunch of them are.

For roadies, there are two types of tech travel planners most of us depend on:

- **GPS standalone navigators:** The major companies are Garmin, Magellan, and Tom-Tom. They work well for many RVers, but in our experience, once you're in rural areas, the system can fail and give you wrong information. Many campgrounds will ask that you ignore GPS, and take your directions from them.

- **Smartphone navigation systems:** Usually these apps employ Google Maps. In distant BLM land, and even in the national parks, cellphone service can be spotty or nonexistent, so if you're relying on your phone for navigation, you may be up a creek.

Both types of devices can have signal loss, not just cellphones. In a nutshell, the best advice is not to be too dependent on any one electronic navigation system or app. Especially in the backcountry, have a good off-road paper map. Look for anything called a "recreation map" or an "adventure map." Depend on your cellphone or GPS device as long as you can, but be ready to switch over to paper when it goes dead on you.

A paper map is often your best way to find the road less traveled, particularly in the planning stage of your trip. For one thing, states are a natural point of reference when an RVer is planning a trip, and cellphone apps can tend to see the world in small, difficult to discern chunks. In the FreeRoam app, for example, it's hard to see what state you're in, as you search areas. The app is great at finding campgrounds, but you'll need to anchor yourself to keep from roaming out of your target area.

National Geographic maps are terrific, especially for hikers, but we also like Benchmark maps — their recreation atlases cover all relevant backcountry details, but they're pretty large and cost around $25. For an RVer, a good alternative is the Benchmark recreation map for a particular state. It's an old-fashioned fold-up map, and at $7.95 it's a gold mine of information, with all public lands marked, as well as campgrounds and local points of interest. Along with the major boondocking states, they have some popular highway route maps, like the Blue Ridge Parkway through Shenandoah and the Great Smoky Mountains. Paper maps are easier for two people to look at together. Plus, you can tack them to the wall and use Post-it flags or pins to mark out your potential route and plan other sights to see.

# Attending to the Necessities of Life

Agencies like the BLM and USFS have long taught the Seven Principles of Leave No Trace (https://lnt.org/why/7-principles), techniques of minimal-impact camping:

>> Plan ahead and prepare.

>> Travel and camp on durable surfaces.

>> Dispose of waste properly.

>> Leave what you find.

>> Minimize campfire impacts.

>> Respect wildlife.

>> Be considerate of other visitors.

The first principle — to plan ahead and be prepared — is a deceptively simple key to boondocking. People who aren't prepared can make bad choices that wreck the landscape, not to mention choices that endanger their own lives.

So, before you head out to boondock, think about what you'll need far from any campground services — what you'll *really* need, apart from toys and general junk. You'll need food, of course, and that one's fairly simple — when all else fails, get the can opener. But the two most problematic needs are power and water. Each has its own hassles, and its own triumphs.

## Power me up

For some reason, being able to run your AC is the holy grail of boondocking, everyone's target. In fairness, most camping goes on in summer, and air-conditioning is the biggest power hound in your RV, which makes "Can I run my AC?" sort of a watermark for the discussion. But everyone's power needs and desires are different. Campers in a mini-teardrop aren't far removed from tent camping, but someone in a luxury rig who wants all the comforts while free of shore power has a very different set of power priorities.

That's what boondocking is about, priorities, and what you're willing to invest in order to achieve them.

If you're in a motorhome, you probably have a built-in generator. They're getting popular in fifth wheels, which often come with at least a compartment for one, making for an easy upgrade. But if your trailer has a standard pair of lead-acid batteries and a power inverter, you can probably boondock for at least one night. Test it in your own driveway. (The neighbors may give you funny looks, but that's okay.)

Disconnect the power and water, and pretend you're camping. Run through a list of everything you'd want to do. Then try boondocking for one night just to see how many hours you can get out of your batteries. Be sure to turn on your inverter switch, which tells your batteries to run the 110-volt stuff (or at least the 110-volt stuff plugged into the marked inverter circuits). Some things are fussy on battery power, and others won't run at all (typically your microwave, electric tea kettle, and toaster). Any appliance that generates heat is a power hog and typically exceeds the capacity of a factory-installed inverter. Our Airstream did fairly well on batteries that, at the time, weren't even the superior absorbed glass mat (AGM) batteries (see Chapter 14).

If you're content to boondock no more than a single night at a time, it may be the best system for you. Of course, the biggest challenge to camping unplugged is weather — boondocking isn't practical in the withering desert heat or the bitter cold when the fan on your gas furnace can burn through your batteries in four or five hours.

If you want to boondock for an extended time, you essentially have two choices for power:

» **Portable generator, running on gas or propane:** A generator is the cheaper ticket to independence from shore power. We've worked with generators in the past, and we choose not to camp with one due to the weight, noise, and smell (not to mention the hassle of hauling gasoline). These complaints are common ones that manufacturers are trying to address, however. (For a detailed discussion of your options in generators and batteries, see Chapter 14.)

» **Solar panels:** A briefcase solar panel can be a nice addition to give your rig's batteries a boost, but that's its limits. If you want to go completely solar, you'll need a *lot* of panels, as well as a bank of high-performance batteries fed by them. And yes, you can run your AC with this system, but you'll still probably have limits, like only running it for a few hours and only one unit of a dual system.

The brightest future for boondocking is probably better and smaller solar panels, combined with improving battery technology. For now, there's still no free lunch. Lithium RV batteries are making major leaps, but they're expensive, as is the conversion you'll need to use them. To talk about "free energy" with an all-solar installation can be a little like crowing that you got free wine on a first-class flight to Paris. The best sources of info we've seen, in the mass of videos out there, are on the dependable YouTube channel *The Long Long Honeymoon:*

● "We've Gone All in with RV Solar — Here's What We Got" (https://youtu.be/_m2K1LqKCaM)

● "RV Solar — Installation & Costs" (https://youtu.be/tEc6DwBMGwA)

These videos are a detailed and honest examination of going solar to boondock, including the cost. Their total upgrade bill was more than $16,000. Although you may argue that you'll make this money back in what you don't pay to a campground, it's going to be a long wait, unless you're a full-timer.

WARNING

In a trailer, you can plug into your tow vehicle to get power, but this is for an emergency situation. The seven-way trailer connector to your tow vehicle transmits the truck's power to the trailer. Start the engine, and it becomes a generator that will slowly recharge your RV. But with the engine off, the RV can drain your truck's battery, and you may not get your engine started again.

# Water: Finding it, storing it, conserving it, dumping it

If your boondocking weather is temperate, no freezing cold or miserable heat, then there's no question at all — it's easier to get by without power than without water. Of course, you'll start your dry camping with full freshwater tanks and empty blackwater and graywater tanks. But sooner or later, you'll need to handle extending your water supply or finding more.

## Finding water

If you've run dry on the road and haven't got a divining rod handy, the easiest way to refill your freshwater tanks is to spend a night in a pay campground. But many boondockers resist this, and some of them simply can't afford it, at least on a regular basis. Advice on finding places to fill your tanks at low or no cost can't be absolute — you may have to be creative because sources vary, depending on where you are.

Truck stops are a good place to get water. Little America has RV service lanes, and Pilot Flying J is currently remodeling more locations to include RV fuel lanes and dump stations. Most of them have potable water spigots. Sometimes the spigot will be in the truck lanes.

**WARNING**

If you spot a spigot around a wastewater dump station, look for signs warning that it's not potable water. Hoses at dump sites are intended to clean out the sewage lines. Don't get your fresh water from them!

**TIP**

Some apps, like FreeRoam, allow you to search for the nearest available water. Boondockers Welcome (www.boondockerswelcome.com) is an inexpensive club that unites boondockers with those who will host them. There are many such mutual-aid groups for individual RVers; search out one for your rig.

We know some boondockers just hook up to any spigot they can find (in places like gas stations) and help themselves, but we don't encourage that. It wasn't a huge deal in the past, but there are lots more RVers now. People have to pay for water, and in places like California, they pay a lot. We don't want to see RVers become a plague and a nuisance.

If you're dry, with no RV services near, ask the local business that has a spigot if you can fill or top off your water tank. Try to buy something from them first. Perhaps offer them a few dollars. They'll probably let you.

If you're a boondocker, you may be getting your potable water from some dicey sources, out of an aged and battered spigot. So, it's a good idea to carry something called a Water Bandit with you. It's a cheap little rubber adaptor that fits over a spigot with a stripped connection or no threads at all. You still need to use a proper white or blue water hose for drinking water, not a garden hose, and you may consider putting a filter on it. Yes, filters are a small hassle, but when you're boondocking you'll be getting water from all sorts of sources, and some are a little bit hinky, like well water with all kinds of rust and metals, even sand and tiny rocks in it.

## Storing water

A typical RV water tank is 30 gallons, but lots of them are even stingier, just 15 to 20 gallons. Our Class B had a piddling 5-gallon tank. Our current rig has a 54-gallon tank, with another 6 gallons in the water heater that can be drained if we need it. You can upgrade to a bigger water tank, but even if you can fit it, it may be too much weight on your chassis when it's full. If you've got a big Class A, the heaviest cross you have to bear when you're boondocking is your low clearance on crummy roads, but the biggest advantages you've got are the built-in generator and the size of your water tanks; 100-gallon tanks are fairly common in Class A motorhomes.

Of course you can, and should, bring extra water when you boondock. But remember how heavy water is — over 8 pounds per gallon. We have an inexpensive plastic water storage container that holds 5 gallons, and it weighs over 40 pounds full, as much as a small generator. There are several other varieties of water storage containers, including some that can be collapsed when empty and others that are durable enough to be tied on the back end of your rig, like old-fashioned jerry cans.

We've seen some large-scale commitments to water storage. For example, you can buy a large water tank for the back of your pickup, plus a hose line and a 12-volt pump to refill the RV tanks when they've run dry. Landscaping companies often use these things. You can store a couple hundred gallons this way, if your truck can take the weight. It's an inexpensive option, as long as you don't mind the space you'll lose.

## Conserving water

For the RVer committed to a long stay in a wilderness area, the object of the game is to conserve water. And when you're enjoying a perfect campsite you fought your way to, watching the water gauge drop is annoying. There are all sorts of ways to conserve water and tons of online videos about it. The methods range wide, and they can get a little kooky. Here are the basics:

>> **Limit showers.** They're the number-one water waster. How long you can do without a shower is a personal matter. Substituting with things like baby wipes (or Dude Wipes, if you prefer) could help extend your time between showers. You may also consider a "birdbath," the kind that was the norm in the 19th century, washing with a large basin and a sponge or washcloth while you stand on something relatively waterproof, probably your shower stall. When people had to haul their wash water in a heavy jug up a flight of stairs, conservation was a way of life. When we didn't shower, our 54-gallon tank lasted a surprisingly long time. We didn't curtail any other activities, and we went four days before it was an issue.

TIP

If you're in a trailer you can unhitch, or if you have a toad, there are all sorts of shower options without breaking camp. You can go to the nearest truck stop and pay to shower there, or buy a national gym or YMCA membership. If there's one in the nearest town, you can go there to shower, without tearing down your campsite.

>> **Limit dish washing.** The easiest way is to use paper plates and cups, and burn them. This also cuts down on the trash you'll have to haul out. We use plastic ware (knives are the hardest to find — try Party Central). And hey, you can use them more than once! Just wipe them off. Rethink the meaning of the word *dirty*.

>> **Cook over a campfire when possible and use single-pot recipes.** Look online for easy camp-stove recipes that can be cooked in a Lodge Dutch oven. You'll never eat better.

>> **Limit hand washing.** We get tired of the liquid hand sanitizer and use wipes instead. Our favorite brand of wipes is Purell. They cost a bit more, but they're easy on your skin, and with their mild, sort of foaming action, it's the closest you'll come to feeling like you washed your hands.

>> **Limit toilet flushing.** We find this tip the least palatable, but boondocking websites love it. You can get a twofer by draining buckets of water off your graywater tank and using them to flush the toilet. Other sites recommend putting no water down, just urine and waste, but we don't agree. Your blackwater tank will probably be the last one to fill up anyway, and if you put no water down it, you'll get all sorts of problems, including a dreadful smell. And if you put toilet paper down your tank, while withholding water, you're going to have sludge problems.

» **Do your business in the glories of nature.** Whether you use a trash can with a toilet seat or lean against a tree, with this option, your waste will have to be buried. You can't leave it out like bear scat. Backpackers call this a *cat hole*, for obvious reasons. Use a small garden trowel to dig a hole 6 to 8 inches deep in an inconspicuous place, and make your deposit. Some websites recommend taking your used toilet paper with you, which seems an odd notion. Why not burn it? According to the USFS, there's nothing illegal about peeing freely in the wilderness. Men everywhere will rejoice.

» **Install a composting toilet.** This expensive upgrade is growing in popularity. If you go this route, you'll develop an even closer relationship with your waste than you had with the blackwater system. Compost systems use no water. They separate urine from feces, and both will need to be dumped, the urine far more often. Of course, you'll still be coping with graywater, which fills up faster than the blackwater tanks of a typical RV anyway.

WARNING

If you're hyper-focused on water conservation, you may be limiting how much you drink without even realizing it. Dehydration is dangerous — don't go there.

## Dumping wastewater

Sooner or later, you'll need to break camp and dump your wastewater tanks. Public land campgrounds aren't KOAs, and often there won't be a dump station. Allstays and other apps will tell you where the nearest dump station is to you, as will RV Dump Stations (www.rvdumps.com). If all else fails, Google "RV dump station near me." They're out there, many of them in odd places like local water treatment plants. There will usually be a small fee to use them.

Is it legal to dump your graywater on BLM land? Yes, but only on BLM land, not on any other federal land, and it's not encouraged. Regulations vary, and you need to be aware that the area you're in may regulate against it. Developed camp areas will forbid it, but they may not have a dump station. Ask any park ranger or manager you can find for help with the issue.

On a long-term boondock, people do it whether it's legal or not. Our best advice is to use common sense. With a blackwater tank, the answer is clear: You break camp, and you dump it in a proper station and *nowhere else.* But there are lots of gray areas with graywater. After all, a tent camper or backpacker is "dumping" their graywater, tossing wash water aside in a campsite, but RVers take the flak.

If you're really pressed, draw off a couple of buckets, and dump it in a rocky or sandy area, never in any body of water. Most Americans overuse soap, and the fats in the soap could make it more difficult for the soil to absorb water, thereby affecting plant life. Be a good camper, and try to follow the rules.

# 6

# The Part of Tens

**IN THIS PART . . .**

Avoid ten typical RV catastrophes.

Equip yourself with ten must-have RV phone apps to make life on the road easier.

Discover ten great attractions across the United States that are just off the highway.

» **Getting wrecked by a ham sandwich**

» **Handling a supercell**

Chapter **21**

# Ten Potential RV Catastrophes and How to Avoid Them

n this chapter, we offer a list of ten fairly common disasters and tell you how to keep them from happening to you. Some can threaten your sanity, some can threaten your rig, and one or two can threaten your life.

## Destroying Your Jack

If you're pulling a trailer, *always* make sure your stabilizers are up before you raise your front-end hitch jack in order to hitch up. If your stabilizers are still down, you'll be using the considerable force of your jack against your stabilizers. The poor things are only trying to do their job by keeping your trailer level and, well, stable. The jack may or may not win this contest; the stabilizers, which don't look nearly as strong, may cop the prize, but they'll annihilate one another with major repair costs.

Remember the scene in *The Long, Long Trailer*, with "Trailer brakes first!" That's for driving. For breaking camp, you might put these words on your whiteboard: *Stabilizers first!* We raise the stabilizers before doing anything else when breaking camp.

By the way, if you're traveling in the cold, be careful putting down your stabilizers if there's lot of moisture. You can easily freeze them to the ground. A few buckets of warm water should solve it, but if they go deep into ice that's formed overnight, you could do some damage trying to lift them before you realize it. Some people travel with wooden blocks to put under the feet in winter — that's one answer. Another is to just do without stabilizers if conditions warrant it.

# Watching Your Rig Roll Away

No, we're not contradicting ourselves. When you're breaking camp, it's *stabilizers first.* When you're making camp, it's *chocks first.* This job takes about 30 seconds, and eventually you'll do it without thinking about it. As soon as you're lined up on your campsite, put your chocks on your wheels. If you're in a trailer or fifth wheel, do it before you unhitch.

Chocks help your stabilizers keep your rig steady when you walk in it, but their main purpose is to keep your RV sitting on your campsite. Yes, your RV can decide to roll away and maybe pick up speed on the hill down to the road.

It seems like a trailer would be more susceptible to a rollaway, but Chris had it happen with a 40-foot Class A motorhome he mistakenly left in Neutral. They seem so substantial, but motorhomes will get it in their heads to leave, too. Looking back, it was funny, but he wasn't laughing at the time, racing after it and leaping inside like Keanu Reeves in *Speed.* Chris was younger then. And it's all so easy to avoid when you drop your chocks.

# Tangling with Wildlife

Don't put garbage outside your rig, *ever.*

No matter how late it is and how tired you are after the barbecue, all your garbage needs to be put under cover. If you're boondocking, without access to a dumpster, the garbage may start piling up, but you have to keep it in your RV or tow vehicle. If you have a dog, and you don't want them getting into the chicken parts you threw away, and it's cold and dark outside, and the dumpster seems miles away, you may be tempted to just toss the bag of garbage outside the door until morning. We did that once when we were newbies.

Coyotes, wolves, and bears are just some of the animals that will descend on your campsite with astonishing speed if you have any food out. So, did we open the door to a grizzly? Nothing so dramatic. We got a family of raccoons. They urinated all over everything, as they'll do when marking territory, and their urine has an ungodly smell. We hate to admit how cute they are, and it's harder to admit we used to hand-feed a pair of them in our backyard. Don't get suckered by a pretty face. Raccoons can be carriers of rabies, and if your child or pet tangles with one, you could be in trouble. Plus, raccoon feces commonly carry ringworm, which can be transmitted to humans. Enough said. Finally, they're absolute marauders in your campsite, unbelievably destructive. And, yes, a raccoon can open a cooler. Aren't they cute? Stow it inside at night.

# Running on Empty

Running out of gas is something that makes you feel *really* dumb, but it's not as dumb as it sounds. We only have a 30-gallon tank in our Chevy Suburban, which is annoying in a supposed "tow package." This means a full tank will take us roughly 270 miles when towing, often less. We've been in many stretches, in Texas, New Mexico, and Arizona, where gas stations were rare, and we got very nervous. Sometimes a kindly sign warns you that there are no gas stations for the next 120 miles, and sometimes not. Easterners and Midwesterners just aren't used to this. No, we haven't been stranded yet, but once it was pure luck, and we rolled into the truck stop on fumes. So, when you get below half a tank, top off, especially out West.

**TIP**

Have we said "Plan ahead" often enough in this book? When traveling in the alien corn, consult your handy *Pocket Truck Stop Guide* early in the day. It takes only a few seconds. All the truck stops on the stretch of interstate you're traveling are laid out, and you can easily see if there are few truck stops, separated by lots of miles.

# Causing Your Own Power Failure

Lead acid batteries are like azaleas; if you don't water them, they die.

So, you park for the night, plug into shore power, and go inside to turn on the main power switch. And the lights start madly flickering or maybe don't come on at all. You can hear the click of a solenoid somewhere in the wall, but power is zip.

When it happened to us, we were trying to outrun a snowstorm, and the temperatures were dropping into the teens. It was a lousy moment to lose our power. We thought it was either the park's power post or our power line until we finally thought to check the monitor panel on the wall. Healthy batteries should read between 12.4 and 12.8. Ours were reading 5, practically dead.

REMEMBER

There's a natural tendency to think of batteries as a power backup, to think that if you're plugging into shore power, it's just like plugging in a toaster. So what if the batteries don't work? You should still be getting full electricity from the pole. But RVs don't work that way. The *converter* in a trailer is taking all that 110-volt pole power and converting it into 12 volts so that your trailer can use it. This is confusing at first and counterintuitive. Want to get more confused? If your trailer, like ours, has an inverter for camping without shore power, it's taking the 12-volt power and turning it back into 110 volts, only coming out two plugs marked "Inverter." It takes time to adjust your thinking to this.

You don't need to be neurotic about it, but check your lead acid coach batteries a couple times a season, removing the caps to see if one or more cells look dry. (Other types don't need the attention — absorbed glass mat [AGM] batteries are sealed and lithium doesn't use water.) We had been using shore power every night for a long time, which can overheat and even boil your batteries, cooking off the electrolyte fluid. If there's even a single cell that's dry, the electric current can't pass through the body of the battery. So, we watered the batteries, and the system fixed itself almost immediately.

TIP

If you open the battery caps and see any of the gray lead plates without liquid completely covering them, top them off with distilled, mineral-free water. (We always keep a gallon in the back of the SUV.) If the pure stuff isn't available, any water will do in an emergency. Just fill until the cell plates are covered, not to the top.

# Dancing on an Uninsured Ledge

Routine RV tasks you do every day will usually become second nature and are rarely forgotten. But anything you need to do "once in a while" is more problematic. And anything you need to do in the tiring chaos of packing up for a major road trip is just begging to be forgotten.

Many RV insurance companies offer "seasonal" insurance, a storage option that allows you to skip paying for accident coverage when your rig is in long-term storage, usually longer than 30 days. (You can keep the comprehensive part of your insurance at a reduced rate, so you're still protected from things like theft, vandalism, or falling tree limbs.) It has the potential to save you a great deal of money;

this trick shaves about half off of our annual premiums. But you must notify the insurance company when the rig comes out of storage and when it goes back in again. If you forget to do it, you run the risk of an accident not being covered.

Our policy with Good Sam (issued by National General) gives you a short grace period, if, say, you have an accident on the day you leave, and you forgot to tell them. But this isn't something you should ever depend on.

# Losing Your Own Trailer

When RV insurance companies list the reasons for accidents, the majors aren't surprising: speeding, high winds, overloading, driving tired, or driving distracted. (We cover all of them in Chapter 11.) But being tired or distracted isn't a great way to get ready to hit the road either, and it can cause mistakes, particularly in hitching. Sloppy, incompetent, or just plain mistaken hitching is a major cause of accidents.

Make certain you go over your hitch with your dealer or installer. Take videos of the process. Then, when you're comfortable, don't blow all that knowledge by hitching up in the dark, or in a hurry, or when you're tired.

For example, if you're not careful, the coupler may not seat properly over the hitch ball when you lower your hitch jack. In most of these cases, the latching lever on top of the coupler won't completely flip closed, and a hitch pin won't go through its hole if this has happened. But if you blow off that one little hitch pin, you may kill someone when your trailer breaks away on the road.

The hitch mistake we once made was forgetting to attach the weight distribution and anti-sway bars. We were in the Texas Panhandle, where it often seems windy, but it wasn't *that* bad, and we wondered for an hour or so why the ride felt funny. Until a truck blew past us, and sway struck like the hand of God, so we pulled off to check the hitch. You'll find out quickly how valuable anti-sway bars are when you forget to use them.

# Flooding Your Rig

Once, long ago, we were in the landlord business. Really dumb. We were haunted by the fear of fire in our apartments. We did have one once, and it was terrible. But all the old hands were right: Though fires happen, water was the far more likely culprit for major damage. The same is true of RVs.

One of the handful of RV disasters that will see your rig totaled out by the insurance company is, believe it or not, a leak. And the most dangerous time for one is when it's in storage and exposed to rain. You take your first spring trip, and there's a funny soft spot in the floor or wall near the slide, and it begins. Any soft or "popcorn-like" area in your rig's wall, floor, or ceiling is a disaster brewing. You need to handle it quickly. Water incursions can get so out of hand that the walls split and virtually collapse, mold or mildew sets in, and it's not worth repairing.

Most common leak hotspots are under sinks, around lines to the icemaker or washer, around the toilet ring on the floor, and the water line connections around the toilet flush valve or pedal. Most of these stem from the constant jostling of the RV's plumbing as it bounces down the road. We've had several of these leaks over the years, and they tend not to be disastrous. That's because when you're in the rig, using it, you find the issue and fix it.

Water travels, and like lightning, it always seeks the ground. Slides with improper seals are a major culprit, but on your roof, all it takes is one screw coming out of the TV antenna mount, and a leak will find a tiny place to enter. This is the cartoon image of a roof leak, dripping on your head, and sometimes it happens that way. But the greatest fear of any RVer is the insidious leak that runs between an outer and interior wall and isn't visible.

TIP

If you can't afford or find interior or covered storage, it's a good idea to buy an RV cover. For us, this is another rig-specific oddity, because you're not supposed to put a cover on an Airstream (aluminum is easily scratched). Your other best weapon is regularly inspecting your slides and inspecting your roof twice a year. There are tons of how-to websites with good instructions for roof inspection. Bring your caulk gun. If you're older or you have any health issues, take it to your dealer for a checkup or hire someone to do it.

And most important, store your rig where you can easily get to it! If it's an hour away, you'll avoid checking on it. *Remember:* Interior storage won't protect you from pest infestations. And if an insidious leak starts, you can open that door months later to find black mold has taken over or your walls have warped, and the rig is probably lost. Find a regular day in the week, or twice a month, to check on your stored RV.

# Swarming Nightmares

We thought this one was bizarre, but found out later it's not that unusual. Like most Class B motorhomes, ours had a tiny refrigerator, down low on the floor. Coming home from a long trip, we thought we'd completely cleaned it out. But half of a ham and cheese sandwich rolled foul to the very back of the top shelf hidden under the freezer section. And even though we didn't store our Class B (we used it as a second car), the consequences were huge. About eight weeks later, when we opened the fridge again, a cloud of fruit flies poured out. They'd hatched from it or from eggs laid in it and kept right on multiplying, and you don't want to know the details.

The bugs had infested the guts of the system, laying eggs everywhere, and it was safer to just buy a new refrigerator. An expensive lesson: Check your fridge and freezer before you store your rig; then check them again. Use bleach wipes on the interior, and brace open both doors to prevent mold. Use the plastic clips in camping stores or just a dishtowel tucked in the hinge.

# Losing It All

Campers may face any sort of natural disaster, but like skiers with avalanches, the most common one an RVer may face is a tornado. And in a tornado, there's nowhere more dangerous to be than in a mobile home or RV.

As an RVer, you need to develop weather awareness. Midwesterners have a leg up on this because all our lives we've learned to watch for the green skies and battling hot and cold fronts that cause tornados. They can happen anywhere at any time, but the high season is in spring and early summer, in the month of May, the kickoff to camping season. The most common time of day is late afternoon and early evening. Being on the lookout for a tornado or severe storm when conditions are ripe and having a sketch plan in your head of what to do at your campsite is the number-one way to protect yourself.

**TECHNICAL STUFF**

The Fujita scale for tornado intensity runs from F1 to F5. A "moderate" F1 can have winds over a hundred miles an hour, enough to overturn any RV. An F3 or F4 would have devastating consequences in an RV park.

In an RV, you need some sort of device that will set off the distinctive wail of a tornado alarm. A weather radio with a National Oceanic and Atmospheric Administration (NOAA) warning system is a great investment, but every cell phone can be set to receive what are called wireless emergency alerts, and they can save your life. The location of tornado alley is debatable, but if you're in the Great Plains or anywhere east of the Rockies and west of the Mississippi, you're at much higher risk. Use a phone app, or Sirius in your tow vehicle, to watch the weather on radar, but favor a system with locality that pinpoints where you are in relation to the storm.

Whether you're boondocking or in a campground, know where you are. What county, what township, and what nearby towns. Weather reports on local TV stations are great for tracking tornados, but like most weather alerts, they often speak of counties and towns you don't know with "a line of storms running east/southeast from Jackson to Kalispell." If all else fails, ask Siri or Alexa what county you're in. Remember that a *tornado watch* means conditions are ripe, while a *tornado warning* is more serious: It means radar and spotters are tracking an actual tornado on the ground. If you hear the word *supercell,* it's a more intense type of rotational thunderstorm that can throw off multiple tornadoes during its longer lifespan, potentially lasting hours.

The scariest tornados come at night. Death tolls always skyrocket when people are asleep. If your alarm has gone off, get up and get dressed. Grab your bug-out bag if you have one (see the nearby sidebar), and *get out.* If you're in a campground, every campground manager knows what to do in this situation, or check your campground map; it may identify tornado shelters. If it's late at night and you're alone, go anyplace solid, preferably a stone or concrete building, which is often the laundry room or bathhouse. Some campgrounds have small concrete shelters scattered across the park. Especially in tornado season, find out where the safest place is when you check in.

In a sudden lightning storm, you're better off hunkering down in your rig. Stay away from windows and power. If you've ever had lightning strike the power pedestal you're plugged into, you will *never* forget it. But if you're wilderness camping, hearing constant advisories on the radio, you're in a weather stewpot — leave your campsite, while you have time to do it! Get to the ranger station or any building that offers shelter. If you're near one, a cave is the ideal shelter. Stay away from power lines and trees. And if circumstances have put you out in the open in a tornado, look for the deepest depression possible, even a ditch. Lie down, and cover your head. The most common cause of tornado deaths is flying debris, and your head is the most vulnerable target.

Planning is the key to surviving any natural disaster, but because RVers are constantly on the move, situational wisdom is your other best weapon, especially when experts don't agree. If you see a tornado, should you pull off the road and get under a highway underpass? It's a traditional tactic, and it's saved lives, but it's still debatable. Wind and debris worsen in the tunnel effect, and the snarl of stopped vehicles can endanger others. Should you try to escape a tornado? As a rule, you shouldn't drive in dangerous weather. But if it's daylight, and you can see the tornado, you may be better off getting in your tow vehicle or toad. Buckle up, and drive away from it, making sure you know its direction. If it seems to be still, it's probably coming directly at you. Move at right angles to it, quickly, and don't ignore what's happening on the road while you're watching the tornado. We've been in this situation, and this was the best action for us. Again, when experts don't agree, use situational wisdom.

# PACKING A BUG-OUT BAG

The possibility of a tornado points out what a good idea it is to keep a bug-out bag because in the worst case, you may not have a rig on its side or even the rubble of one — your rig may be in another county, if not another state. You'll need basic survival supplies.

We keep a bug-out bag in the back of Red Scare, our SUV, an inexpensive waterproof backpack with pretty standard survival basics:

- A radio
- A mini water filtration system, like a Sawyer or a LifeStraw
- A pack of Mylar emergency blankets
- A small first-aid kit
- A fire starter
- A headlamp flashlight
- A quality camping knife
- Some paracord
- A Kelly Kettle (a lightweight camp stove that can boil drinking water with little fuel, just leaves or bracken)

These are things that would stand us in good stead if we found ourselves in the wilderness with a destroyed RV.

*Remember:* Even if you're not alone and in a town, a tornado will cause chaos, and you may not be able to get the things you need. If there's a medication you *must* have, ask your doctor for some extra and keep a three-day supply in your bag. For more advice to get you thinking, survival instructor Creek Stewart has a YouTube video worth watching: https://youtu.be/1cUp402hsPY.

# Chapter **22**

# Ten Smartphone Apps You Can't Live Without

You can find a smartphone app for nearly any activity, service, or research problem you can think up. That's great news for RVers. In fact, there are so many helpful and indispensable apps for RVs and campers that it's tough to narrow the list to just ten, so we cheat a little and include alternatives when they exist.

**REMEMBER**

Meanwhile, don't forget a couple of simple tools that you may already have built into your phone's software: a compass, a bubble level, and a measuring tape.

## Google Maps

You'll be shocked at how many campground websites specifically warn you that GPS can't find them. We've owned at least five standalone GPS navigation units over the years, even a couple that were specifically marketed as being for RVers. But since automakers have worked hard to let smartphones interconnect with dashboard information displays, we've dumped GPS units in favor of Google Maps. It's far more reliable, up to date, and exact, especially when it comes to finding an obscure campground address or business location. Because Google's map system is so widely used, most dashboard systems are made to integrate well with the phone app. Even the voice-activated search feature works well with modern dashboard systems and their built-in microphones.

Apple's Maps app comes preloaded on iPhones, and it's a close second for ease of use and comprehensive information. Many drivers also like Waze, which specifically looks for traffic jams, accidents, road construction, speed traps, and more on the road ahead of you, and then suggests shortcuts around them where possible.

# CoPilot GPS

CoPilot GPS is another navigation app, but it's specifically designed for RVers and truckers. You enter the overall dimensions of your rig, and the app will route you around low bridges, dead-end streets, steep hills, and other potentially problematic road conditions that can make life miserable for drivers of big vehicles. It alerts you to toll roads, shows the shortest versus the fastest routes, displays the current speed limit, and even warns you about annoyances like tunnels that forbid vehicles with propane tanks. You can download CoPilot GPS maps onto your phone in the background so they work even when you can't get a Wi-Fi or cellular connection. That's important in a place like Yellowstone National Park, where there's almost no cell service at all after you pull through the gate.

# Roadtrippers

Roadtrippers is a trip-planning app that helps you find nearby sights to see on your route. If you never get off the interstate, you'll never know what fascinating, quirky, breathtaking, beautiful, historic, or hilarious attractions may be lurking right off the next exit. It also lets you plug in the places you intend to stop along your route, like overnighting in your Aunt Minnie's driveway. For all you know, Aunt Minnie lives just blocks from a great museum or historical site.

If your sightseeing tastes lean to the goofy side, Roadside America is another terrific app for finding weird, wonderful, and crazy things to see and places to visit. Its approach is a bit zanier than Roadtrippers — it points out stuff as wacky as novelty mailboxes, embarrassingly misspelled billboards, noteworthy yard art, rocks shaped like amorous barnyard animals, the world's largest ball of rubber cement, and countless other submissions from fellow connoisseurs of roadside kitsch. If you spot something unique on your own that isn't listed, you can help expand its listings by recommending your own discoveries or posting updates about existing ones.

# GasBuddy

Face it, when you're driving a massive motorhome or hauling a heavy trailer that gets 9 gas-gulping miles per gallon (and only downhill with a stiff tailwind), a few pennies saved per gallon at the gas pump add up fast, especially if you have a 60-gallon fuel tank. GasBuddy lets you search your local area to find the best gas or diesel prices — and that's not always the closest truck stop to the exit.

**WARNING**

One caveat: Before you pull into any gas station driveway, scan the pumps and the lot carefully to make sure your RV roof will clear any overhead canopy and that you have enough room to turn and get your rig back out to the street again when the tank's full. Not every gas station is big-rig friendly. Even the auto lanes at an interstate truck stop may not be easy to extract yourself from because of a narrow parking area or too many close concrete bumper posts and canopy pylons. That's even more important with a motorhome hauling a *toad* (a car or other vehicle), especially if your tow bar won't permit you to back up without unhitching.

# Allstays Camp and RV

When it comes to finding a campground, park, truck stop, services, or just a place to park your RV for the night, many apps are available, and everybody has a favorite. For speed and ease of use, we like Allstays Camp and RV. Enter your location, or just zoom in on the national map to look at the area you're in, and you'll be presented with the campgrounds and parks close by. It lists public and private campgrounds and even military campsites that you can use. The app also points out RV service centers, camping stores, propane vendors, truck stops, dump stations, Walmarts, Cracker Barrels, and Costcos that allow overnight parking for RVs, and lots more. Honestly, no other app comes close to being as comprehensive or useful. Links on listings let you see or leave reviews, go to a site's web page, send directions to Google Maps, or call the campground. Allstays Camp and RV is available in both a free and paid version. Unfortunately, it's only available for iOS, not Android. But it does have a website you can access with an Android phone (www.allstays.com).

Other popular campground planning apps that *do* have Android versions include RV Parks & Campgrounds, RV Parky, and The Dyrt. The Dyrt has free and paid versions (with substantial discount rates at campgrounds available for its paying users). It also identifies free boondocking areas like Bureau of Land Management (BLM), U.S. Forest Service, and National Park System sites. Best of all, its planning maps work offline with the paid version.

Don't forget that Good Sam Camping, Passport America, KOA, Jellystone Park, Harvest Hosts, and Escapees all have their own phone apps with specific information about their affiliated campgrounds, along with links to easily reserve a spot online. And if you have a very long rig and intend on staying overnight in truck stops, most of them have instituted a reservation system to hold a long parking space in their truck lots, so you should have the Pilot Flying J, Love's, and TA/Petro apps on your phone to make that a little easier.

# RA Camping

Many state and local parks with campsites handle all their reservations online. The majority have handed off reservation duties to Reserve America (www.reserveamerica.com) and its RA Camping phone app. A great feature of Reserve America is that it lets you pick a very specific campsite in a campground from a site map, and it usually includes a photo of the space itself to let you actually see where you'll be parking.

Unfortunately, RA Camping doesn't include federal campgrounds in its database. Recreation.gov (www.recreation.gov) does, and it works in a similar way: It lets you search specifically government-owned campsites. If you want to stay in a lot of parks, you should have both apps on your phone.

Of course, there are exceptions. California withdrew its state parks from Reserve America a few years ago and created its own campground reservation system. The website (https://reservecalifornia.com) lets you access and reserve spots in that state's many park campgrounds. Just be aware that there is currently no dedicated phone app for it.

# SkySafari

Most Americans have never seen the night sky the way all of mankind did until the 20th century and the advent of outdoor lighting. To most people, the Milky Way is a quaint term they've heard but something they've never seen. When you can get away from the ambient glow of lights from cities and towns and into those places where the night sky is truly inky black, everything above your head changes. Suddenly, the night sky is filled with so many stars and other objects that it can be overwhelming. On the road, you'll see loads of RVers with telescopes. One of our favorite campgrounds, Butterfield RV Resort & Observatory (www.rv-resort.com) in Benson, Arizona, has its own private observatory, but you'll find "star parties" all over the country.

It took humans thousands of years to identify the objects in the heavens. But smartphones with their built-in compasses and gyroscopes have spawned a wave of apps that now allow you to identify every celestial object in the sky just by aiming at it. SkySafari is one of the top recommended astronomy apps. It features photographs, descriptions, NASA spacecraft images, animation, and more. And it works well even when you can't get a cellular connection. It can send alerts to you to let you know when eclipses, meteor showers, comets, and other events are happening. It can even point you to sights like the International Space Station passing overhead in orbit. It's available in Pro and Plus editions, with more features for more money.

SkySafari is most popular, but Star Chart and Star Walk also have lots of fans. Luminos is actually our longtime personal favorite nighttime stargazing app, but it's only available for iOS, not Android, and it's also one of the priciest.

Regardless of the app you choose, download at least one. You'll find it addictive and a great icebreaker with campground neighbors around the campfire.

# AccuWeather

If you spend more than just occasional weekends hauling around your RV, you need to check the extended weather forecast on a regular basis. Just like private plane pilots, you don't want to be surprised by a freak downpour, snowstorm, tornado, or flash flood. And besides, driving or towing a big rig is just plain nerve-wracking in a white-knuckle windstorm or rainstorm.

Everybody has a favorite weather app, but AccuWeather is the most popular. It comes in a free version with ads and a paid "ad-free" version. Its uncluttered interface is simple and straightforward, and it lets you check the weather at your location or your destination and anywhere in between. You can check the temperature and forecast by the hour or by the day up to two weeks in advance. It also shows predicted average wind speeds and gusts, which are *very* important when you're driving or deploying an awning. And you can quickly check radar maps as well.

Scores of other weather apps are out there if you don't care for AccuWeather's simplicity. MyRadar is a fast and free app that gives you instant, live access to weather radar, along with the forecast. We like Weather Live because it's endlessly customizable, even alerting you when "magic hour" arrives for taking the best sunset or sunrise photos. Weather Underground and The Weather Channel are also excellent. And the NOAA Weather Radio app lets you hear the National Weather Service 24-hour radio broadcast along with live views of the weather radar in the areas you choose.

**TIP**

All these apps let you customize their settings to send you notifications of severe weather alerts. Be sure you set up at least one or two weather apps to access your location and send your phone these emergency warnings.

# RV Pocket Reference

We very much want you to keep our book with you on the road at all times so that you can quickly look up answers to questions. But we know plenty of folks prefer a phone app. The RV Pocket Reference app is a deceptively jam-packed reference guide that helps jog your memory when it comes to driving, towing, hitching, setting up, shutting down, and maintaining your RV. Its very brief explanations and tips are well organized into categories and give you the basics on any topic. You can find explanations of the appliances and major systems found in rigs. It also includes instructions for weighing your rig or towing a toad, capacity and measurement conversion calculators, state RV towing laws, a decent glossary of RV terms, and a whole lot more.

# Ultimate RV Checklist

By the time you've gotten to this chapter, you know there are a vast amount of details you need to remember in order to safely tow, set up, maintain, and store an RV, stuff you had no idea about when you first cooked up the idea of owning one. Driving an RV is not as complicated as flying a 747 to Burkina Faso, but don't forget that pilots have checklists, too, for a very simple reason: No one can remember absolutely everything every time, so don't think that relying on checklists is for wusses and absentminded oldsters.

Fortunately, the Ultimate RV Checklist app provides a bumper crop of checklists to help you. Whether you're hauling a trailer or fifth-wheel or driving a motorhome, the app's premade checklists will guide you through setup, teardown, hitching, unhitching, hooking up, and dealing with a toad. The app also lets you modify its existing checklists to suit your rig's peculiarities or create your own from scratch. And you can export and print the checklists so you can post them inside your rig or stow them in the glove compartment of your tow vehicle.

# Chapter 23

# Ten Great Attractions Just off the Highway

The best part about an RV trip is the slower pace. So, we offer this list of ten nice things to stop and see in no particular order. But with only ten, we've had to be ruthless in our selection.

Each of these can be done in an hour unless you linger. We've left off the World's Largest Rocking Chair–type stops because they're goofy, but they're just not that interesting. It's a great big rocking chair. So get out, stretch your legs, and enjoy a few of these interesting stops if they're on the path you're wandering. For more fun places, visit the terrific Roadside America website (www.roadsideamerica.com).

## National Route 66 Museum

2717 W. 3rd St.
Elk City, Oklahoma
580-225-6266
www.elkcity.com/departments/museums/national-route-66-museum

We had no idea what this place was the first time we stumbled onto it, but it was Sunday, and the whole thing was closed. We wandered through it anyway, impressed by the re-creation of a small roadside town, down to the school, the village green, and the Masonic lodge. It was like a movie set.

It's actually an entire museum complex, with a re-creation of a blacksmith shop, a barn with period farm implements, and the Old Town Museum house, with Western and rodeo artifacts. But the highlight is the Route 66 Museum, with an entire little town from the heyday of the Mother Road and a transportation museum with vintage rides. The living-museum idea works remarkably well here, and the experience flows, more like playing than a wearying walk-through exhibits. You can stay as long as you like and make a day of it, or wrap it up in an hour, at the refreshing museum price of $7 per person, with a reduced rate for children and seniors. And that's to see everything in the entire complex. And it's incredibly easy to get to.

TIP

Across the street is a grocery store a drug store, and a Dollar General (with a nice, big, roomy parking lot!), so it's a great all-purpose stop where you can stock up before hitting the road again.

# Custer Battlefield Museum

I-90, Exit 514
Garryowen, Montana
406-638-1876
http://custermuseum.org

The little town of Garryowen isn't named after the comedian, or the announcer on the old TV show *Laugh-In.* "Garryowen" was an old Irish marching song, one you'd recognize, and it was the marching tune of Custer's Seventh Cavalry.

The Custer Battlefield Museum in Garryowen is a private museum that gets no shower of federal money. We know this is a museum run mostly on love by people with a deep commitment. We stumbled into the place by chance, looking for some coffee, not as odd as it sounds. There's a gas station in the parking lot, with a small restaurant and trading post.

It's on the former site of Sitting Bull's encampment, and the battlefield is all around you. Being book hounds, we spent a long time in the large bookstore section of the gift shop, with a great selection on Western history. You'll pay to get into the actual museum ($8 for adults, under 12 free). There are dioramas of the battle and remarkable artifacts, as well as more than a hundred period photos by D.F. Barry, who the Lakota people called "Little Shadow Catcher." The remains of a trooper found during highway construction in 1926 have been placed here, part of a peace monument and Tomb of the Unknown Soldier, with statues of both Sitting Bull and Custer.

We arrived in Little Big Horn, never having had any particular interest in the battle. We decided to spend the night in Garryowen and lucked into a great campground called the 7th Ranch RV Camp (www.historicwest.com), with incredible vistas from every campsite. There's a remarkable aura in this place, a stillness that makes you want to whisper. That very night we began to read, and the next day we went to the Little Big Horn National Monument. It's the best part of RVing, the way you wander into the nation's history and have the time to make connections, leading to experiences you never forget.

# The Thing

**2631 N. Johnson Rd.**
**Dragoon, Arizona**
**520-586-2581**

During the heyday of 1960s driving trips, huckstering a roadside attraction for hundreds of miles using billboards was an important, if slightly cheesy, part of the cultural fabric of American travel. One of the few remaining establishments still practicing this delightfully insidious form of self-promotion is I-10's The Thing, in Dragoon, Arizona. After staring at nothing but *See the Thing! What is the Thing? Mystery of the Desert!* billboards for a hundred miles, you'll gratefully pull in and plop down five smackers just to satisfy your curiosity.

The Thing has been attracting travelers to this desolate spot since 1965, and the museum underwent a major renovation in 2018. The huge gift shop still has all the goofy roadside tchotchkes you crave. But the new and improved museum is now jam-packed with dinosaurs, aliens, conspiracy theory displays, unidentifiable whatsits, and dioramas asking those open-ended speculative *"Could this be?"* questions that make bad History Channel ancient alien shows so irresistible. Honestly, there *is* a lot to see — lots more things before you get to the actual Thing itself.

No, we won't tell you what the Thing is. Fork over your five clams, and see for yourself. Then fill the tank, grab a Dairy Queen treat, and proudly stick an "I've seen THE THING!" sticker on your RV.

# Cahokia Mounds State Historic Site

30 Ramey St.,
Collinsville, Illinois
618-346-5160
https://cahokiamounds.org

There are Native American "mound" sites all over the Midwest. But just across the Mississippi River from modern-day Saint Louis is one of the most important archeological finds in American history, a major pre-Columbian city. It's the biggest indigenous settlement site ever found in North America, with more than 80 mounds. At its pinnacle in the 12th century, the city covered 6 square miles and had a population of more than 100,000.

The visitor center will give you an understanding of what you're seeing. Eight hundred acres with some beautiful trails are accessible to the public at no cost, though a donation is a good idea. Don't miss climbing Monks Mound to see Woodhenge, the reconstruction of an ancient sun calendar. You're near Saint Louis, so don't forget the mosquito repellent in summer.

# Meteor Crater

I-40, Exit 233
Winslow, Arizona
928-289-5898
https://meteorcrater.com

Here is the greatness of America, the cool and efficient capitalization of a gigantic hole in the ground in the middle of the desert.

A 150-foot-asteroid smacked into the ground 50,000 years ago and blasted apart this 3,900-foot-wide crater. The Moon may be full of them, but Earth doesn't have many well-preserved impact craters, and this one's the biggest.

Thirty-five miles east of Flagstaff, this is the ultimate stretch-your-legs attraction; it's an easy 5 miles off the highway, and you can see it all in an hour, including the gift shop and the polished, admirably brief little film telling the story of the crater. If you like, you can stop for the night in Meteor Crater RV Park, neat, pretty, and well-run, with its office and camp store in a geodesic dome. It's also just off Exit 233 on I-40.

# Wisconsin Dells

I-90, Exits 87 and 92
Between Chicago and Minneapolis
800-223-3557
www.wisdells.com

Neither of us will ever forget stumbling into the Dells for the first time, by car, after dark, surprised by all the hotels around it. But it was late, and we didn't see anywhere to get a brochure in that time before cellphones. That night we called Chris's mother to see if she'd ever heard of it. "Oh, I remember! That's the nutty place in Wisconsin!"

*Dalles* is a French word for a narrows in the rapids, from the *voyageurs* who explored this region. You could easily spend a couple days here, and many RVers do — the waterparks alone take some time. But an hour-long stop for a stroll in the heart of town will give you a taste of this living time capsule and a look at what tourist traps from the 1940s were like. Wander the many shops and attractions, like the unforgettable Ripley's Believe It Or Not! Museum, a shameless monument to kitsch, and note signs for the famed "duck boat" tours, named for the amphibious vessels of World War II. All through the area, you'll also find the classic motor lodge motels from the '40s through the '60s, plenty of which have been lovingly restored to their atomic-age charm.

Head south on Wisconsin Dells Parkway for the other half of the Dells, the numerous attractions with their entertainment architecture: the upside-down White House, the Mayan temple, Mount Olympus, and the Trojan Horse, along with a motel inside a re-creation of the Roman Colosseum. Pure Americana.

If you decide to stay, there are dozens of campgrounds in the immediate area around the Dells, even the Ho-Chunk Casino run by the Winnebago tribe.

# Pedro's South of the Border

**I-95, Exit 1A, across from the Welcome Center**
**Dillon, South Carolina**
www.sobpedro.com

"You're always a wiener at Pedro's!"

This one you have to see for yourself. The pen fails. The border in question is between North Carolina and South Carolina, and Pedro's South of the Border has been the ultimate roadside attraction for more than 70 years. Pedro's sits on I-95, the main north–south artery running down the East Coast. It began life as a beer garden to entice customers from the dry counties of North Carolina just across the border, but the location set it up for future growth.

Both I-95 and I-75 are loaded with roadside attractions for Easterners and Midwesterners fleeing the cold, but Pedro's is in a class by itself, the granddaddy of them all. The enormous sombrero atop the tower is the eye candy that ropes in weary travelers. Moving south, drivers take the first South Carolina exit, just past the Contrary Swamp, to find a slew of souvenir shops, motels, and tamale stands, as well as Pedroland amusement park and the Crocodile Lagoon. Don't miss this one. Put it on your bucket list.

There's also an RV park, called (what else?) Camp Pedro.

# Wall Drug

**510 Main St.**
**Wall, South Dakota**
**605-279-2175**
www.walldrug.com

Wall Drug, in the little town of Wall near Badlands National Park, is something of a South Dakota institution. We love tourist traps, but this is the kind of place that makes even the grumpy love them, too. Ted Hustead and his wife Dorothy purchased it in 1931 when the town had a population of 231 souls. To scare up a little business, his wife had the idea of offering free ice water to travelers on their way to Mount Rushmore, and an institution was born. The store grew from its original modest dimensions into sort of a Wild West theme mall. The Western art in the dining room is original and valuable, decorating an enormous collection of historical artifacts and kitsch, and scattered here and there are the items you'd find in any other drugstore.

We never miss a stop at Wall Drug. You can do a lot of shopping here. It's a welcoming place, too — they've long given free coffee and donuts to active service personal. They still give away more than 20,000 cups of free ice water a day in the hottest part of the tourist season. So famed, there's even a sign for it planted in Antarctica, advertising free ice water . . . in 9,333 miles.

The Sleepy Hollow RV Campground is a short walk from the stores.

# Solvang, California

### U.S. 101, Exit 140A at Buellton, then east 3 miles

In 1911, a group of Danish immigrants living in Iowa decided the winters were too much to endure. (Worse than Denmark?) They packed up and fled to a spot near Santa Barbara, California, in the Santa Ynez Valley, where they established the village of Solvang, the Danish Capital of America.

By the '40s, the Danish Provincial style predominated, and eventually, four wooden windmills decorated the skyline. Town fathers even put up their own Little Mermaid and Hans Christian Andersen statues. Danish restaurants, a school, a Lutheran church, and bakeries and other shops lined the streets, and the locals could feel they hadn't entirely left their native land behind.

After World War II, the tourists poured in. Travelers burning up U.S. Route 101 between Los Angeles and San Francisco would exit for the scores of gas stations in Buellton and grab a bowl of "world-famous split pea soup" at Pea Soup Andersen's. The Valley eventually became a country retreat for the well-to-do, and by the '80s, famous area residents included the decidedly not-Danish Ronald Reagan and Michael Jackson.

Today, Solvang still attracts 1.5 million tourists every year. A visit can take an hour, or it can take all day, with loads of shopping and places to eat. So, after you wash down your *smørrebrød* and *frikadeller* with a pint of Tuborg, shop for chocolates, pet the ostriches, or taste the local wine — the town's loaded with tasting rooms for products from the local vineyards, which has one up on Copenhagen. There's a posh Flying Flags RV Resort in nearby Buellton.

# Star Trek Original Series Set Tour

**112 Montcalm St.**
**Ticonderoga, New York**
**518-503-5497**
www.startrektour.com

It's an uncomfortable thing for people of our age to admit, but we're a pair of unreconstructed Trekkies. Because we're originalists, this museum had to make a place on this list, with its meticulous and dazzling re-creation of the original *Star Trek* interior sets. You'll feel like you passed through the screen into a TV, Friday night on NBC in 1968. You can do the whole tour in about an hour. This is the only moderately expensive stop on the list ($22.50 for an adult, half that for a child, and a senior discount). The genuine Trekkie won't mind paying.

The beautiful Lake George area is loaded with attractions for anyone with any interest in history; if you can, visit nearby restored Fort Ticonderoga.

**TIP**

Truly dedicated Star Trek aficionados may also want to visit the site of Captain James Tiberius Kirk's future birth in 2228. You'll find a commemorative marker at 51 First St. W. in Riverside, Iowa, about a dozen miles south of Iowa City. A stone marker behind a hair salon commemorates the spot.

# Index

first-aid kit, 161–162

Fish and Wildlife Service
   (FWS), 345

5 percent grade, 117

flashlights, 154

flat towing, 334–338
   safety systems, 335–338
      safety cables, 335
      supplemental brakes,
         336–338
      tail lights, 335–336
   tow bars, 335

Flex Tape, 155

float sensors, 293

flooding, 363–364

floor plans, 61–62, 101

Flush King, 276

FMCA (Family Motor Coach
   Association), 175

food
   food grade hoses, 144, 251
   removing for storage, 319
   safety, 170

foot pedals, 260

forced arbitration clauses, 105

Ford, 116

Ford F-150 Electric, 125

Forest River, 87, 328

Foretravel, 90

formaldehyde, 277

four down towing. *See* flat
   towing

four-way pivot head, 128

four-wheel drive (4WD), 32,
   35, 124

FreeRoam app, 344, 352

freestanding dump sites,
   268–269

freezing, 330–331. *See also*
   winter

freon, 306

freshwater system, 250–259
   from campsite, 250–251
   defined, 248
   filling tank, 252–253
   potential issues, 254–257
   water heaters, 257–259
      propane/electric, 258–259
      tankless/on-demand, 259
   water pump, 253–254
   winterizing, 321

Froli system, 319

front to back leveling, 214

fuel. *See also* diesel pushers;
   gasoline
   generators, 243
   running out of, 361
   stabilizing chemical
      additives, 325

Fujita scale, 365

full-size (half-ton) trucks,
   118–119

Fulltime Families, 14

full-timers, 12–14

full-wall slides, 62–63

furnace, 282

fuse panel, 239–241
   12V fuses, 239–240
   120V circuit breakers, 240–241

fuses, 154

fusible link, 240

FWS (Fish and Wildlife
   Service), 345

## G

galley, 193

gap insurance, 79

garbage, 360

GasBuddy app, 371

gasoline, 27–28, 113–114, 325

gauze, 162

GAWR (gross axle weight
   rating), 115

GCWR (gross combined weight
   rating), 115, 171

Geico insurance, 82

generators, 241–245
   for boondocking, 351
   campground etiquette, 225
   checking, 199
   fuel, 243
   maintenance, 244–245
   motorhomes, 57–58
   noise, 243–244
   power output, 242
   security, 245
   weight, 243

gig economy, 13

Girl Camper, 16

glampers, 16, 47

*Glamping with MaryJane*
   (Butters), 16

gloves, 151, 155, 263

GM OnStar system, 223

GMC Hummer EV, 125

*Going RV* (TV show), 71

Gone With the Wynns show, 94

Good Sam, 82, 108, 117, 203

*Good Sam Campground &
   Coupon Guide*, 203

Google Maps, 369–370

gooseneck hitches, 120

gozintas, 149–151

GPS standalone navigators, 348

grades, 190

Grand Design Reflection, 65

gravel, 341

graywater, 248, 270, 354

green machines, 15–16

grills, 124, 157, 169

gross axle weight rating
   (GAWR), 115

gross combined weight rating (GCWR), 115, 171
gross trailer weight (GTW), 133
gross vehicle weight rating (GVWR), 115, 171
Gulf Stream, 59
gypsies, 17
*The Gypsies* (Yoors), 17

# H

hair dryers, 331
half-ton (full-size) trucks, 118–119
hammer, 153
hard water, 255
hardware stores, 296
Hartford insurance, 82
Harvest Hosts, 205
hazard lights, 190
head, 193
Heartland, 328
Heat My RV website, 309
heat pumps, 304–307
heaters
   electric space heaters, 157, 310–311
   propane space heaters, 311–312
   water, 197, 257–259
      propane/electric, 258–259
      tankless/on-demand, 259
   for winter RVing, 329
heating. *See* HVAC system
heavy-duty (three-quarter-ton) trucks, 119
height, 179–180
hex wrenches, 153
Highway 101, 22
hills, driving, 190–191
history, roads, 18–19
hitch ball, 131
hitch pin, 131
hitches, 127–137

avoiding catastrophes with, 363
factory tow packages, 123–124
gooseneck, 120
hitch receiver, 129–130
overview, 127–128
parts of, 130–132
preventing thefts, 326
sizes, 132–133
unhitching, 212–214
weighing RV, 134–137
weight-carrying and weight-distributing, 133–134
holding tanks
   filling up, 252–253
   monitor, 262–263
   overview, 248–249
homeowner's association (HOA), 82
homeschooling, 14
hooks, 163
hookup, built-in tank washout, 272–275
Horizons RV, 88
horsepower, 28, 152
hoses
   heated, 331
   sewer drain, 145–146
   water, 144
hot side, 231
hotspots, 199–200, 222
house power, 230, 324
housecleaning, 318–320
   fighting humidity, 318–319
   pests, 319–320
   removing food, 319
"How to Back in a 5th Wheel" (video), 178
humidity, 318–319
*The Hunt for Red October* (Clancy), 16
Husky Towing Products, 335
HVAC system, 196, 301–312

air conditioners, 304–307
alternative heating methods, 309–312
   electric space heaters, 310–311
   propane space heaters, 311–312
awnings, 302
heat pumps, 304–307
hydronic heating, 309
propane furnace, 307–308
rooftop fans, 303–304
hydraulic stablizers, 326
Hydro-Hot, 309
hydronic heating, 309
HyperVent, 319

# I

I-495, 181
ice
   ice makers, 157
   washing out blackwater tanks, 275
*Ice Road Truckers*, 332
icons, used in this book, 4
ignition spark, 283
IKEA, 163
Imodium, 161
imperial measurements, 152
in parallel batteries, 233
in series batteries, 234
incline brake assist, 123
inertia brakes, 336
inspection requirements, propane tanks, 290
Instant Pot, 157
insurance, 81–82, 362–363
interest, 78
interior space, 60–67
   traveling with kids, 64–65
   traveling with pets, 65–66
   working from road, 67

Vistabule, 88
volt meter, 154
voltage, 231

# W

walkie-talkies, 175, 210
Wall Drug, 380–381
wall space, 165
warranties, 77, 101, 106–108
washers, 68–69, 258
washing blackwater tanks,
    272–276
  built-in tank washout hookup,
    272–275
  manually, 275–276
  using ice and water softener or
    detergent, 275
wastewater system,
    260–278
  checking holding tank monitor,
    262–263
  defined, 248
  emptying tanks, 263–272
    at campsites, 263–268
    at freestanding dump sites,
      268–269
    options for, 269–272
  maintenance of, 276–277
    deodorizing tank, 276–277
    toilet paper, choosing, 277
  RV toilet, 260–262
  washing out blackwater tanks,
    272–276
    built-in tank washout
      hookup, 272–275
    manually, 275–276
    using ice and water
      softener or detergent, 275
  winterizing, 322
Water Bandit, 353

water heaters
  propane gas system, 283
  water system, 257–259
  winterizing, 322
water hoses, 144
water pump, 197
water system, 247–278.
    *See also* leaks
  boondocking, 352–355
    conserving water, 353–355
    finding water, 352–353
    storing water, 353
  checking, 196
  freshwater, 250–259
    from campsite, 250–251
    filling tank, 252–253
    potential issues, 254–257
    water heaters, 257–259
    water pump, 253–254
  heating blankets for, 331
  overview, 248–250
  setting up campsites,
    217–218
  wastewater system, 198,
    260–278
    checking holding tank
      monitor, 262–263
    emptying tanks, 263–272
    maintenance of, 276–277
    RV toilet, 260–262
    washing out blackwater
      tanks, 272–276
  in winter, 278
wattage, 231, 242
WD-40 spray lubricant, 155
weather
  avoiding catastrophes with,
    365–366
  awnings and, 302

winter RVing, 328–332
winterizing RV, 316–327
wedges, 143
weekenders, 11
weight
  cosmetic features on
    trucks, 124
  diesel engines and, 28
  generators, 243
  packing and, 171
  of RV, 134–137
  terms, 115
  toy haulers and, 45
  truck campers, 54
  water, 353
weight-carrying hitches,
    133–134
weight-distributing (load-
    equalizing) hitches, 129,
    133–134, 363
well water, 253, 255
wet bath, 37, 59
wet bay, 252–253
wet cell batteries, 234
wheel chocks, 143, 212, 360
Wheeler, Bob, 89
*Who Killed Roger Rabbit?* 20
width, 180
Wi-Fi, 199, 222–223
Wikipedia, 86
wildlife, 360–361
wind
  driving and, 183
  sensors for awnings, 302
windows, 329
Winegard, 223
Winnebago company, 87

## About the Authors

**Christopher Hodapp:** Chris is the author of *Freemasons For Dummies* (Wiley), the world's best-selling guide to the Masonic fraternity. Before becoming an author, Chris spent more than 20 years as a commercial filmmaker. He is the founding editor emeritus of the *Journal of the Masonic Society* and is presently the associate director of the Masonic Library and Museum of Indiana. His other books include *Solomon's Builders* and *Heritage Endures.*

**Alice Von Kannon:** Alice is an author and historian, and she's been RVing since the age of 16. Before becoming an author, she worked for many years in advertising as a writer and broadcast producer. Alice released her most recent historical romance novel, *Heart's Blood,* in 2020.

Together, the couple has cowritten *The Templar Code For Dummies* (Wiley) and *Conspiracy Theories & Secret Societies For Dummies* (Wiley). They have both appeared many times on programs for the History, Discovery, National Geographic, truTV, and American Heroes channels, most recently on *Codes and Conspiracies, The Curse of Oak Island,* and *America: Facts vs. Fiction.* Chris and Alice have owned motorhomes and trailers for more than 15 years. Although they call Indianapolis their home, they spend as much time as possible crisscrossing the country in their 30-foot Airstream Flying Cloud with their traveling companion, Sophie the Flying Poodle. So far, they have visited and camped in 44 of the 50 states in literally hundreds of campgrounds and parks.

## Dedication

To Loralyn Bailey, who inspired us to write this book in the first place by suddenly selling her house and worldly possessions to buy a motorhome and becoming a full-time RVer. "What I really need now is a *For Dummies* book about RVs," she idly said one afternoon. We are happy to grant her wish.

# Authors' Acknowledgments

We'd like to thank Mike and Mary Brumback for their friendship, wisdom, and experience.

We are indebted to many companies, organizations, and individuals in the RV business who helped us with our research: the Recreational Vehicle Industry Association; Airstream, Inc. in Jackson Center, Ohio; the management and staff at Braun's Fun Time Campers, Mount Comfort RV, and Camping World of Indianapolis; Lazydays RV in Phoenix, Arizona; Eric Davis and Aaron Jones at Mark Wahlberg Airstream and RV in Columbus, Ohio; SportChassis in Clinton, Oklahoma; and the RV/MH Hall of Fame in Elkhart, Indiana.

Our deep appreciation goes out to Steven Hayes at Wiley and our project editor, Elizabeth Kuball, for patiently putting up with our calamitous road trip delays as our manuscript slowly trickled in. With the insanity of everything else in the year 2020, we considered ourselves lucky that the Great Meteor didn't strike on New Year's Eve just to get in under the wire.

A very special hat tip goes to Brienne Ropp at Luxe Luxury Fifth Wheels for serving as our technical editor.

And finally, we especially want to thank the hundreds of RVers we've met across the country and the scores of dedicated RV writers, reporters, bloggers, vloggers, and forum folks who share their indispensable knowledge, insights, successes, catastrophes, and triumphs online every single day. It is their experience, dedication, and love of the lifestyle that truly helps unite us all into one vast community of fellow travelers and adventurers.

We'll see you down the road.

## Publisher's Acknowledgments

**Executive Editor:** Steven Hayes

**Project Editor:** Elizabeth Kuball

**Copy Editor:** Elizabeth Kuball

**Technical Editor:** Brienne Ropp

**Production Editor:** Tamilmani Varadharaj

**Cover Photos:** © Jupiterimages/Stockbyte/ Getty Images